AF761795

UNITED NATIONS LAW, POLITICS, *and* PRACTICE

United Nations Law, Politics, *and* Practice

Alexandre Tavadian

IRWIN LAW

United Nations Law, Politics, and Practice

Published in 2021 by

Irwin Law Inc.
Suite 206, 14 Duncan Street
Toronto, ON M5H 3G8

www.irwinlaw.com

ISBN: 978-1-55221-557-9 | e-book ISBN: 978-1-55221-558-6

Cataloguing in Publication available from Library and Archives Canada

Title: United Nations law, politics, and practice / Alexandre Tavadian.
Names: Tavadian, Alexandre, author.
Description: Includes bibliographical references and index.
Identifiers: Canadiana (print) 20200415905 | Canadiana (ebook) 20200415921 | ISBN 9781552215579(softcover) | ISBN 9781552215586 (PDF)
Subjects: LCSH: United Nations.
Classification: LCC KZ4986 .T38 2020 | DDC 341.23—dc23

Ontario Media Development Corporation
Société de développement de l'industrie des médias de l'Ontario

Printed and bound by CPI Group (UK) Ltd, Croydon, CR0 4YY

1 2 3 4 5 25 24 23 22 21

To Vassiléna

DISCLAIMER

While all care was taken, the responsibility for any errors or omissions, and all views expressed herein, remain with the author and cannot and should not be attributed to the United Nations, UNHCR, or NATO.

SUMMARY TABLE OF CONTENTS

DETAILED TABLE OF CONTENTS

PREFACE

One of the most rewarding aspects of my work as a lawyer in the United Nations was coaching and mentoring interns and young professionals. I was fortunate enough to work with students, university graduates, and young lawyers from different continents, legal systems, and cultures who shared my passion for public international law and the United Nations. Despite their diverse background, they all asked me to recommend a book that could provide a holistic overview of the United Nations as an institution. They were particularly interested in a textbook that could provide a multidisciplinary approach to the study of the UN rather than an exclusively legal or political analysis and survey. My research revealed that there was a need for a comprehensive yet accessible book on the United Nations apparatus, covering the legal, political, and practical aspects of the organization's functioning and activities. The main problem I encountered when looking for suitable books on the UN was that none of them addressed the topics and issues that I thought were important. Some excellent books, including the Oxford Handbook on the United Nations, study the UN from an international relations perspective. Other great resources, such as Bruno Simma's *Commentary on the UN Charter* and *Oppenheim's International Law* are too detailed to be used as a textbook or a reference manual for the uninitiated. Both works consist of two large volumes and are accessible mostly to legal experts conducting research. They also have a prohibitive retail price.

This book is different from those currently available on the market in many respects. First, it presents a detailed historical account of important events that shaped the United Nations under different Secretaries-General. Second, it covers not only legal aspects of the organization but also its politics and practice from an insider's viewpoint. Third, it is intended for a diverse audience. Students, professors, lawyers, diplomats, international public servants, people aspiring to work for the United Nations, or those with any interest in the world organization, international relations, or international law will find this book useful.

The documents consulted and relevant developments noted are those up to and including May 2020.

ACKNOWLEDGEMENTS

I owe my wife a great debt of thanks for her valuable advice, support, and encouragement while I was writing this book. She spent countless hours reading my manuscript at different stages and providing tremendously helpful feedback. I would like to express my gratitude also to all those who contributed ideas or reviewed some chapters of the book. In particular, I am grateful to Hasmik Egian, Director of the Security Council Affairs Division of the UN Secretariat; Brian Gorlick, former UN and UNHCR official and lecturer at University of London; François Olivier Bouchard, Associate Legal Advisor of NATO Support and Procurement Agency; Rafael Ruschel, Associate in DeBrauw Blackstone Westbroek; and Marjorie Langlois, Associate and National Representative in Unifor. I also would like to thank those who made this book possible by exposing me to UN law, politics, and practice. More specifically, I am grateful to my friends and former supervisors, Brian Gorlick and Elizabeth Brown, from whom I learned a great deal about the United Nations system. I am equally grateful to my former colleagues in the internal justice system of the UN and in the UNHCR.

INTRODUCTION

The United Nations is the result of a three-hundred-year experiment. Between 1648 and 1945, nations made three major attempts to establish a new world order. These three unsuccessful attempts occurred in: (a) 1648 at the Peace of Westphalia after the Thirty Years' War; (b) 1815 at the Congress of Vienna after the Napoleonic Wars; and (c) 1919 in Paris after World War I. The international community of states drew valuable lessons from these failures. To understand the United Nations, one must consider the events that led to its establishment.

A. FIRST ATTEMPT: WESTPHALIA PEACE PROCESS (1648)

No historic overview of international relations, politics, or law can be complete without a study of the Thirty Years' War and of the Westphalia peace process that marked its end. The Thirty Years' War was a series of destructive hostilities in Europe between 1618 and 1648. The conflict emerged as a religious clash between Protestant and Catholic states and gradually developed into a broader struggle of European powers for political pre-eminence.

The Thirty Years' War began when the Roman Emperor Ferdinand II attempted to curtail the religious freedom of his subjects, sparking a rebellion among the Protestant aristocrats of Bohemia and Austria. The rebellion was successfully repressed after a five-year struggle, but it did not end the persecution of Protestants. In the meantime, some states took advantage of the volatile situation and invaded neighbouring countries. For instance, Denmark and Sweden invaded Germany. Poland attacked Russia. Gradually, destructive battles occurred over most of Europe, redrawing its geopolitical maps. The conflict lasted until 1648.

In 1648, the contending powers finally met in the German province of Westphalia and agreed to end the bloodshed. The Thirty Years' War ended with the treaties of Osnabrück and Münster[1] that were part of the wider peace agreement called the Peace of Westphalia. This treaty had significantly changed the balance of power[2] in Europe. The Netherlands had gained independence from Spain. Switzerland had gained independence from Austria. Spain had lost its status as a great power whereas France had acquired vast territories and the status of the new superpower in Europe. The Holy Roman Empire collapsed. It was then that it became obvious that Protestantism was going to stay. Finally, the essential structure of modern Europe as a community of sovereign states was established.

Most historians regard the Westphalian settlement or deal as the fundamental constitution of Europe's political system.[3] It created a balance of power that prevented any subsequent religious or imperialist conflicts in the region. Of course, the Westphalia peace process did not remain the basis of Europe's political system forever. Nevertheless, it achieved important lasting effects.[4] Scholars and historians generally agree that the Westphalia peace process was the bedrock of international relations because it engendered the concept of state

---

1 It is noteworthy that several separate bilateral treaties were signed between various parties in relation to the same war because in those times, the technique of multilateral or collective treaties was unknown. Consequently, one treaty could not be used where there were more than two parties.

2 Balance of power refers to the interrelation between great powers, with each balancing off against the others to prevent the rise of a single great power to the status of a dominant hegemon vis-à-vis the others.

3 Jean-Jacques Rousseau, "Extrait du projet de paix perpétuelle de Monsieur l'Abbé de St Pierre" (1761) in *Œuvres complètes de Jean-Jacques Rousseau* (Paris: Éditions de la Pléiade, 1964) vol III at 572.

4 Geoffrey Parker, *The Thirty Years' War*, 2d ed (New York: Routledge, 1997) at 182.

sovereignty.[5] The notion of the modern sovereign state emerged because of the Westphalia peace process. Indeed, it was at Westphalia that the contending states agreed to respect each other's right to choose their own religion, to determine their domestic politics without foreign interference, and to preserve complete sovereignty within their territorial borders. The Westphalian sovereignty recognized the autonomy of domestic power structures and rejected authoritative external influences.[6] These principles became the fundamental characteristics of a Westphalian state as we know it today. Although the geopolitical map of Europe continued to evolve and borders continued to shift, the Westphalia peace process was a transformational and significant diplomatic event that introduced fundamental rules that would later form the foundation of the international legal order.

B. SECOND ATTEMPT: CONGRESS OF VIENNA (1814–1815)

Although the concept of state sovereignty began to take form in the seventeenth century, it took major European powers two more centuries to fully understand that respecting each other's sovereignty and territorial integrity would require some form of cooperation. This realization occurred surprisingly late in history. The trigger was Napoleon Bonaparte's military campaigns against neighbouring countries, which constituted a breach of the principle of inviolability of territorial integrity agreed upon in the Westphalia peace process.

Following the battle of Paris of 1814, Napoleon was forced to abdicate and go into exile. Eight states signed the *Treaty of Paris* to settle the war with France and to restore the French territorial borders of 1792. Then, they agreed to meet in Vienna (at the Congress of Vienna) to settle other outstanding matters pertaining to the restoration of the

---

5 Daniel Philpott, *Revolutions in Sovereignty: How Ideas Shaped Modern International Relations* (New Jersey: Princeton University Press, 2001); Hans J Morgenthau, *Politics Among Nations: The Struggle for Power and Peace* (New York: AA Knopf, 1973).

6 Stephen D Krasner, "Problematic Sovereignty" in Stephen D Krasner, ed, *Problematic Sovereignty: Contested Rules and Political Responsibilities* (New York: Columbia University Press, 2001) at 2.

European balance of power. Like Westphalia, the Congress of Vienna is an iconic event in the history of European politics and diplomacy. The great powers wanted to ensure that no single state would dominate in Europe. The four triumphant great powers of the time—Austria, Prussia, Russia, and the United Kingdom—agreed to play the role of guardians of the established international legal order by maintaining and improving the balance of power in Europe. Although France was the defeated party, it also managed to secure a place at the table of allied powers. Before these great powers had time to agree on the way to preserve the balance of power in Europe, Napoleon unexpectedly returned from exile and grabbed power again. When he was finally defeated at Waterloo, triumphant states realized that simply agreeing on principles was insufficient. They needed to create an alliance tasked with guaranteeing the implementation of what had been decided in Vienna and Paris. To monitor the implementation of the measures that each state had to take, the allied powers agreed to meet at regular intervals. That is how multilateral conferences and follow-up conferences came into existence. In contrast to the seventeenth and eighteenth centuries when bilateral diplomacy was the exclusive means of conflict resolution, in the nineteenth century, diplomacy was conducted primarily by multilateral conferences. Multilateral conferences played a significant role in the appearance of permanent intergovernmental institutions. They were, in fact, the embryonic foundation of contemporary international organizations.

In the early nineteenth century, European nations were experimenting with multilateral conferences. Since they proved to be an effective way to reach international agreements and to ensure compliance, such conferences had significantly increased in frequency towards the end of the nineteenth century. These conferences received secretarial services either from the civil service of a host country or from an improvised team composed of several participating states.[7] Secretarial services included production and filing of documents, recording of decisions, translation and editing services,

7 Leon Gordenker, *The UN Secretary-General and Secretariat*, 2d ed (New York: Routledge, 2010) at 4–5.

and other housekeeping tasks. At one stage, multilateral conferences became so frequent that the only logical outcome was to institutionalize them by establishing permanent organizations with staff to service them. Thus, international organizations, also known as intergovernmental organizations,[8] began appearing as a direct result of this progressive institutionalization of multilateral conferences. They were "little more than an attempt to recognize that international conferences were becoming a regular and frequently recurring part of international practice."[9]

Initially, international organizations had a primitive structure. The earliest forms of international organizations were river commissions and international public unions. They were fora for international cooperation on very specific and technical issues and matters. The first such commissions and unions were the Danube River Commission, the International Telegraph Union, followed by the Universal Postal Union. States established these organizations because they came to the realization that international institutions would enable them to attain their goals more efficiently by facilitating cooperation through their technical expertise, through the specialized knowledge they would acquire over time, as well as through ordinary secretariat functions they would perform.

At the beginning of the twentieth century, the idea of a universal organization was beginning to ripen. Many states had already met on several occasions in international conferences relating to peace. For instance, in 1899 and 1907, at the initiative of the Russian Czar Nicholas II, many states gathered in The Hague to establish the Permanent Court of Arbitration for the peaceful resolution of disputes and to adopt multilateral conventions that addressed, *inter alia*, the conduct

---

8 Intergovernmental organizations should not be confounded with non-governmental organizations (NGOs). Intergovernmental organizations are normally formed by international treaties between states or between states and other international organizations. However, NGOs are normally established under the national legislation of the state where they operate. This also applies to international NGOs or NGOs that carry out activities in more than one state.

9 Charles Howard-Ellis, *The Origin, Structure and Working of the League of Nations* (London: George Allen & Unwin, 2003) at 67.

of warfare. The parties were supposed to meet in The Hague one last time in 1915; however, this third conference never took place due to the outbreak of World War I.

The establishment of the Permanent Court of Arbitration in 1899 yielded positive results within only a few years of its existence.[10] The benefits of establishing permanent international organizations were becoming obvious. Anti-war movements in the United States and the United Kingdom campaigned for a new international system whereby the use of force would be justified to preserve peace.[11]

C. THIRD ATTEMPT: PARIS PEACE CONFERENCE

During the First World War, plans for an international peace organization were emerging in different countries, including in the United States, Britain, and France. Influential groups were urging the creation of an international organization because intellectuals and politicians alike acknowledged that peace could only be achieved if it was actively and jointly promoted. The United States' President Woodrow Wilson strongly favoured the idea as a means of preventing another destructive world conflict. He set up an independent inquiry to develop his ideas on a peace settlement, which resulted in *Wilson's Fourteen Points*, with the last point being the establishment of a general association of nations. In January 1917, two months before the United States declared war against Germany, President Wilson addressed the US Senate and appealed for a definitive resolution of the war. This address, known as the *Peace without Victory* speech,[12] placed an emphasis on

---

10 For instance, in 1905, the Court resolved the diplomatic conflict between Russia and Britain that arose because of the Hull incident, also known as the Dogger Bank incident. The crisis occurred in October 1904, during the Russo-Japanese war, when the Russian fleet mistook British fishing boats in the North Sea for the Japanese Navy force and torpedoed them. The British and the Russian governments agreed to submit the issue to the international commission of inquiry, which resulted in an award of compensation to the British fishermen.

11 Anique HM van Ginneken, *Historical Dictionary of the League of Nations* (Maryland: Scarecrow Press, 2006) at 3.

12 Lewis Copeland, Lawrence W Lamm & Stephen J McKenna, *The World's Great Speeches*, 4th ed (Mineola: Dover Publications, 1999) at 352:

having a "community of power" without undermining the neutrality of the United States.[13]

The end of World War I, marked by the capitulation of Germany, led to the six-month-long Paris Peace Conference negotiations, which culminated in the *Treaty of Versailles*.[14] One of the outcomes of the *Treaty of Versailles* was the creation of an international organization called the League of Nations—the predecessor of the United Nations.

The League of Nations was founded in January 1920. Its objective was to promote international cooperation and to achieve international peace and security. The allies at the Paris Peace Conference signed a League Covenant, incorporating the principles of collective security, peaceful resolution of international disputes, and reduction of armaments. The Covenant established the League's three principal organs: an Assembly composed of representatives of all member states; a Council composed of permanent representatives of the leading allied powers and additional rotating members; and a Secretariat presided over by a Secretary-General with its seat in Geneva.

The chief decision-making organ of the League of Nations was the Council. The Council initially had four permanent members: France, Italy, Japan, and the United Kingdom. Germany joined as a fifth permanent member from 1926 to 1933 and was subsequently replaced by the Soviet Union from 1934 to 1939. The Council also had four

---

> Victory would mean peace forced upon the loser, a victor's terms imposed upon the vanquished. It would be accepted in humiliation, under duress, at an intolerable sacrifice, and would leave a sting, a resentment, a bitter memory upon which terms of peace would rest, not permanently, but only as upon quicksand. Only a peace between equals can last. Only a peace the very principle of which is equality and a common participation in a common benefit. The right state of mind, the right feeling between nations, is as necessary for a lasting peace as is the just settlement of vexed questions of territory or of racial and national allegiance.

13 The United States could no longer remain neutral when Germany began indiscriminately torpedoing American tankers in the Atlantic Ocean. As soon as the United States became aware of the secret telegram in which Germany sought Mexico's support against the United States, President Wilson declared war against Germany. The US involvement in the war was undoubtedly the turning point.

14 The treaty required Germany to compensate for the losses of the Allied nations by conceding territory and paying reparations.

non-permanent members elected by the Assembly for a period of three years. This number was subsequently increased when the League's membership grew. Two of the Council's seats were semi-permanent or eligible for re-election encumbered by Poland and Spain.[15] Seven non-permanent seats were to be distributed among countries from Latin America, Asia, and the Commonwealth, for the former neutral states and the Little Entente.[16] Unanimity was required for the Council to adopt decisions.

The Assembly was another important organ of the League. Unlike the Council, it consisted of all member states. It was the plenary and democratic organ of the League where smaller states also had a voice. The Assembly was not a popular organ in the eyes of the big powers because small states whose interests were disregarded in the Council could voice their grievances before the Assembly. The Assembly convened once a year for a period of three weeks. Its meetings were public. In addition to plenary meetings, the Assembly conducted its work through specialized committees.[17] The voting procedure in the Assembly was perhaps its biggest flaw because decisions could be adopted only unanimously, unless they pertained to procedural matters or to the admission of new members, in which case a two-thirds majority was sufficient.

The permanent Secretariat modeled on the British civil service was the administrative organ of the League of Nations. It was headed by a Secretary-General and was based in Geneva. The first Secretary-General was Sir Eric Drummond, a former British public servant. In 1933, a French national and former banker Joseph Avenol succeeded Drummond. The Secretary-General of the League had one deputy and three Under-Secretaries-General who represented the big powers. They were

15 Ginneken, above note 11 at 9.

16 The Little Entente refers to an alliance formed in 1920 and 1921 by Czechoslovakia, Romania, and Yugoslavia, directed against Hungarian and German domination and military oppression.

17 The first committee dealt with the organization of the League; the second with economic, social, and technical questions; the third with the Permanent Court of International Justice; the fourth with the budget and staff of the Secretariat; the fifth with admission of new member states; the sixth with political questions, mandates, and minorities.

in charge of the internal administration, political affairs, and cooperation. The Secretariat also employed a small group of international public servants. It began its work with approximately 120 staff members in 1920 and increased its workforce to over 700 in 1930.

The League of Nations was a fragile international organization at its inception for several reasons. First, although the United States was the pioneer of the League of Nations, its Congress refused to ratify the Covenant; therefore, it never became a member state.

The Refusal of the United States to Ratify the Covenant of the League of Nations

In his 1796 farewell address, George Washington had cautioned Americans against permanent alliances with foreign states:

> Europe has a set of primary interests which to us have none; or a very remote relation. Hence she must be engaged in frequent controversies, the causes of which are essentially foreign to our concerns. Hence, therefore, it must be unwise in us to implicate ourselves by artificial ties in the ordinary vicissitudes of her politics, or the ordinary combinations and collisions of her friendships or enmities. . . .
>
> It is our true policy to steer clear of permanent alliances with any portion of the foreign world; so far, I mean, as we are now at liberty to do it; for let me not be understood as capable of patronizing infidelity to existing engagements. I hold the maxim no less applicable to public than to private affairs, that honesty is always the best policy. I repeat it, therefore, let those engagements be observed in their genuine sense. But, in my opinion, it is unnecessary and would be unwise to extend them.[18]

Article 10 of the League of Nations Covenant provided that "the Members of the League undertake to respect and preserve as against external aggression the territorial integrity and existing political independence of all Members of the League. In case of any such

18 Lewis Copeland, Lawrence W Lamm & Stephen J McKenna, *The World's Great Speeches*, 4th ed (Mineola: Dover Publications, 1999) at 256–57.

aggression or in case of any threat or danger of such aggression the Council shall advise upon the means by which this obligation shall be fulfilled."

This article placed an obligation on all member states not only to respect the territorial integrity of other member states but also to ensure that other member states or third parties respected it. The United States' legislature believed that by ratifying the treaty the United States would lose the ability to decide whether it should get involved in a conflict. Essentially, the United States did not want to be compelled to take hostile measures, such as imposing an economic embargo or severing diplomatic relations, against another state with which it had no issues. This legal obligation enshrined in Article 10 of the Covenant was seen to be inconsistent with the long-standing foreign policy of the United States. Consequently, the US Congress strongly opposed President Wilson's plea to ratify the *Treaty of Versailles*.

The second reason for the League's vulnerability was the non-committal nature of its Covenant. Member states of the League had no obligation to defend other members of the League against an armed aggression. The only obligation expressed in clear and absolute terms was to apply economic and communications sanctions against a recalcitrant member state that was waging war in violation of the Covenant. If sanctions failed, member states had no obligation to take more robust measures, even if the Council recommended such measures. It also meant that sanctions were ineffective when the biggest economic powers did not cooperate with the League.

The third fatal defect was the requirement of unanimity for a resolution to pass in the Assembly and in the Council on any important question. Essentially, each member of the League had a veto in both organs of the organization and could therefore single-handedly block any proposal.

Although the Covenant also established the Permanent Court of International Justice, this body was an independent entity as opposed to an organ of the League of Nations. The Court held its inaugural sitting in 1922 and was dissolved in 1946. Pursuant to Article XIV of the Covenant, its mandate was "to hear and determine any dispute of an international character which the parties thereto submit to it." The Assembly appointed the Court's judges and deputy judges. The Court's Statute also provided for an "optional clause," which allowed any state to accept the compulsory jurisdiction of the Court. Although the adherence to the optional clause was voluntary, over forty states had signed it.

The League's Covenant also provided for a mechanism whereby colonies in Asia and Africa would be distributed among the Allied Powers (Mandatories) in the form of mandates. A mandate was a power conferred by the League of Nations to a country to administer on behalf of the League the territory of another country that was not prepared to form its own government.

The League of Nations began experiencing difficulties in the 1930s. The precursor of its demise was Brazil's withdrawal of its membership in 1928 when it was denied a permanent seat on the Council. In March 1933, Japan withdrew from the League when the Assembly adopted a report condemning it for its invasion of Manchuria. In October 1933, ten months after Adolf Hitler came to power, Germany also withdrew its membership from the League. In 1935, Italy, led by Mussolini, invaded Ethiopia, which caused other member states to impose sanctions against the aggressor. For this reason, Italy also withdrew from the League in 1937. Finally, at the last meeting of the League's Assembly and Council in November 1939, the members of the League expelled the USSR from the organization for attacking Finland. Without Germany, Italy, Japan, and the Soviet Union, the League lacked political and economic power to enforce compliance and to maintain international peace and security. These events led to the collapse of the League of Nations and its structurally flawed collective security system designed by the international community at the end of World War I. President Wilson's prophecy "that within another generation there will be another world war" materialized.[19]

Although the official dissolution of the League of Nations occurred in April 1946 (when the United Nations organization was already

---

19 Stephen Schlesinger, *Act of Creation: The Founding of the United Nations* (Cambridge: Westview Press, 2003) at 25.

active)[20] it had ceased its operations in 1940 immediately after the expulsion of the USSR from the League. Many historians and scholars regard the League of Nations as a complete failure. This simplistic view ignores the fact that the League was the first universal organization with a political vocation. It had no precedents or earlier institutions as models; it was humanity's first attempt of this magnitude. Against all odds, the League's achievements during its brief two decades of existence were remarkable. It is true that the League of Nations failed to prevent the Second World War. Nevertheless, the international community of states learned a great deal from the League's challenges. These lessons were instrumental when nations decided to create the United Nations. As an American diplomat rightly observed:

> [W]e should abandon the notion, sometimes held, that in 1945 the United Nations sprang into being from nowhere, like Minerva from the brow of Zeus. The analogy, rather, should be the Phoenix arising from its own ashes. For while many felt it wise in 1945 to avoid dwelling on antecedents, those who laboured to create the United Nations would have had an extremely difficult time without the precedents of the League of Nations to guide them.[21]

D. WHAT IS THIS BOOK ABOUT AND WHOM IS IT FOR?

The main purpose of this book is to provide readers with sufficient information on the UN's evolution, institutional structure, functioning, and activities in order to enable them to form their own views about the strengths, weaknesses, successes, and failures of the UN. This book examines how the organization strives to achieve its primary goal "to maintain international peace and security" and its secondary goal "to reaffirm faith in fundamental human rights; to establish conditions under which justice and respect for the obligations arising from treaties and other sources of international law can

---

20 Benedetto Conforti, *The Law and Practice of the United Nations* (Leiden: Martinus Nijhoff, 2005) at 1.

21 Francis O Wilcox, "The United Nations in the Mainstream of History" (1956) 50 *Am Soc'y Int'l L Proc* 187.

be maintained; and to promote social progress and better standards of life in larger freedom."[22] "Knowledge and understanding of the aims and activities of the United Nations and its related agencies contribute to the fostering ... of the ideas of peace and international cooperation."[23] Therefore, soon after the UN was established, the General Assembly recommended that the governments of all countries "take measures at the earliest possible date to encourage the teaching of the *Charter of the United Nations* (also referred to as the *UN Charter* throughout this book) and the purposes and principles, the structure, background and activities of the United Nations in the schools and institutes of higher learning of their countries, with particular emphasis on such instruction in elementary and secondary schools."[24]

This book neither vaunts the merits of the United Nations nor plays down its flaws; it describes historical developments and the performance of the organization from the author's perspective. It focuses on both what happened and why it happened.

The book is designed for professors, lecturers, and students of international law and international relations, legal practitioners working for international organizations and NGOs, UN personnel, diplomats and delegates representing governments in the United Nations, and other individuals with an interest in international politics, international law, or the United Nations.

E. EXPLAINING THE TITLE

The title of the book contains four terms that need to be defined. They are the United Nations, [UN] Law, [UN] Politics, and [UN] Practice. At first sight, the United Nations is not a term that needs to be defined

---

22 *Charter of the United Nations*, Can TS 1945 No 7 at Preamble, art 1.1.

23 *Teaching of the purposes and principles, the structure and activities of the United Nations and its related agencies*, GA Res 1511 (XV), UNGAOR, 15th Sess, UN Doc A/Res/1511(XV) (1960) 22.

24 *Teaching of the purposes and principles, the structure and activities of the United Nations in the schools of Member States*, GA Res 137 (II), UNGAOR, 2nd Sess, UN Doc A/Res/137(II) (1947) 45. See also ESC Res 748 (XXIX), UNESCOR, 1960, UN Doc E/Res/748(XXIX).

or explained. Various types of media outlets regularly mention the UN in daily news broadcasts and newspaper articles. The organization features in several films and fictional books. Even Lego construction toys have a set for building the UN headquarters in New York City. However, a closer analysis shows that the *United Nations* is by far the most elusive term of the title. The academic literature draws a distinction between two, and sometimes three identities of the UN. Professor Inis Claude described the two distinct identities of the organization as follows:

> [I]t is first necessary to distinguish between the two identities of the UN, which I shall call the "First UN" and the "Second UN." These two "institutions" are closely intertwined and mutually dependent, but they are nonetheless quite different and have distinctive capabilities. It is therefore of the greatest importance to be clear about which of them we have in mind when we discuss their appropriate tasks.
>
> The First UN is constituted by its staff, an international secretariat or bureaucracy located in New York, Geneva, and other regional headquarters. Its leader, chief, and most authoritative official spokesperson, is the Secretary-General. Most discussions of the intentions, hopes, and plans of the UN refer in fact to the will of this First UN, as expressed by the Secretary-General or his or her subordinate officials.... Theoretically, states control this UN, although the extent of their actual control and direction is limited and variable. At the least, however, the member states exercise very considerable influence. The UN's member states are the First UN's sponsors, suppliers, supporters, and directors, its clients and customers, the beneficiaries of most of its activities. But they are not, and cannot be, this First UN. It is a corporate entity, existing alongside the member states, something other than and different from a state, separate from but dependent on and useful to the states that are listed as its members.
>
> The Second UN is a collectivity formed by almost all the states of the world; it consists of its member states, who employ an international secretariat to support their joint deliberations and activities. Various states exercise leadership from time to time, in particular

> areas of policy. Most notably, the major powers tend to be its leaders, and for many of its most important functions the world's most prominent state, the United States, is the indispensable leader of this Second UN, while the Secretary-General is its chief employee. (One might say that the Secretary-General is the general in command of the First UN and the secretary of the Second UN.) The roles of the Secretariat and the member states are reversed in the two organizations: the staff constitutes the First UN and works for the Second UN, while the states support the First UN and constitute the Second UN. From the point of view of the member states, the First UN requires the third-person pronoun and the Second UN takes the first-person—the former is "they" or possibly "it," while the latter is "we."[25]

At a more granular level, however, Inis Claude's definition is incomplete. The first UN may itself have two meanings. In the strict sense of the word, the term "UN" refers to the United Nations organization only, which consists of its six main organs (and their subsidiary organs). This narrow meaning of the term excludes other UN agencies and entities, such as UNICEF, UNHCR, WFP, and WHO. In the broader sense of the term, the UN refers to all entities of the UN family, including UN Funds, Programmes, Research Institutes, UN Specialized Agencies, and Related Organizations. This network of UN agencies and entities is known as the UN system. In this book, we will study the first and second UNs as defined by Professor Claude. However, when studying the first UN, we will focus primarily on the United Nations organization and its main and subsidiary organs. Other entities of the UN system will be examined only briefly.

---

25 Inis L Claude, Jr, "Peace and Security: Prospective Roles for the Two United Nations" (1996) 2:3 *Global Governance* 289 at 290–91. Other academics suggest a "third UN," consisting of NGOs, academics, consultants, experts, and independent commissions. See in particular: Thomas G Weiss, Tatiana Carayannis & Richard Jolly, "The 'Third' United Nations" (2009) 15:1 *Global Governance* 15; Roger A Coate, "The John W Holmes Lecture: Growing the Third UN for People-Centered Development—The United Nations, Civil Society, and Beyond" (2009) 15:2 *Global Governance* 153.

The term "[UN] law" refers to a body of rules established by the *UN Charter*, treaties, international customs, judgments, advisory opinions, resolutions, and other documents that regulate the functioning of the United Nations and its various organs and bodies. It also includes rules and principles that UN member states are expected to comply with when interacting with one another in UN organs. An example of UN law is the rule requiring that all permanent members of the Security Council cast a positive vote in favour of a proposal for it to become a resolution. The *UN Charter* does not specify whether the resolution would fail if a permanent member of the Security Council abstains from voting. The answer to this question can be found in the jurisprudence of the International Court of Justice. UN law also seeks to answer other questions pertaining to the organization's functioning. For instance, which UN organs and specialized agencies and related organizations are authorized to request an advisory opinion from the International Court of Justice? Does the Secretary-General or the UN Secretariat have the power to seek an advisory opinion? Is it lawful for a member state to intervene in the recruitment of staff members by the Secretary-General? These are all examples of legal norms and rules that this book calls UN law.

The term "politics" in the title of this book was rather inevitable. Even though international law and international politics are different fields of academic study, no scholar of either field can reasonably deny the intrinsic relation between these two fields. International legal scholars who rebuff politics and try to focus on purely legal solutions to international problems are idealists. It is therefore not surprising that an impressive body of literature studies the relation between international law and international politics. Lawyers practising public international law in ministries of foreign affairs, IGOs, and some NGOs know only too well that they can never disregard the political dimensions of a legal problem. This is particularly true in the United Nations where the understanding of a legal concept may vary dramatically from country to country and depend heavily on local or regional politics. This does not mean that international politics always take precedence over international law or that international law is a fiction; it simply means that when choosing two possible legal solutions to a problem, a prudent international legal practitioner will opt for the solution that is not only legally sound but also politically acceptable for all interested parties. International law requires a delicate equilibrium between legal and political considerations. The excessive dominance of legal considerations would make international law too rigid, politically unacceptable, and therefore dysfunctional, while the excessive dominance of political interests would make law malleable and validate reprehensible conduct. That is why UN law cannot be separated from UN politics. An example of UN politics is the parliamentary dynamics in the deliberative organs of the UN. As we will see in the chapter on the General Assembly, small nations and developing countries form voting coalitions and pressure groups to improve their numerical advantage and to counter the influence of wealthier industrialized states that control the UN's purse. Other examples of UN politics include the exercise of the veto right in the Security Council, voting patterns of small states that heavily rely on neighbouring superpowers in various organs, and the appointment of senior officials of the UN.

The last word of the title of this book is "practice." UN practice refers to the usual and habitual way of doing things in the United Nations. It describes how member states and UN organs adhere to certain principles and rules. Practice is not law, even though it may ultimately lead to the formation of a customary rule and become law. Practice is not politics either because it has no influence on policy. One example of a practice is the two-term limit to the Secretary-General's appointment. Neither the *UN Charter* nor the General Assembly resolution governing the election of the Secretary-General prohibit a third term. In fact, some Secretaries-General have been considered for a third term, even though none was eventually elected. With time, this restriction crystallized into an accepted practice. This practice has not yet become an international customary rule and may change anytime. It is entirely possible that some day, member states will be so satisfied by a Secretary-General that they might elect that individual for a third term. Another practice that is neither expressly permitted nor prohibited by any rule is the splitting among two contending states of a two-year non-permanent membership in the Security Council.

Practice may also refer to the frequency with which a specific legal rule has been applied or followed. This type of practice is significant because it allows the assessment of the importance or relevance of a legal rule. For example, Article 6 of the *UN Charter* permits the expulsion of a member state from the United Nations for persistently violating the principles contained in the *UN Charter*. Although many UN member states repetitively breached the principles of the *UN Charter*, none have been expelled from the organization. By examining the practice of the United Nations, one can determine that this provision has never been applied and is therefore dead letter.

F. STRUCTURE OF THE BOOK

This book consists of seven chapters. The first chapter of the book deals with the history of the UN and the conferences that preceded its establishment. This chapter is split into two different periods. The first period covers the conferences that led to the establishment of the United Nations. The second and main part of Chapter One focuses on the history and evolution of the organization. It explores the history of the UN in periods that correspond to the mandates of all nine Secretaries-General, starting with Trygve Lie and ending with Antonio Guterres. Since providing a comprehensive account of all events was not possible, only the most salient moments relevant to the UN are covered under each period.

Chapter Two explores in detail the four purposes of the United Nations and the seven principles that all member states are required to uphold. At the time of creating the world organization, the founding fathers knew from previous unsuccessful experiences with the League of Nations that to maintain international peace and security and to take effective collective measures for the prevention and removal of threats to the peace, they had to agree on and respect a number of principles. These principles include the sovereign equality of states, the obligation to act in good faith, a duty to resolve disputes through peaceful means, the prohibition to use force or threaten to use force, and the proscription to intervene in domestic affairs of other countries. It is not possible to understand the United Nations and how governments of states interact with one another, if one does not fully grasp these basic tenets of international law and international relations.

Chapter Three discusses the General Assembly, the only plenary and the main deliberative organ of the United Nations. This chapter explains how states can become members of the General Assembly (and of the United Nations) and what conditions they need to meet to be admitted as UN members. Chapter Three also explores how a state's membership may end or be suspended. It describes other participatory rights, including the observer status granted to entities that are not recognized as states by the international community. The same chapter describes various types of meetings of the General Assembly and its voting procedure. It covers the subsidiary bodies of the General Assembly, in particular its six main committees. With regard to the Assembly's powers, Chapter Three focuses on three main roles and responsibilities: the residual responsibility in maintaining international peace and security; the power to generate international law; and the budgetary power. It also briefly examines the parliamentary dynamics or voting blocks and pressure groups in the General Assembly.

Chapter Four deals with the Security Council, which is often referred to as the executive organ of the United Nations. This chapter examines the types of membership, drawing a distinction between permanent and non-permanent members. It explains how states are elected as non-permanent members of the Council. Chapter Four also examines the voting procedure with particular emphasis on the veto power. It describes the format of Security Council meetings and identifies circumstances when its members *may* abstain from voting and when they *must* abstain from voting. This chapter also touches upon the important, yet often neglected and not well-understood role of the Security Council president. The vast powers of the Security Council make up an important part of Chapter Four. A distinction is drawn between compulsory and non-compulsory measures and a further distinction is made between compulsory measures that do not entail any use of force (i.e., sanctions) and measures that may require the use of force. Peacekeeping, peace enforcement, and peacebuilding operations are also part of Chapter Four.

Chapter Five is about the Economic and Social Council (ECOSOC). It briefly reviews its history and membership. It then describes its functioning, including the voting procedures and participation by non-members, types of meetings and sessions, presidency and vice-presidency, and the ECOSOC secretariat. A small portion of Chapter Five is dedicated to ECOSOC's subsidiary bodies such as functional commissions, regional commissions, and standing committees. A larger part of the chapter analyses the ambiguous relationship of ECOSOC with the General Assembly and describes the institutional relationship and reporting lines between ECOSOC and various organizations and agencies that are part of the UN system. It explains the difference between UN Funds and Programmes, specialized agencies such as the World Bank, the IMF, and UNESCO and related organizations, such as the International Atomic Energy Agency and the International Criminal Court. The consultative status of NGOs also features in Chapter Five.

The topic of Chapter Six is the International Court of Justice, the main judicial organ of the United Nations. This judicial body is one of six main organs of the United Nations. However, it is different from other UN organs in many respects. It is not a forum for political deliberations, it is not composed of delegates, and its functions are limited to judicial settlements of disputes. The ICJ is not a supreme court "empowered to pass judgment on the legal rights and duties of all States from a position of superiority and supervision."[26] It is a dispute settlement mechanism that nations may decide to have recourse to on a voluntary basis. Nevertheless, when the ICJ settles disputes brought before it, it generates a body of jurisprudence that is crucial to the development of public international law. The purpose of Chapter Six is to provide a full picture of how the Court operates. In particular, it covers the composition of the Court and the election of its judges. It explains the roles and responsibilities of *ad hoc* judges, the Court's president, and Registry. It also explores the contentious and advisory jurisdictions of the ICJ. Specifically, it analyses various

26 Hugh Thirlway, *The International Court of Justice* (Oxford, UK: Oxford University Press, 2016) at 3.

ways in which states can accept the jurisdiction of the Court or agree to have specific disputes settled by it. It also identifies the limits to the Court's jurisdiction. Chapter Six also canvasses the Court's advisory jurisdiction by identifying UN bodies that can seek advisory opinions and the legal effect that these advisory opinions produce. The last part of Chapter Six focuses on sources of international law applied by the World Court. In domestic legal systems, lawyers are not required to give much thought to the concept of sources of law, because what constitutes law and how legal norms come into existence are obvious. The same question is less evident in international law since there is no parliament or legislature.[27] The power to promulgate legal norms or laws has not been given to any central authority. Hence, the concept of law or sources of law is an important one.

The topic of Chapter Seven is the UN Secretariat, the administrative organ of the United Nations. This last chapter begins by explaining why member states decided to establish the UN Secretariat in New York. It then identifies the roles and responsibilities of the Secretary-General and its staff. An explanation of the confusing hierarchical structure of the UN is an important part of Chapter Seven. In particular, the reader will find information on how the Secretaries-General are appointed and what their conditions of service are. It also explains the difference between various types of UN staff members, including political appointees, staff in the professional and higher categories, staff in the field service category, and staff in the general services and related categories. Chapter Seven describes how UN staff are recruited, what their conditions of service are, what rights and obligations they have, and what privileges and immunities they enjoy. Finally, this chapter explores the dispute resolution mechanisms for work-related conflicts that occasionally arise between the UN and some of its staff.

Although the Trusteeship Council, which is another main organ of the United Nations, played an important role in the history and development of the UN during the colonial era, a separate chapter is

---

27 Hugh Thirlway, *The Sources of International Law* (Oxford, UK: Oxford University Press, 2019) at 2.

not dedicated to it, primarily because this body fell in desuetude by ceasing its activities on 1 November 1994, a month after Palau, the last United Nations Trust Territory, became an independent state.

Chapter 1

HISTORY OF THE UNITED NATIONS

Any narrative that purports to be a historical account of certain events is merely a perspective of the person narrating it. History is constructed from evidential traces of the past. As new sources of information surface, chronicles are revisited, and history is reconstructed. It is therefore natural that different historians and scholars interpret historical data differently and propose several variations of the same event or period. For this reason, in international relations, controversy is the norm and a universally agreed version of important historical events is the exception.

This chapter is not a comprehensive history of the United Nations and even less of international relations; it is a glimpse of the events that gradually shaped the organization, its law, politics, and practice. This chapter is concerned primarily with the history of the organization's central responsibility—the maintenance of peace and security. Other important areas of the UN's work, in particular the work of its multiple funds, programs, specialized agencies, and related organizations are mentioned only in passing.

A. THE CREATION OF THE UNITED NATIONS

Like the League of Nations, the establishment of the United Nations was the initiative of the United States. While the League of Nations was President Wilson's idea, the United Nations came into existence under the leadership of President Franklin D Roosevelt, who had instructed his government to begin researching and exploring global security plans as early as 1939. The United States successfully worked behind the scenes to secure the consent of the USSR and the United Kingdom for the creation of a global peace organization. Six years and five conferences later, the United Nations Organization was born.

1) The First Conference—Arcadia Conference (1941)

The first conference, called "Arcadia," took place between December 1941 and January 1942. Twenty-six governments, including the "Big Four" (United States, USSR, United Kingdom, and China), gathered in Washington, DC, and signed the Declaration by United Nations. In this document, "each government pledge[d] itself to employ its full resources, military or economic, against"[1] the Axis powers and "not to make separate armistice or peace with the enemies."[2] Nations also agreed to "subscribe to a common program of purposes and principles embodied in . . . the Atlantic Charter," which included the "establishment of a wider and permanent system of general security."[3]

The establishment of a permanent international organization, such as the United Nations, to replace the League of Nations was not explicitly envisaged in the United Nations Declaration.[4] It is noteworthy that the adjective "United" in the United Nations as used in the Declaration did not refer to an international organization. The term came from the Atlantic Charter of 1941 and referred to nations *united* in war against the Axis powers.[5] This had a historical significance, because three years later, only states that had declared war on Germany and Japan and had subscribed to the United Nations Declaration were invited to San Francisco to take part in the final conference.

1 Declaration by United Nations (1 January 1942) at para 1.

2 *Ibid* at para 2.

3 *Atlantic Charter* (14 August 1941) at para 8.

4 Benedetto Conforti, *The Law and Practice of the United Nations* (Leiden: Martinus Nijhoff, 2005) at 1.

5 Brian Urquhart, *A Life in Peace and War* (New York: Harper and Row Publishers, 1987) at 93.

2) The Second Conference—Moscow and Tehran Conferences (1943)

It was only in October 1943 at the Moscow Conference that the establishment of an international organization was officially envisaged and its basis defined.[6] The four major allies who participated in the Moscow Conference recognized "the necessity of establishing at the earliest practicable date a general international organization, based on the principle of the sovereign equality of all peace-loving States and open to membership by all such States, large and small, for the maintenance of international peace and security."[7]

The Moscow negotiations continued in Tehran. In November 1943, when the major allies of World War II met in Tehran, they agreed on the American idea of "four policemen," which would require them to act as a global coalition able to deploy military enforcement powers at the head of a world assembly.[8] Each power undertook to keep order within its sphere of influence. The United States was responsible for ensuring peace in the Western Hemisphere. The United Kingdom was to ensure oversight in the British Dominions and in Western Europe. Eastern Europe and Central Asia were assigned to the Soviet Union, whereas China would be responsible for East Asia and the Western Pacific. Under German occupation and with the Vichy regime still in power, France was initially excluded from the group of four; however, at the insistence of British Prime Minister Winston Churchill, the great powers agreed to include France as the fifth member of the group.

3) The Third Conference—Dumbarton Oaks (1944)

The third conference took place at Dumbarton Oaks estate in Washington, DC, in 1944. The purpose of the Dumbarton Oaks conference was to lay the groundwork for the United Nations structure. During this conference, several important issues were decided. In particular, four principal bodies were agreed on, including a General Assembly

---

6 Conforti, above note 4 at 2.

7 The Moscow Declaration on General Security (30 October 1943) at para 4.

8 Norrie MacQueen, *The United Nations, Peace Operations and the Cold War*, 2d ed (New York: Routledge, 2011) at 9.

composed of all the members, a Security Council of eleven members (with five permanent and six elected to hold office for two years), an International Court of Justice, and a Secretariat. An Economic and Social Council was briefly discussed but no mention of trusteeship was made during the Dumbarton Oaks conference. The crux of the agreement reached in Dumbarton Oaks can be summarized as follows.

The Security Council had the primary responsibility for maintaining international peace and security. The plan was to ensure that member states would place armed forces at the disposal of the Security Council so that armed conflicts and acts of aggression could be prevented. The absence of such a force was viewed to be a fatal flaw of the League of Nations. It was also agreed by major powers and proposed to other nations that the General Assembly would study, discuss, and make recommendations in order to promote international cooperation and adjust situations likely to impair welfare. The General Assembly would be empowered to consider problems of cooperation in maintaining peace and security, and disarmament, in its general principles. But it would have no authority to make recommendations on any matter being considered by the Security Council. Moreover, all questions on which action was required had to be referred to the Security Council.

Superpowers were unable to reach a compromise with regard to the voting procedure in the Security Council at Dumbarton Oaks. The Soviet Union wanted permanent members to have an absolute veto power in relation to all matters discussed by the Security Council, even on procedural matters. The Soviets had a legitimate concern that they would be outnumbered in the Security Council and in the General Assembly by Western states and their allies. The United States and the United Kingdom were opposed to the veto. They feared that an absolute veto power would allow the Soviets to abuse it by blocking discussions that pertained to disputes in which the Soviets themselves were involved.

4) The Fourth Conference—Yalta Conference (1945)

In February 1945, the sponsoring powers met in Yalta. In contrast to the Dumbarton Oaks conference where senior diplomats represented states, Yalta was a meeting of the heads of states. The Big Three (United States, United Kingdom, and USSR) agreed on a number of outstanding and new issues, including the current voting formula in the Security Council. One important issue was the organization's membership. The Soviet Union insisted that membership be open only to "peace loving nations," which meant countries that had declared war on the Axis powers before 1 March 1945. Countries that supported the Nazis or remained neutral during the war were not invited to the San Francisco conference to become original members of the organization.

Also on the issue of membership, the Soviet Union asked for two additional seats in the General Assembly for the Soviet Republics of Belarus (formerly Byelorussia) and Ukraine. Since the Soviets had initially asked for sixteen seats, the United States decided to support the request for three seats, subject to the Soviet Union's support for two additional seats for the United States. Russia, Ukraine, and Belarus held the three Soviet seats in the General Assembly. As to the United States, due to constitutional constraints, it could not lawfully designate states that would occupy the two extra seats in the General Assembly. As a result, the United States contented itself with only one seat.

Although the question of trusteeship was extensively discussed, it remained unresolved at the conclusion of the conference in Yalta. The existing mandates from the old League of Nations as well as territories captured from the Axis powers during World War II needed to be administered at least on an interim basis. Nevertheless, Prime Minister Winston Churchill was reluctant to accept any arrangement that could be seen as an interference with the territorial sovereignty of British colonies. Consequently, the only point on which an agreement was reached pertained to the definition of the term "trusteeship," which was defined as "territories mandated under the League of Nations, territories detached from Axis powers and such other territories as any member nation may wish to place in trusteeship."[9] The United States, USSR, and United Kingdom agreed to return to this issue in San Francisco.

---

9 Jean E Krasno, *The United Nations: Confronting the Challenges of a Global Society* (Boulder, CO: Lynne Rienner Publishers, 2004) at 29.

The initial proposal developed in Dumbarton Oaks was amended to reflect the agreements reached in Yalta. The draft document was then circulated among the countries that were invited to meet in San Francisco to finalize the *Charter of the United Nations.*

5) The Fifth and Last Conference—San Francisco Conference (1945)

Fifty nations, 850 delegates, some 2,600 advisers, interpreters, translators, and 2,500 reporters and other observers gathered at the fifth and last conference in San Francisco. The United Nations Conference on International Organization (UNICIO) was a convention of delegations from fifty nations that took place from 25 April to 26 June 1945. The conference was organized into several bodies. At the very top was the Steering Committee, composed of the heads of delegations. This body took decisions in relation to major principles and policy. A two-thirds majority was required to reach a decision. An Executive Committee of fourteen heads of delegations (including the five permanent members of the Security Council) was formed to make recommendations to the Steering Committee. Four commissions were established to consider four different sections of the *UN Charter*. Commission I worked on the general purposes of the organization, its founding principles, the Secretariat, and amendments to the *UN Charter*. Commission II handled the powers and responsibilities of the General Assembly. Commission III dealt with the Security Council. Commission IV worked on a draft Statute of the International Court of Justice. In addition, each committee had twelve technical subcommittees. A coordinating committee responsible for the preparation of the final text was also established (please see the diagram on pages 30–31).

During the conference, a previously unresolved issue arose: the proposed *UN Charter* had no system for administering territories placed under United Nations trusteeship. After much debate, it was recommended that the United Nations would promote the progressive development of the peoples of trust territories towards independence or self-government.

Although the founding members of the United Nations organization debated and negotiated a significant number of issues, admittedly, the veto right of permanent members of the Security Council was the most heated debate. Smaller states considered the veto right to be inconsistent with the principle of sovereign equality of all members. Smaller powers also feared that if one of the "Big Five" threatened the peace, the Security Council would be paralyzed by the veto of that same superpower. Although this was a reasonable concern, it did not gain any traction, because at that time the great powers had already agreed that they would not sign up to any arrangement that did not include a veto power. They were adamant that the right to veto a decision made by the Security Council was essential to their ability to maintain world peace. As this became a decisive point, the smaller powers eventually conceded in the interest of not compromising the establishment of the United Nations.

Another point decided in San Francisco was the jurisdiction of the International Court of Justice. Nations disagreed as to whether the Court was to have a compulsory or optional jurisdiction. Many states wanted the jurisdiction to extend to all member states whereas others insisted that the Court should be competent to adjudicate cases brought before it by member states that voluntarily adhered to its jurisdiction. The conference decided that member nations would not be compelled to accept the Court's jurisdiction but could voluntarily declare their acceptance of compulsory jurisdiction.

As soon as a consensus was reached on all of the issues, the Coordinating Committee began working on the final draft. The fruit of these laborious efforts was a document containing 111 articles divided into nineteen chapters. On 25 June 1945, the final draft of the *UN Charter* was put to a vote. Given the extraordinarily important nature of the document, nations agreed to depart from the customary method of voting. Instead of showing hands, delegates rose and remained standing. As soon as it was announced that the *UN Charter* had been passed unanimously, approximately 5,000 people gave a standing ovation.

The following day, delegates gathered around the table on which they were to sign the *UN Charter* and the Statute of the International Court of Justice. As a symbolic gesture, and in recognition of its enduring fight against aggression, China was asked to affix its signature first. The USSR, the United Kingdom, and France followed. Then, the remaining founding states proceeded in alphabetical order, with the United States signing last as the host nation.

UNITED NATIONS CONFERENCE ON INTERNATIONAL ORGANIZATION (SAN FRANCISCO CONFERENCE)

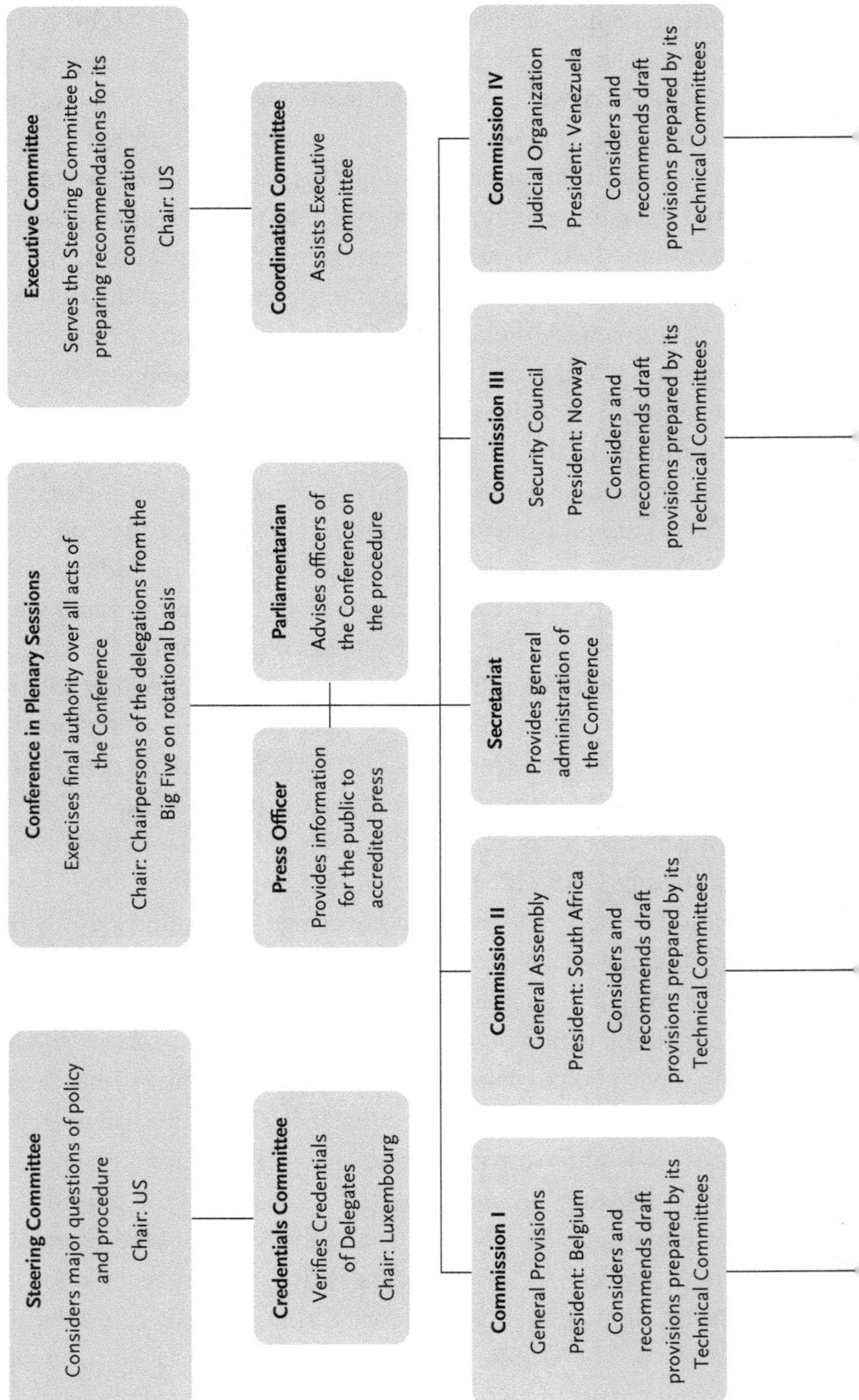

Technical Committee 1
Prepares draft provisions on Preamble, Purposes and Principles

Technical Committee 2
Prepares draft provisions on membership, principal organs, methods of amendment, and the Secretariat of the UN

Technical Committee 1
Prepares draft provisions on the structure and procedures of the General Assembly of the UN

Technical Committee 2
Prepares draft provisions on the political and security functions of the UN

Technical Committee 3
Prepares draft provisions on arrangements for international economic and social cooperation

Technical Committee 4
Prepares draft provisions on principles and mechanism of a system for dependent territories placed under trusteeship.

Technical Committee 1
Prepares draft provisions on the structure and procedures of the Security Council of the UN

Technical Committee 2
Prepares draft provisions on methods for peaceful settlement of disputes

Technical Committee 3
Prepares draft provisions of the prevention and suppression of aggression

Technical Committee 4
Prepares draft provisions on regional arrangements

Technical Committee 1
Prepares draft provisions on the International Court of Justice

Technical Committee 2
Prepares draft provisions on legal questions connected with the functionning of the UN

UN PHOTO/MCLAIN

The San Francisco Conference, 25 April–26 June 1945: China Signs the United Nations Charter *(26 June 1945). Permission for use granted by The United Nations.*

B. THE HISTORY OF THE UNITED NATIONS

Every major political event that occurred after the creation of the United Nations had some impact on the organization. The opposite is also true; hardly any part of the world escapes the influence of the United Nations. It would have been an impossible task to provide a comprehensive account of all-important historical events during the relevant period in a few pages. The principal challenge faced in this part concerned the degree of importance to be accorded to specific events. Inevitably, a difficult choice had to be made when deciding which events would be mentioned or discussed and which ones would be left out. Often, political developments or events that on the surface had little to do with the United Nations are explained because they had a great impact on the organization's evolvement and activities. The history of the United Nations is divided into chronological periods that correspond to the mandates of nine Secretaries-General.

1) Period Under Trygve Lie's Leadership: 1945–1952

The first Secretary-General of the United Nations was Trygve Lie, a Norwegian labour lawyer and politician.[10] Lie served as Norway's foreign minister from 1940 to 1945 while the Norwegian government was in exile in London. He earned a reputation as a pragmatic diplomat, which may have played a role in the decision to appoint him on 1 February 1946 as the chief administrative official of the United Nations. In his memoirs, Trygve Lie recollects that he had not applied for or expressed an interest in the position of the Secretary-General. Therefore, he was very surprised to learn that the Security Council had recommended his candidacy to the General Assembly:

> I had been nothing less than catapulted into the Secretary-Generalship of this new international organization, to preserve peace and promote progress in a world beset by unrest, poverty, and great power rivalry. It was a challenge beyond my wildest dreams; but it was a nightmare as well. I hardly dared to think of the days ahead. Instead, I asked myself again and again, why had this awesome task fallen to a labor lawyer from Norway?[11]

The reason this task had fallen to Trygve Lie is simple and unflattering. As was the case for most Secretaries-General succeeding him, Lie was appointed not because he was the most suitable candidate for

---

10 UNGAOR, 1st Sess, 20th Plen Mtg, UN Doc A/PV.20 (1946) and unnumbered resolution in UN Doc A/64.

11 Trygve Lie, *In the Cause of Peace: Seven Years at the United Nations* (New York: Macmillan, 1954) at 17.

the post but rather because he was the least objectionable candidate to the permanent members of the Security Council. In fact, "there was no consideration of who might be the best qualified for the job."[12] The preferred candidate for the position of the Secretary-General was the Canadian diplomat Lester B Pearson, who subsequently became the prime minister of Canada. Pearson's nomination was blocked by the Soviet Union because, as a Canadian, he was perceived to be too close to the United States.[13] The USSR wanted an Eastern European Secretary-General. In the end, the Security Council had to reach a compromise and identify a candidate agreeable to all. Trygve Lie happened to be the least objectionable candidate at the time because he was from a political and geographic background that both the United States and USSR could live with. "Lie was regarded by both sides as politically a safe bet"[14] and was therefore appointed as the Secretary-General. Sir Brian Urquhart, who was appointed as Lie's personal assistant, recalls that Lie was not a suitable Secretary-General. He describes Lie as an unsophisticated man who relied more on peasant shrewdness than on intellectual effort or hard diplomatic work.[15]

a) Iranian Imbroglio (1946)

The *Charter of the United Nations* envisioned an international system in which the United Nations played a central role. Multilateralism was a condition *sine qua non* for the adequate functioning of the newly established world order. The organization's purposes, principles, and rules revolve around this fundamental requirement. The doctrine of unilateralism and the pursuit of imperialism were notions inconsistent with the basic scheme of the *UN Charter*. Unfortunately, the practice that emerged significantly differed from the intended purpose. The superpowers exhibited distrust towards each other and jealously guarded their sovereignty, unwilling to empower the newly created organization. Permanent members of the Security Council did not intend to give any significant role to the UN and even less

12 Urquhart, above note 5 at 99.

13 Lie, above note 11 at 16.

14 Urquhart, above note 5 at 99.

15 *Ibid* at 100.

to its Secretary-General. For the United States and USSR, the UN was merely a forum for meetings, discussions, and debates. The two superpowers were using the UN as a stage to sway public opinion on specific political topics.

The UN Secretary-General's first confrontation with the superpowers occurred during the Iranian crisis. One of Trygve Lie's first tasks was to prompt the withdrawal of Soviet troops from Iran. During World War II, the Allied forces had placed their troops in Iran to ensure a supply route for the Soviet Union and to prevent German troops from reaching its oil fields. In a tripartite treaty of 1942, it had been agreed that both sides would withdraw their troops from Iran within six months of the end of hostilities. Although the Western countries complied with their treaty obligations, the Soviet Union kept delaying the evacuation of its troops. With the assistance of the United States, Iran managed to include this point on the agenda of the Security Council. The Council scheduled a debate on the Iranian question, which led to the first walkout by a Soviet delegate from the Security Council. Before the debate took place, Moscow and Tehran had resolved their dispute by agreeing on a specific date of withdrawal. As a result, the USSR requested the removal of the Iranian question from the Security Council's agenda. The majority of the Security Council members voted against this proposal. They were determined to pursue the matter in order to set an embarrassing precedent for the Soviet Union. Trygve Lie agreed with the Soviet position, seeing no point in maintaining a moot issue on the agenda of the Security Council. He circulated to the members of the Security Council a memorandum prepared by his legal counsel in which he argued that the issue had become moot and its continued presence on the Security Council's agenda was unwarranted.[16] Some member states protested, arguing that the Secretary-General had no right to make comments on political

16 UNSCOR, 1st Year, 33rd Mtg, UN Doc S/PV.33 (1946); see also *The Iranian Question*, SC Res 2 (1946), UNSCOR, 1st Year, UN Doc S/RES/2 (1946) 1, *The Iranian Question*, SC Res 3 (1946), UNSCOR, 1st Year, UN Doc S/RES/3 (1946) 4, *The Iranian Question*, SC Res 5 (1946). UNSCOR, 1st Year, UN Doc S/RES/5 (1946) 3.

issues.[17] In his memoirs, Lie recollected that when he handed out the memorandum to the president of the Security Council (the Chinese delegate) in the Security Council hall, he indignantly ignored him and refused to take the document.[18] Lie's seemingly innocent and well-intentioned action was the first political initiative undertaken by a UN Secretary-General. Although it engendered a lot of debate in the Security Council, it also set an important precedent that led to further developments in the Secretary-General's prerogatives.

b) Korean War (1950–1953)

Trygve Lie had another run-in with a superpower during the Korean War, this time upsetting the Soviets. In June 1950, North Korea invaded South Korea. During this period, the Soviet Union was boycotting Security Council meetings because the majority of member states of the UN were refusing to recognize the communist government in Beijing as the legitimate representative of China. The USSR had erroneously assumed that its presence in the Security Council was required for any resolution to be adopted. As a result, it did not attend an important session of the Security Council, during which Trygve Lie declared the North Korean aggression against South Korea as a threat to international peace. Based on Lie's declaration, the Security Council adopted a resolution authorizing UN armed forces, consisting primarily of US troops, to assist the Republic of Korea. As the Soviet representative was absent during the vote, the Soviet Union did not cast a vote. The resolution was nevertheless adopted without the Soviet participation. Despite vigorous protests by the USSR, the majority of the members of the Security Council concluded that a permanent member's absence from the meeting room could not prevent the Security Council from discharging its functions, an interpretation that still prevails.[19] The USSR chastised the Secretary-General

17 Andrew W Cordier & Wilder Foote, *Public Papers of the Secretaries General of the United Nations*, vol 1 (New York: Columbia University Press, 1969) at 40; see also Lie, above note 11 at 85.

18 *Ibid* at 83.

19 The International Court of Justice endorsed this view in *Legal Consequences for States of the Continued Presence of South Africa in Namibia (South West Africa)*

for what it believed to be taking sides. It even vetoed Lie's re-election for a second term.[20] The Americans threatened to do the same in relation to any other candidate.[21] To circumvent the Soviet veto and to prevent an impasse, the General Assembly extended Lie's term for three years without formal re-election.[22] The USSR refused to deal with Lie as the Secretary-General for the remainder of his mandate. It addressed its letters and other communications to the Secretariat rather than to the Secretary-General.

The Korean War provided incontrovertible proof that collective security and a cold war were incompatible. Unfortunately, the Cold War shaped the foreign policy of the United States and USSR and dominated international relations for forty-five years. During this period, the Security Council was practically paralyzed.

c) Containment[23] and Marshall Plan[24]

In May 1945, when Germany formally surrendered to the Red Army, the USSR quickly absorbed the Baltic states of Estonia, Latvia, and Lithuania—territory that Germany had occupied from 1941 to 1945.[25] Communism soon expanded to Bulgaria and Romania. In the fall of 1945, a Soviet-backed regime had taken control of Poland. It was only a matter of time before the USSR had absorbed into its sphere of influence Hungary and the former Czechoslovakia. The United

notwithstanding Security Council Resolution 276 (1970), Advisory Opinion, [1971] ICJ Rep 16 at para 22.

20 Lie, above note 11 at 376.

21 *Ibid* at 379–81.

22 *Continuation in office of the Secretary-General of the United Nations*, GA Res 492 (V), UNGAOR, 5th Sess, UN Doc A/RES/492(V) (1950).

23 See, generally, Henry Kissinger, *Nuclear Weapons and Foreign Policy* (New York: Harper Brothers, 1957).

24 See, generally, William I Hitcock, "The Marshall Plan and the Creation of the West" in Melvin P Leffler & Odd Arne Westad, eds, *The Cambridge History of the Cold War, Volume 1: Origins* (Cambridge: Cambridge University Press, 2010) at 154–74.

25 See Lauri Malksoo, *Illegal Annexation and State Continuity: The Case of the Incorporation of the Baltic States by the USSR* (Leiden: Martinus Nijhoff Publishers, 2003); see also John Hiden, Vahur Made & David J Smith, eds, *The Baltic Question During the Cold War* (New York: Routledge, 2008).

States and Western Europe perceived the positioning of Soviet military power in Eastern Europe as a serious threat to Western Europe's security. The United States government was particularly concerned with this rapid expansion of the Soviet empire and decided to reverse this trend. It developed a plan to halt the expansion of communism and experimented with Greece and Turkey,[26] where the USSR was attempting to replace the pro-Western governments with regimes favourable to communism. President Truman requested that the US Congress approve $400 million in economic and military aid for the two nations.[27] This intervention proved effective and both Turkey and Greece remained in the Western sphere of influence. This experiment led to the development of a broader plan known as the "Containment Policy," which entailed sending financial aid to countries where the expansion of communism and a Soviet takeover was a real threat. Although the real purpose of the aid was to contain communism within its current borders, the announced aim of the European Recovery Plan, also known as the Marshall Plan, was purely humanitarian. The Marshall Plan had an immense impact on Western European industries. From a political viewpoint, the plan produced the expected result of containing the expansion of communism in Western Europe. However, the economic progress achieved by the Marshall Plan did not resolve the political or ideological conflict. The relationship between the Soviet Union and the United States worsened. For the United Nations, this meant a clear division of the world into Eastern and Western blocs based almost exclusively on ideological differences. The East–West rivalry dominated most aspects of the UN's history and of international politics for forty-five years.

d) Western Domination of UN Politics

Before the outbreak of World War II, there were six great powers: the United States, the USSR, France, Great Britain, Germany, and Japan. The result of the Second World War was a drastic decline of the British and French empires and the collapse of the German and

---

26 Hitcock, above note 24 at 155–56.

27 Lie, above note 11 at 104.

Japanese powers. This marked the end of the European era and the rise to dominance of two superpowers, the United States and the Soviet Union. The United States had a distinct advantage over the Soviet Union. Whereas the war had cost the USSR 27 million lives (approximately 10 percent of its population) and had wiped out a significant part of its prewar wealth, already crippled by communism, it had almost doubled the US economy and had transformed it into the world's manufacturing and technological leader of the time.[28] This superiority of the West over the Eastern Bloc was also initially reflected in international politics.

Throughout the 1950s, the Western Bloc dominated the United Nations. The United States and its allies had the majority of the votes in the Security Council and the General Assembly. If a resolution was vetoed by the USSR in the Security Council, it would be passed, where possible, before the General Assembly. For instance, in 1950, the USSR was blocking any decision by the Security Council with regard to proposed measures against North Korea for its armed aggression against South Korea. Initially, the Security Council had been able to recommend to the members of the United Nations to "furnish such assistance to the Republic of Korea as may be necessary to repel the armed attack and to restore international peace and security in the area."[29] As we have already seen, this resolution passed only because the USSR was absent from the Security Council during the vote. In response to this resolution, the representative of the USSR returned to the Security Council and began casting negative votes on any resolution condemning North Korea's defiance of the principles of the *UN Charter*. To overcome this strategy, the United States convinced the General Assembly to take on a subsidiary responsibility with regard to international peace and security. Specifically, where the Security Council fails to exercise its primary responsibility for the maintenance of international peace and security as a result of a veto by one of its permanent members, the issue is brought before the General Assembly for a

---

28 David S Painter, *The Cold War: An International History* (New York: Routledge, 1999) at 5.

29 *Complaint of aggression against the Republic of Korea*, SC Res 83 (1950), UNSCOR, 5th Year, UN Doc S/RES/83 (1950).

decision on behalf of the Council.[30] This General Assembly resolution became known as the *Uniting for Peace* resolution.

2) Period Under Dag Hammarskjöld's Leadership: 1953–1961

After the USSR refused to deal with Lie as the Secretary-General, and after the United States accused him of recruiting communists, Trygve Lie resigned in November 1952.[31] To replace him, the Security Council recommended the appointment of Dag Hammarskjöld, the son of a former Prime Minister of Sweden and the chairman of the Swedish delegation to the General Assembly.[32] Just like Trygve Lie, Dag Hammarskjöld had neither lobbied nor applied for the position of the Secretary-General. He reluctantly accepted the appointment, writing in a cablegram to the president of the Security Council, "With a strong feeling of personal insufficiency, I hesitate to accept candidature, but I do not feel I could refuse the task imposed upon me." Trygve Lie had warned his successor that he was about to take over "the most impossible job on earth."

> Any Secretary-General will find it so if he tries to be the kind of officer that I think the San Francisco Charter envisaged. Should his [Dag Hammarskjöld's] conception be the same as mine, he will find

30 In November 1950, the General Assembly adopted Resolution 377 A (V) *Uniting for Peace*, UN Doc A/RES/377A(V) (1950). This resolution was a result of the USSR's practice of vetoing decisions by the Security Council, especially with regard to proposed measures against North Korea. To overcome the impasse in the Security Council caused by the East–West rivalry, the General Assembly, at the initiative of the United States and its allies, adopted the *Uniting for Peace* resolution, granting itself a subsidiary responsibility with regard to maintaining international peace and security. The purpose of this resolution was to ensure that where the Security Council failed to exercise its primary responsibility for the maintenance of international peace and security as a result of a veto vote by one of its permanent members, the General Assembly would seize itself of the matter.

31 For Trygve Lie's resignation speech, see UNGAOR, 7th Sess, 392d Plen Mtg, UN Doc A/PV.392 (1952).

32 *Appointment of the Secretary-General of the United Nations*, UNGAOR, 7th Sess, 392d Plen Mtg, UN Doc A/PV.423 (1952).

> it impossible to avoid the displeasure of one or more of the greater or smaller states during the years to come. He will be the target of criticism from right, left and center.[33]

Lie had correctly predicted Hammarskjöld's fate as the Secretary-General. Although Hammarskjöld was a determined and courageous leader, he was unable to avoid the displeasure of the superpowers. Hammarskjöld knew well that such confrontations were risky and could result in difficulties. Nevertheless, he did not hesitate to confront the superpowers on major political issues.

a) First Official Mission of a UN Secretary-General

Arguably, the United Nations experienced its most apparent transformation during Dag Hammarskjöld's mandate. Hammarskjöld tried to expand the political powers of the Secretary-General. When the Security Council requested Hammarskjöld to "consider ... the best ways of strengthening the Truce Supervision Organization" relating to the armistice agreement between Jordan and Israel,[34] he offered to be the mediator during the conference between these two states. A Secretary-General had never been requested or allowed to undertake any political function. Member states did not feel the need to change this practice and therefore summarily rejected the Secretary-General's offer. This, however, did not discourage Hammarskjöld from trying to broaden the political powers of his office. He continued volunteering his good offices. His perseverance paid off when, during the Korean War, the Chinese forces captured, tried, and convicted eleven American pilots who were under UN command on charges of spying. No government could secure the release of the American prisoners. The General Assembly requested Hammarskjöld to negotiate the release of American airmen.[35] This request marked the first time a

---

33 Lie, above note 11 at 417.

34 *The Palestine Question*, SC Res 101 (1953), UNSCOR, 8th Year, UN Doc S/3139/Rev.2 (1953) 1.

35 *Complaint of detention and imprisonment of United Nations military personnel in violation of the Korean Armistice Agreement*, GA Res 906 (IX), UNGAOR, 9th Sess, UN Doc A/RES/906(IX) (1954).

Secretary-General of the United Nations was specifically asked to play an important political role by a member state.

The request was an extraordinarily challenging task because the Chinese courts had already convicted the American soldiers under China's national law. Any attempt to secure their release or to vacate the verdict could have been perceived as interference in the internal affairs of a sovereign state. In addition, Western member states of the United Nations had antagonized the government of the People's Republic of China by not recognizing the communist government as the legitimate representative of China. There was no official or formal channel of communication between the United Nations and the Chinese government.

Despite the extremely delicate nature of this mandate, Dag Hammarskjöld agreed to mediate the release of the American prisoners of war. Without offering anything in exchange to the Chinese Government, Hammarskjöld managed to convince the Chinese authorities to release the prisoners.[36] This historic success was decisive in broadening the political role of future Secretaries-General.

b) Appearance of the First UN Peacekeeping Force

Immediately after this successful mission, Dag Hammarskjöld faced another major challenge, which marked the beginning of a watershed period in UN history. In July 1956, Egypt nationalized the Suez Canal Company and pressed for evacuation of the joint British–French enterprise that had owned and operated the Suez Canal since its construction in 1869. In October 1956, with the blessing of France and the United Kingdom, Israeli forces launched an attack on Egypt and occupied the Sinai and Gaza Strip. British and French troops followed suit and took control of the Suez Canal. The Security Council was unable to adopt any decision owing to the vetoes of France and the United Kingdom. The matter was then referred to the General Assembly under the *Uniting for Peace* resolution. The Assembly established

36 Brian E Urquhart, "The Evolution of the Secretary-General" in Simon Chesterman, ed, *Secretary or General: The UN Secretary-General in World Politics* (New York: Cambridge University Press, 2007) 15 at 19–20.

the United Nations Emergency Force (UNEF) to secure and supervise the cessation of hostilities.[37] Following the dispatch of the Emergency Force to the area, the French, British, and Israeli forces withdrew.

UNEF was the first armed UN peacekeeping force. It represented an important innovation. Although the UN had already deployed several observer missions prior to 1956, their mandates were limited to observing and monitoring ceasefires after an agreement to cease all hostilities had already been concluded.[38] UNEF was not a mere observer mission. Its deployment occurred before the parties had reached an agreement to cease the hostilities. This was a new type of UN-led peacekeeping operation.

c) Shift in the Balance of Power

The Western domination of the United Nations continued during the mandate of Dag Hammarskjöld. As U Thant, the third Secretary-General, wrote in his memoirs:

> [I]n the early years of the United Nations, it was obvious that whenever the Security Council was deadlocked over a question because of Big-Power disagreement, the United States was able to muster the required majority in the General Assembly. For a decade, when the membership of the United Nations did not exceed sixty, there were more than forty members that generally supported the United States position on major issues.[39]

---

37 The idea to create UNEF is attributed to Canada's then Minister of Foreign Affairs Lester B Pearson, who received the Nobel Prize for it in 1957. It was Pearson who had suggested the actual notion of the UN-led peacekeeping force to the special emergency session of the General Assembly on 2 November 1956. In his speech to the General Assembly, Pearson argued for "a truly international peace and police force ... large enough to keep these borders at peace while a political settlement is being worked out."

38 The United Nations Truce Supervision Organization (UNTSO), formed in 1948 to supervise the truce in Palestine in the aftermath of the Arab–Israeli war, and the United Nations Military Observer Group in India and Pakistan (UNMOGIP), established in 1949 to supervise the ceasefires between India and Pakistan, are examples of such missions.

39 U Thant, *View from the UN* (London: David & Charles Publishing, 1978) at 34.

Decolonization changed the composition of the UN membership as well as the character and the agenda of the General Assembly, bringing to numerical majority the emerging Third World. As of 1955, the United States could no longer easily secure the required two-thirds majority in the General Assembly.[40] The year 1960 marked an important shift in the balance of power. The leader of the USSR, Nikita Khrushchev "realized that the emergent Third World provided a major bargaining counter in achieving a balance between the two superpower groups.... [H]e had seen how much political capital could be made from the split between the west and these new nations over the issue of colonialism."[41] Hence, during his 1960 address to the General Assembly, Khrushchev proposed the adoption of a declaration concerning the decolonization of the remaining dependent territories.[42] Three weeks after this speech, Khrushchev had his famous outburst in the General Assembly during which he took off his shoe and pounded it on the desk.[43] Although the decolonization movement was already well underway since the 1940s, Khrushchev's address in the General Assembly had "struck a spark among the representatives of the former colonies."[44] In September 1960, the United Nations admitted seventeen new members, the biggest increase in membership in any one year.[45] Former colonies were emerging as independent states

---

40 *Ibid.*

41 Kurt Waldheim, *In the Eye of the Storm: The Memoirs of Kurt Waldheim* (London: George Weidenfeld & Nicolson, 1985) at 28.

42 UNGAOR, 15th Sess, 869th Plen Mtg, UN Doc A/PV.869 (1960) at 68–84.

43 Khrushchev lost his temper when the head of the Philippines' delegation stated that the Soviet Union's domination of Eastern Europe was not better than colonialism or Western imperialism. Khrushchev retorted, calling the Filipino diplomat "a jerk, a stooge and a lackey of imperialism." He then banged his shoe on the desk.

44 Waldheim, above note 41 at 28.

45 Because of this increase in membership, the *Charter of the United Nations* was amended three times between 1963 and 1973. The first amendment expanded the membership of the Security Council from eleven to fifteen and increased the number of votes necessary to pass a resolution from seven to nine; it also expanded the membership of the Economic and Social Council (ECOSOC) from eighteen to twenty-seven. The second amendment corrected the amendment procedures themselves in order to reflect the increased size of the

and seeking membership in the UN. By 1961, the UN had more than doubled its membership (from 51 to 104 states) within sixteen years.[46] As a result "[t]he balance of power ha[d] fallen into the hands of the newly admitted nonaligned and uncommitted states."[47] A large number of these newly formed states, unwilling to become proxy battlefields of the United States or the USSR, sided with neither Eastern nor Western blocs. An essentially bipartite parliamentary structure was giving way to a multipartite system. This was the beginning of a new era in UN politics. The East–West divide had to make space for a new type of rivalry between the industrialized and developing states.

d) The Conflict in the Congo Transforms UN Peacekeeping

Although decolonization was generally a positive development, it nevertheless produced some perverse consequences. It resulted in many civil wars nurturing proxy conflicts between the two main rivals in the Cold War. The United States and the Soviet Union were involved in most armed conflicts, usually supporting opposing factions for ideological reasons. The Congolese crisis of 1960 was one of many such unfortunate situations. The present-day Democratic Republic of the Congo was a former Belgian colony. In June 1960, under the leadership of Patrice Lumumba—a political leader and the first democratically elected president of the country—the Congo declared independence. The former colony was unprepared for independence because Belgian colonialism was very exploitative. Its primary goal was commercial profit for colonial investors through exploitation of natural resources. Colonial powers generally, but Belgium in particular, did not believe in transmitting expertise. According to Secretary-General U Thant, "there were at that time only seventeen

---

Council. The new rule required nine (instead of seven) members to support a call for a General Conference of member states for the purposes of reviewing the *UN Charter*. The third amendment further increased the membership of ECOSOC from twenty-seven to its current size of fifty-four.

46 Thomas G Weiss, David P Forsythe & Roger A Coate, *The United Nations and Changing World Politics*, 3d ed (Boulder, CO: Westview, 2001) at 263.

47 Thant, above note 39 at 35.

Congolese university graduates and not a single doctor or engineer.[48] Under the colonial regime, no African could enlist as an officer in the army or hold important positions in the administration. Thus, the newly established country had no elite to form a competent government. Not surprisingly, in the days that followed the declaration of independence, civil unrest broke out. Belgium immediately sent its troops to the Congo, without the agreement of the Congolese Government, under the pretext of restoring law and order. Patrice Lumumba, acting on behalf of the Congolese Government, sought the assistance of the United Nations against the Belgian aggression. In July 1960, the Security Council established the United Nations Operation in the Congo (Opération des Nations Unies au Congo, ONUC).[49]

The initial mandate of ONUC was to ensure the withdrawal of Belgian forces. It was subsequently broadened to include maintaining the territorial integrity and political independence of the Congo, preventing the occurrence of civil war and securing the removal of all foreign military, paramilitary, and advisory personnel not under the United Nations Command, and all mercenaries. This was considerable progress in comparison with UNEF, whose troops were authorized to fire only in self-defence. ONUC troops were authorized to use force in order to implement their mandate. ONUC was the first peacekeeping mission to be based entirely within the borders of one state. This was yet another type of peace operation established during Dag Hammarskjöld's term.

---

48 *Ibid* at 104.

49 *The Congo Question*, SC Res 143 (1960), UNESCOR, 15th Year, UN Doc S/4387 (1960), wherein the Council authorized the "Secretary-General to take the necessary steps, in consultation with the Government of the Republic of the Congo, to provide the Government with such military assistance as might be necessary until, through that Government's efforts with United Nations technical assistance, the national security forces might be able, in the opinion of the Government, to meet fully their tasks." Two subsequent resolutions, 161 (1961) of 21 February 1961 and 169 (1961) of 24 November 1961, expanded the mandate of the mission, allowing the UN troops to use force if necessary to prevent clashes or to detain foreign military and paramilitary personnel and mercenaries. The latter resolution was adopted in response to the murder of thirteen Italian airmen working in ONUC.

ONUC also marked a milestone in the history of United Nations peacekeeping in terms of the responsibilities it was required to assume, the size of its operational area, and the number of personnel involved. The peacekeeping force comprised approximately 20,000 military personnel. ONUC was one of the first triumphs of the United Nations. It succeeded in suppressing a secession attempt in the Congolese province of Katanga. After the Katanga province had been reintegrated into the national territory of the Congo, ONUC began withdrawing.

e) Sudden Death of Dag Hammarskjöld (1961)

During the last year of Dag Hammarskjöld's mandate, "the Soviet Union had been boycotting the Secretary General, treating him as functioning illegally, mainly because of Hammarskjöld's interpretation and active implementation of the Security Council resolutions on the Congo."[50] "Nikita Khrushchev believed that Hammarskjöld was acting in the Congo on behalf of Western interests,"[51] and that the United Nations had to withdraw from the Congo after the assassination of Patrice Lumumba in 1961. The USSR was also blaming the UN for Lumumba's assassination,[52] demanding Hammarskjöld's resignation. Khrushchev wanted the position of the Secretary-General to "be replaced by a troika: three equal Secretaries General—one representing the East, one the West, and one representing nonaligned countries."[53] The practice in the Security Council had already demonstrated that if this recommendation were to be implemented, the entire system would be brought to a standstill because three heads of equal rank representing different ideologies would likely disagree on every serious political issue. This was the type of deadlock that had paralyzed the Security Council.

---

50 Thant, above note 39 at 3.

51 *Ibid* at 4.

52 In his memoirs, U Thant pondered whether the UN peacekeeping troops turned a blind eye to Lumumba's arrest and murder. "To my knowledge, there was no rational explanation why ONUC troops failed to intervene [when they saw Lumumba being placed on a lorry and taken away]." *Ibid* at 122.

53 *Ibid* at 4.

In a speech that triggered a standing ovation, the Secretary-General responded the same day to the Soviet demand during the plenary meeting of the General Assembly. He explained his refusal to step down as follows:

> I said the other day that I would not wish to continue to serve as Secretary-General one day longer than such continued service was considered to be in the best interests of the Organization. The statement this morning seems to indicate that the Soviet Union finds it impossible to work with the present Secretary-General. This may seem to provide a strong reason why I should resign. However, the Soviet Union has also made it clear that if the present Secretary-General were to resign now, it would not wish to elect a new incumbent but insist on an arrangement which ... would make it impossible to maintain an effective executive. By resigning I would, therefore at the present difficult and dangerous juncture throw the Organization to the winds. I have no right to do so because I have a responsibility to all those Member States for which the Organization is of decisive importance—a responsibility which overrides all other considerations. It is not the Soviet Union or indeed any other Big Power who need the United Nations for their protection: it is all the others. In this sense, the Organization is first of all their Organization, and I deeply believe in the wisdom with which they will be able to use it and guide it. I shall remain in my post during the term of my office as a servant of the Organization in the interest of all those other nations, as long as they wish me to do so. In this context the representative of the Soviet Union spoke of courage. It is very easy to resign. It is not so easy to stay on. It is very easy to bow to the wishes of a Big Power. It is another matter to resist. As is well to all members of this Assembly, I have done so before on many occasions and in many directions. If it is the wish of those nations who see in the Organization their best protection in the present world, I shall now do so again.[54]

---

54 UNGAOR, 15th Sess, 883d Plen Mtg, UN Doc A/PV.883 (1960).

On 18 September 1961, the Secretary-General died in a fatal airplane crash while on mission in the Congo. Recent reports suggest that this was not an accident but a planned assassination.[55] However, there may still be insufficient evidence to corroborate this version.[56] Hammarskjöld—the most venerable Secretary-General of the United Nations—is remembered as a true visionary.

3) Period Under U Thant's Leadership: 1961–1971

Picked to succeed Dag Hammarskjöld was U Thant, Burma's (present-day Myanmar) permanent delegate to the United Nations.[57] U Thant was a devout Buddhist, which is said to have shaped his worldview and ethical principles.[58] He had an unassuming demeanour and the amazing ability to remain composed in most extreme situations.[59] U Thant inherited the post during the most turbulent period of the Cold War.

---

55 Emma Graham-Harrison, Andreas Rocksen & Mads Brügger, "RAF veteran admitted 1961 killing of UN secretary general" *The Guardian* (12 January 2019), online: www.theguardian.com/world/2019/jan/12/raf-veteran-admitted-killing-un-secretary-general-dag-hammarskjold-in-1961#:~:text=New%20evidence%20has%20emerged%20linking,simply%20as%20a%20Belgian%20pilot.

56 The Hammarskjöld Commission, *Report of the Commission of Inquiry on whether the evidence now available would justify the United Nations in reopening its inquiry into the death of Secretary-General Dag Hammarskjöld, pursuant to General Assembly Res 1759 (XVII) of 26 October 1962*, UNGAOR, 68th Sess, UN Doc A/68/800 (2014); see also Colum Lynch, "U.N. to Probe Whether Iconic Secretary-General Was Assassinated" Foreign Policy (1 August 2016); Susan Williams, *Who Killed Hammarskjöld?: The UN, the Cold War and White Supremacy in Africa* (London: C Hurst & Co Publishers, 2011); see also *Report of the Independent Panel of Experts established pursuant to General Assembly Res 69/246*, UNGAOR, 70th Sess, UN Doc A/70/132 (2015).

57 U, pronounced [oo], is not a first name, but an honorary title equivalent to mister in Burmese. U Thant was initially appointed as Acting Secretary-General in *Appointment of an Acting Secretary-General*, GA Res 1640 (XVI), UNGAOR, 60th Sess, UN Doc A/RES/1640 (XVI) (1961) 64. He was appointed as Secretary-General in *Appointment of the Secretary-General of the United Nations*, GA Res 1771 (XVII), UNGAOR, 70th Sess, UN Doc A/RES/1771 (XVII) (1962) 72.

58 A Walter Dorn, "U Thant: Buddhism in Action" in Kent J Kille, ed, *The UN Secretary-General and Moral Authority: Ethics and Religion in International Leadership* (Washington, DC: Georgetown University Press, 2007) at 143.

59 *Ibid* at 150.

Indeed, in late 1961, the German Democratic Republic put up the Berlin Wall—the symbol of the East–West divide and the world was on the verge of a nuclear war between the United States and the USSR.

a) The Cuban Missile Crisis (1961)

During U Thant's mandate, the world faced the most hazardous turning point it had ever witnessed—the Cuban missile crisis. This incident began evolving with the failed invasion of the Bay of Pigs. In an attempt to topple Fidel Castro, who had overthrown the dictator Fulgencio Batista in January 1959, the United States devised a plan to invade Cuba without a direct involvement. The US government trained some 1,500 exiled Cubans as paramilitary troops and sent them to invade Cuba, rally the Cuban population, and overthrow the Castro regime. The attempted coup was a monumental failure. The Cuban government captured and imprisoned the invasion force and publicly humiliated the United States.

Soviet leader Nikita Khrushchev decided to defend the island against any future American aggression by installing on Cuban territory medium- and intermediate-range ballistic missiles capable of reaching the eastern United States within a few minutes. American spy planes flying over Cuba had detected the presence of Soviet missiles. Intense negotiations ensued between Kennedy and Khrushchev. U Thant facilitated the dialogue on several occasions. On 28 October 1961, a deal was brokered. Khrushchev promised Kennedy that the missiles already in Cuba would be returned to the Soviet Union. In return, Kennedy committed the United States to never invade Cuba and secretly promised to withdraw the US nuclear missiles from Turkey.

The Cuban missile crisis marked the closest point that the world had ever come to nuclear war. Although no credit has been given to the United Nations for the prevention of this catastrophe, President Kennedy himself admitted that the Secretary-General's role in the resolution of the conflict was decisive: "U Thant has put the whole world in his debt."[60] In his memoirs, U Thant also attributes the merit for resolving the dispute to the United Nations:

---

60 *Ibid.*

> The settlement was an eloquent illustration of the usefulness of the United Nations to member states as a place for peaceful settlement of international conflicts. It is clear that direct, and almost daily, communication between President Kennedy and Chairman Khrushchev was mainly responsible for bringing to an end a most frightening confrontation between the two nuclear giants.[61]

b) From Proxy Wars to Full-Fledged Invasions

As of 1960, the United States and the Soviet Union were no longer attempting to conceal their true intentions, either from each other or from the rest of the world. Both superpowers were prepared to go to great lengths to preserve complete control in their respective spheres of influence. In 1965 the United States invaded the Dominican Republic and then in 1983 the tiny island of Grenada, in efforts to forestall communist regimes. In 1968, the USSR invaded Czechoslovakia, crushing a brief period of liberalization in that country called the "Prague Spring." Between 1961 and 1969, the United States conducted a large-scale intervention in the Vietnam War, for the purpose of combatting the spread of communism. At the same time, the United Nations was dealing with other supremely important conflicts, including the Six Day War in the Middle East in June 1967,[62] and the two Indo-Pakistani wars over Kashmir in 1965 and 1971.

Soviet and American interventions in post-colonial state-making took increasingly intrusive and militarized turns not only in Vietnam, but also in Angola, Mozambique, Ethiopia, Central America, Afghanistan, Nicaragua, and many other countries.[63] Although the UN's

---

61 Thant, above note 39 at 191.

62 Many Western diplomats blamed Secretary-General U Thant for withdrawing the United Nations Emergency Force (UNEF) established under the leadership of Dag Hammarskjöld in 1956, which had effectively served as a buffer between Egypt and Israel. U Thant, however, ordered the withdrawal of the troops at the request of the Egyptian Government since any peacekeeping operation required the consent of the host state.

63 Mark Philip Bradley, "Decolonization, Global South, and the Cold War, 1919–1962" in Melvin P Leffler & Odd Arne Westad, eds, *The Cambridge History of the Cold War, Volume 1: Origins* (Cambridge, UK: Cambridge University Press, 2010) 464 at 484.

inability to prevent these conflicts in the 1960s cannot be attributed solely to then Secretary-General U Thant, his restrictive understanding and rigid approach to the role of the Secretary-General may have contributed to these failures. As U Thant's successor, Kurt Waldheim, put it, "where Hammarskjöld had stretched the powers of his office with risky dynamism, U Thant had been criticized for excessive passivity."[64] U Thant's unconditional deference to the United States and USSR may have empowered their governments to act lawlessly. His approach and views of his role stood in stark contrast to those of Dag Hammarskjöld. U Thant was of the view that it was not in the interests of his office and function to alienate the superpowers by openly criticizing their actions. History proved U Thant wrong.

Nevertheless, the frustration over the failures of the UN in several important conflicts compelled the organization to adapt. It coped with the threat of annihilation by shifting its focus from mainly political vocation to such matters as food, environment, population, development, trade, and other global problems not envisaged by the drafters of the *UN Charter* at the inception of the United Nations. Unanticipated by the founders of the United Nations, this rapid expansion of the organization's mandate resulted in a proliferation of complex subsidiary organs, funds, programs, and other technical and specialized international organizations. Between 1961 and 1971, a dozen major institutions of the United Nations System, such as the World Food Programme (WFP), the UN Development Programme (UNDP), and the UN Population Fund (UNFPA), were created to carry out the new functions and responsibilities of the organization.[65]

---

64 Kurt Waldheim, *In the Eye of the Storm: The Memoirs of Kurt Waldheim* (London: George Weidenfeld & Nicolson Limited, 1985) at 39.

65 In 1963, the World Food Programme (WFP) came into existence as the UN's food aid organization; in 1964, the International Trade Centre (ITC) and the United Nations Conference on Trade and Development (UNCTAD) were set up; in 1965, the General Assembly established the United Nations Development Programme (UNDP) to reduce poverty, promote democratic governance, prevent and recover from crises, protect the environment, and combat climate change; in 1966, the General Assembly established the United Nations Capital Development Fund (UNCDF) to create new opportunities for poor people and their communities by increasing access to microfinance and investment

4) Period Under Kurt Waldheim's Leadership: 1972–1982

U Thant's successor was Kurt Waldheim, an Austrian career diplomat, minister of foreign affairs, and Austria's permanent representative to the UN. When Waldheim acceded to the Secretary-General's post on 21 December 1971,[66] the political climate was conducive to the easing of the Cold War tensions between the United States and the Soviet Union. Both sides stood to gain from improved relations. America was suffering an ignominious defeat in Vietnam and was exhausted from a decade of social pandemonium caused by the war. American activists and political commentators, such as Noam Chomsky, who criticized the United States for its involvement in the conflict, were now gaining a wider audience. A larger portion of the United States population began realizing that with its increasingly global intolerance towards any collectivist ideology, the United States had caused and perpetuated the Cold War to at least as high a degree as the Soviet Union had.[67] The Vietnam debacle was viewed as a confirmation that perhaps the United States was simply not suited to be a leader abroad, especially when it was unable to rectify internal injustices based on race, gender, education, and income levels.[68] Thus, mending relations with the USSR became a means for the US government to improve public image and to avoid other costly conflicts.

---

capital; also in 1966, the United Nations Industrial Development Organization (UNIDO) was established; in 1969, the United Nations Population Fund (UNFPA) was established to assist countries in improving reproductive health and family planning services, as well as in formulating population policies for sustainable development; In 1970, the World Intellectual Property Organization (WIPO) was created to promote the protection of intellectual property and the United Nations Volunteers (UNV) was set up to support peace, relief, and development initiatives in more than 130 countries.

66 Kurt Waldheim was appointed in General Assembly Resolution 2903 (XXVI), UNGAOR, 26th Sess, UN Doc A/Res/2903 (XXVI) (1971) 18.

67 Odd Arne Westad, "The Cold War and the International History of the Twentieth Century" in Melvin P Leffler & Odd Arne Westad, eds, *The Cambridge History of the Cold War, Volume 1: Origins* (Cambridge, UK: Cambridge University Press, 2010) 1 at 4.

68 *Ibid.*

The USSR could gain as much as the United States from the thawing of the Cold War. It was facing an increasingly hostile relationship with the Chinese communist government, which viewed the Soviet Union and its expansionist aspirations as the biggest threat to China. The intensification of the Sino-Soviet rivalry forced the USSR to compromise with the United States.[69] Also, in the aftermath of the Cuban missile crisis, both sides realized that their mutual destruction would be assured if they allowed rivalry to slip out of control.

a) Short-Lived Détente

With both sides prepared to see a general warming of relations, a new era commonly known as "détente" began in the late 1960s or early 1970s and lasted for a decade. In May 1972, US President Nixon visited the leader of the USSR, Leonid Brezhnev, becoming the first US president to visit Moscow.

In practical terms, this period was a time of increased trade and cooperation between the two superpowers. The precursor of détente was the signing of the *Treaty on the Non-Proliferation of Nuclear Weapons* in 1968. The détente led to further agreements on arms control, including the *Anti-Ballistic Missile Treaty*.[70] The security of Europe also became a topic of discussions. The Conference on Security and Cooperation in Europe that had started in 1973 culminated in the seminal agreement Helsinki Final Act, which recognized political borders, created opportunities for trade and cultural exchanges, and promoted human rights. Great hopes were pinned on the process of détente. The United Nations interventions were becoming, if not successful, at least possible. The improved relations allowed for a more effective United Nations relief operation in Bangladesh. Also, although following the 1974 coup in Cyprus, the United Nations did not resolve the conflict, it was able to put an end to the hostilities and maintain the peace on the

---

69 Henry Kissinger, *White House Years* (London: Simon & Schuster, 2011) at 79.

70 During the late 1960s, the Soviet Union began building up a massive arsenal of Intercontinental Ballistic Missiles (ICBM) in order to reach parity with the United States. It had also begun to construct a limited anti-ballistic missile defence system around Moscow. Such a system allows one side to launch a strike and prevent the other side from retaliating by shooting down incoming missiles.

island. With the fall of Saigon in 1975, the Vietnam war came to an end at last. The accession to independence of the Portuguese colonies in 1974, and of Zimbabwe in 1980, brought the process of decolonization nearer to a conclusion. The independence of Namibia was the only outstanding issue in this area.

In 1979, when the Soviet Union invaded Afghanistan, the détente decade ended and the relations between the East and the West cooled again. In response to this invasion, the United States imposed an embargo on grain shipments to the USSR and boycotted the Moscow Olympics. The renewal of the Cold War triggered a number of major political conflicts around the world.

b) Intensification of the North–South Divide

During the détente period, while the East–West tensions were easing, a new type of rivalry was emerging in the international arena, particularly in the General Assembly, between industrialized countries and the Third World. This clash, known as the North–South divide, was about a fair redistribution of wealth or the socio-economic gap between the two poles.

Developing countries understood the importance of consolidating their voices. Yet, they supported neither the Eastern nor the Western bloc. They had different concerns, priorities, and worldviews. As a result, they established two powerful coalitions. The first organization, called the Non-Aligned Movement, emerged from the Bandung (Indonesia) conference of April 1955. It focused mainly on geopolitical issues and kept aloof from the East–West alliances. The group got off the ground in 1961.[71] The second coalition, known as the Group of 77 or G-77, was composed of former colonies and developing countries. Initially composed of seventy-seven states, this organization currently has over 130 member states. It is now better known as "G-77 and China." While the Non-Aligned Movement focuses on geopolitical issues, G-77 pursues an agenda of economic

---

71 David M Malone & Lotta Hagman, "The North-South Divide at the United Nations: Fading at Last?" (2002) 33:4 *Security Dialogue* 399 at 400.

and social development and redistribution of wealth.[72] Post-colonial states were of the view that their precarious economic condition was the product of the colonial policies of the past and the power politics of the present. They had missed the industrial revolution and, as a result, fell behind for decades. Accordingly, they demanded a new international economic order[73] without offering the Western states anything in exchange.[74] They saw "the redressing of wrongs, and economic and social development, not as an aspiration but as a right to which they were entitled."[75] The creation of the UN Conference on Trade and Development (UNCTAD) in 1964, the UN Development Programme (UNDP) in 1965, and the UN Industrial Development Organization (UNIDO) in 1967 was the direct result of the pressure exercised by developing countries on their First World counterparts.[76] The North–South divide still defines to a great extent the terms of political debate in the UN.[77]

c) Civil War in Lebanon (1975–1990)

A major political and humanitarian crisis the United Nations was dealing with in the 1970s during Waldheim's mandate was the civil war in Lebanon. Following the collapse of the Ottoman Empire, which had ruled in the Middle East for four centuries, the territory that is now Syria and Lebanon fell to France. In those times, and according to a 1932 census, Lebanon's population consisted predominantly of three major religious groups: Maronite Christians, Sunni Muslims, and Shia Muslims. Lebanon had other religious groups, such as Druse and

---

72 *Ibid.*

73 See, *Declaration on the Establishment of a New International Economic Order*, GA Res 3201 (S-VI), UNGAOR, 6th Sess, UN Doc A/RES/S-6/3201 (1974) 3.

74 Kurt Waldheim, *In the Eye of the Storm: The Memoirs of Kurt Waldheim* (London: George Weidenfeld & Nicolson Limited, 1985) at 113.

75 *Ibid.*

76 Thomas G Weiss, David P Forsythe, & Roger A Coate, *The United Nations and Changing World Politics*, 3d ed (Boulder, CO: Westview, 2001) at 263–65; Waldheim, above note 74 at 112.

77 Soo Yeon Kim & Bruce Russett, "The New Politics of Voting Alignments in the United Nations General Assembly" (1996) 50:4 *International Organization* 629 at 339–40.

Orthodox Christians. In 1932, 51 percent of the population was Christian and 49 percent was Muslim. In 1943, these different religious groups with opposing interests managed to reach an unwritten agreement, which became known as the National Pact. In accordance with this agreement, the president of Lebanon is always a Maronite, the prime minister is always a Sunni, and the president of the Parliament is always a Shia Muslim. In the 1970s, this arrangement became less attractive to the Muslim constituents because, with a steadier demographic growth, Muslims represented two-thirds of the Lebanese population, yet the power was still held primarily by Maronites. Muslims began demanding constitutional reforms, including an expansion of the role of a Muslim prime minister. Maronites had no intention of surrendering their power. They resisted by forming private militias. As tensions were heating up between Muslims and Christians, a catalyst—the conflict between Palestinians and Jews—was introduced to a highly explosive situation in Lebanon. Palestinian militias, chased by the Jordanian army for upsetting Jordan's King Hussein, were fleeing refugee camps in Amman and were arriving in large numbers into refugee districts of Beirut. Muslim Lebanese welcomed the arrival of fellow Arabs because they realized that they could use Palestinian guerrillas against militias formed by Maronites.[78] In April 1975, a provocative terrorist attack killed four Christians, marking the beginning of a twenty-year-long war. The United Nations became involved in Lebanon in 1978 when Israel intervened militarily in southern Lebanon. The UN established the United Nations Interim Force in Lebanon (UNIFIL), still in existence today.

d) Modern Terrorism Motivated by Extreme Islamist Movements

In the late 1960s and early 1970s, the United Nations also began dealing with the phenomenon of modern terrorism.[79] Before 1960, ter-

78 James R Stocker, *Spheres of Intervention: US Foreign Policy and the Collapse of Lebanon, 1967–1976* (Ithaca: Cornell University Press, 2016) at 11.

79 In its Resolution 1566 of 8 October 2004 (UN Doc S/RES/1566 (2004)) the Security Council defined the term terrorism as "Criminal acts, including [those] against civilians, committed with the intent to cause death or serious bodily injury, or taking of hostages, with the purpose to provoke a state of

rorism was primarily a revolutionary strategy perpetrated against the colonial powers. From 1960 to 1980, terrorism developed into a type of weapon for waging a war. It became a means of struggle for secular nationalist and neo-Marxist groups, such as FLNC,[80] FARC,[81] IRA,[82] PFLP,[83] ETA,[84] and the Red Brigades.[85] Also, during these two decades, and in particular after the humiliating blow inflicted by Israelis on the Arab World during the Six-Day War, Palestinians began availing themselves of terrorism as a measure of last resort. Several terrorist attacks took place immediately after the Six-Day War. For instance, in July 1968, an Israeli civilian aircraft was hijacked. Its crew and passengers were kept hostage in Algeria for two months. Similarly, in February 1970, another flight carrying Israeli passengers crashed as

---

terror in the general public or in a group of persons or particular persons, intimidate a population or compel a government or an international organization to do or to abstain from doing any act, which constitute offences within the scope of and as defined in the international conventions and protocols relating to terrorism, are under no circumstances justifiable by considerations of a political, philosophical, ideological, racial, ethnic, religious or other similar nature."

80 Formed in 1976, the Corsican National Liberation Front (or Front de Libération Nationale de la Corse in French) was the most powerful and violent Corsican nationalist movement that sought autonomy for Corsica through armed struggle and terrorism.

81 Active since 1964, the Revolutionary Armed Forces of Colombia (or Fuerzas Armadas Revolucionarias de Colombia in Spanish) is a guerrilla movement known to employ terrorism for the purposes of promoting its Marxist-Leninist political platform.

82 The Irish Republican Army was a paramilitary organization seeking the establishment of a republic, the end of British rule in Northern Ireland, and the reunification of Ireland. From 1969 until the Belfast Agreement, the IRA carried out many bombings and assassinations.

83 The Popular Front for the Liberation of Palestine claimed responsibility for a series of bombings, armed and suicide attacks, and airplane hijackings.

84 ETA is the abbreviation of a separatist organization in Spain called "Basque Euskadi Ta Askatasuna," which means Basque Homeland and Freedom. Initially, this group emerged as a student resistance fighting against General Franco's repressive dictatorial regime. However, in mid-1970, it began using terrorism exclusively in support of its campaign for an independent Basque state.

85 Inspired by the Latin American urban guerrilla movements, Red Brigades was an Italian militant neo-Marxist organization whose primary purpose was to undermine the Italian state and bring about a socialist political system. It gained notoriety in the 1970s for terrorist attacks, kidnappings, and assassinations.

a result of a planted explosive. In September 1970, Palestinian terrorists hijacked four aircraft and exploded three of them in Amman. The most infamous attack, however, occurred in September 1972, with the assassination of eleven Israeli athletes at the Munich Olympics. Regrettably, terrorism proved to be an effective method of an armed struggle. In November 1974, two years after the Munich massacre, Yasser Arafat was invited to address the United Nations General Assembly as the chairman of the Palestine Liberation Organization (PLO).[86] A few days after, the General Assembly adopted a resolution reaffirming the right of the Palestinian people to self-determination and granting the PLO observer status.[87] The real or perceived success of the Palestinians led to a proliferation of terrorist acts around the world because other militant groups were inspired by the ability of the Palestinians to attract international attention and sympathy for their cause through terrorism. Moreover, as the Palestinian militant groups had acquired an international reputation for their expertise in aircraft hijacking,[88] they began exporting their expertise by spreading techniques of terrorism worldwide.[89]

Whereas from the early 1960s to late 1970s, terrorism was a means for a militant group—typically a weaker party—to wage a war against its perceived "oppressor," in the early 1980s, terrorism motivated by extreme Islamist movements was gradually emerging.[90] It is believed that this trend was attributable to the Iranian revolution and the Iranian hostage crisis:

> A common inspiration in the rise of these movements was the Iranian Islamic revolution, led by Ayatollah Khomeini, which overthrew the Shah in 1979 and attempted to construct a new Islamic republic based on fundamentalist principles. The Iranian revolution attracted growing admiration not only among Shi'ite Islamic

---

86 UNGAOR, 29th Sess, 2282th Plen Mtg, UN Doc A/PV.2282 and Corr1 (1974).

87 *Question of Palestine*, GA Res 3236 (XIX), UNGAOR, 29th Sess, UN Doc A/RES/3236 (XIX) (1974) 4.

88 Paul Wilkinson, *Terrorism versus Democracy: The Liberal State Response*, 2d ed (New York: Routledge, 2006) at 245.

89 *Ibid* at 25.

90 *Ibid* at 30.

> communities but also among the Sunnis, who form the overwhelming majority of Muslims. The leaders of the Iranian revolution were seen as having struck a humiliating blow against the United States.[91]

This type of terrorism continues to take centre stage in the United Nations today, particularly after the 9/11 terrorist acts.

e) Iran Hostage Crisis (1979–1981)

Kurt Waldheim's last assignment was to help secure the release of the American hostages held by the Iranian students in Tehran with the blessing of the newly formed religious regime. Unfortunately, the Secretary-General's efforts were unsuccessful. This hostage situation began on 4 November 1979 when the American embassy in Tehran was stormed by a very large mob primarily composed of students. The group took more than sixty American hostages. The immediate cause of this terrorist act was President Carter's decision to allow Iran's deposed Shah, a pro-Western autocrat who had been expelled from his country some months before, to come to the United States for cancer treatment. This was merely the straw that broke the camel's back. The real source of the problem was misappropriated profits from Iranian oil. American and British corporations had controlled a large part of the Iranian petroleum reserves for decades. In 1951, a newly elected prime minister, Muhammad Mossadegh, announced a plan to nationalize Iran's oil industry. To retain control over Iranian petroleum resources, the American and British intelligence services were instructed by their respective governments to devise a plan to replace Mossadegh with Mohammed Reza Shah Pahlavi, a secular, anti-communist and pro-Western leader. When Mossadegh was deposed and Shah took office, the new government returned 80 percent of Iran's oil reserves to the American and British stakeholders. Iranians never forgave the Americans for this blatant interference in their domestic affairs.

In July 1979, the Ayatollah Khomeini returned from exile and staged a revolution, forcing Shah to flee to Egypt. At the time of his escape from Iran, Shah had a malignant cancer and needed advanced

---

91 *Ibid* at 30–31.

medical care. The United States allowed Shah to receive treatment in an American hospital. This triggered a public outcry among Iranians who perceived Shah as a traitor and US puppet.

The Iranian hostage crisis lasted for two years. In the meantime, the United States tried to resolve the dispute through legal, economic, and military means. First, it froze all Iranian assets and imposed an embargo. Then, it instituted proceedings against Iran before the International Court of Justice and obtained a favourable judgment.[92] Finally, as a measure of last resort, the United States attempted an unsuccessful hostage-rescue mission known as Operation Eagle Claw. It failed, resulting in the death of eight American airmen.[93] The humiliated US government expended great efforts to repatriate the bodies of these soldiers to the United States.

The only remaining option was diplomacy. The United States had asked a number of allies to exert pressure on the Iranians. Nonetheless, Iran remained intransigent. The decisive point may have been the unexpected war with Iraq in 1980. Iran was unable to get support from any third country without releasing the American hostages. Consequently, it softened its stance. In 1981, the United States and Iran entered into the Algiers Accords, creating the Iran-United States Claims Tribunal[94] to resolve existing disputes between the two countries and their nationals.

f) Kurt Waldheim's Past Is Revealed

In 1986, after Waldheim had concluded his second five-year term as Secretary-General of the United Nations and while he was campaigning for the presidency of Austria, allegations emerged that he had participated in ethnic cleansing in the Balkans when serving as an officer in the German Army during World War II. Despite these

---

92 *United States Diplomatic and Consular Staff in Tehran (United States of America v Tehran)*, [1980] ICJ Rep 3 at 3.

93 Marc A Selmer, *Terrorism, US Strategy and Reagan Policies* (New York: Greenwood Press, 1987) at 68.

94 The Tribunal sits in The Hague and is comprised of nine arbitrators: three appointed by Iran, three by the United States, and three by the party-appointed members acting jointly or, in absence of agreement, by an appointing authority.

allegations, Waldheim was elected as Austria's ninth president. In 1987, the United States government placed Kurt Waldheim's name on the US Immigration and Naturalization Service's list of undesirable aliens prohibited from entering the United States. This decision gave rise to a delicate situation; Waldheim was the head of a friendly country with which the United States maintained full diplomatic relations. Barring Waldheim from entering the United States, even for the purposes of attending the fiftieth anniversary of the United Nations, was unprecedented. It is generally recognized that Waldheim significantly diminished the respect and authority commanded by the position of Secretary-General.[95]

5) Period Under Javier Pérez de Cuéllar's Leadership: 1982–1992

None of the Secretaries-General who preceded Kurt Waldheim had lobbied for their appointments nor for their reappointments for a second term. Trygve Lie wrote in his memoirs that he "had been nothing less than catapulted into Secretary-Generalship."[96] Dag Hammarskjöld was surprised by his nomination and accepted the appointment reluctantly.[97] U Thant tried to resist a renewal for a second term and categorically refused a third term.[98] Kurt Waldheim, on the other hand, vigorously lobbied for a third term.[99] When China persistently vetoed his re-election for a third mandate, Kurt Waldheim felt compelled to withdraw his candidacy.[100] As a result, the Security Council began

95 Marcus Franda, *The United Nations in the Twenty-First Century* (Lanham: Rowman & Littlefield Publishers, 2006) at 27.

96 Lie, above note 11 at 17.

97 Thant, above note 39 at 6.

98 *Ibid.*

99 *Ibid* at 230–57.

100 In April 2001, the CIA released declassified material on the former Secretary-General and Austrian President Kurt Waldheim. These documents confirmed that the British and American intelligence services knew as early as 1945 that Waldheim was a junior Wehrmacht officer in a Nazi intelligence unit in the Balkans, which was renowned for its brutalities. However, the document had been forgotten or misplaced when Waldheim was recommended for the position of the UN Secretary-General.

searching for another docile and non-intrusive Secretary-General. Javier Pérez de Cuéllar, a Peruvian diplomat with strong ties to the United Nations, seemed to fit the bill, as he "was unlikely to make international waves as head of the United Nations."[101]

a) End of the Cold War

Pérez de Cuéllar took over during a decisive period.[102] Communist states had been mired in stagnation. Their economies were paralyzed by a lack of innovation and productivity. An extremely poor economic performance in the 1980s, especially in contrast with the West, had discredited communism. As the world began experiencing the benefits of a new information technology revolution, communist regimes had difficulty keeping up. In 1980s, the Soviet Union was also running out of steam after years of a stagnating economy under Leonid Brezhnev's tenure.[103] Hence, it was perhaps inevitable that the USSR would turn inward to face the internal problems of its deeply flawed system.

In 1985, Mikhail Gorbachev came to power, becoming the last leader of the USSR. He initiated substantial reforms of the Soviet political and economic systems. Two of his major policies brought down the Soviet empire, thereby ending the Cold War. First, under his policy known as "glasnost" (meaning "openness"), freedom of expression and information were markedly expanded. The press was allowed unprecedented candour. Gorbachev's second policy, called "perestroika" (meaning "restructuring"), was an attempt to democratize the Soviet political system and introduce free-market mechanisms into the Soviet economy.

Gorbachev's foreign policy promoted warmer relations and trade with the developed nations. In December 1987, Gorbachev and US

---

101 Barbara Ann Rieffer-Flanagan & David P Forsythe, "Religion, Ethics and Reality: A Study of Javier Perez de Cuellar" in Kent J Kille, ed, *The UN Secretary-General and Moral Authority, Ethics and Religion in International Leadership* (Washington, DC: Georgetown University Press, 2007) 229.

102 Javier Pérez de Cuéllar was appointed through General Assembly Resolution 36/137, UNGAOR, 36th Sess, UN Doc A/RES/36/137 (1981) 38.

103 Mark Sandle, "Brezhnev and Developed Socialism: The Ideology of Zastoi?" in Edwin Bacon & Mark Sandle, eds, *Brezhnev Reconsidered* (New York: Palgrave Macmillan, 2002).

President Ronald Reagan signed a treaty agreeing to destroy their countries' existing stocks of intermediate-range nuclear-tipped missiles. Gorbachev pulled out Soviet troops from Afghanistan after a nine-year occupation of that country.

The end of the Cold War triggered a significant number of important changes in the political landscape of the World. The most visible symbol of the East–West division, the Berlin Wall, was brought down, allowing the reunification of the Democratic Republic of Germany and the Federal Republic of Germany. Democratically elected governments began replacing communist regimes across Eastern and Central Europe. In most countries, except in Romania where events turned violent, the transition was peaceful.

Unfortunately, in some parts of the world, the fall of communism had disastrous consequences. Although communist regimes were undemocratic, they managed to suppress deep-rooted antagonisms and nationalism. Ethnic, cultural, religious, and linguistic diversities were held in check by political suppression or by the threat of Soviet intervention. When these restraints disappeared, ethnic and religious conflicts as well as secessionist movements erupted in many parts of the world.

For the United Nations, the collapse of the Soviet Union had the immediate effect of considerably increasing its membership. The transition from one era to another was symbolized by the wave of new states seeking admission to the UN. In 1992, countries that had just gained independence, including Armenia, Azerbaijan, Bosnia and Herzegovina, Croatia, Georgia, Kazakhstan, Kyrgyzstan, the Republic of Moldova, San Marino, Slovenia, Tajikistan, Turkmenistan, and Uzbekistan, took their seats in the General Assembly for the first time. Between 1990 and 2014, 34 new countries emerged and sought membership in the UN. The dissolution of the USSR, Yugoslavia, and Czechoslovakia caused the creation of most of the newly independent states.

The thawing of the Cold War strengthened the UN's role in the area of international peace and security for several reasons. First, the conflicts that were erupting during this period were no longer ideological and therefore had little or no strategic relevance to the Great Powers. Nevertheless, the humanitarian consequences of these conflicts had to be addressed and the UN was viewed as the ideal candidate for the task. Second, Gorbachev was now stressing the importance of international cooperation and multilateralism because he understood that by strengthening the UN, where the Soviet Union had a permanent seat and veto power, he could soften the blow to the superpower's declining prestige and influence in world politics. Third, in January 1989, the change in the American administration was viewed from the UN as another promising event. Unlike the Reagan administration that believed in unilateralism and was critical of the United Nations, President George HW Bush was a former US ambassador to the UN and held a more favourable view of the world organization.

As a result of these significant changes in the world, many armed conflicts and proxy wars ended in 1989. For instance, as soon as the Cold War had ebbed, the internal conflict that devastated Mozambique during the 1980s ended, Cuban troops withdrew from Angola, Soviet troops withdrew from Afghanistan, Vietnamese troops withdrew from Cambodia, Namibia gained independence from South Africa, Iran and Iraq ceased hostilities, and so on. Superpowers had lost interest in most of these countries. Pouring substantial financial resources into military equipment and weapons made no sense in most of these destitute states. The disengagement of the superpowers left an enormous gap to be filled. This gave the United Nations an ideal opportunity to fulfill its core mandate. The ensuing post-Cold War era began with high (but short-lived) hopes for new world order marked by cooperation and multilateralism with the UN at its core. The Persian Gulf War was a foretaste of what a new world order could have been like. The UN handled this first crisis extremely well.

b) The Gulf War (1990–1991)—Short-Lived Hope of Cooperation in the Security Council

During the Cold War, it would have been unimaginable for the Security Council to adopt almost unanimously resolutions condemning an aggression and swiftly authorizing measures under Chapter VII of the *UN Charter*.[104] Indeed, between 1948 and 1988, the United Nations

104 Stanley Meisler, *United Nations: A History* (New York: Grove Press, 1995) at 261.

had managed to establish only thirteen peacekeeping missions, most of which had very limited ceasefire observing functions. During the following decade—that is between 1988 and 1998—thirty-six new robust peacekeeping operations had been launched. The Gulf War was the first element that marked the transformation of the Security Council.

In early August 1990, Iraqi president Saddam Hussein ordered the invasion and occupation of neighbouring Kuwait. To justify this aggression, Saddam Hussein "asserted a longstanding Iraqi claim to sovereignty over Kuwait on the ground that Kuwait had been a part of the province of Basra when the area was under the Ottoman Empire, and Basra wound up as part of Iraq when the area was divided into states."[105] Essentially, the Iraqi position was that Kuwait was an artificial state carved out of the Iraqi territory by Western colonialist regimes. The Security Council adopted a series of resolutions condemning Iraq for aggression and demanding its withdrawal from Kuwait,[106] imposing embargoes to force compliance,[107] authorizing a naval blockade,[108] and authorizing member states "to use all necessary means to uphold and implement resolution 660 and all subsequent relevant resolutions and to restore international peace and security in the area."[109] At the same time, Secretary-General Pérez de Cuéllar also made serious diplomatic efforts to resolve the conflict peacefully. But the Iraqi leader was incomprehensibly unwavering. Saddam Hussein reminded the Secretary-General that the Security Council had not acted for one month when Iraq had invaded Iran.[110] On 17 January 1991, a US-led coalition of military forces attacked Iraq

---

105 John Quigley, "The United States and the United Nations in the Persian Gulf War: New Order or Disorder" (1992) 25 *Cornell Int'l LJ* 1 at 2.

106 *The Situation Between Iraq and Kuwait*, SC Res 660 (1990), UNSCOR, 45th Year, UN Doc S/RES/660 (1990) 19.

107 *Ibid.*

108 *The Situation Between Iraq and Kuwait*, SC Res 665 (1990), UNSCOR, 45th Year, UN Doc S/RES/665 (1990) 21.

109 *The Situation Between Iraq and Kuwait*, SC Res 678 (1990), UNSCOR, 45th Year, UN Doc S/RES/678 (1990) 27.

110 Javier Pérez de Cuéllar, *Pilgrimage for Peace: A Secretary-General's Memoir* (New York: St. Martin's Press, 1997) at 237.

with overwhelming force. Iraq surrendered and was subjected to a very harsh ceasefire deal.

Although the military intervention was very successful, the subsequent measures had severe humanitarian consequences. The Security Council resolution offering peace was very onerous for Iraq.[III] Unfortunately, the comprehensive sanctions imposed by the Security Council did not produce the desired effect. They not only set Iraq back several decades, but they also had disproportionate and indiscriminate human costs. Another perverse effect of the sanctions was the infamous Oil-for-Food program.

c) Oil-for-Food Scandal (1995–2004)

The Security Council established the Oil-for-Food program in response to complaints that the population of Iraq was disproportionately affected by the international economic sanctions aimed at the demilitarization of Saddam Hussein's regime. The program allowed the sale of Iraqi oil in exchange for basic necessities such as food and medicine. The program was designed to offer humanitarian assistance to the Iraqi population without allowing Saddam Hussein's regime to boost its military power. After eight years of operation, it became clear that the Oil-for-Food program did not produce the desired effect; the embargo continued to adversely affect the Iraqi economy and population but not Saddam Hussein's regime.

The scandal emerged in the beginning of 2004 after official documents of the Iraqi Oil Ministry were leaked to the media. These documents revealed that hundreds of high-ranking officials, including UN personnel, and organizations had received kickbacks from the Iraqi government. People who were allegedly involved in the scheme included a former French interior minister, a British Member of Parliament, an Indian foreign minister, Russian politicians, the oil companies Total, Lukoil, and Gazprom, and, ironically, the son of then Secretary-General Kofi Annan. It was alleged that some members of the Russian Orthodox Church and the Vatican were involved in the illicit oil trade as well.

III SC Res 687 (1991), UNSCOR, 46th Year, UN Doc S/Res/687 (1991) 1.

The scheme was relatively straightforward. Individuals and organizations were awarded contracts to sell Iraqi oil on the international market. The seller kept a small transaction fee of USD$0.50 per barrel of oil sold. In order to secure a contract, some sellers agreed in advance to refund a part of the commission to the Hussein administration as a kickback. Similarly, contracts for buying humanitarian goods through the program were offered to those companies that agreed in advance to return a percentage of their profits to the Hussein regime as a bribe.

When the scandal erupted, UN Secretary-General Kofi Annan set up a seventy-five-member independent inquiry committee, presided over by Paul Volker, the former chief of the US Federal Reserve. Following the release of the committee's final report, two UN staff members were prosecuted, fined, and convicted for corruption. A US Senate investigative body concluded that the Oil-for-Food program had allowed the Hussein administration to sell over USD$13 billion worth of oil in violation of the embargo. Billions more were collected by the Iraqi regime through illegal commissions, bribes, and kickbacks through the program. The Oil-for-Food program had seriously dented the image of the United Nations.

6) Period Under Boutros Boutros-Ghali's Leadership: 1992–1996

When Pérez de Cuéllar's second term expired, "it was Africa's turn to select someone for the job."[112] Boutros Boutros-Ghali, a seasoned diplomat, a lawyer with a strong international law background, and fluent in English, French, and Arabic, seemed to be a suitable candidate for many African leaders. Boutros-Ghali was appointed as the sixth Secretary-General of the United Nations in December 1991.[113]

Boutros-Ghali held office during particularly turbulent times. Ethnic, religious, cultural, and linguistic conflicts were spreading in many

112 Boutros Boutros-Ghali, *Unvanquished: A US–UN Saga* (London: IB Tauris Publishers, 1999) at 7.

113 Boutros-Ghali was appointed in General Assembly Resolution 46/21, UNGAOR, 46th Sess, UN Doc A/RES/46/21 (1991), 22 and UNGAOR, 46th Sess, 59th Mtg, A/46/PV.59 (1991).

corners of the globe. These were not traditional interstate conflicts where the UN peacekeeping forces were asked to separate national armies of two neighbouring states. Nor were these conflicts where the UN deployed peacekeeping troops with the consent of the warring parties. Rather, these were intricate armed struggles and civil strife occurring *within* states. The founders of the UN had not foreseen that internal conflicts or collapse of state structures could become the primary threat to international peace. In fact, the *Charter of the United Nations* explicitly prohibits the organization from intervening in these matters, which are essentially within the domestic jurisdiction of any state. The UN was facing a dilemma. On the one hand, its primary function was to maintain international peace, but, on the other hand, it had no authority to intervene in internal conflicts.

Traditionally, UN peacekeeping operations were based on three key principles. First, the consent of the parties to the conflict was a precondition to any UN military intervention. Peacekeepers were allowed to be present in a conflict with the consent of the concerned parties.[114] Second, the UN peacekeepers had an obligation to be impartial. They could neither assist nor hinder either side in a conflict. Third, peacekeepers could not proactively use force. They could engage in hostilities only in self-defence or in order to protect their mission.[115] Respecting these three principles allowed the UN peacekeepers to gain the trust of both sides and expect a reasonable degree of cooperation.[116] In the aftermath of the Cold War, the UN could no longer count on the presence of these three key requirements. UN peacekeeping forces were often being deployed into failed states with no central authority or legitimate government that could authorize or consent to their presence. Also, the UN could not always remain

114 In May 1967, the Secretary-General U Thant directed the United Nations Emergency Force (UNEF) to pull out from the United Arab Republic because President Nasser withdrew his consent for the force's presence on the Egyptian territory.

115 Devon Whittle, "Peacekeeping in Conflict: The Intervention Brigade, MONUSCO, and the Application of International Humanitarian Law to United Nations Forces" (2014–2015) 46 *Geo J Int'l L* 837 at 838.

116 Norrie MacQueen, *The United Nations, Peace Operations and the Cold War*, 2d ed (New York: Routledge, 2011) at xiv.

neutral, particularly when one of the belligerent parties was committing crimes against humanity or targeting civilians. UN forces were no longer confronting regular uniformed armed forces but a multitude of loosely organized militias, guerrillas, or rebels with conflicting interests. Finally, UN peacekeeping troops were now moving into position when no ceasefire was yet in place; therefore, there was no peace to keep. UN forces had to secure a cessation of fighting and forcefully restore peace as opposed to monitor pre-existing ceasefires.

The UN had some familiarity with this type of peacekeeping operation. Military interventions in internal (or intrastate) conflicts had been conducted before the Cold War, too. In particular, the peacekeeping missions in the Democratic Republic of the Congo, Cyprus, and Lebanon were essentially interventions in civil conflicts, even though they had international dimensions to them. However, a long time had passed since these peacekeeping missions were set up. In addition, the scope of activities the UN was expected to carry out in post-Cold War conflicts was much greater. Troop-contributing countries were required to make available to the UN a large number of military and support personnel with varied expertise beyond the primarily infantry functions. Also, the UN was expected to carry out a wide range of new functions such as disarming, demobilizing, reintegrating combatants back into the community, and organizing or monitoring elections.

It is against this backdrop that Secretary-General Boutros-Ghali produced his report, *An Agenda for Peace*,[117] where he identified and explained four consecutive phases of international action to prevent or resolve conflicts. These phases are: (a) preventive diplomacy; (b) peacemaking (pacific settlement of disputes pursuant to Chapter VI of the *UN Charter*); (c) peacekeeping (deployment of UN peacekeeping troops); and (d) peacebuilding (measures to help strengthen peace in order to avoid a relapse into conflict). Boutros-Ghali's proposed concept of peacekeeping would significantly broaden the scope of peacekeeping missions. These proposals were not well received by all. Small

---

117 *An Agenda for Peace, Report of the Secretary-General pursuant to the statement adopted by the Summit Meeting of the Security Council on 31 January 1992*, UNGAOR, 47th Sess, UN Doc A/47/277 (1992) 1.

nations viewed the proposal allowing preventive deployment of troops even in the absence of hostilities as a threat to their sovereignty.[118] The permanent members of the Security Council were fearful of the proposal to establish a permanent rapid deployment force under the command and authority of the Secretary-General. Western countries were concerned about the Secretary-General's expansive definition of peacekeeping, which entailed a greater degree of risk to their personnel and higher costs of peacekeeping. The crisis in Somalia confirmed that their fear, at least in relation to risk of physical harm, was objectively well-founded.

a) Somalian Fiasco

Somalia is strategically located on the Horn of Africa with an extensive coastline on the Indian Ocean. It became a victim of the Cold War as a result of the USSR's support of a revolutionary regime in neighbouring Ethiopia in the 1970s and 1980s. To prevent a Soviet expansion in East Africa, the United States backed the Somali regime of Siad Barre. However, with the end of the Cold War, superpowers lost interest in the region and withdrew their support. The corrupt and unpopular government of Somalia was vulnerable without American support. When the Somali government was deposed at the beginning of 1991, the country had no central authority. Rival opposition parties, led primarily by warlords, began to fight for power.

Initially, the UN became involved in the horrid conflict in Somalia for humanitarian reasons. It was the first time the peacekeeping force had been used for humanitarian intervention. In 1992, 1.5 million people (or a quarter of the Somali population) were at risk of starvation. Approximately five thousand people were dying daily. Consequently, in April 1992, the Security Council established a mission with the task of furnishing humanitarian assistance to the population. The United States agreed to send American combat troops to protect aid workers. After a Somali ambush and killing of a group of Pakistani blue helmets, the Security Council expanded the mandate of the peacekeeping

118 Marcus Franda, *The United Nations in the Twenty-First Century* (Lanham: Rowman & Littlefield Publishers, 2006) at 65.

mission, authorizing it to take any measure against all those responsible for the armed attacks.[119] In an attempt to capture the warlord responsible for the attack perpetrated against Pakistani peacekeeping troops, a small assault team of US commandos staged an unexpected attack that did not go as planned. Somali guerrillas captured several American soldiers and paraded their mutilated bodies through the streets of Mogadishu. The US public was shocked by the televised images of Somalis dragging the corpses of American soldiers and demanded the withdrawal of US troops from Somalia. The reaction of the Clinton administration was the promulgation of the Presidential Directive, which significantly limited American participation in UN peace-enforcement operations. Many Western countries followed suit by largely withdrawing support for peacekeeping. Unfortunately, it is in this climate that the peacekeeping mission in Rwanda was established.

b) Rwandan Genocide

The first negative consequence of the Security Council's disengagement due to the Somali fiasco was the failure of the international community to offer troops during the genocide in Rwanda in 1994.[120] The UN Security Council ignored evidence that the genocide was planned and refused to act once it had started. Approximately 2,500 UN peacekeepers were withdrawn after the murder of ten Belgian soldiers. In one case, the peacekeeping forces left hundreds of Tutsis to their fate when a shelter where they were hiding was attacked. The root causes of the hostilities were summarized by Canadian General Roméo Dallaire, who served as Force Commander of UNAMIR, the ill-fated UN peacekeeping force for Rwanda:

> When the Belgians chased the Germans out of the territory in 1916, they discovered that two groups of people shared the land.

---

119 SC Res 837 (1993), UNSCOR, 48th Year, UN Doc S/Res/837 (1993) (1993) 1 at para 5.

120 For a thorough analysis of the Rwandan genocide see the *Report of the Independent Inquiry into the Actions of the United Nations during the 1994 Genocide in Rwanda*, UNSCOR, 54th Year, UN Doc S/1999/1257 (1999) 3.

> The Tutsis, who were tall and quite light-skinned, herded cattle; the shorter, darker Hutus farmed vegetable plots. The Belgians viewed the minority Tutsis as closer in kind to Europeans and elevated them to positions of power over the majority Hutu.[121]

In 1962, the Tutsi "dominance of the colonial era was overturned during a violent power struggle that accompanied decolonization of the Belgian rule."[122] A popular uprising slaughtered or drove out the Tutsi elite and installed a Hutu-dominated government.[123] Over the next decade, Hutus continued persecuting Tutsis and Tutsis continued fleeing to neighbouring countries (Burundi, Democratic Republic of the Congo, and Uganda), where they struggled as stateless refugees. As a result of this precarious existence, Tutsi refugees decided to forcefully return to Rwanda and formed the Rwandese Patriotic Front (RPF). This armed group would subsequently become a formidable force. In October 1990, the RPF, consisting primarily of Tutsis, launched an assault from neighbouring Uganda against the government led by Hutus. Since Rwanda's independence, Hutus had always been fearful of a return of Tutsi hegemony. This fear nearly materialized with the unexpected invasion of the RPF in October 1990. Without military support from France, the Hutu government forces would have been unable to repel the attack.[124]

In August 1993, under pressure from Belgium, France, and the United States, the belligerent parties signed a peace agreement and requested the Security Council of the United Nations to establish a peacekeeping mission.[125] France was the only permanent member of the Security Council willing to intervene in Rwanda. There was "little appetite among permanent members of the Security Council for mandating a new peacekeeping force in so distant and, to many, so

121 Roméo Dallaire, *Shake Hands with the Devil: The Failure of Humanity in Rwanda* (London: Arrow Books, 2004) at 47.

122 Kofi Annan, *Interventions: A Life in War and Peace* (London: Penguin Books, 2012) at 48.

123 Dallaire, above note 121 at 47.

124 Annan, above note 122 at 49.

125 Boutros Boutros-Ghali, *Unvanquished: A US–UN Saga* (London: IB Tauris Publishers, 1999) at 129; and Annan, *ibid.*

obscure a country—especially when they were so preoccupied with other complicated, sizable, and deeply troubled missions in Somalia and Bosnia."[126] The members of the Security Council reached a compromise whereby France agreed to support a peacekeeping force in Haiti (to please the United States) and in Georgia (to satisfy Russia) in exchange for their support of a peacekeeping mission in Rwanda. Nevertheless, the peacekeeping force established in Rwanda was clearly inadequate in strength and number of troops. It is therefore not surprising that when Roméo Dallaire warned the UN leadership of an imminent ethnic cleansing, he was not authorized to take any action to prevent it. A mere three months after Dallaire's code cable, approximately 800,000 people, predominantly Tutsis, were killed. The trigger was the plane crash carrying the presidents of Rwanda and Burundi (both Hutus). A controversy still surrounds this incident. "Opponents of the current regime and some academics insist that RPF rebels shot [the plane] down, while the RPF and other regional experts maintain that it was extremists within the Habyarimana [Hutu] government"[127] who "were opposed to the concessions that the two Hutu presidents had been making to the Tutsis in Rwanda and Burundi."[128] However, Hutu leaders blamed Tutsis for the assassination and incited violence, which resulted in a brutal slaughter of civilians. Although the government organized the massacre, the Hutu civilian population carried it out using grenades, guns, machetes, clubs, swords, knives, drowning, arson, sticks, rocks, and bare hands.[129] In the meantime, the UN peacekeepers either fled or helplessly witnessed the massacre of innocent civilians. What brought the genocide to an end was not the intervention of a United Nations peacekeeping force, a superpower, or an adjacent country; it was RPF's victory over the former government of Rwanda.

---

126 *Ibid.*

127 Jason K Stearns, *Dancing in the Glory of Monsters: The Collapse of the Congo and the Great War of Africa* (New York: Public Affairs, 2011) at 14, n 1.

128 Boutros-Ghali, above note 125 at 131.

129 Scott Straus, "How many perpetrators were there in the Rwandan genocide? An estimate" (2004) 6:1 *Journal of Genocide Research* 85 at 88.

c) Democratic Republic of the Congo (DRC)

When the Hutu regime in Rwanda crumbled, the Tutsi Rwandan Patriotic Front, led by Paul Kagame (current president of Rwanda) took power. Fearful of reprisals, over a million Hutus, including the perpetrators of the massacres against Tutsis, fled across the border into neighbouring Congo. This however did not end the civil war in Rwanda. Hutus had the intention of waging a war from the DRC, whereas Paul Kagame was determined to root out the *génocidaires*, even if that meant encroaching on the territorial sovereignty of a neighbouring country. Kagame knew that Mobutu—then president of the Democratic Republic of the Congo—had sent troops to support the Hutu regime in Rwanda in its fight against the Tutsi Rwandan Patriotic Front. He also knew that Mobutu was harbouring Hutus who had organized and carried out massacres against Tutsis. Therefore, President Kagame did not hesitate to send Rwandan soldiers and death squads across the border. The president of Rwanda was not the only leader of a neighbouring country upset with the Congolese president. Aspiring to become the leader of a regional power, Mobutu had angered several countries in the region by welcoming dissident armed groups of other states. Therefore, in 1996, a regional military coalition led by Angola, Rwanda, and Uganda formed to overthrow the Congolese military dictator.[130] The coalition triumphed within a few months. In May 1997, the first Congolese war ended with the toppling of Mobutu Sese Seko. Laurent-Désiré Kabila, an experienced rebel and former supporter of Patrice Lumumba, was installed as the new president of the DRC.

Rwanda had used the war to topple Mobutu as an opportunity to exterminate all traces of Hutu resistance in the Congolese refugee camps right across the border. In the process, the Rwandan army had also killed a large number of Congolese civilians. Even after Laurent Kabila was sworn into office, Rwandan fighters remained in the Congo and continued committing abuses against the Congolese population. The extrajudicial killings of and sexual abuses perpetrated against refugee and civilian populations generated a great public outcry among

---

130 Stearns, above note 127 at 7.

the Congolese population. Eventually, Kabila's regime yielded to the public pressure and he turned against those who helped him grab power. Kabila began recruiting and training Hutu fighters hiding in the DRC who were part of the Rwandan army during the genocide. Kabila's decision infuriated Rwanda. For the Congo's tiny neighbour, Kabila's decision to strengthen Hutu armed groups posed a serious threat. This triggered the second Congolese war. In August 1998, Rwanda and Uganda agreed to invade eastern Congo for a second time, in an attempt to replace Kabila with a friendlier leader. This invasion precipitated the second Congolese war. This time, however, Rwanda and Uganda had made a strategic mistake; they were so confident in success that they had found it unnecessary to seek Angola and Zimbabwe's assent before attacking the Congo. Yet, these two countries were satisfied with the newly appointed President Kabila. Therefore, they deployed troops to help Kabila repel the Rwandan and Ugandan invasion. At the same time, the DRC exerted political pressure against Rwanda and Uganda by instituting proceedings against them before the International Court of Justice.

Although the war officially ended in 2003, the fighting in the eastern parts of the Congo continues to this day. This armed conflict has claimed millions of lives and produced an even larger number of refugees and internally displaced persons.

d) Bosnian Peacekeeping Disaster

During the same decade, the United Nations confronted an equally macabre war in the former Yugoslavia where the traditional precondition for a successful peace operation—a responsive host state—was absent.

In the 1990s, Yugoslavia was a complex mix of ethnicities and religions. It consisted of Serbia, Croatia, Bosnia-Hercegovina, Macedonia, Montenegro, Slovenia, and Kosovo. The country's population included Sunni Muslims, Catholics, and Orthodox Christians. This ethnically and religiously diverse area became a federal state after the Second World War.

During World War II, Joseph Broz Tito led a major communist resistance movement against Nazis in the Balkans. When the Axis powers were defeated, Tito became the leader of a united Yugoslavia during the post-war period and held power for almost four decades. Although Yugoslavia was a communist state, it entertained good relations with the United States and Western Europe. It was also a thriving state with stable economic growth. However, it was politically vulnerable because any internal strife or revolt could lead to a Soviet invasion similar to the one in Czechoslovakia in 1968 under the pretext of restoring order. Such external intervention would have deprived Yugoslavia of all forms of political autonomy. Therefore, Tito ruthlessly oppressed any nationalist tendencies. Tito's death in 1980 coincided with a decline in Yugoslavia's economy. Nationalistic sentiments were flowering all across the country. In 1986, the idea of creating a Greater Serbia appealed to many nationalist Serbs. Nationalism was also growing in Kosovo, where a predominantly Albanian population was no longer content with Serbian political supremacy and domination.

The emergence of a Serb nationalist leader with a strong personality like Slobodan Milošević was sufficient to spark ethnically fuelled violence. Milošević annulled Kosovo's status as an autonomous province and forcibly suppressed Albanian Kosovars' protests. These actions caused concern among the other republics of Yugoslavia. In 1991, Croatia, Slovenia, and Bosnia declared independence and violence spread throughout the country in the following months. Troops of the Serbian-dominated regular army and militias took over a third of Croatia's territory in their attempt to block Croatian secession. In December 1991, Bosnia's president formally appealed to the United Nations Security Council to deploy peacekeeping forces to reduce the risk of a serious outbreak of ethnic violence.

Although the UN deployed peacekeeping troops, Serbia did not stop its brutal bombing campaigns on the civilian population. In July 1995, the infamous Srebrenica massacre took place, during which the Bosnian Serb forces slew over 8,000 Bosnian Muslim men and boys and expelled 20,000 civilians from the area. This was an important failure for the UN because it transpired under the watch of Dutch peacekeeping troops.

At the heart of the UN's inability to protect the safe areas in Bosnia was the refusal of Security Council members to authorize enough troops to carry out the mandate of the peacekeeping mission. Secretary-General Boutros-Ghali had requested 34,000 troops, whereas the Security Council authorized only 7,400. Despite this, the United States government blamed the Secretary-General for the UN's failure and even vetoed his re-election for a second term. Boutros-Ghali became the first Secretary-General of the UN not to be re-appointed for a second term.

The events in Somalia, Rwanda, and Bosnia confirmed that the UN was not prepared to deal with the new generation of conflicts. Thus, UN member states initiated several important reforms of UN peacekeeping.

7) Period Under Kofi Annan's Leadership: 1997–2006

Appointed on 17 December 1996, Kofi Annan became the first black Secretary-General of the United Nations.[131] He was also the first Secretary-General appointed from within UN ranks. Kofi Annan began his international public service career as a junior professional in the World Health Organization and gradually climbed up the hierarchical pyramid of the UN apparatus. All Secretaries-General before and after him were diplomats or politicians in their countries of nationality before their appointments to the UN.

Determined not to repeat the dramatic failures of UN peacekeeping in the 1990s, one of the earliest reforms that Kofi Annan set in motion when he took office related to peacekeeping. He asked a high-level group of experts, composed of individuals experienced in conflict prevention, peacekeeping, and peacebuilding, to assess the UN system's shortcomings and to make frank and realistic recommendations for change.

The panel presented its recommendations in a seminal document known as the "Brahimi Report,"[132] named after the chairman

131 Kofi Annan was appointed in *Appointment of the Secretary-General of the United Nations*, GA Res 51/200, UNGAOR, 51st Sess, UN Doc A/RES/51/200 (1997), and UNGAOR, 51st Sess, 88th Mtg, A/51/PV.88 (1996) 1.

132 *Report of the Panel on United Nations Peace Operations*, UNSCOR, 55th Sess, UN Doc. A/55/305 and S/2000/809 (2000).

of the panel, Lakhdar Brahimi, an Algerian diplomat. Having noted that UN peacekeeping operations were not properly resourced and equipped, and were not given clear, credible, and achievable mandates, the Brahimi Report called for renewed political commitment on the part of member states, increased financial support commensurate with the peacekeeping mandate, as well as significant institutional changes. The UN implemented the recommendations of the Brahimi Report, enhancing its ability to fulfill its peacekeeping and peacebuilding mandates. As a result of this report, UN peacekeeping missions gained credibility and strength.

a) Millennium Development Goals

Although collective security continues to be at the core of the UN mandate, the security threats have substantially changed. The proliferation of civil strife in the Middle East, the ethnic conflicts in Africa, the rise of powerful transnational crime syndicates and terrorist organizations such as al-Qaeda and IS support the conclusion that in the twenty-first century, civil wars, terrorism, and mass migration of refugees are much more likely to disrupt global security than conventional interstate wars. Similarly, small arms, improvised exploding devices, or "dirty bombs" may cause as many (if not more) casualties than missiles and warheads.

Nevertheless, the major threat to life of billions of people is not violence or conflict; it is extreme poverty, the spread of infectious diseases, inequality, forced migration, climate change, environmental degradation, and shortage of water.[133] These are known as "soft threats." Consequently, the UN could not tackle security concerns in isolation. These issues needed to be addressed alongside security as central objectives. Thus, if any one goal can be said to have dominated the period during Kofi Annan's two consecutive mandates, it must surely be development.

A notable contribution of the United Nations under Kofi Annan's leadership is the landmark Millennium Declaration, adopted in 2000

---

133 Paul Heinbecker & Patricia Goff, *Irrelevant or Indispensable: The United Nations in the 21st Century* (Waterloo, ON: Wilfred Laurier University Press, 2005) at 1.

by all member states, and the 2005 World Summit Outcome document. These General Assembly resolutions reflect the commitment of member states to reach specific goals to attain peace, security, disarmament, development, poverty eradication, safeguarding of human rights, rule of law, preservation of the environment, satisfying the special needs of Africa, and so on. The Millennium Declaration set out within a single framework the key challenges facing humanity in the new millennium and proposed a response to these challenges through concrete measures. For assessing performance, there was a set of commitments, goals, and targets on development, governance, peace, security, and human rights.

In order to translate this commitment into action, the Millennium Development Goals (MDGs) were developed. The eight MDGs range from halving extreme poverty rates to halting the spread of HIV/AIDS and providing universal primary education by the target date of 2015. The MDGs have spurred efforts to meet the needs of the world's poorest and most vulnerable. In many parts of the world, the MDGs allowed the international community to address extreme poverty in its many dimensions—low income, hunger, disease, lack of adequate shelter, and exclusion. Although not every goal has been met, an enormous progress has been made in all areas.[134] In 2016, these goals were extended to seventeen Sustainable Development Goals with 169 associated targets to be met by 2030.[135]

Significant gaps remain in improving maternal and reproductive health; achieving gender equality; achieving full and productive employment, especially for women and youth; halting and reversing the alarming global rate of deforestation; and accelerating progress in least developed countries.

b) Afghanistan

During Kofi Annan's mandate, international terrorism reached new dimensions. The hijacking and crashing of four American passenger

---

134 *Report of the Secretary-General on the work of the Organization*, UNGAOR, 70th Sess, UN Doc A/70/1 (2015).

135 *Transforming our World: The 2030 Agenda for Sustainable Development*, GA Res 70/1, UNGAOR, 70th Sess, UN Doc A/RES/70/1 (2015) 1.

airplanes on 11 September 2001 brought instant attention to al-Qaeda and Afghanistan. The ultraconservative political and religious faction called Taliban ruled Afghanistan between 1996 and 2001 and provided sanctuary for perpetrators of the attacks of 11 September 2001. In late 2001, invoking its right of self-defence, the United States, with the assistance of the United Kingdom, invaded Afghanistan in order to overthrow the regime and to dismantle the terrorist organization al-Qaeda. Although the coalition managed to oust the Taliban within a few months, the war against al-Qaeda and Islamic fundamentalism never ended. The alliance of states that agreed to combat terrorism was drawn into a protracted war and occupation of Afghanistan. The Bush administration had underestimated the stamina of Afghan fighters. By the time the military intervention led by the United States in Afghanistan formally ended in December 2014, the war in Afghanistan had become the longest armed conflict ever fought by the United States. However, in 2003, the US administration had not foreseen that the war would last thirteen years. After toppling the Taliban regime in Afghanistan, the morale of the US administration was still high. In 2003, it turned its attention to regime change in Iraq as part of the second phase of what it called the Global War on Terror.

c) Invasion of Iraq (2003)

In 1990, after the end of the Cold War, US President George Bush asserted that the rule of law would supplant the rule of the jungle in international politics and prompted the United Nations to fulfill its long-promised role as the guardian of international peace and security. The magnanimous rhetoric of George HW Bush was short-lived. It is somewhat ironic that in 2003, his son, George W Bush, authorized the invasion of Iraq without a Security Council approval and on the basis of seemingly inaccurate information. Specifically, the American and British governments were advised by their respective intelligence services that Iraq possessed chemical and biological weapons and the means to deliver them. It was also alleged that Saddam Hussein had the intention of further building up his arsenal. On the basis of this flawed intelligence, the United States and the United Kingdom invaded Iraq without the assent of the UN Security Council.

Before the invasion, the UK government had convinced the US administration to seek international support for military intervention in Iraq. In November 2002, the Security Council unanimously adopted Resolution 1441,[136] giving Iraq a final opportunity to disarm or face serious consequences. It also provided for any further breaches by Iraq to be reported to the Security Council for assessment. The weapons inspectors returned to Iraq later that month. However, the US administration had already decided that further weapons inspections were futile and that Saddam Hussein needed to be removed from power. To satisfy the wishes of his British ally, President Bush agreed to seek a further UN resolution determining that Iraq had failed to take its final opportunity to comply with its obligations. However, the United States was unable to secure a majority support for a second resolution. Without evidence of new Iraqi violations or reports from the inspectors that Iraq was failing to cooperate, France and Russia were not convinced that peaceful options to disarm Iraq had been exhausted and that military action was therefore justified.

Nevertheless, the United States and the United Kingdom launched a joint military attack against Iraq without a UN Security Council resolution authorizing the use of force. The consequences of this action were in many respects disastrous. Iraq became a failed state and the ensuing chaos resulted in the creation of major terrorist organizations, including the Islamic State (IS), that were responsible for the deaths of thousands of people.

This substantially undermined the idea of collective security in a world dominated by a single superpower. The US-led invasion of Iraq also set a precedent for permanent members of the Security Council to violate international law with impunity. Russia's annexation of Crimea and large-scale intervention in Ukraine in 2014 and 2015 is only one recent consequence of this precedent.

d) Canal Hotel Bombing—UN Becomes a Target of Terrorist Attacks

Since the establishment of the United Nations, its logo and flag have been much more than means of identification for the United Nations

136 SC Res 1441 (2002), UNSCOR, 57th Year, UN Doc S/Res/1441 (2002) 1.

personnel and vehicles in areas of trouble and conflict. The UN flag and logo were aspirational symbols; they represented hope, peace, unity, and neutrality. This changed when, in August 2003, the United Nations became the target of a terrorist plot. On 23 August 2003, a suicide bomber drove a truck filled with explosives into the Canal Hotel of Baghdad, where the United Nations had its headquarters, killing twenty-two people, and injuring hundreds. This bombing marked a profound change in the way the UN and other humanitarian organizations operate today. This terrorist attack blurred the separation line between military and humanitarian workers. Just two months after the Canal Hotel bombing, terrorists also bombed the offices of the International Committee of the Red Cross (ICRC) in Baghdad, which had always commanded the utmost respect worldwide.

Although the United Nations had condemned the US–UK invasion of Iraq as illegal, the deployment of hundreds of UN aid workers immediately after that of the US troops may have given the impression to the radical elements of Iraq that the UN was operating alongside the United States. The fact that the sanctions authorized by the UN Security Council, which the Iraqi population resented so much, were enforced and implemented by the United Nations may have added to the confusion. Secretary of State Colin Powell's remarks describing humanitarian agencies as an important part of the American combat team only reinforced this erroneous belief. The recorded speech of the terrorist group that was televised after the Canal Hotel bombing confirmed that the terrorists regarded the UN as an accomplice of the American military campaign in Iraq.

The Canal Hotel bombing set a terrible precedent. Since then, the UN has been the subject of terrorist attacks in many parts of the world, including Afghanistan, Pakistan, Syria, Iraq, Mali, Somalia, and Algeria. The division between the military and humanitarian personnel no longer exists in many parts of the world where the United Nations has a peacekeeping mission. Humanitarian and aid workers are now obliged to use armoured vehicles, carry radio transmitters, wear bulletproof vests and helmets, and be accompanied by armed security teams. Today, the humanitarian aid is compelled to militarize to fulfill its mission.

8) Period Under Ban Ki Moon's Leadership: 2007–2016

On 1 January 2007, Ban Ki Moon, a national of South Korea, became the eighth Secretary-General of the UN.[137] The decade following his appointment proved that the world is indeed a global village; the events in one country may have repercussions in other countries. The European Union continued to welcome new members from Eastern Europe. The mortgage crisis in the United States affected the global economy. Protests in Tunisia led to a series of revolutions in the Middle East and North African region.

a) The Arab Spring

The profound transformation in the Middle East and North African region began on 17 December 2010, when a Tunisian street vendor, Mohammed Bouazizi, set himself on fire in an act of protest against humiliation by local police for not having a permit to sell vegetables. This suicide was followed by mass anti-government protests. In January 2011, the president of Tunisia, Ben Ali, bowed to the pressure and fled to Saudi Arabia. This ignited a spark that would subsequently be known as the "Arab Spring." From Tunisia, the spark then moved to Egypt, where Egyptians held a coordinated mass protest demanding Mubarak's resignation after three decades in power. During the same month, January 2011, similar protests erupted in Yemen and Sudan. In February 2011, as soon as Mubarak announced his resignation, the Arab Spring spilled over into Bahrain, where thousands demanded substantial reforms. Within two days, protesters took to the streets in Benghazi, Libya, demanding Gaddafi's resignation. A violent crackdown triggered a destructive civil war in Libya. The Security Council passed a controversial resolution authorizing the use of "all necessary measure" to protect civilians. Russia, China, and Germany were

137 SC Res 1715 (2006), UNSCOR, 61st Year, UN Doc S/RES/1715 (2006) (2006) and UNSCOR, 61st Year, 5547th Mtg, S/PV.5547 (2006); *Appointment of the Secretary-General of the United Nations*, GA Res 61/3, UNGAOR, 61st Sess, UN Doc A/RES/61/3 (2006) and UNGAOR, 61st Sess, 31st Plen Mtg, A/61/PV.31 (2006).

among the countries that voiced their concerns and abstained from voting. On the basis of the broad language of the Security Council resolution, NATO carried out a full-scale bombing campaign. The intervention by NATO significantly weakened the Libyan army and allowed the rebels to capture and execute Gaddafi in October 2011. Gaddafi's death created a political vacuum and subsequently resulted in violence between political factions. Libya became a failed state and breeding ground for international terrorists.

In the meantime, in March 2011, the Syrian population revolted against its regime as well. By June 2012, the uprising in Syria had transformed into a war. The Security Council tried to intervene again; however, this time, Russia and China were opposed to any use of armed force in Syria. Russia took a hard stance against any resolution intended to topple sitting leaders. Considering Libya's current situation, this objection was not without basis. The war in Syria has cost hundreds of thousands of lives and has caused the displacement of millions of refugees. Syria can be regarded today as a failed state too.

Unfortunately, the Arab Spring was not followed by an Arab summer. Countries where regimes were toppled are neither more democratic nor more developed. In Tunisia, soon after Ben Ali resigned, several high-profile politicians were assassinated. The political situation in the country remains unstable. The same applies to Egypt; the Muslim Brotherhood, an oppressive and undemocratic regime, replaced President Mubarak. The Muslim Brotherhood was also overthrown within one year of taking power and replaced by a military regime. Yemen, Syria, and Libya became failed states. Bahrain managed to oppress its dissidents by soliciting the military assistance of Saudi Arabia and the United Arab Emirates. Libya and Syria will require decades to be rebuilt. The UN Economic and Social Commission for Western Asia (UN-ESCWA) estimated in a report that the Arab Spring led to a net loss of over USD$600 billion in economic activity, which represents 6 percent of the region's GDP.

The United Nations has a large number of political and peacekeeping missions in the Middle East and North African region. The proliferation of internal conflicts in the region, and the world in general, combined with the UN's limited, and lately shrinking, resources, makes it impossible for the organization to focus on any one of these conflicts. Instead of concentrating its efforts on preventing armed conflicts by addressing their underlying issues in a timely manner, the UN is forced to operate in a constant state of emergency by putting out fires.

b) Ukraine

If there were still some doubts about the inefficiency of the Security Council after the civil wars in Libya and Syria, the limitations of the UN collective security system became apparent with the crisis in Ukraine. This conflict confirmed once again that the organization is helpless when one of the recalcitrant parties is a superpower with a permanent seat in the Security Council.

In November 2013, Ukraine was scheduled to sign association agreements aimed at expanding political and economic ties with the European Union. One week before the summit, Ukraine's pro-Russian president, Victor Yanukovych, announced that Ukraine would suspend negotiations with the EU in order to concentrate efforts on strengthening its relationship with Russia. Mass protests erupted in Kiev and other cities across Ukraine. An estimated 100,000 Ukrainians who supported the deal with the EU gathered in Maidan, Kiev's independence square. A confrontation between the protesters and the police force caused hundreds of deaths. This violent crackdown resulted in larger demonstrations that took place in December 2013 and January 2014. Eventually, the popular protest ousted the pro-Russian president from office. An interim pro-Western government seized power.

In the meantime, in March 2014, militia affiliated with the Russian army took control of the autonomous republic of Crimea, which was historically part of Russia. Crimea's self-proclaimed parliament voted to secede from Ukraine and organized a Crimea-wide referendum, during which the majority of the population, primarily people of Russian ethnicity, voted in favour of joining Russia. The majority of UN member states condemned Russia's interference in Ukrainian domestic affairs and its use of force. A draft resolution declaring illegal the referendum regarding the independence of Crimea was vetoed by Russia in the Security Council.[138] It is noteworthy that China abstained on the basis that Russia's military intervention in Ukraine, though unlawful, was prompted by foreign interference in Ukraine.

Unable to condemn Russia's actions in the Security Council, member states took the issue to the General Assembly, which adopted a resolution calling upon all states, international organizations, and specialized agencies not to recognize any alteration of the status of the autonomous Republic of Crimea on the basis of the referendum and to refrain from recognizing Russia's annexation of Crimea.[139] However, the General Assembly resolution is only symbolic and cannot be enforced. Consequently, member states had to resort to individual or collective sanctions outside the statutory framework of the *UN Charter*.

c) Refugee Crisis

In 2015, a significant displacement of populations posed enormous challenges for the international community and the United Nations. Wars, armed conflicts, lawlessness, increasingly frequent natural disasters (floods, earthquakes, hurricanes, tsunamis, and forest fires), extreme poverty, and other types of socio-economic deprivation (the lack of food, water, education, and basic health care) were the main reasons forcing people to flee their countries.[140] A high number of these migrants, mainly from the Middle East and Africa, undertook perilous journeys to reach European shores. By the end of 2016, over five million asylum seekers were at the EU's doorstep. In the process, thousands, including women and unaccompanied children, perished or went missing in search of safety.

In March 2016, the European Union entered into a controversial agreement with Turkey in order to prevent migrants from entering

---

138 SC Draft Res S/2014/136, UNSCOR, 69th Year, 7138th Meeting, UN Doc S/PV.7138 (2014) 2.

139 *Territorial Integrity of Ukraine*, GA Res 68/262, UNGAOR, 68th Sess, UN Doc A/Res/68/262 (2014) 1.

140 The *Convention Relating to the Status of Refugees*, 28 July 1951, 189 UNTS 137 (entered into force 22 April 1954) recognizes as refugees only those individuals who flee persecution for reasons of race, religion, nationality, membership of a particular social group, or political opinion.

the EU. The deal required Turkey to block border crossings by migrants into the EU. In exchange, the EU promised to give Turkish nationals access to the Schengen passport-free zone, to provide financial aid, and to resume negotiations for Turkey's bid to join the EU. Human rights groups and civil society strongly criticized the deal, especially after televised images of drowned children floating to the shores of Greek islands shocked the public. Consistent with his style, Secretary-General Ban failed to take a strong stance and voice more assertively the UN's concern on this issue.

9) Period Under Antonio Guterres's Leadership: 2017–

When Ban Ki Moon's mandate expired, it was believed that the most suitable successor would be a female from an Eastern European country, since no woman has ever been elected Secretary-General and the Eastern European Group was the only regional group never to have held the office of Secretary-General.[141] A male candidate from Western Europe—a regional group that has already held the office three times—was an unlikely pick. Despite all odds, the General Assembly appointed Antonio Guterres of Portugal, a seasoned politician who served as Portugal's prime minister and as the UN High Commissioner for Refugees.

a) Revival of Nuclear Threat

During Antonio Guterres's first term, three separate incidents significantly increased the threat of nuclear proliferation.

First, in 2017, North Korea successfully tested its first intercontinental ballistic missile. During the same year, it carried out another test of a weapon that it claimed was a thermonuclear missile. Its increasingly sophisticated nuclear weapons and ballistic missile program, combined with its extreme poverty, represents an immense threat, particularly for South Korea. In addition, North Korea is also believed

141 Irina Bokova from Bulgaria, the former Director General of UNESCO, seemed to fit the bill. Another outstanding female candidate for the position was former Prime Minister of New Zealand and former Administrator of UNDP Helen Clark.

to possess biological and chemical weapons. UN Secretary-General Guterres recalled that non-proliferation remains a fundamental pillar of global nuclear security and must be preserved, and invited North Korea to resume a dialogue aimed at bringing about the complete denuclearization of the Korean Peninsula.

Second, in May 2018, the Trump administration announced that the United States was withdrawing from a nuclear agreement among the five permanent members of the Security Council, Germany, and Iran, named the Joint Comprehensive Plan of Action. Celebrated by the UN as a major achievement of nuclear non-proliferation, this 160-page agreement was signed in July 2015 and endorsed by the Security Council.[142] The purpose of the deal was to ensure that Iran's nuclear program was exclusively peaceful. Iran's compliance with this obligation was subject to verifications by the International Atomic Energy Agency (a UN-related organization). In return, Iran obtained phased sanctions relief. President Trump abandoned the deal and reinstated sanctions on Iran, claiming that Iran was persistently breaching its obligations under the pact. In an attempt to salvage the deal, European states remained parties to the agreement and took measures to alleviate the consequences that the unilateral decision of the United States produced on Iran. Nevertheless, in April 2019, allegations that Iran was developing missiles capable of delivering nuclear warheads surfaced on social media.

Third, in August 2019, the United States pulled out of the *Intermediate-Range Nuclear Forces Treaty* (INF) signed in 1987 by President Reagan and Soviet leader Mikhail Gorbachev. This treaty memorialized an arms control deal that banned short- and medium-range (between 500 and 5,500 km) nuclear and non-nuclear missiles. The treaty also allowed both countries to inspect each other's installations in order to ensure that they were complying with their obligations. The agreement was a major success; by 1991, the United States and Russia had destroyed approximately 2,700 missiles. In 2019, the United States and its NATO allies accused Russia of violating the agreement by developing a new type of missile, which prompted the US

142 SC Res 2231 (2015), UNSCOR, 70th Year, UN Doc S/Res/2231 (2015) 1.

withdrawal. Antonio Guterres deplored the decision to terminate the INF treaty, pointing out that "the world will lose an invaluable brake on nuclear war."

b) Myanmar

The Rohingya, believed to be descendants of Arab traders, are an ethnic and religious minority living in the Rakhine state of Myanmar to the south of Bangladesh. At the start of 2017, approximately one million Rohingya lived in Myanmar, representing the largest Muslim minority group in Myanmar, with the majority living in Rakhine state. This ethnic group has its own language and culture. The government of Myanmar, a predominantly Buddhist country, sees them as illegal immigrants from Bangladesh and refuses to recognize them as citizens of Myanmar. Secretary-General Guterres described the Rohingya as "people [who] have always been one of, if not the, most discriminated people in the world, without any recognition of the most basic rights starting by the recognition of the right of citizenship by their own country—Myanmar."[143] Deep-rooted tensions between the Buddhist majority and the Rohingya minority living in Rakhine state have led to violent skirmishes in the past. However, the situation significantly worsened in August 2017, when a group of Rohingya militants[144] launched attacks on police stations, killing several members of the security forces. The authorities reacted with a disproportionate crackdown against the entire Rohingya population, including women and children.

The Human Rights Council established an independent fact-finding mission to investigate allegations of human rights violations by military and security forces of Myanmar.[145] The mission released its report in September 2018, concluding that the Myanmar security

---

143 Unofficial transcript of Secretary-General's remarks at a press encounter with president of the World Bank, Jim Yong Kim, on his visit to Cox's Bazar, Bangladesh, on 2 July 2018.

144 The group responsible for the attacks is known as Arakan Rohingya Salvation Army (ARSA), which claims to protect the Rohingya against state-led repression.

145 *Situation of Human Rights in Myanmar*, HRC Res 34/22, UNHRCOR, 31st Sess, UN Doc A/HCR/Res/34/22 (2017) 1.

forces, particularly the military, committed serious violations of international humanitarian law that amount to the gravest crimes under international law. It established that Myanmar's armed forces deliberately targeted civilians and the government of Myanmar promoted a culture of impunity.[146]

China halted any decisive action by the Security Council against Myanmar, arguing that this was a development and poverty issue.[147] In November 2019, The Gambia, a small West African state, supported by the Organisation of Islamic Cooperation, instituted proceedings against Myanmar before the International Court of Justice, alleging violations of the Convention on the Prevention and Punishment of the Crime of Genocide. Pending the outcome of the case, The Gambia asked the ICJ to make an emergency ruling on its request for provisional measures and order the cessation of violence against Rohingya. On 23 January 2020, the ICJ granted the request and ordered Myanmar to do all it could to prevent the perpetration of genocidal crimes against Rohingya.[148] In February 2020, some member states of the Security Council attempted to explore ways to ensure Myanmar's compliance with the order for provisional measures issued by the ICJ, but discussions on this matter were once again blocked by China.

c) Pandemic

In 2020, the UN was confronted with a different type of threat to global peace and security. The COVID-19 pandemic forced most nations to impose complete lockdowns, causing the greatest disruption to global economic activity since the Second World War. The economic impact is particularly disproportionate in developing countries and states torn by armed conflict. This creates instability and a breeding ground for conflict in many parts of the world, especially in and near refugee camps sheltering particularly vulnerable persons. The

---

146 *Report of the independent international fact-finding mission on Myanmar*, UNHRCOR, 39th Sess, UN Doc A/HRC/39/64 (2018).

147 *The situation in Myanmar*, UNSCOR, 74th Year, 8477th Mtg, UN Doc S/PV.8477 (2019).

148 *Application of the Convention on the Prevention and Punishment of the Crime of Genocide (The Gambia v Myanmar)*, Provisional Measures, [2020] ICJ Rep 1.

pandemic also created a risk of civil unrest in countries where the authorities mishandled the crisis, postponed elections, used the opportunity to adopt controversial laws, or to crack down on individual freedoms and the press.

Chapter 2

PURPOSES AND PRINCIPLES

Delegations from fifty states worked on the final text of the *Charter of the United Nations* (*UN Charter*) during the San Francisco conference. A large number of people were split into committees and subcommittees that worked simultaneously on specific parts or topics of the *UN Charter*. One of these technical committees had the responsibility to prepare draft provisions of the Preamble, Purposes, and Principles. This part sets the tone for the entire *UN Charter*. The Preamble needed to have a "language and tone which [would] lead its way to the hearts of men, [would] awaken the imagination of the common man to the points at issue, kindle his feelings and move him."[1] The most difficult part of this task was to conceive a text that not only had "literary sense of harmony, rhythm and appealing moral beauty" but also "juristic consideration of precision and logical sequence."[2] The other difficulty was to draw up a sharp and clear-cut distinction between what should be included under the Preamble, Purposes, and Principles. "Some questions were transferred during the deliberations from the Preamble to Purposes, from Purposes to Principles and from Principles back to the Preamble."[3]

1 United Nations Conference on International Organizations, Commission I, General Provisions, Verbatim Minutes of First Meeting of Commission I, Doc 2006 I/6 (15 June 1945) at 1 [Conference on International Organizations].

2 *Ibid.*

3 *Ibid* at 16.

A. PREAMBLE

It is noteworthy that, initially, the founders of the UN did not plan to insert a preamble in the *UN Charter*. The chief delegate of South Africa, Field Marshal Smuts, proposed the inclusion of the preamble, arguing that,

> [W]hatever efforts we might make to define the Organization—could only hope to succeed if it found support in the public opinion of mankind all over the world. Because of that, it was essential that it should not only be drafted in as precise terms as we could find, but that there should be great warmth and simplicity, at least in the first lines, so that we may hope to find an answer in the hearts of humanity.[4]

The Preamble of the *UN Charter* is the ideology of the organization. It sets forth the declared common intentions that brought countries together in San Francisco to harmonize, organize, and regulate their international action.[5] It differs significantly from the style of preambular clauses of international agreements and conventions. It is drafted in the name of the peoples of the United Nations as opposed to in the name of states, making it clear that the UN is not so much about states and their governments as it is about its peoples who have endured the horrible experience of World War II. It expresses the hopes of mankind to be preserved forever from the repetition of such horrors. A US delegate to the San Francisco conference stated that the text of the Preamble was intended to "express the intentions, the ideals, and the emotions which animate the nations as we join together in this great new world Organization. It is a sort of preface, and probably many millions of people will read it and it alone, and not read further into the more complicated parts of the *UN Charter*. We had hoped that the Preamble might be so simple and clear and moving that it might hang upon the wall of every home in all our member nations, and be understood by common man everywhere,

4 *Ibid* at 13.
5 *Ibid* at 17.

and warm their hearts and strengthen them after the long exhaustion and sorrow of war."[6] The Preamble of the *UN Charter* reads as follows:

WE THE PEOPLES OF THE UNITED NATIONS DETERMINED

- to save succeeding generations from the scourge of war, which twice in our lifetime has brought untold sorrow to mankind, and
- to reaffirm faith in fundamental human rights, in the dignity and worth of the human person, in the equal rights of men and women and of nations large and small, and
- to establish conditions under which justice and respect for the obligations arising from treaties and other sources of international law can be maintained, and
- to promote social progress and better standards of life in larger freedom.

AND FOR THESE ENDS

- To practice tolerance and live together in peace with one another as good neighbours, and
- To unite our strengths to maintain international peace and security, and
- To ensure, by the acceptance of principles and the institution of methods, that armed force shall not be used, save in the common interests, and
- To employ international machinery for the promotion of the Economic and social advancement of all peoples,

HAVE RESOLVED TO COMBINE OUR EFFORTS TO ACCOMPLISH THESE AIMS

- Accordingly, our respective Governments, through representatives assembled in the city of San Francisco, who have exhibited their full powers found to be in good and due form, have agreed to the present Charter of the United Nations and do hereby establish an international organization to be known as the United Nations.

Normally, preambular clauses are not an integral part of a legal instrument; it may be useful for the purposes of teleological

6 *Ibid* at 19.

interpretation only.[7] This was not the intended role of the *Charter's* Preamble. The Rapporteur of the Technical Committee I pointed out that there were no grounds for supposing that the Preamble had less legal validity than the two succeeding chapters. Therefore, unlike preambular clauses of most agreements, the Preamble of the *UN Charter* has a legally binding effect. From a practical perspective, however, the language of the Preamble is more political and aspirational than legal. No legal rule or norm can be derived from or identified in the Preamble.

B. PURPOSES

Article 1 of the *UN Charter* identifies four purposes of the United Nations. These purposes constitute the raison d'être of the organization. They are the aggregation of those common ends on which all founding members of the organization agreed. They are the cause and object of the *UN Charter*. These purposes are:

1. To maintain international peace and security, and to that end: to take effective collective measures for the prevention and removal of threats to the peace, and for the suppression of acts of aggression or other breaches of the peace, and to bring about by peaceful means, and in conformity with the principles of justice and international law, adjustment or settlement of international disputes or situations which might lead to a breach of the peace;
2. To develop friendly relations among nations based on respect for the principle of equal rights and self-determination of peoples, and to take other appropriate measures to strengthen universal peace;
3. To achieve international co-operation in solving international problems of an economic, social, cultural, or humanitarian character, and in promoting and encouraging respect for human rights and for fundamental freedoms for all without distinction as to race, sex, language, or religion; and

7 *Case concerning the application of the Convention of 1902 governing the Guardianship of Infants (Netherlands v Sweden)*, [1958] ICJ Rep 55 at 67.

4. To be a centre for harmonizing the actions of nations in the attainment of these common ends.

The maintenance of international peace and security referred to in the first sentence of paragraph 1 was the chief purpose for creating the United Nations. As the International Court of Justice pointed out, this "primary place ascribed to international peace and security is natural, since the fulfilment of the other purposes will be dependent upon the attainment of that basic condition."[8] All other purposes that follow this paragraph are directly or indirectly related to it. The General Assembly recognized that international peace is a sacred right of all peoples.[9] What does the phrase "international peace and security" really mean? It is a universal ideal[10] and a notion infinitely broader than the mere absence of war. We often erroneously assume that wars erupt in hostile environments. The reality is that wars result from the absence of conditions and factors safeguarding peace. To prevent wars, the international community must nurture circumstances and environments essential to maintaining peace. Over the past seven decades, the General Assembly identified some conditions and factors that promote peace and security. They include the obligation of all states:

a. not to threaten or use force;[11]
b. not to use propaganda for wars or aggression;[12]
c. to take prompt united action to meet aggression whenever it arises;[13]
d. to respect each other's sovereignty, equality and territorial integrity;

---

8 *Certain expenses of the United Nations (Article 17, paragraph 2 of the Charter)*, Advisory Opinion, [1962] ICJ Rep 151 at 168.

9 *Declaration on the Right of Peoples to Peace*, GA Res 39/11, UNGAOR, 39th Sess, UN Doc A/Res/39/11 (1984) 22.

10 *Proclamation of the International Year of Peace*, Annex to GA Res 40/3, UNGAOR, 40th Sess, UN Doc A/Res/40/3 (1985) 15 [*International Year of Peace*].

11 *Essentials of peace*, GA Res 290 (IV), UNGAOR, 4th Sess, UN Doc A/Res/290(IV) (1949) [*Essentials of peace*].

12 *Declaration on the Preparation of Societies for Life in Peace*, GA Res 33/73, UNGAOR, 33rd Sess, UN Doc A/Res/33/73 (1978) 55 [*Preparation of Societies*].

13 *Peace through deeds*, GA Res 380 (V), UNGAOR, 5th Sess, UN Doc A/Res/380(V) (1950) 13 [*Peace through deeds*].

e. not to intervene in one another's internal affairs;
f. not to impair the freedom, independence or integrity of another state;[14]
g. to eliminate all forms of colonialism and apartheid;[15]
h. not to form civil strife or subvert the will of the people in any state;[16]
i. to settle international disputes by peaceful means;[17]
j. to control atomic energy and prohibit atomic weapons;[18]
k. to eliminate all weapons of mass destruction;[19]
l. to reduce to a minimum their armaments;[20]
m. to eliminate the threat inherent in the arms race;[21]
n. to carry out in good faith their international agreements;[22]
o. to allow peaceful expression of political opposition;[23]
p. to allow the exercise of religious freedom and the other fundamental rights;[24]
q. to regulate conventional armaments;[25]
r. to develop peaceful and tolerant relations among states based on mutual respect and benefit;
s. to broaden international cooperation and develop friendly relations;[26]
t. to promote mutually advantageous and equitable political, economic, social and cultural cooperation with other states;[27]

---

14 *Essentials of peace*, above note 11.
15 *Preparation of Societies*, above note 12.
16 *Essentials of peace*, above note 11.
17 *Ibid.*
18 *Ibid.*
19 *Peace through deeds*, above note 13.
20 *Ibid.*
21 *Preparation of Societies*, above note 12.
22 *Essentials of peace*, above note 11.
23 *Ibid.*
24 *Ibid.*
25 *Ibid.*
26 *Peaceful and neighbourly relations among States*, GA Res 1236 (XII), UNGAOR, 12th Sess, UN Doc A/Res/1236(XII) (1957) 5.
27 *Preparation of Societies*, above note 12.

u. to eliminate incitement to hatred and discrimination against other peoples;[28]
v. to eliminate injustice or advocacy of violence;[29]
w. to maintain the outer space for peaceful uses;[30]
x. to protect the environment;
y. to eliminate economic and social threats including poverty, infectious disease;[31]
z. to prevent inter-state conflicts, terrorism, and transnational organized crime.[32]

Most of the purposes contained in Article 1 of the *UN Charter* were not new. The first purpose—to maintain international peace and security through effective collective measures—was inherited from the League of Nations. The Covenant of the League of Nations provided that an act of aggression against one member of the League was deemed to be an act of war against all other members. It is through this collective security system that the League was able to impose sanctions on Italy for its invasion of Ethiopia and to expel the Soviet Union from the organization for its aggression against Finland. Although the collective security system of the League was structurally flawed and operationally dysfunctional it became the precedent or point of reference for the UN's collective security system. The *UN Charter* merely improved an existing system.

Similarly, the peaceful settlement of international disputes, also mentioned in the first purpose of the *UN Charter*, derives from the Hague Conventions of 1899 and 1907 and the Covenant of the League of Nations, which contained an obligation to settle international disputes through peaceful means. Between 1900 and 1945, the international community had extensively experimented with peaceful settlement of international disputes, mainly through the Permanent

28 *Ibid.*
29 *Ibid.*
30 *International Year of Peace*, above note 10.
31 *Ibid.*
32 *A More Secure World: Our Shared Responsibility*, Secretary-General's Report, UNGAOR, 59th Sess, UN Doc A/59/2005 (2005) 3.

Court of Arbitration and the Permanent Court of International Justice. As this proved to be an effective way of resolving many conflicts without use of force, it made perfect sense to include it in the purposes of the United Nations.

The second purpose of the *UN Charter*, which mandates the respect for self-determination of peoples, was already a subject of contention and discord between the United States and Soviet Union on the one hand and Great Britain and France on the other. Britain and France, two other key players in the creation of the United Nations, were the largest colonial powers of the time. Colonialism and self-determination of peoples are mutually exclusive concepts. Both the United States and the Soviet Union opposed colonialism. President Roosevelt felt strongly about the right to self-determination for all colonial peoples. He believed that colonialism was the major post-war problem. Roosevelt's position became even firmer when he visited The Gambia on his way to the 1943 Casablanca conference. While in The Gambia, Roosevelt fell ill. He attributed his illness to the insalubrious conditions of the British colony. He was so appalled by the poverty and disease he witnessed there that he wrote to Churchill describing the territory as a "hell-hole."[33] Once Roosevelt finally reached Casablanca, he also upset the French by telling the Moroccan Sultan that Morocco was entitled to self-determination like any other colony,[34] thereby hinting that the United States would support Moroccan aspirations for independence.

The third purpose of the *UN Charter* is to achieve international cooperation in economic, social, and humanitarian fields. It was already known that the Great Depression caused panic and resentment that led to fascism and war. Prominent economists and politicians argued that economic cooperation would allow nations to understand and appreciate the benefits of peace. This idea led to the establishment of the Bretton Woods institutions (the World Bank Group and the International Monetary Fund) only two months after the inception of the UN. The Bretton Woods agreements envisaged

---

33 Martin Meredith, *The Fate of Africa: A History of the Continent Since Independence* (New York: Public Affairs, 2011) at 9.

34 *Ibid.*

the creation of a third institution, known as the International Trade Organization, but this organization never saw the light of day because the US Congress refused to ratify its charter.[35] During the conceptual stages of the UN, the USSR wanted to limit the purpose of the organization strictly to direct threats of war, such as armed aggressions. The Soviet government was opposed to broadening the purposes of the organization beyond its main objective—the maintenance of international peace and security. Stalin was concerned that if the UN were allowed to play a role in economic, social, and humanitarian spheres, it would interfere in matters that fell within the exclusive jurisdiction of member states. However, the period between 1920 and 1945 had left no doubt that to prevent another world conflict the international community had to tackle not only acts of aggression but also the root causes of wars. Therefore, despite the Soviet opposition, it was decided that the UN would address the underlying causes of armed conflicts and aggressions, such as inequality, colonialism, and human rights violations.

The fourth purpose mentioned in the *UN Charter*—to be a centre for harmonizing the actions of nations in the attainment of these common ends—was new. The founders of the UN most probably did not suspect that they were setting up an organization that would grow from a few hundred staff members and a very modest budget into an organization with an impressive network of agencies and entities employing over 110,000 staff members in over 600 duty stations with an annual budget of USD$48 billion in 2015.[36] During the last seven decades of its existence, the United Nations system has been constantly growing. As we will see in subsequent chapters, the UN system has a multitude of funds, programs, specialized agencies, and related organizations. This complex web of some forty international

---

35 The *General Agreement on Tariffs and Trade* (GATT), established in the wake of the Second World War, became a *de facto* international organization dealing with the global rules of trade between nations. In January 1995, the World Trade Organization (WTO) came into being as a successor to GATT.

36 *Statistical Report of the United Nations System Chief Executives Board for Coordination on the Budgetary and Financial Situation of the Organizations of the United Nations System*, UNGAOR, 71st Sess, UN Doc A/71/583 (2016) 3.

institutions has indeed become the centre for harmonizing the actions of nations. There is hardly any area or field for which the UN does not have a fund and program or specialized agency.

C. PRINCIPLES

Immediately after setting out the purposes of the United Nations in its Article 1, the *UN Charter* provides in Article 2 the principles that should guide the conduct of all member states in pursuit of the purposes. Unless member states act in accordance with these principles, the purposes of the United Nations cannot be attained. The distinction between purposes and principles is not obvious. Purposes normally entail an improvement in economic, political, social, or other aspects of the international community. Principles, on the other hand, are standards that must be observed, not because it will advance or secure an economic, political, or social situation deemed desirable, but primarily because it is a requirement of justice or fairness or some other dimension of morality.[37] Principles are not rules; they underlie, explain, or provide reasons for rules. Where rules answer the question *what*, principles answer the question *why*.[38] Principles act as a guide in the process of interpreting rules. Article 2 of the *UN Charter* sets out seven principles in accordance with which member states shall act. Most of these principles have become the cornerstones of public international law. Each principle is canvassed below in a separate section.

1) First Principle—Sovereign Equality of Member States

As early as 1943, the governments of the United States, the United Kingdom, the Soviet Union, and China jointly declared that they recognized "the necessity of establishing at the earliest practicable

37 Ronald Dworkin, *Taking Rights Seriously* (Cambridge: Harvard University Press, 1977) 25.

38 Gerald Fitzmaurice, "The General Principles of International Law Considered from the Standpoint of the Rule of Law" (1957) 92 *Recueil des Cours de l'Académie de Droit International* 7.

date a general international organization, based on the principle of the sovereign equality of all peace-loving States, and open to membership by all such States, large and small, for the maintenance of international peace and security."[39] This declaration is now part of paragraph 1 of Article 2 of the *UN Charter*, which provides as follows:

> The Organization is based on the principle of the sovereign equality of all its Members.

Sovereignty denotes not being answerable to any authority above oneself.[40] The term derives from the Latin word *superanus* through the French term souveraineté, which in the ordinary popular sense means supremacy or supreme power. Sovereignty is not limited to the idea of actual power. It must be understood as a title to exercise absolute control. A state's sovereignty is not affected by its system of government or statehood. Saudi Arabia, which is a monarchy, is as sovereign as France, which is a republic. Similarly, a state's wealth or strength has no impact on its sovereignty. For example, although Madagascar is militarily and economically weaker than Russia, it is not, at least in theory, less sovereign. The practical reality of international relations is an important caveat to the principle of equal sovereignty of all states.

The *UN Charter* refers to the principle of sovereign equality of member states without providing a definition or an explanation of the term. During the San Francisco conference, the Rapporteur of the Commission who presented Article 2, paragraph 1, explained that the term "sovereign equality" was new terminology and meant to include the following four elements: (1) states are juridically equal; (2) each state enjoys the right inherent in full sovereignty; (3) the personality, territorial integrity, and political independence of a state are respected; and (4) states must comply under international law with their international duties.[41] In several resolutions, the General Assembly identified various elements that form the concept of *sovereign equality*. In

39 Hans Kelsen, "The Principle of Sovereign Equality of States as a Basis for International Organizations" 53:2 *The Yale Law Journal* 207.

40 See, generally, Robert Jackson, *Sovereignty* (Cambridge: Polity Press, 2007).

41 Conference on International Organizations, above note 1 at 69.

particular, equally sovereign states have equal rights and duties and are equal members of the international community, notwithstanding differences of an economic, social, political, or other nature.[42] In a legal order that is based on sovereign equality, states are judicially equal. This means that all states have the same legal capacity to accept international rights and obligations. It also means that international legal rules apply to all states equally without discrimination. For instance, the obligation not to use force applies as much to superpowers as it does to microstates. Similarly, sovereign equality entails the enjoyment of rights inherent in full sovereignty. One example of an application of this principle of equality is that no state has jurisdiction over another state without the latter's consent. Each state has absolute freedom to choose its preferred form of government, to establish judicial institutions, and to enact internal laws. No state can impose its national laws on another state or on nationals of another state. In addition, sovereign equality gives each state the assurance that other states will respect its personality, territorial integrity, and political independence. The respect for territorial integrity entails an absolute prohibition to acquire territory through use or threat of force. The respect for political independence means that a state may make its own decisions on its domestic and foreign policy. It has the right to choose freely and develop its political, social, economic, and cultural systems. Any attempt to interfere with this power would be a violation of the principle of sovereign equality. Sovereign equality implies not only rights but also obligations. Each state has the duty to comply fully and in good faith with its international obligations and to live in peace with other states. When a state chooses to limit its sovereignty by accepting international obligations, it actually exercises its sovereignty. Once it accepts an international obligation, it must comply with it. Its failure to comply with its international obligations undermines not only its credibility but also the international legal order.

---

42 *Declaration on Principles of International Law concerning Friendly Relations and Co-operation among States in accordance with the Charter of the United Nations*, Annex to GA Res 2625 (XXV), UNGAOR, 25th Sess, UN Doc A/RES/2625(XXV) (1970) 121 [*Declaration on Principles of International Law*].

It is interesting to note, however, that even though sovereign equality is an essential principle of the international legal order, it is not absolute in the United Nations. Recall that in the League of Nations, "States met as equals, and decisions could not be adopted that would somehow place obligations on States which had indicated their dissent."[43] Each member of the League of Nations had one vote and a single member state could block any proposal. There are still many important international organizations where decisions are made unanimously, by consensus or reverse consensus. The North Atlantic Treaty Organization (NATO) and the World Trade Organization (WTO) are just two such examples. In principle, any member of these organizations, irrespective of its size, wealth, or military power, may block any decision. This is a very strong expression of the principle of equal sovereignty. However, you will recall that unanimity proved to be a major flaw in the decision-making process of the League of Nations. Thus, the drafters of the *UN Charter* made a deliberate choice to move away from the unanimity rule. Today, for a resolution on an important question to be adopted by the General Assembly, a two-thirds vote of those present and voting suffices. A resolution on all other questions requires a simple majority.[44] How can this "tyranny of the majority" be compatible with the principle of sovereign equality? One possible explanation is that General Assembly resolutions do not normally give rise to direct legal obligations for member states. They are generally recommendatory. Another

---

43 Nigel D White, *The Law of International Organizations*, 2d ed (Manchester: Manchester University Press, 2005) at 131.

44 Article 18.2 of the *UN Charter* lists a few examples of important questions, which include: recommendations with respect to the maintenance of international peace and security, the election of the non-permanent members of the Security Council, the election of the members of the Economic and Social Council, the admission of new members to the United Nations, the suspension of the rights and privileges of membership, the expulsion of members, questions relating to the operation of the trusteeship system, and budgetary questions. An example of decisions on other or "non-important" questions mentioned in Article 18.3 is the determination of additional categories of questions to be decided by a two-thirds majority. In other words, the designation of a question as "important" is itself not an important question and may be decided by simple majority.

explanation is that the majority rule does not negate the fact that each member state of the UN, irrespective of its size or power, has one vote in the General Assembly, which is the most obvious manifestation of the principle of sovereign equality. A third possible explanation is that this was a necessary compromise to avoid the mistakes of the past and ensure that the decision-making process in the UN is not paralyzed by a few member states.

It is infinitely more difficult to reconcile the principle of sovereign equality of states with the membership and voting procedure in the Security Council. Indeed, the membership and voting procedure in the Security Council are perhaps the most notable exceptions to the principle of sovereign equality. Although each member of the Security Council has one vote, only five members (China, France, Russia, the United Kingdom, and the United States) have a permanent seat and veto power in the Security Council. Their permanent membership in the Security Council and their veto power symbolize a status of superiority. The only explanation for this unequal membership status and voting privilege is historical. The Big Five had made it clear that they would not sign the *UN Charter* if the veto right was not included and a permanent seat was not guaranteed.

While the voting procedure in the General Assembly whereby each state has one vote appears to be democratic, it certainly has its drawbacks. Indeed, approximately 5 percent of the world population carries 50 percent of the votes in the General Assembly simply because the vast majority of member states have a population of less than ten million. A reasonable question is whether it is fair that large states like China and India with almost 40 percent of the world's global population have the same voting rights in the General Assembly as member states with a negligible population, such as Tuvalu and Palau? Put differently, slightly less than 40 percent of the world's population holds only 1 percent of the votes in the General Assembly. The alternative, of course, is the voting procedure of the Council of the European Union,[45]

45 The Council of the European Union should not be confused with the Council of Europe. The European Union and the Council of Europe are two entirely different organizations. The Council of Europe is a legal and cultural alliance of European nations that was born after the Second World War. It has forty-seven

with a formula of a qualified majority, or the weighted voting system of the Bretton Woods organization (the World Bank and the IMF), where high-income countries hold approximately 60 percent of voting power. It is almost certain that such a weighted voting procedure in the UN would not have been accepted by most nations.

In practice, and despite the principle of equal sovereignty, countries with small populations do not have the luxury of voting autonomously and independently.[46] Their economic, military, and political dependence on larger states often dictates the way they exercise their voting rights in the United Nations. For instance, under the Compact of Free Association, the United States has full authority and responsibility for security and defence of the Marshall Islands, Micronesia, and Palau. These islands' economies heavily depend on US foreign aid. Thus, the voting pattern of these microstates in the General Assembly is very similar to the voting pattern of the United States. Even on the most controversial issues, such as the General Assembly resolution calling for an end to the United States' economic, commercial, and financial embargo against Cuba, these islands were the only states (except Israel) that either voted against or abstained.[47]

Monaco and Andorra are also examples of microstates that do not have full control over their foreign policy. "Monaco is obliged to consider the political, economic and military interests of France; and Andorra is bound by a trilateral treaty with both France and Spain, in which it commits itself to French and Spanish foreign policy interests."[48] In fact, in accordance with Andorra's Constitution, the President of France is

---

member states. The European Union, on the other hand, is an economic and political alliance of some twenty-seven states. All members of the European Union belong to the Council of Europe, but not all members of the Council of Europe are part of the European Union.

46 James R Vreeland & Axel Dreher, *Political Economy of the United Nations Security Council: Money and Influence* (New York: Cambridge University Press, 2014).

47 See General Assembly Resolutions 47/19, 48/16, 49/9, 50/10, 51/17, 52/10, 53/4, 54/21, 55/20, 56/9, 57/11, 58/7, 59/11, 60/12, 61/11, 62/3, 63/7, 64/6, 65/6, 66/6, 67/4, and 68/8.

48 Baldur Thorhallsson, "Small States in the UN Security Council: Means of Influence?" (2012) 7 *The Hague Journal of Diplomacy* 135 at 145.

a Coprince of Andorra.[49] Hence, the principle of sovereign equality is a fiction for many member states that are unable to resist the political influence of their powerful neighbours.

2) Second Principle—Good Faith Fulfillment of Obligations

Paragraph 2 of Article 2 of the *UN Charter* states that all "Members, in order to ensure to all of them the rights and benefits resulting from membership, shall fulfill in good faith the obligations assumed by them in accordance with the present Charter." Long before the *UN Charter* came into existence, it was well established that "the mechanism for co-operation between States is governed by the principle of good faith."[50] The requirement to act in good faith is "one of the basic principles governing the creation and performance of legal obligations, whatever their source."[51] A state does not have to accept an international obligation, but when it does, it has a duty to comply with it in good faith.

Good faith is generally understood to be a standard of ethical behaviour. In both international and municipal law, including civil law and common law traditions, the principle of good faith introduces superior moral considerations such as equity, fairness, and justice into legal norms. Some specific applications of the principle of good faith have already crystallized into customary rules or have been

---

49 Article 43 of Andorra's Constitution reads as follows:

> 43.1 In accordance with the institutional tradition of Andorra, the Coprinces are, jointly and indivisibly, the Head of State, and they assume its highest representation.
>
> 43.2 The Coprinces, an institution which dates from the Pareatges and their historical evolution, are in their personal and exclusive right, the Bishop of Urgell and the President of the French Republic. Their powers are equal and derive from the present Constitution. Each of them swears or affirms to exercise their functions in accordance with the present Constitution.

50 *Pulp Mills on the River Uruguay (Argentina v Uruguay)*, [2010] ICJ Rep 14 at para 145 [*Pulp Mills*].

51 *Nuclear Tests Case (Australia v France)*, Merits, [1974] ICJ Rep 253 at para 46 [*Nuclear Tests Case*].

codified in international treaties. For example, many rules on how to interpret international treaties found in the *Vienna Convention on the Law of Treaties* derive from the principle of good faith. They include the rule requiring states to refrain from acts which would defeat the object and purpose of a treaty, to perform their international obligations under a treaty in good faith, and to interpret treaties in good faith in accordance with the ordinary meaning to be given to the terms. A well-known customary rule that compels states to refrain from adopting positions and views inconsistent with those adopted in the past in relation to the same matter is also rooted in the principle of good faith.

States have an obligation to act in good faith at all times. This obligation applies even before they reach an agreement or sign a treaty. The principle of good faith governs the conduct of states during negotiations that might or might not lead to an agreement. States have an obligation "so to conduct themselves that the negotiations are meaningful."[52] Although the negotiating parties are not obliged to reach an agreement, where an obligation to negotiate exists or where they decide to commence negotiations, they must pursue them as far as possible with a view to concluding an agreement.[53] A party who enters into or continues negotiations despite its intention not to reach an agreement acts in bad faith. Also, a state that misleads the other party either by misrepresenting facts or by concealing facts that should have been disclosed does not negotiate in good faith.

The principle of good faith also requires states to act consistently and to honour their promises even where such promises are not contained in an international treaty or convention. As the International Court of Justice noted, "trust and confidence are inherent in international co-operation, in particular in an age when this co-operation in many fields is becoming increasingly essential."[54] In 1973, Australia instituted proceedings before the ICJ with the view to compelling France to cease atmospheric nuclear tests in the South Pacific.

---

52 *North Sea Continental Shelf (Federal Republic of Germany/Denmark; Federal Republic of Germany/Netherlands)*, [1969] ICJ Rep 3 at para 85 [*North Sea Continental Shelf*]; see also *Pulp Mills*, above note 50 at para 146.

53 *Railway Traffic between Lithuania and Poland* (1931), PCIJ (Ser A/B) No 42 at 116.

54 *Nuclear Tests Case*, above note 51 at para 46.

Before the Court adjudicated the dispute, France made several public statements in 1974, announcing its intention to cease the conduct of such tests. Although Australia intended to pursue the case and obtain a final judgment, the Court refused to entertain the case. The ICJ found that Australia's objective had in effect been accomplished, in as much as France had undertaken the obligation to hold no further nuclear tests in the atmosphere in the South Pacific. The Court concluded that various public declarations made by France in 1974 produced legal effects similar to those deriving from a treaty:

> [I]nterested States may take cognizance of unilateral declarations and place confidence in them, and are entitled to require that the obligation thus created be respected.[55]

The principle of good faith precludes a state from acting in contradiction with its own previous representations or conduct, particularly when another state has relied on them. Even a tacit acquiescence may be interpreted as an undertaking or promise. For instance, if a state tacitly accepts a situation, it cannot subsequently change its position and question the legality of the situation.[56] The territorial dispute between Cambodia and Thailand with regard to the Temple of Preah Vihear illustrates this principle. The temple is an archaeologically important sanctuary, situated on the Dangrek Mountains between Cambodia and Thailand. The origins of this dispute could be traced to 1904 when France, acting on behalf of its former protectorate Cambodia, signed a treaty with Siam (present day Thailand), establishing a mixed commission to conduct a delimitation of the frontiers. The commission had produced a large number of maps placing the temple on the territory of Cambodia. Although Thailand's monarchy and government were aware of these maps, they raised no objections. Almost five decades later, in the 1950s, when the temple became an attractive tourist destination, Thailand asserted its sovereignty over it, claiming that the temple was situated on its territory.

---

55 *Ibid.*

56 *Case concerning the Temple of Preah Vihear (Cambodia v Thailand)*, Merits, [1962] ICJ Rep 39.

Cambodia instituted proceedings against Thailand before the International Court of Justice. The Court found that Thailand's failure to object over a period of several decades to the maps placing the temple in Cambodia could be construed as a tacit acquiescence of the fact that the temple was situated on the territory of Cambodia. Therefore, Thailand was precluded from adopting a contradictory position. Consistent conduct is an integral part of the good faith principle.

The obligation to act in good faith also applies when states exercise their right to vote under the *UN Charter*. Between 1945 and 1955, the admission of new members to the United Nations was a highly politicized topic. The USSR was opposing the admission of Western states to membership unless the same number of states from the Eastern Bloc were admitted at the same time.[57] In other words, the USSR made the admission of Western states contingent on the admission of its own allies. To resolve this disagreement between the USSR (the principal representative of the East) and the United States (the principal representative of the West), the General Assembly decided to request an advisory opinion from the International Court of Justice. The Court had to determine whether the Soviet Union was entitled to veto the admission of new members on the basis of a condition not mentioned in the *UN Charter*. The Court ruled that factors and criteria not expressly mentioned in the *UN Charter* could be taken into account so long as they can reasonably and in good faith be connected with one or more of the five conditions. This advisory opinion confirmed that states must act in good faith even when they exercise a highly political and discretionary right, such as voting in the Security Council.

This raises an interesting question about voting patterns of some permanent members of the Security Council. There have been many instances where one or several permanent members of the Security Council vetoed draft resolutions proposing military intervention by the United Nations' peacekeeping forces. As a result of the veto, some armed conflicts turned into ethnic cleansing or genocide. The most notorious examples are: (a) the United States' position in the Security

57 David I Efevwerhan, "Kosovo's Chances of UN Membership: A Prognosis" (2012) 4:1 *Goettingen Journal of International Law* 93 at 106–7.

Council in relation to the Palestinian question, and in particular the construction of a wall in the Palestinian territories;[58] and (b) Russia's veto of a proposed intervention to protect the population of Bosnia from the Serbian troops. A more flagrant example is the Rwandan genocide. With the exceptions of Nigeria, New Zealand, and the Czech Republic, no other members of the Security Council argued for a military intervention. They refused to recognize the events of 1994 in Rwanda as genocide until hundreds of thousands of people had lost their lives. And even after the Security Council agreed to call the massacres genocide, it failed to assemble an intervention force.[59]

It can be reasonably argued that when a permanent member of the Security Council exercises its veto right arbitrarily or excessively or fails to support a draft resolution proposing a humanitarian intervention, it abuses its power or right conferred by the *UN Charter*. After all, an important privilege such as a veto right comes with responsibilities. A permanent member does not act in good faith when it obstructs collective action by exercising its veto right. Good faith is frequently associated with the theory of abuse of rights or abus de droit.[60] When a right is exercised with the intent of injuring another or in an excessive and unreasonable manner, it is contrary to the requirements of good faith and may give rise to international responsibility warranting reparations.

3) Third Principle—Peaceful Resolution of Disputes

Pursuant to paragraph 3 of Article 2 of the *UN Charter*, all members of the United Nations "settle their international disputes by peaceful

58 See *Legal Consequences of the Construction of a Wall in the Occupied Palestinian Territory*, Advisory Opinion, [2004] ICJ Rep 136 [*Construction of a Wall in the Occupied Palestinian Territory*].

59 Michael Barnett, *Eyewitness to a Genocide: The United Nations and Rwanda* (Ithaca: Cornell University Press, 2002) at 20.

60 See United States—*Import Prohibition of Certain Shrimp Products* (*Complaint by the United States*) (1998), WTO Doc WT/DS58/AB/R, AB-1998-4 (Appellate Body Report), online: https://docs.wto.org/dol2fe/Pages/FE_Search/FE_S_S006.aspx?DataSource=Cat&query=@Symbol=WT/DS58/AB/R&Language=English&Context=ScriptedSearches&languageUIChanged=true.

means in such a manner that international peace and *security*, and justice, are not endangered." For this provision to apply, there must be an international dispute. The international nature of the dispute requires a transnational dimension. Internal conflicts, such as civil strife or revolutions, do not trigger the application of this principle. As to the term "dispute," it should not be confounded with the term "situation." The *UN Charter* draws a clear distinction between disputes and situations.[61] A situation may include tension between states that has not yet escalated to a dispute. The jurisprudence of the Permanent Court of International Justice and that of its successor, the International Court of Justice, define a dispute as a disagreement on a point of law or fact, a conflict of legal views or of interests between parties. In order for a dispute to exist, it "must be shown that the claim of one party is positively opposed by the other."[62] The opposing sides must "hold clearly opposite views concerning the question of the performance or non-performance of certain international obligations."[63]

A significant number of bilateral and multilateral treaties (some of regional and others of universal application) aimed at the peaceful settlement of disputes have been concluded.[64] The *UN Charter* devotes an entire chapter to the pacific settlement of disputes. In addition, the General Assembly adopted a number of resolutions regarding the pacific settlement of disputes.[65]

---

61 See, in particular, Articles 24, 35.1, and 36.1 of the *Charter of the United Nations*, 26 June 1945, Can TS 1945 No 7 [*Charter of the United Nations*].

62 *South West Africa (Ethiopia v South Africa; Liberia v South Africa)*, Preliminary Objections, Judgment, [1962] ICJ Rep 319 at 328.

63 *Alleged Violations of Sovereign Rights and Maritime Spaces in the Caribbean Sea (Nicaragua v Colombia)*, Preliminary Objections, Judgment, [2016] ICJ Rep 3 at para 50; see also *Interpretation of Peace Treaties with Bulgaria, Hungary, and Romania*, First Phase, Advisory Opinion, [1950] ICJ Rep 65 at 74.

64 The most notable examples are the 1899, 1907, and 1928 General Act and 1949 Revised General Act for the Pacific Settlement of Disputes, the 1948 *American Treaty on Pacific Settlement of Disputes*, and the 1957 *European Convention for the Peaceful Settlement of Disputes*.

65 *Manila Declaration on the Peaceful Settlement of International Disputes*, GA Res 37/10, UNGAOR, 37th Sess, UN Doc A/Res/37/10 (1982) 261 [*Manila Declaration*]; *United Nations Model Rules for the Conciliation of Disputes between States*, GA Res 50/50, UNGAOR, 50th Sess, UN Doc A/Res/50/50 (1995) 1; *Declaration*

International disputes may be resolved peacefully through a number of mechanisms. Article 33.1 of the *UN Charter* lists the main methods for resolving disputes. This provision provides that "the parties to any dispute, the continuance of which is likely to endanger the maintenance of international peace and security, shall, first of all, seek a solution by negotiation, enquiry, mediation, conciliation, arbitration, judicial settlement, resort to regional agencies or arrangements, or other peaceful means of their own choice." These methods are not set out in an order of priority and are not exhaustive; disputes may be settled through other mechanisms as well. Also, the parties may have recourse to more than one method at the same time. States may negotiate and litigate simultaneously. Generally, dispute resolution mechanisms fall under the following two categories: diplomatic and judicial mechanisms.

a) Diplomatic Mechanisms

As its name suggests, diplomatic mechanisms for settling disputes entail a degree of diplomacy. The word "diplomacy" derives from the Greek word "diploma," which means paper folded in two. Traditionally, diplomacy was viewed as inalienable from a documented or written agreement. In many cases, this still holds true today. Conflicts resolved through diplomatic means are generally memorialized or documented in a written agreement. Normally, diplomacy is entrusted to professional diplomats, such as delegates representing their governments in international organizations, ambassadors and other qualified embassy personnel, negotiators, officials of international organizations, and politicians handling foreign affairs.

The way diplomacy is pursued is very often as important as its subject matter. If the mechanism for carrying out diplomacy is chosen poorly, the dispute is not likely to be resolved. Below, we will explain different approaches that parties can opt for in pursuing diplomacy. Negotiations, consultations, good offices, enquiry, mediation, and conciliation are among diplomatic methods of dispute settlement.

---

on the Prevention and Removal of Disputes and Situations Which May Threaten International Peace and Security and on the Role of the United Nations in This Field, GA Res Res 43/51, UNGAOR, 43rd Sess, UN Doc A/Res/43/51 (1988) 276.

i) Negotiation

Negotiation is the oldest and primary method by which states resolve their disputes.[66] The vast majority of international disputes are resolved through negotiation. It is therefore not surprising that negotiation and diplomacy are often used interchangeably or as synonyms.[67] Its flexibility and effectiveness make negotiation by far the most successful dispute settlement method. It is flexible because it can be applied to all types of disputes, including political, legal, or technical. Also, as opposed to judicial proceedings (in which they have little control), the parties have full control over the duration, frequency, location, and scope of the negotiations. Negotiations are effective not only because there is a high likelihood of resolving a dispute but also because disputes are resolved speedily. Negotiations require at the very least a genuine attempt by one of the disputing parties to engage in discussions with the other disputing party, with a view to resolving the dispute.[68]

Normally, negotiations precede all other forms of dispute settlement methods. Most of the time, negotiations are optional. Negotiations are said to be optional when there is no requirement to have recourse to them prior to instituting judicial proceedings. A state may seize an international court or tribunal by submitting the dispute for adjudication without first attempting to resolve it through negotiation.[69] When negotiations are optional, a state may pursue negotia-

---

66 John Collier and Vaughan Lowe, *The Settlement of Disputes in International Law* (New York: Oxford University Press, 2000) at 20; see also *North Sea Continental Shelf*, above note 52 at para 86.

67 See in particular the 1949 *Revised General Act for the Pacific Settlement of International Disputes*, 28 April 1949, 71 UNTS 101 (entered into force 20 September 1950) and the 1948 *Charter of the Organization of American States*, 30 April 1948, 119 UNTS 3 (entered into force 13 December 1951).

68 *Application of the International Convention on the Elimination of All Forms of Racial Discrimination (Georgia v Russian Federation)*, Preliminary Objections, Judgment, [2011] ICJ Rep 70 at para 157 [*Georgia v Russian Federation*].

69 *Land and Maritime Boundary between Cameroon and Nigeria (Cameroon v Nigeria)*, Preliminary Objections, Judgment, [1998] ICJ Rep 275 at 303: "Neither in the Charter nor otherwise in international law is any general rule to be found to the effect that the exhaustion of diplomatic negotiations constitutes a precondition for a matter to be referred to the Court."

tions and at the same time institute judicial or arbitral proceedings.[70] In case the negotiations are successful and result in the settlement of the dispute, the aggrieved state may discontinue judicial or arbitral proceedings.[71] In addition, where negotiations are optional, a state may refuse to enter into negotiations with another party. A number of reasons may explain a state's refusal to accept another state's invitation to negotiate. The most common reason for a state's refusal to negotiate is its unwillingness to give the other party the required legitimacy or recognition as a sovereign entity. Two conflicting states may be invited to engage in negotiation either by the General Assembly,[72] the Security Council, the Secretary-General, or the International Court of Justice.[73]

In many circumstances, negotiations are mandatory. The word "mandatory" does not imply that a state can be compelled to negotiate as soon as it receives an invitation to do so. It simply means that the aggrieved state cannot have recourse to other dispute settlement mechanisms without first inviting the other party to enter into negotiations. Typically, the obligation to negotiate is contained in a bilateral or multilateral treaty or agreement signed by the concerned states. There are many treaties that place on the states' parties thereto an obligation to carry out negotiations, consultations, or exchanges of views whenever a controversy arises in connection with a particular treaty to which they are both signatories.[74] For instance, in the *International Conven-*

---

70 *Aegean Sea Continental Shelf (Greece v Turkey)*, [1978] ICJ Rep 3 at para 29.

71 See *Trial of Pakistani Prisoners of War (Pakistan v India)*, [1973] ICJ Rep 347.

72 See Article 12 of the *Manila Declaration*, above note 65.

73 *Fisheries Jurisdiction (United Kingdom v Zeeland)*, Merits, Judgment, [1974] ICJ Rep 3 at para 75: "[T]he obligation to negotiate thus flows from the very nature of the respective rights of the Parties; to direct them to negotiate is therefore a proper exercise of the judicial function." [*United Kingdom v Zeeland*].

74 Examples of such treaties are: the 1979 Agreement Governing the Activities of States on the Moon and Other Celestial Bodies, 1363 UNTS 3; the 1975 *Vienna Convention on the Representation of States in their Relations with International Organizations of a Universal Character*, UN Doc A/Conf67/16; the *International Convention for the Suppression of the Financing of Terrorists*, 2178 UNTS 197; the 1982 *United Nations Convention on the Law of the Sea*, United Nations, 1833 UNTS 3; and the 1959 *Antarctic Treaty*, United Nations, 402 UNTS 71.

tion for the Suppression of the Financing of Terrorism,[75] states agreed to prosecute persons who provide or collect funds in order to carry out acts of terrorism. If a state refuses to take any action vis-à-vis an individual who funds terrorism, the aggrieved state cannot immediately commence arbitral proceedings. It must first attempt to convince the recalcitrant state to comply with its treaty obligations through negotiations. It is only if negotiations fail that the aggrieved state can submit the dispute to arbitration. A similar obligation may exist in a bilateral treaty.[76]

The conduct of negotiations does not, however, require the reaching of an actual agreement between the disputing parties.[77] Unfortunately, on the international arena, negotiations are often undertaken under false pretense or for the wrong reasons. As Lon Fuller remarked, negotiation is a means to an end:

> [i]t is the road the parties must travel to arrive at their goal of mutually satisfactory settlement. But like other means, negotiation is easily converted into an end in itself; it readily becomes a game played for its own sake and a game played with so little reserve by those taken up with it that they will sacrifice their own ultimate interests in order to win it.[78]

This excerpt accurately describes the reason for the failure of so many highly political international negotiations. When negotiations do not take place or fail, other methods of settling disputes, including consultations, exchange of views, mediation, good offices, and conciliation, remain available to the parties.

---

75 The *International Convention for the Suppression of the Financing of Terrorism*, 10 January 2000, 2178 UNTS 197 (entered into force: 10 April 2002), adopted by the General Assembly of the United Nations in Resolution 54/109, UNGAOR, 54th Sess, UN Doc A/RES/54/109 (1999) 1.

76 See *Pulp Mills*, above note 50.

77 *Georgia v Russian Federation*, above note 68 at para 158.

78 Lon Fuller, *Anatomy of the Law* (New York: Praeger, 1968) at 128.

ii) Consultations and Exchange of Views

Often, the term negotiation is used loosely to include consultations and exchange of views. These are known to be different forms of negotiation. For instance, Article 4 of Annex II to the Agreement Establishing the World Trade Organization, which governs the settlement of trade disputes within the WTO, and Article 283 of the *United Nations Convention on the Law of the Sea*, make bilateral consultations between the parties the first stage of the formal dispute settlement mechanism. Thus, before one state can institute legal proceedings against another state, it must first invite that state to consultations.

Negotiations, consultations, or exchanges of views are similar but not identical. The main difference is in the degree or intensity of the compromises expected from the parties. Negotiations may require a party to make significant concessions in order to obtain something in exchange. Consultations and exchange of views, on the other hand, appear to be an opportunity for one party to hear out and take into consideration the position of the other party:

> When a Government anticipates that a decision or a proposed course of action may harm another state, discussions with the affected party can provide a way of heading off a dispute by creating an opportunity for adjustment and accommodation. Quite minor modifications to its plans, of no importance to the state taking the decision, may be all that is required to avoid trouble, yet may only be apparent if the other side is given a chance to point them out.[79]

iii) Fact-Findings and Inquiries

A distinct dispute settlement method that has recently gained importance is inquiry or fact-finding. Fact-findings are akin to investigations. This approach is used when the facts are both decisive and disputed. Its purpose is to facilitate "a solution by elucidating the facts through an impartial and conscientious investigation."[80]

---

79 JG Merrills, *International Dispute Settlement*, 3d ed (Cambridge: Cambridge University Press, 2000) at 3.

80 *Convention for the Pacific Settlement of International Disputes (The Hague Convention I)*, 26 September 1928, 93 LNTS 343, art 9 (entered into force 16 August

The inquiry first appeared in 1898 as a means to resolve a conflict between the United States and Spain during the Cuban War of Independence. The unexplained explosion of an American battleship, the *USS Maine* on its way to Cuba, led to two separate national inquiries undertaken by the United States and Spain. The American and Spanish inquiries resulted in two diametrically opposed conclusions as to the reasons for the ship's demise. This exacerbated the already acrimonious relationship between the two countries. To ensure that the fact-finding was impartial, Russian diplomats proposed the establishment of an independent inquiry commission to establish the cause of the explosion.

A number of subsequent bilateral and multilateral treaties, including the Covenant of the League of Nations and the *UN Charter*, expressly provided for inquiry as a means of settlement of disputes. In his report *An Agenda for Peace*,[81] Secretary-General Boutros-Ghali emphasized the importance of fact-finding as a tool for preventive diplomacy and as part of an early warning system, and encouraged an increased resort to fact-finding by the UN main organs. The impartial and independent establishment of facts and circumstances that give rise to an international dispute leads to a better understanding of events and is supposed to prevent the exacerbation of a conflict. An inquiry may also facilitate the task of judges or arbitrators required to adjudicate a dispute in case it is not resolved through diplomatic mechanisms. However, it is important to point out that inquiries and fact-finding exercises should be limited to statements of fact and not read as an indictment or disguised arbitral award, as this would defeat the purpose of this exercise and antagonize the parties.[82]

1928).

81 *An Agenda for Peace, Report of the Secretary-General pursuant to the statement adopted by the Summit Meeting of the Security Council on 31 January 1992*, UNGAOR, 47th Sess, UN Doc A/47/277 (1992) 1 at paras 23–25.

82 In contrast, paragraph 27, article 5, of Annex VIII to the 1982 *United Nations Convention on the Law of the Sea* (1833 UNTS 3) recognizes an inquiry procedure whose outcome or findings of fact, unless the parties otherwise agree, are to be considered conclusive by the parties to the dispute.

Inquiries and fact-findings may be used not only as a way of settling interstate disputes but also to address global threats and problems. In the *Declaration on Fact-finding by the United Nations in the Field of Maintenance of International Peace and Security*, member states confirmed that the Security Council, the General Assembly, and the Secretary-General have the power to undertake fact-finding activities.[83] These three main organs of the United Nations have often resorted to inquiries and fact-finding activities.[84] The Security Council and the General Assembly established investigative mechanisms to identify individuals, groups, or governments involved in the use of chemical weapons in Syria.[85] Also, in 1987, the Security Council requested the Secretary-General Javier Pérez de Cuéllar to conduct a similar fact-finding regarding the use of chemical weapons in the Gulf War between Iran and Iraq.[86]

iv) Mediation

Mediation is a means of peaceful settlement of an international dispute where a third party intervenes to reconcile the claims of the contending parties and to advance his or her own proposals aimed

---

83 *Declaration on Fact-finding by the United Nations in the Field of the Maintenance of International Peace and Security*, GA Res 46/59, 46th Sess, UN Doc A/Res/46/59 (1991) 290.

84 See SC Res 780 (1992) regarding former Yugoslavia, UNSCOR, 47th Year, UN Doc S/RES/780 (1992); SC Res 885 (1993) regarding Somalia, UNSCOR, 48th Year, UN Doc S/RES/885 (1993) 1; SC Res 935 (1994) regarding Rwanda, UNSCOR, 49th Year, UN Doc S/RES/935 (1994) 1; *An international investigation into the conditions and circumstances resulting in the tragic death of Mr. Dag Hammarskjöld and of members of the party accompanying him*, GA Res 1628 (XVI), UNGAOR, 16th Sess, UN Doc A/RES/1628 (XVI) (1961) 63; *The situation in the Republic of the Congo [and the circumstances resulting in the death of Patrice Lumumba]*, GA Res 1601 (XV), UNGAOR, 15th Sess, UN Doc A/RES/1601 (XV) (1961) 18; *International, Impartial and Independent Mechanism to Assist in the Investigation and Prosecution of Persons Responsible for the Most Serious Crimes under International Law Committed in the Syrian Arab Republic since March 2011*, GA Res 71/248, UNGAOR, 71st Sess, UN Doc A/RES/71/248 (2016) 1 [*Syrian Arab Republic*].

85 SC Res 2235 (2015), UNSCOR, 70th Sess, UN Doc S/Res/2235 (2015) 1; *Syrian Arab Republic*, above note 84.

86 SC Res 598 (1987), UNSCOR, 42nd Year, UN Doc S/RES/598 (1987) 5.

at a mutually acceptable compromise or solution.[87] The purpose of mediation is to facilitate a dialogue between parties and to soothe hostilities and tensions in order to find an amicable solution to an international dispute.

Most universal and regional multilateral instruments, such as the *Charter of the United Nations, Hague Conventions for the Pacific Settlement of International Disputes,* the *Pact of the League of Arab States,* the *Charter of the Organization of American States,* and the *American Treaty on Pacific Settlement of 1948,* include mediation as one of primary means of settlement of international disputes.

In the United Nations, the office responsible for mediating international disputes is the Department of Political Affairs established in 1992. Recognizing the importance of mediation in resolving international disputes,[88] the General Assembly and the Security Council requested that the Secretary-General enhance the UN's capability to support mediation efforts. In response to this request, in 2006 the Secretary-General established the Mediation Support Unit under the auspices of the Department of Political Affairs. This unit provides advisory, financial, and logistical support to peace processes. Its primary task is to strengthen the mediation capacity of regional and sub-regional organizations involved in finding solutions to political or armed conflicts. The Mediation Support Unit also serves as a repository of mediation policy, expertise, guidance, lessons learned, and best practices.

Mediation is a convenient dispute resolution method because, unlike judicial settlement, it is flexible. One fundamental characteristic of mediation is its informal nature. Generally, there are no pre-established mediation procedures. The contending parties have the freedom to conduct mediation as they see fit. Mediation is also

---

87 United Nations Office of Legal Affairs, *Handbook on the Peaceful Settlement of Disputes between States* (New York: United Nations Publication, 1992), UN Doc OLA/COD/2394 at para 123.

88 See, in particular, SC Res 2171 (2014), UNSCOR, 69th Year, UN Doc S/RES/2171 (2014) 1 at para 11; *Strengthening the role of mediation in the peaceful settlement of disputes, conflict prevention and resolution,* GA Res 70/304, UNGAOR, 70th Sess, UN Doc A/RES/70/304 (2016) 1.

confidential. Irrespective of the outcome, all parties to a mediation process are expected to preserve the confidentiality of their discussions during mediation even if the process proves to be unsuccessful.

Mediators can be states, international organizations, non-governmental organizations, or individuals. For instance, in 1965, the Soviet Union, acting as mediator between India and Pakistan over Kashmir, secured a ceasefire when war had already broken out.[89] In 1978, Cardinal Antonio Samoré acted as mediator on behalf of the Roman Catholic Church in a dispute between Chile and Argentina over the possession of three islands in the Beagle Channel.

v) Good Offices

In addition to mediation, when states parties to a dispute are unable to settle it directly between themselves, they may seek a third party's good offices as a means of preventing further exacerbation of the conflict and as a method of facilitating efforts towards a peaceful settlement of the dispute. Good offices are a third-party influence that facilitates one party's dealings with another. It generally implies that the third party uses his or her reputation or prestige (or those of his office) to convince the disputing parties to resolve their disagreement peacefully. The third party exercising good offices must be acceptable to all the parties to the dispute. Good offices can be offered or performed by a single state, a group of states, an individual, or an organ of a universal or regional international organization. For example, Algeria offered and pursued a good offices role in the hostage crisis dispute between Iran and the United States. The possibility to have recourse to good offices may be expressly provided for in a bilateral or multilateral treaty.[90]

The exercise of good offices constitutes a substantial part of the Secretary-General's workload.[91] Secretaries-General of the United Nations have frequently used their good offices to resolve highly

89 Merrills, above note 79 at 29.

90 See, in particular, Article 5, paragraph 6 of the *Understanding on Rules and Procedures Governing the Settlement of Disputes*, Annex II to the Agreement Establishing the WTO, 1867 UNTS 3.

91 U Thant, *View from the UN* (London: David & Charles Publishing, 1978) at 49.

political crises or disputes such as the Cuban missile crisis, the Arab–Israeli war of 1967, the invasion of the Dominican Republic by the United States, the Iran hostage crisis, the Soviet withdrawal from Afghanistan, the conflict in Namibia, etc. In his memoirs, U Thant, the third Secretary-General, described good offices as "a useful method of preventing differences between states from developing into major crises or of getting results on sensitive problems before they reach the insoluble stage."[92] Good offices by the Secretary-General can be effective only if the parties to the dispute have "courage and vision as well as confidence in the discretion and integrity of the Secretary-General."[93]

The primary role of the party exercising good offices is to provide the disputing parties with a channel of communication so that they can resume negotiations. In some instances, the third party is authorized to go beyond the traditional limitations and to take active part in the dispute settlement process by proposing specific solutions and conducting shuttle diplomacy with the parties to the dispute to discuss such proposals individually. In these cases, the distinction between good offices and mediation becomes very blurred.

vi) Conciliation

Conciliation is a more recent dispute settlement mechanism that evolved as a result of a resolution adopted by the League of Nations in 1922, inviting states to resolve their disputes through conciliation commissions.[94] Subsequently, states resumed a practice of including conciliation in multilateral treaties as an important third-party mechanism for settlement of international disputes. Conciliation is a more institutionalized form of mediation. It typically combines the elements of both inquiry and mediation. A conciliation commission first undertakes an objective investigation and evaluation of all aspects of the dispute and provides the parties with a better understanding of

---

92 *Ibid* at 44.

93 *Ibid.*

94 United Nations Office of Legal Affairs, *Handbook on the Peaceful Settlement of Disputes between States* (New York: United Nations Publication, 1992), UN Doc OLA/COD/2394 at para 141.

each other's case. Then, it issues a report with its recommendations. Unless otherwise agreed by the parties, these recommendations are normally not binding, which is indicative of the diplomatic nature of this dispute settlement mechanism. In many regional human rights systems, courts or commissions tasked with adjudicating complaints submitted by individuals against states have an obligation to make attempts to find friendly settlements through conciliation.

b) Judicial Mechanisms

States may have recourse to a wide range of international courts and tribunals in order to resolve international disputes in a peaceful manner. Some of these courts and tribunals are universal whereas others are regional. Some courts and tribunals are related to the United Nations while others are entirely independent. For instance, the International Court of Justice is a principal organ of the UN and is a judicial dispute settlement mechanism with universal jurisdiction. Similarly, the International Tribunal for the Law of the Sea is another judicial body with a universal jurisdiction established to adjudicate disputes arising out of the interpretation and application of the *UN Convention on the Law of the Sea*. It is related to the UN. However, the Court of Justice of the European Union has a regional jurisdiction and is unrelated to the United Nations.

The judicial means of settling international disputes can be classified into the following two categories: arbitration and judicial settlement. Historically, arbitration preceded international judicial institutions. When arbitration first appeared, the concept of a permanent international court or tribunal with compulsory jurisdiction was a fantasy. Arbitration provided the much-needed inspiration for the creation of permanent judicial institutions.[95]

i) Arbitration

Arbitration is "the determination of a difference between States (or between a State and a non-State entity) through a legal decision of one or more arbitrators and an umpire, or of a tribunal other than the

95 Merrills, above note 79 at 88.

International Court of Justice or other permanent tribunal."[96] The origins of modern arbitration are dated to the *Treaty of Amity, Commerce, and Navigation,* commonly known as the Jay Treaty, signed between the United States and Great Britain in 1794.[97] The purpose of this Treaty was to resolve outstanding disputes since the *Treaty of Paris* of 1783, which ended the American revolutionary war.

Arbitration can be public or private. It can also be permanent (institutionalized) or *ad hoc.* Arbitration is public when it is set up by states to decide a dispute between them. It is private where corporations or individuals are parties to the arbitral proceedings. Arbitration is said to be *ad hoc* where it is established for the settlement of a specific dispute. It is permanent or institutionalized for the settlement of a class of disputes, such as the Iran–US Claims Tribunal or the International Centre for the Settlement of Investment Disputes (ICSID).

There are two ways in which states can trigger arbitral proceedings. The first method is to agree in advance to submit any future dispute arising from a treaty to arbitration. For instance, two or more states sign a free trade agreement. They include in the treaty a clause for settling future disputes that may arise from it. The clause provides that in case of any dispute regarding the interpretation or application of the free trade agreement, the parties agree to submit it to arbitration. The parties can agree in advance which arbitral tribunal will have jurisdiction and which set of rules will apply to arbitral proceedings.

The second way of triggering arbitration is to negotiate an agreement for the purposes of submitting to arbitration a dispute which has already arisen. Imagine a situation where two states have a territorial or maritime boundary dispute. As this type of dispute arises unexpectedly, it is unlikely that the two states have agreed in advance on the way to settle such disputes. Therefore, they will have to negotiate an agreement in order to submit the dispute to arbitration. This type of agreement is called a compromise.

---

96 John Collier & Vaughan Lowe, *The Settlement of Disputes in International Law: Institutions and Procedures* (Oxford, UK: Oxford University Press, 1999) at 31.

97 *Ibid.*

The main practical difference between arbitration and judicial settlement is the extent of control the parties to the dispute have over the proceedings. In arbitral proceedings, the parties can choose the arbitrator, the applicable law and the procedural rules that will govern the proceedings. In judicial proceedings, the parties do not have any control over such factors, as they are predetermined.

Also, whereas international courts and tribunals adjudicate disputes that arise primarily between states (international criminal courts are an exception), arbitration is open to non-state actors such as armed opposition groups or foreign investors. For instance, in June 2008, the government of Sudan and the Sudan People's Liberation Movement/Army agreed to submit their dispute concerning the boundaries of the oil-rich Abyei region to the Permanent Court of Arbitration in The Hague. The area was important for the 2011 referendum on independence of South Sudan. Similarly, investment arbitrations are open to private entities, including multinational corporations dissatisfied with the treatment they receive by the government of the country where they operate.

ii) Judicial Settlement

Judicial settlement involves the referral of a dispute to a permanent tribunal for a legally binding decision.[98] Since the Second World War, the international community has witnessed a proliferation of permanent international tribunals. Some of these tribunals, such as the International Criminal Tribunals for Rwanda and the former Yugoslavia, as well as the Special Tribunal for Lebanon, were set up for a finite period of time and for a specific mandate. These judicial institutions are also known as *ad hoc* tribunals. Other courts and tribunals are permanent in nature. They include the International Court of Justice, discussed in Chapter 6; the World Trade Organization dispute settlement mechanism; the International Tribunal for the Law of the Sea; and the International Criminal Court.

International courts and tribunals can be universal (open to all states regardless of their geographical location) or regional (open to a

98 Merrills, above note 79 at 121.

limited number of states that belong to the same geographical or geopolitical region). There are dozens of regional courts and tribunals. The European Court of Justice, the European Court of Human Rights, the African Court on Human and Peoples' Rights, the East African Court of Justice, and the Inter-American Court of Human Rights are only a few examples of regional judicial dispute settlement mechanisms.

It is important to emphasize that an international court's universal jurisdiction does not necessarily imply that all states have an obligation to appear before it or comply with its judgments. Since state sovereignty still constitutes the cornerstone of public international law, the state's consent to be bound by the judgments of an international court or tribunal is required. None of the universal courts listed above has competence to hear or adjudge a dispute involving a state that did not accept its jurisdiction. This applies even to the main judicial organ of the United Nations, the International Court of Justice, which cannot entertain a case where one of the parties to the dispute does not accept its jurisdiction.

Not every international court or tribunal adjudicates disputes between states. Some courts and tribunals were set up for the sole purpose of prosecuting individuals accused of war crimes or crimes against humanity. Other international tribunals, such as the United Nations Dispute Tribunal, the United Nations Appeals Tribunal, and the ILO Administrative Tribunal, were set up to hear work-related grievances submitted by staff members of international organizations. The ICJ, the International Tribunal for the Law of the Sea, the Dispute Settlement Panels and Appellate Body of the WTO are judicial organs adjudicating disputes between states.

4) Fourth Principle—Prohibition to Threaten or to Use Force

The most frequently raised principle in the *UN Charter* is the prohibition to use force enshrined in Article 2.4:

> All Members shall refrain in their international relations from the threat or use of force against the territorial integrity or political

independence of any state, or in any other manner inconsistent with the Purposes of the United Nations.

The obligation to refrain from using force is no longer considered as only a conventional norm. It has come to be recognized as *jus cogens*—an overriding and unmodifiable prohibitory norm.[99] *Jus cogens* norms are fundamental principles accepted by the international community of states as a norm from which no derogation is permitted.[100] It is an obligation owned to the international community as a whole. Therefore, any state, regardless of whether it has been injured or not, is entitled to invoke the responsibility of the violating state on the basis of a *jus cogens* norm. The prohibition applies not only to the actual use of force but also to the threat to use force. At the same time, the provision admits of exceptions by stating that there may be circumstances where the threat or the actual use of force is consistent with the purposes of the *UN Charter*.

In this part, we will first examine what constitutes a use of force or a threat within the meaning of Article 2.4 of the *UN Charter*. We will then explore circumstances where a threat or the actual use of force may be consistent with the *UN Charter*.

a) What Constitutes Use of Force?

Traditionally, a violation of Article 2.4 for use of force required an act of aggression. While aggression remains the most obvious type of use of force, it is not the only way of using force. The *UN Charter* does not provide a definition of the terms "use of force" or "act of aggression." This omission was intentional. The delegates at the San Francisco conference feared that a specific definition would provide an easy escape for a potential aggressor and be used as a list of actions that should be avoided.[101] Therefore, it was felt that it would be wiser

---

99 *Case Concerning Military and Paramilitary Activities in and against Nicaragua (Nicaragua v United States of America)*, Merits, Judgment, [1986] ICJ Rep 14 at para 190 [*Nicaragua v United States*].

100 *Vienna Convention on the Law of Treaties*, 23 May 1969, 1155 UNTS 331, art 53 (entered into force 27 January 1980).

101 US, *The Charter of the United Nations: Hearings before the Senate Comm on Foreign Relations*, 79th Cong, 1st Sess 51 (1945) (Statement by Leo Pasvolsky,

to leave it to the determination of each particular case on the facts and circumstances at the time. In fact, when the *UN Charter* was being drafted, several delegations proposed and advocated for a specific definition of the term "aggression"; however, these proposals were not retained.[102] Based largely on precedents, there appears to be a consensus among nations that a number of actions deemed unfriendly, including espionage, unfavourable trade practices, severance of diplomatic relations, economic competition, sanctions and embargoes, and economic and political coercion, do not rise to the threshold of use of force.

Throughout the years, the Security Council, the General Assembly, and the International Court of Justice dealt with situations and controversies that compelled them to make specific determinations as to what constitutes use of force or an act of aggression. As a result, it is now well established in international law that the following conducts constitute an act of aggression or a form of force envisaged in Article 2.4 of the *UN Charter*:

a) Invasion by a state of the territory of another state;
b) Temporary or permanent military occupation of another state;
c) Annexation by the use of force of the territory of another state;
d) Use of any weapons by a state against the territory of another state;
e) Blockade of the ports or coasts of a state by another state;
f) Use of armed forces of one state which are within the territory of another state with the agreement of the receiving state, in contravention of the conditions provided for in the agreement of their presence in such territory;
g) Allowing another state to use its territory for perpetrating an act of aggression against a third state;
h) Propaganda for wars of aggression;

Special Assistant to the Secretary of State for International Organization and Security Affairs).

102 Daniel W Abbott, "The United Nations and Interstate Conflict: A Legislative History of Article 39 of the *United Nations Charter*" (2002) 8 *UC Davis J Int'l L & Pol'y* 276 at 287.

i) Any forcible action depriving peoples of their right to self-determination, freedom and independence;
j) Organizing or encouraging the organization of irregular forces or armed bands including mercenaries, for incursion into the territory of another state;
k) The attack on a vessel of another state in international waters provided the vessel flies the flag of that state;
l) Instigating, assisting or participating in acts of civil strife or terrorist acts in another state or acquiescing in organized activities within its territory directed towards the commission of such acts.[103]

i) Invasion by a State of the Territory of Another State

An invasion is a military incursion by one state into the territory of another state. A number of reasons may justify a state to invade another state. The ultimate objective of an invasion can be to conquer and annex territory, to liberate another state, to re-establish political control over a territory, to partition a country, to replace a government, to obtain concessions from the victim state, or to capture and bring to justice terrorists or criminals who take refuge in another state.

Since the establishment of the United Nations, the world has witnessed a large number of invasions, including the Soviet invasion of Hungary in 1956 and of Czechoslovakia in 1968, the American invasion of Cuba in 1961, of Dominican Republic in 1965, and of Panama in 1989, Israeli invasion of Lebanon in 1978 and 1982, Iraq's invasion of Iran in 1980, and the Argentine invasion of the Falkland Islands in 1982 to name a few. In a post-Cold War era, the most notable examples are Iraq's invasion of Kuwait in 1990, the US–UK invasion of Iraq in 2003, the invasion of Lebanon by Israel in 2006, and Russia's invasion of Ukraine in 2014. In most cases, a military invasion leads to a forcible change of regime, temporary military occupation, or annexation.

103 On 21 December 1988, a bomb exploded on board a Pan Am flight over the town of Lockerbie, Scotland, causing the death of 270 people. Several investigations established that two Libyan government officials (alleged intelligence officers) were responsible for this terrorist act.

ii) Temporary or Permanent Military Occupation of Another State

The term "occupation" can be defined as the effective control of a power over a territory to which that power has no sovereign title, without the volition of the sovereign of that territory.[104] When a territory is placed under the authority of a hostile army it becomes occupied. Whether or not the occupation is met with armed resistance is irrelevant. Occupation may be the result of a threat to use force or of a peace agreement. An occupying state may exercise its authority over the occupied territory either by administering it directly or by establishing a lackey government to conceal the belligerent nature of its presence.

Military occupation can be total or partial, short term or long term. An occupation that is total entails control over the entire territory of another state. Syria's occupation of Lebanon from 1976 to 2005 and South Africa's occupation of Namibia until 1990 are examples of total and long-term occupations. An example of a partial occupation was Armenia's military control of swathes of Azeri territory around the mountainous enclave of Nagorno-Karabakh.[105] In late September 2020, military hostilities resumed again.

The occupation of Guantanamo Bay by the United States is undoubtedly a long-term occupation. An example of a much shorter military occupation was the political and military crisis between Russia and Georgia. In August 2008, South Ossetia and Abkhazia, two separatist provinces that are officially part of Georgia and supported by Russia, declared independence. When Georgia refused to recognize their cessation, violent confrontations took place across the country. To protect the interests of its proxies, Russia invaded Georgia and temporarily occupied the country. This occupation ended within a few days.

---

104 Eyal Benvenisti, *The International Law of Occupation* (Princeton: Princeton University Press, 2004) at 5.

105 The fighting between Armenia and Azerbaijan dates back to 1988, when the ethnic Armenian population of Nagorno-Karabakh attempted to secede from Azerbaijan. The conflict grew into a full-scale war. A ceasefire brokered by Russia in 1994 left Nagorno-Karabakh, as well as parts of Azeri territory (used by Armenia as a security belt) around the enclave, under the control of Armenia. In late September 2020, military hostilities resumed again.

iii) Annexation by the Use of Force of the Territory of Another State

Annexation is the forcible acquisition by one state of another state's territory. Annexation and military occupation are two different notions. Occupation is temporary in nature; the occupying power makes no claims for permanent sovereignty over the occupied territory. Annexation, on the other hand, is permanent. Annexation allows the belligerent state to extend its sovereignty over the territory of another, usually weaker, state. Also, unlike occupation, annexation requires the belligerent state to confer citizenship rights upon the subjugated population.[106]

The annexation of Crimea by Russia in 2014 following the Ukrainian revolution is perhaps the most recent illustration of such use of force. Following the annexation, Russia replaced the Ukrainian system of administration on the peninsula with its own governmental structures and granted Russian citizenship to the entire population of Crimea. As a result of this annexation, many countries, including the United States, Canada, European Union, and Australia, imposed economic sanctions on Russia.

Although the intended purpose of annexation is to acquire territory on a permanent basis, the situation may be reversed. For instance, in 1976, the former Portuguese colony of East Timor gained independence. Civil war broke out between those who favoured independence and those who aspired to be part of Indonesia. Indonesia intervened militarily and absorbed the island as its twenty-seventh province. The General Assembly and the Security Council condemned the annexation and demanded Indonesia's immediate withdrawal. In 1999, the Security Council established a peacekeeping mission. Shortly thereafter, Indonesia gave in and withdrew completely from East Timor.

iv) Use of Weapons by a State Against the Territory of Another State

A state can use force against another state without any military incursion into the territory of the other state. For example, ballistic missile bombings and drone strikes do not require troops on the ground

---

106 Peter MR Stirk, *Politics of Military Occupation* (Edinburgh: Edinburgh University Press, 2012) at 44.

and may be carried out from another state. Such attacks have become more frequent in the last two decades. They are not any different from strikes launched from manned aircrafts such as fighter jets or helicopters. Essentially, like airplanes and helicopters, drones enable the delivery of force from a distance. The use of drones may be more advantageous for tactical reasons. In particular, drones are cheaper to produce than manned aircrafts. They do not pose any risk to the lives of pilots and their strikes can be inconspicuous. Nevertheless, drone strikes are not more lawful than other types of armed attack; they are just another form of prohibited use of force. However, it is important to point out that not all drones are armed or used in combat. The majority of drones are unarmed surveillance vehicles used to gather and transmit information on the location and identification of enemy targets. Under principles of international law, the utilization of this type of drone does not constitute prohibited use of force.

In May 1960, the United States sent a manned aircraft into Soviet territory to carry out a reconnaissance mission. The American U-2 plane was unarmed but equipped with several surveillance cameras. The aircraft was detected by Soviet radar and shot down. The American pilot was captured and sentenced. This incident triggered a diplomatic row between the United States and the USSR. The United States argued that sending a single-engine unarmed aircraft with one pilot does not constitute aggression. The Soviet delegation tabled a draft resolution before the Security Council characterizing the US reconnaissance flight over USSR territory as an act of aggression. In support of this resolution, the Soviet representative raised the following argument:

> The United States Government asserts ... that the penetration of a single aircraft—and at that an unarmed, single-engine aircraft manned by one airman—into Soviet Territory, is not an aggressive act. These are peculiar and absurd arguments. Perhaps the United States Government will explain for our benefit how many aircraft it takes to make a violation of the frontiers of another State—and a premeditated violation into the bargain—an act of aggression. It appears that a violation of frontiers by a single aircraft does not

> constitute aggression. But if two, three or four aircraft were involved, would that be aggression or not? In a word, what is the minimum number of aircraft which must take part to make a violation of the frontiers of another State an act of aggression? Who will answer this question?[107]

However, the draft resolution was not adopted, having failed to obtain the affirmative votes of seven out of eleven members.[108] The majority of Security Council members did not view a reconnaissance mission as an act of aggression. Nevertheless, two decades later, the International Court of Justice strongly implied that the violation of another country's airspace constitutes a threat of force.[109]

v) Blockade of the Ports or Coasts of a State by Another State

A naval blockade is a belligerent operation to prevent vessels and aircraft of all nations, enemy or neutral, from entering or exiting specified ports or coastal areas belonging to or under the control of an enemy nation. Such actions may constitute acts of aggression.[110]

In January 2009, Israel imposed a naval blockade on the coast of Gaza. On 31 May 2010, a flotilla of six vessels was approaching the coast of Gaza. The Turkish-registered vessels were carrying people and humanitarian supplies. The flotilla had been directed to change course by the Israeli forces. When the convoy of vessels disobeyed the orders, Israeli Defense Forces boarded and took over the vessels seventy-two nautical miles from land (in high seas). In the process, nine passengers lost their lives and many others were wounded. Both Turkey and Israel conducted separate investigations and inquiries. Different panels and commissions reached inconsistent conclusions. The Secretary-General established the Panel of Inquiry, known as the Palmer Panel, to investigate the incident. The Palmer Panel report, released in September 2011, found that Israel was entitled to impose

---

107 UNSCOR, 15th Year, 860th Meeting, UN Doc S/PV.860 (1960) at para 7.

108 This incident occurred before the *UN Charter* was amended to expand the membership of the Security Council from eleven to fifteen states.

109 *Nicaragua v United States*, above note 99.

110 *Ibid.*

a naval blockade as a legitimate security measure in order to prevent weapons from entering Gaza by sea and its implementation complied with the requirements of international law. The panel also concluded that the conduct of passengers of the convoy was provocative. However, the panel blamed Israel for boarding the vessels with such substantial force at a great distance from the blockade zone. Its approach was viewed to be excessive and unreasonable. Israel was unable to explain the deaths of five passengers. Forensic evidence showed that these passengers were shot multiple times, including in the back or at close range. The panel also found that there was significant mistreatment of passengers by Israeli authorities after the take-over of the vessels had been completed through to their deportation. This included physical mistreatment, harassment and intimidation, unjustified confiscation of belongings, and the denial of timely consular assistance. Israel's actions were held to constitute prohibited use of force.

vi) Use of Armed Forces of One State Which Are Within the Territory of Another State with the Agreement of the Receiving State, in Contravention of the Conditions Provided for in the Agreement of Their Presence in Such Territory

This scenario arose in the *Armed Activities on the Territory of the Congo* case.[111] In 1997, Laurent-Désiré Kabila, who was at the time a Congolese rebel leader of a group supported by Uganda and Rwanda, succeeded in overthrowing the then president of Zaire, Mobutu Sese Seko. When Kabila was formally sworn in as president, he granted Uganda and Rwanda substantial benefits in the DRC in the military and economic fields as a token of appreciation for their support. He then sought a gradual reduction in influence of these two states over the DRC's internal affairs. Rwanda and Uganda tried to protect their interests and decided to overthrow the new president. Rwandan and Ugandan armed forces invaded parts of the DRC and fought against the Congolese army. In June 1999, the DRC instituted proceedings before the International Court of Justice against Uganda for acts of

---

111 *Armed Activities on the Territory of the Congo (Democratic Republic of the Congo v Uganda)*, [2005] ICJ Rep 168 [*Democratic Republic of the Congo v Uganda*].

armed aggression perpetrated by it on the territory of the DRC. Uganda argued, *inter alia*, that the presence of its armed forces was a direct result of President Kabila's own request memorialized in an agreement between Uganda and DRC. The International Court of Justice found that the consent that had been given to Uganda to place its forces in the DRC, and to engage in military operations, was not open-ended. DRC accepted that Uganda could act, or assist in acting, against rebels on the eastern border and in particular to stop them operating across the common border. This consent was limited in time and restricted to certain geographic locations. It also found that this consent was subsequently withdrawn. Therefore, the Court concluded that Uganda had been using its armed forces within DRC in contravention of the conditions provided for in the agreement of their presence in the DRC.

vii) Allowing Another State to Use Its Territory for Perpetrating an Act of Aggression Against a Third State

The first judgment rendered by the International Court of Justice dealt with this form of aggression.[112] In October 1946, a squadron of four British warships were navigating through a channel in the North Corfu Strait in Albania's territorial waters. Two British vessels struck mines and were heavily damaged. Forty-four British marines died or sustained injuries. The United Kingdom filed an application against Albania and sought monetary compensation. The International Court of Justice had to determine whether Albania was responsible for the act. The Court found that Albania did not have the required capability to lay mines, as it had no navy. The United Kingdom produced evidence establishing that two Yugoslav war vessels were seen carrying the same type of mines to the Corfu Channel a few days before the explosion. On this basis, the United Kingdom tried to prove that the Yugoslav vessels were responsible for laying the mines. The Court was of the view that the evidence was too circumstantial to draw such a conclusion. Nevertheless, the Court determined that there was no need to establish the identity of the perpetrator. Albania could be held

112 *Corfu Channel Case (United Kingdom v Albania)*, Merits, Judgment, [1949] ICJ Rep 4 [*Corfu Channel Case*].

liable because the minefield, which caused the explosions, could not have been laid without the knowledge of the Albanian government. The Court held that by allowing another state to use its territory to perpetrate acts of aggression against another state, Albania breached its obligations under international law. It is important to point out, however, that the unlawful act or knowledge of such an act cannot be imputed to the state by reason merely of the fact that it occurred on its territory or in its waters. This is a question of evidence and requires a case-by-case determination.

viii) Propaganda for Wars of Aggression

States are under a legal obligation to refrain from spreading warmongering or subversive propaganda hostile to the government of a foreign country in time of peace. Warmongering is a propaganda designed to provoke or encourage aggression, civil unrest, violence, or revolution. There can be no doubt that this prohibition is part of international customary law.[113] The proposition that propaganda in aid of an aggressive war is an international offense was confirmed in the Nuremberg trials.[114]

In a letter addressed to the then Secretary-General U Thant in February 1966, Fidel Castro unsuccessfully attempted to convince the international community that any country has the inherent right to aid revolutionary movements in other countries. Castro argued that the so-called liberation movements were permitted to use force against the government in power. This triggered a very strong objection from several Latin American countries. Today, there can be no doubt that aiding or abetting revolutionary movements in other states is prohibited by the *UN Charter*.

---

113 Arthur Larson, "The Present Status of Propaganda in International Law" (Summer 1966) 31 *Law and Contemporary Problems* 439.

114 *Ibid* at 445.

ix) Any Forcible Action Depriving Peoples of Their Right to Self-Determination, Freedom, and Independence

The case of *Legal Consequences for States of the Continued Presence of South Africa in Namibia*[115] dealt with this type of situation. From 1884, Namibia was a German colony. After the First World War and the German surrender, the newly created League of Nations had to determine the fate of freed colonies and occupied territories such as Namibia. It created a mandates system that consisted of entrusting the administration of such colonies and territories to states that had functional governments called "mandatories." Namibia became South Africa's protectorate. After decades of administering Namibia, South Africa decided to annex it in violation of the terms of its mandate. Its government contended that the mandate was no longer legally in force, and that South Africa had essentially conquered Namibia. South Africa disregarded Security Council resolutions urging it to leave Namibia. In 1970, the Security Council sought an advisory opinion from the International Court of Justice.[116] The Court determined that the continued presence of South Africa in Namibia was illegal and that South Africa was obligated to withdraw its administration from Namibia immediately and thus put an end to its occupation of the territory. South Africa did not comply with its obligation until 1989.

x) Organizing or Encouraging the Organization of Irregular Forces or Armed Bands, Including Mercenaries, for Incursion into the Territory of Another State

In the *Case Concerning Military and Paramilitary Activities in and against Nicaragua*,[117] the International Court of Justice found that the United States had breached its obligations under Article 2.4 of the *UN Charter* and had used force against Nicaragua by conducting unauthorized military activities on its territory. The Court determined that certain forms of indirect aggression — such as organizing, recruiting, training,

---

115 *Legal Consequences for States of the Continued Presence of South Africa in Namibia (South West Africa) notwithstanding Security Council Resolution 276 (1970)*, Advisory Opinion [1971] ICJ Rep 16.

116 SC Res 284 (1970), UNSCOR, 25th Year, UN Doc S/RES/284 (1970).

117 *Nicaragua v United States*, above note 99.

supplying, directing, and controlling a mercenary army, paramilitary group, or guerrilla forces for the purposes of overthrowing a government—were use of force prohibited by Article 2.4 of the *UN Charter*. If the attacks perpetrated against a state cannot be linked or attributed to another state, Article 2.4 of the *UN Charter* will not apply. This is a matter of evidence. For instance, in the case concerning *Armed Activities on the Territory of the Congo*,[118] the International Court of Justice examined whether a paramilitary group (MLC) operating in the Congo (Democratic Republic of) was an organ of Uganda or an entity exercising elements of governmental authority on its behalf. Having found no evidence that MLC was acting on the instructions of, or under the direction or control of, Uganda, the Court reached the conclusion that the aggression could not be attributed to Uganda. However, having found evidence that Uganda was giving training and military support to a military wing of the MLC, the Court concluded that Uganda had violated its obligations under international law.

xi) The Attack on a Vessel of Another State in International Waters Provided the Vessel Flies the Flag of That State

In the case of *Oil Platforms*,[119] the ICJ examined whether an attack on a vessel constitutes an armed aggression. The actions giving rise to this case occurred during the armed conflict that opposed Iran and Iraq in the Persian Gulf, which is an important international commercial route. In 1984, Iraq commenced attacks against Iranian ships carrying oil in the Persian Gulf. Iran retaliated by exploding Iraqi ships and oil tankers. Between 1984 and 1988, a number of commercial vessels and warships of various nationalities, including neutral vessels, were attacked by aircraft, helicopters, missiles, or warships, or struck by mines in the waters of the Persian Gulf. This became known as the "Tanker War." The United States attributed responsibility for certain incidents to Iran, whereas Iran argued that Iraq was responsible for them. One sunk tanker belonged to the United States. It accused

118 *Democratic Republic of the Congo v Uganda*, above note 111.

119 *Oil Platforms (Islamic Republic of Iran v United States of America)*, [2003] ICJ Rep 161 [*Oil Platforms*].

Iran of exploding it and retaliated by attacking Iranian offshore oil production installations, claiming to be acting in self-defence. The International Court of Justice held that, in order to establish that the United States was legally justified in attacking the Iranian oil platforms in exercise of the right of individual self-defence, the United States had to show that Iran was responsible for the explosion of its tanker and that the attack was of such a nature as to be qualified as armed aggression. The Court found that the United States failed to meet this burden. Nevertheless, the Court pointed out that an attack on a US-flagged ship (as opposed to US-owned) could be an armed aggression justifying self-defence.

xii) Instigating, Assisting, or Participating in Acts of Civil Strife or Terrorist Acts in Another State or Acquiescing in Organized Activities Within its Territory Directed Towards the Commission of Such Acts

From 1996 to 2001, Afghanistan was ruled by an ultraconservative political and religious faction known as the Taliban. The Taliban was effectively the government of Afghanistan. This regime provided sanctuary for terrorists and drug lords. It also harboured the perpetrators of the attacks of 11 September 2001. This was viewed by the international community as a prohibited use of force by one state against another. It is important to recall that although the perpetrators of the attacks were non-state actors, they received assistance from the Taliban regime. On this basis, the United States invoked its right to self-defence and invaded Afghanistan in retaliation for 9/11.

xiii) Cyber-attacks

A cyber-attack aims at altering, disrupting, deceiving, degrading, or destroying computer systems, networks, information, data, or programs. It has now become an important component of what is known as "hybrid warfare," which describes a combination of means, including military and technological, to wage a war. It is important to note at the outset that although some cyber-attacks may constitute use of force, not all cyber-attacks can be regarded as such. First and foremost, to be an act prohibited under Article 2.4 of the *UN Charter*, cyber-attacks must be attributable to a state actor. In the cases of *Military and*

Paramilitary Activities in and against Nicaragua and *Armed Activities on the Territory of the Congo*, the International Court of Justice developed a relatively simple test for determining whether the recalcitrant party is acting under the direction or control of a state or government.

Second, to determine whether a cyber-attack constitutes a use of force, one must examine the objective of the attack and the effect it produces. If the purpose of the cyber-attack is similar to those of an armed attack, the cyber-attack will amount to a use of force. For instance, a cyber-attack by any state actor on the Pentagon's information technology systems and networks for the purposes of disabling US defence capabilities would be characterized as an armed aggression. Conversely, if a cyber-attack has an effect similar to government-initiated coercive or harmful actions that are generally not viewed as a use of force, it would probably not be regarded as use of force.[120] Such actions include economic sanctions, espionage, or covert actions such as planting information or influencing elections.

In 2016, allegations arose that the Russian Government intended to influence the US presidential elections through a series of cyber-attacks. Assuming that these cyber-attacks can be positively linked to the Russian government, do they constitute use of force? On the one hand, if the cyber-attacks had a direct impact on the outcome of the presidential elections, they were akin to a staged coup, which can be regarded as an armed aggression prohibited by the *UN Charter*. On the other hand, Russia's alleged actions were limited to gathering and disseminating objectively verifiable information. There were no attempts to disable systems or to cause material or physical harm. This can hardly be described as use of force within the meaning of the *UN Charter*. Either way, such actions constitute interference in the domestic affairs of another state, which is a breach of another UN principle, discussed below.

---

120 Michael Schmitt, "Computer Network Attack and the Use of Force in International Law: Thoughts on a Normative Framework" (1999) 37 *Colum J Transnational L* 885; Herbert S Lin, "Offensive Cyber Operations and the Use of Force" (2010) 4 *J Nat'l Sec L & Pol'y* 63.

b) Authority to Determine What Constitutes Use of Force

The Security Council has the primary responsibility to determine whether a particular act or a series of acts constitutes an aggression.[121] However, the Security Council only rarely makes such determinations because this would amount to a condemnation, whereas the Security Council is a political body that tries to find diplomatic solutions to problems. The Security Council's authority to make determinations under Article 2.4 of the *UN Charter* is not exclusive. The General Assembly and the International Court of Justice have also played an important role in qualifying acts of aggression or use of force. For instance, the General Assembly defined aggression as "the use of armed force by a State against the sovereignty, territorial integrity or political independence of another State"[122] and provided examples of aggression in other resolutions.[123]

The International Court of Justice also adjudged several cases and issued advisory opinions on the same topic. The most notable examples are the *Corfu Channel Case*,[124] the *Case Concerning Military and Paramilitary Activities in and against Nicaragua*,[125] and the *Case concerning Armed Activities on the Territory of the Congo*.[126]

c) What Constitutes Threat to Use Force

The delegates at the San Francisco conference did not consider in depth the notion of "threat of force" or when such a threat is prohibited.[127] The jurisprudence of the International Court of Justice is also scant on this subject. Normally, any serious or credible threat could be construed as a threat to use force. When the state making the threat has the ability to carry it out, the threat should be perceived as credible. For instance, if the government of Samoa threatened to

---

121 *Charter of the United Nations*, above note 61, art 39.

122 *Definition of Aggression*, GA Res 3314 (XXIX), UNGAOR, 29th Sess, UN Doc A/RES/3314(XXIX) (1974) 142.

123 *Declaration on Principles of International Law*, above note 42.

124 *Corfu Channel Case*, above note 112.

125 *Nicaragua v United States*, above note 99.

126 *Democratic Republic of the Congo v Uganda*, above note 111.

127 Nikolas Stürchler, *The Threat of Force in International Law* (Cambridge, UK: Cambridge University Press, 2012) at 35.

invade and conquer China, its threat would not be credible because Samoa cannot possibly carry out such a hypothetical threat. Consequently, it would be unreasonable for China to take pre-emptive steps in self-defence by attacking Samoa. If, however, we inversed the roles, the threat would become very credible and serious as China has the military capability to carry out the threat.

While imminence of use of force is a strong indicator of an unlawful threat, it is not a condition *sine qua non* for its existence. Although the bar is lower to qualify as a threat of force than an actual use of force, in practice, threats are frequently veiled or implied, which makes them difficult to establish. It is even more difficult to determine from a veiled threat how imminent the use of force is.

There is no longer any doubt that "if the envisaged use of force is itself unlawful, the stated readiness to use it would be a threat prohibited under Article 2, paragraph 4" of the *UN Charter*.[128] In other words, the threat cannot be lawful unless carrying out the threat would be lawful. For instance, "it would be illegal for a State to threaten force to secure territory from another State, or to cause it to follow or not follow certain political or economic paths."[129] Also, a threat to use chemical weapons would be unlawful regardless of the circumstances because the use of chemical weapons itself is prohibited. With regard to nuclear weapons, the law is more nuanced. In the advisory opinion on the *Legality of the Threat or Use of Nuclear Weapons*, some states argued that possession of nuclear weapons is itself a threat to use force. The International Court of Justice addressed this argument as follows:

> Possession of nuclear weapons may indeed justify an inference of preparedness to use them. In order to be effective, the policy of deterrence, by which those States possessing or under the umbrella of nuclear weapons seek to discourage military aggression by demonstrating that it will serve no purpose, necessitates that the intention to use nuclear weapons be credible. Whether this is a "threat" contrary to Article 2, paragraph 4, depends upon whether

128 *Legality of the Threat or Use of Nuclear Weapons*, Advisory Opinion, [1996] ICJ Rep 226 at para 47.

129 *Ibid.*

> the particular use of force envisaged would be directed against the territorial integrity or political independence of a State, or against the Purposes of the United Nations or whether, in the event that it were intended as a means of defence, it would necessarily violate the principles of necessity and proportionality. In any of these circumstances the use of force, and the threat to use it, would be unlawful under the law of the Charter.[130]

In this case, the ICJ was asked an extremely difficult question. On the one hand, nuclear weapons can cause significantly more damage than any other weapon. Nuclear weapons are also incapable of distinguishing civilian from military targets. The destructive power of nuclear weapons cannot be contained in either space or time. On the other hand, the possession of nuclear weapons by the five founding superpowers of the UN has always been tolerated, if not accepted, by other states for decades. The *Treaty on the Non-Proliferation of Nuclear Weapons* prohibits the use of nuclear weapons but does not bar their possession. These can be the reason for the ICJ's ambivalent and non-assertive advisory opinion.

For a risk to constitute a threat to use force, physical harm or destruction is not required. A mere credible threat that another state could use force would generally be sufficient. The International Court of Justice held that violations of airspace by military aircrafts, violations of territorial waters by military or armed vessels, and demonstration of force for the purpose of exercising political pressure are viewed as threats.[131] Verbal threats, initial troop movements, initial movement of ballistic missiles, massing of troops on a border, use of fire control radars, and interference with early warning or command and control systems could also constitute threats. Conversely, measures undertaken to enhance a state's self-defence capabilities do not constitute threats. For instance, piling up of armaments and forming military alliances cannot be regarded as threats within the meaning of Article 2.4 of the *UN Charter*.

---

130 *Ibid* at para 48.

131 *Nicaragua v United States*, above note 99.

d) Circumstances Permitting a Use of Force or a Threat Thereof[132]

There are two recognized exceptions to the prohibition to use force under Article 2.4 of the *UN Charter*. The first exception is military measures authorized by the Security Council under Chapter VII, which will be canvassed in Chapter 4 on the Security Council. The second exception is the right of self-defence provided for in Article 51 of the *UN Charter*:[133]

> Nothing in the present Charter shall impair the inherent right of individual or collective self-defence if an armed attack occurs against a Member of the United Nations, until the Security Council has taken measures necessary to maintain international peace and security. Measures taken by Members in the exercise of this right of self-defence shall be immediately reported to the Security Council and shall not in any way affect the authority and responsibility of the Security Council under the present Charter to take at any time such action as it deems necessary in order to maintain or restore international peace and security.

This second exception is relied upon very frequently in international law. When states use force against other states, they almost invariably invoke self-defence. Self-defence can be individual or collective. In the *Case Concerning Military and Paramilitary Activities in and against Nicaragua*, the International Court of Justice specified that in the language of Article 51 of the *UN Charter*, the inherent right that any state possesses in the event of armed attack covers both collective and individual self-defence. Nevertheless, Article 51 of the *UN Charter* may justify a use of force in self-defence only within the strict confines laid down therein. It does not allow the use of force by a state to protect perceived security interests beyond these parameters. Other means are available to a concerned state, including recourse to the Security Council.[134]

---

132 See, generally, James A Green, *The International Court of Justice and Self-Defence in International Law* (Oxford, UK: Hart Publishing, 2009).

133 High-level Panel on Threats, Challenges and Change, *A More Secure World: Our Shared Responsibility*, UNGAOR, 59th Sess, UN Doc A/59/565 (2004).

134 *Democratic Republic of the Congo v Uganda*, above note 111 at para 148.

The right of self-defence is temporary; it can be exercised only until the Security Council steps in. A state that invokes the right to collective self-defence must make a declaration of being the victim of an armed attack and a request for collective self-defence.[135] Once the Security Council is notified of the situation, it must determine whether or not the aggrieved state was justified to use force in self-defence. While the Security Council is considering or deliberating on the situation, the injured state can use force based on its own unilateral assessment of whether or not it is acting in self-defence. If the Security Council subsequently determines that the state was not entitled to use force in self-defence, any use of force (past or future) becomes unlawful. In such a case, the aggrieved state cannot continue using force on the basis of its own determination that it is acting in self-defence. Conversely, if the Security Council determines that the injured state was justified to use force in self-defence, the Council must step in and take collective measures on behalf of the international community. As soon as the Security Council steps in and takes measures, the right to use force in self-defence ceases. In this sense, the Security Council is the arbiter of the use of force.

The right to use force in self-defence is permissible if force is necessary and proportionate. Force is necessary if the injured party has no other alternative to repel an aggression or prevent an imminent threat. The use of force is proportional if the amount of force used was necessary to achieve the desired legitimate ends. In cases where the requirements of necessity and proportionality are not met, the Security Council is likely to determine that the use of force is an aggression and not justified under the principle of self-defence.

Some states invoked the right to self-defence to justify use of force when none was necessary. For instance, during the Falkland Islands war in 1982, Argentina invoked the right to use force against the United Kingdom by rationalizing its aggression as a self-defence action.[136] The Security Council rejected Argentina's claim of self-

135 *Nicaragua v United States*, above note 99.

136 Atsushi Tago, "Why Do States Formally Invoke the Right of Individual Self-Defence? Legal, Diplomatic and Aid-Politics to Motivate States to Respect International Law" (2013) 30:2 *Conflict Management and Peace Science* 161 at 162.

defence because it was the aggressor and the United Kingdom was the aggrieved state. Similarly, in 1981, Israel attempted to argue that its strikes against civilian targets in Lebanon were justified as self-defence. The Security Council determined that such use of force was unnecessary because there was no imminent danger to the security of Israel. The Council strongly condemned Israel and demanded the cessation of the attacks.[137]

It is also important to point out that the right of individual self-defence must be exercised with restraint. The amount of force used must be proportionate to the action taken by the other side. The excessive use of force by a state invoking self-defence can be construed as a violation of the prohibition to use force. Such a scenario arose in the *Oil Platforms* case referred to above.[138] In 1980s, during the Iraq-Iran war, a number of tankers carrying oil were sunk in the Persian Gulf. One sunk tanker belonged to the United States. The United States accused Iran of exploding its tanker and retaliated against it by attacking Iranian offshore oil production installations, claiming to be acting in self-defence. The International Court of Justice held that in order to establish that it was legally justified in attacking the Iranian platforms in exercise of the right of individual self-defence, the United States had to show that Iran was responsible and that those attacks were of such a nature as to be qualified as "armed attacks" within the meaning of that expression in Article 51 of the *UN Charter*. The Court further stated that the United States must also show that its actions were necessary and proportional to the armed attack made on it, and that the platforms were a legitimate military target open to attack in the exercise of self-defence. The Court found that the United States had failed to meet this burden.

The right to self-defence was also unsuccessfully invoked by Israel in the case of the *Construction of a Wall in Palestine*.[139] The Court noted that Article 51 of the *UN Charter* recognized the existence of an inherent right of self-defence in the case of an armed attack by one state

137 SC Res 508 (1982), UNSCOR, 37th Year, UN Doc. S/Res/508 (1982) 5.
138 *Oil Platforms*, above note 119.
139 *Construction of a Wall in the Occupied Palestinian Territory*, above note 58.

against another state. The Court observed that since the alleged attacks against Israel were not imputable to a foreign state, and that the threat justifying the construction of the wall originated within its territory, Article 51 of the *UN Charter* had no relevance in this case. Therefore, it opined that both the wall and the associated regime that had been imposed on the Palestinian inhabitants were contrary to international law.

In other cases, the use of force in self-defence was either endorsed or condoned by the Security Council. In particular, during the Persian Gulf War in 1990 and 1991, Saudi Arabia invoked the right of self-defence for its border protection and deployed military forces to counter Iraq's manoeuvres. Similarly, after the 9/11 terrorist attacks on the United States in 2001, the United States invoked Article 51 to start military operations against the Taliban and al-Qaeda. In both cases, there was a consensus that self-defence warranted the use of force.

5) Fifth Principle—Duty to Give the United Nations Assistance and Duty to Refrain from Giving Assistance to Recalcitrant States

In the early 1930s, two events served to show the League's inability to successfully impose sanctions. In both situations, the members of the League did not act collectively in their attempts to suppress the aggressor nation. The first event was Japan's invasion of Manchuria in 1932. It took the League one year to produce a report from a fact-finding commission condemning Japan's conduct. The second event is known as the Abyssinia crisis and relates to Italy's invasion of Ethiopia in 1935. The emperor of Ethiopia personally went to the League to ask for help. The League agreed to impose sanctions, but they did not produce any practical effect. Far from imposing sanctions on Italy, Britain and France tried to make a secret pact to give Ethiopia to Italy.

The founders of the UN were determined to rectify this problem. Article 2.5 of the *UN Charter* makes it mandatory for all "members [to] give the United Nations every assistance in any action it takes in accordance with the present *Charter*, and [to] refrain from giving assistance to any state against which the United Nations is taking preventive or enforcement action." This principle ensures that individual states do not undermine the efficiency and credibility of the collective security system of the United Nations. The equivalent provision in the Covenant of the League of Nations was not worded in such strong terms.

This paragraph contains one mandatory or positive obligation and one prohibitive or negative obligation. The positive obligation compels states to give the UN *every* assistance in *any* action it takes. The prohibitive obligation forbids states to provide assistance to another state against which the UN is taking preventive or enforcement action.

The obligation to provide assistance in any action taken by the United Nations can range from providing financial assistance to supplying military equipment and troops. It can include imposing sanctions, enforcing no-fly zones and making its territory accessible to UN peacekeeping troops. The text of the provision, namely the words "every assistance" and "any action," is sufficiently broad for the UN to request any type of reasonable assistance.

The second half of Article 2.5 prohibits member states from providing assistance to any state against which the United Nations is taking preventive or enforcement action. The UN may have recourse to a range of enforcement measures to compel a recalcitrant state to correct its behaviour in the interests of international peace and security. The two major categories of enforcement actions that the Security Council can impose are those that involve the use of armed force and those that do not. Article 41 of the *UN Charter* allows the Security Council to impose measures that do not involve the use of armed force, including complete or partial interruption of economic relations and of rail, sea, air, postal, telegraphic, radio, and other means of communication, and the severance of diplomatic relations or an arms embargo. In accordance with Article 42 of the *UN Charter*, where measures provided for in Article 41 would be inadequate or have proved to be inadequate, the Security Council may take more robust measures such as use of force. Measures belonging to this category may include demonstrations, blockade, and other operations by air, sea, or land forces of members of the United Nations. Regardless of whether the Security Council takes actions involving the use of armed force or imposes measures not involving the use of force, all states have an obligation to refrain from giving assistance to the country that is the target of Security Council enforcement measures.

6) Sixth Principle—Application of the Principles to Non-member States

Paragraph 2.6 of the *UN Charter* provides that the "Organization shall ensure that states which are not Members of the United Nations act in accordance with these Principles so far as may be necessary for the maintenance of international peace and security." This provision appears to be devoid of any legal force for two reasons.

First, it is important to recall that only those states that had, by March 1945, declared war on Germany and Japan and subscribed to the United Nations Declaration were invited to San Francisco to take part at the final conference. When the United Nations came into existence, it had only fifty founding members. Many states were initially excluded from the organization. Therefore, it was felt that paragraph 2.6 would allow member states to ensure that non-members did not attempt to sabotage or undermine world peace and security. However, as the UN membership grew, this provision became redundant. In 1961, the UN had more than doubled its membership (from 51 to 104 member states). In 2017, with its 193 member states, the United Nations is the most international organization. There are only three sovereign states that are not members of the United Nations: the Holy See (Vatican City),[140] the Cook Islands, and Nuie. There are other territories, such as Taiwan, Palestine, and Kosovo, that are not

140 The term "Holy See" refers to the supreme authority of the Roman Catholic Church. The Holy See became a Permanent Observer State at the United Nations on 6 April 1964, and since then has always been invited to participate in the meetings of all the sessions of the General Assembly. Vatican City is the physical or territorial base of the Holy See. Although the State of Vatican City itself possesses a personality under international law, it is the Holy See that represents Vatican City State on the international arena. The UN entertains diplomatic relations with the Holy See and not with Vatican City.

UN members; however, these territories do not yet enjoy the status of sovereign states.

Second, this provision is also redundant because it does not clarify how the United Nations can ensure that non-members comply with its instructions and act in accordance with international obligations that they have never accepted. In other words, this provision neither provides possible sanctions for a non-member's refusal to act in accordance with the principles of the United Nations nor equips the United Nations with tools for enforcing this obligation.

It is also unfortunate that Article 2.6 of the *UN Charter* refers only to states. A number of important non-state actors, such as regional organizations (NATO, League of Arab States, African Union, European Union, etc.), opposition groups, or multinational corporations may, if they choose to do so, adversely affect the maintenance of international peace and security. It is as important for these actors as it is for any state to conduct their affairs in accordance with UN principles.

7) Seventh Principle—Prohibition to Intervene in Matters Within Domestic Jurisdiction

Article 2.7 of the *UN Charter* provides that "Nothing contained in the present *Charter* shall authorize the United Nations to intervene in matters which are essentially within the domestic jurisdiction of any state or shall require the Members to submit such matters to settlement under the present *Charter*; but this principle shall not prejudice the application of enforcement measures under Chapter VII." The principle of non-intervention involves the right of every sovereign state to conduct its affairs without outside interference.[141] It is part and parcel of customary international law.[142] The rationale for this principle is simple: only strong states can afford intervening without fear into domestic affairs of weaker states.[143] This would promote the survival of the fittest.

---

141 *Nicaragua v United States*, above note 99 at para 202.

142 *Ibid.*

143 See the discussion in *Corfu Channel Case*, above note 112 at 35.

The Covenant of the League of Nations had a similar provision. Article 15, paragraph 8 of the Covenant provided that "if the dispute ... is found by the Council, to arise out of a matter which by international law is solely within the domestic jurisdiction of that party, the Council shall so report, and shall make no recommendation as to its settlement." The prohibition to intervene in domestic affairs was addressed to the Council of the League of Nations. The *UN Charter* broadened the application of this prohibition not only to the Security Council but to all UN organs. The principle of non-intervention in domestic matters applies to the United Nations as an organization as well as to individual member states. Essentially, any organ of the United Nations, including the General Assembly, the Security Council, and the Secretariat, have a duty to abstain from intervening in domestic affairs of another state. The General Assembly and the International Court of Justice confirmed that this prohibition applies also to member states.[144]

a) Matters Essentially Within the Domestic Jurisdiction

The *UN Charter* does not define the phrase "matters which are essentially within the domestic jurisdiction of any state." This was not accidental. At Dumbarton Oaks, when this provision first appeared, it contained language that would have allowed member states to determine what falls within the domestic jurisdiction of a state. However, the US delegation objected, arguing that a precise definition could lead to an intrusion on domestic jurisdiction.[145] Therefore, what constitutes matters "which are essentially within the domestic jurisdiction of any state" was purposefully left vague. It is fair to assume that the phrase refers to the concept of sovereignty. To understand what falls within the domestic jurisdiction of a state, one needs to canvass the ambit of a state's sovereignty. The inherent attributes of sovereignty

144 *Declaration on the Inadmissibility of Intervention in the Domestic Affairs of States and the Protection of their Independence and Sovereignty*, GA Res 2131 (XX) [*Declaration on the Inadmissibility*], UNGAOR, 20th Sess, UN Doc A/RES/2131(XX) (1965) 11, and *Nicaragua v United States*, above note 99.

145 Stephen Schlesinger, *Act of Creation: The Founding of the United Nations* (Cambridge: Westview Press, 2003) at 236.

are: (1) an exclusive jurisdiction over a territory and the permanent population living there, and (2) the right not to be bound by international obligations arising from customary law and treaties without consenting to them. The first attribute relates to the state's domestic jurisdiction and is discussed immediately following this paragraph. The second attribute of sovereignty pertains to a state's international jurisdiction, which will be examined below in Section 7(a)(ii).

i) Domestic Attributes of Sovereignty

In 1928, Max Huber, a Swiss lawyer, former judge of the Permanent Court of International Justice and arbitrator, attempted to define sovereignty in the *Island of Palmas* case involving a territorial dispute between the Netherlands and the United States over an island. In adjudicating the dispute in his capacity as the arbitrator of the Permanent Court of Arbitration, Max Huber proposed the following definition:

> Sovereignty in the relations between States signifies independence. Independence in regard to a portion of the globe is the right to exercise therein, to the exclusion of any other State, the functions of a State. The development of the national organisation of States during the last few centuries and, as a corollary, the development of international law, have established this principle of the exclusive competence of the State in regard to its own territory in such a way as to make it the point of departure in settling most questions that concern international relations. . . . [I]t may be stated that territorial sovereignty belongs always to one, or in exceptional circumstances to several States, to the exclusion of all others.[146]

The most fundamental attribute of sovereignty is the exclusive jurisdiction over a specific territory and population. The International Court of Justice held that "respect for territorial sovereignty is an essential foundation of international relations."[147] Exclusive jurisdic-

---

146 *Island of Palmas Case (or Miangas) (United States v Netherlands)*, Award, (1928) II RIAA 829, ICGJ 392 (PCA 1928).

147 *Corfu Channel Case*, above note 112 at 35.

tion over a territory and the population living there empowers the state to regulate its domestic or internal affairs as it sees fit. The state can determine with absolute freedom its political, economic, and social systems, its state religion, establish its desired form of government and judicial organs. States have the exclusive authority to exercise legislative functions, such as enacting laws and regulations that apply to their subjects. For instance, a state can settle by its own legislation the rules governing the acquisition of its nationality[148] or real estate. The right to legislate, however, does not mean that domestic legislation will be opposable to third parties or other states.[149] Where a state's legislation is inconsistent with its international obligations, it will not be opposable to other states. Also, a state cannot legislate extraterritorially. An illustration of extraterritorial legislation is the United States regulations relating to sanctions against Cuba. The US regulations prohibited dealings with Cuba by any person subject to the "jurisdiction of the United States."[150] The phrase "subject to the jurisdiction of the United States" was so broad that the regulations applied to any subsidiaries of US companies organized outside the United States or to companies only partially owned by US citizens. Some countries, such as Canada, reacted strongly to these regulations by issuing their own laws prohibiting their nationals from complying with US extraterritorial regulations.[151]

In addition to their power to exercise legislative functions, states also have the authority to perform executive functions (i.e., enforce and implement the laws) and judicial functions on their territory as long as they do not breach another state's international rights.[152]

---

148 *Nottebohm Case (Liechtenstein v Guatemala)*, Second Phase, Judgment, [1955] ICJ Rep 4 at 20.

149 *United Kingdom v Zeeland*, above note 73.

150 *Cuban Assets Control Regulations*, 31 CFR Part 515 (2019).

151 *Foreign Extraterritorial Measures Act*, RSC 1985, c F-29.

152 In the case *Avena and Other Mexican Nationals (Mexico v United States of America)*, [2004] ICJ Rep 12, Mexico instituted proceedings against the United States for arresting, detaining, trying, convicting, and sentencing to death fifty-two Mexican nationals without informing them or the Mexican consulate of their rights as mandated by Article 36.1 and 36.2 of the Vienna Convention on Consular Relations. Although the United States tried and convicted the

Sovereignty grants states the inalienable right to freely dispose of their natural wealth and resources in accordance with their national interests.[153] Any attempt by another state to intervene in such matters will be construed as a violation of the principle of non-intervention in domestic issues.

ii) International or External Attributes of Sovereignty

From an international perspective, a sovereign state is the direct and immediate subject of international law. This direct and immediate application of international law does not exist for entities that are not sovereign powers. For instance, a federated state (i.e., Connecticut in the United States), province (i.e., Province of Ontario in Canada), or a canton (i.e., canton de Vaud in Switzerland) is not an immediate subject of public international law even if in domestic law it may possess a degree of sovereignty. Therefore, in the eyes of public international law, federated entities are not sovereign.

Sovereign states are deemed to have the unrestricted authority to manage their external affairs, including diplomatic and economic relations with other states. A state may voluntarily limit its sovereignty by accepting international obligations vis-à-vis other states or third parties. International obligations arise when a state concludes a treaty or an international agreement with other states.[154] International obligations may also arise when a state decides to join an international organization and delegate to it some of its sovereign powers. Such self-imposed restriction of its sovereignty is entirely compatible with the notion of sovereignty itself. The right to enter into international

---

fifty-two Mexican nationals in accordance with its national laws, which is a legitimate exercise of its sovereignty, it failed to comply with its international obligations under the Vienna Convention on Consular Relations. This case is an illustration of how international obligations can limit a state's sovereignty.

153 *Permanent sovereignty over natural resources*, GA Res 1803 (XVII), UNGAOR, 17th Sess, UN Doc A/RES/1803 (XVII) (1962) 15.

154 For analyses of the impact of international legal commitments on state sovereignty, see Oona A Hathaway, "International Delegation and State Sovereignty" (2008) 71 *Law & Contemp Probs* 115, and Jack L Goldsmith & Eric A Posner, *The Limits of International Law* (Oxford, UK: Oxford University Press, 2007).

engagements is an important attribute of state sovereignty.[155] It is by exercising this attribute that a state chooses to accept international obligations and restrict its own sovereignty.

Nonetheless, this does not mean that where a state did not accept an international obligation it can transgress it. The sovereignty of a state may be restricted by international obligations that it did not expressly accept. Certain international obligations arise from general principles of law, binding judgments, Security Council resolutions, *erga omnes* obligations,[156] or *jus cogens* norms.[157] For instance, war crimes or crimes against humanity often override state sovereignty. When the Security Council establishes a criminal court for the purposes of trying war criminals, the consent of the accused's country of nationality is not required.[158] All states have an obligation to cooperate with an international criminal tribunal set up by the Security Council. States also have an obligation to comply with Security Council resolutions adopted under Chapter VII of the *UN Charter*. As we will see in Chapter 4 on the Security Council, measures that fall into this category include arms embargoes or trade sanctions.

---

155 *Case of the SS "Wimbledon" (France, Italy, Japan, and UK v Germany)* (1923) PCIJ (Ser A) No 1.

156 Black's Law Dictionary defines an *erga omnes* obligation as a country's duties that concern issues affecting the international community at large, not just the country's neighbouring states. At paragraph 33 of its judgment *Barcelona Traction, Light and Power Company, Limited (Belgium v Spain); Second Phase*, [1970] ICJ Rep 3, the International Court of Justice explained the difference between regular obligations and *erga omnes* obligations: "In particular, an essential distinction should be drawn between the obligations of a State towards the international community as a whole, and those arising vis-à-vis another State in the field of diplomatic protection. By their very nature the former are the concern of all States. In view of the importance of the rights involved, all States can be held to have a legal interest in their protection; they are obligations *erga omnes*."

157 Black's Law Dictionary defines *jus cogens* as a mandatory or peremptory norm of general international law accepted and recognized by the international community as a norm from which no derogation is permitted. Such norms are not the result of practice. They are the product of strong common consensus. Rules prohibiting crimes against humanity or genocide constitute *jus cogens* norms.

158 On the subject of how human rights affect state sovereignty, see Louis Henkin, "Human Rights and State 'Sovereignty'" (1995–1996) 25 *Ga J Int'l & Comp L* 31.

b) Intervention Within the Meaning of Paragraph 2.7 of the *UN Charter*

Paragraph 2.7 prohibits the organization to intervene in matters of domestic jurisdiction without specifying what qualifies as an intervention. The word "intervene" within the meaning of the *UN Charter* may be given a broad or narrow interpretation. In its broad sense, the word "intervention" includes mere discussions or recommendations pertaining to a domestic matter. Even a simple proposal to include an exclusively domestic matter in the agenda of the General Assembly may be construed as an unlawful intervention. A fact-finding or an inquiry pertaining to domestic matters may also constitute an intervention prohibited by paragraph 2.7 of the *UN Charter*.

According to a narrower interpretation, an intervention would become unlawful only if the organization took measures, including use of force, threat, subversion, or collective sanctions, to address exclusively domestic matters. The act of using or encouraging the use of economic, political, or any other type of measures to coerce another state in order to obtain from it subordination of the exercise of its sovereign rights or secure from it advantages of any kind constitutes an intervention within the meaning of the *UN Charter*.[159] This narrow interpretation of intervention does not prohibit mere discussions and recommendations in relation to matters that fall within the domestic jurisdiction of a state.

c) Humanitarian Interventions

Some argue that humanitarian interventions constitute an exception to the prohibition to intervene in matters that are essentially within the domestic jurisdiction of another state. At the outset, it is important to distinguish between humanitarian assistance and humanitarian intervention. Humanitarian assistance is the provision of humanitarian aid, such as food and medicine. It does not entail any use of force and is therefore legitimate. Humanitarian interventions, on the other hand, involve a threat or use of armed force against another state motivated by humanitarian considerations. This political concept is

---

159 *Declaration on the Inadmissibility*, above note 144 at para 2.

known as "responsibility to protect." It appeared in response to the tragedies in Rwanda and the Balkans in the 1990s. The monumental failure of the Security Council to protect the civilian population from massacres and genocide compelled the international community to seriously debate how to react effectively in future humanitarian crises. The fundamental question that the international community of states was battling with was whether states have unconditional sovereignty or whether the international community has the right to intervene in a country on humanitarian grounds. To find an answer to this question, in December 2001 the Canadian government set up the International Commission on Intervention and State Sovereignty (ICISS). The commission was asked to present proposals on the way the international community must react in future humanitarian crises. The commission's final report, titled "Responsibility to Protect," found that sovereignty not only gave a state the right to control its affairs but also conferred on the state primary responsibility to protect its people. The report proposed that when a state is unable or unwilling to protect its people, the responsibility shifts to the international community. In 2004, a high-level panel appointed by Secretary-General Kofi Annan approved the newly emerged principle of "responsibility to protect" and recommended its adoption. In 2005, at the World Summit, member states endorsed the concept and confirmed that when a state fails to protect its civilian population from atrocities, the international community has a collective responsibility to intervene. This however was not a carte blanche for any state to intervene militarily as it sees fit. Member states made it clear that the UN Security Council must authorize humanitarian interventions on a case-by-case basis.

The norm "responsibility to protect" was the basis of several interventions carried out by the Security Council. Specifically, in August 2006, the Security Council made reference to the responsibility to protect when it authorized the deployment of UN peacekeeping troops to Darfur, Sudan.[160] In 2011, the Security Council authorized member states to take all necessary measures to protect the civilian

---

160 SC Res 1706 (2006), UNSCOR, 61th Year, UN Doc S/RES/1706 (2006) 1.

population in Libya.[161] On the basis of this resolution, NATO planes bombed Libya's military. Also, following the post-election violence in Côte d'Ivoire in 2011, the Security Council, relying on the principle of responsibility to protect, authorized the UN peacekeeping force to use all necessary means to protect life and property.[162] This use of force was instrumental in saving many lives. Similar uses of this principle allowed UN interventions in South Sudan and Central African Republic. Thus, the interpretation of Article 2.7 of the *UN Charter* has been expanded. The new interpretation of this provision grants the UN the authority to intervene in a wide range of scenarios that were once regarded as infringements of sovereignty. Threats to the peace came to include protracted civil wars and armed interference with humanitarian assistance in emergencies.

The practical application of this concept still poses difficulties. In what circumstances is the international community justified to intervene? Who determines whether a state is unwilling or unable to protect its citizens? How is a state expected to deal with powerful guerrilla or revolutionary forces without adversely affecting the civilian population? What is the role of the international community in rebuilding the country once it successfully intervened?

In 2005, Kofi Annan had proposed an objective way of determining whether a humanitarian intervention was justified. In a report called "In Larger Freedom," he suggested that a list of criteria, including seriousness of the threat, proportionality, and chance of success, be applied when deciding whether the Security Council should authorize the use of force. This recommendation did not attract a lot of interest in the Security Council and was eventually abandoned. Nevertheless, in the 2005 World Summit Outcome, the General Assembly made the following undertaking:

> The international community, through the United Nations, also has the responsibility to use appropriate diplomatic, humanitarian and other peaceful means, in accordance with Chapters VI and VIII of the Charter, to help to protect populations from genocide,

---

161 SC Res 1973 (2011), UNSCOR, 66th Year, UN Doc S/RES/1973 (2011) 1.
162 SC Res 1975 (2011), UNSCOR, 66th Year, UN Doc S/RES/1975 (2011) 1.

> war crimes, ethnic cleansing and crimes against humanity. In this context, we are prepared to take collective action, in a timely and decisive manner, through the Security Council, in accordance with the Charter, including Chapter VII, on a case-by-case basis and in cooperation with relevant regional organizations as appropriate, should peaceful means be inadequate and national authorities are manifestly failing to protect their populations from genocide, war crimes, ethnic cleansing and crimes against humanity.[163]

There can be no doubt that unless the Security Council authorizes the use of force or an intervention in a country for the purposes of protecting its population, humanitarian interventions would be unlawful. The travaux préparatoires for Article 2.4 of the *UN Charter* confirm that the drafters of the *UN Charter* never contemplated humanitarian interventions. Allowing a state or a group of states to determine unilaterally when humanitarian intervention is justified without the assent of the Security Council—the primary custodian of collective security measures—runs counter to the spirit of the *UN Charter*. It is important to recall that several blatantly unlawful invasions, including the US invasion of the Dominican Republic in 1965 and of Panama in 1989, were justified under the pretense of humanitarian interventions.

163 *2005 World Summit Outcome*, GA Res 60/1, UNGAOR, 60th Sess, UN Doc A/Res/60/1 (2005) at para 139.

Chapter 3

THE GENERAL ASSEMBLY

The United Nations consists of six principal organs: the General Assembly, the Security Council, the Economic and Social Council, the Trusteeship Council, the International Court of Justice, and the Secretariat.[1] This chapter is focused on the General Assembly. The remaining principal organs (except the Trusteeship Council, to which no separate chapter is dedicated) will be examined in the subsequent four chapters. Since the Trusteeship Council ceased its activities in November 1994, it is mentioned only in passing.

The General Assembly is arguably the most important organ of the organization. It is the only body that comprises all member states of the UN and discusses any question or matter within the scope of the *UN Charter*. In the General Assembly, member states deliberate and make policy decisions in political, economic, humanitarian, social, and legal areas. US President Harry Truman called it the world's supreme deliberative body.[2] Others have described it as the open conscience of the world. Decisions made in the General Assembly have had a direct impact on the lives of billions of people. These decisions often culminate in significant declarations or lead to international conventions on matters relevant to our day-to-day life.

---

1 *Charter of the United Nations*, 26 June 1945, Can TS 1945 No 7, art 7 [*Charter of the United Nations*].

2 Alger Hiss, "General Assembly of the United Nations" (1946–1947) 41:5 *NW UL Rev* 591.

In the first section of this chapter, we examine the membership of the General Assembly. We survey different types of membership and explore how states acquire and lose the status of a UN member. In the second section, we canvass the functioning of the General Assembly, including its voting procedures. The third section of this chapter focuses on the Assembly's main powers. The fourth section explores the dynamics between various regional alliances, political or economic coalitions, and other interest groups.

A. MEMBERSHIP AND OTHER STATUSES

All members of the United Nations are necessarily members of the General Assembly and vice versa. The General Assembly is a universal organ where each member state, irrespective of its might, size, or prosperity, has a voice. The *UN Charter* draws a distinction between founding members (original members) and adhering members of the United Nations. The founding members are those states that took part in the San Francisco conference or had previously signed the Declaration by United Nations[3] of 1 January 1942, and subsequently ratified the *UN Charter*.[4] Any member of the UN that is not a founding member is by default an adhering member. The adhering members are "all other peace-loving states which accept the obligations contained in the present Charter and, in the judgment of the Organization, are able and willing to carry out these obligations."[5] There is

---

3 For the Declaration by United Nations, see Chapter 1.

4 *Charter of the United Nations*, above note 1, art 3. This second alternative was a compromise reached for Poland. Poland was unable to participate in the San Francisco conference because at the time of convening the San Francisco conference, sponsoring powers (China, USSR, United Kingdom, and United States) were still debating who should be recognized as the legitimate representative of Poland. No consensus was reached before the conference and Poland did not receive an invitation. However, it would have been unfair to penalize Poland. That is why Article 3 of the *UN Charter* provides that even if a state was unable to take part in the San Francisco conference, it can nevertheless be a founding member if it had signed the Declaration by United Nations on 1 January 1942. As Poland met this requirement, and ratified the *UN Charter*, it was allowed to become the 51st original member of the organization.

5 *Charter of the United Nations*, above note 1, art 4.1.

no practical difference between the status of a founding member and that of an adhering member.[6] Both categories of members have the same rights, privileges, and obligations.

1) Admission of New Members

At its inception, the United Nations had only fifty-one members. Since 1945, its membership has grown fourfold. With the admission of South Sudan in June 2011, the organization currently has 193 members. The founding fathers of the United Nations designed the criteria of admission of new members to ensure inclusiveness. The organization was set up to be universal and open to all peace-loving states. A few international organizations have such an open admission policy. Paradoxically, no international organization has faced nearly as many difficulties as the UN in respect of admission of states to membership. To increase its membership from 51 states in 1945 to 193 states in 2020, the United Nations had to overcome a significant number of obstacles. The issue of membership happened to be a highly political and sensitive matter.

a) Criteria of Admission

Two provisions of the *UN Charter* (Articles 4.1 and 4.2) govern the admission of new members. They read as follows:

> 4.1 Membership in the United Nations is open to all other peace-loving states which accept the obligations contained in the present Charter and, in the judgment of the Organization, are able and willing to carry out these obligations.
>
> 4.2 The admission of any such state to membership in the United Nations will be effected by a decision of the General Assembly upon the recommendation of the Security Council.

Whereas Article 4.1 provides the conditions that a potential member must meet to accede to membership, Article 4.2 sets out the procedure

6 Jan Klabbers, *An Introduction to International Institutional Law*, 2d ed (New York: Cambridge University Press, 2009) at 93.

of admission. Any state wishing to become a member of the United Nations organization must meet four conditions. First, the candidate must be a state. Second, the candidate must be "peace-loving." Third, it must accept the obligations contained in the *UN Charter*. Fourth, it must be able and willing to carry out the obligations contained in the *UN Charter*. The following pages discuss the five conditions that a state seeking admission to UN membership must satisfy.

i) First Requirement: Candidate Must Be a State

The most important criterion a candidate for membership must meet is statehood. The *UN Charter* does not provide any mandate to either the General Assembly or the Security Council to recognize a sovereign state or to determine whether a particular territory meets the requirements to be a sovereign state. It is left to individual governments to determine whether they recognize a specific territory as a sovereign state. The four requirements for statehood are: (a) a permanent population; (b) a defined territory; (c) an effective government; and (d) capacity to enter into relations with other states.[7]

There are dozens of territories that aspire to become states as a result of unilateral secession. Abkhazia, Nagorno Karabakh, Kosovo, Palestine, South Ossetia, Taiwan, and Transnistria are only a few examples of territories not recognized as states by the international community. For these territories, admission to membership of the United Nations would be the ultimate goal. When a country accedes to the UN as a member, it necessarily implies that the international community recognizes it to be a sovereign state, notwithstanding the objections by some states, as most Arab states do to Israeli statehood.[8] The opposite is also true but only to a limited extent: when entities have not been admitted into the UN, it is indicative of the fact that their statehood has not yet been settled in the opinion of the international community.[9]

---

7 See *Montevideo Convention on the Rights and Duties of States 1933*, 26 December 1933, 165 UNTS 19, art 1 (c) (entered into force 26 December 1934).

8 David I Efevwerhan, "Kosovo's Chances of UN Membership: A Prognosis" (2012) 4:1 *Goettingen J of Intl L* 93 at 110.

9 An admission to the UN membership is not the only way of giving credence to a nation's claim that it is a sovereign state. There are other decisions of the UN

Therefore, it is not uncommon for states to oppose the admission of other territories as members of the UN on the basis of the statehood criterion. For instance, Morocco attempted to block Mauritania's admission, arguing that Mauritania was not a sovereign state but part of Morocco, split by the French during colonial rule.[10] Similarly, Iraq objected to Kuwait's admission, contending that it was an integral part of Iraq.[11] More recently, there have been three controversial applications for membership in the United Nations. In 2006, China blocked Taiwan's application for admission.[12] In 2007, Russia threatened to veto Kosovo's application for membership. In 2011, the United States threatened to veto Palestine's application for admission.[13] It is noteworthy that all three territories are full-fledged members of at least one specialized agency or related organization. For instance, as of June 2009, Kosovo is a member of the International Monetary Fund and the World Bank. As of October 2011, Palestine is a member of UNESCO. Taiwan is a member of World Trade Organization (WTO).[14]

The fact that a candidate state is not recognized by some UN member states is not a decisive factor. As long as the required majority in the Security Council (including all of the permanent members) and in the General Assembly view the candidate as a state, the admission to membership is guaranteed. If, however, a permanent member of the

---

organs or actions by the Secretary-General that may lend support to a candidate's claim that it is a sovereign state. For instance, when former colonized territories were gaining independence, the General Assembly would adopt a resolution welcoming the development and congratulating them with the newly acquired sovereignty. (See, for instance, GA Res 3061(XXVIII) of 2 November 1973, where the General Assembly "Welcomed the recent accession to independence of the people of Guinee-Bissau, thereby creating the sovereign State of Republic of Guinee-Bissau.") Such resolutions may provide support to a nation's claim that it has reached the status of an independent state. Similarly, an invitation received from the Secretary-General to a conference open to all states could also be indicative that the country is perceived to be a sovereign state.

10 KP Misra, "Recognition of Mauritania — A Case Study with Particular Reference to India's State Practice" (1964) 20:3 *India Quarterly* 239 at 240.

11 UNSCOR, 16th Year, 957th Mtg, UN Doc S/PV.957 (1961).

12 David I Efevwerhan, "Kosovo's Chances of UN Membership: A Prognosis" (2012) 4:1 *Goettingen J Int'l L* 93 at 100.

13 *Ibid.*

14 Taiwan is designated as a Separate Customs Territory and not as a state.

Security Council does not recognize the candidate as a state, it can veto the recommendation for membership of that state. This is the primary reason why Kosovo, Palestine, and Taiwan are not members of the UN.

ii) Second Requirement: Candidate Must Be Peace-Loving

The second eligibility requirement for becoming a UN member is to be a *peace-loving* state. The notion of a peace-loving state is very subjective. Objections based on this factor were raised mainly at the very beginning of the United Nations' history. At the San Francisco conference, the USSR opposed the inclusion of Argentina as a founding member of the United Nations on the basis that it could not be regarded as a peace-loving state, having sided with Germany until almost the end of World War II. The USSR was also determined to exclude from membership the defeated states of World War II (Germany and Japan) and Franco's Spain.[15] In 1947, the USSR vetoed the admission of Ireland and Portugal to membership of the United Nations on the ground that the two nations remained neutral during World War II and therefore, were not "peace-loving" nations. To overrule the Soviet objection, the General Assembly resubmitted the applications of both countries to the Security Council with a resolution expressly declaring these countries to be peace-loving states within the meaning of Article 4.1 of the *UN Charter*.[16]

With time, nations realized that international peace and security could only benefit from inclusiveness and stopped objecting on this ground. The qualification of peace-loving state gradually lost its relevance. Today, member states show a high degree of deference vis-à-vis other states' internal politics and ideologies, even when they do not approve of their regime or democratic values.

iii) Third Requirement: Accept the Obligations Contained in the UN Charter

Any state wishing to become a member of the United Nations must submit with its application to the Secretary-General a formal

15 Gerry Simpson, "Two Liberalisms" (2001) *Eur J Int'l L* 537 at 556.

16 *Admission of new members*, GA Res 113 C and D (II), UN Doc A/Res/113(II) (1947).

declaration that the state in question accepts the obligations contained in the *UN Charter*.[17] There is no specific formulation of such a declaration. The adhering member must accept the obligations contained in the *UN Charter* without reservation.[18] In the UN practice, this requirement never prompted any issues or controversies. In fact, a state has never been denied admission even when its conduct was not entirely consistent with the obligations set out in the *UN Charter*.

iv) Fourth Requirement: Candidate Must Be Able and Willing to Carry Out Its Obligations

To become a UN member, it is not enough for a state to accept the obligations contained in the *UN Charter*. The candidate state must also demonstrate that it is able and willing to carry out its *UN Charter* obligations. This requirement became particularly relevant in the 1960s when, as a result of the decolonization process, many small islands and entities began emerging as independent states and sought membership in the UN. When the application for membership of the Maldives Islands was being considered, the delegations of the United States and France raised a concern that some small states may be unable to carry out their *UN Charter* obligations because their economic resources and population size would simply not permit them to contribute to the work of the organization however much they are willing to do so.[19] This was not the first time a similar concern had been raised. Membership in the League of Nations was denied to microstates (often referred to as Lilliputian states), such as Liechtenstein, on the ground that they were too small to carry out their obligations under the League's Covenant.

In 1967, Secretary-General U Thant suggested that the competent organs undertake a thorough and comprehensive study of the criteria

---

17 Rule 134 of the General Assembly Rules of Procedure, UN Doc A/520/Rev.18 [General Assembly Rules of Procedure], and Rule 58 of the Provisional Rules of Procedure of the Security Council, UN Doc S/96/Rev.7 [Provisional Rules of Procedure of the Security Council].

18 See *Letter dated 9 July 2011 from the president of the Republic of South Sudan to the Secretary-General*, UN Doc A/65/900; S/2011/418, Annex I.

19 Roberto Adam, "Micro-States and the United Nations" (1976) 2 *Italian YB Int'l L* 80.

for membership in the United Nations, with a view to laying down the necessary limitations on full membership while also defining other forms of association that would benefit both the microstates and the United Nations.[20] The UN was unable to carry out this proposal. The UN legal counsel opined that none of the amendments could be implemented without altering the *UN Charter*. More importantly, a microstate's membership could not be limited or restricted because this would be contrary to the core principle of sovereign equality of all states.[21] Denying or restricting membership to microstates would have also triggered practical difficulties. For instance, what characterizes a microstate: a small territory, a small population, or a tiny economy? Approximately thirty-five member states of the United Nations have a population of one million or fewer.[22] Also, a state's population may either increase or decrease over time. It would be inconceivable to expel a state whose population drops under a certain threshold. If, on the other hand, in deciding which countries are microstates, we take into account the nominal GDP of a member state, then some Lilliputian states are wealthier than average-sized countries.

In addition, the microstate's ability to meet its financial burden can also be a genuine concern. In particular, although Kiribati, Tonga, and Tuvalu established their independence in the 1970s, they sought admission as UN member states in 1999 and 2000. The reason for this long delay was their lack of financial resources necessary to participate in the United Nations. When a state struggles to make its mandatory contributions to the UN, it is unlikely to contribute in a meaningful way to the maintenance of international peace and security. Nevertheless, the international community has thus far been inclusive and has admitted many states that have difficulty meeting

---

20 *Introduction to the Annual Report of the Secretary-General on the Work of the Organization, 16 June 1966–15 June 1967*, UNGAOR, 22nd Sess, UN Doc A/7601/Add.1 (1967) at paras 163–67.

21 Baldur Thorhallsson, "Small States in the UN Security Council: Means of Influence" (2012) 7:2 *Hague J of Diplomacy* 135 at 145.

22 United Nations, Department of Economic and Social Affairs, Population Division. *World Population Prospects 2019, Volume I: Comprehensive Tables* (ST/ESA/SER.A/426).

their basic financial obligations vis-à-vis the UN. For these reasons, the ability and willingness of a candidate state to carry out its obligations under the *UN Charter* is also a criterion that is no longer relevant in practice.

v) Other Requirements Not Expressly Stated in the UN Charter

Are the four requirements described above the only conditions that a candidate state must meet in order to accede to a full membership of the organization? Can the General Assembly or the Security Council impose additional conditions on some or all candidates? Can a permanent member of the Security Council veto the admission of a state that meets all four conditions? Can a permanent member of the Security Council veto the admission of a new state without providing any reason? These questions arose in 1947 when the USSR opposed the admission to membership of Italy and Finland. The Soviet Union demanded that Hungary, Romania, and Bulgaria be admitted at the same time, failing which it would veto the admission of Italy and Finland.[23] Was it lawful for the USSR to make the admission of Italy and Finland contingent on the admission of states that it considered to be its allies? To resolve this stalemate between the East Bloc and the West Bloc, the General Assembly requested an advisory opinion from the International Court of Justice. The Court was asked to provide an answer to the following two questions:

> Is a member of the United Nations which is called upon to vote, either in the Security Council or in the General Assembly, on the admission of a State to membership in the United Nations, legally entitled to make its consent to the admission dependent on conditions not expressly provided in the Charter? In particular, can such a Member, while it recognizes the conditions set forth in that provision to be fulfilled by the State concerned, subject its affirmative vote to the additional condition that other States be admitted to membership in the United Nations together with that State?

---

23 Efevwerhan, above note 12 at 106–7.

The USSR argued that the Security Council was a political organ and, as such, had authority to take into account political considerations that are not expressly mentioned in the *UN Charter*. The Court rejected this argument, noting that the powers of the Security Council are not unlimited. The political character of the Security Council does not give rise to powers not granted by the *UN Charter*. The Court ruled that in order to become a member of the United Nations a state must only meet the conditions of admission identified in Article 4.1 of the *UN Charter*.[24] Consequently, the Soviet Union could not make its consent to the admission of another state dependent on the admission of other states. The Court held that every application for admission should be examined and voted on separately and on its own merits. Factors and criteria not expressly mentioned in Article 4.1 of the *UN Charter* could be taken into account so long as they could reasonably and in good faith be connected with the conditions set out in Article 4.1.

The advisory opinion of the ICJ did not resolve the issue; the deadlock concerning the admission of new members continued until the mid-1950s. The United Nations was unable to admit new states because the permanent members of the Security Council could not agree on states to be admitted first. The USSR vetoed the admission of states that belonged to the Western Bloc and the United States vetoed the admission of states that belonged to the Eastern Bloc. Hence, a system designed to have a universal membership was paralyzed due to this divide in the Security Council.

To overcome this impasse, the General Assembly explored the possibility of circumventing the Security Council by admitting a candidate without its recommendation. The main obstacle was the explicit requirement contained in Article 4.2 of the *UN Charter* requiring a recommendation from the Security Council before any state could be admitted as a new member of the UN. The General Assembly sought a second advisory opinion from the International Court of Justice on

24 *Conditions of Admission of a State to Membership in the United Nations (Article 4 of the Charter)*, Advisory Opinion, [1948] ICJ Rep 57.

the subject of membership.[25] This time, the Assembly asked the ICJ to address the following question:

> Can the admission of a state to membership in the United Nations, pursuant to Article 4, paragraph 2, of the Charter, be effected by a decision of the General Assembly when the Security Council has made no recommendation for admission by reason of the candidate failing to obtain the requisite majority or of the negative vote of a permanent Member upon a resolution so to recommend?

The Court concluded that a recommendation from the Security Council was as essential as the decision to admit by the General Assembly. The phrase "upon the recommendation" of the Security Council contained in Article 4.2 of the *UN Charter* implies that the recommendation of the Security Council is the foundation of the decision to admit and is therefore indispensable to form the judgment of the organization. Consequently, the General Assembly's attempt to circumvent the Security Council in the decision-making process was unsuccessful.

This deadlock was eventually resolved in 1955, when the East and the West agreed to recommend the admission of sixteen states belonging to both sides (with some non-aligned states). This agreement is commonly known as the Compromise Package or the Package Deal of 1955. Subsequent "package deals" were made to admit other members. The Federal Republic of Germany and the Democratic Republic of Germany were admitted simultaneously.[26] The Republic of Korea and the Democratic Republic of Korea were also admitted as a package deal.[27]

---

25 *Competence of Assembly regarding admission to the United Nations,* Advisory Opinion, [1950] ICJ Rep 4.

26 *Admission to the Commonwealth of the Bahamas to membership in the United Nations,* GA Res 3050 (XXVIII), UNGAOR, 28th Sess, UN Doc A/RES/3050(XXVIII) (1973) 2.

27 *Admission of the Democratic People's Republic of Korea and the Republic of Korea to membership in the United Nations,* GA Res 46/1, UNAGOR, 46th Sess, UN Doc A/RES/46/1 (1991) 12. See Tullio Treves, "The Expansion of the World Community and Membership of the United Nations" (1995) 6 *Finnish YB Int'l L* 248, 253.

Such arrangements were the only viable solution to the membership problem that persisted until the end of the Cold War.[28]

b) Procedural Steps for Admitting New Members

As a first step, an aspiring candidate must submit its application to the Secretary-General who then places it on the Security Council's provisional agenda. Normally, the application is submitted to the Committee on the Admission of New Members, comprised of a representative of each Security Council member.[29] The Committee on the Admission of New Members issues a report. The Security Council reviews the report and then votes either in favour or against the state's admission as a new member. Permanent members of the Security Council can exercise their veto right when deciding whether a new member must be recommended. If, after taking into consideration the conditions laid down in Article 4.1 of the *UN Charter*, the Security Council recommends the admission of the state to membership, the application with the recommendation of the Security Council is transmitted to the General Assembly. The *UN Charter* requires that admission decisions be made by a two-thirds majority of the General Assembly members present and voting.[30] In theory, the General Assembly may either approve or reject the recommendation of the Security Council. In practice, the General Assembly always approves the recommendation of the Security Council. The approval of the General Assembly is a mere formality. Decisions regarding admission to membership are really made in the Security Council.

2) Becoming a UN Member Through Succession of States

A succession of states occurs when one or more states replace another state. The term succession in public international law should not be confounded with the notion of succession in municipal law. State

---

28 Eric Ting-Lun Huang, "Taiwan's Status in a Changing World: United Nations Representation and Membership for Taiwan" (2003) 9 *Annual Survey of Int'l & Comparative L* 55 at 73.

29 Provisional Rules of Procedure of the Security Council, above note 17 at Rule 59.

30 *Charter of the United Nations*, above note 1, art 18.2.

succession in public international law does not necessarily presuppose continuity or inheritance of legal personality. Therefore, when a succession of one or more states occurs, there is no presumption that the membership of the predecessor state would devolve to the successor state.

State successions occur frequently. For instance, the dismemberment of the Soviet Union led to the creation of fifteen separate states in 1991. Similarly, in the 1990s, the former Yugoslavia was split into six independent states. Two new countries were created as a result of Czechoslovakia's dissolution in 1993. State succession also occurs as a result of a cessation, decolonization, annexation, or absorption of a state or a merger of two states.

When a state is replaced by one or more states, it is important to determine what happens to the legal rights and obligations of the predecessor state, and in particular to its membership in the UN. The *UN Charter* does not regulate issues of membership in cases of succession. Therefore, when the USSR split into fifteen sovereign states, difficult membership questions arose for the United Nations. The most sensitive question was the devolution of the permanent seat in the Security Council. Fortunately, some general rules governing admission to or transfer of membership in the United Nations derive from practice and from the *Vienna Convention on Succession of States in respect of Treaties* of 1978.[31]

In cases of state succession, the lawfulness of the succession under the international law is of paramount importance. International law does not recognize a succession of states that does not occur in conformity with international law and, especially, the principles of international law embodied in the *UN Charter*.[32] When determining whether the newly created state "inherits" the membership of its predecessor in the UN, several factors must be taken into account, including the existence of a prior agreement among the entities affected by the state succession.

---

31 *Vienna Convention on Succession of States in respect of Treaties*, 23 August 1978, 1946 UNTS 3 (entered into force 6 November 1996).

32 *Ibid*, art 6.

In cases of decolonization, a former colony or an occupied state that gains independence must apply for membership as a new member if it wishes to do so. The status of the occupying state does not change and it continues to be a member of the international organization. However, when a member state breaks apart or splits into several states, three scenarios can govern the devolution of its membership.[33] First, all of the successor states (that used to be one country) may be allowed to succeed to the former state's membership by automatically becoming UN members.[34] Second, all of the successor states may be required to apply for membership as new members.[35] Finally, one of the successor states may be allowed to continue the predecessor state's membership while the remaining states may be

---

33 Michael P Scharf, "Musical Chairs: The Dissolution of States and Membership in the United Nations" (1995) 28 *Cornell Int'l LJ* 29 at 33.

34 In February 1958, Egypt and Syria, original members of the United Nations, had merged into a single state. It had resulted in the establishment of the United Arab Republic, with Cairo as its capital, and in the election of President Gamal Abdel Nasser as president of the new republic. The government of the United Arab Republic declared that the newly formed state was a single member of the United Nations, bound by the provisions of the *UN Charter*, and that all treaties and agreements concluded by Egypt or Syria with other countries would remain valid within the regional limits prescribed on their conclusion and in accordance with the principles of international law. On 8 October 1961, three years after the formation of the union, Syria seceded from Egypt. The General Assembly allowed Syria to resume its membership without being required to apply for admission as a new member.

35 In 1991 and 1992, Slovenia, Croatia, Macedonia (now North Macedonia), and Bosnia and Herzegovina declared their secession from former Yugoslavia. In April 1992, Serbia and Montenegro created a new federation called the Federal Republic of Yugoslavia. Instead of applying for new membership, this newly created federation claimed to be an automatic continuation of the legal existence of the former Yugoslavia. In its resolution 777(1992), the Security Council noted that former Yugoslavia ceased to exist and therefore the Federal Republic of Yugoslavia could not automatically continue its membership. The General Assembly endorsed this view in its resolution 47/1 and requested that the Federal Republic of Yugoslavia apply for membership. In the case of Czechoslovakia, the Czech Republic and Slovakia had both signed a devolution agreement and agreed that none of the resulting states would contend to Czechoslovakia's membership in the UN. They each applied for a fresh membership.

required to apply for new membership.[36] The practice of the United Nations has been inconsistent.

The situation is much simpler when two member states merge or when a large member state absorbs a smaller state (irrespective of whether the small state is a member or not). In these scenarios, the membership of one of these states (or both if applicable) devolves onto the newly created state.

3) Legitimate Representation of the Government

Distinct from the issue of admitting new members is that of determining the representation of states that are already members. The question of who represents a member state of the United Nations is not a membership issue. It is important to highlight that states and not governments are members of the United Nations. Governments are merely the representatives of their respective states. Under international law, "once a state has come into existence it continues until it is extinguished by absorption or dissolution. A government, the instrumentality through which a state functions, may change from time to time ... without affecting the continuity or identity of the state as an international person."[37] Each state has the exclusive right to determine the form of its government. Of course, other states have no obligation to recognize a government of which they do not approve. However, the refusal to recognize a particular state's government as a legitimate representative of a country does not affect the state's membership in the United Nations. In fact, a state may be admitted as a new member of the United Nations even if the identity

36 When the Soviet Union dissolved, Russia was allowed to continue the membership of USSR whereas the remaining republics had to seek admission. In principle, other members of the United Nations could have objected to Russia's automatic admission to the Security Council as a permanent member. However, this would have necessitated a fundamental review of the *UN Charter*. It was helpful that former Soviet republics had entered into a devolution agreement that provided for the USSR's membership in the United Nations and related bodies to devolve on Russia.

37 Green Hackworth, *Digest of International Law* (Washington: Government Printing Office, 1940) Vol 1 at 127.

of its legitimate representative is unclear. Recall that "effective government" is one of the criteria for a state to exist. If the legitimate representative of a state is unknown, one can argue that it has no effective government and therefore cannot be regarded as a sovereign state. The practice of the United Nations suggests differently. The acceptance of Poland as a founding member of the United Nations even though its government was not recognized or ascertainable is evidence of the fact that a state may become a member of the United Nations even when its legitimate representative is unknown.[38]

The General Assembly encountered challenges in cases where, as a result of a revolution, two different and competing governments claimed to be the legitimate representatives of the same country. This situation arose in relation to China. The Republic of China (ROC) joined the UN in 1945. Its government lost the Chinese Civil War and relocated to Taipei, Taiwan.[39] In October 1949, the People's Republic of China (PRC) was established. Many members of the United Nations did not recognize the communist government of PRC as a legitimate representative of China in the UN. The question with regard to the legitimate representation of China was on the General Assembly's agenda for two decades. In the meantime, China's seat remained unoccupied. In 1971, the General Assembly could no longer avoid the question and had to make a decision on which group it considered to be the legitimate representatives of China. With the support of member states with communist and socialist regimes and some Western European countries, the People's Republic of China was finally recognized as the only lawful representative of China to the United Nations.[40] On this basis, the status of China as the founding member was retroactively restored to the People's Republic of China.

---

38 LC Green, "Representation versus Membership: The Chinese Precedent in the United Nations" (1972) 10 *Can YB Int'l L* 102 at 110.

39 Su Wei, "Some Reflections on the One-China Principle" (2000) 23:4 *Fordham Intl LJ* 1169 at 1171.

40 *Restoration of the lawful rights of the People's Republic of China in the United Nations*, GA Res 2758 (XXVI), UNAGOR, 26th Sess, UN Doc A/RES/2758(XXVI) (1971) 2: "deciding to restore all its rights to the People's Republic of China and to recognize the representatives of its Government as the only legitimate representatives of China to the United Nations, and to expel forthwith the representatives

A completely different situation emerged in the case of South Africa. There was no rivalry between governments. South Africa had only one government that claimed to represent the people of South Africa. However, many member states did not consider the government of South Africa to be representative of its people because the apartheid policy alienated four-fifths of the population by depriving them of their most fundamental rights.[41] As a result, these states argued that the representatives of the government of South Africa could not legitimately claim that they represented the people of South Africa in the United Nations. The proposals to expel South Africa or suspend its membership were vetoed by France, the United Kingdom, and the United States.[42] Consequently, in September 1974 the General Assembly adopted a resolution[43] rejecting the credentials of the South African delegation to the UN.[44] This resolution could be adopted without a vote from the Security Council. The rejection of credentials resulted in a *de facto* suspension of South Africa because its delegates were no longer able to participate in the sessions of the General Assembly.[45] Between 1974 and 1994, South Africa was effectively banned from participating in the work of the General Assembly. The legitimacy of this action is questionable.[46] The approval of credentials of a state's representatives is a formality and is considered a

---

of Chiang Kai-shek from the place which they unlawfully occupy at the United Nations and in all the organizations related to it."

41 Gerhard Erasmus, "The Rejection of Credentials: A Proper Exercise of General Assembly Powers or Suspension by Stealth?" (1981) 7 *S Afr YB Int'l L* 40 at 41.

42 *Relationship between the United Nations and South Africa*, UNSCOR, 29th year, 1808th meeting, UN Doc S/PV.1808 (1974).

43 *Credentials of representatives to the twenty-ninth session of the General Assembly*, GA Res 3206 (XXIX), UNAGOR, 29th Sess, UN Doc. A/Res/3206(XXIX) (1974) 2.

44 Delegates to international organizations must produce a letter, called credentials, from the Minister of Foreign Affairs or head of state proving that they are authorized to represent their countries. The organ of the General Assembly mandated to verify the credentials of delegations is the Credentials Committee, which is a subsidiary organ of the General Assembly. The Credentials Committee verifies the credentials and transmits a report with its findings to the General Assembly. The final decision is within the purview of the General Assembly.

45 Erasmus, above note 41 at 42.

46 *Ibid* at 40.

procedural matter. It cannot be used to circumvent the provisions of the *UN Charter* that expressly deal with suspension of membership.

4) Withdrawing from the Organization

The *UN Charter* contains no provision governing withdrawals from the organization. This omission was deliberate. At the San Francisco conference, delegates of founding member states extensively discussed whether the *UN Charter* should expressly allow member states to withdraw from the UN. The arguments against the right to withdraw were the following: (a) withdrawal from the organization would undermine the concept of universality; (b) withdrawal from the UN would give recalcitrant members the possibility of securing concessions from the organization by threatening to leave; and (c) withdrawal would be a means of escape from fulfilling international obligations by leaving the organization. Furthermore, the founders of the UN did not want to repeat the mistakes of the past. A significant number of states had withdrawn from the League of Nations, which led to its demise. At the same time, delegates were mindful that not providing for the possibility to leave the organization would be contrary to the notion of sovereignty. It was decided that the *UN Charter* should not make express provisions either to permit or to prohibit withdrawal from the Organization:

> The Committee deems that the highest duty of the nations which will become Members is to continue their co-operation within the Organization for the preservation of international peace and security. If, however, a Member because of exceptional circumstances feels constrained to withdraw, and leave the burden of maintaining international peace and security on the other Members, it is not the purpose of the Organization to compel that Member to continue its co-operation in the Organization. It is obvious, particularly, that withdrawal or some other forms of dissolution of the Organization would become inevitable if, deceiving the hopes of humanity, the Organization was revealed to be unable to maintain peace or could do so only at the expense of law and justice. Nor would a Member be bound to remain in the Organization if its rights and obligations

> as such were changed by Charter amendment in which it has not concurred and which it finds itself unable to accept, or if an amendment duly accepted by the necessary majority in the Assembly or in a general conference fails to secure the ratification necessary to bring such amendment into effect.[47]

It is for these reasons that the *UN Charter* is silent on the question of withdrawing from the organization. Thus far, there has been only one case of withdrawal. In January 1965, Indonesia left the United Nations in protest of Malaysia's election as a non-permanent member of the Security Council.[48] Indonesia considered that Malaysia did not meet the eligibility requirements for a seat in the Security Council. Two years later, Indonesia restored its membership without formally applying for membership.[49]

5) Expulsion from the UN or Suspension of a Member's Rights and Privileges

A member of the United Nations can be expelled, suspended or lose its right to vote. The expulsion of a member is governed by Article 6 of the *UN Charter*, which provides that a state that "has persistently violated the Principles contained in the present *Charter* may be expelled from the Organization by the General Assembly upon the recommendation of the Security Council." This provision has already been invoked against Israel and South Africa but was not implemented due to a veto by permanent members of the Security Council. The *UN Charter* also provides for the less draconian measure of suspension. In accordance with Article 5 of the *UN Charter*, a member "against

---

47 United Nations Conference on International Organizations, Commission I "General Provisions," Committee 2 *Membership, Amendment and Secretariat*, Summary Report of Twenty-Eighth Meeting of Committee I/2, Doc 1086 I/2/77 (19 June 1945), at 1.

48 *Letter dated 20 January 1965 from the First Deputy Prime Minister and Minister for Foreign Affairs of Indonesia to the Secretary-General*, UN Doc. A/5857 and S/6157 (21 January 1965).

49 *Telegram dated 19 September 1966 from the Ambassador of Indonesia to the United States of America addressed to the Secretary-General*, UN Doc A/6419 and S/7498 (19 September 1966).

which preventive or enforcement action has been taken by the Security Council may be suspended from the exercise of the rights and privileges of membership by the General Assembly upon the recommendation of the Security Council." For this provision to apply, the following three requirements need to be satisfied:

a. preventive or enforcement action has to be taken by the Security Council against the member state concerned;
b. the Security Council has to recommend to the General Assembly that the member state concerned be suspended from the exercise of the rights and privileges of membership;
c. the General Assembly has to act affirmatively on the foregoing recommendation by a two-third vote.[50]

Article 5 of the *UN Charter* has also been invoked but never applied. As discussed earlier in this chapter, attempts were made to suspend or expel South Africa from the UN for its apartheid policy. These attempts failed because three permanent members of the Security Council vetoed the proposal.[51] To circumvent the Security Council's veto, the General Assembly rejected the credentials of the South African delegation, preventing the South African delegates from participating in the sessions of the General Assembly.[52]

---

50 "Scope of Credentials in Rule 27 of the Rules of Procedure of the General Assembly in Selected Legal Opinions of the Secretariats of the United Nations and Related Intergovernmental Organizations" in *United Nations Juridical Yearbook*, Part II, Chapter VI, at 169–70.

51 Draft Security Council Resolution, 29th Year, Supplement for October–December 1974, UN Doc S/11543 at 34–35 vetoed by France, United Kingdom, and United States on 30 October 1974.

52 The United Nations legal counsel advised the General Assembly that rejecting the credentials of the South African delegation for the apartheid policy was inconsistent with the *UN Charter*. The legal counsel opined that a delegation's credentials could be withheld when two different delegations claim to be the legitimate representatives of the same member state. Since a member state may be represented by only one delegation, the credentials of one of the two delegations must be rejected. Nevertheless, where there is no question of rival claimants, rejecting credentials in order to exclude a member state from participation in meetings has the effect of suspending a member state from the exercise of rights and privileges of membership in a manner not foreseen

Relying on the South African precedent, Kuwait, in its capacity as the Chair of the Group of Arab States, proposed that a similar measure be taken against Israel.[53] The proposed measure did not receive the requisite number of votes; therefore, the proposal was defeated.

A state may retain its full membership but lose the right to vote. Article 19 of the *UN Charter* states that a member which is in arrears in the payment of its financial contributions to the organization loses its right to vote in the General Assembly if the amount of its arrears equals or exceeds the amount of the contributions due for the preceding two years.[54] This loss of vote occurs automatically and does not require a separate decision by the Assembly.[55] The General Assembly

---

by the *UN Charter*. The UN legal counsel concluded, "suspension of this right through the rejection of credentials would not satisfy the foregoing requirements and would therefore be contrary to the Charter."

53 UNGOAR, 40th Sess, General Assembly Provisional Verbatim Record of the thirty-seventh meeting, UN Doc A/40/PV.37 (1985), at 8–10:

> In the light of this outrageous Israeli record, which shows its lack of the prerequisites for membership of the United Nations, its violation of the principles of and its commitments under the Charter and its unparalleled breach of international agreements and treaties, the Arab States signing this amendment believe that Article 6 of the Charter, on the suspension of membership, should be applied to Israel. . . . Notwithstanding the unequivocal applicability to Israel of this Article, the delegations sponsoring this amendment are aware of the difficulties of its application because the stipulated recommendation by the Security Council cannot be achieved, not for legal or moral reasons but rather for political reasons relating to the umbrella of protection provided to Israel by a major Power which blocks any resolution or deterrent measure against Israel. In view of the preceding facts, we thought that the General Assembly, which represents the international community and the world conscience and which has proved its inability, as a result of the use of the veto, to pursue the course of suspending the membership should resort to a less effective method by rejecting the credentials of the delegation of Israel.

54 *Charter of the United Nations*, above note 1, art 19.

55 Question whether the first sentence of Article 19 of the *UN Charter* concerning the loss of vote in the general assembly of member states two years in arrears in the payment of their contributions has automatic application or is subject to a prior decision of the Assembly, Opinion of the Legal Counsel No 4, *United Nations Juridical Yearbook* (1968) at 186.

may nevertheless permit such a member to vote if it is satisfied that the failure to pay is due to conditions beyond the control of the member.[56]

6) Observer Status

Apart from full membership in the organization, the UN General Assembly provides for other forms of participation in its activities. Although not provided for in the *UN Charter* or its Rules of Procedure, the General Assembly has developed a practice of admitting states and certain other entities and organizations to observer status. This practice began in 1946, when Switzerland was reluctant to join the United Nations for fear of losing its neutrality. The UN granted Switzerland the status of Permanent Observer to the United Nations. Switzerland kept this status until September 2002 when it became a full-fledged member of the United Nations.

Today, the status of permanent observer in the General Assembly is confined to states as well as to intergovernmental organizations and entities whose activities cover matters of interest to the Assembly.[57] The request for the granting of observer status must be submitted by a UN member state in the form of a letter to the Secretary-General containing a request for the inclusion of an item in the agenda of the General Assembly. The non-member state or intergovernmental organization that seeks to obtain such a status cannot apply for it independently. It needs a member state to sponsor its application. The request must first be considered by the General Assembly's Sixth Committee.[58] If the Sixth Committee determines that the observer status should be granted, it forwards a recommendation to that effect to the General Assembly for a final decision.

---

56 See for example *Scale of assessments for the apportionment of the expenses of the United Nations: Requests under Article 19 of the Charter*, GA Res 72/2, UNGAOR, 77th Sess, UN Doc A/Res/72/2 (2017).

57 *Question of criteria for the granting of observer status in the General Assembly*, GA Dec 49/426, UNGAOR, 49th Sess, UN Doc A/49/49 (Vol 1) (20 September–23 December 1994) at 341.

58 *Observer status for the International Union for the Conservation of Nature and Natural Resources in the General Assembly*, GA Res 54/195, UNGAOR, 54th Sess, UN Doc A/Res/54/195 (2000) at para 2.

There are different categories of observer status. The first category is that of non-member states having received a standing invitation to participate as observers in the sessions and the work of the General Assembly and maintaining permanent offices at headquarters. Currently, there are two non-member observer states: the Holy See and the State of Palestine.[59] The second category of permanent observers includes intergovernmental organizations who hold a standing invitation to participate as observers in the sessions and the work of the General Assembly and maintaining permanent offices at headquarters.[60] There are approximately seventy such organizations. The third category of observers includes entities that are neither states nor international organizations such as the Inter-Parliamentary Union, the International Committee of the Red Cross, and the Sovereign Order of Malta.[61]

Within each category, different observers may have different rights of participation. To determine the breadth of its participatory rights and privileges, it is important to examine the decision or resolution conferring that observer its participatory rights. For instance, the participatory rights of the Holy See and Palestine are identical.[62] They include the right to participate in the general debate of the General Assembly, to make interventions, to reply, to co-sponsor draft resolutions and decisions that make reference to the Holy See or Palestine (as the case might be), to have its communications relating to the sessions and work of the General Assembly issued and circulated directly, and without intermediary, as official documents of the Assembly, to raise points of order relating to any proceedings involving the Holy See or Palestine, and to be seated after member states

59 *Permanent Missions to the United Nations* (commonly known as the UN Blue Book) No 306 of November 2017, UN Doc ST/PLS/SER.A/306 at 356–57.

60 *Ibid* at 359.

61 *Ibid* at 391.

62 *Participation of Palestine in the work of the United Nations*, GA Res 52/250, UNGAOR, 52nd Sess, UN Doc A/Res/52/250 (1998) 1. Palestine's status of permanent observer was upgraded from the status of entity to the status of State of Palestine in GA Res 67/19, UNGAOR, 67th Sess, UN Doc A/Res/67/19 (2012) 1. *Participation of the Holy See in the work of the United Nations*, GA Res 58/314, UNGAOR, 58th Sess, UN Doc A/Res/54/314 (2004) 1.

but before the other observers with the allocation of six seats in the General Assembly Hall.

In the second category of permanent observers, the European Union probably enjoys the most enhanced participatory rights. In its Resolution 65/276,[63] the General Assembly established modalities of participation to enable the European Union to represent its positions in the sessions of the General Assembly consistent with the terms of the Lisbon Treaty. The resolution grants the EU an enhanced observer status providing it greater rights and privileges of participation than had previously been conferred to an international organization. In particular, the EU has the right to speak in debates and to submit proposals and amendments. It has the right of reply and may raise points of order and circulate documents. The resolution also specifies limitations of this participation in the General Assembly, its committees, and their working groups. Like all three categories of observers, the EU cannot vote on or sponsor independently General Assembly resolutions.

7) Consultative Status

Nongovernmental organizations (NGOs) are extremely important actors in the international arena and play a pivotal role in supporting the UN at the national, sub-regional, regional, and international levels. The breadth of these organizations' expertise and their capacity to implement the activities of the United Nations on the ground are unquestionable. It is for this reason that in addition to full membership and observer status, the UN established a more limited status for nongovernmental organizations, known as consultative status. Unlike the status of a permanent observer, the consultative status is granted not by the General Assembly but by the Economic and Social Council, another principal organ of the UN. Consequently, the rights and privileges deriving from this consultative status can be exercised only before the Economic and Social Council and its subsidiary bodies. This status gives no rights or privileges to NGOs during General Assembly

---

63 *Participation of the European Union in the Work of the United Nations*, GA Res 65/276, UNGAOR, 65th Sess, UN Doc A/Res/65/276 (2011) 1.

sessions. Its purpose is to encourage the participation and involvement of nongovernmental organizations in the decision-making process. Currently, approximately 6,000 nongovernmental organizations enjoy this privileged status. Since consulting with all of them would be an unmanageable task, the Economic and Social Council developed three categories of consultative statuses and some criteria that nongovernmental organizations must satisfy in order to be granted such a status.[64]

B. FUNCTIONING OF THE GENERAL ASSEMBLY

It is important to recall that the United Nations has two facets. On the one hand, the UN is a forum where national delegations of member states deliberate, discuss, debate, and make decisions. In this sense, the UN is just a building (or a set of buildings) with no autonomy or freedom of action independent from its member states. However, once delegates of member states collectively decide to do something, they are not the ones to implement their own decisions. They entrust the implementation or execution of their wishes to the UN. Decisions to be carried out may involve the distribution of food in conflict areas or natural disaster zones, immunization of children, provision of shelter to displaced populations, investigation of human rights violations, and so on. Thus, the UN can also be an independent actor with its own legal personality and ability to carry out activities autonomously. These activities are planned and carried out by UN staff members, consultants, contractors, and other types of personnel employed in the Secretariat of the Organization—another main organ of the UN—or personnel of UN Funds, Programmes, Specialized Agencies, and Related Organizations. Consequently, where the General Assembly is the incarnation of the UN in its first aspect—the forum where member states discuss and decide, the UN Secretariat is the embodiment of the UN in the second form—an independent actor. In this section, we will be focusing much less on what the UN does as an autonomous participant and more on what and how member

---

64 *Consultative relationship between the United Nations and non-governmental organizations*, ESC Res 1996/31, UNESCOR, 1996, UN Doc E/1996/96, 54, para 9.

states deliberate and make decisions when they meet in the General Assembly Hall.

1) Voting Procedures

Voting at international meetings on political matters is a relatively recent practice. At conferences that preceded the League of Nations, states did not vote except on procedural points.[65] This practice was formally codified in the Covenant of the League of Nations where decisions of both the Assembly and the Council were to be subject to the unanimity rule on all non-procedural questions. The only exception to the unanimity rule was recognized by the Permanent Court of International Justice in its advisory opinion, which dealt with a territorial dispute between Turkey and the United Kingdom. The Court held that the League's Council could make decisions by a majority in specific cases, only if express provision was made for this power by treaty stipulations.[66] In comparison with the practice of international conferences and the League of Nations, the voting rules in the General Assembly are considerably more advanced.

For a debate on any issue or topic to occur in the General Assembly, at least one-third of UN member states must be present. If at least one-third of UN member states are not present, the president of the General Assembly cannot declare a General Assembly meeting open. Moreover, the presence of one-third of member states in the General Assembly is insufficient for a decision or resolution to be adopted. For any decision to be taken, at least the majority of the members must be present.[67] Decisions or resolutions of the General Assembly on important questions require the positive vote of the two-thirds majority of the members present and voting.[68] Important questions include

65 FA Vallat, "Voting in the General Assembly of the United Nations" (1954) 31 *Brit YB Int'l L* 273.

66 *Interpretation of Article 3, paragraph 2 of the Treaty of Lausanne* (1925), Advisory Opinion, PCIJ (Ser B) No 12 at 30.

67 General Assembly Rules of Procedure, above note 17 at Rule 67.

68 The phrase "members present and voting" means members casting an affirmative or negative vote. Members who abstain from voting are considered as not voting.

recommendations pertaining to the maintenance of international peace and security, the election of the non-permanent members of the Security Council, the admission of new members to the United Nations, the suspension of the rights and privileges of membership, the expulsion of members, and budgetary questions. Decisions on other questions, which essentially means unimportant or less important questions, including the determination of additional categories of questions to be decided by a two-thirds majority, are made by a majority of the members present and voting.[69] A vote in the General Assembly normally takes place by show of hands or by standing, but any representative may request a roll call. The roll call is taken in the English alphabetical order of the names of the members, beginning with the member whose name is drawn by lot by the president. When the name of a member state is called in a roll call, one of its representatives must reply "yes," "no," or "abstention."[70] Voting by secret ballot is also possible but may occur only when decisions pertain to elections.[71]

A historical review of resolutions reveals that the General Assembly adopted by a simple majority only an insignificant proportion of decisions. The vast majority of decisions were adopted either by the affirmative vote of at least two-thirds of the members or by consensus without a vote. A vote by consensus is possible with respect to uncontroversial matters or when the proposed resolution represents the lowest common denominator of all 193 states. If any state or coalition of states is opposed to the contents of the proposed resolution, the decision is likely to be put to a vote.

In accordance with the principle of sovereign equality, each member state of the UN has one vote in the General Assembly.[72] However, a member state that is in arrears in the payment of its financial contributions to the organization can be prevented from voting in the General Assembly if the amount of its arrears equals or exceeds the amount of the contributions due from it for the preceding two full years.[73] The

---

69 *Charter of the United Nations*, above note 1, art 18.

70 General Assembly Rules of Procedure, above note 17 at Rule 87.

71 *Ibid* at Rule 92.

72 *Charter of the United Nations*, above note 1, art 18.

73 *Ibid*, art 19.

General Assembly may, nevertheless, permit such a member to vote if it is satisfied that the failure to pay is due to conditions beyond the control of the member. Although each member state has one vote, its delegation may consist of up to five representatives and five alternate representatives and as many advisers, technical advisers, experts, and persons of similar status as may be required by the delegation.[74]

2) Types of General Assembly Sessions

UN member states can meet in the General Assembly in three types of sessions: (a) regular sessions; (b) special sessions; and (c) emergency special sessions. For all three types of meetings, the quorum[75] for opening a General Assembly meeting is one-third of the member states. The quorum for adopting resolutions or decisions is a simple majority of member states.

Regular sessions of the General Assembly are annual. They open on Tuesday of the third week of September and run for one entire year. Regular sessions consist of two portions. The first and more important portion of this session runs from mid-September to the end of December. During this period, the General Assembly debates controversial issues and passes resolutions on important topics. It begins every year with the "General Debate" or "high-level week," at which heads of state and government attend and give televised speeches. Each year the President of the General Assembly chooses a theme for the debate.

The second and less important portion of a regular session runs from January to September. It is known as the "resumed part" of the regular session. During this period, delegates of member states hold thematic debates, meet in various working groups, and carry out work

74 General Assembly Rules of Procedure, above note 17 at Rule 25.

75 The term "quorum" refers to the number of member states that need to be present for the president of the General Assembly to open a meeting. It may also refer to the number of member states that need to be present for the General Assembly to adopt decisions or resolutions.

required for the following session.[76] The resumed part runs until all issues on the General Assembly's agenda have been addressed, which is often just before the beginning of the following session. Hence, the General Assembly is practically always in session.

Regular sessions necessitate a great deal of preparatory work, especially by the UN Secretariat. For instance, at least sixty days before the opening of a regular session, the Secretary-General prepares a provisional agenda and communicates it to the member states.[77] The provisional agenda of a regular session always includes the Secretary-General's report on the work of the organization as well as reports from the principal bodies of the UN, subsidiary organs of the General Assembly, and the specialized agencies. The preparation of this report requires thousands of hours of work. The agenda of a regular session must also include items ordered by the General Assembly at a previous session and those proposed by any member state.[78]

Regular sessions are not the only format for meetings. General Assembly meetings may also be held in special sessions as occasion may require. A special session of the General Assembly can be

---

76 General Assembly sessions are numbered consecutively. The first regular session opened in 1946, the second session opened in 1947, the third session opened in 1948, and so on. The reference number of a General Assembly resolution normally reveals the session (and therefore the year) during which it was adopted. For instance, General Assembly Resolution A/Res/68/135 refers to a resolution adopted at the 68th session, which opened in September 2013. The numeral 135 refers to the sequence in which resolutions were adopted during that session. This particular one was the 135th resolution adopted during the 68th session or in 2013. The following year, in 2014, the first resolution would start from 1 and has the number A/Res/69/1. Older resolutions had a different numbering system. Until the thirtieth regular session or the year 1975, General Assembly resolutions were identified by an Arabic numeral followed in parenthesis by a Roman numeral indicating the session. For example, the number A/Res/292(IV) reveals that it is a General Assembly resolution adopted during the fourth session or in 1949. The Arabic numeral of the old numbering system showed the sequence of General Assembly resolutions from the UN's inception as opposed to its sequence during a particular year or session. In other words, the number A/Res/3541(XXX) shows that this was the 3541st resolution adopted by the General Assembly since the UN was set up.

77 General Assembly Rules of Procedure, above note 17 at Rule 12.

78 *Ibid* at Rule 13.

convened either at the request of the qualified majority of the Security Council or a majority of member states in the General Assembly. Usually, special sessions are high-level events with the participation of heads of state or ministers. There have been approximately thirty special sessions to date. Typically, special sessions are short and last from one to five days. Their agenda normally contains only one item. The last special session was held in April 2016 and the only item on the agenda was the world's drug problem. A special session often leads to the adoption of outcome documents such as a declaration, action plan, or strategy.

In addition to special sessions, there are also "emergency special sessions." They are a subcategory of special sessions with some particularities. They began in 1950 when the General Assembly adopted the *Uniting for Peace* resolution. An emergency special session can be convened within twenty-four hours to consider a matter that is before the UN Security Council. In fact, an emergency special session is the only time the General Assembly can take decisions on issues that are within the exclusive purview of the Security Council. It is convened in the same manner as a special session. To date, there have been ten emergency special sessions. Out of these ten sessions, six dealt with the situation in the Middle East. An emergency special session may remain open for several years and have many successive meetings over a prolonged time period.

3) Presidency and Vice-Presidency of the General Assembly

The General Assembly has one president and twenty-one vice-presidents.[79] The president of the General Assembly is elected by a simple majority vote of the General Assembly at least three months before formally assuming office.[80] The term of the presidency is one year and cannot be extended or renewed. The election usually occurs in June of each year, which allows the president to prepare and to assemble a team before the General Assembly session begins in September.

79 *Ibid* at Rule 30.
80 *Ibid.*

The president cannot be a national of one of the five permanent members of the Security Council as this would give the permanent five a disproportionately high concentration of power. The presidency normally rotates among the five regional groups, namely the Group of Asian States, the Group of Eastern European States, the Group of Latin American and Caribbean States, the Group of African States, the Western European and other States Group.[81] To avoid a vote by secret ballot, the states of the regional group agree on presenting one candidate. This approach enables the General Assembly to elect its president by acclamation.

The president of the General Assembly is elected in his or her personal capacity and cannot vote in the General Assembly.[82] The president represents the membership as a whole. The president has limited procedural and symbolic powers only. The president's primary role is to ensure that the General Assembly Rules of Procedure are respected. The *UN Charter* refers to the function of the president but does not specify his or her exact role and mandate. These responsibilities have been defined in the General Assembly Rules of Procedure and General Assembly resolutions.[83] The President opens and closes each General Assembly plenary meeting, directs the discussions in plenary meetings by managing the list of speakers, rules on points of order, proposes adjournment or suspension of a meeting, organizes thematic debates, enhances the public image of the General Assembly regularly meets with the Secretary-General and the president of the Security Council, etc.

Also in June of each year, after the election of the president, the General Assembly elects twenty-one vice-presidents for the next session. The five permanent members of the Security Council are always among the vice-presidents; however, when the president is absent,

---

81 *Question of the composition of the relevant organs of the United Nations: amendment to Rules 31 and 38 of the rules of procedure of the General Assembly*, GA Res 33/138, UNGAOR, 33rd Sess, UN Doc. A/Res/33/138 (1978) 75.

82 General Assembly Rules of Procedure, above note 17 at Rule 36.

83 Mandates assigned to the president of the General Assembly by individual resolutions can pertain to the organization of events, such as high-level meetings, the negotiation of outcome documents, or consultations on a specific topic.

they cannot assume the role of the acting president. To ensure balanced geographical representation, the remaining sixteen vice-presidencies are distributed among the regional groups as follows: six members from the Group of African States; five members from the Group of Asian States; one member from the Group of Eastern European States; three members from the Group of Latin American States; and two members from the Western European or other States Group.[84]

4) Main Committees of the General Assembly

The General Assembly debates and adopts resolutions on a wide spectrum of topics that often require an inordinate amount of time and technical expertise. For this reason, the General Assembly was empowered to establish such committees as it deems necessary for the performance of its functions.[85] The General Assembly relies on six main committees that roughly correspond to the major fields of its mandate. They consider agenda items referred to them by the General Assembly at the beginning of its session and submit recommendations and draft resolutions for adoption by the Assembly. The main committees consist of all member states of the General Assembly. The practices and working methods of the main committees are very similar to the rules of procedure and practices of the General Assembly. Each main committee is headed by a bureau, which consists of an elected chairperson, three vice-chairpersons, and a rapporteur.[86] In all six main committees, a simple majority suffices for a recommendation to proceed to the General Assembly. However, this does not change the voting rule in the General Assembly itself, where a two-thirds majority is required for "important questions" and a simple majority is sufficient for all other questions.

---

84 Although the list adds up to twenty-two, there is no inconsistency. There are only twenty-one vice-presidents because the regional group putting forward the president loses one vice-presidential seat.

85 General Assembly Rules of Procedure, above note 17 at Rule 96.

86 *Amendment to rule 103 of the rules of procedure of the General Assembly*, GA Res 52/163, UNAGOR, 52nd Sess, UN Doc A/Res/52/163 (1997).

a) First Committee—Disarmament and International Security Committee

The Disarmament and International Security Committee, also known as the First Committee, deals with the following topics: nuclear weapons, other weapons of mass destruction, disarmament aspects of outer space, conventional weapons, regional disarmament and security, other disarmament measures and international security, and the disarmament machinery. It considers all disarmament and international security matters within the scope of the *UN Charter* or relating to the powers of any other organ of the United Nations. It handles matters relating to the general principles of cooperation in the maintenance of international peace and security, as well as principles governing the regulation of armaments. It promotes cooperative arrangements and measures aimed at strengthening stability through lower levels of armaments. This committee works in close cooperation with the United Nations Disarmament Commission and the Conference on Disarmament. For instance, during its sixty-ninth session, the General Assembly adopted a resolution requesting the Conference on Disarmament to commence negotiations in order to reach an agreement on an international convention prohibiting the use or threat of use of nuclear weapons based on a recommendation made by the First Committee.[87] Similarly, the very first General Assembly resolution, titled *Establishment of a Commission to Deal with the Problems Raised by the Discovery of Atomic Energy*, was adopted on recommendation by the First Committee on 24 January 1946. Also, the landmark Resolution 1378 (XIV) of 20 November 1959, in which the General Assembly "expressed the hope that measures leading towards the goal of general and complete disarmament under effective international control will be worked out in detail and agreed upon in the shortest possible time," was also adopted on the recommendation of the First Committee. The work of this committee generally does not exceed six weeks and ends in October or November.

---

87 *Convention on the Prohibition of the Use of Nuclear Weapons*, GA Res 69/69, UNGAOR, 69th Sess, UN Doc A/Res/69/69 (2014).

b) Second Committee—Economic and Financial Committee

The Economic and Financial Committee (also known as the Second Committee), deals with issues relating to economic growth and development, including international trade, international financial system, external debt sustainability, sustainable development, human settlements, poverty eradication, globalization and interdependence, operational activities for development, and information and communication technologies for development. It considers issues relating to the Least Developed Countries (LDCs) and Landlocked Developing Countries (LLDCs). Understandably, the G-77 and China Group is very active in this committee, tabling a large portion of its resolutions. This committee holds a dialogue with ECOSOC and the five Regional Commissions of the United Nations. The governing bodies of the UN Environment Programme, UN Habitat, UNCCC, and UNCCD report to the General Assembly through the Second Committee. The Economic and Financial Committee begins its work in October and completes it in November or December.

c) Third Committee—Social, Humanitarian, and Cultural Committee

The Social, Humanitarian, and Cultural Committee (Third Committee) of the General Assembly has on its agenda items relating to a range of social and humanitarian affairs and human rights issues that affect people all over the world. A considerable part of the committee's work focuses on the examination of human rights questions such as the advancement of women, the protection of children, indigenous issues, treatment of refugees, promotion of fundamental freedoms through the elimination of racism and racial discrimination, and the right to self-determination. The committee also addresses important social development questions, such as issues related to youth, family, ageing, persons with disabilities, crime prevention, criminal justice, and international drug control. It interacts with special rapporteurs, independent experts, and chairs of working groups as mandated by the Human Rights Council. This committee is supported by the Office of the High Commissioner for Human Rights (OHCHR). The Third Committee meets annually for approximately eight weeks in October and November, overlapping with UNGA's annual regular session, also known as "main part," which runs from September to December.

d) Fourth Committee—Special Political and Decolonization Committee

Initially, the Fourth Committee dealt with only decolonization questions. An additional Main Committee, the Special Political Committee (SPC), handled political questions. In 1993, the General Assembly merged the SPC and the Fourth Committee and called it the Special Political and Decolonization Committee (Fourth Committee).[88] The Fourth Committee or the Special Political and Decolonization Committee deals with issues that fall under the following categories: the effects of atomic radiation, review of peacekeeping operations and of special political missions, Palestinian refugees, and international cooperation in the peaceful uses of outer space. It frequently interacts with the UN Agency for Palestinian Refugees in the Near East (UNRWA) and with the First Committee on issues relating to outer space. It also reviews reports from the Special Committee on Peacekeeping Operations (known as the C-34 Committee). The work of this committee begins in September, breaks in November, and resumes again in the spring for the purpose of making recommendations to the General Assembly on peacekeeping.

e) Fifth Committee—Administrative and Budgetary Committee

The Fifth Committee is allocated agenda items related to administrative and budgetary matters. The committee meets in three sessions throughout the year. The second resumed session deals exclusively with administrative and budgetary aspects of peacekeeping. The committee reviews reports of Secretary-General, ACABQ,[89] and other bod-

88 *Revitalization of the work of the General Assembly*, GA Res 47/233, UNGAOR, 47th Sess, UN Doc A/Res/47/233 (1993) 7.

89 The General Assembly established the Fifth Committee on Administrative and Budgetary Questions by Resolution 14 (I) of 13 February 1946. The ACABQ is appointed by the General Assembly and consists of sixteen members (the General Assembly enlarged ACABQ's membership to twenty-one members as of 1 January 2021 in its 2 of 17 January 2020), including at least three financial

ies regarding budget and finances and reports to the plenary. It always has before it the budget estimates and the information annexed to them by the Secretary-General, as well as all relevant reports from the ACABQ. The Fifth Committee prepares resolutions to be adopted by the General Assembly on the appropriation of the budget and apportionment for each member state. This is where the scale of assessment is determined every three years. It considers the biennial program budget prepared by the Secretariat, the annual peacekeeping budgets, and human resources issues. The Fifth Committee is also responsible for administrative matters. It considers management reform, governance, oversight, and accountability issues.

f) Sixth Committee—Legal Committee

Pursuant to Article 13 of the *UN Charter*, the General Assembly has an express mandate to promote the progressive development and codification of public international law. The General Assembly carries out this mandate through the Sixth Committee, which meets every year from late September to late November, in parallel with the General

---

experts of recognized standing. No two members of the ACABQ can be nationals of the same member state and all members are selected on the basis of broad geographical representation, personal qualifications, and experience. Major donors and superpowers, such as the United States, Japan, and Russia, are always represented in the ACABQ. The role of the ACABQ is described in Rule 157 of the General Assembly Rules of Procedure as follows:

> The Advisory Committee on Administrative and Budgetary Questions shall be responsible for expert examination of the programme budget of the United Nations and shall assist the Administrative and Budgetary Committee (Fifth Committee). At the beginning of each regular session at which the proposed programme budget for the following biennium is to be considered, it shall submit to the General Assembly a detailed report on the proposed programme budget for that biennium. It shall also submit, at such times as may be specified in the applicable provisions of the Financial Regulations and Rules of the United Nations, a report on the accounts of the United Nations and all United Nations entities for which the Secretary-General has administrative responsibility. It shall examine on behalf of the General Assembly the administrative budgets of specialized agencies and proposals for financial and budgetary arrangements with such agencies. It shall perform such other duties as may be assigned to it under the Financial Regulations of the United Nations.

Assembly's annual session. At the beginning of the session, the General Assembly assigns to the Sixth Committee a list of agenda items to be discussed. Those items may include such matters as the annual reports of the International Law Commission, the United Nations Commission on international trade law, legal issues relating to terrorism, rule of law, the internal justice system of the United Nations, and so on. Following a formal discussion of specific proposals, the Sixth Committee adopts a recommendation that is then submitted to the plenary of the General Assembly for its adoption. The Sixth Committee is also responsible for making recommendations to the General Assembly regarding applications for an observer status. As discussed above, admitted observers have a standing invitation to participate in the sessions and the work of the General Assembly.

g) General Committee

In addition to its six main committees, the General Assembly also has a General Committee and a Credentials Committee. Normally, setting and adopting the agenda of the General Assembly precedes any other order of business. The first draft of the General Assembly agenda is prepared by the UN Secretariat. It is the role of the General Committee to review the draft agenda proposed by the Secretariat and make recommendations to the General Assembly. It makes recommendations to the General Assembly on the inclusion or rejection of new items and the allocation of included items to the main committees. It also makes recommendations on organizational issues and on issues pertaining to the conduct of meetings and meeting records. The General Committee, chaired by the president of the General Assembly, consists of the twenty-one vice-presidents and the six chairpersons of the main committees. It does not deal with political questions.

h) Credentials Committee

Before a member state can participate in the General Assembly, it must submit credentials and obtain accreditation for its delegation.[90]

---

90 *Permanent Missions to the United Nations*, GA Res 257(III), UNGAOR, 3rd Sess, UN Doc A/Res/257(III) (1948) 171.

Credentials normally inform the Secretary-General of the name of the individual appointed as permanent representative of the state to the UN. The permanent representative is authorized to designate a substitute to act temporarily on its behalf after due notice to the Secretary-General.[91]

By approving the credentials of a delegation, the General Assembly formally acknowledges the representative of member states. It is the role of the Credentials Committee to review the credentials and make recommendations to the General Assembly as to whether or not a delegation should be recognized as a legitimate representative of that member state. The Credentials Committee consists of nine members proposed by the president of the General Assembly for their appointment.

C. POWERS AND RESPONSIBILITIES OF THE GENERAL ASSEMBLY

The powers of the General Assembly fall into two unofficial categories: "soft" and "hard." The *UN Charter* does not refer to the terms "soft" and "hard." This terminology is used in international relations to describe the legally binding nature of decisions. In particular, a soft power may give rise to decisions that carry a persuasive or political weight but cannot be enforced. Conversely, a hard power may lead to decisions that are legally binding and enforceable.

Most of General Assembly's powers are soft. A cursory review of Articles 10–22 of the *UN Charter* reveals that the General Assembly mostly "discusses," "considers," "makes recommendations," "calls the attention of the Security Council," and "refers to the Security Council questions." None of these verbs and phrases evoke legally binding and enforceable decisions. Nevertheless, the General Assembly does have hard powers as well, particularly in relation to the budget of the UN.

The Assembly's broadest power derives from Article 10 of the *UN Charter*. This provision states that "the General Assembly may discuss any questions or any matters within the scope of the present *Charter* or relating to the powers and functions of any organs provided

91 United Nations Protocol and Liaison Service, "United Nations Manual of Protocol," online: https://protocol.un.org/dgacm/pls/site.nsf/xpManual.xsp.

for in the present *Charter*, and, except as provided in Article 12, may make recommendations to the members of the United Nations or to the Security Council or to both on any such questions or matters." The General Assembly may rely on this catch-all provision when the remaining provisions do not empower it to act.[92] Article 10 makes it clear that if an organ of the UN has a power to do or decide something, the General Assembly can discuss and make recommendations on it. By virtue of Article 10, almost all sectors of international relations fall under the purview of the General Assembly. This provision renders the powers of the General Assembly universal and gives rise to a wide overlap of functions between the General Assembly and the Security Council, subject only to certain restrictions.

An exhaustive analysis of General Assembly's functions and powers is beyond the scope of this chapter. Instead, we will briefly examine the three most important roles of the General Assembly. They are: (a) the residual role of the General Assembly in the maintenance of international peace and security; (b) the legislative powers of the General Assembly; and (c) the budgetary powers of the General Assembly.

1) Powers Relating to Maintenance of International Peace and Security

The primary responsibility for maintaining peace is conferred on the Security Council.[93] Disarmament and the regulation of armaments are also within the province of the Security Council. Nevertheless, the founders of the UN decided to vest in the General Assembly powers that belong primarily to the Security Council. Accordingly, the General Assembly has a residual role in matters relating to international peace and security.[94] In cases where the Security Council is unable to agree on a solution, the General Assembly can fill the void and make

---

92 Article 11.4 of the *UN Charter* supports the interpretation that Article 10 of the *UN Charter* is a catchall provision as opposed to an introductory article to the remaining powers of the General Assembly.

93 2005 *World Summit Outcome*, GA Res 60/1, UNAGOR, 60th Sess, UN Doc A/Res/60/1 (2005) 1 at para 80.

94 *Ibid.*

decisions on questions that are within the primary responsibility of the Security Council. Hence, the functions of the two organs in these fields are at least partly concurrent.

Recall that in 1950, the Security Council was paralyzed due to the East–West rivalry and continuous exercise of the veto power by its permanent members. Noting the Security Council's failure to discharge its primary responsibility under the *UN Charter*, the General Assembly adopted the Resolution *Uniting for Peace*,[95] granting itself a subsidiary responsibility with regard to maintaining international peace and security. This resolution provides that where the Security Council fails to exercise its primary responsibility for the maintenance of international peace and security as a result of a veto by one of its permanent members, the General Assembly will seize itself of the matter. The resolution sets out the procedural requirements for the General Assembly to be properly seized of the matter. First, the Assembly must be in regular session[96] or convened through an emergency special session.[97] Second, the session must have as an objective the making of recommendations for collective measures that may include the use of force. However, the resolution specifies that the Assembly can only make recommendations, which do not have any binding legal force.[98]

This resolution may appear to be inconsistent with Article 12.1 of the *UN Charter*, which states that "while the Security Council is exercising in respect of any dispute or situation the functions assigned

95 *Uniting for Peace*, GA Res 377 A (V), UNGAOR, 5th Sess, UN Doc A/Res/377A(V) (1950) 10.

96 See *Declaration of the Assembly of Heads of State and Government of the Organization of African Unity on the Aerial and Naval Military Attack against the Socialist People's Libyan Arab Jamahiriya by the Present United States Administration in April 1986*, GA Res 41/38, UNGAOR, 41st Sess, UN Doc A/RES/41/38 (1986) 34.

97 An emergency special session can be convened by a vote of majority in the Security Council. This is a procedural question; therefore, the veto by some permanent members is insufficient to prevent an emergency session. An emergency special session may also be convened by the General Assembly. The request must emanate from a member state and be addressed to the Secretary-General. This request must be seconded by a majority in the General Assembly.

98 Larry D Johnson, "'*Uniting for Peace*': Does It Still Serve Any Useful Purpose" (2014–2015) 108 *AJIL Unbound* 106.

to it in the present *Charter*, the General Assembly shall not make any recommendation with regard to that dispute or situation unless the Security Council so requests." The rationale behind this rule is that when both the General Assembly and the Security Council are seized of the same question, contradictory solutions may be proposed by each of these two organs.[99] Nevertheless, the International Court of Justice held that the prohibition of simultaneous action has been superseded by practice.[100] Today, the General Assembly may make recommendations with regard to a dispute or situation even if the same dispute or situation is being considered by the Security Council.

A crucial role that the General Assembly may play in relation to international peace and security is the establishment of UN peacekeeping missions. As we will see in the chapter on the Security Council, peacekeeping forces as they currently exist were not envisaged in the *UN Charter*. Traditional peacekeeping forces appeared in 1956, when Israel (supported by the United Kingdom and France) invaded Egypt in response to its nationalization of the Suez Canal.[101] In order to restore peace in the region, the General Assembly authorized a peacekeeping force. Normally, such an action should have been authorized by the Security Council. However, since the vetoes of the United Kingdom and France made it impossible for the Security Council to agree on a resolution, the General Assembly intervened under its residual role and deployed peacekeeping troops to Suez. This action sparked a debate over whether the General Assembly has the power to authorize

---

99 Juraj Andrassy, "Uniting for Peace" (1956) 50:3 *Am J Int'l L* 563 at 566.

100 *Legal Consequences of the Construction of a Wall in the Occupied Palestinian Territory*, Advisory Opinion, [2004] ICJ Rep 136 at paras 27–28.

101 Although the UN had already deployed several observer missions prior to 1956, their mandates were limited to observing and monitoring ceasefires after an agreement had been concluded. The United Nations Truce Supervision Organization (UNTSO) formed in 1948 to supervise the truce in Palestine in the aftermath of the Arab–Israeli war, and the United Nations Military Observer Group in India and Pakistan (UNMOGIP), established in 1949 to supervise the ceasefires between India and Pakistan, are examples of such missions. UNEF was not a mere peace-enforcement operation; it was a peacekeeping operation requiring the consent and the cooperation of the parties to the conflict. Also, its deployment occurred before the parties had reached an agreement to cease the hostilities. This was a new generation of peacekeeping operations.

the establishment of a peacekeeping mission and whether such action constitutes an enforcement measure. Even though the Soviet Union wanted the United Kingdom and France out of the Suez, it opposed the idea of establishing a peacekeeping force. The General Assembly submitted this matter to the International Court of Justice and sought from it an advisory opinion. The Soviet delegation argued that only the Security Council is authorized to decide on any action relating to the maintenance of international peace and security. The Court rejected this argument, noting that the responsibility conferred to the Security Council in matters of international peace and security is primary, but not exclusive. The Court pointed out that the Security Council has the power to impose an explicit obligation of compliance and require enforcement by coercive action against an aggressor. However, the General Assembly also has a role to play in relation to international peace and security. It can recommend measures for the peaceful adjustment of a situation that it deems likely to impair the general welfare or friendly relations among nations. The Court determined that the *UN Charter* empowers the General Assembly, by means of recommendations to member states or the Security Council, or to both, to organize peacekeeping operations, at the request, or with the consent, of the states concerned.[102] It is important to note, however, that according to the International Court of Justice, the General Assembly could establish peacekeeping forces only if such forces did not have the power to enforce peace. In other words, unlike peacekeeping missions established by the Security Council, peacekeeping forces established by the General Assembly were not authorized to act against the host state. The Court's reasoning implies that the General Assembly does not have the power to authorize the most robust types of peace operations.

2) Legislative Powers

When the required majority of member states present in the General Assembly vote in favour of a proposal, they adopt a declaration, resolution, or decision. From a legal point of view, there is no difference

---

102 *Certain expenses of the United Nations (Article 17, paragraph 2, of the Charter)*, Advisory Opinion, [1962] ICJ Rep 151 [*Certain expenses of the United Nations*].

between these three types of actions; they all have the same legal status. From a political or symbolic viewpoint, they are different. General Assembly declarations connote a high political importance and almost invariably embrace particularly significant legal principles.[103] General Assembly resolutions are just another form of decisions by the General Assembly. Although they may also express important legal principles, the majority of resolutions deal with relatively routine matters. Resolutions are more common than declarations. General Assembly decisions deal with procedural questions such as elections, appointments, time, and place of future sessions. They may also be used to record the adoption of a text representing the consensus of the members of a given organ. Decisions have the lowest symbolic importance among the three types of decisions that the General Assembly makes.

General Assembly declarations, resolutions, and decisions are normally not binding on member states and do not set legal norms. They are not regarded as a formal source of international law.[104] In the vast majority of cases, General Assembly resolutions are recommendatory in nature. However, their political value cannot be underestimated. Major powers go to great lengths to have weightier support for their proposed resolutions because they realize that the legitimacy of General Assembly recommendations is directly proportional to the number of favourable votes these recommendations receive in the General Assembly.

---

103 In a memorandum issued on 2 April 1962, the Office of the Legal Affairs of the United Nations explained that in United Nations practice, a "declaration" is a formal and solemn instrument suitable for rare occasions when principles of great and lasting importance are being enunciated. It opined that "in view of the greater solemnity and significance of 'declaration,' it may be considered to impart, on behalf of the organ adopting it, a strong expectation that Members of the international community will abide by it. Consequently, insofar as the expectation is gradually justified by State practice, a declaration may by custom become recognized as laying down rules binding upon states." (UN Doc E/CN.4/L.610 at para 4).

104 Pursuant to Article 38.1(a) of the Statute of the International Court of Justice, the only formal sources of international law are: international conventions, international custom, general principles of law, and judicial decisions and the teachings of the most highly qualified publicists of the various nations, as subsidiary means for the determination of rules of law.

While declarations, resolutions, and decisions of the General Assembly are often recommendatory, the General Assembly may adopt, in specific cases within the framework of its competence, resolutions that make determinations or have operative design.[105] There are matters on which a vote in the General Assembly may become binding, either alone or together with a decision or recommendation of the Security Council. In particular, the General Assembly elects the non-permanent members of the Security Council[106] and the members of the Economic and Social Council.[107] The Assembly admits new members to the United Nations on the recommendation of the Security Council.[108] The General Assembly may suspend the rights and privileges of membership or expel members.[109] It approves the budget of the organization and apportions the expenses among UN member states.[110] These decisions are not mere recommendations; they have a direct effect on the rights and obligations of member states. They produce specific legal consequences and are binding for the members of the UN. Similarly, the General Assembly may adopt resolutions establishing subsidiary bodies or organs. Such resolutions produce concrete legal effects.

In addition, even though General Assembly resolutions are not formal sources of international law, they often lead to the formation of international rules in two different ways. First, a General Assembly resolution can lead to the adoption of international conventions. For example, the Universal Declaration of Human Rights of 10 December 1948 is an important General Assembly declaration. In its initial form, it was not a legally binding instrument, but it led to a series of legally binding conventions, such as the International Covenant on Civil and Political Rights and the International Covenant on Economic, Social, and Cultural Rights. Similarly, several resolutions on the question of

---

105 *Legal Consequences for States of the Continued Presence of South Africa in Namibia (South West Africa) notwithstanding Security Council Resolution 276 (1970)*, Advisory Opinion, [1971] ICJ Rep 16 at 50.

106 *Charter of the United Nations*, above note 1, art 23.

107 *Ibid*, art 61.

108 *Ibid*, art 4.

109 *Ibid*, arts 6–7.

110 *Ibid*, art 17.

peaceful use of outer space[111] resulted in an international treaty on the same topic.[112] Second, declarations and resolutions can help crystallize an emerging customary international law or trigger the formation of new customary international norms.[113] They can even become customary rules themselves if member states adopt a uniform and consistent practice of complying with them and feel compelled to respect them.[114] In many cases, the International Court of Justice relied on General Assembly resolutions in support of its conclusions that some norms have become customary international rules.[115]

The General Assembly also has an indirect role in developing and codifying international law. Specifically, paragraph 13(a) of the *UN Charter* mandates the General Assembly to initiate studies and make recommendations for the purpose of "encouraging the progressive development of international law and its codification." To discharge this responsibility, in 1947 the General Assembly established the International Law Commission (ILC).[116] The ILC consists

---

111 *Question of the Peaceful Use of Outer Space*, GA Res 1348 (XIII), UNGAOR, 13th Sess, UN Doc A/Res/1348(XIII) (1958) 5; *International Cooperation in the Peaceful Use of Outer Space*, GA Res 1472 (XIV), UNGAOR, 14th Sess, UN Doc A/Res/1472(XIV) (1959) 5; *International Cooperation in the Peaceful Use of Outer Space*, GA Res 1721 (XVI), UNGAOR, 16th Sess, UN Doc A/Res/1721(XVI) (1961) 6; *International Cooperation in the Peaceful Use of Outer Space*, GA Res 1802 (XVII), UNGAOR, 17th Sess, UN Doc A/Res/1802(XVII) (1962) 3; *Declaration of Legal Principles Governing the Activities of States in the Exploration and Use of Outer Space*, GA Res 1962(XVIII), UNGAOR, 18th Sess, UN Doc A/Res/1962(XVIII) (1963) 15.

112 *Treaty on Principles Governing the Activities of States in the Exploration and Use of Outer Space, Including the Moon and Other Celestial Bodies*, Annex to the GA Res 2222(XXI), UNGAOR, 21st Sess, UN Doc A/Res/2222(XXI) (1966) 13.

113 See Ian Brownlie, *Principles of Public International Law*, 7th ed (New York: Oxford University Press, 2008) at 15.

114 The Latin term *opinio juris* is used to describe a situation where states recognize that a certain practice is obligatory or required by prevailing international law. It refers to a sense of legal obligation as opposed to moral obligation or mere courtesy. *Opinio juris* is an element required for a legal norm to be recognized as a customary rule.

115 See *Review of the Role of the International Court of Justice*, GA Res 3232 (XXIX), UNGAOR, 29th Sess, UN Doc A/Res/3232(XXIX) (1974) 141 at Preamble.

116 *Establishment of an International Law Commission*, GA Res 174(II), UNGAOR, 2nd Sess, UN Doc A/Res/174(II) (1947) 105. As a document simply annexed to

of thirty-four members elected by the General Assembly from a list of candidates nominated by the governments of member states. ILC members must be "persons of recognized competence in international law." They are recognized experts or practitioners in both doctrinal and practical aspects of international law. They are selected from various segments of the international legal community, such as academia, the diplomatic corps, national governments, and international organizations. The members of the commission sit in their individual capacity and not as representatives of their governments. The role of the International Law Commission includes the preparation of draft conventions on subjects that have not yet been regulated by international law or where the law has not yet been sufficiently developed by state practice. The ILC also has the responsibility to formulate and systematize rules of international law in fields where there has already been long state practice. The work of the ILC has led to the creation of a number of extremely important treaties and other instruments of international law, including the *Vienna Convention on the Law of Treaties*, the *Vienna Convention on Succession of States in respect of Treaties*, the *Vienna Convention on Diplomatic Relations*, and the Draft Articles on the Responsibility of States for Internationally Wrongful Acts.

3) Budgetary Powers

Three primary organs of the UN—the General Assembly, the Security Council, and the ECOSOC—have the authority to make policy decisions. However, no policy decision can be implemented unless member states agree to pay for it. For instance, establishing a peacekeeping mission or creating an *ad hoc* international criminal tribunal are very expensive endeavours that require substantial financial resources. The UN also has running costs that include the salaries and travel expenses of its personnel, rent and public utility services

a resolution of the General Assembly, the Statute of the ILC does not have the status of a treaty. Hence, it may be amended by a subsequent resolution of the General Assembly.

for its premises, acquisition and maintenance of official vehicles and office furniture, operation of the UN library and archives, and so on. It is the responsibility of the General Assembly to approve the budget detailing the UN's anticipated expenditures. The approval of the UN budget may appear to be a purely financial matter. In reality, it is a complex political game. Wealthy nations who contribute the most often exert pressure by delaying the payment of their dues. Some member states go as far as withholding their shares of the contribution until their demands are fully satisfied. Of course, such political blackmail is entirely inconsistent with the *UN Charter*. It is interesting to note that countries that use this strategy make sure that they do not lose their right to vote in the General Assembly under Article 19 of the *UN Charter* by keeping the amount of their arrears below the amount of the contributions they owe for the preceding two full years. In other words, when a member state delays the payment of its contributions for twelve months (or even twenty-three months) as opposed to twenty-four months, Article 19 of the *UN Charter* does not apply. Other wealthy nations exercise a lot of influence by determining which projects or programs the UN must prioritize.

The United Nations Organization, UN Funds and Programmes, and UN Specialized Agencies have different ways of financing their activities and operations. The funding of the UN System falls into two major categories: assessed contributions and voluntary contributions.

Assessed contributions refer to the amount of money that the General Assembly determines should be "assessed" to finance the approved appropriation, which is shared among member states to pay for the expenses of the organization. Arguably, UN activities that are funded through assessed contributions are less vulnerable to political influences of member states, because once member states agree on the overall amount of the budget, the apportionment among various countries is mathematical and not overly controversial. Of course, agreeing on the budget requires a prior agreement on the activities to be carried out by the UN. This is where the line between politics and funding gets blurred. For example, some member states may want to scale down certain peacekeeping missions while other states might be willing to strengthen them. Similarly, some countries may wish to focus on migration and refugee issues while others may want to tackle development questions. These divergent political agendas have a direct financial impact on the final amount of the budget that the General Assembly will have to consider and approve. States with opposing views normally engage in extensive negotiations in order to find the middle ground or a compromise. Assessed contributions are used for three types of funding: the UN Regular Budget, UN Peacekeeping Operations Budget, and UN Specialized Agencies Budgets.

Voluntary contributions are used to finance almost all of the activities of UN Funds and Programmes and a large part of activities of Specialized Agencies. Activities funded through voluntary contributions are more vulnerable to political influences primarily because the donor state can legitimately control the manner in which the UN fund or program should use its portion of the contribution. The diagram below illustrates various types of funding sources.

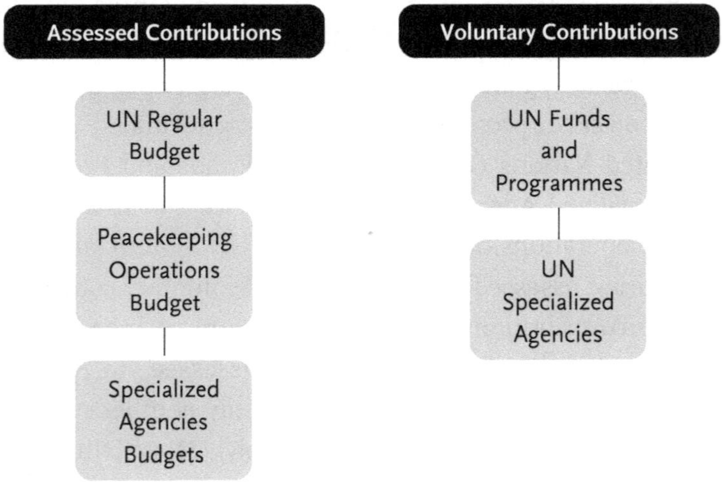

In this part, we will address only the regular budget of the UN. The peacekeeping operations budget will be examined in the chapter that deals with the Security Council.

a) General Assembly's Power to Consider and Approve the Organization's Budget

Paragraph 17.1 of the *UN Charter* empowers the General Assembly to consider and approve the budget of the organization. The UN's budget is a complex process. The budget cycle of the UN has three phases and is spread over a period of five years. The three phases are planning, implementation, and evaluation. The planning phase begins two years before the start of a biennium and lasts approximately two years.[117] For instance, the planning for the biennium 2020–2021 begins in 2018. As the Chief Administrative Officer of the United Nations,[118] the Secretary-General is responsible for planning and preparing the budget.[119] The planning of the budget requires the participation of all departments and offices of the UN. UN Financial Rules require heads of departments of the UN to prepare program budget proposals for the forthcoming budget period for their respective departments and transmit them to the Secretary-General so that they can be compiled into a single document.[120]

---

117 For the biennium 2020–2021, the Secretary-General issues the first planning documents for the General Assembly's consideration as early as 2018. The first documents include the proposed Strategic Framework and the proposed Budget Outline. The Strategic Framework sets out the anticipated activities of the organization to fulfill its mandates and the Budget Outline lists the anticipated budget requirements for the biennium. The difference between the Strategic Framework and the Budget Outline is simple: the Strategic Framework answers the questions "what will the organization do during the upcoming biennium" whereas the Budget Outline addresses the question "how much the organization will need to complete these activities." The planning phase for the biennium 2020–2021 continues the following year—that is in 2019. The Secretary-General produces the Proposed Programme Budget, which details the anticipated activities and the corresponding resource requirements. According to Financial Regulation 2.5, UN Doc ST/SGB/2013/4, at least twelve weeks prior to the opening of the regular session of the General Assembly, the Secretary-General is expected to submit, in the second year of a budget period, his proposed program budget for the following budget period to the ACABQ. He must submit to the General Assembly, at least five weeks prior to the opening of the regular session, the budget estimates for the following financial year.

118 *Charter of the United Nations*, above note 1, art 97.

119 In accordance with Rule 153 of the General Assembly Rules of Procedure, above note 17, "no resolution involving expenditure shall be recommended by a committee for approval by the General Assembly unless it is accompanied by an estimate of expenditures prepared by the Secretary-General."

120 United Nations, *Financial Regulations and Rules of the United Nations*, UN Doc ST/SGB/2013/4. After preparing their respective portions of the proposed program budget, departments submit their part of the budget to the Office

The second phase of a UN budget cycle—known as the implementation phase—is the core of the cycle. This is the period during which the funds are actually spent. The implementation phase for the UN regular budget is based on a "biennium," which refers to a two-year period during which the budget is expended.[121] The implementation phase for peacekeeping operations is based on an annual budget that runs from 1 July to 30 June. The Secretary-General has a duty to ensure that the UN does not incur unauthorized expenses during the implementation phase.

The third and final phase of the UN budget cycle consists of evaluating the UN's financial performance. This phase begins at the end of the first year of the biennium and concludes one year after the end of the biennium. In other words, for the UN regular budget, the implementation phase and the evaluation phase overlap during the fourth and fifth years of the cycle. During this final phase, the Secretary-General produces performance reports focusing on the financial performance of the UN. A performance report is issued at the end of each year of the biennium listing the activities carried out during the relevant period. During the same phase, a financial report and audited financial statements are issued in relation to the same biennium.

Due to an emergency or unforeseen circumstance, the UN may occasionally incur expenses that have not been authorized by the General Assembly. In such cases, can the General Assembly refuse to honour the financial obligations of the organization if it did not authorize them in advance? This question arose in the 1950s when the General

---

of Programme Planning, Budget and Accounts (OPPBA), which carries out activities pertaining to the financial and budgetary operations of the organization. OPPBA is part of the Department of Management and is headed by the Controller, who has the level of an Assistant Secretary-General. OPPBA is responsible for establishing and applying budgetary and accounting policies and procedures. It is responsible for the financial management of all resources of the organization, for accounting and reporting, as well as for facilitating intergovernmental deliberations on financial and budgetary matters.

121 In its Resolution 72/266, the General Assembly decided to change from a biennial to an annual budget period on a trial basis, beginning with the programme budget for 2020, and requested the Secretary-General to conduct a review of changes to the budgetary cycle in 2022, following the completion of the first full budgetary cycle (UN Doc A/Res/72/266 (24 December 2017) at para 6).

Assembly refused to pay monetary damages awarded by the United Nations Administrative Tribunal against the organization for unlawfully terminating the employment of many UN staff members.

In the late 1940s and early 1950s, US Senator Eugene McCarthy led a series of investigations against US citizens employed in the UN and suspected to be communists. A federal grand jury was set up to investigate the alleged subversive activities by US citizens working in the United Nations. A number of Americans employed by the United Nations appeared before the grand jury. Some of these staff members chose to testify while others invoked their privilege against self-incrimination under the US Constitution. The US government exerted pressure on the then Secretary-General Trygve Lie to terminate the appointment of over twenty American citizens who refused to testify before the federal grand jury. The Secretary-General of the UN yielded to the pressure and dismissed these staff members. The aggrieved individuals sued the UN before the UN Administrative Tribunal and prevailed.[122] The tribunal awarded them a monetary compensation. Since the UN did not have sufficient funds to disburse the awarded damages, the Secretary-General requested the General Assembly to absorb this extraordinary expense by making additional contributions to the UN budget. Some member states felt that this was the sole responsibility of the United States and that other UN member states had no obligation to pay for expenses that they had neither caused nor authorized. The General Assembly sought an advisory opinion from the International Court of Justice. The World Court was required to determine whether the General Assembly could refuse to give effect to an award of compensation made by the UN Administrative Tribunal in favour of UN staff members whose contracts of service had been unlawfully terminated. The Court concluded that as the final judgment of the Administrative Tribunal had binding force on the United Nations, the General Assembly, as an organ of the United Nations, must likewise be bound by the judgment.[123] As a result of

122 United Nations Administrative Tribunal, Judgments No 28–37, A/DEC/28 to A/DEC/37 (21 August 1953).

123 *Effect of awards of compensation made by the UN Administrative Tribunal*, Advisory Opinion, [1954] ICJ Rep 47.

this advisory opinion, it is now settled that the General Assembly has an obligation to apportion expenses incurred by the Secretary-General even if it had not authorized such expenses.

A similar dilemma arose when two permanent members of the Security Council refused to pay their contribution for a peacekeeping mission. In 1956, Egypt angered France and the United Kingdom by nationalizing the Suez Canal Company. Israeli forces used this opportunity to launch an attack against Egypt. British and French troops joined the operations and took control of the Suez Canal. The matter was brought to the attention of the Security Council, but no decision could be adopted owing to the vetoes of France and the United Kingdom. The issue was then picked up by the General Assembly under the *Uniting for Peace* resolution. The General Assembly established the United Nations Emergency Force (UNEF) to secure and supervise the cessation of hostilities[124] and the withdrawal of foreign forces. This peacekeeping mission cost the UN a substantial amount of money. Two permanent members of the Security Council (the USSR and France) refused to pay their contributions, arguing that the General Assembly had no authority under the *UN Charter* to establish a peacekeeping force. According to them, only the Security Council could authorize such an action and no state could be expected to fund unauthorized activities. The General Assembly sought an advisory opinion from the ICJ. The Court held that even though the *UN Charter* did not explicitly regulate expenses that result from peacekeeping activities authorized by the General Assembly, any expenditure that is made for one of the purposes of the UN must be considered an expense of the organization.[125]

---

124 The idea to create UNEF is attributed to Canada's then Minister of Foreign Affairs Lester B Pearson, who received the Nobel Prize for it in 1957. It was Pearson who had suggested the actual notion of the UN-led peacekeeping force to the special emergency session of the General Assembly on 2 November 1956. In his speech to the General Assembly, Pearson argued for "a truly international peace and police force . . . large enough to keep these borders at peace while a political settlement is being worked out."

125 *Certain expenses of the United Nations*, above note 102.

b) Approval Process

The General Assembly does not normally have a sufficient amount of time and the expertise to review the budget proposal of the Secretary-General. It delegates this technically onerous task to its Fifth Committee or the Administrative and Budgetary Committee. The Fifth Committee itself relies on the expert advice of the Advisory Committee on Administrative and Budgetary Questions (ACABQ). This committee is responsible for expert examination of the program budget of the United Nations. In essence, it assists the Administrative and Budgetary Committee (Fifth Committee).[126] The ACABQ consists of sixteen members who are appointed by the General Assembly in their individual capacity and not as representatives of their governments. ACABQ must have, at all times, at least three financial experts of recognized standing. No two members of the ACABQ can be nationals of the same member state and all members are selected on the basis of broad geographical representation, personal qualifications, and experience. Major donors and superpowers, such as the United States, Japan, and Russia, are always represented in the ACABQ.

At the beginning of each regular session of the General Assembly at which the proposed budget for the following biennium is to be considered, ACABQ submits to the General Assembly a detailed report on the proposed program budget. It also submits a report on the accounts of the United Nations and all UN entities for which the Secretary-General has administrative responsibility. It examines on behalf of the General Assembly the administrative budgets of specialized agencies and proposals for financial and budgetary arrangements with such agencies. The recommendations of ACABQ are usually, but not always, approved by the Fifth Committee and subsequently endorsed by the General Assembly.

c) General Assembly's Power to Apportion the Budget Among Member States

Paragraph 17.2 of the *UN Charter* states that UN member states bear the expenses of the organization as apportioned by the General Assembly.

---

126 General Assembly Rules of Procedure, above note 17 at Rule 157.

The regular budget of the organization is apportioned among member states according to the scale of assessments approved by the General Assembly on the recommendation of the Committee on Contributions.[127] The elements of the methodology used in preparing the scale of assessments were initially established by the General Assembly.[128] The Assembly subsequently requested the Committee on Contributions to review the methodology of future scales of assessments based on the principle that the expenses of the organization should be apportioned broadly according to capacity to pay and to prepare the scale of assessments strictly on the basis of reliable, verifiable, and comparable data.[129] The committee produced a detailed report on the methodology for determining the scale of assessment in June 2019.[130]

The scale of assessments for the UN's regular budget covers three years and is based on the following elements and criteria:

(a) Estimates of gross national income;[131]
(b) Average statistical base periods of three and six years;
(c) Conversion rates based on market exchange rates;
(d) The debt-burden approach employed in the scale of assessments for a period of three years;
(e) A low per capita income adjustment of 80 percent;
(f) A minimum assessment rate of 0.001 percent;

---

127 Established by GA Res 14 (I) A, UNGAOR, 1st Sess, UN Doc A/RES/14(I) (1946) 19, the Committee on Contributions advises the General Assembly on the apportionment of the expenses of the organization among the member states according to their capacity to pay. The committee's functions are described in Rules 158 to 160 of the Rules of Procedure of the General Assembly, above note 17.

128 *Scale of assessments for the apportionment of the expenses of the United Nations*, GA Res 55/5B, UNGAOR, 55th Sess, UN Doc A/Res/55/5B (2001).

129 *Scale of assessments for the apportionment of the expenses of the United Nations*, GA Res 73/271, UNGAOR, 73rd Sess, UN Doc A/Res/73/271 (2019) 1 at para 5 [*Scale of assessments 2019*].

130 *Report of the Committee on Contributions*, UNGAOR 74th Session, UN Doc A/74/11 (2019) at para 64.

131 The national income of an economy represents the income of its residents. It is obtained by adjusting the Gross Domestic Product (GDP) with the income of residents from activities abroad and the income of non-residents from activities in the country.

(g) A maximum assessment rate for the least developed countries of 0.01 percent;

(h) A maximum assessment rate of 22 percent (reduced from 25 percent in 2001).[132]

The largest contributor to the UN's budget is the United States of America. It pays 22 percent of the regular budget. Traditionally, Japan and Germany have been the second and third largest contributors, respectively. However, China has recently surpassed both countries, becoming the second largest contributor to the UN's regular budget.

SCALE OF ASSESSMENTS FOR THE APPORTIONMENT OF THE EXPENSES OF THE UNITED NATIONS[133]

Member state	%
Afghanistan	0.007
Albania	0.008
Algeria	0.138
Andorra	0.005
Angola	0.005
Antigua and Barbuda	0.002
Argentina	0.915
Armenia	0.007
Australia	2.210
Austria	0.677
Azerbaijan	0.049
Bahamas	0.018
Bahrain	0.050
Bangladesh	0.010
Barbados	0.007
Belarus	0.049
Belgium	0.821
Belize	0.001

Member state	%
Cambodia	0.006
Cameroon	0.013
Canada	2.734
Cape Verde	0.001
Central African Republic	0.001
Chad	0.004
Chile	0.407
China	12.005
Colombia	0.288
Comoros	0.001
Congo	0.006
Costa Rica	0.062
Côte d'Ivoire	0.013
Croatia	0.077
Cuba	0.080
Cyprus	0.036
Czechia	0.311
Democratic People's Republic of Korea	0.006

132 *Scale of assessments for the apportionment of the expenses of the United Nations*, GA Res 70/245, UNGAOR, 70th Sess, UN Doc A/Res/70/245 (2016) 1.

133 *Scale of assessments 2019*, above note 129.

Member state	%
Benin	0.003
Bhutan	0.001
Bolivia	0.016
Bosnia and Herzegovina	0.012
Botswana	0.014
Brazil	2.948
Brunei Darussalam	0.025
Bulgaria	0.046
Burkina Faso	0.003
Burundi	0.001
Estonia	0.039
Ethiopia	0.010
Fiji	0.003
Finland	0.421
France	4.427
Gabon	0.015
Gambia	0.001
Georgia	0.008
Germany	6.090
Ghana	0.015
Greece	0.366
Grenada	0.001
Guatemala	0.036
Guinea	0.003
Guinea-Bissau	0.001
Guyana	0.002
Haiti	0.003
Honduras	0.009
Hungary	0.206
Iceland	0.028
India	0.834
Indonesia	0.543
Iran	0.398
Iraq	0.129
Ireland	0.371

Member state	%
Congo (Dem. Rep.)	0.010
Denmark	0.554
Djibouti	0.001
Dominica	0.001
Dominican Republic	0.053
Ecuador	0.080
Egypt	0.186
El Salvador	0.012
Equatorial Guinea	0.016
Eritrea	0.001
Lao People's Dem. Rep.	0.005
Latvia	0.047
Lebanon	0.047
Lesotho	0.001
Liberia	0.001
Libya	0.030
Liechtenstein	0.009
Lithuania	0.071
Luxembourg	0.067
Madagascar	0.004
Malawi	0.002
Malaysia	0.341
Maldives	0.004
Mali	0.004
Malta	0.017
Marshall Islands	0.001
Mauritania	0.002
Mauritius	0.011
Mexico	1.292
Micronesia	0.001
Monaco	0.011
Mongolia	0.005
Montenegro	0.004
Morocco	0.055
Mozambique	0.004

Member state	%
Israel	0.490
Italy	3.307
Jamaica	0.008
Japan	8.564
Jordan	0.021
Kazakhstan	0.178
Kenya	0.024
Kiribati	0.001
Kuwait	0.252
Kyrgyzstan	0.002
Oman	0.115
Pakistan	0.115
Palau	0.001
Panama	0.045
Papua New Guinea	0.010
Paraguay	0.016
Peru	0.152
Philippines	0.205
Poland	0.802
Portugal	0.350
Qatar	0.282
Republic of Korea	2.267
Rep. of North Macedonia	0.007
Rep. Moldova	0.003
Romania	0.198
Russian Federation	2.405
Rwanda	0.003
Saint Kitts and Nevis	0.001
Saint Lucia	0.001
St-Vincent and the Grenadines	0.001
Samoa	0.001
San Marino	0.002
Sao Tome and Principe	0.001
Saudi Arabia	1.172

Member state	%
Myanmar	0.010
Namibia	0.009
Nauru	0.001
Nepal	0.007
Netherlands	1.356
New Zealand	0.291
Nicaragua	0.005
Niger	0.002
Nigeria	0.250
Norway	0.754
South Sudan	0.006
Spain	2.146
Sri Lanka	0.044
Sudan	0.005
Suriname	0.005
Swaziland	0.003
Sweden	0.906
Switzerland	1.151
Syria	0.011
Tajikistan	0.004
Thailand	0.307
Timor-Leste	0.002
Togo	0.001
Tonga	0.001
Trinidad and Tobago	0.040
Tunisia	0.025
Turkey	1.371
Turkmenistan	0.033
Tuvalu	0.001
Uganda	0.008
Ukraine	0.057
United Arab Emirates	0.616
United Kingdom	4.567
Tanzania	0.010

Member state	%
Senegal	0.007
Serbia	0.028
Seychelles	0.002
Sierra Leone	0.001
Singapore	0.485
Slovakia	0.153
Slovenia	0.076
Solomon Islands	0.001
Somalia	0.001
South Africa	0.272

Member state	%
USA	22.000
Uruguay	0.087
Uzbekistan	0.032
Vanuatu	0.001
Venezuela	0.728
Viet Nam	0.077
Yemen	0.010
Zambia	0.009
Zimbabwe	0.005

D. PARLIAMENTARY POLITICS OF THE GENERAL ASSEMBLY

On the surface, the decision-making process in the General Assembly seems very simple and straightforward: each member state has one vote and the wishes of the qualified majority prevail. The reality is much more complex. The parliamentary politics of the General Assembly entail more than the voting patterns of member states or televised speeches of world leaders. General Assembly resolutions do not necessarily reflect the power dynamics of international politics. The political process of the General Assembly is elusive even for experienced diplomats. Nevertheless, these parliamentary politics are at the core of the General Assembly's functioning. The two main pressure points in the General Assembly are money and numerical advantage of votes. Powerful and wealthy states control the purse but do not always manage to dictate the terms because less powerful states take full advantage of their arithmetical advantage by agreeing on a common position and voting together on specific issues.

During the Cold War, the General Assembly was initially divided between the East and the West. The East Bloc consisted of the former Soviet Union, its allies in Eastern and Central Europe and other socialist countries around the world. The West Bloc included the United States and its allies, including Canada, Western Europe, Japan, Australia, New Zealand, and Israel. The process of decolonization triggered another type of divide within the General Assembly. In addition to the East–West enmity, a North–South rivalry began emerging between developing and least developed countries and the industrialized countries. With the collapse of the Soviet Union and the end of the Cold War, the East–West divide disappeared, even though it seems to have been re-emerging during the last decade. The North–South divide, on the other hand, intensified. Today, UN member states are organized in formal and informal groups with a huge diversity in purposes and memberships. Some groups are exclusively political. The members of such groups have common interests or positions that transcend geographic boundaries. Other groups are regional or religious. They were set up to represent member states that share the same geographic region, state religion, language, or continent.

1) Non-Aligned Movement (NAM)

In the late 1950s, developing countries showed for the first time an interest in consolidating their voices. The largest developing countries of Asia and Africa, including Indonesia, India, Egypt, and Vietnam, gathered in Bandung, Indonesia, in April 1955 to create a coalition of states not aligned with either the East or the West. These member states considered that the rivalry between the Soviet Union and the United States was paralyzing the UN. It was difficult for any individual member state to resist the political pressure exerted on it by the Soviet Union or the United States, which often obliged these countries to take sides. In order to avoid being enmeshed in the Cold War, these countries formed a coalition known as the Non-Aligned Movement (NAM). NAM is a loose and diverse political group. Throughout its existence, it often had deep internal divisions. It went through its first identity crisis with the end of colonization and through its second crisis with the end of the Cold War. Nevertheless, it managed to survive these setbacks and redefine itself. Today, it remains an important voice in the UN. The members of this group do not consider themselves aligned with any major power bloc. It currently has 118 members and holds summits every three years. In the General Assembly, the group presents a common position on peace and security issues, on disarmament, on the development and codification of international law, as well as on some humanitarian issues. On the question of disarmament, for example, the NAM aspires to a complete disarmament through elimination of nuclear arsenals and all other weapons of mass destruction under effective international control.[134]

2) The Group of 77, Also Known as G-77 and China

G-77 and China was established in 1964 by seventy-seven developing countries, signatories of the "Joint Declaration of the Seventy-Seven Developing Countries" issued at the first session of the United Nations Conference on Trade and Development (UNCTAD) in Geneva. Although today the number of members of the G-77 has reached 133 countries, the group chose to retain its name for symbolic reasons. Unlike the Non-Aligned Movement, the G-77 does not focus on political issues. It was designed to promote its members' collective economic interests and create an enhanced joint negotiating capacity in the United Nations. Indeed, the numerical strength of this bloc of developing countries has served as a counterpoint to the influence of industrialized countries, which, due to their far greater financial resources and ability to fund international organizations, enjoy a significant influence in the UN. Essentially, the G-77 holds the "power of the majority," whereas the industrialized countries hold the "power of the purse." This tension often prevents timely and meaningful consensus on critical issues because the side that needs an international action the most is not the one paying the most for it. While the G-77 would like the General Assembly to play a more prominent role in development and global financial issues, developed countries would like to limit the role of the UN to international peace and security, humanitarian issues, and human rights, arguing that the Bretton Woods institutions, WTO and UNDP, were specifically established to

---

134 See the *Final Document of the 11th Summit of the Heads of State or Government of the Non-Aligned Countries*, Cartagena, Colombia, 18–20 October 1995 at paras 82–83.

deal with development.[135] The G-77 coordinates and presents a joint position on financial, economic, and budgetary issues. The G-77 maintains an office at UN headquarters. The group has a chairman who acts as its spokesman and coordinates the group's actions. The chairmanship is the highest political body within the organizational structure of the group. The chairmanship rotates on a regional basis between Africa, Asia-Pacific, and Latin America, and the Caribbean. A region may hold the office for one year. The supreme decision-making body of the G-77 is the South Summit.

Since most G-77 members are also members of the Non-Aligned Movement, these two groups put in place a Joint Coordination Committee. This committee is a mechanism for coordinating and harmonizing the positions of the Non-Aligned Movement and G-77 in order to avoid unnecessary duplication of work between the two groups.

3) European Union

The European Union is an economic and political partnership between European countries. It has a unique setup. The EU's broad priorities and policies are determined by the Council of the European Union, which is composed of national and EU-level leaders. The European Council is the forum where each member of the European Union defends its country's national interests. The interests of EU citizens are represented by the members of the European Parliament elected directly by EU citizens. The executive body of the European Union is the European Commission whose members are appointed by national governments.

The EU has a diplomatic service and a permanent office in the United Nations distinct from those of its member states. The EU coordinates on the entire range of UN activities. However, for the European Union to have a common position, consensus must have been previously reached among all EU member states. The EU delegation to the UN continuously holds intensive meetings to reach a

---

135 Lydia Swart, "The Voice of the Majority: The Role of the Group of 77 in the UN General Assembly" (2014) 51:1 *United Nations Chronicle* 39 at 40.

common EU position. Every year the Council of the European Union adopts the EU priorities at the UN General Assembly, taking into account the UN's agenda and global issues. These priorities determine the EU's work for the upcoming year. For instance, for the seventy-third session of the General Assembly, the Council of the EU identified as its key priority "to boost multilateralism and to stand behind the UN in a volatile and unpredictable world." Its areas of focus for the relevant cycle are: (a) peace and conflict prevention; (b) human rights; and (c) climate change. Furthermore, in accordance with the *Treaty on the European Union*, any EU member that sits on the Security Council[136] has an obligation to request that the EU High Representative for Foreign Affairs be invited to present the EU's position to the Security Council (provided the EU has a common position on the relevant matter).[137] The EU member states collectively are the largest financial contributor to the UN system. It is therefore not surprising that the European Union is a powerful player in the General Assembly.

4) African Union

The African Union (AU) was a derivative of the Organisation of African Unity (OAU), established in 1963 to unite African states in the struggle against colonialism.[138] In September 1999, the heads of African states adopted the Sirte Declaration announcing the creation the African Union.[139] The AU is an intergovernmental organization with

136 After the United Kingdom left the European Union, the only EU member state with a permanent seat in the Security Council is France.

137 *In fine* of the *Treaty on European Union*, 7 February 1992, 1759 UNTS 3, art 34, para 2 (entered into force 1 November 1993).

138 Mohammed Bedjaoui, "Brief Historical Overview of Steps to African Unity" in Abdulqawi A Yusuf & Fatsah Ouguergouz, eds, *The African Union: Legal and Institutional Framework* (Leiden: Martinus Nijhoff, 2012) at 17.

139 Paragraph 6 of the Sirte Declaration reads as follows:

> In order to cope with those challenges and to effectively address the new social, political and economic realities in Africa and in the world, we are determined to fulfill our peoples' aspirations for greater unity in conformity with the objectives of the OAU Charter and the Treaty establishing the

many structural similarities to the UN. For instance, it has among other organs an assembly, which is its deliberative organ, the Peace and Security Council, and a secretariat (called the Commission). The African Union is an important actor in the international arena, as it represents a bloc of fifty-four votes. The AU plays a particularly important role in the area of peace and security because many large-scale armed conflicts are concentrated on the African continent. In fact, the *Protocol Relating to the Establishment of the Peace and Security Council of the African Union* explicitly addresses cooperation of the African Union with the United Nations and other international organizations.[140] Indeed, the United Nations and the African Union frequently cooperate in matters of peace and security.[141]

> African Economic Community. It is also our conviction that our Continental Organization needs to be revitalized in order to be able to play a more active role and continue to be relevant to the needs of our peoples and responsive to the demands of the prevailing circumstances. We are also determined to eliminate the scourge of conflicts, which constitutes a major impediment to the implementation of our development and integration agenda.

140 Article 17 of the Protocol provides as follows:

> 1. In the fulfilment of its mandate in the promotion and maintenance of peace, security and stability in Africa, the Peace and Security Council shall cooperate and work closely with the United Nations Security Council, which has the primary responsibility for the maintenance of international peace and security. The Peace and Security Council shall also cooperate and work closely with other relevant UN Agencies in the promotion of peace, security and stability in Africa.
> 2. Where necessary, recourse will be made to the United Nations to provide the necessary financial, logistical and military support for the African Unions' activities in the promotion and maintenance of peace, security and stability in Africa, in keeping with the provisions of Chapter VIII of the *UN Charter* on the role of Regional Organizations in the maintenance of international peace and security.
> 3. The Peace and Security Council and the Chairperson of the Commission shall maintain close and continued interaction with the United Nations Security Council, its African members, as well as with the Secretary-General, including holding periodic meetings and regular consultations on questions of peace, security and stability in Africa.

141 The cooperation in peacekeeping operations between the African Union and the United Nations can take three forms. It can be a purely African operation receiving support from the UN. The mission in Somalia is an example of that. It

The African Union has observer status and maintains a permanent office in New York. The AU and the Group of African States[142] work closely together on General Assembly issues. It is usually the Group of African States that speaks in the General Assembly on behalf of the African Union and its member states.

5) Organisation of Islamic Cooperation

The Organisation of Islamic Cooperation (OIC) (formerly the Organization of the Islamic Conference) is an intergovernmental organization with fifty-seven member states spread over four continents. It is the second largest international organization after the United Nations.[143] It is believed that the reason for the creation of the OIC was the need for Muslim solidarity following two events in modern history: the Arab loss of the Six Day War in 1967 and the 1969 arson in the Al-Aqsa Mosque, a holy site in Jerusalem.[144] The principal deliberating organ of the OIC is the Islamic Summit, composed of kings and heads of state and governments of member states. This organ is the supreme authority of the organization. It convenes once every three years to deliberate and develop the institutional policy. The organization also has the Council of Foreign Ministers. The council meets once a year and determines the manner in which the implementation

---

can be an African operation that is eventually replaced by a UN operation. This occurred in Burundi and Mali. It can also be a hybrid deployment of AU and UN operations. The mission in Darfur is an example of such a hybrid cooperation.

142 The regional groups were formed to facilitate the equitable geographical distribution of seats among the member states in different UN bodies. There are currently five regional groups. They are the Group of African States, the Group of Asian States, the Group of Eastern European States, the Group of Latin American and Caribbean States, and the Group of Western European and Other States. Although these regional groups exist for electoral and ceremonial purposes, some, including the Group of African States, choose to coordinate on substantive issues and/or use the group structure to share information.

143 Salim Farrar, "The Organisation of Islamic Cooperation: Forever on the Periphery of Public International Law" (2014) 13:4 *Chinese J of Int'l L* 787.

144 Azin Tadjdini, "The Organisation of Islamic Cooperation and Regional Challenges to International Law and Security" (2012) 4:2 *Amsterdam L Forum* 36 at 37.

of the general policy of the organization will take place. The third principal organ of the OIC is the General Secretariat. It is the executive organ of the organization, entrusted with the implementation of the decisions of the two preceding bodies.

The OIC has a permanent observer status and delegation to the United Nations in New York. The organization's primary goal is to promote and represent the interests of Muslims around the world. Issues of interest for this group include a wide array of questions such as Palestine, Islamophobia, Human Rights in Islam, emergency relief to Muslims, and terrorism.

6) League of Arab States

The League of Arab States, also called the Arab League, is an association of Arab states. The League holds an observer's status in the United Nations General Assembly. It was formed in Cairo in March 1945 with six members. It currently has twenty-two member states. The main aims of the League are to strengthen relations and to coordinate collaboration between member states. The highest body of the League is the Council, which is composed of representatives of each state. Each member has one vote and decisions are binding only on states that voted for them. The League has a secretariat that administers its operation and day-to-day activities. It is headed by a Secretary-General appointed by the Arab League Council every five years. The member states of the UN who are also members of the League represent a particularly important bloc of votes when the General Assembly discusses the situation in the Middle East, and more specifically with regard to the Palestinian question.

7) Other Coalitions and Interest Groups

There are many other coalitions and interest groups in the General Assembly, including:

- The Alliance of Small Island States (AOSIS), composed of forty-two small island states and low-lying coastal countries;

- The Association of Southeast Asian Nations (ASEAN);
- CAN where Canada, Australia, and New Zealand coordinate their positions and may authorize one among them to speak or negotiate on behalf of all three;
- The LDCs or Least Developed Countries, whose membership is based on a set of criteria defined by the GA;
- Nordic Countries involving Denmark, Finland, Iceland, Norway, and Sweden as well as the three autonomous areas.

To strengthen their individual voices, member states will continue to adopt and defend collective positions through coalitions and interest groups. Understanding the interests and positions of these various groups and coalitions is key to successfully navigating the UN's diplomatic waters.

Chapter 4

THE SECURITY COUNCIL

To explain the role of the Security Council, many scholars and academics draw an analogy between the UN and national governments. They then equate the Security Council to the executive branch of a government. Such comparisons are confusing and not helpful. Any attempt to understand the UN or the Security Council through the prism of domestic constitutional law is doomed to failure.

With a wide range of powers, the UN Security Council is considered to be the most influential organ of the United Nations, vested foremost with the primary responsibility for the maintenance of international peace and security.[1] In comparison with the Council of the League of Nations, the Security Council is a ground-breaking arrangement.

First, the Council of the League of Nations was unable to attract all of the major powers of the time. Indeed, the United States never joined the League and most other powerful states of the time held a seat on the Council only temporarily. Germany, Italy, and Japan withdrew from the League at different times for different reasons, while

1 *Charter of the United Nations*, 26 June 1945, Can TS 1945 No 7, art 24 [*Charter of the United Nations*].

the Soviet Union was expelled for its invasion of Finland. France and the United Kingdom were the only powerful states that remained in the Council throughout the League's existence. However, they were colonial powers with doubtful credibility. They lacked the required legitimacy to represent weaker nations against strong aggressors. Their unethical secret pact with Italy after its invasion of Ethiopia only confirmed their unsuitability for the role of guardians of peace.

Second, decisions made by the League Council required unanimity. It meant that each member of the League Council, including non-permanent members, could unilaterally veto any proposed action. As the Council's membership gradually increased, it became more difficult for the Council to reach unanimity.

Third, the Covenant of the League of Nations empowered the Council to act in cases of aggression only. Actions to pre-empt aggression or to prevent breaches of peace were not permitted. When aggression did arise, the Council could only impose economic measures. It could neither implement military action nor compel or oblige other states to use force in order to restore international peace.

The founders of the UN learned from past mistakes and decided to address the League's flaws. First and foremost, the major powers of the time had together designed the structure of the Security Council, thereby ensuring that the proposal would be acceptable to all. Second, only permanent members of the Security Council have a veto right. Non-permanent members of the Security Council cannot single-handedly block a resolution of the Security Council. Third, the Security Council has the authority to deal not only with aggression but also with a wide range of security problems and threats to international peace and security. This allows the Security Council to take preventive measures. Moreover, the Security Council can do more than merely recommend military action and count on member states to carry it out. The Security Council is empowered to use force in its own right. However, the most innovative addition of the *UN Charter* was the provision giving the Security Council access to armed forces so that it could intervene efficiently and promptly. Unfortunately, this proved to be too innovative for the times. Member nations of the UN did not entrust the organization with its own armed forces.

A. MEMBERSHIP

It is important to recall that in 1945, the membership of the UN was not universal. The organization was founded by fifty-one states. Initially, the Security Council consisted of eleven member states, of which five were permanent members and the remaining six were non-permanent members. The eleven members of the Security Council represented more than 20 percent of the UN's initial membership of fifty-one states. When decolonization resulted in a significant number of admissions into the organization, the Security Council could no longer claim to adequately represent the world. In fact, most former colonies were Asian and African states that did not participate in developing the *UN Charter*. They were not represented at the San Francisco conference and, therefore, played no role in determining the composition of the Security Council. They successfully argued that the Security Council had to be enlarged to ensure a more equitable representation. In 1963, the General Assembly decided to amend the *UN Charter* in order to enlarge the membership of the Security Council from eleven to fifteen members as of 31 August 1965.[2]

Today, the Security Council consists of fifteen members. Five of these member states hold a permanent seat on the Security Council. Frequently referred to as the P5, the permanent members of the Security Council are China, France, Russia, the United Kingdom, and the United States. The remaining ten states are non-permanent members of the Security Council. These members are elected by the General Assembly for a term of two years. Each year, the General Assembly conducts staggered elections for five seats of the Security Council. The elections take place in June, but the terms begin in January of the following year. A retiring non-permanent member of the Security Council is not eligible for immediate re-election. In other words, no country can serve a term exceeding two consecutive

---

2 *Question of equitable representation on the Security Council and the Economic and Social Council*, GA Res 1991 A (XVIII), UNGAOR, 18th Sess, UN Doc A/Res/1991(XVIII) (1963) 21, enlarging the membership of the Security Council from eleven to fifteen and changing the required majority for its decisions from seven to nine.

years. Generally, countries wait for two full years before proposing their candidacy again. Governments may announce their candidacy one or several years in advance of elections just as they may do so during the elections.

What happens when the General Assembly cannot agree on the election of a non-permanent member of the Security Council? In theory, such a scenario should not occur because the General Assembly Rules of Procedure[3] require the voting to continue until all vacancies are filled. Nevertheless, the General Assembly has already faced such a deadlock. In 1979, Colombia and Cuba were competing for the last seat as a non-permanent member of the Security Council. After numerous inconclusive rounds of balloting, neither of these two states was able to obtain the two-thirds majority of votes in the General Assembly to secure a seat in the Security Council. Hence the Security Council remained short one member. Some delegations argued that the Security Council was not legally constituted and therefore could not lawfully convene or deliberate. A legal opinion was sought from the UN legal counsel, who opined that while the failure of the General Assembly to elect a non-permanent member of the Security Council was neither desirable nor consistent with Article 23 of the *UN Charter*, it could not affect the functioning and the legal constitution of the Council or the validity of its decisions:

> [A]n act of omission or the failure of the General Assembly to fulfil its constitutional obligations cannot be held to produce legal consequences so fundamental to the Organization as the paralysis of a principal organ. To argue otherwise would be to effect a constitutional amendment of the Charter through extra-constitutional means. Such a paralysis could have the gravest consequences for the whole system of the preservation of international peace and security, including a potential shift of well-established powers between the Security Council and the General Assembly.[4]

---

3 General Assembly Rules of Procedure, UN Doc A/520/Rev 18 at Rule 94 [General Assembly Rules of Procedure].

4 *Elections to fill vacancies in principal organs*, UNGAOR, 34th Sess, 118th Meeting, Agenda Item 15, UN Doc A/34/PV.118 (1979) at paras 31–32.

The deadlock was resolved when both Colombia and Cuba withdrew their candidacies and Mexico was elected as the fifteenth member of the Council.[5]

1) Election of Non-permanent Members

When electing non-permanent members of the Security Council, Article 23 of the *UN Charter* requires that due regard be given to two considerations. The first consideration is the proposed candidate's contribution to the maintenance of international peace and security and the second consideration is the equitable geographical distribution.

a) First Consideration: Contribution to the Maintenance of International Peace

The *UN Charter* does not specify the factors that should be taken into account when assessing a member state's contribution to the maintenance of international peace and security. From practice, it is known that countries facing UN sanctions[6] and countries involved in interstate or intrastate conflict[7] are less likely to be elected as non-permanent members of the Security Council. States with poor human rights records also have lower chances of being elected. In fact, human rights groups often lobby against such a country's election to the Security Council. Nevertheless, economic muscle and strategic partnerships still play an important role, which often results in the election of countries with a poor human rights record.

A state's inability to contribute to the maintenance of international peace and the high cost of campaigning for a Security Council seat may also be factors against its election. Some 63 out of 193 member states of the United Nations have never been elected as non-permanent members of the Security Council. Conversely, countries with solid

---

5 W Michael Reisman, "The Case of the Nonpermanent Vacancy" (1980) 74:4 *Am J Int'l L* 907.

6 James R Vreeland & Axel Dreher, *The Political Economy of the United Nations Security Council* (New York: Cambridge University Press, 2014) at 130–31.

7 *Ibid* at 145.

democratic regimes and spotless human rights records as well as countries that regularly contribute troops to UN peacekeeping missions have higher chances of being elected.[8] Similarly, countries with large populations or high GDP per capita are also more likely to be elected.

These considerations are not assessed by the General Assembly. As we will see below, candidates for a non-permanent membership in the Security Council are nominated by regional electoral groups. An assessment of a candidate's contribution to the maintenance of the peace is also done by the regional group of countries. Once these regional alliances have identified a suitable candidate for a Security Council membership, the General Assembly's role is generally reduced to a symbolic rubber-stamping exercise.

Although the ten rotating members of the Security Council do not have a veto right, they can nevertheless wield a lot of power and influence. For one, the Security Council often proceeds by consensus. Consensus-based decisions can be significantly influenced by debates. Therefore, even a small country can wield considerable influence over the outcome of a question if it presents cogent arguments in support of its position. Also, Security Council resolutions on non-procedural matters require at least nine affirmative votes (and no vetoes) to pass. Therefore, seven non-permanent members acting together have the ability to block Security Council decisions. It is not uncommon for resolutions to attract fewer than nine affirmative votes. This is particularly true in recent years due to a divide between Russia and China on the one hand and Western powers on the other related to the conflict in Syria. When the permanent members are divided, non-permanent members tend to emerge as a more powerful force. Finally, non-permanent members of the Security Council inevitably hold the presidency, which allows them to steer the agenda of the Security Council for the month. For these reasons, the election process of non-permanent members may generate strong reactions from UN member states. For instance, in 1965, Malaysia's election to the

8 Axel Dreher, Matthew Gould, Matthew D Rablen & James Raymond Vreeland, "The Determinants of Election to the United Nations Security Council" (2014) 158:1/2 *Public Choice* 51–83.

Security Council led to Indonesia's withdrawal from the UN membership as a sign of protest, even though it sought readmission two years later after the expiration of Malaysia's two-year term. Similarly, in October 2013, Saudi Arabia rejected a seat on the Security Council as a sign of protest, citing the double standards of the Security Council, namely its failure to take a clear stance in the conflict in Syria, to tackle the Israeli–Palestinian conflict and its inability to control the proliferation of weapons of mass destruction in the Middle East.

b) Second Consideration: Equitable Geographical Distribution

As described above, before 1966, there were only six non-permanent members of the Security Council. These six seats were typically distributed as follows: two seats were reserved for Latin American countries, one seat belonged to a country from the Middle East, one seat was attributed to Eastern Europe, and the remaining two were shared among the British Commonwealth countries.[9] In 1963, member states agreed to enlarge the Security Council and specified in broad terms the geographic distribution of non-permanent seats. Five seats were given to Asian and African states. Two seats were allocated to Latin American countries and two other seats were reserved for the Western Europe and Other States group.[10] Eastern European countries obtained one seat.

Since the Asian continent already had a permanent seat in the Security Council, African and Asian states informally agreed to divide their lot of five seats into three seats for Africa and two seats for Asia. Another informal agreement was reached in order to ensure that Arab countries were also represented at all times. Therefore, one seat was attributed to an Arab state with Asia and Africa taking turns every second year to provide an Arab seat from its divided lot.

The regional groups do not elect members of the Security Council; they only nominate candidates if all countries of the same region

9 Sam Daws, "The Origins and Development of UN Electoral Groups" in Ramesh Thakur, ed, *What Is Equitable Geographical Representation in the Twenty-First Century* (Tokyo: United Nations University, 1999) at 11–29.

10 The group called Western Europe and Other States includes Australia, Canada, New Zealand, Israel, and Turkey.

reach a consensus. Countries can nominate themselves without any regional support. This, however, is not likely to lead to favourable results for these countries. Essentially, regional groups control the process by nominating one candidate for the seat allocated to that region, thereby guaranteeing the election of their preferred candidate. When a regional group cannot agree on one single candidate, two contenders may agree to split the two-year term between themselves. In the 2017–2018 elections, Italy and the Netherlands were contesting a non-permanent seat in the Security Council. After five inconclusive rounds of balloting, with the fifth round deadlocked at ninety-five votes each, the two states agreed to split the two-year term. Their regional group—Western European and Others Group (WEOG)—endorsed the agreement and the General Assembly elected them for a one-year term each.

The practice of splitting terms began in 1955, when, after thirty-five rounds of inconclusive voting in the contest between the Philippines and former Yugoslavia, the president of the General Assembly convinced the two contenders to agree to a split term in order to break the impasse. The order in which each state assumed its half of the term was decided by drawing lots. Since the *UN Charter* does not expressly permit the splitting of a term, member states had to be creative. The Philippines agreed to withdraw from the current election and in return Yugoslavia promised to resign after one year, at which point the Philippines would run as the only candidate for the vacant seat. Similar arrangements were made during the 1960–1961 term when Turkey shared its term with Poland, during the 1961–1962 term when Ireland shared a term with Liberia, during the 1962–63 term when Romania shared a term with the Philippines, and in 1964–1965 when Czechoslovakia split a term with Malaysia.

The election of the non-permanent members of the Security Council is an important decision that requires a two-thirds majority of the members present and voting in the General Assembly. The Security Council is not involved in the election of its non-permanent members. Consequently, the permanent members of the Security Council cannot veto the election of non-permanent members. Nevertheless, permanent members of the Council "may have enough informal influence to occasionally block truly distasteful candidates from winning" the election process.[11] They influence the selection process in other ways in order to prevent the election of an unfriendly state or to ensure the election of an ally. The ultimate decision belongs to a two-thirds majority of the General Assembly.

B. FUNCTIONING OF THE SECURITY COUNCIL

This part examines the voting procedures of the Security Council, the way it holds its sessions and meetings, and its subsidiary bodies. It also discusses the role and powers of the Security Council president and the Secretariat.

1) Voting Procedures

The voting procedure in the Security Council has been a controversial topic even before the UN was created. During the Dumbarton Oaks conference held in 1944, it became clear that the veto would have to be included in the *UN Charter* if the major powers were to be parties to it.[12] Initially, the superpowers were unable to reach a compromise with regard to the voting procedure in the Security Council. The USSR wanted permanent members to have an absolute veto power in relation to all matters, including procedural questions, discussed by the Security Council. The USSR also wanted each permanent member to have the right to veto a proposal that concerned a dispute to which the permanent member was a party. The Soviets were concerned that they would be outnumbered in the Security Council and in the General Assembly by Western states and their allies. Therefore, they tried to retain the ability to block single-handedly a resolution in the Security Council. The United States and the United Kingdom were opposed to an absolute veto because they feared that it would allow Moscow to block any attempt to discuss disputes in which the

11 James R Vreeland & Axel Dreher, *The Political Economy of the United Nations Security Council* (New York: Cambridge University Press, 2014) at 94.

12 Frederic L Jr Kirgis, "The Security Council's First Fifty Years" (1995) 89:3 *Am J Int'l L* 506 at 507.

USSR was involved. They also believed that a permanent member should not be permitted to cast a vote when the Security Council was considering a dispute to which it was a party. Therefore, they reached a compromise agreeing that a permanent member would be able to veto a decision of the Security Council on non-procedural matters. They also included a mandatory abstention from voting on a dispute to which the permanent member was a party. Many small states were unhappy with this compromise. Although they were prepared to accept a permanent membership of the Big Five in the Security Council, they were reluctant to agree to a veto right reserved exclusively to permanent members. To reassure smaller states, the P5 states pointed out that non-permanent members of the Council acting collectively also had a veto power since they could jointly block any proposal under consideration. The founding states grudgingly accepted this compromise. The modalities of voting are set out in Article 27 of the *UN Charter*, which reads as follows:

1. Each member of the Security Council shall have one vote.
2. Decisions of the Security Council on procedural matters shall be made by an affirmative vote of nine members.
3. Decisions of the Security Council on all other matters shall be made by an affirmative vote of nine members including the concurring votes of the permanent members.

The first paragraph merely states the obvious: each member has one vote. Any other arrangement would have been inconsistent with the principle of sovereign equality of states enshrined in paragraph 2.1 of the *UN Charter*. The provisional Rules of Procedure of the Security Council contain only one provision relating to the voting procedure. This provision provides that "voting in the Security Council shall be in accordance with the relevant Articles of the *Charter* and of the Statute of the International Court of Justice." It is known from the practice of the Security Council that its members generally vote by a show of hands unless the vote relates to elections, such as the election of the Secretary-General and members of the International Court of Justice, in which case, the voting is conducted by secret ballot. Members of the Security Council can abstain, vote in favour, or vote against a resolution. They may choose to refrain from voting altogether or even be absent.

The second and third paragraphs of Article 27 of the *UN Charter* deal with the requirements for adopting decisions. Paragraph 2 deals with procedural questions. It specifies that a qualified majority of nine votes is required for decisions on procedural matters. The veto right of permanent members of the Security Council does not apply to decisions on procedural matters. Put differently, a permanent member cannot block the adoption of a resolution on a purely procedural matter. Paragraph 3, on the other hand, deals with substantive questions. It requires nine votes, which must include an affirmative vote of the permanent members on all matters that are not procedural. The exact phrase that the *UN Charter* uses in paragraph 3 of Article 27 is "other matters," which refers to non-procedural or substantive questions. The phrase "affirmative vote of the permanent members" refers to the veto power that China, France, Russia, the United Kingdom, and the United States have. In fact, the *UN Charter* does not expressly use the term "veto." All five permanent members have exercised the right of veto at one time or another. The veto power exists for two reasons. First, it was a way to incentivize the Big Powers to be part of the organization. Important responsibilities must be accompanied by corresponding rights or benefits. Second, the veto power ensures that the Security Council does not authorize action against any of its permanent members or their close allies. At first glance, the Security Council's inability to mandate action against a permanent member is a major handicap. However, a more thoughtful analysis reveals that it is a distinct advantage. The veto power may have been a decisive factor in preventing another world war, because instead of using force against each other, the superpowers can veto any proposed collective action against them. Without the veto power, superpowers would be compelled to resist collective action with force.

In order to determine whether the Security Council should vote in accordance with paragraph 2 or paragraph 3 of Article 27, members of the Security Council first need to decide whether the proposal they are voting on is procedural or substantive. The following question then arises: when voting on the preliminary question whether a matter is procedural or non-procedural, should the Council consider this question itself procedural or substantive? The answer to this question was provided in the authoritative statement by the four sponsoring governments on voting procedure in the Security Council[13] of 7 June 1945. Relying on the theory of "chain of events," the sponsoring governments argued that they could veto a decision as to whether a particular matter is procedural or substantive in nature. Essentially, permanent members of the Security Council appropriated the right to have a double veto. First, they could veto the determination that a draft resolution is procedural in nature in order to render it substantive and then veto it again, thereby blocking its adoption. Permanent members argued that because a preliminary question could trigger a chain of events that may eventually require the Council to resort to measures of enforcement under Chapter VII of the *UN Charter*, it requires the unanimity of the permanent members. They feared that substantive decisions would be falsely identified as procedural for the purposes of depriving permanent members of their veto power.

Although permanent members may veto a preliminary decision qualifying a matter as procedural, they are expected to exercise this right in good faith. In April 1949, noting the difficulties faced by the Security Council in agreeing on what constitutes procedural questions, the General Assembly offered a long list of matters that should normally be regarded as procedural.[14] Certain matters enumerated in the General Assembly resolution are unambiguously procedural, including the following questions:

- the inclusion or removal of an item in or from the agenda;
- the establishment of an order of items on the agenda;
- adjournment of a meeting;
- invitation of a non-member to participate in a discussion pursuant to Article 31 of the *Charter*.[15]

---

13 It was issued as a Security Council document on 4 May 1946 (S/Procedure/79).

14 *The Problem of Voting in the Security Council*, GA Res 267(III), UNGAOR, 3rd Sess, UN Doc A/Res/267(III) (1949) 7.

15 Article 31 of the *Charter of the United Nations* states that "Any Member of the United Nations which is not a member of the Security Council may participate,

Other matters listed in the resolution can have political repercussions. Specifically, the decision to submit to the General Assembly a question relating to the maintenance of international peace and security, the approval of credentials of representatives of Security Council members, the request to the Secretary-General to convene a special session of the General Assembly, and the appointment of a subsidiary committee[16] are not necessarily procedural. Imagine a resolution in which the Security Council decides to establish a fact-finding mission to investigate allegations of crimes against humanity that may have been committed during an armed conflict. While the establishment of the fact-finding mission may appear procedural, the characterization of its mandate appears to be a substantive matter. With time, the characterization of which questions are purely procedural lost a lot of its importance because consistent practice emerged, and permanent members of the Security Council have informally agreed on issues that should be qualified as procedural questions. The decision to include an agenda item, to convene or suspend a meeting, to call for an emergency session of the General Assembly, and to invite a concerned state to participate in Council meetings are deemed to be procedural.

Security Council resolutions and decisions may be adopted with or without a vote.[17] As we have already seen above, for any resolution or decision to be adopted by a vote, at least nine affirmative votes are required. Many resolutions are adopted unanimously, which gives the resolution a higher political legitimacy. A resolution or decision may also be adopted without a vote, in which case it is adopted either by consensus or by acclamation. For a resolution to be adopted by consensus or acclamation, the president of the Security Council must be satisfied that all members of the Security Council support the

without vote, in the discussion of any question brought before the Security Council whenever the latter considers that the interests of that Member are specially affected." This provision is under a section titled "Procedure."

16 Article 29 of the *Charter of the United Nations* reads: "The Security Council may establish such subsidiary organs as it deems necessary for the performance of its functions." This provision is under a section titled "Procedure," which strongly suggests that the matter is procedural.

17 Loraine Sievers & Sam Dows, *The Procedure of the UN Security Council*, 4th ed (Oxford, UK: Oxford University Press, 2014) at 336.

proposal and have agreed not to hold a formal voting process. Consensus and acclamation are also a sign of strong agreement or unanimity among Council members. In the Security Council's recent practice, resolutions are more frequently adopted without a vote.[18] Behind-the-scenes negotiations take place with the hope of reaching consensus. In cases where it becomes apparent that a permanent member of the Security Council is not likely to support the proposal, the member sponsoring the draft resolution will not bring it to a formal vote in order not to prompt a negative vote or veto. In some circumstances, where a permanent member of the Security Council threatens to veto a proposal, the sponsor of the draft resolution may nevertheless bring it to a vote. The reason for this strategy is to compel the permanent member to make a choice between obstructing an important proposal, thereby facing public embarrassment, or abstaining from voting in order to avoid public embarrassment. This strategy is known in international relations as "shaming," which has been defined as "moral criticism intended to induce a change in some state behavior without reliance on formal, legal processes."[19] Shaming efforts seek to convince permanent members that they should support a proposal, which in most cases relates to a humanitarian intervention, because of the embarrassment that they will suffer if they block action by willing states.[20] For instance, when the former dictator of Libya, Muammar Gaddafi, publicly declared that his army would show no mercy or compassion in fighting against the supporters of the Libyan revolution, it became obvious that the Security Council could either idly watch another massacre similar to Rwanda and Srebrenica take place in Libya or intervene on humanitarian grounds. The Arab League and the African Union were in favour of an intervention in Libya. Russia and China—who are against humanitarian interventions by the Security Council—opposed military action in Libya. It was by using the

---

18 Security Council Report, "In Hindsight: Consensus in the Security Council" (20 December 2013), online: www.securitycouncilreport.org/monthly-forecast/2014-01/in_hindsight_consensus_in_the_security_council.php.

19 Saira Mohamed, "Shame in the Security Council" (2013) 90:4 *Wash U L Rev* 1191 at 1200.

20 *Ibid* at 1194.

shaming strategy that other members of the Security Council were able to ensure that China and Russia abstained from voting on Resolution 1973.[21] Nevertheless, both states publicly voiced their concern about the decision to intervene in order to save face.[22]

a) Mandatory Abstention of a Member of the Security Council

There are two types of abstentions from voting in the Security Council. The first type is a voluntary abstention, which means that the member of the Security Council chooses not to cast a vote on a specific issue. In some cases, a voluntary abstention signals a lack of interest in a particular proposal. In other cases, the abstaining state does not agree with the proposal but does not want to be seen as an obstruction.

The second type of abstention is a mandatory abstention. It is the only limitation in the *UN Charter* imposed on a Security Council member participating in a vote. This limitation is found in Article 27.3, which states that "in decisions under Chapter VI, and under paragraph 3 of Article 52, a party to a dispute shall abstain from voting." In accordance with this provision, a Security Council member has an obligation to abstain from voting if the following conditions are met: (a) the proposed resolution is made pursuant to Chapter VI or paragraph 52.3 (in Chapter VIII) of the *UN Charter*; (b) the Security Council determined that a dispute (as opposed to a "situation") exists;[23] (c) the Security Council member concerned is party to the dispute; and (d) the decision the Security Council is about to make is not purely procedural.

This provision applies to all Council members including the five permanent members. It is not by chance that this restriction was placed in the same paragraph that grants the permanent members of the Council the veto right. This restriction was intended to remind the Big Five that they should not abuse their veto power by blocking

21 SC Res 1973 (2011), UNSCOR, 66th Year, UN Doc S/Res/1973 (2011) 1.

22 *Explanation of vote*, UNSCOR 6498th Meeting, UN Do. S/PV.6498 (2011).

23 *Legal Consequences for States of the Continued Presence of South Africa in Namibia (South West Africa) notwithstanding Security Council Resolution 276 (1970)*, Advisory Opinion, [1971] ICJ Rep 16 at para 26 [*Continued Presence of South Africa in Namibia*].

draft resolutions that adversely affected their interests. As a Chilean diplomat put it, paragraph 27.3 *in fine* "seeks to prevent a member of the Council from acting as judge in its own case."[24] In most cases, member states adhered to this obligation by abstaining when they were a party to the dispute. For example, in 1947, the United Kingdom abstained from voting on the Corfu Channel question when the Security Council recommended that the governments of Albania and the United Kingdom refer their dispute to the International Court of Justice.[25] From 1950 to 1952, India and Pakistan both abstained from participating in the vote on decisions that addressed their dispute. Argentina abstained from voting when the Security Council was considering the Eichmann question. However, at least on one occasion, a permanent member of the Security Council disregarded this restriction and vetoed a resolution that was averse to its interests. This occurred in 1948 when the USSR vetoed a resolution calling for an investigation of the Soviet aggression against the former Czechoslovakia. Article 27.3 does not require a Security Council member who is a party to a dispute to abstain when the Council takes decisions under Chapter VII of the *UN Charter*. For instance, the United Kingdom participated in the vote that resulted in the adoption of Security Council Resolution 502 (1982), which dealt with the Falkland Islands war between the United Kingdom and Argentina.

b) Voluntary Abstention of a Permanent Member of the Security Council

Under Article 27.3 of the *UN Charter*, decisions of the Security Council on all other matters shall be made by an affirmative vote of nine members, *including the concurring votes of the five permanent members.* Does the abstention of a permanent member of the Security Council during the vote preclude the Security Council from making a decision under paragraph 27.3 of the *UN Charter*? A literal interpretation of this rule, particularly the phrases "affirmative vote" and "concurrent votes" contained in the provision, would strongly suggest that unless

24 UNSCOR, 3rd Year, 303d Meeting, UN Doc S/PV.303 (1948) at 35.

25 SC Res 22 (1947), UNSCOR, 2nd Year, UN Doc S/Res/22 (1947).

all permanent members cast an affirmative vote, a decision under this provision cannot be made. A more pragmatic and purposeful interpretation of the rule would lead to a different conclusion. In particular, there is no reason for a permanent member of the Security Council not to veto a decision that it wishes to block. The failure to exercise its veto power suggests that the permanent member lacks interest in the matter to be decided or attempts to sabotage the functioning of the Security Council. Hence, an abstention should not be regarded as a negative vote.

In an advisory case on the legality of South Africa's continued presence in Namibia, South Africa challenged the validity of a Security Council resolution on the basis that two permanent members abstained from voting. South Africa contended that the resolution was invalid because it was not adopted by an affirmative vote of nine members, including the concurring votes of the permanent members, as required by Article 27.3 of the *UN Charter*. The Court dismissed this objection and held that the practice of voluntary abstention by a permanent member does not constitute a bar to the adoption of resolutions:

> However, the proceedings of the Security Council extending over a long period supply abundant evidence that presidential rulings and the positions taken by members of the Council, in particular its permanent members, have consistently and uniformly interpreted the practice of voluntary abstention by a permanent member as not constituting a bar to the adoption of resolutions. By abstaining, a member does not signify its objection to the approval of what is being proposed; in order to prevent the adoption of a resolution requiring unanimity of the permanent members, a permanent member has only to cast a negative vote. This procedure followed by the Security Council, which has continued unchanged after the amendment in 1965 of Article 27 of the *Charter*, has been generally accepted by Members of the United Nations and evidences a general practice of that Organization.[26]

26 *Continued Presence of South Africa in Namibia*, above note 23 at para 22.

c) Absence of a Permanent Member of the Security Council

The *Namibia* advisory opinion dealt with the *abstention* of a permanent member of the Security Council from voting. It did not deal with the *absence* of a permanent member during a vote. There may be circumstances where a permanent member of the Security Council is simply absent from the proceedings and could not have cast a vote. Such a situation first arose in 1946 when the Soviet representative decided to boycott the proceedings of the Security Council by not attending its meetings in relation to the Iranian complaint.[27] The USSR was operating under the erroneous assumption that its absence from the Security Council meetings would make it impossible for the Security Council to adopt any substantive resolution. However, despite the absence of the Soviet delegation, the Security Council continued adopting resolutions on the grounds that the absence was equivalent to an abstention from voting by a permanent member, and that the Council had no rule relating to a necessary quorum. In 1950, the representative of the USSR again boycotted a Security Council meeting because he was protesting against the participation of the representative of China.[28] However, this time, the USSR's absence would prove to be a costly mistake. During that specific meeting, the Security Council discussed the question of aggression against the Republic of Korea by North Korea. The Security Council adopted a resolution unfavourable to the USSR and its ally North Korea. The USSR challenged the legality of the resolution on the basis that it had not been adopted in conformity with Article 27 since the Soviet representative was absent. The remaining members of the Security Council disagreed with the Soviet position and upheld the validity of the resolution, concluding that the absence of a permanent member was not equivalent to a negative vote (or veto) under Article 27.3 of the *UN Charter*. They recalled that in 1946 it had been agreed that an absence from a meeting during the voting was tantamount to an abstention. It is now settled law that

---

27 For a detailed account of the Iranian complaint, see Chapter 1.

28 The Republic of China (ROC) joined the UN in 1945. Its government lost the Chinese Civil War and relocated to Taipei, Taiwan. The USSR did not recognize the government of the Republic of China as a legitimate representative of China in the UN.

unless a permanent member casts a negative vote, the veto right is not exercised under Article 27.3 of the *UN Charter*. A mere abstention from voting or absence from the meeting during a vote is not enough to block a decision by the Security Council.

While unanimity is not required for a resolution to be adopted, a unanimous vote increases the legitimacy and authoritative value of a Security Council resolution.[29] That is why some states invest a lot of effort and resources in trying to convince and sometimes exert pressure on other member states to vote in support of resolutions favourable to their interests or against resolutions adverse to their interests.

2) Types of Security Council Meetings

Unlike the General Assembly and the Economic and Social Council where a meeting can resume only if at least one third of the members are present, the Security Council does not have a quorum for a meeting to be convened. In theory, the president may open a meeting even if several members are absent. As long as nine members are present, they can vote in favour of a proposal that will then be adopted as a resolution. In practice, however, the president of the Security Council normally refrains from opening a meeting until all fifteen members are present in the Council Chamber. "In the rare instances when it has been necessary to proceed before all representatives are assembled, it has been the practice that a meeting may start with a small number of seats unfilled, on the assumption that those delegations have merely been delayed and will arrive shortly."[30] Three provisions of the *UN Charter* deal with the convening of meetings by the Security Council. These provisions provide:

Article 28

1. The Security Council shall be so organized as to be able to function continuously. Each member of the Security Council shall

---

29 Susan Hulton, "Council Working Methods and Procedure" in David Malone, ed, "The UN Security Council: From the Cold War to the 21st Century" (Boulder, CO: Lynne Rienner Publishing, 2004) at 237.

30 Sievers & Dows, above note 17 at 234.

for this purpose be represented at all times at the seat of the Organization.

2. The Security Council shall hold periodic meetings at which each of its members may, if it so desires, be represented by a member of the government or by some other specially designated representative.
3. The Security Council may hold meetings at such places other than the seat of the Organization as in its judgment will best facilitate its work.

The requirement to "be so organized as to be able to function continuously" does not mean that the Security Council must be in continuous meetings. It simply means that the Council must be able to convene a meeting at any time and on short notice. Security Council meetings are either regular or periodic.[31] Regular meetings are convened either at the request of a Security Council member or when a dispute or situation is brought to the attention of the Security Council under specific provisions of the *UN Charter*. Periodic meetings are supposed to be held twice a year but, in practice, such meetings are not held.[32]

The Security Council can meet either in formal or informal meetings. Formal meetings are normally open whereas informal meetings are closed.[33] In 2019, the Council held 243 public meetings and fifteen private meetings. Of these fifteen private meetings, thirteen were held with troop- and police-contributing countries and two were devoted to a briefing by the president of the ICJ and the situation in the Middle East. The Council also held a total of 135 consultations in 2019.[34] There is an official record of public meetings and these meetings are also covered by UNTV, UN webcam, and public media. Public meetings can be held under the following four formats:

---

31 Provisional Rules of Procedure, UN Doc S/96/Rev7 at Rules 1 and 4 [Provisional Rules of Procedure of the Security Council].

32 Sievers & Dows, above note 17 at 39–41.

33 Provisional Rules of Procedure of the Security Council, above note 31, art 48, states that "Unless it decides otherwise, the Security Council shall meet in public."

34 United Nations Security Council, "Highlights of Security Council Practice," online: www.un.org/securitycouncil/content/annual-highlight.

- "Open debate": briefings may or may not be conducted, and Council members may deliver statements. Non-members of the Council may also be invited to participate in the discussion upon their request under Rule 37 and other entities may be permitted to participate under Rule 39 of the Provisional Rules of Procedure;
- "Debate": briefings may be conducted, and Council members may deliver statements; non-Council members that are directly concerned or affected or have a special interest in the matter under consideration may be invited to participate in the discussion upon their request under Rule 37 of the Provisional Rules of Procedure;
- "Briefing": briefings are conducted, and Council members may deliver statements following briefings. Concerned Member States may, at their request, be invited to participate under Rule 37 of the Provisional Rules of Procedure;
- "Adoption": Council members may or may not deliver statements (known as explanation of vote) before or after adopting, *inter alia*, resolutions and presidential statements; non-Council members may or may not be invited to participate in the discussion upon their request under Rule 37 of the Provisional Rules of Procedure.[35]

For public meetings, the Security Council may invite states that are not members of the Council to participate, without the right to vote.[36] The Council may also invite individuals to participate in a meeting.[37]

The Security Council may also hold formal but private meetings. Such meetings are held infrequently (fewer than twenty per year)[38] and the minutes for these meetings are not accessible to the public.

---

35 Note by the president of the Security Council, UN Doc S/2017/507 (2017) [Note by the president of the Security Council].

36 Provisional Rules of Procedure of the Security Council, above note 31 at Rule 37.

37 Provisional Rules of Procedure of the Security Council, above note 31 at Rule 39.

38 Security Council Report, "Monthly Forecast October 2019" (30 September 2019) at 2, online: www.securitycouncilreport.org/atf/cf/%7B65BFCF9B-6D27-4E9C-8CD3-CF6E4FF96FF9%7D/2019_10_forecast.pdf.

Nevertheless, the Council issues a communiqué. The function of private meetings is to conduct discussions or take actions without the attendance of the public or the press. The only instance in which the Provisional Rules of Procedure require a private meeting is in connection with the Council's recommendation to the General Assembly regarding the appointment of the Secretary-General.[39] Private meetings are also held when discussing politically sensitive issues such as meetings with troop-contributing countries to UN peacekeeping missions. The annual briefing by the President of the International Court of Justice is also held in private. During private meetings, briefings and debates are carried out in a manner similar to that of public meetings. Council members may deliver statements and other UN member states or members of the Secretariat may be invited to be present or to participate in the discussion, including for the purpose of giving briefings to the Council, in accordance with Rule 37 or 39 of the Provisional Rules of Procedure.[40] Irrespective of whether the meeting is public or private, any formal meeting of the Security Council is entitled to verbatim coverage,[41] although access to the written record varies depending on whether the meeting was public or private.

In order to allow for frank briefings and discussions, the Council also holds informal meetings producing no official records. On the one hand, this confidentiality increases the efficiency of the meetings because member states can openly and freely voice their real concerns and reach common ground more quickly. On the other hand, the lack of transparency associated with these meetings affects their legitimacy. Between 2017 and 2019, there was a sharp increase in formal open meetings and a decrease in closed consultations. This trend has not been regarded as a positive development, as open formal meetings are frequently used for public posturing and playing to the gallery rather than for constructive discourse. This has given rise

39 Provisional Rules of Procedure of the Security Council, above note 31 at Rule 48, states that the appointment of the Secretary-General is a question that "shall be discussed and decided at a private meeting."

40 Note by the president of the Security Council, above note 35 at 8.

41 The preparatory work for formal meetings is conducted in informal consultations for which no public record exists.

to extensive debates among Council members to find a better balance between transparency on the one hand and effectiveness on the other.

The participation in informal meetings is strictly limited to the members of the Security Council, which deprives the Security Council of an opportunity to hear the views of interested parties and the wider membership. In 1994, to promote an exchange of ideas and information between Council members and other member states of the United Nations, the Security Council agreed to have recourse to open meetings, in particular at an early stage in its consideration of a subject.[42]

UN PHOTO/KIM HAUGHTON
A wide view of the Security Council meeting on security challenges in the Mediterranean (17 November 2017). Permission for use granted by The United Nations.

Security Council meetings are normally held in the Security Council Chamber at UN headquarters in New York or in the Security Council Consultations Room. The Council may decide to meet in another conference room or even away from headquarters. Under

42 Statement by the president of the Security Council, UN Doc: S/PRST/1994/81 (1994).

Article 28.3 of the *UN Charter*, the "Security Council may hold meetings at such places other than the seat of the Organization as in its judgment will best facilitate its work." Meetings away from headquarters are very infrequent.

In 1992, another form of an informal meeting was devised by the former Permanent Representative of Venezuela, Diego Arria. During the armed conflict in the former Yugoslavia, a Croatian priest arrived in New York and requested a face-to-face meeting with Security Council members. Only Ambassador Arria, who during the relevant period held the presidency of the Security Council, agreed to meet him. Impressed with the priest's account of the events, Arria wanted other members of the Security Council to hear the story. However, testimonies from individuals were not permissible in any format of the Security Council's meetings. Therefore, Arria organized an informal gathering to which he invited the interested members of the Council. This practice was institutionalized. Today, the Security Council regularly meets in Arria-formula meetings. The main characteristics of Arria-formula meetings are the following: (a) these meetings do not constitute an activity of the Security Council; (b) attendance is entirely optional for Security Council members; (c) Arria meetings are convened by those who organize it and not by the Secretariat; (d) Arria meetings take place in conference rooms as opposed to the Security Council Consultation Room.[43] Initially, these meetings were confidential and open only to invitees. The format of Arria meetings changed in August 2016, when a meeting on Syria was webcast live for the first time. Since then, all Arria meetings are webcast.

3) Presidency of the Security Council

The presidency of the Security Council is limited in terms of time and authority. Each member of the Security Council holds the presidency for a period of one calendar month in the English alphabetical order of their names.[44] The main benefits for such a short mandate

---

43 Sievers & Dows, above note 17 at 76.

44 Provisional Rules of Procedure of the Security Council, above note 31 at Rule 18.

are: an opportunity for each member to highlight its priorities and an opportunity to learn how the Council functions. This enhanced understanding lasts long after a presidency has ended, and thus, month by month, the presidential rotation strengthens the proficiency of the Council as a whole.[45]

The powers of the president of the Security Council are set out in the Provisional Rules of Procedure of the Security Council, in various decisions of the Security Council or derive from its unwritten practice. These powers fall into two categories.

First, the president is responsible for the conduct and running of the Security Council meetings. In essence, he or she presides over meetings of the Council. The president has the authority to call a meeting of the Council at any time he or she deems necessary, enjoying a degree of discretion as to the times at which such meetings are held. He or she also approves the provisional agenda prepared by the Secretary-General for each Security Council meeting. The president invites representatives in the order in which they have expressed their desire to speak. He or she may also rule on a point of order raised by a representative. If two or more amendments to a motion or draft resolution are proposed, the president may rule on the order in which they are to be voted on. The president also has the authority to make statements when a decision is adopted without a vote. In such cases, the president reads a carefully prepared statement confirming that the Security Council reached a consensus and unanimously adopted a decision. The president would not make such a statement without ascertaining beforehand that all Security Council members have agreed to support it.

Second, the president is the spokesperson and representative of the Security Council in its relations with other organs, member states of the United Nations, or parties to a dispute.[46] The Security Council may explicitly or implicitly require its president to undertake

45 Sievers & Dows, above note 17 at 111.

46 Provisional Rules of Procedure of the Security Council, above note 31 at Rule 19, provide that the president, "under the authority of the Security Council, shall represent it in its capacity as an organ of the United Nations."

consultations, mediation, or good offices on its behalf in order to propose a means for a peaceful settlement of disputes. The president represents the Council in the General Assembly, in ECOSOC, and in interactions with the Secretary-General of the UN. Written communications from and to the Security Council are signed by or addressed to the president. Public statements on Security Council-related matters are also part of the president's responsibility.

4) Subsidiary Bodies of the Security Council

Under Article 29 of the *UN Charter* and Rule 28 of its Provisional Rules of Procedure, the Security Council is authorized to establish subsidiary bodies as needed for the performance of its functions. The *UN Charter* does not define the term "subsidiary organs." This phrase may be construed restrictively or broadly. The narrow meaning of the term refers to "bodies which are under the Council's direct authority and composed of some or all Council members."[47] A broader interpretation of the same term would "include peacekeeping operations, tribunals, commissions, special representatives, good offices missions, an ombudsperson, sanctions monitoring groups, and other individuals or groups requested to perform specified tasks."[48] The Military Staff Committee is the only subsidiary body that is mentioned in the *UN Charter*. The Security Council creates additional subsidiary organs through resolutions. It established a number of subsidiary bodies that are under its direct authority and are composed of some or all Council members. Some bodies are called committees while others are called working groups. There is no hierarchy between the two categories of subsidiary bodies.[49] The legal status of both types of subsidiary organs is identical and they both arrive at their decisions

47 Sievers & Dows, above note 17 at 460.

48 *Ibid.*

49 *Ibid* at 463.

by consensus. The mandate of subsidiary organs can range from purely procedural matters[50] to substantive issues.[51]

Other subsidiary bodies of the Security Council are international criminal tribunals. Although *ad hoc* international criminal tribunals, such as the ICT for Rwanda[52] and ICT for Yugoslavia,[53] were subsidiary bodies of the Security Council and were dependent on the UN for administrative and financial support, they were nevertheless judicial entities and entirely independent of any one state or group of states, including the Security Council. Another category of subsidiary bodies are peace operations, which consist of either peacekeeping missions or (special) political missions.[54]

---

50 For instance, in 1993, the Security Council established an "Informal Working Group on Documentation and Other Procedural Questions" to improve the process by which the Council addresses issues concerning its documentation and other procedural questions.

51 Subsidiary bodies that deal with substantive issues include the Counter-Terrorism Committee, established in 2001 pursuant to the Security Council Resolution 1373 (2001); the Committee on non-proliferation of nuclear, biological, and chemical weapons, established pursuant to Resolution 1540 (2004); the multitude of Sanctions Committees; the Working Group on Children and Armed Conflict established pursuant to Resolution 1612 (2005), etc.

52 The Security Council established the International Criminal Tribunal for Rwanda (ICTR) in 1994 to prosecute individuals responsible for genocide and other serious violations of international humanitarian law committed in Rwanda and on the territory of neighbouring states between 1 January and 31 December 1994. This tribunal became the first international court to hand down a verdict and sentence on the crime of genocide.

53 The Security Council created the International Criminal Tribunal for the former Yugoslavia (ICTY) in 1993 to prosecute individuals responsible for massive violations of humanitarian law during the armed conflict in the former Yugoslavia. This tribunal became the first international court to prosecute international war crimes since the Nuremberg and Tokyo tribunals at the end of the Second World War.

54 While peacekeeping missions are led by the UN Department of Peacekeeping Operations, political missions are led by the UN Department of Political and Peacebuilding Affairs.

5) Secretariat of the Security Council

Direct support to the Security Council is provided by the Security Council Affairs Division (SCAD), which is the largest organizational unit of the Department of Political and Peacebuilding Affairs (DPPA). The mandate of the SCAD is to facilitate the deliberations of and decision making by the Council. The division's responsibilities include (a) provision of secretariat services during formal and informal meetings of the Security Council; (b) processing of Security Council records and documents, such as volumes of resolutions, letters from or to the President of the Security Council, the provisional program of work, the daily program and agenda; (c) provision of substantive support to expert groups, including guidance on the scope of their mandates and applicable evidentiary standards; (d) preparation of procedural briefs, annual reports, and the Repertoire of the practice of the Security Council; and (e) provision of advice on rules of procedure, protocol, and practice of the Security Council and its subsidiary organs, such as the sanctions committees and the Counter-Terrorism Committee. The division also provides guidance to the Security Council's rotating monthly presidency, ensures that draft resolutions and presidential statements are ready for adoption in all official languages, publishes and disseminates letters and decisions, and performs any other function that an effective functioning of the Security Council may require. The division holds the institutional memory of the Security Council. Headed by a director at the D-2 level, it employs approximately 100 staff members and over sixty experts on behalf of Security Council Sanctions Committees. The SCAD consists of the following branches: the Security Council Secretariat Branch; the Security Council Subsidiary Organs Branch; the Security Council Practices and *Charter* Research Branch; and the Military Staff Committee Secretariat.

C. POWERS AND RESPONSIBILITIES OF THE SECURITY COUNCIL

The Council's primary responsibility is to maintain or restore international peace and security. It is by virtue of this responsibility that the Security Council has broad powers. The *UN Charter* empowers the Council to impose legally binding mandatory measures, commonly known as "sanctions," to call for cease fires, to authorize military action on behalf of the UN and all member states, and to set up international criminal tribunals to prosecute war crimes and crimes against humanity. The Council has other important powers that it shares with the General Assembly. These include the admission of a country as a new member state of the UN, the appointment of the Secretary-General, and the election of judges to the International Court of Justice. Some powers held by the Security Council are implied, which means that they are not expressly provided for in the *UN Charter* but are nevertheless necessary to fulfill the Security Council's primary responsibility to maintain international peace and security.[55] For example, the *UN Charter* does not envisage the establishment of *ad hoc* international criminal tribunals and does not confer the responsibility to appoint judges and prosecutors to the Security Council. The *UN Charter* does not contain any provision expressly authorizing the Security Council to deploy peacekeeping troops. These powers "arise by necessary intendment out of the Charter."[56]

It is interesting to note that the powers of the Security Council are mostly directed at the parties to a dispute or conflict. For instance, in accordance with Article 33.2 of the *UN Charter*, the Security Council *shall*, when it deems necessary, call upon the parties to a dispute to settle it by peaceful means. Pursuant to Article 40 of the *UN Charter*, it may call upon the parties to a dispute to comply with such provisional measures as it deems necessary or desirable. Also, Articles 36.1 and 37.2 of the *UN Charter* empower the Council to recommend at any stage of a dispute or a situation of like nature appropriate procedures or methods of adjustment or such terms of settlement as it may consider appropriate. The Council may also make recommendations or decide on measures not involving the use of armed force under Articles 39 and 41 of the *UN Charter*. It may decide on such military

55 See *Reparation for Injuries Suffered in the Service of the United Nations*, Advisory Opinion, [1949] ICJ Rep 174 at 180, 184 [*Reparation for Injuries*], and *Effect of awards of compensation made by the UN Administrative Tribunal*, Advisory Opinion, [1954] ICJ Rep 47 at 57.

56 *Reparation for Injuries*, above note 55 at 184.

action as may be necessary to maintain or restore international peace and security under Articles 39 and 42 of the *UN Charter*.

While the Security Council has extensive powers, it also has important responsibilities. Nonetheless, unlike its powers (which are directed at the parties), its responsibilities are owed to the UN wider membership. More specifically, the obligations that the Security Council has towards all member states of the UN include the responsibility to act on behalf of all UN member states in carrying out its duties for the maintenance of international peace and security,[57] the obligation to submit to them plans for the establishment of a system for the regulation of armaments,[58] the obligation to ensure continuous functioning of the Security Council, the duty to convene periodic meetings, and determine the venue of its meetings.[59]

Vis-à-vis the General Assembly, the Security Council has some recommendatory powers and some procedural obligations. Measures in connection with the General Assembly include the power to bring before the General Assembly questions relating to the maintenance of international peace and security,[60] the power to make recommendations to the General Assembly about the admission, suspension, or expulsion of Members,[61] the obligation to submit annual and special reports to the General Assembly, the power to make recommendations on the appointment of the Secretary-General,[62] etc.

All of the Security Council's powers derive from its primary responsibility to maintain international peace and security.[63] In exercising this power, the Security Council has the authority to determine the existence of any threat to the peace, breach of the peace, or act of aggression.[64] It has an unlimited discretion to determine what constitutes a threat to international peace. Once it determines that a particular situation

57 *Charter of the United Nations*, above note 1, art 24.1.
58 *Ibid*, art 26.
59 *Ibid*, art 28.
60 *Ibid*, art 11.2.
61 *Ibid*, arts 4–6.
62 *Ibid*, art 97.
63 *Ibid*, art 24.1.
64 *Ibid*, art 39.

constitutes a threat to international peace and security, the Security Council may either make recommendations or decide on measures to be taken in accordance with Articles 41 and 42 of the *UN Charter* in order to maintain or restore international peace and security.[65]

1) Making Recommendations Under Chapter VI of the *UN Charter*

When exercising powers under Chapter VI of the *UN Charter*, the Security Council may "call upon the parties to settle their dispute"[66] peacefully, "investigate any dispute, or any situation which might lead to international friction or give rise to a dispute, in order to determine whether the continuance of the dispute or situation is likely to endanger the maintenance of international peace and security,"[67] "recommend appropriate procedures or methods of adjustment" for resolving a dispute or situation through peaceful means,[68] and recommend terms of settlement of a dispute.[69] Decisions and recommendations listed in Chapter VI are not legally enforceable. This does not mean these resolutions are not legally binding or have no legal effect. The International Court of Justice ruled that

> [t]he language of a resolution of the Security Council should be carefully analysed before a conclusion can be made as to its binding effect. In view of the nature of the powers under Article 25, the question whether they have been in fact exercised is to be determined in each case, having regard to the terms of the resolution to be interpreted, the discussions leading to it, the Charter provisions invoked and, in general, all circumstances that might assist in determining the legal consequences of the resolution of the Security Council.[70]

To determine whether a resolution is legally binding or mandatory in nature, one must always have recourse to techniques of

65 *Ibid.*
66 *Ibid*, art 33.2.
67 *Ibid*, art 34.
68 *Ibid*, art 36.1.
69 *Ibid*, art 37.2.
70 *Continued Presence of South Africa in Namibia*, above note 23 at para 114.

statutory interpretation. The literal meaning of the terms used in the resolution is important. For instance, it is clear that if the Security Council resolution uses such terms as "demands," "requires," "requests," and "decides," the relevant portion of the resolution has a legally binding effect. Where some parts of the resolution use such terms as "urges," "calls upon," or "encourages," that portion of the resolution is not intended to produce a binding effect. Nevertheless, a prudent reader must always examine the context in which the resolution was proposed, negotiated, and adopted. The exact provisions of the *UN Charter* to which the resolution makes reference are also important considerations in determining the binding nature of the decision. Typically, a resolution may occasionally refer to Chapter VI or Chapter VII. Resolutions adopted under Chapter VI normally contain non-binding measures and recommendations, except for investigations carried out under Article 34 of the *UN Charter.*

Member states are normally expected to follow voluntarily Security Council recommendations. If, however, a member state disregards the recommendation, the Security Council would be unable to enforce it. The only way to ensure full compliance with a Security Council recommendation is to pass a new resolution under Chapter VII or include in the text of the resolution some imperative language, thereby converting the recommendation into a binding decision. However, even legally binding resolutions of the Security Council are not self-executing in the sense that they cannot be directly enforced by the Security Council within the jurisdiction of UN member states.[71] For a resolution to become enforceable in the internal legal order of a state, it needs to be translated into domestic law in accordance with the legal system of each nation. In the constitution of some states (known as monist states), international law does not need to be transposed into national law. In monist legal systems, international law automatically becomes part of the national legal order. However, this

71 See "*Question whether a transnational corporation is legally obligated to comply with or to observe a United Nations resolution—Legal character of United Nations resolutions*" in Selected Legal Opinions of the United Nations Secretariat and related intergovernmental organizations, *United Nations Juridical Yearbook*, part 2, chapter 5 (New York: UN, 1983).

direct application is limited to treaties and international customary law and does not extend to Security Council resolutions. Consequently, even monist states need to incorporate Security Council resolutions into their domestic law so that they become not only binding but also enforceable.

In some cases, even a mere recommendation of the Security Council may be legally binding. Specifically, the Council's recommendations on the admission of new members or on the appointment of a Secretary-General are mandatory and cannot be ignored. The UN practice leaves no doubt that such recommendations have always been followed by the General Assembly and have a binding effect.

2) Taking Measures Not Involving Use of Armed Force[72]

To maintain or restore international peace and security, the Security Council has the authority to impose measures not involving the use of armed force. This power is found in Chapter VII of the *UN Charter*, which means that the measures are binding on all member states and can be enforced. To impose enforcement measures not involving armed force, the Security Council does not need to determine that a breach of the peace or an aggression has occurred. A mere threat to international peace and security is sufficient. Thus, measures can be (and have been) taken pre-emptively. The provision that empowers the Security Council to take such measures is Article 41 of the *UN Charter*, which provides as follows:

> The Security Council may decide what measures not involving the use of armed force are to be employed to give effect to its decisions, and it may call upon the Members of the United Nations to apply such measures. These may include complete or partial interruption of economic relations and of rail, sea, air, postal, telegraphic, radio, and other means of communication, and the severance of diplomatic relations.[73]

---

72 The author would like to acknowledge and express his gratitude for Rafael Ruschel's contribution to the section on measures taken by the Security Council.

73 *Charter of the United Nations*, above note 1, art 41.

During the Cold War, the Security Council was able to impose enforcement measures under Article 41 of the *UN Charter* only twice, because the five permanent members of the Council rarely agreed on any important issue.[74] Between 1945 and 1990, measures were imposed against Southern Rhodesia and South Africa only.[75] However, after the fall of the Soviet Union, the Security Council intensified its use of measures under Article 41 of the *UN Charter*. Since 1990, it has imposed sanctions to support peaceful transitions, deter non-constitutional changes, constrain terrorism, protect human rights, and promote non-proliferation of nuclear weapons. With the end of the Cold War, collective enforcement measures increased not only in frequency but also in variety. Acting under Article 41 of the *UN Charter*, the Security Council determined the responsibility of states for breaching Article 2.4 of the *UN Charter*,[76] set up frameworks for the interim administration of Kosovo,[77] established compensation commissions[78]

---

74 Malcolm Shaw, *International Law*, 5th ed (Cambridge, UK: Cambridge University Press, 2003) at 4.

75 In 1966 the Council adopted a mandatory embargo against the Rhodesian regime opposing the Unilateral Declaration of Independence from the United Kingdom by the white minority regime, and in 1977 the Council approved a mandatory arms embargo against South Africa in response to the maintenance of apartheid, as well as the South African government's acts of aggression against neighbouring states.

76 *Charter of the United Nations*, above note 1, art 2.4: "The Organization and its Members, in pursuit of the Purposes stated in Article 1, shall act in accordance with the following Principles. (. . .) 4. All Members shall refrain in their international relations from the threat or use of force against the territorial integrity or political independence of any state, or in any other manner inconsistent with the Purposes of the United Nations." In its Resolution 687 (1991), UN Doc S/RES/687(1991), the Security Council reaffirmed Iraq's liability under international law for any direct loss or damage, including environmental damage and the depletion of natural resources, or injury to foreign governments, nationals, and corporations, resulting from Iraq's unlawful invasion and occupation of Kuwait.

77 SC Res 1244 (1999), UNSCOR, 54th Year, UN Doc S/Res/1244 (1999) 1 [SC Res 1244 (1999)].

78 SC Res 692 (1991), UNSCOR, 46th Year, UN Doc S/Res/692 (1991) (establishing the United Nations Compensation Fund to pay compensation for claims that resulted from direct loss or damage, including environmental damage and the depletion of natural resources, or injury to foreign governments, nationals

and *ad hoc* international criminal tribunals,[79] demarcated maritime boundaries,[80] froze assets of and imposed travel bans on individuals,[81] introduced a limit for importing refined petroleum products,[82] imposed a ban on all member states to issue work permits to nationals of the recalcitrant party,[83] to name just a few. The Security Council has used its Article 41 powers under the *UN Charter* to impose enforcement measures approximately thirty times since the end of the Cold War. Currently, the following fourteen sanctions regimes are in force.

No	Sanctions Regime	Description	Target of Sanctions	Date
1.	Somalia	Arms embargo, assets freeze, travel ban, charcoal ban.	Individuals who undermine peace, security, or stability of Somalia, obstruct the delivery of humanitarian aid, recruit children in armed conflicts, target civilians, support al-Shabaab, or misappropriate financial resources in Somalia.	1992–
2.	Al-Qaeda, ISIL	Arms embargo, assets freeze, travel ban.	Individuals and entities associated with al-Qaeda and ISIL.	1999–
3.	Iraq	Arms embargo and assets freeze.	Individuals or entities who were related to or associated with Saddam Hussein's regime.	2003–
4.	Democratic Republic of the Congo	Arms embargo, assets freeze, travel ban.	Non-governmental armed groups and individuals operating in DRC territory.	2003–

and corporations, resulting from Iraq's unlawful invasion and occupation of Kuwait).

79 See SC Res 827 (1993) establishing the International Criminal Tribunal for the former Yugoslavia, UNSCOR, 48th Year, UN Doc S/Res/ 827 (1993) 1; see also SC Res 955 (1994), UNSCOR, 49th Year, UN Doc S/Res/955 (1994) 1.

80 See SC Res 833 (1993), UNSCOR, 48th Year, UN Doc S/Res/833 (1993) 1.

81 See SC Res 1718 (2006), UNSCOR, 61st Year, UN Doc S/Res/1718 (2006) 1.

82 SC Res 2375 (2017), UNSCOR, 72nd Year, UN Doc S/Res/2375 (2017) 1.

83 *Ibid.*

No	Sanctions Regime	Description	Target of Sanctions	Date
5.	Sudan	Arms embargo, assets freeze, travel ban.	Individuals who impede the peace process or constitute a threat to stability in Darfur and the surrounding region. Individuals who commit violations of international humanitarian or human rights law or other atrocities.	2005–
6.	Lebanon	Assets freeze, travel ban.	Individuals suspected of involvement in the 14 February 2005 terrorist bombing that killed the Lebanese prime minister Rafiq Hariri.	2005–
7.	Democratic People's Republic of Korea (North Korea)	Embargo on arms and related materiel, coal, minerals, fuel, food and agricultural products, earth, stone, wood, industrial machinery, transportation vehicles, seafood, textiles, and luxury goods. Restrictions on DPRK's access to energy sources, financial sanctions, a travel ban, and assets freeze. Ban on providing work authorizations for DPRK nationals as well as a ban on procuring statues from the DPRK.	DPRK and designated individuals.	2017–

No	Sanctions Regime	Description	Target of Sanctions	Date
8.	Libya	Arms embargo, travel ban, assets freeze, illicit export of petroleum.	Individuals and entities involved in or complicit in ordering, controlling, or otherwise directing the commission of serious human rights abuses against persons in Libya, including by being involved in or complicit in planning, commanding, ordering, or conducting attacks, in violation of international law, including aerial bombardments on civilian populations and facilities.	2011–
9.	Taliban	Arms embargo, assets freeze, travel ban.	Individuals associated with the Taliban and who constitute a threat to the peace, stability, and security of Afghanistan. Specifically, individuals, groups, and entities who support the activities of the Taliban.	2011–
10.	Guinea-Bissau	Travel ban.	Individuals seeking to prevent the restoration of the constitutional order or taking action that undermines stability in Guinea-Bissau, in particular those who played a leading role in the coup d'état of 12 April 2012.	2012–
11.	Central African Republic	Arms embargo, assets freeze, travel ban.	Individuals and entities who violate human rights and humanitarian law, commit sexual offenses and gender-based violence, recruit child soldiers, provide support to armed groups and criminal networks, obstruct delivery of humanitarian aid, plan or take part in attacks against the UN, etc.	2013–

No	Sanctions Regime	Description	Target of Sanctions	Date
12.	Yemen	Assets freeze and travel ban.	Individuals and entities engaging in or providing support for acts that threatened the peace, security, or stability of Yemen.	2014–
13.	South Sudan	Arms embargo, assets freeze, travel ban.	Individuals who attempt to perpetuate the conflict, undermine the political process, jeopardize the transitional agreements, target civilians, commit sexual offenses, obstruct the activities of the international community, and recruit child soldiers.	2015–
14.	Mali	Assets freeze, travel ban.	Individuals and entities engaging in hostilities and hindering the implementation of the Agreement on Peace and Reconciliation in Mali, signed in 2015. Individuals who target civilians, commit sexual offenses, obstruct the activities of the international community, and obstruct delivery of humanitarian aid, and recruit child soldiers.	2017–

A sanctions regime imposed by the Security Council can be comprehensive or targeted, also known as smart. Comprehensive sanctions refer to measures that seek to prevent the flow of all commodities and products to and from a specific state. In other words, they are general trade embargoes affecting the entire population of the country. In most cases, the Security Council exempts from comprehensive sanctions the import of humanitarian supplies such as medicine, educational material, and petroleum. Comprehensive sanctions are broad-spectrum measures that produce an impact on all economic sectors. During the 1990s, comprehensive economic sanctions proved to be ineffective and often had unintended adverse consequences on the most vulnerable segments of the targeted state's population. The impact of the Security Council sanctions on the civilian populations of Iraq and Haiti sparked a debate on their appropriateness. To yield the desired effects without causing collateral damage to civilians, the Security Council had to revise its approach to sanctions not involving force. It replaced comprehensive broad-spectrum sanctions with more targeted and sectoral sanctions. The purpose of targeted sanctions is to exert pressure on the belligerents and policymakers most directly responsible for reprehensible acts and policies. Generally, the target of the new generation of sanctions is the elite of the recalcitrant country or the leaders of terrorist groups as opposed to the entire population of the country.[84] Also, smart sanctions are sectoral in the sense that they prohibit other states from exporting to the target state a specific category of commodities or products. Specific items covered by such sanctions have included arms, weapons, aircrafts, diamonds, financial services, and travel bans, as well as the severance of diplomatic relations. Normally, several measures are used together to strengthen a sanctions regime. Typically, arms embargoes, asset freezes, and travel bans are almost invariable part of measures currently in force. Security Council measures under Article 41 of the *UN Charter* can be directed not only against states and their governments but also against non-state actors such as terrorist organizations, rebel groups, and individual politicians or policymakers of the target state.

The objective of arms embargoes is to deny to warring parties weapons, ammunition, and hardware required to engage in armed conflict. The purpose of commodity sanctions is to deprive states, entities, and individuals of an important source of income that may be used to finance hostilities. Financial sanctions may include asset freezing and restrictions on financial transactions targeting certain individuals or entities. Their intended purpose is to deny to the banks

---

84 David Cortright, George A Lopez & Linda Gerber-Stellingwerf, "The Sanctions Era: Themes and Trends in UN Security Council Sanctions since 1990" in Vaughan Lowe, Adam Roberts, Jennifer Welsh & Dominik Zaum, eds, *The United Nations Security Council and War: The Evolution of Thought and Practice since 1945* (Oxford, UK: Oxford University Press, 2008) at 213.

of a targeted state access to international financial markets, foreign currency, and liquidity. Travel bans may include measures denying visas, bans on all flights, imposition of no-fly zones prohibiting the use of airspace.

Even though the terms "measure" and "sanction" are used interchangeably, a measure within the meaning of Article 41 of the *UN Charter* is not always a sanction. The word "sanction" denotes a punitive measure imposed for a breach of a legal norm. However, a measure under Article 41 of the *UN Charter* does not always require a breach of any legal norm and is not necessarily punitive in nature. Some measures are taken to give effect to Security Council's decisions. For instance, in case of an internal armed conflict, the Security Council may decide to impose an arms embargo on all concerned parties. The purpose of an arms embargo is not punitive; it is to deny the parties the tools of war. Such a measure cannot be regarded as a sanction because it is a preventive measure necessary to restore peace or to de-escalate violence.

It is also important not to confound measures that the Security Council imposes under Article 41 of the *UN Charter* on behalf of the international community with sanctions, countermeasures, and reprisals that individual member states adopt to address an international wrong. Unilateral sanctions can be imposed by one state against another state or by several states against one or several other states. Such measures are not taken on behalf of the international community; they are unilateral or multilateral actions. They do not require the Security Council's approval. The most widely used forms of unilateral or multilateral sanctions are trade restrictions in the form of embargoes or boycotts and the interruption of financial and investment flow between the sanctioning state and the target country.

Unless a measure is authorized by the Security Council, it is not adopted in accordance with the *UN Charter*. For instance, the Security Council did not authorize sanctions imposed by the United States, Canada, Australia, and many European states on Russia for its annexation of Crimea. Such sanctions would not have been authorized by the Security Council because Russia would have vetoed any proposed collective action or measure against it. In April 2020, Russia tabled a resolution pledging "not to apply any unilateral coercive measures undertaken without the mandate of the Security Council."[85] But this resolution was defeated.

In the eyes of the *UN Charter*, imposing sanctions on another state without the Security Council approval is a form of unilateralism. The question of whether unilateral sanctions, countermeasures, or retaliation are legal is controversial. On the one hand, they are not expressly prohibited by the *UN Charter*. On the other hand, they are inconsistent with the spirit of the *UN Charter* and the international legal order as it currently exists. Powerful nations frequently employ sanctions not authorized by the Security Council in order to impose their will on smaller or economically weaker states. This constitutes political bullying and has no legitimacy in international law. In some cases, imposing unilateral sanctions or reprisals against another state may constitute a manifest violation of an international obligation. For instance, all signatories of the *Charter of the Organization of American States* agreed not to use or encourage the use of coercive measures of an economic or political nature in order to force the will of another state.[86] Any signatory of the OAS *Charter* would breach this international obligation by imposing sanctions against another signatory of the same treaty. Similarly, economic sanctions not authorized by the Security Council can potentially be inconsistent with several provisions of the GATT,[87] including the provisions known as "the Most-Favoured-Nation Treatment"[88] and "the National Treatment."[89]

---

85 *Declaration of solidarity of the United Nations in the face of the challenges posed by the coronavirus disease 2019 (COVID-19)*, UNGAOR, 74th Sess, Agenda Item 126, UN Doc A/74/L.51 (2020) 1 at para 7.

86 Article 20 of the *Charter of the Organization of American States* signed in Bogota in 1948 and amended by the Protocol of Buenos Aires in 1967, by the Protocol of Cartagena de Indias in 1985, by the Protocol of Washington in 1992, and by the Protocol of Managua in 1993.

87 *General Agreement on Tariffs and Trade 1994*, Annex 1A to the Marrakesh Agreement Establishing the World Trade Organization, 15 April 1994, 1867 UNTS 154 (entered into force 1 January 1955).

88 The Most Favoured Nation is a treaty obligation to treat goods imported from one member state no less favourably than goods imported from another member state. Imposing economic sanctions (embargoes) on a member state inevitably results in a less favourable treatment of that state's goods.

89 Under this principle, a member state cannot treat goods from another member state less favourably than domestic goods. By imposing economic sanctions

By contrast, sanctions authorized by the Security Council would be lawful under the GATT.[90]

Another point worth mentioning under this topic is the monitoring mechanisms that are part of any modern sanctions regime. These monitoring mechanisms started appearing in the 1990s, when the UN realized that a sanctions regime can be circumvented and can be disproportionately harmful to the civilian population without some sort of continuous monitoring and fine-tuning. In 1992, the Security Council established, for the first time, a committee to ensure an effective implementation of the embargo on all deliveries of weapons and military equipment to Somalia.[91] This practice has been extended to most subsequent sanctions regimes. Today, these monitoring bodies are known as sanctions committees. Composed of the same fifteen Security Council member states, they supervise the implementation of measures instructed by Security Council resolutions.

In 2000, the Security Council began reinforcing further its sanctions regimes. In addition to sanctions committees, the Security Council also established panels of experts.[92] Normally, a panel of experts assists the sanctions committee in carrying out its mandate by gathering, examining, and analyzing information from states, UN bodies, and other parties regarding the implementation of the measures. Based on the information received from a panel of experts, the sanctions committee then determines whether there have been incidents of non-compliance with Security Council resolutions. A panel of experts also makes recommendations on actions that the Security Council should take to improve the implementation of the measures. There are currently ten such panels for fourteen sanctions regimes. The effectiveness of measures taken under Article 41 of the *UN Charter*

---

against a member state, the goods from the targeted state will be treated less favourably than domestic goods.

90 Article XXI(c) of the GATT provides that "Nothing in this Treaty shall be construed . . . (c) to prevent any contracting party from taking any action in pursuance of its obligations under the *Charter of the United Nations* for the maintenance of international peace and security."

91 SC Res 751 (1992), UNSCOR, 47th Year, UN Doc S/Res/751 (1992) 51 at para. 11

92 See, for instance, SC Res 1591, UNSCOR, 70th Year, UN Doc S/Res/1591 (2005) 1.

is determined not only by the type and scope of the measures but also by the institutional structure of monitoring mechanisms. Specifically, a set of measures without any monitoring mechanism is institutionally weaker than measures accompanied by a Sanctions Committee. Similarly, measures accompanied by a sanctions committee are weaker than a regime equipped with a sanctions committee and a panel of experts.

The Security Council sanctions regimes have often been criticized for being undemocratic. Specifically, it is argued that they lack transparency and do not give their targets a procedurally fair recourse to challenge the sanctions before an independent judicial or quasi-judicial body. When states that are adversely affected by measures imposed under Article 41 of the *UN Charter* on a neighbouring state, they can seek an exemption from the Security Council. Article 50 of the *UN Charter* states that

> If preventive or enforcement measures against any state are taken by the Security Council, any other state, whether a Member of the United Nations or not, which finds itself confronted with special economic problems arising from the carrying out of those measures shall have the right to consult the Security Council with regard to a solution of those problems.[93]

The Security Council and its sanctions committees may grant partial or limited exemptions permitting certain transactions with the target state for specific commodities or services of crucial importance to neighbouring countries.[94] For instance, when the Security Council imposed sanctions on the former Yugoslavia, the measures had a

---

93 *Charter of the United Nations*, above note 1, art 50.

94 See *Report of the Secretary-General on the implementation of the provisions of the Charter of the United Nations related to assistance to third States affected by the application of sanctions*, UNGAOR, 50th Sess, UN Doc A/50/361 (1995) 1 at paras 30–38); and *Reports of the Secretary-General on economic assistance to States affected by the implementation of the Security Council resolutions imposing sanctions on the Federal Republic of Yugoslavia*, UNGAOR, 50th Sess, UN Doc A/50/423 (1995) 1 at paras 5–17, and *Reports of the Secretary-General on economic assistance to States affected by the implementation of the Security Council resolutions imposing sanctions on the Federal Republic of Yugoslavia*, UNGAOR, 51st Sess, UN Doc A/51/356 (1996) 1 at paras 9–11.

direct impact on its neighbouring countries. The Security Council received and approved requests for exemptions from Albania (for transit of electric energy), Hungary (for supply of fuel for icebreakers), Romania (for oil deliveries for the Iron Gates I system on the Danube), and the former Yugoslav Republic of Macedonia (for transit traffic). However, these states do not have any recourse before an independent body to contest the validity of the sanctions that have a direct impact on them. The International Court of Justice has no jurisdiction to review the validity or the lawfulness of the Security Council sanctions regime. The only way to seek the intervention of the ICJ is to obtain a sufficient number of votes in the General Assembly in order to seek an advisory opinion on this question. Nevertheless, an advisory opinion is not binding.

What is even more problematic is that the *UN Charter* does not provide any remedy equivalent to Article 50 of the *UN Charter* to non-state actors. The vulnerability of non-state actors was further compounded by the absence of any guidelines or standards that the Security Council was required to follow in proposing names and entities to be included on a sanctions list. The process was for all means and purposes arbitrary and not subject to any review. In the *2005 World Summit Declaration*, the General Assembly requested the Security Council to ensure that fair and clear procedures are in place for the imposition and lifting of sanctions measures.[95] In response to this request, the Council adopted a special procedure that any individual or entity who is listed in a resolution imposing enforcement measures can use to seek a remedy.[96] This recourse is called "delisting." In 2009, the Security Council established an ombudsman's office whose main task is to examine requests for delisting from certain sanction regimes and making recommendations to the Security Council.[97] This mechanism is often criticized as falling short of minimum standards of procedural equity and due process. A European court had an opportunity to review the delisting procedure of the Security Council in a

95 *2005 World Summit Outcome*, GA Res 60/1, UNGAOR, 60th Sess, UN Doc A/Res/60/1 (2005) 1 at para 109.

96 SC Res 1730 (2006), UNSCOR, 61st Year, UN Doc S/Res/1730 (2006) 1.

97 SC Res 2368 (2017), UNSCOR, 72nd Year, UN Doc S/Res/2368 (2017) 1.

case where an individual complained that his assets had been frozen due to a Security Council sanction regime targeting al-Qaeda and the Taliban.[98] The court concluded that the delisting procedure provided for some procedural guarantees. However, it was not sufficiently transparent to allow the European authorities to determine whether the reasons invoked in support of the sanctions were well founded.

3) Taking Measures Involving the Use of Armed Force

It is important to recall that one of the most fundamental principles of the legal order that the *UN Charter* introduced was to prohibit the unilateral use of force.[99] The only permissible exception is the use of force in self-defence:

> Nothing in the present Charter shall impair the inherent right of individual or collective self-defence if an armed attack occurs against a Member of the United Nations, until the Security Council has taken measures necessary to maintain international peace and security. Measures taken by Members in the exercise of this right of self-defence shall be immediately reported to the Security Council and shall not in any way affect the authority and responsibility of the Security Council under the present Charter to take at any time such action as it deems necessary in order to maintain or restore international peace and security.[100]

This provision of the *UN Charter* lays down the procedure that needs to be followed when a state exercises its right of self-defence. Specifically, when a state claims to act in self-defence, it must immediately report the situation to the Security Council. The purpose of this notification is to ensure that the Security Council steps in and takes collective measures to maintain or restore international peace and

---

98 *Commission, Council, United Kingdom v Yassin Abdullah Kadi*, Judgment in Joined Cases C-584/10 P, C-593/10 P, and C-595/10 P [2014] All ER (EC) 123, [2013] All ER (D) 411, GC [*Kadi*].

99 *Charter of the United Nations*, above note 1, art 2.4. For an explanation of what can be regarded as use of force, see Chapter 2.

100 *Ibid*, art 51.

security. As soon as the Security Council intervenes, the wronged state must cease its use of force in self-defence. Thus, the right to use force in self-defence is provisional and operates only until the Security Council takes appropriate measures.

How does the Security Council take measures? As we have already seen in the previous section, it can take measures that do not involve any use of force, including a "complete or partial interruption of economic relations and of rail, sea, air, postal, telegraphic, radio, and other means of communication, and the severance of diplomatic relations."[101] Where such measures fail or are unlikely to produce the desired effect, the Security Council can take more serious measures that entail using force. Article 42 of the *UN Charter* states that,

> Should the Security Council consider that measures provided for in Article 41 would be inadequate or have proved to be inadequate, it may take such action by air, sea, or land forces as may be necessary to maintain or restore international peace and security. Such action may include demonstrations, blockade, and other operations by air, sea, or land forces of Members of the United Nations.

The Security Council can use force without even attempting measures not involving force, such as economic sanctions. A mere suspicion that measures not involving force would be ineffective is sufficient for the Council to take more serious measures that require a certain extent of force. When the Security Council authorizes measures involving the use of force, it does not actually use force itself. The UN does not have a standing army and, therefore, is not equipped to use force. It can only authorize the use of force and call on UN member states or regional organizations to use all necessary means to maintain or restore international peace and security. In other words, by taking measures that entail the use of force, the Security Council does nothing more than give legitimacy to the use of force.

---

101 *Ibid*, art 41.

a) The UN Does Not Have Its Own Armed Forces

It is a widespread yet erroneous belief that the UN peacekeeping troops (often referred to as Blue Helmets because of the light blue colour of their helmets) are part of a permanent UN army. The UN has no standing army or police force of its own. It relies on member states to contribute military and police personnel required for each peace operation. During the Moscow and Tehran conferences held in 1943, the four major allies of World War II (China, the United Kingdom, the United States, and the USSR)[102] agreed to be the "four policemen" by acting "as a global coalition able to deploy military enforcement powers at the head of a world assembly."[103] Each power undertook to keep order within their spheres of influence. At the Dumbarton Oaks conference in 1944, these allies agreed to establish the Security Council and to place at its disposal armed forces so that conflicts and acts of aggression could be prevented or handled expeditiously. The absence of such a force was viewed to be a fatal flaw of the League of Nations. This agreement was memorialized in Articles 43.1 and 45 of the *UN Charter*, which placed an obligation on all member states of the United Nations to make available to the Security Council armed forces and air-force contingents ready to be deployed on call. Articles 46 and 47 of the *UN Charter* provide for the Military Staff Committee to advise and assist the Council in fulfilling its role. These provisions were never implemented.[104]

In 1946 and 1947, the newly created UN Military Staff Committee, composed of the five permanent members of the Security Council, examined the feasibility of contributions of armed forces to the Security Council. The initial proposal was to equip the Security Council with armed forces from the best-trained and best-equipped units or formations of member nations. The size of the formations would

---

102 France was initially excluded from the group of four; however, at the insistence of British Prime Minister Winston Churchill, the great powers agreed to include France as the fifth member of the group.

103 Norrie MacQueen, *The United Nations, Peace Operations and the Cold War*, 2d ed (New York: Routledge, 2011) at 9.

104 Aiyaz Husain, "The United States and the Failure of UN Collective Security: Palestine, Kashmir, and Indonesia, 1947–1948" (2007) 101:3 *Am J Int'l L* 581.

have been determined by the Security Council (with the assistance of the Military Staff Committee) and would have depended on the armed conflict the Council needed to address. The initial contribution of armed forces was supposed to be made in large part by the permanent members of the Security Council. The intention was to gradually increase this force as the contributions of other UN nations became available. The armed forces made available to the Security Council would have been deployed only by the decision of the Security Council and only for the period necessary for the fulfillment of the tasks set out in Article 42 of the *UN Charter*.

Although the permanent members of the Security Council agreed that equipping the Security Council with armed forces was desirable, they could not agree on the size of their contingents. The USSR insisted that all five permanent members of the Security Council had to contribute armed forces and weapons equal in quantity and quality. The Soviet delegation was concerned that if any one permanent member contributed more troops than the others, it would give the appearance of superiority to that member. However, the Soviet delegation was also opposed to making a large number of troops available to the Security Council.[105] Other permanent members of the Security Council considered this proposal utopian. Due to these irreconcilable differences among the permanent members as to the size of the force and the contribution that each permanent member would make, no agreement was reached and the Security Council was never equipped with standing armed forces.

Since 1948, UN Secretaries-General have stressed the importance of establishing a standing force and giving the Security Council access to it.[106] The existence of a standing force under the direct command

---

105 *Letter from the Chairman of the Military Staff Committee to the Secretary-General Dated 30 April 1947* and *Enclosed Report on General Principles Governing the Organization of the Armed Forces Made Available to the Security Council by Member Nations of the United Nations*, UN Doc S/336 (1947), reproduced in 1946–47 *UN Yearbook* at 424–43.

106 See *A UN Rapid Deployment Brigade: A Preliminary Study*, Annex to a letter of 7 April 1995 from the Permanent Representative of the Netherlands to the United Nations to the Secretary-General, UN Doc A/49/886 and S/1995/276 (1995); *Report of the Working Group on a Multinational United Nations Stand-by*

of the Security Council could have saved hundreds of thousands of lives in 1994, especially in the southern and western parts of Rwanda, where the massacres started after the Security Council agreed that measures were needed but was unable to amass the required armed forces to intervene. This prompted then Secretary-General Boutros-Ghali to make a more ambitious proposal for a UN rapid reaction force almost five decades after Trygve Lie's unsuccessful attempt to set up a UN Guard Force:

> In these circumstances, I have come to the conclusion that the United Nations does need to give serious thought to the idea of a rapid reaction force. Such a force would be the Security Council's strategic reserve for deployment when there was an emergency need for peace-keeping troops. It might comprise battalion-sized units from a number of countries. These units would be trained to the same standards, use the same operating procedures, be equipped with integrated communications equipment and take part in joint exercises at regular intervals. They would be stationed in their home countries but maintained at a high state of readiness. The value of this arrangement would of course depend on how far the Security Council could be sure that the force would actually be available in an emergency. This will be a complicated and expensive arrangement, but I believe that the time has come to undertake it.[107]

This proposal was also abandoned because states have always been reluctant to hand over to the Security Council full command

---

Forces High Readiness Brigade, Annex to a letter of 29 February 1996 from the Permanent Representative of Denmark to the United Nations to the Secretary-General, UN Doc A/51/75 and S/1996/166 (1996); *Comprehensive review of the whole question of peacekeeping operations in all their aspects: Identical letters dated 21 August 2000 from the Secretary-General to the president of the General Assembly and the president of the Security Council,* General Assembly, UN Doc A/55/305 and S/2000/809 (2000); *Annual Report of the Secretary-General on the Work of the Organization: 1 July 1947—30 June 1948,* UNGAOR, 3rd Session, UN Doc A/565 (5 July 1948) at xvii and xviii.

107 *Supplement to An Agenda for Peace: Position Paper of the Secretary-General on the Occasion of the Fiftieth Anniversary of the United Nations,* UNGAOR, 50th Sess, UN Doc A/50/60 (1995) 1 at para 44.

and control (exercise of authority and direction over troops) over their armed forces. Consequently, UN peacekeeping operations appeared as *ad hoc* surrogates for UN enforcement actions after the failure of the Security Council to enter into agreements entrusting command of member states' military forces to the UN Military Staff Committee.[108]

b) UN Peace Operations

UN peace operations is a term used to describe various types and categories of peacekeeping missions carried out by the United Nations in a conflict area. It is a generic term that may include peacekeeping, peace enforcement, or peacebuilding missions. Some legal scholars and authors divide peacekeeping missions into consecutive generations. Such a taxonomy is not always helpful or accurate because the mandate and scope of a peace operation may evolve throughout its existence, and because each armed conflict is unique, each requires a peace operation tailored to its specific needs.

Below, we will explore the evolution of peace operations and compare five different configurations of peace operations. It is important to emphasize that while some peace operations may fall squarely within one of these five configurations, other peace operations may be a combination of two or of several configurations.

The most primitive forms of peace operations were traditional interposing forces. These were unarmed or lightly armed contingents wearing UN blue helmets and positioned as a buffer force between two opposing armies. The main objective of these missions was to reduce contact between the forces and to decrease the probability of escalation. Such peacekeeping forces could be tasked to monitor borders, verify demilitarized zones, and perform other tasks aimed at creating political space for negotiation or mediation. These military observers were typically deployed in interstate conflicts (as opposed to intrastate conflicts). The first UN peace operation of this type was formed in 1948 to supervise the truce in Palestine in the aftermath of the Arab–Israeli war.

108 Husain, above note 104 at 582.

UN PHOTO/BZ

UN Peacekeeping Force in Cyprus (UNFICYP). Finland soldiers on their way to Nicosia from Dhekelia — a distance of 120 miles by road (1 May 1964). Permission for use granted by The United Nations.

In the late 1940s, the United Kingdom decided to relinquish the mandate to administer Palestine entrusted to it by the League of Nations in 1923 after the fall of the Ottoman Empire. The UK government began exploring a solution that would be acceptable to both Arab and Jewish communities of Palestine. During this period, approximately two-thirds of Palestine's population were Arabs and one-third were Jews. Both communities claimed control over the entire territory. Unable to find a compromise acceptable to both parties, the British government sought the intervention of the UN General Assembly. The Assembly adopted a resolution partitioning the territory into an Arab state and a Jewish state and creating a special international regime for the City of Jerusalem.[109] Clashes broke out almost immediately between Jews and Arabs in Palestine. On 14 May 1948, the United Kingdom ceased administering Palestine and

109 *Future Government of Palestine*, GA Res 181 (II), UNGAOR, 2nd Year, UN Doc A/Res/181(II) (1947) 131.

withdrew completely. The leaders of the Jewish community proclaimed the state of Israel. The violence intensified during the following two weeks. On 29 May 1948, the Security Council adopted a resolution giving the parties an ultimatum to either cease fighting for four weeks or face consequences under Chapter VII of the *UN Charter*.[110] In the same resolution, the Council decided that the truce should be supervised by the UN mediator assisted by a group of military observers. This group of military observers, which has become known as the United Nations Truce Supervision Organization (UNTSO), began its activities in June 1948. The mandate of this UN peace operation was limited to monitoring ceasefire arrangements that had already been agreed. This primitive form of peace operations is possible only if the fighting ceases following a truce or ceasefire. It is not the type of peacekeeping that can be established while hostilities are still ongoing. The sole objective of these peace operations is to create an environment conducive to efforts at peaceful conflict resolution by the belligerents. The United Nations Military Observer Group in India and Pakistan (UNMOGIP)—established in 1949 to supervise the ceasefires between India and Pakistan—is another example of this primitive type of peace operation.

A more robust configuration of peacekeeping forces appeared with the sending of the United Nations Emergency Force (UNEF) to the Suez to oversee the withdrawal of foreign troops from Egypt. In July 1956, the Egyptian government nationalized the Suez Canal Company. In October 1956, with the blessing of France and the United Kingdom, Israeli forces launched an attack on Egypt. Israel occupied Sinai and the Gaza Strip. British and French troops followed suit and took control of the Suez Canal. The Security Council was unable to adopt any decision owing to the vetoes of France and the United Kingdom. The matter was then referred to the General Assembly under the *Uniting for Peace* resolution.[111] The Assembly established the United

---

110 SC Res 50 (1948), UNSCOR, 3rd Year, UN Doc S/Res/50 (1948) 20 at paras 1 and 11.

111 In November 1950, the General Assembly adopted Resolution 377 A (V) *Uniting for Peace*, UN Doc A/RES/377A(V) (1950). This resolution was a result of the USSR's practice of vetoing decisions by the Security Council, especially with

Nations Emergency Force (UNEF) to secure and supervise the cessation of hostilities.[112] Following the dispatch of the Emergency Force to the area, the French, British, and Israeli forces withdrew. UNEF was the first fully armed United Nations peacekeeping force with 6,000 troops. UNEF was established under Chapter VI of the *UN Charter* and was deployed before the parties had reached an agreement to cease the hostilities. This was an important innovation because the military contingents were fully armed and could become operational while hostilities were still ongoing. Secretary-General Dag Hammarskjöld issued detailed regulations that set out the international character of UN peacekeepers, authorized the troops to use the UN flag and other distinctive UN markings, and conferred on them privilege and immunities.[113] The regulations also granted full authority to the Force Commander over the force and to the Secretary-General over all administrative, executive, and financial matters affecting the force.[114] This type of peace operation may include non-military activities, such as the organization of elections, disarmament, demobilization, and reintegration (DDR), promotion of human rights, delivery of humanitarian aid, and government capacity-building. They may also be accompanied by a deployment of police forces either as part of

---

regard to proposed measures against North Korea. To overcome the impasse in the Security Council caused by the East–West rivalry, the General Assembly, at the initiative of the United States and its allies, adopted the *Uniting for Peace* resolution, granting itself a subsidiary responsibility with regard to maintaining international peace and security. The purpose of this resolution was to ensure that where the Security Council failed to exercise its primary responsibility for the maintenance of international peace and security as a result of a veto vote by one of its permanent members, the General Assembly would seize itself of the matter.

112 The idea to create UNEF is attributed to Canada's then Minister of Foreign Affairs Lester B Pearson, who received the Nobel Prize for it in 1957. It was Pearson who had suggested the actual notion of the UN-led peacekeeping force to the special emergency session of the General Assembly on 2 November 1956. In his speech to the General Assembly, Pearson argued for "a truly international peace and police force . . . large enough to keep these borders at peace while a political settlement is being worked out."

113 *Regulations for the United Nations Emergency Force*, UN Doc ST/SGB/UNEF/1 (1957) at paras 5–10.

114 *Ibid* at paras 11–17.

a training or to keep law and order. Missions that appear to fall into this category were the United Nations Transition Assistance Group (UNTAG) in Namibia,[115] the United Nations Operation in Mozambique (UNOMOZ),[116] and the United Nations Observer Group in El Salvador (ONUSAL).[117] Three fundamental conditions had to be met for such peacekeeping forces to be authorized: (a) the consent of the host nations; (b) impartiality of UN troops; and (c) the prohibition to use force except in self-defence.

A more robust configuration of peace operations appeared after the three failures of peacekeeping in Somalia, Rwanda, and Bosnia. The Security Council authorized military contingents to use force not only to keep the peace but also to enforce it. These missions are often referred to as "peace-enforcement" operations. Such operations have more expansive rules of engagement, which means that they have a greater ability to use force in order to successfully carry out their missions. The UN first experimented with such a mission in 1999 by deploying UNAMSIL to Sierra Leone.[118] The Security Council broadened the language of its resolution so that peacekeepers could be authorized to use force not only in self-defence but also to protect civilians and their mission.[119] The legal justification for departing from the requirement of prohibition to use force except in self-defence was humanitarian grounds. The three conditions required for a peace operation force to be deployed were significantly loosened. Specifically,

---

115 The United Nations Transition Assistance Group in Namibia was established by Security Council Resolution 632 (1989) of 16 February 1989, UN Doc S/Res/632 (1989) on the basis of *Further Report of the Secretary-General's Concerning the Implementation of Security Council Resolutions 435(1978) and 439 (1978) Concerning the Question of Namibia*, UNSCOR, 44th Year, UN Doc S/20412 (1989) 1.

116 The United Nations Mission in Mozambique was established by Security Council Resolution 797 (1992), UN Doc S/Res/797 (1992) (16 December 1992) on the basis of the *Report of the Secretary General on the United Nations Operation in Mozambique* (ONUMOZ), UNSCOR, 47th Year, UN Doc S/24892 (1992) 1.

117 The United Nations Observer Mission in El Salvador was established by Security Council Resolution 693 (1991), UNSCOR, 46th Year, UN Doc S/Res/693 (1991).

118 The United Nations Mission in Sierra Leone was established by Security Council Resolution 1270 (1999), UNSCOR, 54th Year, UN Doc S/Res/1270 (1999) 1.

119 Stephen Mathias, "UN Peacekeeping Today: Legal Challenges and Uncertainties" (2017) 18:2 *Melbourne J Int'l L* 138 at 140.

UN PHOTO/MARCO DORMINO

Togolese peacekeepers from the United Nations Multidimensional Integrated Stabilization Mission in Mali (MINUSMA) patrol Menaka (6 May 2018). Permission for use granted by The United Nations.

the forces could be deployed without the consent of the host state, especially since in many conflicts, there may be no effective government to give consent on behalf of the state. Also, peace operations were permitted to use targeted offensive force against one of the parties, which is not entirely consistent with the notion of neutrality or the prohibition to use of force except in self-defence. For instance, in 2013, the Security Council authorized the UN Organization Stabilization Mission in the Democratic Republic of the Congo (MONUSCO) to neutralize an armed group known as the "23 March Movement" or "M23" by carrying out combat operations in collaboration with the armed forces of the Democratic Republic of the Congo.[120] Of course, one could reasonably argue that this was a preventive use of force

120 SC Res 2098 (2013), UNSCOR, 68th Year, UN Doc S/Res/2098 (2013) 1 at para 12(b), which read as follows: Authorizes MONUSCO to neutralize armed groups through its intervention brigade, either unilaterally or jointly with the FARDC, in strict compliance with international law, including international humanitarian law and with the human rights due diligence policy on UN-support to non-UN forces (HRDDP).

for the purposes of protecting civilians. The United Nations Multidimensional Integrated Stabilization Mission in Mali (MINUSMA) is also authorized "to use all necessary means to carry out its mandate, within its capabilities and its areas of deployment."[121]

The most potent peace operations are those that exercise a part of the host country's sovereignty. Peace operations that belong to this configuration have extensive powers and rules of engagement. They also have a very robust civilian component. These peace operations are commonly known as "peacebuilding operations." They combine a broad mandate to use force with intrusive measures to control important governmental functions or take over all governmental structures. For instance, when establishing the UN Interim Administration Mission in Kosovo (UNMIK), the Security Council vested the mission with authority over the territory and people of Kosovo, including all legislative and executive functions.[122] Similarly, when the Security Council set up the UN Transitional Administration in East Timor (UNTAET), it gave the mission the overall responsibility for the administration of East Timor and empowered it to exercise all legislative, executive, and judicial functions. The peace operation was mandated, among other things, to maintain law and order, to develop civil and social services, and to build capacity for self-government.

The fifth and last configuration of peace operations is known as partnership peacekeeping or hybrid missions.[123] These missions deploy troops and police personnel under mixed command, with both the UN and relevant regional organizations deploying troops to the same missions under distinct chains of command and different mandates. The UN has already partnered, with varying degrees of success, with the Organization of American States (OAS) in the Dominican Republic, with the Economic Community of West African States (ECOWAS) in Sierra Leone, with the African Union (AU) in Burundi, Central African Republic, Mali, Somalia, and Sudan, and

121 SC Res 2423 (2018), UNSCOR, 73rd Year, UN Doc S/Res/2423 (2018) 1 at para 32.

122 SC Res 1244 (1999), above note 77.

123 See *Partnering for Peace: Moving Towards Partnership Peacekeeping*, Report of the Secretary-General to the Security Council, UNSCOR, 70th Year, UN Doc S/2015/229 (2015).

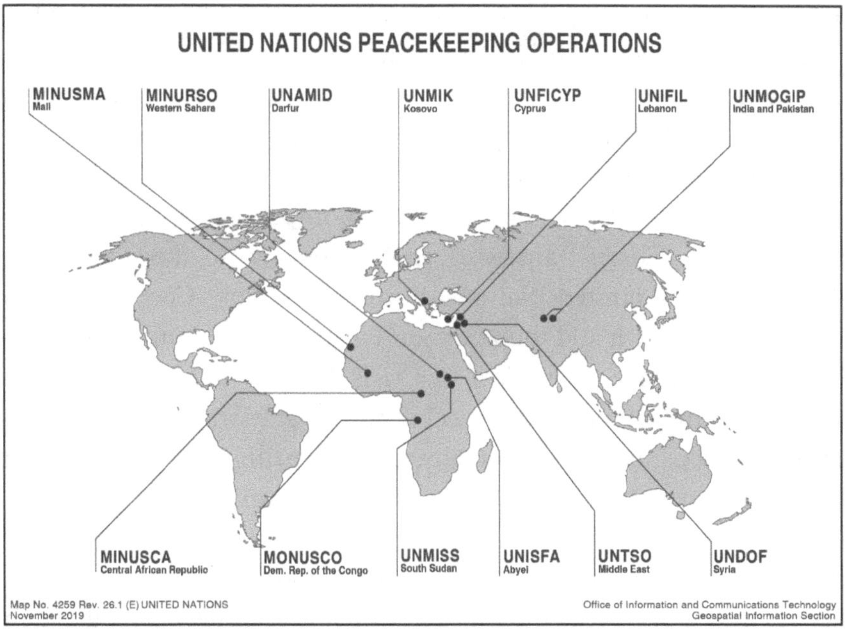

MINURSO	United Nations Mission for the Referendum in Western Sahara	established: 1991
MINUSCA	United Nations Multidimensional Integrated Stabilization Mission in the Central African Republic	established: 2014
MINUSMA	United Nations Multidimensional Integrated Stabilization Mission in Mali	established: 2013
MONUSCO	United Nations Organization Stabilization Mission in the Democratic Rep. of the Congo	established: 2010
UNAMID	African Union-United Nations Hybrid Operation in Darfur	established: 2007
UNDOF	United Nations Disengagement Observer Force	established: 1974
UNFICYP	United Nations Peacekeeping Force in Cyprus	established: 1964
UNIFIL	United Nations Interim Force in Lebanon	established: 1978
UNISFA	United Nations Interim Security Force for Abyei	established: 2011
UNMIK	United Nations Interim Administration Mission in Kosovo	established: 1999
UNMISS	United Nations Mission in South Sudan	established: 2011
UNMOGIP	United Nations Military Observer Group in India and Pakistan	established: 1949
UNTSO	United Nations Truce Supervision Organization	established: 1948

PERMISSION FOR USE GRANTED BY THE UNITED NATIONS.

with the European Union in DRC, Chad, and Mali. Central to the appearance of this type of mission were the following two elements. First, the establishment of the Peace and Security Council of the African Union in December 2003 substantially strengthened the powers of the African Union in conflict resolution. Since then, the African Union has been increasingly taking initiatives on peace and security, and its role has been growing both qualitatively and quantitatively. As a result, the partnership between the United Nations and the African Union has evolved significantly. Normally, cooperation entails the provision of support by the UN to the African Union during the planning phases, followed by an initial deployment of AU forces. Then, a transition from an African Union-led operation to a UN operation occurs. Second, the European Union decided to play a role in peacekeeping operations only in 2003. The UN and the EU established a strategic framework for their cooperation in peacekeeping and crisis management. These framework instruments were the 2003 Joint Declaration on United Nations–European Union Cooperation in Crisis Management and the 2007 joint statement on United Nations–European Union Cooperation in Crisis Management. Cooperation with the European Union in peacekeeping operations is usually based on a clear separation of tasks, aimed at ensuring the most efficient use of the capacities and resources of each organization.

c) Legal Basis for Establishing Peace Operations

Normally, the Security Council establishes peace operations through Security Council resolutions. In exceptional cases, the General Assembly may also establish a peace operation with a more limited mandate under the *Uniting for Peace* resolution. Historically, resolutions authorizing the deployment of peacekeeping troops did not refer to any specific provision of the *UN Charter* or the Chapter under which peace operations were established. Since the *UN Charter* does not expressly grant either the Security Council or the General Assembly such a power, the legality of a resolution authorizing the deployment of peacekeeping troops was challenged by some member states in the 1960s. At the request of certain nations, the General Assembly sought from the International Court of Justice an advisory opinion on the question of whether or not the expenses incurred by peacekeeping operations could be regarded as expenses of the United Nations as a whole or as the expenses of those nations that contributed to the peacekeeping operation. In addressing this question, the World Court felt compelled to examine first whether the General Assembly and the Security Council had the power to establish peace operations. The ICJ determined that the *UN Charter* implicitly grants both organs the power to deploy peacekeeping troops. While the Security Council's power in this field is primary, it is not exclusive. The

General Assembly also has a responsibility for international peace and security.[124] For these reasons, the Court held that expenses stemming from peacekeeping activities are the expenses of the United Nations. Hence, the General Assembly could apportion them among all member states. As a result of this advisory opinion, it is now settled that both the General Assembly and the Security Council have the power to establish peace operations.[125]

The Court did not point to the exact provision or chapter of the *UN Charter* that authorizes the Security Council to deploy troops. Some scholars have associated peace operations with Chapter VI of the *UN Charter,* which deals with the pacific settlement of disputes. Others describe traditional peace operations as falling between Chapters VI and VII and therefore call them Chapter 6½ or 6 *bis* activities. This debate is unnecessary and only adds to the confusion. It is not prudent to refer to a specific chapter of the *UN Charter* when drafting a resolution authorizing the establishment of a peace operation because this may give rise to ambiguities, inconsistencies, or opposing views when planning and implementing a specific mission. The scope of a peacekeeping mission must be clearly articulated in the mandate of the Security Council, in the Rules of Engagement for the military component, and Directives for the Use of Force for police contingents.

d) Challenges That UN Peace Operations Face

In recent years, the peacekeeping function of the United Nations has been facing some difficulties. The chief challenge the UN is facing in the field of peace operations is the shortage of well-trained, adequately equipped, and sufficiently motivated troops. During the Cold War, the Security Council authorized only thirteen peacekeeping missions, most of which had limited ceasefire observing functions or similar mandates. Supplying these peace operations with personnel and equipment was relatively easy. The end of the Cold War marked

---

124 *Certain expenses of the United Nations (Article 17, paragraph 2, of the Charter)* Advisory Opinion, [1962] ICJ Rep 151 [*Certain expenses of the United Nations*].

125 Vaughan Lowe, Adam Roberts, Jennifer Welsh & Dominik Zaum, eds, *The United Nations Security Council and War: The Evolution of Thought and Practice since 1945* (Oxford, UK: Oxford University Press, 2008) at 7.

the beginning of a new era for peacekeeping. Between 1988 and 1998, thirty-six new peace operations were established. Peace operations grew not only in number but also in size. Military contingents composed of several thousand troops were becoming the norm. In addition, the nature of conflicts was also changing from traditional interstate armed conflicts to chaotic intrastate wars where dozens of non-state armed groups had different interests. The UN was not fully prepared for such a drastic increase in the number, size, and complexity of peace operations. It did not have enough experience to assess and mitigate risks. The organization had to learn through trial and error, including costly errors in Somalia, Rwanda, and Bosnia. As fatalities in peace operations increased, Western states began withdrawing their support for UN peace operations. They remained in some relatively low-risk missions, such as UNFCYP[126] and UNIFIL,[127] but were present only in small numbers in high-risk missions. At the same time, the number and complexity of conflicts continued to grow and casualties to UN peacekeepers consistently increased, reaching 3,890 fatalities in 2019. The UN became overstretched in Africa and was compelled to rely on any military support it could possibly get. The reluctance of member states with large armies to provide soldiers to UN peace operations left a void that was quickly filled by developing nations[128] whose armies desperately needed additional sources of revenue. They viewed peace operations as a lucrative income-generating opportunity. The unintended consequence of this shift was that states participating in peace operations for financial reasons are not likely to make a substantial investment in pre-deployment training of their troops or in advanced equipment. Since troop-contributing countries receive reimbursement per soldier and per piece of equipment, quantitative considerations override qualitative considerations. As a result, poorly prepared and equipped peacekeeping troops often face

---

126 United Kingdom, Argentina, and Slovakia are the largest troop-contributors to UNFCYP.

127 Italy contributes 1,082, France 668, Spain 629, Ireland 467, and Germany 121 troops to UNIFIL.

128 Ethiopia, Bangladesh, Rwanda, India, Nepal, Pakistan, Egypt, Indonesia, Ghana, and China were top troop-contributing countries in 2019.

embarrassing incidents that discredit not only their defence capabilities but also the UN peacekeeping function. For instance, in 2010, Nepalese peacekeepers stationed in Haiti contaminated a river, thereby causing the largest cholera epidemic in the world with 750,000 cases and almost 9,000 deaths. This could have been avoided if the troops had received adequate logistical support. In 2014, Fijian peacekeepers who were part of the UN Disengagement Observer Force (UNDOF) stationed in the Golan Heights were kidnapped by al-Nusra fighters (al-Qaeda's Syrian affiliate). In 2016, Chinese, Nepalese, and Ethiopian peacekeepers refused to engage while aid workers were raped and tortured in South Sudan. In addition, each year, the UN receives a disconcerting number of allegations of sexual exploitation and abuse by peacekeeping troops. It is unclear what consequences, if any, these troops face when they are repatriated to their home countries. The Security Council requested the Secretary-General to ensure that troop-contributing countries whose personnel are the subject of an allegation of sexual exploitation and abuse take appropriate steps to investigate the allegation and to hold perpetrators accountable. If the Secretary-General determines that the troop-contributing state failed to take appropriate steps to investigate and hold accountable perpetrators, that state may not be permitted to participate in future peace operations.[129] However, the UN already has difficulty attracting military and police contingents and cannot be fastidious when choosing troop-contributing states.

Blue Helmets need to attract well-trained and well-equipped forces from countries that do not engage in peacekeeping for exclusively financial reasons. The UN should not agree to deploy contingents whose past performance has been unsatisfactory. States with powerful militaries have a moral obligation to re-engage in peacekeeping activities. A renewed engagement need not necessarily consist of contributing troops. It can consist of offering experienced commanders, military planners, and highly specialized personnel, providing credible and robust pre-deployment training to troops or

---

129 SC Res 2272 (2016), UNSCOR, 71st Year, UN Doc S/Res/2272 (2016). See also SC Res 2436 (2018), UNSCOR, 73rd Year, UN Doc S/Res/2436 (2018).

equipping military and police contingents with the required weapons and defence materiel. Regional organizations with adequate resources, including the EU and NATO, may also play an important role by providing the UN with some technical assistance, such as pre-deployment training programs and, if necessary, logistical support.

The inadequate command and control arrangements between the UN and troop-contributing states exacerbates this problem. In peacekeeping operations, the Special Representative of the Secretary-General (SRSG) (assisted by two Deputies Special Representative of the Secretary-General (DSRSG)) is the highest ranking official responsible for ensuring that the mandate of the mission is fulfilled. In most peace operations, the SRSG is a civilian diplomat with no military background. For tactical or military operations, the SRSG relies on a Force Commander who leads the contingents from one or several troop-contributing countries. The Force Commander may be a national of a country that does not have any troops in that specific mission. Therefore, the authority of the Force Commander can be easily challenged by the military authorities of troop-contributing countries. In particular, when military interventions go beyond a purely defensive engagement, the threat faced by peacekeeping troops is obviously higher. Some troop-contributing states are unwilling to participate in high-risk operations and may instruct their contingents to disregard the orders of the Force Commander or to stand down. This puts at risk the entire peacekeeping operation because the unity of the force is broken.

e) Funding of Peacekeeping Activities[130]

Since the *UN Charter* contains no provisions for establishing peacekeeping forces, it does not provide a methodology for apportioning the expenses of peacekeeping operations. This lacuna gave rise to a dispute among member states of the UN in the 1950s. France and USSR refused to pay their respective shares of the expenses for the

---

130 See Christopher Leck, "International Responsibility in United Nations Peacekeeping Operations: Command and Control Arrangements and the Attribution of Conduct" (2009) 10:1 *Melbourne J of Intl L* 346, and Paolo Palchetti, "The Allocation of Responsibility for Internationally Wrongful Acts Committed in the Course of Multinational Operations" (2013) 95:891/892 *Int'l Rev Red Cross* 727.

peacekeeping missions in Suez (UNEF I) and Congo (ONUC). The General Assembly requested the International Court of Justice to give an Advisory Opinion on the obligation of all member states to pay for peace and security operations carried out by a limited number of nations. The International Court of Justice determined that the phrase "expenses of the Organization" found in Article 17 of the *UN Charter* must be understood as "the amounts paid out to defray the costs of carrying out its purposes [including] the political, economic, social, humanitarian, and other purposes of the United Nations."[131] The Court then concluded that peacekeeping activities are within the scope of the UN functions. Consequently, financing such activities is an ordinary expense that all member states must bear. As a result of this advisory opinion, it is no longer disputed that the financing of peace operations is the collective responsibility of all member states of the UN.[132] Under Article 17.2 of the *UN Charter*, the obligation of a member state to pay its share of the expenses is not just moral but also legal.

Peace operations are very costly endeavours. The UN reimburses troop-contributing countries for the military and police personnel, contingent-owned equipment, and logistical services required to support the operation. For each soldier on the ground, the UN reimburses troop-contributing countries USD$1,428, and for each piece of equipment, the UN reimburses the country a pre-determined amount.[133] With 90,000 Blue Helmets on the ground, the approved budget for UN Peacekeeping operations for the fiscal year 1 July 2019 to 30 June 2020 is USD$6.5 billion.[134]

The assessment rates for the financing of peacekeeping operations is based on the scale of assessments for the regular budget of the

---

131 *Certain expenses of the United Nations*, above note 124 at 158.

132 *Scale of assessments for the apportionment of the expenses of United Nations peacekeeping operations*, GA Res 55/235, UNGAOR, 55th Sess, UN Doc A/Res/55/235 (2001) 1 [*Scale of Assessments*]. See also *Certain expenses of the United Nations*, above note 124.

133 See *Letter dated 8 February 2017 from the Chair of the 2017 Working Group on Contingent-Owned Equipment to the Chair of the Fifth Committee*, UN Doc A/C.5/71/20 (2017).

134 *Approved resources for peacekeeping operations for the period from 1 July 2019 to 30 June 2020*, Note by the Secretary General, UN Doc A/C.5/73/21 (2019).

United Nations with some adjustments.[135] The methodology for apportioning the expenses generated by peacekeeping operations takes into account a country's capacity to contribute, namely its per capita gross national product. While economically more developed countries can make relatively large contributions to peacekeeping operations, the less developed countries have a limited capacity to contribute towards such activities. Additional adjustments may be made for states that are victims of, or otherwise involved in, the events or actions that lead to a peacekeeping operation. Also, due to the privileged position and special responsibilities of the permanent members of the Security Council for the maintenance of peace and security, they are expected to pay more to peacekeeping operations. Consequently, permanent members of the Security Council are assessed for peacekeeping activities at a higher rate than for the activities funded through the regular budget of the United Nations. There are ten categories or levels of contribution for peacekeeping ranging from Level A (permanent members of the Security Council that pay a premium) to Level J (least developed countries that get a 90 percent discount on their contributions). Countries may voluntarily decide to move to another category and contribute at a higher rate.[136] In 2019, the top ten contributors to UN peacekeeping operations were the United States (27.9 percent), China (15.2 percent), Japan (8.6 percent), Germany (6.1 percent), the United Kingdom (5.8 percent), France (5.6 percent), Italy (3.3 percent), Russia (3 percent), Canada (2.7 percent), and Korea (2.3 percent).[137]

The amount of funds required for a peacekeeping operation depends on its scope. It is the Secretary-General's responsibility to prepare the operational plan and budget proposals for various

---

135 *Scale of assessments*, above note 132 at para 4.

136 See *Voluntary movements in connection with the apportionment of the expenses of United Nations peacekeeping operation*, GA Res 55/236, UNGAOR, 55th Sess, UN Doc A/RES/55/236 (2001).

137 *Effective rates of assessment for peacekeeping operations, 1 January 2019 to 31 December 2021, based on the scale of assessment adopted by the General Assembly in its Resolution 73/271 and the composition of levels endorsed by the Assembly in its Resolution 73/272*, Annex to *Implementation of General Assembly Resolution 55/235 and 55/236*, Report of the Secretary-General, UNGAOR, 73rd Sess, UN Doc A/73/350/Add.1 (2018) 1.

peacekeeping operations. The budget estimates are based on the findings by the survey mission sent to the area of the peacekeeping operation. The Secretary-General transmits his budget proposal to the Advisory Committee on Administrative and Budgetary Questions (ACABQ). ACABQ reviews the proposal and makes a recommendation to the Fifth Committee of the General Assembly. If the Fifth Committee approves the proposal, the budget is then submitted to the General Assembly for its endorsement.

f) Responsibility of the UN for the Actions of Peacekeepers

Another interesting and increasingly relevant topic is the responsibility of the United Nations for the actions of its peacekeepers. It is important to recall that while UN peacekeeping missions operate under the operational authority of the UN, the military personnel that form the UN peacekeeping mission remain organs of the states from which they are contributed. The United Nations has limited operational control over the troops. The troop-contributing state retains command over its military contingents.[138] Therefore, when determining whether the UN must be held liable for the actions of its peacekeeping troops, the decisive question is whether members of peacekeeping forces are to be regarded as UN officials or as public officials of their home states.

As a rule, peacekeepers enjoy immunity from legal process in any other state, including the host state and transit states.[139] Immunity does not mean impunity. Immunity from legal process simply means that the host state or transit states cannot prosecute members of a peacekeeping force for offenses committed on their territory in the performance of their duties. Customary international law entitles sending states to exercise this power vis-à-vis their own troops.[140] The

---

138 See Terry D Gill, "Legal Aspects of the Transfer of Authority in UN Peace Operations" (2011) 42 *Netherlands Y of Int'l L* 37.

139 *Jurisdictional Immunities of the State (Germany v Italy: Greece intervening)*, [2012] ICJ Rep 99 [*Jurisdictional Immunities of the State*].

140 See also revised *Model Memorandum of Understanding between the United Nations and States contributing resources to the United Nations Peacekeeping Operation*, UN Doc A/C.5/60/26 Chapter 9 and A/61/19 (Part III).

main purpose of this rule is to prevent external interference in the activities of the peacekeeping mission and to ensure an impartial and effective performance of its mandate.[141] In addition, the absence of immunity in the host state would discourage other states from contributing troops to peacekeeping missions. Of course, contributing states always have the option of waiving the immunity and allowing the host state to prosecute a perpetrator; however, this option is generally not exercised. The criminal liability of the troops is a question entirely separate from the question of whether the international responsibility of the UN or of the troop-contributing state is engaged and whether it has an obligation to make reparation.[142]

In addition to criminal and disciplinary responsibility of its individual members, a peacekeeping mission established under the auspices of the United Nations may also face claims for reparation for the damage caused by the troops. This is known as third-party liability. The types of loss or injury most commonly encountered in the practice of United Nations operations include non-consensual use and occupancy of premises,[143] personal injury[144] and property loss or damage arising from the ordinary operation of the force, and such injury and damage as result from combat operations.[145] According to a well-established general principle of law, damage caused in breach of an international obligation that can be attributed to a state or to an international organization entails the international responsibility of

---

141 Dieter Fleck, "Securing Status and Protection of Peacekeepers" in Roberta Arnold & Geert-Jan Alexander Knoops, eds, *Practice and Policies of Modern Peace Support Operations Under International Law* (New York: Transnational Publishers, 2006) 141 at 155.

142 *Jurisdictional Immunities of the State*, above note 139 at para 100.

143 See for instance *Attorney General v Nissan*, [1969] UKHL 3 at page 646 [*Nissan*]; *NK v Austria*, 77 IRL 470 (1979) (Oberlandesgericht Wien) [*NK*].

144 *Georges v United Nations*, 834 F3d 88 (2nd Cir Ct App 2016) [*Georges*] for actions of the United Nations Stabilization Mission in Haiti (MINUSTAH); *Mothers of Srebrenica et al v State of The Netherlands and the United Nations*, C-10/4437, [2012] 160 ILR 58 [*Mothers of Srebrenica*].

145 *Administrative and budgetary aspects of the financing of the United Nations peacekeeping operations: financing of the United Nations peacekeeping operations*, Report of the Secretary-General to the General Assembly, UNGAOR, 51st Sess, UN Doc A/51/903 (1997) at para 2.

that state or of that organization and triggers an obligation to compensate.[146] Being liable for the activities of UN peacekeeping forces is an attribute of the UN's international legal personality and its capacity to bear international rights and obligations.[147] In most cases, the UN assumes its liability for damage caused by members of its forces in the performance of their duties. In fact, paragraph 51 of the Model Status-of-Forces Agreement[148] requires the UN to have a mechanism in place in order to settle claims resulting from damage caused by members of the force in the performance of their official duties and which for reasons of immunity of the organization and its members could not have been submitted to local courts.

Nevertheless, the UN will not assume liability if the contributing state had effective control over the peacekeeper who committed the tortuous act. The UN's position on this point was articulated in the Secretary-General's report to the General Assembly in 1996:

> The international responsibility of the United Nations for combat-related activities of United Nations forces is premised on the assumption that the operation in question is under the exclusive command and control of the United Nations. Where a Chapter VII-authorized operation is conducted under national command and control, international responsibility for the activities of the force is vested in the State or States conducting the operation. The determination of responsibility becomes particularly difficult, however, in cases

---

146 *Draft articles on responsibility of international organizations, with commentaries*, Report of the International Law Commission, UNGAOR, 63rd Sess, UN Doc A/66/10 and Add.1 (2011) at Chapter V; *Financing of the United Nations Protection Force, the United Nations Confidence Restoration Operation in Croatia, the United Nations Preventive Deployment Force and the United Nations Peace Forces headquarters*, Report of the Secretary-General to the General Assembly, UNGAOR, 51st Sess, UN Doc A/51/389 (1996) para 6.

147 *Financing of the United Nations Protection Force, the United Nations Confidence Restoration Operation in Croatia, the United Nations Preventive Deployment Force and the United Nations Peace Forces Headquarters*, Report of Secretary-General to the General Assembly, UNGAOR, 51st Sess, UN Doc A/51/389 (1996) at para 6 [*Financing the United Nations Protection Force*].

148 *Model Status-of-Forces Agreement for Peacekeeping Operations*, Report of the Secretary-General, UNGAOR, 45th Sess, UN Doc A/45/594 (1990).

> where a State or States provide the United Nations with forces in support of a United Nations operation but not necessarily as an integral part thereof, and where operational command and control is unified or coordinated. This was the case in Somalia where the Quick Reaction Force and the US Rangers were provided in support of the United Nations Operation in Somalia (UNOSOM II), and this was also the case in the former Yugoslavia where the Rapid Reaction Force was provided in support of the United Nations Protection Force (UNPROFOR).
>
> In joint operations, international responsibility for the conduct of the troops lies where operational command and control is vested according to the arrangements establishing the modalities of cooperation between the State or States providing the troops and the United Nations. In the absence of formal arrangements between the United Nations and the State or States providing troops, responsibility would be determined in each and every case according to the degree of effective control exercised by either party in the conduct of the operation.[149]

Essentially, whether unlawful acts committed by peacekeepers can be attributed to the UN depends on the extent to which the peacekeeping force was under the command and control of the UN. This is a question of fact. Unlawful acts committed by peacekeeping forces will be attributed to the UN only where the UN exercised effective command over the troops and control over the commission of the unlawful act. This position is consistent with the jurisprudence of domestic courts. In the case of *Netherlands v Nuhanovic*, the Supreme Court of the Netherlands found the Government of the Netherlands responsible for the death of three men from Srebrenica even though the wrongful act was committed by the Dutch battalion as part of a UN peacekeeping force. The Court determined that the conduct was attributable to the Netherlands because Dutch authorities had effective control over the relevant conduct.[150] The UK House of Lords adopted a similar reasoning when adjudicating a claim for

149 *Financing of the United Nations Protection Force*, above note 147 at paras 17–18.

150 *The State of the Netherlands v Hasan Nuhanovic*, C-12/03324, [2013] 160 IRL 629.

compensation. Specifically, in the case of *Attorney General v Nissan*,[151] the plaintiff was a British national who owned a hotel in Cyprus. The British troops stationed in Cyprus became part of a UN peacekeeping force. While performing its official functions, the British contingent took over and occupied the hotel, causing material damages to the property. The British Government argued that its troops were acting on behalf of the United Nations and their conduct could not be attributed to the United Kingdom. The Court rejected this argument, ruling that the British Crown bore the primary responsibility for the actions of its troops even though they were participating in peacekeeping efforts.

In some instances, victims of wrongful acts committed by peacekeepers are deprived of any recourse because they can sue neither the troop-contributing nation nor the UN. For instance, the Nepalese peacekeeping troops stationed in Haiti as part of the United Nations Stabilization Mission in Haiti (MINUSTAH) caused a cholera outbreak in Haiti by discharging human waste from their military base into a river. Approximately 750,000 people around the military base became seriously ill and almost 9,000 people died. The victims sued the UN before New York courts, but due to the UN's immunity from every form of legal process, their lawsuit was dismissed as not receivable.[152] After several years of refusing to compensate the victims, the UN carried out an investigation that concluded beyond any doubt that the Nepalese peacekeepers were directly responsible for the outbreak. The UN finally admitted liability and decided to make reparations.[153] This case demonstrates that unless the state that contributes troops has a credible, independent, and impartial judicial system, victims of wrongful acts by peacekeeping troops may have no meaningful recourse.

---

151 *Nissan*, above note 143; see also *NK*, above note 143.

152 See for instance the cases of *Georges*, above note 144, for actions of the United Nations Stabilization Mission in Haiti (MINUSTAH); *Mothers of Srebrenica*, above note 144, for actions of Dutch peacekeeping troops in Bosnia and Herzegovina.

153 Jonathan M Katz, "UN Admits Role in Cholera Epidemic in Haiti" *New York Times* (18 August 2016) A1.

D. ACCOUNTABILITY OF THE SECURITY COUNCIL

It is settled law that the Security Council has a duty to observe the treaty provisions established by the *UN Charter* when they constitute limitations on its powers or criteria for its judgment.[154] What can be done when the Security Council obviously exceeds its powers? During the creation of the United Nations, the Belgian delegation proposed to include in the *UN Charter* a provision that would empower the International Court of Justice to review recommendations and decisions made by the Security Council. The proposed provision read as follows:

> Any State, party to a dispute brought before the Security Council, shall have the right to ask the Permanent Court of International Justice whether a recommendation or a decision made by the Council or proposed in it infringes on its essential rights. If the Court considers that such rights have been disregarded or are threatened, it is for the Council either to reconsider the question or to refer the dispute to the Assembly for decision.[155]

This proposal failed. The USSR argued that the Security Council should receive full confidence of the members of the organization, especially since there was no reason to believe that the Security Council might wish to infringe the rights of a sovereign nation. To this, Colombia replied that full confidence in the Security Council does not exclude full confidence in the International Court of Justice. The Soviet delegation also expressed the view that the Belgian proposal would have the effect of weakening the authority of the Council to maintain international peace and security. It added that a mechanism for judicial review of the Council's decision would inhibit its ability to carry out its functions and might even transform the Security Council

---

154 *Conditions of Admission of a State to Membership in the United Nations (Article 4 of the Charter)*, Advisory Opinion, [1948] ICJ Rep 64.

155 United Nations Conference on International Organizations, Dumbarton Oaks Proposals Concerning the Establishment of a General International Organization: Amendments Submitted by the Belgian Delegation, G/7 (k)(1) at 335–36.

into a defendant before the International Court of Justice.[156] The US and French delegations also opposed this proposal on the basis of redundancy. They argued that the Security Council was bound to act in accordance with international law and, therefore, could not act in violation of another state's sovereign rights. They did not see any necessity to include such a provision in the *UN Charter*. The United Kingdom opposed the amendment on completely different grounds. The British delegate contended that reviewing Security Council decisions would compel the International Court of Justice to make not only legal but also political determinations. He added that a review by the International Court of Justice would cause delay and place a "powerful weapon" in the hands of a state contemplating aggression.[157] As a result, Belgium withdrew its proposal and the *UN Charter* remained silent on this point.

No national or supranational body or organ of the United Nations, including the International Court of Justice and the General Assembly, has been endowed with a power similar to that enjoyed by a national constitutional court. As the International Court of Justice recalled, the legality of the Security Council's decisions cannot be reviewed by anyone:

> In the legal systems of states, there is often some procedure for determining the validity of even a legislative or governmental act, but no analogous procedure is to be found in the structure of the United Nations.... As anticipated in 1945, therefore, each organ must, in the first place at least, determine its own jurisdiction.[158]

In its advisory opinion on Namibia, the ICJ explicitly conceded that "the Court does not possess powers of judicial review or appeal in respect of the decisions taken by the United Nations organs

156 United Nations Conference on International Organizations, Commission III, Committee II *Peaceful Settlement*, Summary Report of Seventh Meeting of Committee III/2, UN Doc III/2/15 Doc 433.

157 United Nations Conference on International Organizations, Commission III, Committee II *Peaceful Settlement*, Summary Report of Ninth Meeting of Committee III/2, UN Doc III/2/15 Doc 498.

158 *Certain expenses of the United Nations*, above note 124 at 168.

concerned."[159] Although the *UN Charter* authorizes the ICJ to provide an advisory opinion on any legal question, including the legality of the Security Council's decisions, the Court cannot exercise this power *proprio motu* or of its own volition. The Court cannot give advisory opinions on the request of a UN member state either. The Court may exercise this power only if either the General Assembly or the Security Council requests it to do so. Other organs of the UN and specialized agencies may also request an advisory opinion with a prior authorization from the General Assembly and under certain conditions.[160]

It is highly unlikely that the Security Council will seek an advisory opinion on the legality of its own decisions. Therefore, unless the General Assembly requests the Court to review the legality of decisions made by the Security Council, potential *ultra vires* decisions of the Security Council may remain unchallenged. It is worth mentioning that even if the General Assembly requests an advisory opinion from the Court on the legality of a decision adopted by the Security Council, the legal effect of this advisory opinion would be limited, since it is not binding. An advisory opinion holding that a Security Council decision is illegal or is *ultra vires* will not have the effect of invalidating that decision (and even less the action based on that decision).

UN member states and their national courts also do not have the authority or power to question the legality of Security Council resolutions. On the contrary, UN member states have an international legal obligation to carry out binding decisions of the Security Council even if they view such decisions as *ultra vires*. Nevertheless, in recent years, the implementation of Security Council resolutions has been challenged before national courts. Individuals and entities adversely affected by Security Council resolutions do not seek to invalidate

---

159 *Continued Presence of South Africa in Namibia*, above note 23 at para 89.

160 In its advisory opinion on the *Legality of the Use by a State of Nuclear Weapons in Armed Conflicts*, Advisory Opinion, [1996] ICJ Rep 66 at para 10, the International Court of Justice specified that "three conditions must be satisfied in order to found the jurisdiction of the Court when a request for an advisory opinion is submitted to it by a specialized agency: the agency requesting the opinion must be duly authorized, under the Charter, to request opinions from the Court; the opinion requested must be on a legal question; and this question must be one arising within the scope of the activities of the requesting agency."

Security Council resolutions but to make them inoperative. While national courts do not have jurisdiction to review the lawfulness of Security Council resolutions, they are entitled to review the acts of their governments designed to give effect to Security Council resolutions.[161] Consequently, domestic courts may order their national governments not to implement Security Council resolutions if the implementation would breach national legislation. For instance, the Court of Justice of the European Union invalidated a European Community Regulation adopted in connection with the implementation of a Security Council resolution that required UN member states to take measures to freeze the funds of individuals and entities identified by the Security Council Sanctions Committee.[162] The Court held that the regulation did not give the individuals listed by the Sanctions Committee minimal procedural guarantees. The Federal Court of Canada also ruled that the listing procedure of the al-Qaeda and Taliban Sanctions Committee violated the right to procedural fairness of targeted individuals. The Federal Court ordered the Government of Canada not to give effect to a travel ban imposed by the Security Council on a Canadian citizen of Sudanese descent.[163] Similarly, the European Court of Human Rights held that Switzerland violated the rights of an Italian citizen of Egyptian descent when it implemented the travel ban imposed by the Sanctions Committee of the Security Council.[164] While national courts do not have jurisdiction to review the legality of Security Council resolutions, they can produce an equivalent effect by ordering national governments not to implement problematic Security Council resolutions. Such orders effectively render Security Council resolutions ineffective or inoperative. This erodes and undermines the authority of the Security Council.

One way of preserving the authority of the Security Council without perpetuating its lack of accountability would be to establish a subsidiary

161 *Youssef Nada v State Secretariat for Economic Affairs and Federal Department of Economic Affairs, Administrative appeal judgment*, C-1A 45/2007; ILDC 461 (CH 2007); BGE 133 II 450 (14 November 2007).

162 *Kadi*, above note 98.

163 *Abdelrazik v Canada (Minister of Foreign Affairs)*, 2009 FC 580.

164 *Nada v Switzerland*, No 10593/08, [2012] ECHR 1 (GC).

organ responsible for reviewing and adjudicating complaints of member states affected by Security Council actions or decisions. The same body would have jurisdiction to advise the Security Council in advance whether a proposed course of action is legal and *intra vires.* The same body would be authorized to make a recommendation to the General Assembly to seek an advisory opinion from the ICJ on the legality of a Security Council decision or action. To be fully effective, this subsidiary organ must be completely independent from the Security Council. The main advantage of this proposal is that it does not require an amendment of the *UN Charter* or of the Statute of the ICJ.

Chapter 5

THE ECONOMIC AND SOCIAL COUNCIL

The Covenant of the League of Nations contained only two provisions that dealt with international cooperation in the economic and social fields. These were the first paragraph of the Preamble and Article 23 of the Covenant. The Preamble vaguely established a link between international cooperation on the one hand and international peace and security on the other: "In order to promote international cooperation and to achieve international peace and security." Article 23 was limited in scope, dealing mostly with the protection of employment rights of workers, just treatment of the native inhabitants, prevention of human smuggling and drug trafficking, supervision of the trade in arms and ammunition, maintenance and protection of freedom of communications, equitable transit and treatment of members in relation to commercial relations, and prevention and control of disease.

The limited scope of international cooperation was due to the fact that not all nations agreed on the necessity to mention in the Covenant of the League cooperation in the economic and social spheres. In particular, while the United States and France recognized that international cooperation in all areas was important to prevent another war, they believed that the League of Nations was supposed to be a collective security arrangement only. Great Britain and Italy, on the other hand, favoured a broader role for the League and advocated for the inclusion of provisions dealing with economic and social cooperation.

Thus, the diluted and noncommittal text found in Article 23 of the League's Covenant was a compromise:

> **Article 23**
> Subject to and in accordance with the provisions of international conventions existing or hereafter to be agreed upon, the Members of the League:
> (a) will endeavour to secure and maintain fair and humane conditions of labour for men, women, and children, both in their own countries and in all countries to which their commercial and industrial relations extend, and for that purpose will establish and maintain the necessary international organisations;
> (b) undertake to secure just treatment of the native inhabitants of territories under their control;
> (c) will entrust the League with the general supervision over the execution of agreements with regard to the traffic in women and children, and the traffic in opium and other dangerous drugs;
> (d) will entrust the League with the general supervision of the trade in arms and ammunition with the countries in which the control of this traffic is necessary in the common interest;
> (e) will make provision to secure and maintain freedom of communications and of transit and equitable treatment for the commerce of all Members of the League. In this connection, the special necessities of the regions devastated during the war of 1914–1918 shall be borne in mind;
> (f) will endeavour to take steps in matters of international concern for the prevention and control of disease.

It is interesting to note that the Preamble of the Covenant used the verb "achieve" in relation to peace and security and the verb "promote" in relation to international cooperation. This was a clear indication that achieving peace and security was the organization's primary goal whereas international cooperation was a mere ideal. This perception gradually changed. The nexus between international peace and security and the human condition became abundantly obvious during World War II. The framers of the *UN Charter* understood that peace and security were inseparable from economic development.[1] Hence, the idea of international cooperation in economic and social spheres had ripened at the time of setting up the United Nations. During the Dumbarton Oaks conference, the four allies (China, the United Kingdom, the United States, and the USSR)

> reflected the idea that the United Nations should be involved in economic and social cooperation, albeit within a broader international order which contemplated the International Bank for Reconstruction and Development, the International Monetary Fund and the International Trade Organization (which of course became the much watered-down General Agreement on Trade and Tariffs).[2]

The proposals worked out at Dumbarton Oaks "envisioned the creation of an Economic and Social Council ... as a subsidiary body of the General Assembly."[3] During the San Francisco Conference, the nations decided to set up ECOSOC as a principal organ of the organization as opposed to as a subsidiary organ of the General Assembly.[4] The rationale for this recommendation was:

> The Committee agreed unanimously to recommend to Committee E/1 that the Economic and Social Council be listed as a Principal Organ of the Organization. This decision expressed the opinion of the Committee that economic and social cooperation was of the utmost importance to the success of the Organization as a whole, and that the Charter should not give the impression that these objectives were in any way subordinate to the other principal objectives of the Organization.[5]

---

1 *Report of the High-level Panel on Threats, Challenges and Change*, UNGAOR, 59th Sess, UN Doc A/59/565 (2004) at para 274 [*Report of the High-level Panel*].

2 Gert Rosenthal, "The Economic and Social Council of the United Nations: Ann Issues Paper" February 2005, No 15, *Dialogue on Globalization* at 8.

3 *Ibid.*

4 *Charter of the United Nations*, 26 June 1945, Can TS 1945 No 7, art 7.1 [*Charter of the United Nations*].

5 *United Nations Conference on International Organizations*, Commission II, Committee 3, Economic and Social Cooperation, Report of the Rapporteur Doc 861 II/3/55 (1945) at 229.

Despite this, the *UN Charter* strongly implies that even though ECOSOC is a principal organ, it is subject to the authority of the General Assembly and the Security Council. For instance, the responsibility for the discharge of the international economic and social cooperation functions of the UN are vested in the General Assembly and, under the authority of the General Assembly, in the Economic and Social Council.[6] If the General Assembly and ECOSOC are both principal organs of the UN, then one should not exercise authority over the other. Similarly, the *UN Charter* states that ECOSOC "shall assist the Security Council upon its request,"[7] which implies that the Security Council has authority over ECOSOC.[8] In 1953, the Lebanese delegation raised the question of whether the phrase "shall assist the Security Council upon its request" placed an obligation on ECOSOC or allowed for some discretion to decide whether or not it should comply with the Security Council's request for assistance.[9] ECOSOC Rules of Procedure seem to suggest that the Council is obligated to comply with requests emanating from the General Assembly and the Security Council.[10]

A. MEMBERSHIP

The Economic and Social Council has a limited membership. Initially, it consisted of eighteen member states. As the membership of the United Nations increased, the General Assembly approved the enlargement of ECOSOC from eighteen to twenty-seven member states in

---

6 *Charter of the United Nations*, above note 4, art 60.

7 *Ibid*, art 65.

8 The French version of Article 65 of the *UN Charter* implies that ECOSOC may assist the Security Council upon its request without, however, having an obligation to do so: "Le Conseil économique et social peut fournir des informations au Conseil de sécurité et l'assister si celui-ci le demande."

9 *Repertory of Practice of the United Nations Organs*, 1945–1954, Vol 3, Article 65 at 418.

10 Rules of Procedure of the Economic and Social Council, UN Doc E/5715/Rev.2 at Rule 4.1(c) [Rules of Procedure of the Economic and Social Council].

1963.[11] This resolution came into effect on 31 August 1965. Of these nine additional seats, seven were given to Asian and African states, one to a Latin American state, and one to Western European or other states. In 1971, the General Assembly approved a second expansion of ECOSOC's membership from twenty-seven to fifty-four members.[12] This resolution came into effect on 14 September 1973. The seats are distributed in accordance with this pattern: (a) fourteen members are African states; (b) eleven members are Asian states; (c) ten members are from Latin American states; (d) thirteen members are from Western European and other states; and (e) six members are from Eastern European states.[13] ECOSOC members are elected by the General Assembly for a term of three years.[14] To ensure continuity, staggered elections of eighteen members take place each year. A retiring member is eligible for immediate re-election. Three of the five permanent members of the Security Council have been continuously re-elected, mainly because they provide funding for most of ECOSOC's budget, but also because of their special status. China has also continuously held a seat on the ECOSOC since the restoration of its seat in the UN in 1971 and Russia did not have a seat in ECOSOC between 2010 and 2014. Important contributors to the UN budget such as Japan and Germany also almost continuously hold a seat on the ECOSOC.[15] Membership carries the right to participate in the Council's deliberations and the right to vote.

What happens if the General Assembly fails to elect all fifty-four members of the Council? This question arose in 1983, when the Office of Legal Affairs was asked to explain legal and constitutional consequences that could arise from the General Assembly's inability to elect an ECOSOC member. This was not an entirely unfamiliar

11 *Question of equitable representation on the Security Council and the Economic and Social Council*, GA Res A 1991 (XVIII), UNGAOR, 18th Sess, UN Doc A/Res/1991(XVIII) (1963) 21.

12 *Enlargement of the Economic and Social Council*, GA Res 2847 (XXVI), UNGAOR, 26th Sess, UN Doc A/Res/2847(XXVI) (1971) 67.

13 *Ibid.*

14 *Charter of the United Nations*, above note 4, arts 61.1–61.2.

15 Since 1974, Germany has been continuously represented in ECOSOC, with the exception of 2008 and 2013.

terrain for the UN legal counsel; a similar scenario had arisen four years earlier when the General Assembly failed to elect a non-permanent member of the Security Council. Member states had once again turned to the UN legal counsel for an authoritative interpretation of the *UN Charter* by asking him whether the incomplete composition of the Security Council had an effect on the validity of its resolutions. While acknowledging that such a scenario is neither legally nor constitutionally desirable, the UN's top lawyer opined that "while the failure of the General Assembly to elect a non-permanent member of the Security Council would be inconsistent with Article 23 of the *UN Charter*, such an act of omission could not produce legal consequences for the functioning of the Security Council, which is the organ primarily responsible for the maintenance of international peace and security."[16] In such cases, resolutions of the Security Council taken in accordance with the relevant provisions of Article 27 of the *UN Charter* remain valid. The UN legal counsel applied this same reasoning to the General Assembly's failure to elect a member of ECOSOC:

> While the functions of the Economic and Social Council are of course different, it cannot be said, certainly not as a matter of law, that they are of lesser significance [than those of the Security Council], and in any event both Councils are, by virtue of paragraph 1 of Article 7 of the Charter, "principal organs" of the Organization. Consequently, the reasoning of the 1979 opinion in respect of the Security Council is equally applicable to a failure of the General Assembly to complete an election of members of the Economic and Social Council.[17]

---

16 "Legal consequences of an inability of the General Assembly to elect a non-permanent member of the Security Council" in *United Nations Juridical Yearbook* (New York: UN, 1979) at 164.

17 "Legal and constitutional consequences that would arise from a possible inability of the General Assembly to elect a member of the Economic and Social Council" Legal opinion prepared at the request of Under-Secretary-General for Political and General Assembly Affairs, in *United Nations Juridical Yearbook* (New York: UN, 1983) at 183.

Each member of the Economic and Social Council may have one accredited representative[18] who may choose to be accompanied by such alternative representatives and advisers as may be required.[19] The credentials of representatives and the names of alternate representatives and advisers must be submitted to the Secretary-General at least three days before the first meeting they are to attend.[20]

B. FUNCTIONING OF THE ECONOMIC AND SOCIAL COUNCIL

In accordance with Article 72 of the *UN Charter*, ECOSOC shall adopt its own rules of procedure, including the method of selecting its president, and shall meet as required in accordance with its rules, which shall include provision for the convening of meetings on the request of a majority of its members.

> After the Charter was signed, a Preparatory Commission of the UN was formed, with an executive committee of 14 members, and provisional arrangements were made for the first sessions of all organs. The Committee prepared draft rules of procedure for all of the organs, including ECOSOC, and these were approved by the General Assembly on 29 January 1946 and adopted, without changes, by ECOSOC during its first session, held in London from January 23 to February 18.[21]

ECOSOC's Rules of Procedure contain eighty-six articles that regulate its sessions, agenda, representation of member states, presidency, bureau and secretariat, subsidiary bodies, languages, types of meetings, records, conduct of business, voting and elections, participation of non-members, and consultation with NGOs. Below, we will examine only a few of these topics, including the voting and elections, sessions and meetings, presidency and the bureau, the secretariat, and subsidiary bodies.

---

18 *Charter of the United Nations*, above note 4, art 61.4.

19 Rules of Procedure of the Economic and Social Council, above note 10 at Rule 16.

20 *Ibid* at Rule 17.

21 Rosenthal, above note 2 at 9.

1) Voting, Elections, and Participation

The president may declare a meeting of ECOSOC open and permit the debate to proceed when the quorum is met, which requires the presence of representatives of at least one-third of the members of the Council. However, the presence of representatives of a majority of the members is required for any decision to be taken.[22] Each member of the Council has one vote.[23]

Decisions of ECOSOC are made by a majority of members present and voting.[24] The phrase "present and voting" means members casting an affirmative or negative vote. Members who abstain from voting are considered as not voting.[25] Except in cases of elections, which are held by secret ballot,[26] unless the Council decides to proceed without taking a ballot on an agreed candidate or "slate," the Council normally votes by show of hands. Any representative may, however, request a roll call. In such a case, the names of member states are called in the English alphabetical order of their names, starting with the member whose name is drawn by lot by the president of the Council. When a member's name is called, the representative is expected to reply "yes," "no," or "abstention."[27] The representatives are allowed to make brief statements to explain their votes before the commencement of the vote or after its completion.[28] The state sponsoring the proposal or motion is not permitted to explain its vote unless the proposal has been amended. Nevertheless, no representative is allowed to interrupt the voting by making statements or offering explanations as soon as the president announces its commencement.[29]

---

22 Rules of Procedure of the Economic and Social Council, above note 10 at Rule 41.

23 *Charter of the United Nations*, above note 4, art 67.1 and Rules of Procedure of the Economic and Social Council, above note 10 at Rule 58.

24 *Charter of the United Nations*, above note 4, art 67.2 and Rules of Procedure of the Economic and Social Council, above note 10 at Rule 60.1.

25 Rules of Procedure of the Economic and Social Council, above note 10 at Rule 60.2.

26 *Ibid* at Rule 68.

27 *Ibid* at Rule 61.1.

28 *Ibid* at Rule 62.

29 *Ibid* at Rule 63.

ECOSOC and its subsidiary bodies are expected to invite any member state of the United Nations (which is not a member of ECOSOC or of its relevant subsidiary body) to participate, without vote, in its deliberations on any matter of particular concern to that member state.[30] ECOSOC has the discretion to decide whether a matter is of particular concern to the state seeking an invitation to participate in the Council's session.[31] For example, when socialist states accused some countries of violating trade-union rights, the president of ECOSOC expressed the importance of giving these states the opportunity of answering the charges brought against them.[32] The scope of the participation of a state not a member of the Council does not include the right to vote, but consists of the right to intervene in the discussions and to make proposals that may be put to the vote at the request of any member of the Council.[33]

It may also "make arrangements for representatives of the specialized agencies to participate, without vote, in its deliberations and in those of the commissions established by it, and for its representatives to participate in the deliberations of the specialized agencies."[34] The subsidiary bodies of ECOSOC may even permit the participation of national liberation movements, such as the Palestine Liberation Organization.[35]

Another way of participating in ECOSOC's activities is through consultations. The *UN Charter* draws a clear distinction between the right to participate in the deliberations and the right to be consulted. Only states (not members of ECOSOC) and specialized agencies are permitted to participate without vote in the deliberations of the

---

30 *Charter of the United Nations*, above note 4, art 69.

31 Repertory of Practice of United Nations Organs, above note 9 at para 11.

32 *Ibid* at para 23.

33 *Ibid* at para 13.

34 *Charter of the United Nations*, above note 4, art 70.

35 "Participation of national liberation movements in sessions of the Sub-Commission on Prevention of Discrimination and Protection of Minorities – Rule 70 of the Rules of Procedure of the Functional Commissions of the Economic and Social Council – Practice of the Economic and Social Council in the Application of Rule 73 of the Council's Rules of Procedure" in *United Nations Juridical Yearbook* (New York: UN, 1983) at 189.

Economic and Social Council. Non-governmental organizations do not take part in deliberations—they may be consulted only. This consultative status gives NGOs more limited rights of participation than those accorded to states not members of ECOSOC and to specialized agencies. These restricted participation rights are due to practical considerations. There are over 6,000 NGOs that enjoy a consultative status. If each NGO had been accorded the right to participate in the Council's deliberations, ECOSOC would be paralyzed by continuous and never-ending discussions. Hence, ECOSOC was given the discretion to determine which NGOs should be invited to provide advice on matters and questions within its competence. Participation rights associated with a consultative status may include the ability of an NGO to propose that certain agenda items be placed in the provisional agenda of the Council and its subsidiary bodies, to submit to the Council and its subsidiary bodies written statements, and make oral statements during a plenary.

To be granted this status, an NGO must be concerned with matters falling within the competence of ECOSOC or its subsidiary bodies. The aims and purposes of the NGO applying for a consultative status must be consistent with the purposes and principles of the *UN Charter*. The NGO must demonstrate that it can support the work of the UN and promote knowledge of its principles and activities. In considering applications for consultative status, ECOSOC strives to achieve participation of NGOs from all regions and areas of the world, and particularly from developing countries. To be granted a consultative status, the NGO must have an established headquarters, an executive officer, a democratically adopted constitution, a governing body, and an executive organ.[36]

2) Types of ECOSOC Sessions and Segments

The annual cycle of work of the Economic and Social Council begins in July and ends in July of the following year. During this cycle, the

36 *Consultative relationship between the United Nations and non-governmental organizations*, ESC Res 1996/31, UNESCOR, 1996, UN Doc E/1996/96, 1 at 54.

Council holds two types of sessions: organizational and substantive.[37] During the organizational session, which is held in New York, member states discuss and agree on ECOSOC's Programme of Work, elect the Council's president and the bureau (the role of which will be outlined below in this Chapter).[38] The Council's annual program of work is based on a main theme that is "determined at the beginning of its cycle, selected taking into account the role of the Council in promoting the balanced integration of the economic, social and environmental dimensions of sustainable development, as well as the post-2015 development agenda, decided by the Council based on inputs from its subsidiary bodies, as well as Member States."[39] The main theme provides guidance on the work of all coordinated agencies, organizations, and entities while respecting the agenda, diversity of mandates, and specialized expertise of the various subsidiary bodies. It should enable the Council to promote system-wide coherence and coordination of issues requiring the effective response of the United Nations system.[40] In 2018, the theme of the session was "From global to local: supporting sustainable and resilient societies in urban and rural communities." The theme of the 2019 session was "Empowering people and ensuring inclusiveness and equality."

Substantive sessions are held between May and July and normally last four weeks. Their venue alters between New York and Geneva. To prepare for its substantive session, ECOSOC holds short sessions, meetings, and discussions throughout the year. Substantive sessions consist of many segments, forums, and meetings, including the High-Level Segment, the Integration Segment, Operational Activities Segment, and Humanitarian Affairs Segment. Each segment may have its own theme. The themes of various segments focus on a particular aspect of the main theme, bearing in mind their respective functions, and reflect the integrated, indivisible, and interlinked nature of the

37 Rules of Procedure of the Economic and Social Council, above note 10 at Rule 2.

38 *Ibid.*

39 *Review of the implementation of General Assembly resolution 61/16 on the strengthening of the Economic and Social Council*, GA Res 68/1, UNGAOR, 68th Sess, UN Doc A/Res/68/1 (2013) 1 at para 7.

40 *Ibid.*

sustainable development goals and the three dimensions of sustainable development (economic, social, and environmental).[41]

The most important segment of a substantive session is the High-Level Segment attended by ministers and other high-ranking officials of member states. It represents the culmination of ECOSOC's annual cycle of work and serves as a forum to discuss key international issues such as economic, social, and sustainable development. The outcome of the High-Level Segment is a negotiated ministerial declaration.[42]

The Integration Segment is held for one day immediately before the High-Level Segment. This segment brings together senior officials of member states, subsidiary bodies of ECOSOC, various entities of the UN system, international organizations, NGOs, academia, and even the private sector. The mandate of the Integration Segment was recently redefined by the General Assembly and reads as follows:

> The integration segment will be held for one day immediately before the high-level political forum. It will discuss and consolidate all the inputs of Member States, including case studies and lessons learned, the subsidiary bodies of the Economic and Social Council, the United Nations system and other relevant stakeholders to promote the balanced integration of the three dimensions of sustainable development. This segment will thus bring together the key messages from the subsidiary bodies of the Council and the United Nations system on the main theme, develop action-oriented recommendations for follow-up and feed into the high-level political forum. It will also coordinate the work of the subsidiary bodies of the Council, promoting a clearer division of labour among them, and the policies and activities of the specialized agencies relating to the Sustainable Development Goals and other internationally agreed development goals. The Secretary-General will present to the Council the annual overview report of the United Nations System Chief Executives Board for Coordination. Heads of United Nations system

41 *Review of the implementation of General Assembly resolution 68/1 on the strengthening of the Economic and Social Council*, GA Res 72/305, UNGAOR, 72nd Sess, UN Doc A/Res/72/305 (2018), Annex at paras 4, 6.

42 *Ibid* at para 12.

> entities, Chairs of the subsidiary bodies of the Council and the Executive Secretaries of the regional commissions will also be invited to participate. A dedicated effort will be made in 2019 to improve the role, functioning and impact of the segment along these lines. This will be reviewed as part of the broader review of Council segments and meetings at the seventy-fourth session of the General Assembly along with the high-level political forum.[43]

This segment concludes with adoption of agreed conclusions containing concrete recommendations for action to be taken by relevant actors of the UN system. In the subsequent year, ECOSOC member states follow up on the implementation of these recommendations.

During the Management Segment, which used to be called Coordination and Management Meeting,[44] ECOSOC reviews and approves reports from its subsidiary and expert bodies in economic, social, environmental, and related fields. These reports pertain to a wide range of issues from drugs and crime to health. Some meetings may focus on particular situations in specific countries or on topics that are relevant to a specific region, but which nevertheless require concerted efforts and discussions. This segment lasts no more than two days, twice per cycle, and attracts participants not only from UN member states but also from ECOSOC's substantive and regional commissions, UN development agencies, and UN funds and programs.

The Operational Activities for Development Segment aims at improving the quality and impact of the UN's operational activities for development and at ensuring an integrated approach in this field. It is a platform to ensure "accountability for, and acceleration of, system-wide performance and results in relation to the 2030 Agenda and provide guidance to and overall coordination of the United Nations development system."[45] The work of this segment gives an opportunity to policy-makers and representatives of the UN development system to discuss and consult with each other on international development cooperation issues through panels and interactive

43 *Ibid* at para 11.

44 The meeting was renamed by the General Assembly in *ibid*.

45 *Ibid*, at para 14.

dialogues. The Development Segment is also an opportunity for ECOSOC to exercise oversight over UN funds and programs by receiving from them annual reports and by holding with their executive heads an interactive dialogue session. The Development Segment leads to the adoption of decisions and resolutions.

The Humanitarian Affairs Segment focuses on the activities of UN organs and specialized agencies in the field of emergency humanitarian assistance. Its objective is to strengthen the coordination and effectiveness of UN humanitarian assistance and to support and complement international efforts aimed at addressing humanitarian emergencies, including natural disasters.[46] During the Humanitarian Segment session, the UN Office for the Coordination of Humanitarian Assistance (OCHA) briefs the Council on humanitarian issues.

In addition to organizational and substantive sessions, ECOSOC also holds forums, such as the Youth Forum, Partnership Forum, and Financing for Development Forum. Moreover, special sessions may be held by decision of the Council, upon request or with the concurrence of a majority of the Council's members, upon the request of the General Assembly or the Security Council, by decision of the president with the concurrence of the vice-presidents of ECOSOC, upon request of any member state of the UN, or of a specialized agency, as long as the majority of the members concur in the request.[47] ECOSOC's meetings are held in public unless it decides otherwise.[48]

While the official languages of ECOSOC are Arabic, Chinese, English, French, Russian, and Spanish, its working languages are only English, French, and Spanish.[49] The Secretariat has a duty to ensure that speeches made in an official language are interpreted into the other official languages.[50] A delegation is allowed to make a speech in a language other than an official language if it provides an

46 *Strengthening of the Economic and Social Council*, GA Res 61/16, UNGAOR, 61st Sess, UN Doc A/Res/61/16 (2006) 1 at para 13.

47 Rules of Procedure of the Economic and Social Council, above note 10 at Rule 4.

48 *Ibid* at Rule 36.

49 *Ibid* at Rule 32.

50 *Ibid* at Rule 33.1.

interpretation into one of the official languages of the UN.[51] Interpretation into the remaining five official languages is provided by the Secretariat. Records are drawn up in all three working languages. A delegation may request the UN Secretariat to translate a part or the entirety of the record into the other three official languages that are not working languages of ECOSOC (Arabic, Chinese, and Russian).[52] Nevertheless, all resolutions and formal decisions of ECOSOC are published in all six official languages.[53]

3) Presidency and Vice-Presidency (The Bureau)

Each year, at the commencement of its first meeting, the Council elects a president and four vice-presidents from among the representatives of its members.[54] These five elected officials constitute the executive organ of ECOSOC, called "the Bureau."[55] The president is elected on the basis of an equitable geographical rotation of the presidency among the following regional groups: African states, Asian states, Eastern European states, Latin American and Caribbean states, and Western European and other states.[56] The four vice-presidents are also elected on the basis of equitable geographical distribution; however, they must belong to regional groups other than the one to which the president belongs. The president and the vice-presidents hold office until their successors are elected and they are eligible for re-election.[57] If, during a mandate, the president or a vice-president ceases to hold office, a new president or vice-president is elected as a replacement for the remainder of the term.[58] In the meantime, the remaining members of the Bureau designate one of the vice-presidents to assume the presidency until the election of a new president,[59]

---

51 *Ibid* at Rule 33.2.
52 *Ibid at* Rule 34.
53 *Ibid at* Rule 35.
54 *Ibid at* Rule 18.1.
55 *Ibid.*
56 *Ibid.*
57 *Ibid at* Rule 19.
58 *Ibid at* Rule 22.
59 *Ibid at* Rule 20.2.

in which case the vice-president, acting as president, will have the powers and duties of the president.[60] Similarly, if the president is unable to be present at a meeting, one of the vice-presidents will be designated to take their place.[61] The president and vice-presidents do not vote. However, they may delegate their right to vote to another member of their delegation.[62]

The president's role is described in Rules 42 to 48 of the Rules of Procedure of ECOSOC. These rules expressly provide that the president has "complete control of the proceedings of the Council and over the maintenance of order at its meetings."[63] The president's powers include opening and closing plenary meetings, directing the discussions, ensuring the observance of the Rules of Procedure, according the right to speak, putting questions to the vote, announcing decisions, ruling on points of order, proposing to the Council the closure of the list of speakers, proposing a limitation on the time to be allowed to the speakers and the number of times a representative may speak on a specific item, adjourning or closing the debate, and suspending or adjourning a meeting.[64] The president fulfills these functions under the authority of the Council.[65]

At any point during the discussions in the Council, a representative may raise a "point of order," which, in parliamentary proceedings, refers to an alleged violation of procedural rules. A member state that raises a point of order may only invoke procedural arguments and is not allowed to address the substance of the matter under discussion.[66] The president has the authority to rule whether the point raised by the representative is well-founded or without merit. The president's ruling is not final. Any representative may appeal against the decision of the president by requesting a vote of all members present. The

60 *Ibid at* Rule 21.
61 *Ibid at* Rule 20.1.
62 *Ibid at* Rule 23.
63 *Ibid at* Rule 42.1.
64 *Ibid.*
65 *Ibid at* Rule 42.2.
66 *Ibid at* Rule 43.2.

president's ruling stands unless a majority of the members present and voting overrule the decision.[67]

As to the vice-presidents, their special responsibilities are determined by the Council upon the recommendation of the president.[68] Vice-presidents are often asked to chair meetings or specific segments or moderate panel discussions and debates.[69]

4) Secretariat

The UN Secretariat provides secretarial support and services to ECOSOC. Such services include conference and meeting planning and organization; the preparation of the calendar of conferences and meetings; the provision of meeting room facilities and other services, including translation and interpretation into any or all of the official languages; circulation of documents; printing, publishing, and circulating the records of the sessions, resolutions of the Council, and other documentation; filing and archiving of official records; and other arrangements that may be necessary for ECOSOC's meetings.[70]

The entity responsible for servicing the General Assembly and ECOSOC within the UN Secretariat is the Department for General Assembly and Conference Management led by an Under-Secretary-General. Within this large department, less than a dozen UN staff members work in the Economic and Social Council Affairs Branch, which provides conference management services not only to ECOSOC but also to the Second and Third Committees of the General Assembly, which deal with economic and financial matters and humanitarian and cultural questions, respectively. This branch also provides services to UN conferences dealing with economic and social and related matters.

---

67 *Ibid* at Rule 43.1.

68 *Ibid* at Rule 18.2.

69 See *Report of the Economic and Social Council for 2019*, UNGAOR, 74th Sess, UN Doc A/74/3 (2019).

70 Rules of Procedure of the Economic and Social Council, above note 10 at Rules 28–29.

5) Subsidiary Bodies

Article 68 of the *UN Charter* empowers the Economic and Social Council to set up commissions in economic and social fields and for the promotion of human rights, and such other commissions as may be required for the performance of its functions. The *Report of the Preparatory Commission of the United Nations* "emphasized the need for more or less specialized bodies of various types to assist the Council in carrying out its responsibilities" and "recommended the immediate creation of commissions having functions relating to the following fields: human rights, economic and employment matters, statistics, narcotic drugs and social matters."[71] The Preparatory Commission also advised the Council to examine the desirability of establishing other commissions and committees.

Based on this recommendation, ECOSOC established dozens of subsidiary organs. Currently, ECOSOC has six categories of subsidiary commissions, committees, and expert bodies. These are: (a) functional commissions; (b) regional commissions; (c) standing committees; (d) expert bodies composed of government experts; (e) expert bodies composed of members serving in their personal capacities; and (f) other bodies. The term "commissions" is used to designate two types of subsidiary bodies. First, it refers to the eight functional commissions (described below) established to undertake studies and make recommendations to ECOSOC in the relevant fields of activity. Second, it refers to five regional commissions, which have been set up to deal with economic and social problems of a regional character in specific areas of the world.[72]

a) ECOSOC Functional Commissions

Some delegations insisted on the creation of various functional commissions during the San Francisco Conference. In particular, the Brazilian delegation proposed a commission to assist ECOSOC in promoting the rights of women, whereas the United States proposed a

71 *Repertory of Practice of the United Nations Organs*, 1945–1954, Vol 3, Article 68 at 476.

72 *Ibid* at 477.

commission to control the traffic of dangerous drugs and a human rights commission.[73] In total, six functional commissions were created in the first year of ECOSOC's existence in 1946 in the fields of statistics, population, status of women, social development, narcotic drugs, and human rights. Five of these functional commissions still exist today. The Human Rights Commission was replaced by the Human Rights Council. It was removed from ECOSOC's areas of responsibility and placed under the purview of the General Assembly. Additional functional commissions were created after the end of the Cold War, dealing with crime prevention and criminal justice (1992), science and technology for development (1992), and forests (2000). ECOSOC currently has eight functional commissions. They all have their own bureaus composed of their chairperson, vice-chairpersons, and a rapporteur. Functional commissions have different memberships and methods of functioning and meet at different frequencies. The table below provides basic information on these commissions:

Name	Date of Creation	Mandate	Membership
Statistical Commission	1946[74]	This Commission is the most authoritative decision-making body for international statistical activities. It promotes the development of national statistics and the improvement of their comparability, coordinates the statistical work of specialized agencies, advises UN organs on general questions relating to the collection, analysis, and dissemination of statistical information, and promotes the improvement of statistics and statistical methods.[75]	24 member states[76]

73 Fons Coomans et al, eds, *Human Rights from Exclusion to Inclusion* (The Hague: Kluwer Law International, 2000) at 117.

74 *Statistical Commission*, ESC Res 8 (I), UNESCOR, 1946, UN Doc E/30, 128, as amended by *Statistical Commission*, ESC Res 8 (II), UNESCOR, 1946, UN Doc E/76/Rev.1 and E/84/Rev.1, 518.

75 *Coordination of work in the field of statistics*, ESC Res 1566 (L), UNESCOR, 1971 UN Doc E/Res/1566(L), 2.

76 *Enlargement of subsidiary organs of the Council*, ESC Res 1147 (XLI), UNESCOR, 1996 UN Doc E/Res/1147(XLI) 37 [*Enlargement of subsidiary organs*]; see also

Name	Date of Creation	Mandate	Membership
Commission on Population and Development[77]	1946[78]	It provides advice to ECOSOC on "matters affecting or affected by population changes" and assists it on population issues and trends, population and development strategies, policies, and programs.	47 member states[79]
Commission for Social Development[80]	1946[81]	It advises ECOSOC on aspects of social development policy, including the equitable distribution of national income, social exclusion, and other themes of the Copenhagen Declaration.	46 member states[82]
Commission on the Status of Women	1946[83]	It is the principal global policy-making body dedicated to gender equality and the empowerment of women.	45 member states

Election of members of the functional commissions of the Council, Note by the Secretary-General, UNESCOR, 2020, UN Doc E/12020/9, 1.

77 The General Assembly renamed the Population Commission to Commission on Population and Development, *Report of the International Conference on Population and Development*, GA Res 49/128, UNGAOR, 49th Sess, UN Doc A/Res/49/128 (1994) 1 at para 24.

78 *Population Commission*, ESC Res 3 (III), UNESCOR, 1946, UN Doc E/245/Rev.1, 3.

79 *Membership of the Commission on Population and Development*, ESC Dec 1995/320, in Resolutions and Decisions of the Economic and Social Council, UNESCOR, 1995, UN Doc E/1995/95 at 95; *Enlargement of the membership of the Commission on Population and Development: Election of 20 members*, Note by the Secretary-General, UNESCOR, 1996, UN Doc E/1996/9.

80 The ECOSOC renamed the Social Commission to Commission for Social Development in its resolution entitled *Reappraisal of the role of the Social Commission*, ESC Res 1139 XLI, UNESCOR, 1966 UN Doc E/Res/1139(XLI) 9.

81 *Social Commission*, ESC Res 10 (II), UNESCOR, 1946, UN Doc E/Res/10(II) 522.

82 *Enlargement of subsidiary organs of the Council*, above note 76.

83 *Commission on the status of women*, ESC Res 11 (II), UNESCOR, 1946, UN Doc E/Res/11(II), 525.

Name	Date of Creation	Mandate	Membership
Commission on Narcotic Drugs	1946[84]	It is the principal policy-making body in drug-related matters. It develops proposals to strengthen the international drug control system to combat the use and traffic of narcotic drugs worldwide.	53 member states
Commission on Crime Prevention and Criminal Justice	1992[85]	It acts as the principal policy-making body of the United Nations in the field of crime prevention and criminal justice. It formulates policies and recommendations on such issues as human trafficking, transnational crime, and terrorism prevention.	40 member states
Commission on Science and Technology for Development	1992[86]	It provides advice to the General Assembly and the Economic and Social Council and acts as a forum for examining questions relating to science and technology as well as their impact on development. It also formulates recommendations and guidelines on science and technology matters to UN organs.	43 member states
United Nations Forum on Forests	2000[87]	Its objective is to promote the management, conservation, and sustainable development of all types of forests and to strengthen long-term political commitment to this end.	All UN member states

b) Regional Commissions

The United Nations has five regional commissions, which cover every part of the world. The founders of the UN did not intend or envisage

84 *Commission on narcotic drugs*, ESC Res 9 (I), UNESCOR, 1946, UN Doc E/Res/9(I), 129.

85 *Establishment of the Commission on Crime Prevention and Criminal Justice*, ESC Res 1992/1, UNESCOR, 1992, UN Doc A/Res/1992/1.

86 *Establishment of new subsidiary bodies of the Economic and Social Council*, ESC Dec 1992/218, UNESCOR, 1992, UN Doc E/1992/92, 63.

87 *Report on the fourth session of the Intergovernmental Forum on Forests*, ESC Res 2000/35, UNESCOR, 2000, UN Doc E/Res/2000/35.

the creation of such institutions. They emerged one after the other to meet very specific needs of their respective regions. All five regional commissions have different memberships ranging from eighteen to fifty-six member states. Member states are not necessarily located in the region that the commission serves. For instance, Canada and Israel are members of the European Commission for Europe even though they are not European states. Similarly, Libya, Morocco, and Tunisia are African states, but were nevertheless admitted as members of the Economic and Social Commission for Western Asia. Only the Economic Commission for Africa has a membership limited to African states. Many countries are members of more than one regional commission. Canada, France, Germany, and Italy are members of the Economic Commission for Europe as well as the Economic Commission for Latin America and the Caribbean. The United States and the United Kingdom are members of three regional commissions at once.

Regional commissions have two sources of funding. The administrative budget is funded by the United Nations from its regular budget, which is financed by assessed contributions from UN member states. In fact, the budget of regional commissions is adopted as part of the UN regular budget. A much smaller portion of extra-budgetary funds is provided by voluntary contributions from member states and UN funds and programs such as the United Nations Development Programme (UNDP), the United Nations Population Fund (UNFPA), and the United Nations Children's Fund (UNICEF). Usually, these extrabudgetary funds are reserved for specific projects previously agreed upon by the regional commission receiving the funds and the donor.

The primary functions of regional commissions include most or all of the following responsibilities:

a) To promote economic and social development through regional and sub-regional cooperation and integration;
b) To serve as the main economic and social development forum within the United Nations system for their respective regions;
c) To support the development by its member states of norms and standards that facilitate economic relations and integration within the region and into the world economy;

d) To undertake research and analysis and promote policy measures for the economic and social development of member states;
e) To gather and disseminate information and data relating to the economic and social development of the region;
f) To organize conferences and intergovernmental and expert group meetings and sponsor training workshops, symposiums, and seminars;
g) To formulate and promote development assistance activities;
h) To provide technical advisory services and project-specific consultations to governments at their request;
i) To develop and execute programmes of technical cooperation and projects commensurate with the needs and priorities of the region, act as an executing agency for relevant operational projects, and provide technical advisory services and project-specific consultations to governments, intergovernmental organizations, and non-governmental organizations;
j) To coordinate the activities of ESCWA with those of departments and offices of the United Nations Secretariat, other United Nations organizations, and intergovernmental organizations;
k) To provide substantive and secretariat services and documentation for ESCWA and its subsidiary bodies.[88]

In fulfilling these functions, regional commissions are not authorized to take any action in respect of any country without the agreement of its government. Regional commissions report to ECOSOC by producing yearly full reports on their activities and plans, including those of any subsidiary bodies. They also make interim reports at each regular session of the Council.

---

88 See *Organization of the secretariat of the Economic and Social Commission for Asia and the Pacific*, Secretary-General's Bulletin, UN Doc ST/SGB/2005/11 (2005); *Organization of the secretariat of the Economic and Social Commission for Western Asia*, Secretary-General's Bulletin, UN Doc ST/SGB/2010/7 (2010); *Organization of the secretariat of the Economic Commission for Europe*, Secretary-General's Bulletin, UN Doc ST/SGB/2008/9 (2008); *Organization of the secretariat of the Economic Commission for Latin America and the Caribbean*, Secretary-General's Bulletin, UN Doc ST/SGB/2000/5 (2000); *Organization of the Secretariat of the Economic Commission for Europe*, Secretary-General's Bulletin, UN Doc ST/SGB/1998/3 (1998).

The personnel of regional commissions are considered as staff members of the UN Secretariat. The legal framework that applies to the UN Secretariat applies also to regional commissions. This includes UN Staff Rules and Regulations, Secretary-General's Bulletins, Administrative Instructions, and Information Circulars. However, regional commissions carry out their substantive work without any interference from the UN headquarters in New York. They do not seek or receive instructions regarding their substantive work. Each regional commission is headed by an executive secretary who has a rank of an Under-Secretary-General and reports to the Secretary-General of the UN.

The Economic Commission for Europe is the oldest of the five regional commissions. It was created by ECOSOC[89] "to grapple with the larger economic policy questions facing the region" and "to address the longer-run problems of reconstruction and economic development in Europe."[90] Over time, its functions gradually evolved to encompass all developmental issues affecting Europe. The ECE initiates and participates in measures for facilitating concerted action for the economic development and integration of Europe, for raising the level of European economic activity, and for maintaining and strengthening the economic relations of the European countries both among themselves and with other countries of the world.[91] It carries out or sponsors investigations and studies of economic and technological problems of and developments within member countries of the commission. It also undertakes the collection, evaluation, and dissemination of economic, technological, and statistical information. The Commission is empowered to make recommendations on any matter within its competence directly to the governments and the specialized agencies. Its membership consists of fifty-six states in Europe, North America,

89 *Economic Commission for Europe*, ESC Res 36(IV), UNESCOR, 1947, UN Doc E/437, 10.

90 Yves Berthelot & Paul Rayment, "The ECE: A Bridge between East and West" in Yves Berthelot, ed, *Unity and Diversity in Development Ideas* (Indiana: Indiana University Press, 2004) at 56.

91 *Terms of Reference and Rules of Procedure of the Economic Commission for Europe*, 5th ed, UN Doc E/ECE/778/Rev.5 (2009).

and Asia, including Canada, Israel, and the United States. The raison d'être of the ECE is now unclear. The vast majority of ECE member countries are already developed; therefore, the development debate is of little interest to them. Considering its annual budget of USD$65 million, it may be apposite to examine the relevance and usefulness of the ECE, and in particular, whether its remaining meaningful functions could not be transferred to other regional organizations.

The Economic Commission for Asia and the Far East (ECAFE) (the present-day Economic and Social Commission for Asia and the Pacific, or ESCAP) was also established in 1947 for the economic reconstruction of devastated areas in Asia and the Far East.[92] It is noteworthy that in 1945, Afghanistan, China, Iran, Japan, Nepal, and Thailand were the only six sovereign states in Asia.[93] Only three states (China, India, and the Philippines) were UN members and had the capacity to express the demands of the region.[94] What is more, China could not express its demands effectively due to the well-known controversy surrounding its seat in the United Nations.[95] Thus, India and the Philippines were the only two independent states able to represent the interests of the Asian continent in the UN. Other Asian states achieved their independence between 1945 and 1960.[96] Therefore, it is rather extraordinary that Asian countries managed to secure a regional commission as early as 1947. The African continent, which was in a similar position, was able to create an African regional commission only a decade later.

Initially, only three of ECAFE's ten member states were from the region. Between 1947 and 1974, the membership grew from ten to twenty-nine, triggering a change of the Commission's name to ESCAP to reflect both the economic and social aspects of development and

---

92 *Economic Commission for Asia and the Far East*, ESC Res 37(IV), UNESCOR, 1947, UN Doc E/437, 13 (on the recommendation of the General Assembly in its Resolution 46(I), UN Doc A/Res/46(I) (1946)).

93 Leelananda de Silva, "From ECAFE to ESCAP: Pioneering a Regional Perspective" in Yves Berthelot, ed, *Unity and Diversity in Development Ideas* (Bloomington, IN: Indiana University Press, 2004) at 134.

94 *Ibid* at 141.

95 See Chapter 3.

96 de Silva, above note 93 at 134.

the geographic location of its member states.[97] Covering fifty-three states that are home to one-half of the world's population, ESCAP is by far the largest regional commission of the United Nations. Nevertheless, half of the world can hardly be called a region, which explains why the rationale for such a peculiar regional commission is frequently in question. Headquartered in Bangkok, ESCAP has sub-regional offices in Suva, Fiji; Incheon, South Korea; New Delhi, India; and Almaty, Kazakhstan. Its overall objective is to promote inclusive and sustainable economic and social development in the Asia-Pacific region, with a main focus on the implementation of the 2030 Agenda for Sustainable Development and the achievement of the Sustainable Development Goals.

World War II had not affected the Latin American continent to the same extent as it had affected Europe and, to a lesser extent, Asia. Naturally, the reconstruction of South and Central American states was not a real problem. Instead, the region needed to develop measures for facilitating concerted action for dealing with urgent economic problems arising out of the war and to raise the level of its economic activity.[98] Therefore, the creation of the Economic Commission for Latin America (ECLA) in 1948,[99] subsequently renamed the Economic Commission for Latin America and the Caribbean (ECLAC), was triggered by the desire to promote development in the Latin American region rather than reconstruct countries devastated by war. Its current terms of reference include broad objectives such as studying and seeking solutions to problems arising in Latin America and the Caribbean from world economic maladjustment and to other problems connected with the world economy, with a view to the cooperation of the Latin American countries in the common effort to achieve worldwide recovery and economic stability. ECLAC's main offices are in Santiago Chile. It has sub-regional offices in seven other parts of the region.

97 *Change of name from Economic Commission for Asia and the Far East to Economic and Social Commission for Asia and the Pacific*, ESC Res 1895(LVII), UNESCOR, 1974, UN Doc E/Res/1895/(LVII), 5.

98 *Report of the ad hoc Committee on the proposal for an Economic Commission for Latin America*, ESC Res 106 (VI), UNESCOR, 1948, UN Doc E/Res/106(VI), 4.

99 *Ibid*, UN Doc E/777 (1948) at 4.

ECLAC is almost twice as large as ECE in terms of annual budget and number of staff members employed.[100] However, both regional commissions serve approximately the same number of states.

The establishment of the Economic Commission for Africa in 1958 was particularly difficult for political reasons. As did the Asian continent, a large part of the African continent consisted of colonies. Colonial powers did not want any external interference in their territories or colonial affairs. Belgium, France, Great Britain, Portugal, and Spain were all strongly opposed to the idea of an African commission, as they did not believe that the number of independent African states would grow rapidly.[101] Nevertheless, they agreed to create a regional commission of which they were full members and non-independent African states were mere associate members.[102] This reality rapidly changed with decolonization. Today, only African states are members of the commission. The ECA is headquartered in Addis Ababa, Ethiopia, and has satellite offices in Yaoundé, Cameroon; Kigali, Rwanda; Rabat, Morocco; Niamey, Niger; and Lusaka, Zambia.

The youngest regional commission is the Economic and Social Commission for Western Asia (ESCWA). As early as October 1947, the General Assembly invited ECOSOC "to study the factors bearing upon the establishment of an economic commission for the Middle East."[103] Nevertheless, ECWA (which would be renamed to ESCWA) was created only in 1973.[104] Its delayed establishment was largely due to the Arab–Israeli conflict and partly to other armed conflicts in the

---

100 *Proposed programme budget for the biennium 2018–2019, Regional cooperation for development, Section 21 – Economic and social development in Latin America and the Caribbean*, UN Doc A/72/6 (Sect. 21) (2017).

101 Adebayo Adedeji, "The ECA: Forging a Future for Africa" in Yves Berthelot, ed, *Unity and Diversity in Development Ideas* (Bloomington, IN: Indiana University Press, 2004) at 133–34.

102 *Establishment of an Economic Commission for Africa*, ESC Res 671A (XXV), UNESCOR, 1958, UN Doc E/3123, 1.

103 *Study of factors bearing upon the establishment of an economic commission for the Middle East*, GA Res 120 (II), UNGAOR, 2nd Sess, UN Doc A/Res/120(II) (1947) at para 6.

104 *Establishment of an Economic Commission for Western Asia*, ESC Res 1818(XV), UNESCOR, 1973, UN Doc E/Res/1818(XV).

region. Arab states did not want Israel to be a member of the same regional commission, while the UN could not envisage the creation of a regional institution that would discriminate against and exclude one specific member,[105] which is why Israel joined ECE in 1991.

ESCWA's current headquarters is in Beirut, Lebanon. However, it had to move several times, from Baghdad to Beirut, from Beirut to Amman, and back to Beirut, due to armed conflicts in the region. Like ECE, ESCWA is another commission whose continuous existence is frequently questioned. First, it covers a region that is extremely volatile. Several countries of the region are involved in armed conflicts at any given time. Cooperation in social and economic fields is not feasible without peace. Of course, this also applies to the African continent; however, what sets these two regional commissions apart is the wide economic disparity between ESCWA member states. Specifically, the economic priorities of oil-rich countries of the Gulf, such as Saudi Arabia, UAE, Qatar, and Bahrain, are completely different from those of Yemen, Mauritania, and Sudan.

c) ECOSOC Standing Committees

A "standing committee," as opposed to an "*ad hoc* committee," is a subsidiary body established by a deliberative organ, such as the General Assembly, the Security Council, or ECOSOC, which has an open-ended mandate. It usually consists of representatives from member states and assists the parent organ in its work. ECOSOC has three standing committees, which are the Committee for Programme and Coordination, the Committee on Non-Governmental Organizations, and the Committee on Negotiations with Intergovernmental Agencies.

i) Committee for Programme and Coordination

The Committee for Programme and Coordination (CPC) was established in 1962 to keep under review the activities of the United Nations

---

105 Blandine Destremau, "ESCWA: Striving for Regional Integration" in Yves Berthelot, ed, *Unity and Diversity in Development Ideas* (Bloomington, IN: Indiana University Press, 2004) at 308.

and its related agencies in the economic, social, human rights, and related fields and to submit recommendations to ECOSOC on issues and problems in the field of coordination.[106] The committee is composed of thirty-four UN member states elected for three-year terms on the basis of equitable geographical distribution.[107]

To understand the primary role of CPC, it is important to explain how the Secretary-General obtains the approval of the General Assembly when requesting a budget. The Secretary-General submits to the General Assembly a proposed program budget, which consists of major themes (called Parts) split into sections. The most recent proposed program budget has fourteen parts or themes, such as:

- Political Affairs;
- International Justice and Law;
- International Cooperation for Development;
- Human Rights and Humanitarian Affairs; and
- Internal Oversight.

These fourteen parts are broken down into thirty-six sections. For instance, the part on Human Rights and Humanitarian Affairs consists of four sections: (i) human rights; (ii) humanitarian assistance; (iii) Palestinian refugees; and (iv) protection of and assistance to refugees. The part on International Justice and Law is composed of only two sections: (i) International Court of Justice; and (ii) Legal Affairs. The same proposed program budget also divides all UN activities into programs and subprograms. For each program and subprogram, the Secretary-General provides an estimate of financial and human resources required to implement the activities. This voluminous proposal, which often consists of thousands of pages, is scrutinized by several subsidiary bodies, including the CPC, ACABQ, and the

106 *Special Committee on co-ordination with particular emphasis on the United Nations Development Decade*, ESC Res 920 (XXXIV), UNESCOR, 1962 UN Doc E/Res/920(XXXIV), 30.

107 *Broad representation in the Committee for Programme and Co-ordination*, GA Dec 42/450, UNGAOR, 42nd Sess, A/Dec/42/450 (1988) 313.

Fifth Committee, before reaching the General Assembly. The CPC ensures that the programs and activities of the UN are implemented in line with the legislative mandates and that the activities and programs of the UN, its specialized agencies, and entities are compatible and mutually complementary. The CPC makes recommendations to the General Assembly, ECOSOC, and UN agencies on the programs and activities of the UN, and in particular, on measures necessary to achieve coherence and coordination throughout the system.

ii) Committee on Non-Governmental Organizations

ECOSOC's Committee on Non-Governmental Organizations considers applications for consultative status and requests for reclassification submitted by non-governmental organizations. NGOs are extremely important actors on the international arena and play a pivotal role in supporting the UN at the national, sub-regional, regional, and international levels. The breadth of these organizations' expertise and their capacity to implement the activities of the United Nations are undisputable. It is for this reason that in addition to full membership and observer status, the UN established a more limited status for non-governmental organizations known as consultative status. Unlike the status of a permanent observer, the consultative status is granted not by the General Assembly but by the Economic and Social Council through its Committee on NGOs. Consequently, the rights and privileges deriving from this consultative status can be exercised only before the Economic and Social Council and its subsidiary bodies. This status gives no rights or privileges to NGOs in General Assembly sessions. Its purpose is to encourage the participation and involvement of non-governmental organizations in the decision-making process without burdening the General Assembly. Only a small number of non-governmental organizations can obtain this privileged status. Since there are thousands of non-governmental organizations, establishing and maintaining relationships with all of them would be an unmanageable task. Accordingly, the Economic and Social Council developed some criteria that non-governmental organizations must satisfy in order to obtain a consultative status. They must demonstrate that their program of work is of direct relevance to the aims and purposes of the United Nations and that they are of recognized standing within the particular field of their competence.[108]

The arrangements for consultation with each NGO relate to the fields in which the NGO has special competence or special interest. Since NGOs vary in size, financial resources, credibility, and expertise, they may have different consultative statuses. The broadest consultative status is known as "general consultative status." It is reserved for NGOs that are concerned with most of the activities of ECOSOC and its subsidiary bodies and can demonstrate that they can make substantive and sustained contributions to ECOSOC's mandate.[109] Approximately 140 NGOs belong to this category, including Oxfam International, Save the Children International, and the World Wildlife Fund. NGOs that belong to this category have a more privileged position because they may propose that certain agenda items be placed in the provisional agenda of the Council and its subsidiary bodies, submit to the Council and its subsidiary bodies written statements of up to 2,000 words, and make oral statements.

The second and by far the largest category is known as "special consultative status." This category is for NGOs that have a special expertise or interest in only a few of the fields of activity covered by the Council.[110] Over 4,300 NGOs belong to this second category. Amnesty International, Norwegian Refugee Council, Open Society Institute, and the World Jewish Congress are just a few notable examples of NGOs that have a special consultative status. NGOs that belong to this category have less participatory rights than NGOs that enjoy a general consultative status. They cannot propose agenda items either for the Council or for its subsidiary bodies. They may submit written statements; however, such statements must not exceed 500 words if they are intended for the ECOSOC and 1,500 words if they are submitted to a subsidiary body of ECOSOC. This category of NGOs cannot make oral statements before ECOSOC unless there is no subsidiary body with jurisdiction in a field of interest to the NGO.

---

108 *Consultative relationship between the United Nations and non-governmental organizations*, ESC Res 1996/31, UNESCOR, 1996, UN Doc E/1996/96, 53 at para 9.

109 *Ibid* at para 22.

110 *Ibid* at para 23.

Other organizations that do not have general or special consultative status may be included in a list known as the "roster." To be added to the roster, the Council, the Secretary-General of the UN in consultation of the Council, or the Committee on Non-Governmental Organizations must be satisfied that the NGO can make occasional and useful contributions to the work of the Council or its subsidiary organizations.[111] Almost 1,000 NGOs are listed in the roster. Roster NGOs have less participatory rights than those belonging to the first and second categories described above. For example, they do not have an automatic right to participate in meetings. They cannot make oral statements. They may submit written statements only on invitation by the Secretary-General in consultation with the chairperson of the relevant body.

iii) Committee on Negotiations with Intergovernmental Agencies

This committee's role is to carry out negotiations with intergovernmental organizations that express an interest in becoming a specialized agency of the United Nations. The negotiations culminate in an agreement between the organization and ECOSOC by which the agency is brought into relationship with the United Nations in accordance with Articles 57 and 63 of the *UN Charter*. The contents of this agreement and the common characteristics of UN specialized agencies will be examined below in the section "Specialized Agencies."

d) Other Subsidiary Bodies

ECOSOC has a multitude of other types of bodies, including expert bodies composed of government experts, expert bodies composed of members serving in their personal capacities, and boards. As these bodies are not very active nor central to ECOSOC's activities, we will not be examining them.

---

111 *Ibid* at para 24.

C. POWERS AND RESPONSIBILITIES OF THE ECONOMIC AND SOCIAL COUNCIL

The raison d'être of the Economic and Social Council can be found in different parts of the *UN Charter*, including in Chapters I, IX, and X. For instance, Article 1.3 of the *UN Charter* states that one of four purposes of the United Nations is "to achieve international co-operation in solving international problems of an economic, social, cultural, or humanitarian character, and in promoting and encouraging respect for human rights and for fundamental freedoms for all without distinction as to race, sex, language, or religion."[112] Article 55 of the *UN Charter* mandates the UN to promote higher standards of living, full employment, conditions of economic and social progress and development, solutions of international economic, social, health, and related problems, international cultural and educational cooperation, and universal respect for human rights and fundamental freedoms without distinction as to race, sex, language, or religion.[113] The responsibility for the discharge of these functions of the organization "are vested in the General Assembly and, under the authority of the General Assembly, in the Economic and Social Council."[114]

ECOSOC does not make binding decisions. It initiates studies and reports, formulates recommendations, prepares draft conventions, and calls international conferences with respect to matters falling within its competence, which include international economic, social, cultural, educational, health, and humanitarian issues.[115] The recommendations of ECOSOC can take the form of either resolutions or decisions and be addressed to the General Assembly, UN member states, or UN specialized agencies.[116]

The Council shares most of its functions and responsibilities with other UN entities and bodies, which often results in duplications. This overlap in functions is the main source of criticism of ECOSOC.

112 *Charter of the United Nations*, above note 4, art 1.3.
113 *Ibid*, art 55.
114 *Ibid*, art 60.
115 *Ibid*, art 62.
116 *Ibid*.

For instance, the Second Committee of the General Assembly deals with issues relating to economic growth and development, such as macroeconomic policy issues, financing for development, sustainable development, globalization, and interdependence. As early as 1947, international trade was delegated to the *General Agreement on Tariffs and Trade* (GATT), which took the place of the stillborn International Trade Organization that never saw the light of day. GATT continued to be the main forum for international trade until the creation of the World Trade Organization (WTO) in 1995. To make matters worse, in 1965 the General Assembly created yet another institution—the United Nations Conference on Trade and Development (UNCTAD)[117]—with "responsibilities remarkably similar to those of ECOSOC,"[118] including the promotion of international trade and the development of principles and policies on international trade.

International cooperation in the economic and financial sectors, including monetary policy and developmental lending, fall within the competence of the World Bank Group and the International Monetary Fund (IMF). This was not accidental. The economic

> powers emerging from World War II preferred to concentrate global policy-making in the organizations in which their control was at least proportionate to their relative weight in world affairs.... In the area of economic policy-making the weighted voting arrangements at the Bretton Woods Institutions made the World Bank and the IMF far more attractive alternatives to the United Nations General Assembly and ECOSOC, where each sovereign state had only one vote.[119]

---

117 *Establishment of the United Nations Conference on Trade and Development as an organ of the General Assembly*, GA Res 1995 (XIX), UNGAOR, 19th Sess, UN Doc A/Res/1995(XIX) (1964) 1 [*Establishment of the United Nations Conference*].

118 Marcus Franda, *The United Nations in the Twenty-First Century* (Lanham: Rowman & Littlefield Publishers, 2006) at 165.

119 Gert Rosenthal, "Economic and Social Council" in Thomas G Weiss & Sam Daws, eds, *The Oxford Handbook on the United Nations*, 2d ed (Oxford, UK: Oxford University Press, 2018) at 174.

The High-level Panel on Threats, Challenges and Change established by the then Secretary-General Kofi Annan identified this as one of two key institutional problems of ECOSOC:

> The institutional problem we face is twofold: first, decision-making on international economic matters, particularly in the areas of finance and trade, has long left the United Nations and no amount of institutional reform will bring it back; and second, the Charter allowed for the creation of specialized agencies independent of the principal United Nations organs, reducing the role of the Economic and Social Council to one of coordination.[120]

Even in the field of human rights, ECOSOC does not enjoy exclusive jurisdiction. In fact, the majority of the UN's work on human rights is carried out by the Human Rights Council[121] (an intergovernmental body of the UN based in Geneva responsible for promoting and protecting human rights) and the Third Committee of the General Assembly (even though human rights does not appear in its official name of the Social, Humanitarian, and Cultural Affairs Committee). Both of these entities are subsidiary bodies of the General Assembly. This has not always been the case; the Human Rights Council is the successor of the Human Rights Commission, which was initially placed under the authority of ECOSOC as one of its subsidiary bodies.[122] It was only in 2006 that ECOSOC's authority over the Human Rights Commission was transferred to the General Assembly.

The only substantial powers that ECOSOC still has are: (a) to coordinate the activities of specialized agencies; and (b) to act as the

---

120 *Report of the High-level Panel*, above note 1 at para 274.

121 The resolutions adopted by the Human Rights Council during a calendar year are compiled in one document known as the *Report of the Human Rights Council*. Every year, the Third Committee of the General Assembly adopts a resolution on the annual report of the Human Rights Council. Some argue that since the Human Rights Council has a status of a subsidiary body, it should report directly to the General Assembly and not to the Third Committee. However, in its Resolution 65/281 (para 6), the General Assembly decided to continue referring the *Report of the Human Rights Council* to the Third Committee.

122 *Human Rights Council*, GA Res 60/251, UNGAOR, 60th Sess, UN Doc A/Res/60/251 (2006) 1.

UN's interlocutor with NGOs. We have already seen in Section B(5)(c)(ii) above how the consultations with NGOs take place. Below, we will examine the coordination function of ECOSOC.

1) Coordination Function

ECOSOC is not an implementing or executive body; it is a deliberative organ. It can only discuss matters, commission reports and studies, or make recommendations. It does not have an executive body to carry out the activities required to attain international cooperation in any of the fields that fall within its competence. The Council fulfills its mandate mainly with the assistance of "various specialized agencies, established by intergovernmental agreement and having wide international responsibilities, as defined in their basic instruments, in economic, social, cultural, educational, health, and related fields," which are "brought into relationship with the United Nations in accordance with the provisions of Article 63."[123] With the approval of the General Assembly, ECOSOC enters into agreements with UN specialized agencies defining the terms on which they are brought into relationship with the United Nations.[124] Once specialized agencies become part of the UN system, ECOSOC then coordinates their activities through consultation with and recommendations to them and through recommendations to the General Assembly and to the members of the United Nations.[125] ECOSOC also coordinates the activities of the UN Funds and Programmes, related organizations, and various subsidiary organs. The coordination of the activities carried out by a complex web of UN agencies, bodies, and entities is arguably ECOSOC's most important role.

To understand the coordination role of ECOSOC, it is imperative to canvass three main components of the United Nations System.[126]

123 *Charter of the United Nations*, above note 4, art 57.1.

124 *Ibid*, art 63.1.

125 *Ibid*, art 63.2.

126 The term "UN System" should not be confounded with the notion of UN common system. The latter term refers to a coordinated system of salaries, allowances, and other conditions of service. To avoid discrepancies in terms

These are: (a) UN Funds and Programmes; (b) UN specialized agencies; and (c) UN related organizations.

a) UN Funds and Programmes

The United Nations Funds and Programmes were established to meet emerging needs not foreseen by the drafters of the *UN Charter*. They are quasi-autonomous entities subordinate to the United Nations, each specializing in a specific field such as development assistance, international trade policy-making, refugee protection, and food aid. They are created in accordance with Article 7, paragraph 2 of the *UN Charter*, which empowers the UN and its principal organs to establish "such subsidiary organs as may be found necessary." Like other subsidiary organs, Funds and Programmes are established through General Assembly resolutions. This characteristic sets them apart from specialized agencies, which are founded through constituent treaties. Unfortunately, the practice of the General Assembly in creating Funds and Programmes has not been consistent. In some cases, namely the United Nations Fund for Population (UNFPA), the General Assembly expressly designated them as subsidiary organs, while in others, such as United Nations Children's Fund (UNICEF), it granted them certain legal capacities without specifying their particular status within the UN system.[127]

The term "subsidiary organs" has no definition or specific meaning. A variety of bodies and entities may have the status of a subsidiary

---

and conditions of employment among various entities of the United Nations, the United Nations and its specialized agencies agreed to develop common personnel standards. These standards include classification of grades and corresponding salaries, age of retirement and pension benefits, education and rental allowances, and other similar matters. Another reason for creating a common system of personnel management was to facilitate movement of personnel from one entity to another. The International Civil Service Commission, which is an independent expert body established by the United Nations General Assembly, is responsible for regulating and coordinating the conditions of service of staff in the United Nations common system. For more information on the International Civil Service Commissions, see Chapter 7 on the UN Secretariat.

127 "Question of Juridical Personality and Legal Capacity in Relation to the United Nations agencies, funds, and programmes" in *United Nations Juridical Yearbook* (New York: UN, 1994) at 478 [*Question of Juridical Personality*].

organ. The Security Council, the General Assembly, and the ECOSOC each established dozens of subsidiary bodies, including *ad hoc* tribunals, committees, commissions, panels, councils, etc. However, it is important not to confound the UN Funds and Programmes with other types of subsidiary bodies. Funds and Programmes are more autonomous than most subsidiary bodies of the UN and, *a fortiori*, departments and offices of the UN Secretariat, such as the Office of the UN High Commissioner for Human Rights (OHCHR)[128] or the Office for the Coordination of Humanitarian Affairs (OCHA).[129] For instance, unlike most other subsidiary bodies, Funds and Programmes have their own distinct governing bodies, which report to the General Assembly, in some cases through ECOSOC.[130] Their executive heads "are appointed by some device requiring the [Secretary-General] to secure the approval of or at least to consult with some other organ."[131] In addition, Funds and Programmes enjoy a considerable degree of autonomy in appointing and managing personnel. Although Funds and Programmes (with the exception of World Food Programme and UN Relief and Works Agency (UNRWA)) apply the UN Staff Rules and Regulations, they retain full authority to appoint their own staff members. This power is either explicitly granted to the executive heads of a specific Fund or Programme in the resolution establishing it or delegated to it by the UN Secretary-General. Finally, Funds and Programmes have their own peculiar funding methods. For some, a negligible part of their financial resources emanates from the UN's regular budget and the largest portion is financed by voluntary contributions from the states that are able and willing to fund them. For others, the entire budget consists of voluntary contributions. Some nations may earmark voluntary contributions for certain types of projects or regions. This makes Funds and Programmes more vulnerable

---

128 *Organization of the Office of the United Nations High Commissioner for Human Rights*, Secretary-General's Bulletin, UN Doc ST/SGB/1999/8 (1999).

129 *Organization of the Office for the Coordination of Humanitarian Affairs*, Secretary-General's Bulletin, UN Doc ST/SGB/1997/10 (1997).

130 Paul C Szasz, "The Complexification of the United Nations System" (1999) 3 *Max Planck UNYB* 1 at 12.

131 *Ibid* at 8.

to political influences of their member states, and in particular to the largest contributors. ECOSOC has limited control over the activities of Funds and Programmes since it does not fund them.

Although Funds and Programmes are more independent than the vast majority of subsidiary organs (and *a fortiori* departments and offices of the UN Secretariat), they are less autonomous than specialized agencies, such as the International Civil Aviation Organization (ICAO) or the United Nations Educational, Scientific, and Cultural Organization (UNESCO). As mentioned above, the specialized agencies of the UN are set up through constituent treaties, whereas UN Funds and Programmes are established as subsidiary bodies of the UN through General Assembly resolutions. These two methods of establishing an organization have practical implications. First, specialized agencies are *bona fide* international organizations because they are granted a distinct legal personality. Funds and Programmes do not have an independent legal personality. The absence of an international personality separate from that of the UN means that Funds and Programmes "cannot perform international acts or incur international obligations, except as expressly authorized by their parent bodies."[132] When Funds and Programmes contract or institute a legal action in their own names, "the courts have regarded such action as that of the United Nations unless, under the municipal law of the country concerned, the particular subsidiary body has been recognized as having the capacity to contract and to sue."[133] Since Funds and Programmes lack a distinct legal personality, they are not real intergovernmental organizations. According to some authors, only an entity founded by a treaty can be regarded as an international organization;[134] an institution that is established by a General Assembly resolution does not meet this requirement. Thus, according to this school of thought, UNICEF, UNHCR, UNDP, and WFP are not international organizations *stricto sensu*, while FAO, WIPO, and the UN World Tourism Organization (UNWTO) are. One author calls UN

132 *Question of Juridical Personality*, above note 127 at 480.

133 *Ibid.*

134 See Malcolm Shaw, *International Law*, 6th ed (Cambridge, UK: Cambridge University Press, 2008) at 1103.

Funds and Programmes "'international organizations manquées.'"[135] Yet, they are much larger in size, have a greater budget, employ more people, and are better known than most specialized agencies of the UN (which are full-fledged international organizations). Other authors acknowledge that certain entities can be international organizations even if they are created by resolutions.[136]

The fact that Funds and Programmes do not have a distinct legal personality does not mean that they do not have a legal capacity. They all have the right to conclude contracts, to acquire and dispose of property, and to be party to judicial proceedings without having a distinct legal personality. They have a legal capacity because they draw on or share in the legal personality of the United Nations:

> [I]nternational organizations have been recognized to possess the requisite personality to exercise certain legal capacities, as necessary, to carry out their functions. There are equally compelling reasons for recognizing the capacity of defined subsidiary bodies of international organizations, for certain purposes, to perform legal acts and incur legal obligations in the name of their parent body, or in their own names on behalf of such parent body. This is essential in order to enable the subsidiary bodies to discharge their mandates, as well as to protect the parent organizations from liability resulting from the activities of their subsidiaries, which they form purposely separately with independent financial resources. However, not all subsidiaries qualify for such recognition and the capacities they exercise need not be the same.[137]

Furthermore, the legal status, privileges, and immunities of Funds and Programmes are covered by the *Convention on the Privileges and*

135 Szasz, above note 130 at 1, n 43.

136 Jan Klabbers, *An Introduction to International Institutional Law*, 2d ed (Cambridge, UK: Cambridge University Press, 2008); Gerd Droesse, *Membership in International Organization: Paradigms of Membership Structures, Legal Implications of Membership and the Concept of International Organization* (The Hague, Netherlands: TMC Asser Press, 2020) at 66.

137 *Question of Juridical Personality*, above note 127 at 479.

Immunities of the United Nations,[138] which also applies to the United Nations Secretariat. In contrast, the legal status, privileges, and immunities of specialized agencies are covered by the *Convention on the Privileges and Immunities of the Specialized Agencies.*[139]

Another crucial distinction between Funds and Programmes and specialized agencies is the ability to seek an advisory opinion from the International Court of Justice. Article 96(b) of the *UN Charter* authorizes specialized agencies[140] to request, with the authorization of the General Assembly, advisory opinions from the International Court of Justice. The authority to seek an advisory opinion from the ICJ has not been made available to UN Funds and Programmes. Consequently, UNICEF, UNDP, UNHCR, UNEP, UNRWA, UNFPA, WFP, UN Habitat, UNCTAD, UNOPS, and UN Women cannot seek an advisory opinion from the World Court since they are mere Funds and Programmes of the UN.

Nevertheless, Funds and Programmes may be autonomous, to varying degrees. Some entities, such as UN Relief and Works Agency (UNRWA) and WFP, are more autonomous than other Funds and Programmes, while UNEP, UN Habitat, and UNCTAD are less autonomous. For instance, UNRWA and WFP do not apply the UN Staff Rules and Regulations. UNRWA has its own staff rules and regulations, whereas the WFP applies the staff regulations of the Food and Agriculture Organization (FAO, a specialized agency). Neither of these two organizations has recognized the jurisdiction of the United Nations Dispute Tribunal as a conflict resolution mechanism for work-related

---

138 3 February 1946, 1 UNTS 15 (entered into force 17 September 1946).

139 21 November 1947, 33 UNTS 261 (entered into force 2 December 1948) [*Convention on the Privileges and Immunities of the Specialized Agencies*].

140 These specialized agencies are: International Labour Organization (ILO); Food and Agriculture Organization of the United Nations (FAO); United Nations Educational, Scientific and Cultural Organization (UNESCO); International Bank for Reconstruction and Development (IBRD); International Finance Corporation (IFC); International Development Association (IDA); International Monetary Fund (IMF); International Civil Aviation Organization (ICAO); International Telecommunication Union (ITU); International Fund for Agricultural Development (IFAD).

grievances. UNRWA created its own dispute tribunal[141] and its own office of staff legal assistance, whereas WFP chose to remain under the jurisdiction of the ILO Administrative Tribunal. At the other end of the spectrum of autonomy are UNEP, UN Habitat, and UNCTAD, whose staff are considered to be part of the UN Secretariat. These three entities apply not only the UN Staff Rules and Regulations but also all other administrative and statutory issuances promulgated by the Secretary-General of the UN. These statutory instruments include Secretary-General's Bulletins, Administrative Instructions, and Information Circulars. UNHCR, UNICEF, UNDP, UNFPA, UNOPS, and UN Women are somewhere in the middle of the spectrum of autonomy. Specifically, unlike UNRWA and WFP, these six entities apply the UN Staff Rules and Regulations and recognize the jurisdiction of the UN Dispute Tribunal. However, unlike UNEP, UN Habitat, and UNCTAD, they have their own administrative and statutory issuances promulgated by their executive heads.[142] Hence, they do not apply the UN Secretary-General's Bulletins, Administrative Instructions, and Information Circulars. It is noteworthy that when staff members of Funds and Programmes, with the exception of UNRWA and WFP, contest administrative decisions that affect their conditions of service, they sue the Secretary-General of the United Nations as opposed to the executive heads of their fund or program. For instance, a UNDP staff member who wishes to contest before the UN Dispute Tribunal a decision not to promote him is obliged to sue the Secretary-General of the United Nations, even though the decision was made by UNDP and the Secretary-General played no role in the decision-making process.

Funds and Programmes collectively have a much greater budget and employ more people than their parent organization, the United

141 Appeals from the UNRWA Dispute Tribunal are brought before the United Nations Appeals Tribunal.

142 Paragraph 2.3 of the *Procedures for the promulgation of administrative issuance*, Secretary-General's Bulletin 2009/4, UN Doc ST/SGB/2009/4 (2009) states that "[a]dministrative issuances shall not apply to the separately administered funds, organs and programmes of the United Nations, unless otherwise stated therein, or unless the separately administered funds, organs and programmes have expressly accepted their applicability."

Nations. Unlike the UN Secretariat, the activities of UN Funds and Programmes (with the exception of UNCTAD) are primarily operational. Therefore, their personnel are mostly based in the field and often in remote locations. The footprint of Funds and Programmes in headquarter locations is much smaller than that of the UN's departments and offices. For instance, in 2017, the Office of the United Nations High Commissioner for Refugees (UNHCR) employed 9,740 staff members, of whom only 744 were based in its headquarters in Geneva. Similarly, UNICEF employed 12,806 staff members, of whom only 964 were based in its headquarters in New York. The remaining personnel work in the field. Conversely, the UN Secretariat is heavily headquarter-centred, with 6,000 staff members based in New York, 3,100 in Geneva, 1,600 in Nairobi, and 1,100 in Vienna.

The following entities are regarded as UN Funds and Programmes.

i) United Nations Children's Fund (UNICEF)

UNICEF was established in 1946 by the General Assembly resolution on the basis of a recommendation made by ECOSOC.[143] Initially called the UN International Children's Emergency Fund (hence UNICEF), this entity's mandate consisted of providing emergency "assistance to children and adolescents of countries which were victims of aggression in order to assist in their rehabilitation."[144] The General Assembly set up the fund for a limited duration with the idea of dissolving it once the effects of World War II began to wane. However, ECOSOC recommended to extend the fund's activities for three additional years. In 1950, the General Assembly agreed to enlarge the mandate of UNICEF and to include the needs of children in all developing countries and not just those of countries that were victims of aggression.[145] In 1953, when the fund's mandate was on the verge of expiring, the General Assembly commended the organization for

143 *Establishment of an International Children's Emergency Fund*, GA Res 57(I), UNGAOR, 1st Sess, UN Doc A/Res/57(I) (1946) 90.

144 *Ibid.*

145 *Continuing needs of children: United Nations International Children's Emergency Fund*, GA Res 417 (V), UNGAOR, 5th Sess, UN Doc A/Res/417(V) (1950) [*Continuing needs of children*].

its role in the protection of children and extended UNICEF's mandate indefinitely.[146] The General Assembly changed the organization's name to the United Nations Children's Fund but retained the symbol and acronym of UNICEF. Currently, UNICEF is the largest UN entity, employing over 12,000 staff members in 190 countries and territories. Its total revenue in 2017 reached USD$6.6 billion.[147] It carries out activities and implements programs in health, nutrition, education, water and sanitation, child protection, and other fields relevant to children in coordination with governments, local communities, and other NGOs in developing countries and territories. UNICEF's governing body is the executive board, composed of thirty-six states.[148] It is headquartered in New York and reports to ECOSOC, which in turn reports to the General Assembly. The highest ranking official of UNICEF is its Executive Director, who, thus far, has always been an American national.

ii) United Nations Development Programme (UNDP)

The UN Development Programme, also headquartered in New York, was established in 1965 through a merger of the UN Expanded Programme of Technical Assistance (EPTA) with the Special Fund.[149] UNDP is governed by an Executive Board, which consists of thirty-six member states. The same Executive Board also governs the United Nations Population Fund (UNFPA) and the United Nations Office for

146 *United Nations Children's Fund (UNICEF)*, GA Res 802(VIII), UNGAOR, 8th Sess, UN Doc A/Res/802(VIII) (1953) 53.

147 *Statistical report of the United Nations System Chief Executives Board for Coordination on the budgetary and financial situation of the organizations of the United Nations system*, UNGAOR, 73rd Sess, UN Doc A/73/460 (2018) at 13.

148 *Further measures for the restructuring and revitalization of the United Nations in the economic, social, and related field*, GA Res 48/162, UNGAOR, 48th Sess, UN Doc A/Res/48/162 (1993) 1. Paragraph 25 of the Annex of this resolution provides the geographic representation of the Executive Board as follows: eight members from African states, seven from Asian states, four from Eastern European states, five from Latin American and Caribbean states, and twelve from Western European and other states.

149 *Consolidation of the Special Fund and the Expanded Programme of Technical Assistance in a United Nations Development Programme*, GA Res 2029 (XX), UNGAOR, 20th Sess, UN Doc A/Res/2029(XX) (1965) 20.

Project Services (UNOPS).[150] The board operates under the authority of ECOSOC.

UNDP coordinates global and national efforts to reach the sustainable development goals. It operates in 170 countries and territories. In 2017, it employed approximately 7,100 staff members and had a total revenue of USD$5.3 billion.[151] UNDP also administers the United Nations Volunteer Programme, which is the volunteer arm of the UN system. Based in Bonn, this relatively small organization plays a pivotal role. It employs 6,500 volunteers deployed in the field who support peace, relief, and development activities in more than 130 countries.

UNDP used to play another crucial role in the United Nations system by managing the UN's Resident Coordinator system.[152] The Resident Coordinator system was created to coordinate operational activities for development at the country level.[153] A resident coordinator acts as the highest-ranking representative of the United Nations development system, over United Nations country teams, and is responsible for system-wide accountability for implementing the United Nations Development Assistance Framework and supporting countries in their implementation of the 2030 Agenda for Sustainable Development. This official receives a letter of accreditation from the UN Secretary-General and presents it to the head of state or government where this person acts as the primary UN interlocutor with governmental officials. The most senior official of UNDP (known as the resident representative) in a given country used to act as the resident coordinator for that same country. In 2018, the General Assembly endorsed the recommendation of the Secretary-General to separate

---

150 *Renaming of the Executive Board of the United Nations Development Programme/ United Nations Population Fund to include the United Nations Office for Project Services,* GA Res 65/176, UNGAOR, 65th Sess, UN Doc A/Res/65/176 (2010) 1 [*Renaming of the Executive Board*].

151 *Continuing needs of children,* above note 145.

152 *Quadrennial comprehensive policy review of operational activities for development of the United Nations system,* GA Res 67/226, UNGAOR, 67th Sess, UN Doc A/ Res/67/226 (2012) 1 at para 122.

153 *Restructuring of the economic and social sectors of the United Nations,* GA Res 32/197, 32nd Sess, UNGAOR, UN Doc A/Res/32/197 (1997) 121.

the functions of the resident coordinator from those of the resident representative of UNDP.[154]

iii) United Nations High Commissioner for Refugees (UNHCR)

The Office of the UN High Commissioner for Refugees (UNHCR) is a humanitarian organization whose main functions are to provide international protection to refugees and other persons of concern, including stateless people, and to seek durable solutions for them. UNHCR was set up as a successor to the International Refugee Organization (IRO), which was a temporary specialized agency of the UN (dissolved in 1952) to help Europeans displaced by World War II. In 1949, the General Assembly established a High Commissioner's Office for Refugees as of 1 January 1951 and located its headquarters in Geneva.[155] UNHCR was initially given a three-year mandate to complete its work and then disband. However, its mandate continued to be regularly extended for five-year periods. In 2003, the General Assembly finally removed the time limitation on the organization's mandate "until the refugee problem is solved."[156] The functioning of the Office of the UNHCR is regulated by the statute adopted by the General Assembly in 1950.[157] In December 2019, the General Assembly either intentionally or inadvertently referred to the Office of the United Nations High Commissioner for Refugees as a "*Programme* of the United Nations High Commissioner for Refugees" and enlarged

---

154 *Repositioning of the United Nations development system in the context of the quadrennial comprehensive policy review of operational activities for development of the United Nations system*, GA Res 72/279, UNGAOR, 72nd Sess, UN Doc A/72/279 (2018) 1 at para 8.

155 *Refugees and stateless persons*, GA Res 319 (IV), UNGAOR, 4th Sess, UN Doc A/Res/319(IV) (1949) 36.

156 *Implementing actions proposed by the United Nations High Commissioner for Refugees to strengthen the capacity of his Office to carry out its mandate*, GA Res 58/153, UNGAOR, 58th Sess, UN Doc A/Res/58/153 (2003) 1 at para 9.

157 *Statute of the Office of the United Nations High Commissioner for Refugees*, GA Res 428 (V), 5th Sess, UN Doc A/Res/428(V) (1950) 46.

the composition of its governing body, called the Executive Committee, from 102 to 106 states.[158]

iv) United Nations Relief and Works Agency for Palestine Refugees in the Near East (UNRWA)

UNRWA was created to "carry out in collaboration with local governments the direct relief and works programmes as recommended by the Economic Survey Mission" for Palestinian refugees following the 1948 Arab–Israeli armed conflict. It was established by the General Assembly in December 1949 and began operations on 1 May 1950.[159] As were most UN Funds and Programmes, UNRWA was established temporarily until the end of the Palestine refugee problem. However, in the absence of a solution to this problem, the General Assembly has repeatedly extended UNRWA's mandate. The most recent renewal occurred in December 2019, extending the mandate of the agency until 2023.

UNRWA provides essential services to millions of Palestinian refugees. UNRWA employs approximately 30,000 individuals, including schoolteachers. However, only a few hundred of these individuals are UN staff members. UNRWA's governing body is the Advisory Commission, which initially consisted of four members but is now made up of twenty-eight member states and four observers. The head of the agency is the Commissioner-General of UNRWA, who is appointed for a renewable three-year term by the UN Secretary-General after consultation with UNRWA's Advisory Commission. UNRWA's Commissioner-General reports directly to the General Assembly.

During the last three years, UNRWA has been facing serious difficulties. First, its largest single donor, the United States, cut its contributions. President Trump accused Palestinians of not being appreciative

---

158 *Enlargement of the Executive Committee of the Programme of the United Nations High Commissioner for Refugees*, GA Res 74/129, UNGAOR, 74th Sess, UN Doc A/Res/74/129 (2019).

159 *Assistance to Palestine Refugees*, GA Res 302 (IV), UNGAOR, 4th Sess, UN Doc A/Res/302(IV) (1949) 23 at para 7.

of US assistance and of refusing to negotiate with Israel.[160] Although a few states increased their financial contributions in attempt to make up for the loss, UNRWA is still heavily under-resourced. Second, in 2019, UNRWA's Commissioner General resigned as a result of an investigation into allegations of gross mismanagement.[161]

v) United Nations Conference on Trade and Development (UNCTAD)

The leaders of the developing world conceived UNCTAD "to be something of a competitor to ECOSOC that might be able to move the UN in new directions favourable to the concerns of Asia, Africa, and Latin America, and serve as a complement to the Bretton Woods system of international economic organizations."[162] Headquartered in Geneva, UNCTAD employs slightly fewer than 500 staff members and operates with a relatively small budget of approximately USD$110 million. UNCTAD was established to promote international trade, especially with a view to accelerating economic development and integrating developing countries into the world economy.[163] It is not an operational entity; it formulates principles and policies on international trade, with a particular focus on ensuring that national policies and international action complement one another in bringing about sustainable development. The highest decision-making body of UNCTAD is the quadrennial conference, at which member states make assessments of current trade and development issues, discuss policy options, and formulate global policy responses. Nevertheless, it is the Trade and Development Board, a permanent organ composed of 157 member states, that acts as UNCTAD's governing body. The head of the organization is the UNCTAD Secretary-General, who is appointed

---

160 Reuters, "US Ends Aid To Palestinian Refugee Agency UNRWA" (1 September 2018), online: www.bbc.com/news/world-us-canada-45377336.

161 UN News, "Palestine Refugee Agency Chief Resigns Amidst Mismanagement Probe" (6 November 2019), online: https://news.un.org/en/story/2019/11/1050801.

162 Marcus Franda, *The United Nations in the Twenty-First Century* (Lanham: Rowman & Littlefield Publishers, 2006) at 165.

163 *Establishment of the United Nations Conference on Trade and Development as an organ of the General Assembly*, GA Res 1995 (XIX), UNGAOR, 19th Sess, UN Doc A/Res/1995(XIX) (1964) 1.

by the Secretary-General of the UN and endorsed by the General Assembly.

vi) United Nations Environment Programme (UNEP)

The UN Environment Programme (UNEP) was established in 1972 following the Stockholm Conference on the Human Environment[164] to assess global, regional, and national environmental conditions and trends and to develop international environmental instruments, such as conventions and treaties. UNEP addresses such issues as climate change, natural disasters and their impact on conflicts, ecosystem management, adverse effects of chemicals and waste on human health and the environment, environmental governance, and resource efficiency. The United Nations Environment Assembly, with a universal membership of all 193 member states of the UN, is UNEP's governing body. It replaced the Governing Council, which had a more limited membership. The Assembly is also the most authoritative decision-making body on the environment. It meets once every two years in Nairobi, Kenya, and sets priorities for global environmental policies and develops international environmental law. A level below the Assembly is the Committee of Permanent Representatives. Its role is to prepare the meetings of the Environment Assembly, to regularly review the implementation of its decisions and to provide advice to the UN Environment Assembly on policy matters.

UNEP is headquartered in Nairobi, Kenya, on the same compound as the United Nations Office at Nairobi and the UN Habitat. The head of UNEP, the Executive Director, is nominated by the Secretary-General of the UN and elected by the General Assembly. The program has a budget of approximately USD$900 million and employs slightly fewer than 1,000 staff members who are regarded as staff members of the UN Secretariat.[165]

164 *Institutional and financial arrangements for international environmental cooperation*, GA Res 2997 (XXVII), UNGAOR, 27th Sess, UN Doc A/Res/2997(XXVII) (1972) 43.

165 *Programme of work and budget for the biennium 2020–2021— Report of the Executive Director*, UNEPOR, 2nd Sess, UN Doc UNEP/EA.2/16 (2016).

vii) United Nations Settlements Programme (UN-Habitat)

UN-Habitat, previously known as the UN Centre for Human Settlements, was established in 1977 in order to coordinate human settlement activities within the UN system and facilitate the global exchange of information on shelter and sustainable urban development.[166] Also headquartered in Nairobi, Kenya, this program employs slightly over 300 staff members (who, like UNEP staff members, are also regarded as part of the UN Secretariat) and has a small operating budget of USD$250 million. UN-Habitat is headed by an Executive Director who holds the rank of an Under-Secretary-General. Its three-tier governing structure is made up of the UN-Habitat Assembly, the executive board, and the Committee of Permanent Representatives. The Assembly is a universal body composed of the 193 member states of the UN that convenes every four years. The Executive Board is composed of thirty-six member states elected by the Assembly and meets three times a year in order to ensure oversight by member states of UN-Habitat operations. The Committee of Permanent Representatives of the UN-Habitat meets every two years.[167]

viii) United Nations Population Fund (UNFPA)

UNFPA was initially set up under the auspices of UNDP and called the UN Fund for Population Activities (UNFPA). In 1972, the General Assembly converted it into a distinct UN Fund.[168] UNFPA's name was subsequently changed to United Nations Fund Population, but its official abbreviation, UNFPA, remained the same. UNFPA, UNDP, and UNOPS share the same governing body.

UNFPA employs approximately 2,700 staff members, of which 350 work in its headquarters in New York. Its mandate focuses on

---

166 *Institutional arrangements for international cooperation in the field of human settlements*, GA Res 32/162, UNGAOR, 32nd Sess, UN Doc A/Res/32/162 (1977) 98.

167 *Implementation of the outcomes of the United Nations Conferences on Human Settlements and on Housing and Sustainable Urban Development and strengthening of the United Nations Settlements Programme (UN-Habitat)*, GA Res 73/239, UNGAOR, 37th Sess, UN Doc A/Res/73/239 (2018) 1.

168 *United Nations Fund for Population Activities*, GA Res 3019 (XXVII), UNGAOR, 27th Sess, UN Doc A/Res/3019(XXVII) (1972) 51; see also *Renaming of the Executive Board*, above note 150.

three areas of work: reproductive health, gender equality, and population. More specifically, it supports reproductive health care for women, strives to avoid life-threatening complications of pregnancies, facilitates access to modern contraceptives, provides training to health workers to ensure that childbirths occur in adequate conditions, works to prevent gender-based violence, fights against female genital mutilation and child marriages, and collects and analyzes data. It is active in more than 150 countries. UNFPA does not receive funds from the UN regular budget. It is funded by voluntary contributions of UN member states and donations from private sector groups, foundations, and individuals. Its administrative and operating budget exceeds USD$1 billion.

ix) World Food Programme (WFP)

Rome is the UN's food and agriculture hub. It is home to three important organizations: the World Food Programme (WFP), the Food and Agriculture Organization (FAO), and the International Fund for Agricultural Development (IFAD). The difference between these three agencies is not always clear, even for UN staff. First, they were established at different times for different reasons. The FAO came first. It was established as a UN specialized agency in 1945, immediately after the creation of the UN itself. It is an organization that offers technical expertise for international efforts to combat hunger. The WFP came into existence much later, on the recommendation of the Director-General of FAO and the director of US Food for Peace Programme. In 1961, the General Assembly endorsed the recommendation and established the WFP as a joint UN–FAO undertaking.[169] IFAD appeared only in 1977 for the purposes of eliminating rural poverty, hunger, and malnutrition by increasing productivity and income in rural areas. Second, WFP was created by a General Assembly resolution as an entity that belongs to the category of Funds and Programmes. Hence, unlike FAO and IFAD, which were created through an international treaty, WFP does not have a distinct legal personality,

169 *World Food Programme*, GA Res 1714(XVI), UNGAOR, 16th Sess, UN Doc A/Res/1714/(XVI) (1961) 20.

even though it is much larger and better known than its two sister agencies. Third, while all three organizations share a common vision on how to achieve food and nutrition security and sustainable agriculture, they each have a unique mandate. WFP strives to eliminate hunger and malnutrition mostly in the context of political conflicts and natural disasters. It is a humanitarian agency that operates mainly in the field. FAO, on the other hand, is a knowledge organization that plays the role of a forum for negotiating international agreements. IFAD is more of a financial institution. It mobilizes resources for agriculture and rural development.

The executive board, comprising thirty-six member states, is WFP's supreme governing body. The organization is headed by an Executive Director who is appointed jointly by the UN Secretary-General and the Director-General of FAO. WFP employs over 6,000 staff members, of which only 12 percent are based in Rome. It operates a budget that reached USD$6 billion in 2017.

x) UN Women

Formally named the United Nations Entity for Gender Equality and the Empowerment of Women, UN Women was founded in 2010 to provide guidance and technical support to UN member states on gender equality, the empowerment and rights of women, and gender mainstreaming.[170]

The General Assembly transferred to UN Women the mandates and functions of four UN entities that dealt with gender matters: the UN Development Fund for Women (UNIFEM), the Division for the Advancement of Women, the Office of the Special Adviser on Gender Issues, and the UN International Research and Training Institute for the Advancement of Women. The main objectives of UN Women consist of expanding women's voice, leadership, and participation, ending violence against women, strengthening women's economic empowerment, and making gender equality a priority in all nations.

170 *System-wide coherence*, GA Res 64/289, UNGAOR, 64th Sess, UN Doc A/Res/64/289 (2010) 1 at para 49.

The organization's governing body is the executive board made up of representatives from forty-one member states elected to three-year terms by ECOSOC on the basis of equitable geographic distribution. An executive director, with the rank of Under-Secretary-General, is the highest ranking official of the entity. The organization is headquartered in New York and employs approximately 900 UN staff members.

xi) United Nations Office for Project Services (UNOPS)

UNOPS acts as a service provider to the United Nations system agencies, funds, and programs, international and regional financial institutions, intergovernmental organizations, donor and recipient governments, and non-governmental organizations.[171] It is a key resource for the UN system in procurement and contracts management as well as in civil works and physical infrastructure development, including capacity development activities. UNOPS also provides cost-effective services in the area of human resources by managing consultants and contractors employed by other UN Funds and Programmes. For example, UNHCR employs thousands of consultants whose contracts are managed by UNOPS. In exchange, UNOPS charges UNHCR an administrative fee that represents approximately 10 percent of consultants' or contractors' fees. This arrangement allows UNOPS to be a self-financing entity.

UNOPS activities trace back to 1973, even though, initially, it was part of the UNDP. In 1994, on a proposal by Australia and on the recommendation of ECOSOC, the General Assembly made UNOPS a separate entity as of 1 January 1995.[172] With its headquarters in Copenhagen, Denmark, UNOPS employs over 4,400 personnel, of whom only 750 are staff members. The remaining personnel are contractors.[173] The head of UNOPS is the executive director, who holds a rank of under-secretary-general and reports to an executive board that

171 *United Nations Office for Project Services strategic plan*, UNDP/UNFPA/UNOPS Executive Board Decision 2009/25, UNESCOR, 2009 at para 3.

172 *Office for Project Services*, GA Dec 48/501, UNGAOR, 48th Sess, UN Doc A/48/49 [Vol II] (1994) 1 at 59.

173 *Annual Report of the Executive Director*, UN Doc DP/OPS/2019/2 (2019) at para 69.

oversees the operations of three UN Funds and Programmes: UNDP, UNFPA, and UNOPS.

b) Specialized Agencies

The *UN Charter* defines specialized agencies as international organizations established by intergovernmental agreement with wide international responsibilities, as defined in their basic instruments, in economic, cultural, educational, health, and related fields that have been brought into relationship with the United Nations.[174] The modalities for bringing a specialized agency into relationship with the UN are described in Article 63 of the *UN Charter*. They consist of the UN entering into an agreement with the agency, defining the terms on which the agency will become part of the UN system. The agreements that the UN has entered into with its specialized agencies are similar but not identical.[175] They typically contain clauses requiring both parties to cooperate and describing methods and procedures for coordinating their activities. They allow both parties to propose the inclusion of items in each other's agenda. The UN also normally grants permission to the specialized agency to issue UN laissez-passer to its staff and to request advisory opinions from the ICJ. The parties agree to develop and maintain uniform standards for personnel management, thereby absorbing the specialized agency into the UN's common system. These agreements require the approval of the General Assembly. The implementation of these cooperation agreements has not always been straightforward. In 1967, the UN and the International Bank for Reconstruction and Development (IBRD) exchanged razor-sharp legal views on the obligation of a specialized agency to follow the recommendations of the General Assembly. The disagreement arose as a result of the UN's attempt to penalize Portugal and South Africa for their colonial and apartheid policies. In several resolutions, the General

---

174 *Charter of the United Nations*, above note 5, art 57.1.

175 Compare *Agreement concerning the relationship between the United Nations and the International Fund for Agricultural Development*, Annex to GA Res 32/197, UNGAOR, 32nd Sess, UN Doc A/Res/32/107 (1977) 86 and *Agreement between the United Nations and the World Tourism Organization*, Annex to GA Res 58/232, UNGAOR, 58th Sess, UN Doc A/Res/58/232 (2004) 1.

Assembly called upon the specialized agencies to deny to those states any assistance or benefits of membership in their respective organizations. The IBRD disregarded this recommendation and made loans to Portuguese and South African entities, arguing that it is not permitted to take decisions on political grounds and should be guided by economic considerations alone. Legal counsel of both organizations presented opposing legal views and arguments, the executive heads of both organizations failed to reach an agreement, and the governing body of IBRD did not budge.[176] This incident illustrates that the cooperation agreement between the UN and its specialized agencies does not create a hierarchical or subordinate relationship between them. Specialized agencies have different memberships and different governing bodies. Not all members of the United Nations are necessarily members of all UN specialized agencies. A member state of the UN may choose not to become a member of one or several specialized agencies. Similarly, a member state of one specialized agency is not necessarily a member of all other specialized agencies. In addition, each specialized agency has its own charter and legal framework. Specialized agencies promulgate their own rules pertaining to personnel management and do not apply UN staff rules and regulations. This is not surprising, considering that some specialized agencies, such as the Universal Postal Union (UPU) and the International Labour Organization (ILO), have been in existence longer than the United Nations.

The *UN Charter* empowers the General Assembly to consider and approve any financial and budgetary arrangements with specialized agencies and to examine the administrative budgets of such specialized agencies with a view to making recommendations to them.[177] It also allows the UN to make recommendations for the coordination of the policies and activities of the specialized agencies.[178] In practice,

176 *The Policies of Apartheid of the Government of the Republic of South Africa and Question of Territories under Portuguese Administration, Consultation with the International Bank for Reconstruction and Development*, Report of the Secretary-General, UNGAOR, 21st Sess, UN Doc A/6825 (1967).

177 *Charter of the United Nations*, above note 4, art 17.3.

178 *Ibid*, art 58.

the General Assembly does not exercise any direct oversight functions over administrative and budgetary matters of specialized agencies. Like Funds and Programmes, specialized agencies also submit to ECOSOC regular reports on their activities. However, they retain a greater degree of autonomy than Funds and Programmes do. In particular, the executive heads of specialized agencies do not report to the Secretary-General of the UN. Unlike Funds and Programmes, specialized agencies are funded by both voluntary and assessed contributions and their budgets are completely separate from that of the United Nations. Moreover, unlike most Funds and Programmes, specialized agencies do not recognize the jurisdiction of the United Nations Dispute Tribunal in labour law disputes. The majority of specialized agencies recognize the jurisdiction of the ILO Administrative Tribunal. Some specialized agencies, including the World Bank and the IMF, have set up their own administrative tribunals. In short, if Funds and Programmes are UN's siblings, then specialized agencies are its cousins.

There are currently seventeen specialized agencies: Food and Agriculture Organization (FAO), International Civil Aviation Organization (ICAO), International Labour Organization (ILO), International Fund for Agricultural Development (IFAD), International Monetary Fund (IMF), International Maritime Organization (IMO), International Telecommunication Union (ITU), UN Educational, Scientific and Cultural Organization (UNESCO), UN Industrial Development Organization (UNIDO), UN World Tourism Organization (UNWTO), Universal Postal Union (UPU), World Health Organization (WHO), World Meteorological Organization (WMO), World Intellectual Property Organization (WIPO), World Bank Group, which includes the International Bank for Reconstruction and Development (IBRD), International Development Association (IDA), and the International Finance Corporation (IFC). The majority of these specialized agencies are part of the UN common system of staff administration, which is based on common standards, methods, and arrangements being applied to classification of posts, salaries, allowances, and benefits for the staff of the United Nations. The main purpose of the common system is to avoid substantial discrepancies in terms and conditions of employment, to avoid competition in recruitment of personnel and to facilitate the interchange of personnel. The International Civil Service Commission, an independent expert body established by the General Assembly, is responsible for regulating and coordinating the conditions of service of staff in the UN common system. The Bretton Woods institutions, on the other hand, chose not to participate in the UN common system and created a distinct staff administration system for themselves.

c) Related Organizations

If Funds and Programmes are the UN's siblings, and specialized agencies are its cousins, then related organizations are the UN's distant cousins. The term "related organization" does not appear in the *UN Charter*. It is a generic expression used to refer to international organizations whose cooperation agreement with the United Nations has many points in common with that of specialized agencies. The key difference is that unlike the cooperation agreements with specialized agencies, the agreements with related organizations do not refer to Articles 57 and 63 of the *UN Charter*. Related organizations are more independent and are not subject to the direct oversight of the General Assembly or ECOSOC, even though the International Atomic Energy Agency (IAEA) and the Organization for the Prohibition of Chemical Weapons (OPCW) continue to report to the Security Council and General Assembly.

Unlike specialized agencies, related organizations are not authorized to seek an advisory opinion from the ICJ unless their founding treaties specifically provide otherwise. The only related organization whose basic treaty allows it to request advisory opinions from the World Court is the International Atomic Energy Agency (IAEA).[179] Although IAEA is a related organization, for all means and purposes, it operates like a specialized agency.

---

179 *Statute of the International Atomic Energy*, 26 October 1956, 276 UNTS 3 at art XVII (B) (entered into force 29 July 1957).

Moreover, staff members of related organizations (with the exception of IAEA)[180] are not entitled to use the UN laissez-passer. Finally, the legal status, privileges, and immunities of related organizations are not governed by the *Convention on the Privileges and Immunities of the Specialized Agencies.*[181] Related organizations have provisions for privileges and immunities included in their constituent instruments or in separate legal instruments, and, where necessary, are supplemented by multilateral agreements on privileges and immunities.

Some related organizations, including the International Criminal Court (ICC) and the International Organization for Migration (IOM), are part of the UN common system of staff administration while others, such as the WTO, are not.

d) UN System Chief Executive Board

In 1946, the United States delegation to the United Nations proposed the creation of a "standing committee of administrative officers consisting of [the UN Secretary-General], as chairman, and the corresponding officers [Executive Heads] of the specialized agencies brought into relationship with the United Nations" to supervise the implementation of the agreements between the United Nations and the specialized agencies and to promote cooperation between them.[182] The Secretary-General established a Coordination Committee that was renamed the Administrative Committee on Coordination in 1949[183] and the Chief Executive Board for Coordination in 2001.

The vast majority of funds, programs, specialized agencies, including the Bretton Woods institutions (the World Bank and IMF) and related organizations are members of the Chief Executives Board for Coordination (CEB). The board is composed of thirty-one Executive

---

180 *Administrative Arrangement Concerning the Use of the United Nations Laissez-Passer by Officials of the International Atomic Energy Agency*, 26 June 1958.

181 *Convention on the Privileges and Immunities of the Specialized Agencies*, above note 139.

182 *Coordination Committee*, ESC Res 13(III), UNESCOR, 1946, UN Doc E/231 in E/245/Rev.1 (1946) 1 at 24.

183 *Fourth Report of the Administrative Committee on Coordination to the Economic and Social Council*, UNESCOR, 1948, UN Doc E/1076, 1 at 3.

Heads of these organizations. Chaired by the Secretary-General of the United Nations, the board convenes twice a year to consider policy and management issues that affect organizations of the United Nations system. It carries out its role through two high-level committees. The High-Level Committee on Programmes (HLCP) promotes UN-wide cooperation, coordination, and knowledge-sharing in programmatic and operational areas such as development, climate change, drugs and crime, etc. The High-Level Committee on Management (HLCM) identifies and assesses proposals for administrative management reforms to improve efficiency and streamline business practices. It publishes human resources and financial statistics and discusses issues that affect the safety and security of UN staff members worldwide, or HR and procurement practices. The CEB is supported by its own secretariat financed by various UN entities. It is located within the Executive Office of the UN Secretary-General and has a presence in New York and Geneva.

Chapter 6

THE INTERNATIONAL COURT OF JUSTICE

The idea of establishing permanent institutions in order to resolve disputes between governments through peaceful means originated with Russian Czar Nicholas II. In 1898, the czar had sent twenty-six countries of the world an invitation to a conference to discuss limitation of armaments and prevention of armed conflicts.[1] Since the Netherlands was seen as a neutral country, Nicholas II proposed to hold the conference at The Hague. All of the states accepted the invitation and approximately 100 delegates gathered in the Netherlands. The conference opened on 18 May 1899 and lasted a little over two months. Although the participating countries did not reach an agreement on disarmament, they signed the Convention for Pacific Settlement of International Disputes. The real palpable achievement of the 1899 conference was the establishment of the Permanent Court of Arbitration (PCA) as the first universal mechanism for the settlement of disputes between states. In 1907—eight years after the first conference—the countries convened at The Hague for a second conference, during which the American delegation proposed a plan for a permanent court of international justice, to be called the Court of Arbitral

1 Robin Sharwood, "Princes and Peacemakers: The Story of the Hague Peace Conference of 1899" in Timothy LH McCormack, Michael Tilbury & Gillian D Triggs, eds, *A Century of War and Peace: Asia-Pacific Perspectives on the Centenary of the 1899 Hague Peace Conference* (The Hague: Kluwer Law International, 2001) at 9.

Justice.[2] This proposal failed because participating countries did not agree on the method of appointing judges to the court.[3] Big countries wanted to retain the authority to appoint judges proportionate to their size and influence. They were not willing to allow the great numerical preponderance of small countries to override them and make up the court by overwhelming them with their votes.[4] Smaller countries objected on the basis that "the interests of Peace are not promoted by the creation between states, by means of a contractual stipulation, of categories of sovereignty which humiliate some to the advantage of others, undermining the basis of the existence of all, and proclaiming, by a strange paradox, the predominance in law of might over right."[5] Consequently, the participating states limited themselves to revising the Convention for Pacific Settlement of International Disputes signed in 1899.

The name Permanent Court of Arbitration is confusing and unfortunate because the PCA is neither permanent nor a court in the strict sense of the word. It only provides services to arbitration tribunals once they are set up by the parties. The PCA assists the arbitration tribunal with legal research, translation, and other administrative tasks. For all means and purposes, the PCA plays the role of a registrar. In addition, the PCA is not permanent because there are no judges or arbitrators who are always in session permanently, hearing cases or deliberating. Arbitration tribunals are formed by the parties on an *ad hoc* basis only after a dispute arises between them. The parties may agree on the identity of the arbitrator. Some PCA arbitrators may never get an opportunity to preside in a case.

The PCA has an exclusively voluntary jurisdiction. Countries must agree to bring a dispute before the court. However, this was not why states were reluctant to submit their disputes to the PCA.

---

2 James Brown Scott, "The Proposed Court of Arbitral Justice" (1908) 2:4 *Am J Int'l L* 772 at 778.

3 *Ibid* at 802.

4 Elihu Root, "Permanent Court of International Justice" (1921) 9 *Ky LJ* 106 at 109–10.

5 Antonio S de Bustamente y Sirven, "Permanent Court of International Justice" (1924) 9 *Minn L Rev* 122 at 125.

According to Elihu Root,[6] governments did not have much confidence in the PCA:

> [O]ne difficulty about arbitration is that arbitrators too often are apt to treat the cases brought before them as a matter for settlement, for adjustment. They have come to consider, apparently, that their function is to do with the case what seems to them to be the wisest and most expedient thing for all parties and all interests concerned. They tend to act under a sense of judicial obligation. The great difficulty about arbitration has really been not that nations were unwilling to submit questions of law, questions of right, the kind of questions that our courts pass upon as between individuals in municipal law, to impartial judgment, but that they had not much confidence in getting impartial judgment because they found that the arbitrators, when they got together, went into negotiation as diplomats, and no one could tell what would come out of it. The party having no matter how strong a case, no matter how absolutely right upon the question of legal right, might find itself defeated because it seemed to the arbitrators on the whole that it perhaps would be better that it should not have its legal rights, but that the case should be settled as conveniently as possible.[7]

While the PCA had a few success stories, it did not prevent a global armed conflict. The outbreak of World War I in 1914 served to increase the need for an international court with more authority than the PCA. Therefore, when World War I ended and nations gathered for the Paris Peace Conference in January 1919, vague proposals to set up an international court were presented by some nations, including Italy. It would take the international community three full years to set up a new tribunal called the Permanent Court of International Justice (PCIJ) under the auspices of the League of Nations. The Court began operating on 15 February 1922. Its seat was the Peace

6 Elihu Root was an American lawyer who held senior positions under different presidents. He served as the Secretary of State under President Theodore Roosevelt and was personally involved in the negotiations that led to the creation of the Permanent Court of International Justice.

7 Root, above note 4 at 108–9.

Palace in The Hague, originally built to provide a home for the PCA. Both tribunals shared the magnificent building, the construction of which was funded entirely by American steel magnate Andrew Carnegie. Although the PCIJ was created at the initiative of the League of Nations, it was not integrated into the League as one of its organs, but remained a separate entity.

Like the PCA, the PCIJ was a voluntary court in that the consent of the parties was the basis of its jurisdiction. In fact, the PCIJ itself held in several cases that "no State can, without its consent, be compelled to submit its dispute with other States either to mediation or to arbitration, or any other kind of pacific settlement"[8] and that the consent of the respondent was an essential requirement for it to be properly seized of a dispute.[9] The jurisdiction of the PCIJ could be accepted either in advance, before any controversy actually arose, or once a dispute actually arose. In either case, states had to accept the jurisdiction of the Court. Despite its considerable jurisdictional constraint, the PCIJ adjudicated during its eighteen years of existence some twenty-nine contentious cases and issued twenty-seven advisory opinions. It ceased its operations in 1940 but, in order to ensure a continuity and a transfer of archives from the PCIJ to ICJ, it was formally dissolved only after the establishment of the International Court of Justice in 1946.

The International Court of Justice was heavily inspired by the Permanent Court of International Justice. Article 92 of the *UN Charter* expressly states that the ICJ "shall function in accordance with the annexed Statute, which is based upon the Statute of the Permanent Court of International Justice and forms an integral part of the present Charter." The statutes of both courts have striking similarities not only in content but also in numbering of provisions. Changes had to be made to the Statute of the PCIJ to reflect the transition from the League of Nations to the United Nations. Only a few new elements were introduced in the statute of the ICJ. The main difference between the two courts was their organic structures. Unlike the

---

8 *Status of Eastern Carelia* (1923), Advisory Opinion, PCIJ (Ser B) No 5 at 27.

9 See *Mavrommatis Palestine Concessions (Greece v Britain)* (1924), PCIJ (Ser A) No 2 at 16 [*Mavrommatis Palestine Concessions*]; and *Rights of Minorities in Upper Silesia (Minority Schools) (Germany v Poland)* (1928), PCIJ (Ser A) No 15 at 22.

UN PHOTO/ANDREA BRIZZI
General view of the International Court of Justice (ICJ) in session (1 January 1992). Permission for use granted by The United Nations.

PCIJ, which was an entity distinct from the League of Nations, the ICJ was set up as one of the principal organs of the United Nations.[10] The constitution and functioning of the ICJ are regulated by the *UN Charter*; the Statute of the Court, which is an integral part of the *UN Charter*; and the Rules of the Court. The ICJ is not subordinated to any other organ of the United Nations. With its seat in The Hague, it is the only main organ of the UN that is not headquartered in New York. Its official languages are English and French.[11]

Since its creation, the Court has settled disputes in a wide range of legal fields and controversies, including disputes pertaining to land and maritime boundaries, the use of force, the use of nuclear weapons,

---

10 *Charter of the United Nations*, 26 June 1945, Can TS 1945 No 7, arts 7.1 and 92 [*Charter of the United Nations*].

11 Statute of the International Court of Justice, 1945, art 39 [Statute of the International Court of Justice].

genocide, the protection of the environment, and other important matters.

A. ELECTION OF JUDGES

The Court consists of a body of fifteen independent judges elected to nine-year terms of office. They are elected by the General Assembly and the Security Council, where polling takes place simultaneously but independently of one another. In order to be elected, a candidate must obtain a favourable vote from an absolute majority in both bodies. The term "absolute majority" has always been interpreted as meaning a majority of all electors, whether or not they vote or are allowed to vote.[12] Since the total number of electors in the General Assembly is 193 member states, the absolute majority in the General Assembly requires 97 votes. In the Security Council, where the number of electors is fifteen, the absolute majority is eight. No distinction is made between permanent and non-permanent members of the Security Council.[13] This often leads to intense lobbying and may result in several rounds of voting. To ensure continuity in the ICJ, elections for five judges are held triennially. Judges are eligible to stand for re-election at the end of their nine-year mandate.[14] Elections take place during the autumn session of the General Assembly. After the Court is in session, a president and vice-president are elected by secret ballot to hold office for three years. If a judge dies in office, resigns, or becomes incapacitated and unable to perform the official duties, a special election is held to fill the vacancy for the unexpired duration of the tenure.

All UN member states are eligible to propose candidates. To ensure that the selection process is as apolitical as possible, it is not the government of the state concerned that nominates candidates. Instead, candidates are nominated by a national group, which refers to a group of four (or fewer) arbitrators appointed by a country to

---

12 *Election of five members of the International Court of Justice,* Memorandum by the Secretary General, UN Doc A/66/182 – S/2011/452 (2011) at para 8.

13 Statute of the International Court of Justice, above note 11, art 10.2.

14 *Ibid,* art 13.

the Permanent Court of Arbitration (PCA).[15] This procedure can work only for states that are represented in the Permanent Court of Arbitration. The Statute of the ICJ also provides for a parallel procedure for states not represented in the PCA to nominate candidates.[16] The ICJ Statue recommends that before nominating candidates, members of each national group consult their highest national court, national legal faculties, schools of law, and academies. No group may nominate more than four persons, not more than two of whom must be of their nationality. The national group then communicates the names of the candidates to the Secretary-General, who prepares a list of all persons thus nominated.

Judges must be persons of high moral character and possess the qualifications required in their respective countries for appointment to the highest judicial offices or are jurisconsults of recognized competence in international law.[17] The appointment process is also subject to cultural and geographical considerations. In particular, the Court must be representative of the "main forms of civilization and the principal legal systems of the world."[18] Although the ICJ has no formal requirement for geographic distribution among its fifteen judges, in practice, it reflects the composition of the Security Council with all five permanent members maintaining a judge on the bench. Exceptionally, in 2017, after eleven rounds of voting in the General Assembly and the Security Council, the United Kingdom withdrew its candidate, accepting defeat by India. While the British candidate was able to obtain the absolute majority in the Security Council, the Indian candidate secured a significantly higher number of favourable votes in the General Assembly. The United Kingdom could have invoked a little-known provision in the Statute of the ICJ that allows for an arbitration process known as a joint conference to try to break the deadlock.[19]

---

15 See *ibid*, art 4.1. Contracting parties to *The Hague Convention for the Pacific Settlement of International Disputes* of 1907 may appoint up to four potential arbitrators as members of the PCA.

16 *Ibid*, art 4.2.

17 *Ibid*, art 2.

18 *Ibid*, art 9.

19 *Ibid*, art 12.

However, to resolve the impasse without causing a diplomatic row, the United Kingdom preferred withdrawing its candidate and conceding defeat. This was the first time since the establishment of the ICJ that the United Kingdom was left without a British judge on the Court's bench. The only other permanent member who did not have a continuous representation on the Court was China.

Once elected, a judge of the ICJ cannot be dismissed unless, in the unanimous opinion of the other members of the Court, the required conditions have ceased to be fulfilled.[20] In such cases, the Registrar of the Court makes a formal notification thereof to the Secretary-General.[21] This notification automatically makes the place vacant.[22] In the history of the Court, such a scenario has never occurred. As well, a judge who has begun hearing a case must finish it even after being replaced.[23] A case begins with the opening of the oral proceedings and ends when the judgment is issued.[24]

Judges receive an annual salary established by the General Assembly, which may not decrease during their term of office.[25] The emoluments of the judges are free from taxation.[26]

B. PRESIDENCY OF THE COURT

Under Article 21 of the ICJ Statute, the Court shall elect its president and vice-president for three years; they can be re-elected.[27] The elections take place every third year at the same time as the recurrent election of one-third of the members of the Court. The president of the Court is required to reside at the seat of the Court in The Hague[28] and receives a special allowance of USD$25,000 per year for assuming

20 *Ibid*, art 18.1.
21 *Ibid*, art 18.2.
22 *Ibid*, art 18.3.
23 *Ibid*, art 13.3
24 Hugh Thirlway, *The International Court of Justice* (Oxford, UK: Oxford University Press, 2016) at 10 [Thirlway, *Court*].
25 Statute of the International Court of Justice, above note 11, art 32.
26 *Ibid*, art 32.8.
27 *Ibid*, art 21.1.
28 *Ibid*, art 22.2.

additional responsibilities.[29] The president presides over all meetings of the Court, directs the work and supervises the administration of the Court.[30] The president also has representative functions for the Court. He represents the Court when dealing with the host nation (the Netherlands). He is also the Court's spokesperson in all interactions with other organs of the UN, namely the General Assembly and the Security Council.

All cases are decided by a majority of the judges present. However, in the event of an equality of votes, the president or the judge who acts in his or her place has a casting vote.[31] The president's casting vote has had a decisive effect on the outcome of the Court's judgment in very important cases.[32] The president of the Court may play an important role in proceedings seeking provisional measures. When a state party to the proceedings is of the view that some measures are necessary to preserve its legal rights, it may request the Court to indicate provisional measures. To consider this request, the Court needs time to meet, deliberate, and decide. To ensure that in the meantime the other party abstains from any action that can make any provisional measure nugatory or irrelevant, the president of the ICJ has been empowered to "call upon the parties to act in such a way as will enable any order the Court may make on the request for provisional measures to have its appropriate effects."[33]

In cases where the president is of the nationality of one of the parties to a dispute, that president cannot exercise the functions of that

---

29 *Ibid*, art 32.2; *Conditions of service and compensation for officials other than Secretariat officials: members of the International Court of Justice and judges and ad litem judges of the International Tribunal for the Former Yugoslavia and the International Criminal Tribunal for Rwanda*, GA Res 65/258, UNGAOR, 65th Sess, UN Doc A/RES/65/258 (2011) 1 at para 6.

30 Rules of Court, art 12 [Rules of Court].

31 Statute of the International Court of Justice, above note 11, art 55.

32 See, for instance, *South West Africa (Ethiopia v South Africa; Liberia v South Africa)*, Judgment, Second Phase, [1966] ICJ Rep 6 at para 100, and *Legality of the Threat or Use of Nuclear Weapons*, Advisory Opinion, [1996] ICJ Rep 226 at para 105(2)E; *Question of the Delimitation of the Continental Shelf between Nicaragua and Colombia beyond 200 Nautical Miles from the Nicaraguan Coast (Nicaragua v Colombia)*, Preliminary Objection, [2016] ICJ Rep 100 at para 126(1)(b).

33 Rules of Court, art 74.4.

role.[34] These functions are to be exercised by the vice-president or by the next senior judge eligible to be on the bench and hear the case.[35] Nevertheless, when the president is precluded from presiding in a particular case, that person continues to exercise the functions of the presidency for all other purposes and cases, save in respect of that case.

C. *AD HOC* JUDGES OF THE COURT

In addition to elected judges, the ICJ bench may consist of other judges in a given case. When a party to a dispute does not have a judge of its nationality on the bench, the Statute of the International Court of Justice authorizes that party to choose a person to sit as an *ad hoc* judge.[36] The *ad hoc* judge should be chosen preferably from among those persons who have been nominated as candidates for judgeship in the ICJ but not appointed. A judge *ad hoc* does not need to be a national of the member state that designates him or her. For instance, in the case relating to the *Question of the Delimitation of the Continental Shelf between Nicaragua and Colombia*,[37] Nicaragua appointed a Russian national as a judge *ad hoc*.

If there are two or more states that act in the same interest, they are to be reckoned as one party only and are therefore limited to a single judge *ad hoc*.[38] In the *Appeal Relating to the Jurisdiction of the ICAO Council under Article 84 of the Convention on International Civil Aviation*,[39] Bahrain, Egypt, Saudi Arabia, and United Arab Emirates instituted proceedings against Qatar. Only Egypt appointed a judge *ad hoc* on behalf of all applicants. In addition, if one of the parties

---

34 *Ibid*, art 32.1.

35 This occurred in the *Anglo-Iranian Oil Co Case (United Kingdom v Iran)*, Preliminary Objection, Judgment, [1952] ICJ Rep 93 [*Anglo-Iranian Oil Co Case*], where the judge from the United Kingdom transferred the presidency to the vice-president in accordance with Article 13.1 of the Rules of Court.

36 Statute of the International Court of Justice, above note 11, art 31.2.

37 *Question of the Delimitation of the Continental Shelf between Nicaragua and Colombia beyond 200 nautical miles from the Nicaraguan Coast (Nicaragua v Colombia)*, [2016] ICJ Rep 101.

38 Rules of Court, above note 30, art 36.1.

39 "Joint Application Instituting Proceedings" (4 July 2018), [2018] ICJ Pleadings 6.

acting in the same interest has an elected judge of its nationality on the bench, other parties acting in the same interest are automatically deprived of their right to appoint a judge *ad hoc*.[40] The appointment of an *ad hoc* judge became a contentious issue in the *Whaling in the Antarctic* case.[41] Australia and New Zealand intended to jointly institute proceedings against Japan for its large-scale program of whaling. Australia was entitled to appoint a judge *ad hoc* because no Australian national was a member of the Court. However, there was a New Zealander on the bench. Since Australia and New Zealand intended to act in the same interest, they would be regarded as one party and neither one of them would be permitted to appoint a judge *ad hoc*. Australia asked New Zealand not to join the proceedings as a party so that it would not lose its right to appoint a judge *ad hoc*. New Zealand agreed and instead of joining the proceedings as a party, it submitted a request to intervene in accordance with Article 62 of the Statute of the Court. Japan objected to Australia's appointment of a judge *ad hoc* on the basis that New Zealand and Australia were trying to circumvent the safeguards of procedural equality. The Court overruled the objection and held that New Zealand and Australia acted in accordance with the Statute and Rules of the Court.[42]

Ad hoc judges sit on the bench and participate in the deliberations of the Court concerning the case on terms of complete equality with elected judges. Before taking up its duties as an *ad hoc* judge, the individual is required to make the same solemn declaration as an elected judge of the Court. *Ad hoc* judges receive a fee for each day worked on a case under review. In advisory proceedings, the appointment of *ad hoc* judges has not yet been requested or authorized. A party who merely intervenes in contentious proceedings is not entitled to an *ad hoc* judge.

The possibility of appointing an *ad hoc* judge appears to be contrary to the general principle that judges serve in their individual

40 Statute of the International Court of Justice, above note 11, art 31.5.

41 *Whaling in the Antarctic (Australia v Japan: New Zealand intervening)*, [2014] ICJ Rep 226.

42 *Whaling in the Antarctic (Australia v Japan)*, Declaration of Intervention of New Zealand, Order of 6 February 2013, [2013] ICJ Rep 3 at paras 17–22.

capacities and not as representatives of their countries of nationality. In fact, the Statute of the ICJ expressly states that "judges of the nationality of each of the parties shall retain their right to sit in the case before the Court."[43] Since the Statute of the ICJ is based on the premise that the nationality of the judge does not affect impartiality and independence, it is unclear how the appointment of a judge *ad hoc* can assist either party in obtaining greater equality, impartiality, or independence. In fact, it has been suggested that the presence of judges *ad hoc* on the bench distorts the equality of arms and undermines the principle of judicial independence:

> Elected members of the Court not infrequently vote against the State of their nationality, but to date judges ad hoc have nearly always voted on most issues in favour of the State that appointed them; and it is perhaps too much to expect that they should do otherwise.[44]

Judges *ad hoc* may also be appointed in advisory proceedings. Although states are not parties to advisory proceedings, their status may nevertheless be analogous to that of a party to a dispute. For instance, Israel had a direct interest in the advisory proceedings on the *Legal Consequences of the Construction of a Wall in the Occupied Palestinian Territory*.[45] Therefore, although Israel was not a party to the proceedings, it would have been entitled to appoint a judge *ad hoc* if it had participated in the proceedings. However, it chose not to take part in the case and therefore did not invoke its right to appoint a judge *ad hoc*. The decisive criterion in determining whether the Court should permit a state to appoint a judge *ad hoc* is the existence of a real dispute affecting the interests of a state as opposed to of a simple legal question.[46]

---

43 Statute of the International Court of Justice, above note 11, art 31.1.

44 Thirlway, *Court*, above note 24 at 14.

45 *Legal Consequences of the Construction of a Wall in the Occupied Palestinian Territory*, Advisory Opinion [2004] ICJ Rep 136 [*Construction of a Wall in the Occupied Palestinian Territory*].

46 Thirlway, *Court*, above note 24 at 111.

D. REGISTRY OF THE COURT

The ICJ is the only principal organ of the UN that does not receive secretarial assistance from the Secretary-General. The Registry of the Court is the permanent administrative organ of the ICJ. The Registry's primary responsibilities are set out in Article 26 of the Rules of Court. They include the following functions:

(a) be the regular channel of communications to and from the Court . . . ;

(b) keep . . . a General List of all cases, entered and numbered in the order in which the documents instituting proceedings or requesting an advisory opinion are received in the Registry;

(c) have the custody of the declarations accepting the jurisdiction of the Court made by States not parties to the Statute in accordance with any resolution adopted by the Security Council under Article 35, paragraph 2, of the Statute, and transmit certified copies thereof to all States parties to the Statute, to such other States as shall have deposited declarations, and to the Secretary-General of the United Nations;

(d) transmit to the parties copies of all pleadings and documents annexed upon receipt thereof in the Registry;

(e) communicate to the government of the country in which the Court or a Chamber is sitting, and any other governments which may be concerned, the necessary information as to the persons from time to time entitled, under the Statute and relevant agreements, to privileges, immunities, or facilities;

(f) be present, in person or by his deputy, at meetings of the Court, and of the Chambers, and be responsible for the preparation of minutes of such meetings;

(g) make arrangements for such provision or verification of translations and interpretations into the Court's official languages as the Court may require;

(h) sign all judgments, advisory opinions and orders of the Court, and the minutes referred to in subparagraph (f);

(i) be responsible for the printing and publication of the Court's judgments, advisory opinions and orders, the pleadings and statements, and minutes of public sittings in cases, and of such other documents as the Court may direct to be published;

(j) be responsible for all administrative work and in particular for the accounts and financial administration in accordance with the financial procedures of the United Nations;

(k) deal with enquiries concerning the Court and its work;

(l) assist in maintaining relations between the Court and other organs of the United Nations, the specialized agencies, and international bodies and conferences concerned with the codification and progressive development of international law;

(m) ensure that information concerning the Court and its activities is made accessible to governments, the highest national courts of justice, professional and learned societies, legal faculties and schools of law, and public information media;

(n) have custody of the seals and stamps of the Court, of the archives of the Court, and of such other archives as may be entrusted to the Court.

Another critical function of the Registry consists of advising the Court on its Rules of Court, procedures, and precedents. Neither the Registrar nor the staff of the Registry get involved in the Court's deliberations or decision-making process. Only the judges of the Court make the judicial decisions of the ICJ. Nevertheless, the Registrar may exercise some quasi-judicial powers when deciding whether an application or other written proceedings filed by a party complies with the Statute or the rules of procedure.[47]

The most senior official of the Registry is the Registrar. In accordance with Article 21.2 of the ICJ's Statute, the Court appoints a Registrar who is authorized to appoint such officers as may be necessary. The Registrar is appointed through an election by secret ballot from among candidates proposed by the members of the Court. The Registrar is elected for an initial term of seven years and can be re-elected.[48]

---

47 Shabtai Rosenne, *The Law and Practice of the International Court of Justice, 1920–2005*, 4th ed (Leiden: Nijhoff, 2006) at 419.

48 Rules of Court, above note 30, art 22.1.

The candidate who obtains the votes of the majority of the members of the Court is declared elected.[49] The Registrar is responsible for all departments of the Registry, represents the Court before the budgetary authorities of the UN, including before the ACABQ,[50] and holds the rank of an Assistant Secretary-General. The Registrar is assisted by the Deputy Registrar (a staff member at the D-2 level) and a team of over 100 staff working in thirteen departments, divisions, and other organizational units.

The Registrar does not report to the Secretary-General, but is responsible only to the Court in all matters relating to the discharge of official functions. The conditions of service of staff working in the Registry of the ICJ are governed by the Staff Regulations of the Registry, which are different from those applicable to UN staff members. The Rules of Court require the Registrar to draw up Staff Regulations that are "so far as possible in conformity with the United Nations Staff Regulations and Staff Rules," which are approved by the Court.[51] Disputes relating to the conditions of service or terms of employment of Registry staff are settled through the internal justice system of the United Nations. More specifically, the staff of the ICJ Registry may challenge administrative decisions made by the Registrar that affect their employment rights by submitting an application to the United Nations Dispute Tribunal. They also have access to the United Nations Ombudsman and Mediation Services as well as the Office of Staff Legal Assistance.

The Registrar may be removed from office only if, in the opinion of two-thirds of the members of the ICJ, the incumbent has either become permanently incapacitated from exercising the role's functions or has committed a serious breach of duty. Such decisions must be taken by secret ballot.[52]

---

49 *Ibid*, art 22.4.

50 Rosenne, above note 47 at 423.

51 Rules of Court, above note 30, art 28.4.

52 *Ibid*, art 29.

E. CONTENTIOUS JURISDICTION

The ICJ has jurisdiction to decide, in accordance with international law, disputes of a legal nature that are submitted to it by states. This is called contentious jurisdiction and is the subject of this section. The Court also gives advisory opinions on legal questions at the request of the UN organs, specialized agencies, or a related organization authorized to make such a request. This is known as the advisory jurisdiction of the Court, which will be the topic in Section F, below in this chapter.

Before the ICJ can decide to exercise its contentious jurisdiction, it must be satisfied that a real dispute exists between the parties. The Court would exceed its jurisdiction by entertaining a case in which no real dispute exists between the parties. The term "dispute" has been defined as "a disagreement on a point of law or fact, a conflict of legal views or of interests between two persons"[53] or "a situation in which the two sides held clearly opposite views concerning the question of the performance or non-performance of certain treaty obligations."[54] To establish the existence of a dispute "it is not sufficient for one party to a contentious case to assert that a dispute exists with the other party,"[55] just as a mere denial of the existence of the dispute does not prove its inexistence. Also, it is not adequate to show that the interests of the two parties to such a case are in conflict. The applicant must show that the claim of one party is positively opposed by the other.[56] The failure or refusal by the respondent state to dispute the alleged facts or to refute the arguments advanced by the applicant state does not negate the existence of a dispute.[57] The existence of an

---

53 *Mavrommatis Palestine Concessions*, above note 9 at 11; see also *Case concerning the Northern Cameroons (Cameroon v United Kingdom)*, [1963] ICJ Rep 15 at 27–28.

54 *Interpretation of the Peace Treaties with Bulgaria, Hungary and Romania*, Advisory Opinion, [1950] ICJ Rep 65 at 74 [*Interpretation of the Peace Treaties*].

55 *South West Africa (Ethiopia v South Africa; Liberia v South Africa)*, Preliminary Objections, Judgment, [1962] ICJ Rep 319 at 328 [*South West Africa*]; *Nuclear Tests (Australia v France)*, Judgment, [1974] ICJ Rep 253 at para 55 [*Nuclear Tests Judgment*].

56 *South West Africa*, above note 55 at 328.

57 *Applicability to Arbitrate under Section 21 of the United Nations Headquarters Agreement of 26 June 1947*, Advisory Opinion, [1988] ICJ Rep 12 at para 35.

international dispute is an objective determination.[58] The evidential threshold required to prove the existence of a dispute is generally low. If the respondent denies the complaints of fact and law made by the applicant, a dispute is presumed to exist.[59] "Although a formal diplomatic protest may be an important step to bring a claim of one party to the attention of the other, such a formal protest is not a necessary condition" for a dispute to exist.[60] The existence of a dispute may even "be inferred from the failure of a state to respond to a claim in circumstances where a response is called for."[61]

On two separate occasions, the ICJ refused to exercise its contentious jurisdiction where the state that instituted legal proceedings against another state was unable to demonstrate that an international dispute existed between them. The first refusal to adjudicate a case on this basis pertained to an application filed by Australia against France. Australia asked the Court to declare that France was breaching international law rules by carrying out atmospheric nuclear weapon tests in the South Pacific Ocean. Before the Court had time to adjudicate the case, France promised to cease such tests in the South Pacific Ocean. The World Court concluded that as soon as France unilaterally declared that it would discontinue nuclear tests, the dispute became moot and no longer required the intervention of the ICJ.[62] More recently, the World Court refused to adjudicate another

58 *Interpretation of the Peace Treaties*, above note 54 at 74.

59 *East Timor (Portugal v Australia)*, [1995] ICJ Rep 90 at para 22; *Application of the Convention on the Prevention and Punishment of the Crime of Genocide (Bosnia and Herzegovina v Serbia and Montenegro)*, Preliminary Objections, Judgment, [1996] ICJ Rep 595 at para 29; *Certain Property (Liechtenstein v Germany)*, Preliminary Objections, Judgment, [2005] ICJ Rep 6 at para 25.

60 *Alleged Violations of Sovereign Rights and Maritime Spaces in the Caribbean Sea (Nicaragua v Colombia)*, Preliminary Objections, Judgment, [2016] ICJ Rep 3 at para 72.

61 *Application of the International Convention on the Elimination of All Forms of Racial Discrimination (Georgia v Russian Federation)*, Preliminary Objections, Judgment, [2011] ICJ Rep 70 at para 30; *Land and Maritime Boundary between Cameroon and Nigeria (Cameroon v Nigeria)*, Preliminary Objections, Judgment, [1998] ICJ Rep 275 at para 89.

62 *Nuclear Tests Judgment*, above note 55.

application instituted by the Marshall Islands.[63] In 2014, the Marshall Islands instituted legal proceedings against states that hold nuclear weapons, namely, China, France, India, Israel, North Korea, Pakistan, Russia, the United Kingdom, and the United States. In its application filed before the ICJ, the Marshall Islands alleged that these nine states were in violation of their obligation to negotiate in good faith the cessation of nuclear disarmament. Most cases were summarily dismissed because most respondent states had not consented to the jurisdiction of the Court. However, the proceedings against India, Pakistan, and the United Kingdom remained on the Court's docket because these three states recognized the compulsory jurisdiction of the Court. Despite this, the ICJ did not review the merits of the complaint because it determined that there was no dispute between the Marshall Islands and the responding states. The Court acknowledged that "the Marshall Islands, by virtue of the suffering which its people endured as a result of it being used as a site for extensive nuclear testing programs, has special reasons for concern about nuclear disarmament."[64] Nevertheless, the Court noted that the respondent states were unaware that the Marshall Islands was making an allegation that they were in breach of their international obligations. Therefore, there appeared to be no dispute between the parties.

Where the ICJ decides that an international dispute exists, it must then determine whether it has all four bases of jurisdiction to be seized of a dispute. The ICJ has the power to decide on the existence and extent of its own jurisdiction:

> [I]t has been generally recognized, following the earlier precedents, that, in the absence of any agreement to the contrary, an international tribunal has the right to decide as to its own jurisdiction and has the power to interpret for this purpose the instruments which govern that jurisdiction.[65]

---

63 *Obligations concerning Negotiations relating to Cessation of the Nuclear Arms Race and to Nuclear Disarmament (Marshall Islands v India)*, Jurisdiction and Admissibility, Judgment, [2016] ICJ Rep 255.

64 *Ibid* at para 41.

65 *Nottebohm Case (Liechtenstein v Guatemala)*, Preliminary Objection, Judgment, [1953] ICJ Rep 111 at 119.

The first type of jurisdiction required is *ratione personae*, which refers to a court's power to bring a person or party into its adjudicative process. The second category is the court's *ratione materiae* jurisdiction, otherwise known as subject-matter jurisdiction. It refers to the court's authority to decide a particular case or to grant the relief sought. The third category refers to the Court's *ratione temporis* jurisdiction, also known as temporal jurisdiction. The court can lose temporal jurisdiction over a claim in cases where the applicant fails to submit his claim or application within the prescribed time limits. The fourth category of jurisdiction is territorial or *ratione loci*. Specifically, some states may choose to limit the jurisdiction of the ICJ to a specific territory or to exclude from its jurisdiction disputes relating to certain geographic areas.

1) *Ratione Personae* or Personal Jurisdiction in Contentious Cases

Article 34.1 of the Statute of the ICJ provides that only states may be parties in cases before the Court. Individuals, international organizations, NGOs, and corporations do not have standing before the ICJ and, therefore, cannot institute proceedings against states or be sued by states. Several proposals have been made to extend the Court's jurisdiction in contentious proceedings to include disputes between states and international organizations, including the United Nations.[66] The chief argument in favour of these proposals is the fact that the scope of activities of intergovernmental organizations has substantially increased and, therefore, they need a forum for resolving disputes with their member states. Since implementing these proposals necessarily entails an amendment of the *UN Charter* and of the Statute of the ICJ, the General Assembly has repeatedly rejected them.[67] The General Assembly's guidance has consistently been to

66 See *Report of the Special Committee on the Charter of the United Nations and on the Strengthening of the Role of the Organization*, UNGAOR, 52nd Session, UN Doc A/52/33 and A/52/33/Corr.1 (1997) at para 102.

67 *Report of the Special Committee on the Charter of the United Nations and on the Strengthening of the Role of the Organization*, GA Res 52/161, UNGAOR, 52nd Sess, UN Doc A/RES/52/161 (1997) 1.

propose "practical ways and means of strengthening the Court, while respecting its authority and independence, on the understanding that whatever action may be taken as a result of the consideration will have no implications for any changes in the *Charter of the United Nations* or in the Statute of the International Court of Justice."[68]

Although private citizens, corporations, and NGOs also do not have standing before the World Court, they may convince their respective governments to protect their interests by instituting proceedings on their behalf. Indeed, states have occasionally filed cases before the ICJ to protect the interests of their nationals or corporations. In several cases, the ICJ adjudicated disputes between two states that related to individuals. For example, in the *Nottebohm* case,[69] Liechtenstein sought compensation from Guatemala on the ground that the Guatemalan government had unlawfully seized the property of one of its citizens. The Court found Liechtenstein's claim to be inadmissible because Mr Nottebohm's nationality was not based on any genuine prior link with Liechtenstein. In fact, Nottebohm was a German national who had recently acquired citizenship in Liechtenstein—a neutral country in time of war—in order to evade the expropriation of his property. Hence, the Court concluded that Liechtenstein was not entitled to put forward an international claim on behalf of a German national.

In 2010, Guinea instituted proceedings against the Democratic Republic of the Congo for similar reasons.[70] The DRC arrested and detained a Guinean entrepreneur with business interests in Congo, seized his property and bank accounts, and expelled him from its territory. The Court concluded that Guinea could claim monetary compensation from the DRC for causing damages to its national, even if the state of Guinea itself incurred no financial or material losses.[71]

---

68 See *Report of the Special Committee on the Charter of the United Nations and on the Strengthening of the Role of the Organization*, GA Res 53/106, UNGAOR, 53rd Sess, UN Doc A/RES/53/106 (1998) 1 at para 4(e).

69 *Nottebohm Case (Liechtenstein v Guatemala)*, Second Phase, Judgment, [1955] ICJ Rep 4.

70 *Ahmadou Sadio Diallo (Republic of Guinea* v *Democratic Republic of the Congo)*, Merits, Judgment, [2010] ICJ Rep 639.

71 See the analysis in the separate opinion of Judge Cançado Trindade.

In some cases, states have instituted proceedings against other states in an attempt to prevent the execution of their nationals. For example, Germany and Mexico brought two separate cases against the United States in a dispute concerning their nationals who were sentenced to death in some American states. Germany and Mexico both successfully argued that the United States breached its international obligations by arresting and prosecuting foreign citizens without giving the accused consular rights pursuant to the Vienna Convention on Consular Relations of 24 April 1963.[72]

India filed a case against Pakistan in relation to a similar dispute. An Indian national had been sentenced to death by a military court in Pakistan for engaging in espionage activities. India claimed that Pakistan had failed to inform its embassy in a timely manner of the arrest and detention of its national. It also argued that India's consular officers had been denied access to the detained individual while he was in custody and had been unable to converse or correspond with him and arrange for his legal representation. In its judgment of July 2019, the Court ruled that Pakistan was under an obligation to provide effective review and reconsideration of the conviction and sentence of the Indian national, so as to ensure that full weight was given to the effect of the violation of his due process rights under the Vienna Convention on Consular Relations.[73]

States may seek the intervention of the Court even in exclusively commercial disputes. In the *Barcelona Traction* case of 1970,[74] the ICJ acknowledged that a state can act on behalf of not only its citizens but also on behalf of registered companies that have a distinct juridical personality. However, the Court specified that to have standing before the Court, the state must bring a claim on behalf of a company that is incorporated in its jurisdiction or under its national laws. Belgium's claim against Spain was found to be irreceivable because Barcelona Traction Ltd was incorporated in Canada, whereas Canada chose not to

---

72 *LaGrand (Germany v United States of America)*, [2001] ICJ Rep 466; *Avena and Other Mexican Nationals (Mexico v United States of America)*, [2004] ICJ Rep 12.

73 *Jadhav (India v Pakistan)*, [2019] ICJ Rep 419.

74 *Barcelona Traction, Light and Power Company Limited (Belgium v Spain)*; Second Phase, [1970] ICJ Rep 3.

file an application against Spain. Therefore, the Court concluded that Belgium had no legal interest (standing) even if it was representing the interests of Belgian shareholders who had suffered a financial loss.[75]

In 2009, Belgium initiated proceedings against Switzerland for its failure or refusal to recognize a decision made in a Belgian court on the liability of the Swiss shareholders vis-à-vis the Belgian shareholders of the same company. Belgium argued that Switzerland was in breach of its international obligations set out in the Lugano Convention of 16 September 1988 on jurisdiction and the enforcement of judgments in civil and commercial matters. This case was settled out of the Court and the proceedings were discontinued.[76]

The ICJ is by default open to all state parties to the ICJ Statute.[77] In accordance with Article 93.1 of the *UN Charter*, all members of the United Nations are *ipso facto* parties to the ICJ Statute.[78] Currently, 193 internationally recognized states are members of the UN and parties to the ICJ. However, this has not always been the case. In the past, some states could be parties to the ICJ Statute and not be member states of the UN. In particular, Switzerland, Japan, Liechtenstein, San Marino, and Nauru became parties to the ICJ Statute before their admission to the UN. Article 93.2 of the *UN Charter* expressly allows non-members of the United Nations to become parties to the Statute of the Court on conditions determined by the General Assembly upon the recommendation of the Security Council. The three conditions required to become a party to the ICJ are listed in the General Assembly Resolution 91(I): (a) acceptance of the provisions of the ICJ Statute; (b) acceptance of all of the obligations applicable to UN member states under Article 94 of the *UN Charter*;[79] and (c) an undertaking to

---

75 The ICJ identified some exceptional circumstances which could allow a state to file a case against another state on behalf of shareholders.

76 *Jurisdiction and Enforcement of Judgments in Civil and Commercial Matters (Belgium v Switzerland)*, Order of 5 April 2011, [2011] ICJ Rep 341.

77 Statute of the International Court of Justice, above note 11, art 35.1.

78 *Charter of the United Nations*, above note 10, art 93.1.

79 Article 94 of the *Charter of the United Nations* reads as follows:

> 1. Each Member of the United Nations undertakes to comply with the decision of the International Court of Justice in any case to which it is a party.

contribute to the expenses of the court.[80] States that are not members of the UN become parties to the ICJ Statute as soon as they deposit with the Secretary-General of the United Nations the instrument of acceptance of the conditions set out by the General Assembly.

Pursuant to Article 35.2 of the Court's Statute, the ICJ may also be open to other states that are not parties to the ICJ Statute under certain conditions laid down by the Security Council. The conditions for the ICJ to be open to States that are neither UN members nor parties to the ICJ Statute are contained in the Security Council Resolution 9 (1946), which provides as follows:

1. The International Court of Justice shall be open to a State which is not a party to the Statute of the International Court of Justice, upon the following condition, namely, that such State shall previously have deposited with the Registrar of the Court a declaration by which it accepts the jurisdiction of the Court, in accordance with the Charter of the United Nations and with the terms and subject to the conditions of the Statute and Rules of the Court, and undertakes to comply in good faith with the decision or decisions of the Court and to accept all the obligations of a Member of the United Nations under Article 94 of the Charter;
2. Such declaration may be either particular or general. A particular declaration is one accepting the jurisdiction of the Court in respect only of a particular dispute or disputes which have already arisen. A general declaration is one accepting the jurisdiction generally in respect of all disputes or of a particular class or classes of disputes which have already arisen or which may arise in the future. A State, in making such a general declaration, may, in accordance with Article 36, paragraph 2, of the

---

2. If any party to a case fails to perform the obligations incumbent upon it under a judgment rendered by the Court, the other party may have recourse to the Security Council, which may, if it deems necessary, make recommendations or decide upon measures to be taken to give effect to the judgment.

80 *Conditions on which Switzerland may become a Party to the International Court of Justice*, GA Res 91(I), UNGAOR, 1st Sess, UN Doc A/Res/91(I) (1946) 182.

> Statute, recognize as compulsory, ipso facto and without special agreement, the jurisdiction of the Court, provided, however, that such acceptance may not, without explicit agreement, be relied upon vis-à-vis States parties to the Statute which have made the declaration in conformity with Article 36, paragraph 2, of the Statute of the International Court of Justice.[81]

Albania, Japan, Cambodia, Laos, Sri Lanka, Finland, Italy, Vietnam, and the Federal Republic of Germany recognized the compulsory jurisdiction of the Court before they became UN member states or parties to the ICJ Statute.

2) *Ratione Materiae* or Subject-Matter Jurisdiction in Contentious Cases

In the previous section, it was mentioned that only states had standing before the ICJ. It is, however, important to emphasize that to have standing (which means to be eligible to bring a case before the Tribunal) does not necessarily mean that the Court has jurisdiction to adjudicate the dispute. This is particularly true if the other party did not accept the compulsory jurisdiction of the Court. In contentious proceedings, the jurisdiction of the ICJ is based on the consent of not only the applicant state but also of the respondent state. The consent of states can be expressed in different ways as described below.

a) Declaration Accepting the Compulsory Jurisdiction of the ICJ

The most widely used means of accepting the jurisdiction of the Court is through a unilateral declaration known as the "optional clause" made pursuant to Article 36.2 of the ICJ Statute. This provision states that

> The states parties to the present Statute may at any time declare that they recognize as compulsory ipso facto and without special agreement, in relation to any other state accepting the same obligation, the jurisdiction of the Court in all legal disputes concerning:

81 SC Res 9 (1946), UNSCOR, 1st Year, UN Doc S/Res/9 (1946) 14 at paras 1–2.

a. the interpretation of a treaty;
b. any question of international law;
c. the existence of any fact which, if established, would constitute a breach of an international obligation;
d. the nature or extent of the reparation to be made for the breach of an international obligation.

Declarations recognizing the jurisdiction of the Court as compulsory take the form of a unilateral act of the state.[82] There are no statutory requirements that regulate the form and content of declarations recognizing as compulsory the jurisdiction of the Court. Such declarations minimally contain a paragraph conferring jurisdiction to the ICJ and the signature of the official making the declaration on behalf of the state. For example, the declaration of Austria reads as follows:

> [T]he Republic of Austria recognizes as compulsory ipso facto and without special agreement, in relation to any other State which accepts or has accepted the same obligation, the jurisdiction of the International Court of Justice in all legal disputes referred to in paragraph 2 of Article 36 of the Statute of the International Court of Justice.
>
> This Declaration does not apply to any dispute in respect of which the parties thereto have agreed or shall agree to have recourse to other means of peaceful settlement for its final and binding decision.
>
> This Declaration shall remain in force for a period of five years and thereafter until it will be terminated or modified by a written declaration.[83]

Currently, some seventy-two member states have unilaterally subscribed to the compulsory jurisdiction of the International Court of Justice. These declarations are deposited with the Secretary-General of the United Nations. A declaration can be made unconditionally or on condition of reciprocity on the part of several or certain states,

---

82 *Phosphates in Morocco (Italy v France)*, (1938) PCIJ (Ser A/B) No 74 at 23 [*Phosphates in Morocco*].

83 Austria's Declarations recognizing the jurisdiction of the Court as compulsory, 778 UNTS 301 (19 May 1971).

or for a limited time.[84] The vast majority of declarations, including the declaration by Austria reproduced above, are made on condition of reciprocity. Dominica and Haiti, for instance, chose not to make their acceptance of the Court's compulsory jurisdiction conditional. Dominica's declaration reads as follows:

> The Commonwealth of Dominica hereby accepts the compulsory jurisdiction of the International Court of Justice and makes this Declaration under article 36(2) of the Statute of the Court.[85]

Since the recognition of the Court's jurisdiction is strictly consensual, states are free to supplement their declarations with conditions or reservations,[86] as long as they are compatible with the Statute of the Court. It is for each state, in formulating its declaration, to decide on the limits it wishes to place on its acceptance of the jurisdiction of the ICJ.[87] States choose to include in their declarations limitations in order to specify those areas, topics, or periods in relation to which the declaring state does not want to submit a case to the ICJ. Essentially, limitations or reservations operate to define the parameters of the state's acceptance of the compulsory jurisdiction of the Court.[88] Reservations may exclude from the jurisdiction of the Court specific types of controversies, for example, disputes relating to a specific treaty, specific factual situations, or a specific legal field, such as the delimitation of boundaries or environmental protection. Poland's declaration includes a number of such conditions:

> The Republic of Poland shall recognize with the effect as of 25 September 1996, in accordance with the provisions of [article 36] as

84 Statute of the International Court of Justice, above note 11, art 36.3.

85 Dominica's Declarations recognizing the jurisdiction of the Court as compulsory, 2363 UNTS 325 (24 March 2006); see also Haiti's Declaration made under Article 36.2 of the Statute of the Permanent Court of International Justice on 4 October 1921.

86 Reservations are limitations on or exceptions to the commitments contained in the declaration to recognize the jurisdiction of the Court.

87 *Fisheries Jurisdiction (Spain v Canada)*, Jurisdiction of the Court, Judgment, [1998] ICJ Rep 432 at para 44 [*Fisheries Jurisdiction*].

88 *Ibid.*

> compulsory ipso facto and without special agreement, in relation to any other state accepting the same obligation and subject to the sole condition of reciprocity, the jurisdiction of the International Court of Justice in all legal disputes other than:
>
> . . .
>
> b) disputes with regard to the territory or State boundaries;
> c) disputes with regard to environmental protection;
> d) disputes with regard to foreign liabilities or debts.[89]

Some states exclude from the jurisdiction of the Court disputes that the parties agreed to submit to other methods of peaceful settlement. For instance, Peru's declaration contains this type of restriction:

> This declaration does not apply to any dispute with regard to which the parties have agreed or shall agree to have recourse to arbitration or judicial settlement for a final and binding decision or which has been settled by some other method of peaceful settlement.[90]

The most sweeping reservation used is the one contained in the declaration of the United States, which excluded from the compulsory jurisdiction of the Court "disputes with regard to matters which are essentially within the domestic jurisdiction of the United States of America as determined by the United States of America." The United States revoked its declaration in 1985 after the ICJ issued an unfavourable judgment in a case relating to the military intervention by the United States in Nicaragua.

Limitations or restrictions in the declaration accepting the compulsory jurisdiction of the World Court are a double-edged sword. It is important to recall that with the exception of two states (Dominica and Haiti), all member states that have thus far submitted declarations accept the compulsory jurisdiction of the Court on condition of reciprocity. Consequently, reservations are also reciprocal.[91] The

---

89 Poland's Declarations recognizing the jurisdiction of the Court as compulsory, 1918 UNTS 41 (25 March 1996).

90 Peru's Declarations recognizing the jurisdiction of the Court as compulsory, 2219 UNTS 303 (7 July 2003).

91 *Phosphates in Morocco*, above note 82 at 10.

declaring state is precluded from bringing a case against another state in relation to any issue, area, or period excluded in its own declaration through reservations. Any state against which the declaring state brings a case can invoke the declaring state's reservation as a jurisdictional bar. This occurred when Yugoslavia instituted proceedings against NATO member nations for their bombing campaign in 1999. Yugoslavia sought to establish the jurisdiction of the ICJ under Article 36.2. However, it faced one sizeable obstacle. In its declaration accepting the compulsory jurisdiction of the Court, Yugoslavia had included a temporal reservation that excluded any and all disputes that arose before 25 April 1999 (the date of Yugoslavia's declaration). Several NATO member states invoked this temporal limitation and argued that Yugoslavia's application was not receivable because the bombing campaign began before 25 April 1999. The Court declined jurisdiction and rejected Yugoslavia's application.[92]

By accepting the Court's compulsory jurisdiction through a unilateral declaration, a member state assumes an onerous obligation on the manner in which it must resolve disputes with other states. Therefore, it is not surprising that only 72 out of 193 UN member states have thus far accepted the compulsory jurisdiction of the Court.

b) *Compromis* (Special Agreements) and Compromissory Clause

There are other options for adhering to the jurisdiction of the Court. Article 36.1 of the ICJ's Statute states that "the jurisdiction of the Court comprises all cases which the parties refer to it and all matters specially provided for in the *Charter of the United Nations* or in treaties and conventions in force." This paragraph provides for two distinct mechanisms for accepting the jurisdiction of the Court. The first mechanism is a special agreement, commonly known as *compromis*, whereby the parties enter into an agreement referring an existing dispute to the Court. The second mechanism is the "compromissory clause," contained in a bilateral or multilateral treaty that grants the International Court of Justice jurisdiction over a dispute that might

92 *Legality of Use of Force (Yugoslavia v Belgium)*, Order on Provisional Measures, [1999] ICJ Rep 124 [*Legality of Use of Force*].

arise with regard to the interpretation or the application of that particular instrument. Although these two mechanisms are provided for in the same provision of the *UN Charter*, they are fundamentally different. In the interests of clarity, we will examine each of these two options under separate headings.

i) Compromis *or Special Agreements*

Two or more states may conclude special agreements, also known as *compromis*, after the dispute or controversy arises. At the time of submitting the dispute to the ICJ, the parties are well aware of the facts that led to the dispute. They also know the specific legal issues that the Court needs to decide. This allows the parties to circumscribe the jurisdiction of the Court by listing specific questions that they wish to submit to the Court. Special agreements have several distinct advantages over compromissory clauses.

First, when states conclude a special agreement, the Court is seized by all the parties to the dispute as opposed to by the applicant state. As all parties to the same dispute have expressed a genuine interest in the Court settling their dispute, they are not likely to subsequently raise time-consuming and costly jurisdictional objections. Consequently, the proceedings are more expeditious and less confrontational when a dispute is brought to the Court through a *compromis*.

Second, special agreements are indicative of the parties' willingness and preparedness to accept the outcome and to implement the judgment of the Court. Although states often express their dissatisfaction with unfavourable judgments of the Court even if they willingly submit the dispute to it through special agreements, they generally accept and implement the decisions of the ICJ.[93]

Third, special agreements allow for greater flexibility. Indeed, they do not need to comply with any formal or procedural requirements. The parties are free to agree on the order of procedural steps. They can agree on time limits for the filing of their briefs and on the number of

---

93 Eric A Posner & John C Yoo, "Judicial Independence in International Tribunals" 93 *Calif L Rev* 1 (2005); Aloysius P Llamzon, *Jurisdiction and Compliance in Recent Decisions of the International Court of Justice, E.J.I.L.* (2007), Vol 18 No 5, 815–52.

pleadings allowed. They can choose the language to be used in the proceedings and other procedural questions. The ICJ summarized some of the advantages of using special agreements as follows:

> [P]arties to treaties or special agreements are free to make their consent to the seisin of the Court, and hence the Court's jurisdiction, subject to whatever pre-conditions, consistent with the Statute, as may be agreed between them; and secondly, that in principle a State may validly waive an objection to jurisdiction which it might otherwise have been entitled to raise.[94]

Thus, the special agreement is arguably the safest and most efficient way of bringing a dispute to the International Court of Justice. The majority of cases submitted to the Court by way of a special agreement pertain to territorial sovereignty, or delimitations of land or maritime frontiers.[95] States do not normally submit to the ICJ sensitive political controversies through special agreements because they would be unwilling to assume the risk of losing the case. Unfortunately, fewer than twenty cases have been brought to the ICJ by way of a special agreement.

ii) Compromissory Clause

The second mechanism, known as compromissory clause, is contained in a treaty or a convention to which two or more states are parties. There are nearly 250 bilateral or multilateral treaties and conventions that contain a clause conferring jurisdiction on the ICJ. For instance, the *UN Convention against Transnational Organized Crime* and the *UN Convention against Corruption* provide that:

> Any dispute between two or more States Parties concerning the interpretation or application of this Convention that cannot be settled through negotiation within a reasonable time shall, at the request of

94 *Application for Revision and Interpretation of the Judgment of 24 February 1982 in the Case concerning the Continental Shelf (Tunisia/Libyan Arab Jamahiriya)*, [1985] ICJ Rep 192 at 216.

95 *Gabčíkovo-Nagymaros Project (Hungary/Slovakia)*, [1997] ICJ Rep 7 and *Colombian-Peruvian asylum case (Colombia v Peru)*, [1950] ICJ Rep 266 are exceptions.

> one of those States Parties, be submitted to arbitration. If, six months after the date of the request for arbitration, those States Parties are unable to agree on the organization of the arbitration, any one of those States Parties may refer the dispute to the International Court of Justice by request in accordance with the Statute of the Court.[96]

The wording of compromissory clauses may vary from one treaty to another. The jurisdictional clause contained in Article 119.2 of the Rome Statute of International Criminal Court has an entirely different wording:

> Any other dispute between two or more States Parties relating to the interpretation or application of this Statute which is not settled through negotiations within three months of their commencement shall be referred to the Assembly of States Parties. The Assembly may itself seek to settle the dispute or may make recommendations on further means of settlement of the dispute, including referral to the International Court of Justice in conformity with the Statute of that Court.

The compromissory clause is agreed upon before the controversy or the dispute arises. This way of conferring jurisdiction upon the ICJ does not allow the parties to assess their risks beforehand because at the time of signing the treaty or convention containing the compromissory clause, the parties do not know what kind of disagreement or dispute, if any, might arise. They accept the jurisdiction of the Court in advance and have little control over the issues that another state might ask the Court to determine. The compromissory clause is similar to the unilateral declaration made under Article 36.2 of the Statute. The main difference between these two ways of accepting the compulsory jurisdiction of the Court is that the compromissory clause is limited to a dispute that may arise in relation to the specific treaty containing the clause whereas the unilateral declaration may apply to any dispute.

---

96 *United Nations Convention against Transnational Organized Crime*, 15 November 2000, 2225 UNTS 209, art 35.2 (entered into force 29 September 2003) and *United Nations Convention against Corruption*, 31 October 2003, 2349 UNTS 41, art 66.2 (entered into force 14 December 2005).

Not surprisingly, the rate of compliance with the ICJ judgments is lower when the jurisdiction is conferred on it through declarations or compromissory clauses than through special agreements.

c) The Doctrine of *Forum Prorogatum* in Contentious Cases

The doctrine of *forum prorogatum* may apply to a state that has not yet recognized the jurisdiction of the Court but accepts it when another state institutes proceedings against it. For example, in October 1946, when two British ships were damaged by mines with resulting loss of life and injury to their crews in the Strait of Corfu (a narrow channel of water along the coasts of Albania), the United Kingdom attributed this attack to the Albanian government. The Security Council recommended that the United Kingdom and Albania refer the matter to the International Court of Justice.[97] The Albanian government accepted in writing the recommendation of the Security Council. The United Kingdom instituted proceedings against Albania before the ICJ without signing a special agreement with Albania. Although Albania argued in a written communication addressed to the ICJ that the United Kingdom should have waited until the two governments had signed a special agreement, it agreed once again to have the matter decided by the Court for this specific dispute. Despite this, as soon as the proceedings began, Albania raised objections, arguing that the Court had no jurisdiction to entertain the matter because Albania (a) had not filed a declaration accepting the compulsory jurisdiction of the Court; (b) was not party to any bilateral or multilateral agreement that contained a dispute resolution clause compelling the parties to submit their controversy to the ICJ; and (c) had not concluded a special agreement with the United Kingdom formally agreeing to submit the case to the Court. The ICJ noted that Albania had agreed to refer the dispute to the ICJ on two separate occasions and had therefore accepted the compulsory jurisdiction of the tribunal for that particular dispute.[98] This case is an illustration of the doctrine known as *forum prorogatum*.

---

97 SC Res (1947), UNSCOR, 2nd Year, UN Doc S/Res/22 (1947).
98 *Corfu Channel case*, Judgment on Preliminary Objection, [1948] ICJ Rep 15.

Similarly, in 2002, the Republic of the Congo instituted proceedings against France seeking the termination of criminal proceedings before the French courts against senior officials of the Congolese government in relation to allegations of crimes against humanity and torture committed in the Congo. In its application, the Congo stated that it sought to found the jurisdiction of the Court on the consent yet to be given by France.[99] The application was transmitted to the French government. France had no legal obligation to accept the jurisdiction of the Court. In fact, it could have requested the ICJ to decline jurisdiction on the basis of lack of consent. However, France indicated that it "consent[ed] to the jurisdiction of the Court to entertain the Application pursuant to Article 38, paragraph 5" and the case was registered on the Court's docket.[100] This case is another example of *forum prorogatum*.

In some cases, the Court may determine that the consent of the respondent state was implicit. It is nevertheless important to point out that the act of submitting written or oral arguments for the sole purposes of raising jurisdictional objections cannot be regarded as consent:

> The attitude of the respondent State must, however, be capable of being regarded as "an unequivocal indication" of the desire of that State to accept the Court's jurisdiction in a "voluntary and indisputable" manner.[101]

The Statute of the ICJ compels the party filing the application to "specify *as far as possible* the legal grounds upon which the jurisdiction is said to be based."[102] When the applicant proposes to found the jurisdiction of the Court upon a consent thereto yet to be given

---

99 *Certain Criminal Proceedings in France (Republic of the Congo v France)*, Application instituting proceedings filed in the Registry on 9 December 2002 and entered in the Court's General List on 11 April 2003, [2003] ICJ Rep 3.

100 Letter from the Minister for Foreign Affairs of the French Republic (Consent to the Jurisdiction of the Court to Entertain the Application Pursuant to Article 38, paragraph 5, of the Rules of Court) dated 8 April 2003, online: www.icj-cij.org/files/case-related/129/13344.pdf.

101 *Armed Activities on the Territory of the Congo (New Application: 2002) (Democratic Republic of the Congo v Rwanda)*, Jurisdiction and Admissibility, Judgment, [2006] ICJ Rep 6 at 19; see also *Anglo-Iranian Oil Co Case*, above note 35 at 113–14.

102 Rules of Court, above note 30, art 38.2.

or manifested by the state against which the application is made, the application is transmitted to that state so that it can decide whether or not to accept the jurisdiction of the Court.[103] If the respondent state refuses to accept the jurisdiction of the ICJ, the case will not be registered on the Court's docket. If, however, the respondent state decides to accept the jurisdiction of the Court, the proceedings will begin, and the respondent state will not be permitted to argue subsequently that it has not accepted the jurisdiction of the Court.

3) *Ratione Temporis* or Temporal Jurisdiction in Contentious Cases

Neither the Statute of the International Court of Justice nor its Rules provide for a time limit for submission of a dispute to the Court. However, as discussed previously, some states prescribe time limits or other types of temporal conditions in their declarations under Article 36.2 of the Statute where they accept the compulsory jurisdiction of the Court.

Certain declarations contain temporal limitations that exclude disputes that arose prior to a certain date. For example, Japan's declaration excludes the jurisdiction of the ICJ in relation to disputes that arose before 15 September 1958.[104] Guinea's declaration accepts the jurisdiction of the Court in relation to legal disputes arising since 12 December 1958.[105] Similarly, the Marshall Islands accept the jurisdiction of the Court over disputes arising after 17 September 1991.[106] In some cases, there may be a historical reason for limiting the jurisdiction of the Court to a critical date, namely the end of an era such as a dictatorship[107] or communism, or constitutional reforms. In other

---

103 *Ibid*, art 38.5.

104 Japan's Declaration recognizing the jurisdiction of the Court as compulsory as of 6 October 2015.

105 Guinea's Declaration recognizing the jurisdiction of the Court as compulsory, 2121 UNTS 189 (4 December 1998).

106 Marshall Islands' Declaration recognizing the jurisdiction of the Court as compulsory as of 24 April 2013.

107 See Portugal's Declaration recognizing the jurisdiction of the Court as compulsory, 224 UNTS 275 (25 February 2005) excluding from the jurisdiction of the ICJ disputes "arising before 26 April 1974 or concerning situations or facts prior to that date," which precedes the Carnation Revolution, which overthrew the authoritarian Estavo Novo regime.

cases, the date is related to the date of the declaration itself[108] or to the date of a state's independence.[109]

In a few declarations, the time limit is established solely to prevent extremely old disputes. In particular, the Netherlands chose to limit the jurisdiction of the ICJ "over all disputes arising out of situations or facts that took place no earlier than one hundred years before the dispute is brought before the said Court"[110] and Nicaragua excluded matters or claims "based on interpretations of treaties or arbitral awards that were signed and ratified or made, respectively, prior to 31 December 1901."[111]

The time factor is also important in determining whether, in a given case, the ICJ has inherited the jurisdiction of the PCIJ. Article 37 of the ICJ Statute provides as follows:

> Whenever a treaty or convention in force provides for reference of a matter to a tribunal to have been instituted by the League of Nations, or to the Permanent Court of International Justice, the matter shall, as between the parties to the present Statute, be referred to the International Court of Justice.

The ICJ held that this provision was included in the Statute of the Court to ensure an automatic transition from the Permanent Court of International Justice to the International Court of Justice. More specifically, "owing to the decision to create an international court of justice which would in law be a new entity, and not a continuation of the existing Permanent Court, the dissolution of the latter became

108 See Finland's Declaration recognizing the jurisdiction of the Court as compulsory, 303 UNTS 137 (25 June 1958); see also Mexico's Declaration recognizing the jurisdiction of the Court as compulsory, 9 UNTS 97 (28 October 1947).

109 See Nigeria's Declaration recognizing the jurisdiction of the Court as compulsory, 2013 UNTS 507 (30 April 1998), which explicitly refers to "disputes in relation to matters which arose prior to the date of Nigeria's independence"; see also Cyprus's Declaration recognizing the jurisdiction of the Court as compulsory, 2195 UNTS 3 (3 September 2002) as of its date of independence of 16 August 1960.

110 The Netherlands' Declaration recognizing the jurisdiction of the Court as compulsory as of 1 August 1956.

111 Nicaragua's Declaration recognizing the jurisdiction of the Court as compulsory, 2163 UNTS 73 (reservation made on 9 January 2002).

essential, for it would not have been a tolerable situation for two such Courts to be co-existing."[112] However, a very large number of treaties containing jurisdictional clauses providing for recourse to the PCIJ were still in existence. Article 37 of the Statute of the ICJ was designed to preserve as many jurisdictional clauses as possible from becoming inoperative by reason of the prospective dissolution of the Permanent Court of International Justice.

It is entirely irrelevant whether the two states parties to the dispute became parties to the Statute of the ICJ before or after the dissolution of the Permanent Court of International Justice. The only relevant factors are whether the treaty containing the jurisdictional clause is still in force, whether the treaty provides for a referral of the matter to the PCIJ, and whether the dispute is between states, both of which are parties to the Statute of the ICJ.[113]

4) *Ratione Loci* or Territorial Jurisdiction in Contentious Cases

The ICJ has a geographically universal jurisdiction. Therefore, questions pertaining to the territorial jurisdiction of the Court almost never arise. In their declarations accepting the compulsory jurisdiction of the Court, states may limit the jurisdiction of the Court to a specific territory or exclude from its jurisdiction disputes that arise in some locations. For example, the Canadian declaration accepting the compulsory jurisdiction of the ICJ excludes disputes that arise out of, or concern, conservation and management measures taken by Canada with respect to vessels fishing in the NAFO Regulatory Area.[114] This reservation shielded Canada from judicial proceedings before the ICJ in 1995, when Spain attempted to institute proceedings against Canada in relation to a legislative act passed by the Canadian Parliament with a view to preventing foreign vessels from fishing straddling stocks in an area beyond the Canadian Exclusive

112 *Barcelona Traction Light and Power Company Limited (Belgium v Spain)*, Preliminary Objections, Judgment, [1964] ICJ Rep 6 at 31.

113 *Ibid* at 32.

114 Canada's Declarations recognizing the jurisdiction of the Court as compulsory, 1776 UNTS 9 (10 May 1994).

Economic Zone. Spain viewed this act as extraterritorial legislation. It filed an application before the ICJ. Canada argued that Spain's application was not receivable because the Canadian declaration recognizing as compulsory the jurisdiction of the ICJ contained an explicit territorial limitation.[115] The Court refused to entertain the dispute and dismissed Spain's application.[116]

Territorial limitations are very uncommon. States that have skeletons in the closet are more likely to limit the jurisdiction of the Court by imposing time limitations or by excluding disputes that relate to specific subject matters.

5) Jurisdiction to Indicate Provisional Measures

The adjudication of an international dispute before the ICJ is a lengthy process. To preserve the respective rights of either party pending the outcome of a case, the Court may indicate any provisional measure it considers necessary in the circumstances.[117] The purpose of a provisional measure is to preserve the *status quo* pending the final decision of the Court. Thus, a provisional measure may consist of an order directing either party to refrain from certain acts while the Court is hearing or examining the case.

The Court's power to order provisional measures can be found in Article 41.1 of its Statute. This provision provides that the ICJ may use its power "if it considers that circumstances so require," which implies that the power is discretionary. Articles 73–78 of the Rules of the Court provide a procedural guidance on how provisional measures should be requested, considered, and monitored. However, there are no written rules that specify the criteria or legal requirements that must be met for the World Court to order provisional measures. These criteria derive mainly from the Court's jurisprudence.

To exercise its discretionary power and order provisional measures, the Court does not need to satisfy itself in a definitive manner

---

115 *Ibid.*

116 *Fisheries Jurisdiction*, above note 87.

117 Statute of the International Court of Justice, above note 11, art 41.

that it has jurisdiction to examine the merits of the case.[118] The ICJ must be satisfied that it has a *prima facie* jurisdiction to entertain the dispute.[119] The *prima facie* threshold is low; a mere appearance upon initial observation that the Court has jurisdiction should suffice. Put differently, the Court must ensure that the absence of jurisdiction is not manifest. For instance, the Court will refuse to grant provisional measures if the state seeking such measures is attempting to found the jurisdiction of the court on a legal instrument that contains a clear reservation excluding the dispute from the Court's purview.[120]

A related legal requirement for granting a provisional measure is for the Court to be satisfied that the rights asserted by the party seeking the measure are at least plausible.[121] In other words, the Court will be reluctant to order measures that aim at preserving rights that are not likely to be recognized in the final judgment. The likelihood of prevailing on the merits is a decisive consideration.

The existence of urgency and irreparable harm is another requirement for provisional measures to be indicated. There must be a real and imminent risk that irreparable prejudice will be caused before the Court gives its final decision.[122] The imminent execution of an individual who is on death row,[123] the extermination of a minority group,[124] and nuclear tests[125] have been held to constitute irreparable harm. On the other hand, the Court is not likely to grant provisional measures

---

118 *Jadhav (India v Pakistan)*, Provisional Measures, [2017] ICJ Rep 231 at para 15 [*Jadhav 2017*].

119 *Alleged Violations of the 1955 Treaty of Amity, Economic Relations, and Consular Rights (Islamic Republic of Iran v United States of America)*, Provisional Measures, [2018] ICJ Rep 623 at para 24; *Jadhav 2017*, above note 118 at para 15.

120 See *Legality of Use of Force*, above note 92.

121 *Application of the International Convention on the Elimination of All Forms of Racial Discrimination (Qatar v United Arab Emirates)*, Provisional Measures, [2018] ICJ Rep 406 at para 43; *Jadhav 2017*, above note 118 at para 35.

122 *Application of the Convention on the Prevention and Punishment of the Crime of Genocide (The Gambia v Myanmar)*, Provisional Measures, [2020] ICJ Rep 1 at para 65 [*The Gambia v Myanmar*].

123 *Jadhav 2017*, above note 199 at para 51.

124 *The Gambia v Myanmar*, above note 122 at para 73.

125 *Nuclear Tests (Australia v France)*, Provisional Measures, [1973] ICJ Rep 99 at para 26.

if the measures seek to prevent exclusively monetary damages that can be compensated at the end of the proceedings. For instance, the Court refused to order interim measures staying a seismic exploration of a disputed continental shelf because any harm resulting from such exploration could be compensated by appropriate means.[126] The condition of urgency is met when the acts susceptible of causing irreparable prejudice can occur at any moment before the Court makes a final decision on the case.[127]

For a long time, there was uncertainty about whether the provisional measures indicated by the Court were binding and enforceable. The text of Article 41 of the ICJ Statute strongly implies that provisional measures are merely recommendations or suggestions. In the *LaGrand* case, which concerned the execution of a German citizen in the United States, the Court ruled that provisional measures were binding and enforceable. In fact, it is worth recalling that "pending the final decision, notice of the measures suggested [by the Court] shall forthwith be given to the parties and to the Security Council."[128] It is reasonable to assume that the Court has an obligation to notify the Security Council of provisional measures so that they can be enforced. Thus far, no provisional measures have been enforced.

F. ADVISORY JURISDICTION

In addition to its contentious jurisdiction, the ICJ also has an advisory jurisdiction. The authority to give advisory opinions did not appear with the creation of the ICJ. Before the creation of the ICJ, the Permanent Court of International Justice was already vested with the power to give advisory opinions upon any dispute or question referred to it by the Council or the Assembly.[129]

---

126 *Aegean Sea Continental Shelf (Greece v Turkey)*, Provisional Measures, [1976] ICJ Rep 3.

127 *The Gambia v Myanmar*, above note 122 at para 65.

128 Statute of the International Court of Justice, above note 11, art 41.2.

129 Article 14 of the Covenant of the League of Nations reads as follows: "The Council shall formulate and submit to the Members of the League for adoption plans for the establishment of a Permanent Court of International Justice. The Court shall be competent to hear and determine any dispute of an international

The advisory jurisdiction of the ICJ exists because the UN and its various specialized agencies cannot become parties to a contentious case before the Court. Consequently, the *UN Charter* provides for a special procedure known as "'advisory opinion" for some of the UN organs and specialized agencies. As the International Court of Justice itself explained, in some situations, political considerations are so prominent that it may be necessary for an international organization to obtain an advisory opinion from the Court as to the legal principles applicable to the matter under debate, especially when these principles relate to the interpretation of the organization's constitution.[130]

1) *Ratione Personae* or Personal Jurisdiction in Advisory Cases

While the Statute of PCIJ enabled only the League Council and Assembly to request advisory opinions, the *UN Charter* grants the power to request advisory opinions to the General Assembly, the Security Council, and, with the authorization of the General Assembly, to other UN organs, specialized agencies,[131] and the International Atomic Energy Agency.[132] In 1946, the General Assembly authorized

---

character which the parties thereto submit to it. The Court may also give an advisory opinion upon any dispute or question referred to it by the Council or by the Assembly."

130 *Interpretation of the Agreement of 25 March 1951 between the WHO and Egypt*, Advisory Opinion, [1980] ICJ Rep 73 at para 33.

131 These specialized agencies are: International Labour Organization (ILO); Food and Agriculture Organization of the United Nations (FAO); United Nations Educational, Scientific and Cultural Organization (UNESCO); International Bank for Reconstruction and Development (IBRD); International Finance Corporation (IFC); International Development Association (IDA); International Monetary Fund (IMF); International Civil Aviation Organization (ICAO); International Telecommunication Union (ITU); International Fund for Agricultural Development (IFAD).

132 *Statute of the International Atomic Energy Agency*, 26 December 1956, 276 UNTS 3, art XVII (entered into force 29 July 1957) provides as follows:

> A. Any question or dispute concerning the interpretation or application of this Statute which is not settled by negotiation shall be referred to the International Court of Justice in conformity with the Statute of the Court, unless the parties concerned agree on another mode of settlement.

ECOSOC to request advisory opinions of the ICJ on legal questions arising within the scope of its activities.[133] The possibility to seek an advisory opinion from the ICJ is not available to states, UN agencies, and entities not authorized by the General Assembly, or to international organizations unrelated to the UN. Nevertheless, states can participate in advisory proceedings by presenting written and oral arguments related to the question posed to the tribunal. The relevant provision of the *UN Charter* is Article 96, which provides as follows:

> a. The General Assembly or the Security Council may request the International Court of Justice to give an advisory opinion on any legal question.
>
> b. Other organs of the United Nations and specialized agencies, which may at any time be so authorized by the General Assembly, may also request advisory opinions of the Court on legal questions arising within the scope of their activities.

The ICJ has issued twenty-seven advisory opinions. The General Assembly is by far the most frequent user of this procedure, having requested an advisory opinion of the Court sixteen times. The legal questions asked by the General Assembly are diverse, ranging from interpretation of international treaties to independence and sovereignty of states. They include such legal questions as the legal consequences of the construction of a wall in the occupied Palestinian territory, accordance with international law of the unilateral declaration of independence in respect of Kosovo, and the legality of the threat or use of nuclear weapons.

The Security Council, on the other hand, has scarcely made use of the Court's advisory jurisdiction. The only time the Council sought an

---

> B. The General Conference and the Board of Governors are separately empowered, subject to authorization from the General Assembly of the United Nations, to request the International Court of Justice to give an advisory opinion on any legal question arising within the scope of the Agency's activities.

133 *Authorization of the Economic and Social Council to request Advisory Opinions of the International Court of Justice*, GA Res 89(I), UNGAOR, 1st Sess, UN Doc A/RES/89(I) (1946).

advisory opinion was in 1970 in relation to the occupation of Namibia by South Africa.[134] In its resolution referring the legal question to the ICJ, the Council explained that "an advisory opinion from the International Court of Justice would be useful for the Security Council in its further consideration of the question of Namibia."[135] It is, however, unclear why the Security Council thought that this was the only case in which the Court's opinion could be useful.

The Economic and Social Council obtained two advisory opinions, both of which dealt with privileges and immunities of Special Rapporteurs on Human Rights.[136] The Court issued five opinions at the request of specialized agencies.[137] Three requests for an advisory opinion were made by the Committee on Applications for Review of Administrative Tribunal Judgments.[138] This committee was set up by the General Assembly in 1955 after the International Court of Justice had issued its advisory opinion, in which it held that the General Assembly had an obligation to disburse additional funds to the Secretary-General so that he could indemnify staff members to whom

134 *Legal Consequences for States of the Continued Presence of South Africa in Namibia (South West Africa) notwithstanding Security Council Resolution 276 (1970)*, Advisory Opinion, [1971] ICJ Rep 16.

135 SC Res 284 (1970), UNSCOR, 25th Year, UN Doc S/RES/284 (1970).

136 *Applicability of Article VI, Section 22, of the Convention on the Privileges and Immunities of the United Nations*, Advisory Opinion, [1989] ICJ Rep 177; *Difference Relating to Immunity from Legal Process of a Special Rapporteur of the Commission on Human Rights*, Advisory Opinion, [1999] ICJ Rep 62.

137 *Judgments of the Administrative Tribunal of the ILO upon complaints made against the UNESCO*, Advisory Opinion, [1956] ICJ Rep 77; *Interpretation of the Agreement of 25 March 1951 between the WHO and Egypt*, Advisory Opinion, [1980] ICJ Rep 73; *Legality of the Use by a State of Nuclear Weapons in Armed Conflict*, Advisory Opinion, [1996] ICJ Rep 66; *Judgment No 2867 of the Administrative Tribunal of the International Labour Organization upon a Complaint Filed against the International Fund for Agricultural Development*, Advisory Opinion, [2012] ICJ Rep 10; *Constitution of the Maritime Safety Committee of the Inter-Governmental Maritime Consultative Organization*, Advisory Opinion, [1960] ICJ Rep 150.

138 *Application for Review of Judgment No 333 of the United Nations Administrative Tribunal*, Advisory Opinion, [1987] ICJ Rep 18; *Application for Review of Judgment No 273 of the United Nations Administrative Tribunal*, Advisory Opinion, [1982] ICJ Rep 325; *Application for Review of Judgment No 158 of the United Nations Administrative Tribunal*, Advisory Opinion, [1973] ICJ Rep 166.

the United Nations Administrative Tribunal had awarded a monetary compensation.[139] The General Assembly did not like being faced with a fait accompli and wanted to establish a procedure for reviewing the judgments of the Administrative Tribunal.[140] Through an amendment to the Statute of the UN Administrative Tribunal,[141] the General Assembly established a committee whose sole responsibility was to examine applications from a member state, the Secretary-General, or a concerned staff member, and determine whether it should request an advisory opinion from the International Court of Justice on the lawfulness of a judgment rendered by the UN Administrative Tribunal.[142] The committee referred cases to the International Court of Justice only three times. Such referrals to the World Court are no longer possible because neither the UN Administrative Tribunal nor the Committee on Applications for Review of Administrative Tribunal Judgments still exists. Specifically, in 2007, the General Assembly decided to revamp the internal justice system of the UN and to create a new dispute settlement mechanism comprising a first instance tribunal (UN Dispute Tribunal) and an appellate instance tribunal (UN Appeals Tribunal). As a consequence, the UN Administrative

139 *Effect of awards of compensation made by the UN Administrative Tribunal*, Advisory Opinion, [1954] ICJ Rep 47 [*Effect of awards*].

140 *Awards of compensation made by the United Nations Administrative Tribunal: advisory opinion of the International Court of Justice*, GA Res 888 (IX), UNGAOR, 9th Sess, UN Doc A/RES/888(IX) (1954) 43.

141 *Procedure of Review for the United Nations Administrative Tribunal Judgments: Amendments to the Statute of the Administrative Tribunal*, GA Res 957 (X), UNGAOR, 10th Sess, UN Doc A/RES/957/X (1955) 30.

142 Article 11, paragraphs 1, 2, and 4 of the amended Statute of the UN Administrative Tribunal specified that the Committee was authorized to request advisory opinions from the ICJ. The ICJ would be asked to determine whether the Administrative Tribunal exceeded or failed to exercise its jurisdiction, erred on a question of law relating to the provisions of the *UN Charter*, or committed a fundamental error of procedure that has occasioned a failure of justice. Only a member state, the Secretary-General, or the staff member in respect of whom a judgment had been rendered by the Administrative Tribunal could submit an application to the Committee.

Tribunal and the Committee on Applications for Review of Administrative Tribunal Judgments were dissolved.[143]

It is very unfortunate that the UN Secretary-General has not been empowered to request advisory opinions from the Court. Several Secretaries-General have expressed the view that if they had had the authority to request advisory opinions from the ICJ, they would have been much better equipped to carry out their political functions.[144] More specifically, the Secretaries-General argued that if they were authorized to request an advisory opinion, they would offer to the parties their good offices and propose to formulate together the legal questions that they would submit to the Court on behalf of the parties. The Secretaries-General were confident that the power to seek advisory opinions from the World Court would considerably enhance their ability to facilitate the resolution of conflicts through peaceful means.

Indeed, states are often reluctant to submit sensitive and political disputes to the International Court of Justice. Contentious proceedings are inevitably adversarial; in most cases, one of the parties always loses while the other often wins. In some cases, both parties lose even if one of them prevails on the merits of the case. This reality discourages states from submitting their disputes to the Court's contentious jurisdiction. In such cases, advisory proceedings generally seem to be more appropriate. First, they are less adversarial because the parties are not directly involved in the case and do not participate in the proceedings as opposing parties. They are mere observers. Second, an advisory opinion is not addressed to the parties; it is provided to the entity that requested it. Hence the advisory opinion is not binding on the parties.

Those who oppose the idea of extending the advisory jurisdiction of the ICJ to the Secretary-General argue that the General Assembly or the

---

143 *Administration of justice at the United Nations*, GA Res 61/261, UNGAOR, 61st Sess, UN Doc A/RES/61/261 (2007) 1; *Administration of justice at the United Nations*, GA Res 62/228, UNGAOR, 62nd Sess, UN Doc A/RES/62/228 (2008) 1; *Administration of justice at the United Nations*, GA Res 63/253, UNGAOR, 63rd Sess, UN Doc A/RES/63/253 (2009) 1.

144 *Report of the Secretary-General on the Work of the Organization*, UNGAOR, 46th Sess, UN Doc A/46/1 (1991) at 4; *An Agenda for Peace: Report of the Secretary-General*, UNGAOR, 47th Sess, UN Doc A/47/277 (1992) at para 38.

Security Council already have the power to request an advisory opinion. Thus, in their view, nothing prevents either the General Assembly or the Security Council from requesting an advisory opinion of the Court if it can assist the parties. This argument ignores the practical difficulties and hurdles that need to be overcome in both organs before they can agree to refer a matter to the ICJ for an advisory opinion. First and foremost, not all disputes and conflicts are brought to the attention of the General Assembly or the Security Council. When they are brought to the attention of either organ, they are already at an advanced stage where the parties have become entrenched. Second, before the General Assembly or the Security Council can recommend the referral of a question to the ICJ, they must hold open or public debates on this issue, which may exacerbate the dispute. Third, the exact language of the legal question to be transmitted to the ICJ is decided by the required majority of either organ as opposed to the parties to the conflict. The parties to the dispute have little control over the text of the question to be asked. This indiscreet and cumbersome process is not likely to lead to a satisfactory resolution of the dispute. Moreover, the practice of the United Nations clearly shows that neither organ has been eager to exercise this power. Indeed, the number of advisory opinions sought from the ICJ represents a tiny fraction of international disputes that could have benefited from an advisory opinion.

2) *Ratione Materiae* or Subject Matter Jurisdiction in Advisory Cases

When a request for an advisory opinion is submitted to the Court by a specialized agency, the following three conditions must be satisfied in order to found the jurisdiction of the ICJ:

a) the specialized agency requesting the opinion must be duly authorized, under the Charter, to request opinions from the Court;
b) the opinion requested must be on a legal question; and
c) the question must be one arising within the scope of the activities of the requesting agency.[145]

---

145 *Application for Review of Judgment No 273 of the United Nations Administrative Tribunal*, Advisory Opinion, [1982] ICJ Rep 325 at para 21; *Legality of the Use by*

In 1996, the World Health Organization (WHO) requested the Court to provide an advisory opinion on whether the use of nuclear weapons by a state in war or other armed conflict is a breach of a state's obligations under international law. The Court refused to answer this question. It ruled that the mandate of WHO allows it to deal with health effects of nuclear weapons but not the legality of their use. In other words, the organization's functions were not sufficiently connected with the question.[146]

3) Legal Effect of Advisory Opinions

When the ICJ exercises its advisory jurisdiction, it does not render judgments—it issues advisory opinions. An advisory opinion is a judicial opinion that *normally* does not have the effect of adjudicating a specific case; it merely advises on the interpretation of the law. Essentially, an advisory opinion is an authoritative guidance on a question of public international law. It does not require compliance. The only exceptions are cases where an existing legal instrument (either an international treaty or a statute of an administrative tribunal) explicitly states that the advisory opinion of the ICJ shall have a binding effect. Contrary to judgments, the Court's advisory opinions are normally not binding. The UN organ or agency is in theory free to decide, as it sees fit, what effect to give to Court's advisory opinions. In practice, however, even though advisory opinions do not have binding force, they nevertheless carry great legal weight and moral authority. Advisory opinions may serve to prevent the escalation of a conflict.

In some cases, advisory opinions may have a binding force. For example, in case a dispute arises from the application of the *Convention on the Privileges and Immunities of the United Nations*[147] and the *Convention on the Privileges and Immunities of the Specialized Agencies*

---

a State of Nuclear Weapons in Armed Conflict, Advisory Opinion, [1996] ICJ Rep 66 at 71–72 [*Nuclear Weapons in Armed Conflict*].

146 *Nuclear Weapons in Armed Conflict, ibid.*

147 Section 30 of the *Convention on the Privileges and Immunities of the United Nations*, adopted by the General Assembly on 13 February 1946, 1 UNTS 15 provides that

of the United Nations,[148] the parties must seek from the International Court of Justice an advisory opinion and must accept the opinion of the Court as decisive. In the past, the International Court of Justice used to give binding advisory opinions to the UN and its specialized agencies in employment law disputes with their staff. For instance, the Statute of the International Labour Organization Administrative Tribunal (ILOAT) allowed some international organizations of the UN system to challenge a decision of the administrative tribunal before the International Court of Justice by requesting an advisory opinion.[149] This procedure was available to the international organization only; the staff member of the organization did not have a similar or equivalent right. Essentially, this was a right of appeal granted only

---

> All differences arising out of the interpretation or application of the present convention shall be referred to the International Court of Justice, unless in any case it is agreed by the parties to have recourse to another mode of settlement. If a difference arises between the United Nations on the one hand and a Member on the other hand, a request shall be made for an advisory opinion on any legal question involved in accordance with Article 96 of the Charter and Article 65 of the Statute of the Court. The opinion given by the Court shall be accepted as decisive by the parties.

148 Section 32 of the *Convention on the Privileges and Immunities of the Specialized Agencies,* approved by the General Assembly on 21 November 1947, 33 UNTS 261 states

> All differences arising out of the interpretation or application of the present Convention shall be referred to the International Court of Justice unless in any case it is agreed by the parties to have recourse to another mode of settlement. If a difference arises between one of the specialized agencies on the one hand, and a member on the other hand, a request shall be made for an advisory opinion on any legal question involved in accordance with Article 96 of the Charter and Article 65 of the Statute of the Court and the relevant provisions of the agreements concluded between the United Nations and the specialized agency concerned. The opinion given by the Court shall be accepted as decisive by the parties.

149 Statute of the International Labour Organization Administrative Tribunal, art XII, as amended by the International Labour Conference at its 105th Session in June 2016. Article XII of the Statute and article XII of its Annex—which enabled only the defendant organizations to challenge a decision of the ILO Administrative Tribunal before the International Court of Justice—was removed. The provisions had been criticized as being contrary to the principles of equality of access to justice and equality of arms (see *Judgment No 2867 of the*

to one of the parties to the dispute. In an advisory opinion issued in 2012, the ICJ criticized this mechanism as being contrary to the principles of equality of access to justice and equality of arms since the staff member had no procedural rights whatsoever.[150] Consequently, in June 2016, the Statute of the ILOAT was amended and the possibility to seek advisory opinions from the ICJ was removed from it.

4) The Consent of a Concerned State Is Not Required in Advisory Proceedings

Recall that the consent of states, parties to a dispute, is the basis of the Court's jurisdiction in contentious cases. This consent is not required in advisory proceedings even where the request for an opinion relates to a legal question actually pending between states.[151] The ICJ ruled in several cases that the Court's rulings in advisory proceedings are advisory in character and have no binding force. Advisory opinions are not given to the states, but to the organ that is entitled to request it. The ICJ's reply to the request is the participation of the Court, itself an organ of the UN, in the activities of the organization. Therefore, no state "can prevent the giving of an Advisory Opinion which the United Nations considers to be desirable in order to obtain enlightenment as to the course of action it should take."[152] The lack of consent to the Court's contentious jurisdiction by interested states has no bearing on the Court's jurisdiction to give an advisory opinion.[153]

Administrative Tribunal of the International Labour Organization upon a Complaint Filed against the International Fund for Agricultural Development, Advisory Opinion, [2012] ICJ Rep 10).

150 *Judgment No 2867 of the Administrative Tribunal*, *ibid.*

151 *Western Sahara*, Advisory Opinion, [1975] ICJ Rep 12 at para 32 [*Western Sahara*].

152 *Interpretation of Peace Treaties with Bulgaria, Hungary, and Romania*, First Phase, Advisory Opinion, [1950] ICJ Rep 65 at 71 [*Interpretation of Peace Treaties*].

153 *Construction of a Wall in the Occupied Palestinian Territory*, above note 45 at para 47.

This, however, does not mean that the Court is always obliged to give an advisory opinion as soon as a request is submitted to it.[154] The jurisprudence of the ICJ leaves no doubt that Article 65, paragraph 1, of the ICJ Statute, which establishes the power of the Court to give an advisory opinion, is permissive and of a discretionary character.[155] In exercising this discretion, the Court must always be guided by the principle that, as a judicial body, it is bound to remain faithful to the requirements of its judicial character even in giving advisory opinions.[156] The Court has consistently stressed that since its answer to a request for an advisory opinion represents its participation in the activities of the organization, it should normally not refuse to give advisory opinions.[157] By lending its assistance in the solution of a problem confronting the UN, the Court discharges its functions as the principal judicial organ of the organization. Only compelling reasons may justify a refusal.[158] The Court did not elaborate on the circumstances that could be regarded as compelling reasons. Although many states have often raised a variety of creative arguments to persuade the ICJ not to exercise its jurisdiction, the Court has never refused to satisfy a request for advisory opinions. However, it did give one example:

> An instance of this would be when the circumstances disclose that to give a reply would have the effect of circumventing the principle that a State is not obliged to allow its disputes to be submitted to judicial settlement without its consent. If such a situation should arise, the powers of the Court under the discretion given to it by Article 65, paragraph 1, of the Statute, would afford sufficient legal

154 *Legal consequences of the separation of the Chagos Archipelago from Mauritius in 1965*, Advisory Opinion, [2019] ICJ Rep 97 at para 63 [*Chagos Archipelago*].

155 *Interpretation of Peace Treaties*, above note 152 at 72.

156 *Western Sahara*, above note 151 at para 23.

157 *Interpretation of Peace Treaties*, above note 152 at 71.

158 *Accordance with International Law of the Unilateral Declaration of Independence in Respect of Kosovo*, Advisory Opinion, [2010] ICJ Rep 404 at para 30. See also *Judgments of the Administrative Tribunal of the ILO upon Complaints Made against UNESCO*, [1956] ICJ Rep 86.

> means to ensure respect for the fundamental principle of consent to jurisdiction.[159]

Curiously, the scenario described above by the Court arose in the advisory opinion relating to the Chagos Archipelago dispute between Mauritius and the United Kingdom. Although the request for an advisory opinion received from the General Assembly was undoubtedly addressing a bilateral dispute that Mauritius was unable to resolve through the contentious jurisdiction of the Court, the ICJ ruled that there were no compelling reasons to decline jurisdiction. The Court went as far as to rule in a legal opinion that "the United Kingdom's continued administration of the Chagos Archipelago constitutes a wrongful act entailing the international responsibility of that State."[160]

G. SOURCES OF LAW APPLIED BY THE COURT

In national legal systems, it is generally clear whether a certain legal norm is the applicable law. Legal norms and rules are normally created by the legislative branch of the government, interpreted and applied by its judiciary branch, that is to say domestic courts and tribunals, and enforced by its executive branch, which includes the law enforcement apparatus such as the police force. In comparison, the international legal order is anarchical not because it is disorderly, but because it lacks a centralized and structured law-making and law-enforcing authority.[161] More specifically, there is no world parliament and there is no global enforcement agency. The existence of a legal norm or rule is not a simple matter in international law. International courts cannot determine that a specific expected conduct or norm is the law, because that is a legislative function, which courts normally do not possess. Consequently, when countries set up international courts, they specify where the courts can find the applicable law. In

159 *Western Sahara*, above note 151 at para 33.

160 *Chagos Archipelago*, above note 154 at para 177.

161 Mario Prost, "Hierarchy and the Sources of International Law: A Critique" (2017) 39:2 *Hous J Int'l L* 285 at 286.

the case of the ICJ, it is Article 38 of its Statute that specifies the sources of legal norms and obligations that the Court must apply in adjudicating disputes. This provision reads as follows:

> 1. The Court, whose function is to decide in accordance with international law such disputes as are submitted to it, shall apply:
> (a) international conventions, whether general or particular, establishing rules expressly recognized by the contesting states;
> (b) international custom, as evidence of a general practice accepted as law;
> (c) the general principles of law recognized by civilized nations;
> (d) subject to the provisions of Article 59, judicial decisions and the teachings of the most highly qualified publicists of the various nations, as subsidiary means for the determination of rules of law.
>
> 2. This provision shall not prejudice the power of the Court to decide a case *ex aequo et bono*, if the parties agree thereto.

Except for the opening sentence, this text is almost identical to Article 38 of the Statute of PCIJ. At the request of the Chilean delegation,[162] the phrase "to decide in accordance with international law such disputes as are submitted to it" was added to Article 38 of the ICJ Statute. This phrase appears to suggest that by applying the sources enumerated in paragraphs (a) to (d), the ICJ applies international law. Put differently, international law consists of (a) international conventions, (b) international custom, (c) general principles of law, and (d) judicial decisions and the teachings of the most highly qualified publicists.

Article 38 draws a clear distinction between international conventions, customary law, and general principles of law on the one hand and judicial decisions and teachings on the other. The first three paragraphs refer to primary sources, whereas paragraph (d) describes judicial decisions and teachings as subsidiary. This distinction is based on the fact that obligations for states may derive from treaty law,

162 *United Nations Conference on International Organizations*, Commission IV, Committee 1, Chile proposal of 12 May 1945, Vol 13 at 493.

customary law, and general principles of law; however, they can only be clarified or interpreted by judges and highly qualified lawyers and scholars. Consequently, judges and publicists do not create or make law; they merely explain what the law is.

Also, some international law experts believe that Article 38 of the ICJ Statute provides an exhaustive list of sources of international law and that the Court cannot rely on any other source.[163] Others argue that this is an indicative list only.[164] In support of this view, one may rely on judgments or advisory opinions in which the Court invoked unilateral declarations of a state,[165] consistent conduct of a state,[166] or resolutions of the Security Council or those of the General Assembly.[167] This controversy is beyond the scope of this book. Therefore, we will limit our analysis only to those sources that are expressly mentioned in Article 38 of the ICJ Statute.

Another question that has generated a lot of scholarly debate is whether Article 38 enumerates the sources in a predetermined order of importance or preponderance. More specifically, do international conventions prevail over international custom and does the international custom prevail over general principles of law? During the drafting of Article 38 of the Statute, the establishment of a hierarchy among these sources was proposed but expressly rejected.[168] The sources of international law have an equal status and the order in which they are listed is irrelevant.

---

163 See Hugh Thirlway, *The Sources of International Law* (Oxford, UK: Oxford University Press, 2019) [Thirlway, *Sources*].

164 Mohamed Shahabuddeen, *Precedent in the World Court* (Cambridge, UK: Cambridge University Press, 2007) at 81.

165 *Nuclear Tests Case (Australia v France)*, Merits, [1974] ICJ Rep 253 at para 46.

166 *Case concerning the Temple of Preah Vihear (Cambodia v Thailand)*, Merits, [1962] ICJ Rep 39.

167 *Competence of Assembly regarding admission to the United Nations*, Advisory Opinion, [1950] ICJ Rep 4.

168 Mario Prost, "Hierarchy and the Sources of International Law: A Critique" (2017) 39:2 *Hous J Int'l L* 285 at 290.

1) International Conventions

International conventions refer to legal instruments that demonstrate the existence of an agreement between two or more parties. They have played a fundamental role in the history of international relations and have always been one of the most evident ways in which legal rules binding on two or more states come into existence.[169] As the PCIJ pointed out "[f]rom the standpoint of the obligatory character of international engagements, it is well known that such [international] engagements may be taken in the form of treaties, conventions, declarations, agreements, protocols, or exchanges of notes."[170] International agreements may be given a diversity of names; the exact terminology used is relevant but not a decisive factor when determining whether a legal instrument is an international convention or agreement.[171] A legal instrument does not need to comply with any particular formal requirement to become an international agreement or treaty. For instance, the ICJ ruled that minutes for a meeting confirming the acceptance by one state of another state's proposal may constitute proof of an international agreement within the meaning of Article 38.1(a) of the ICJ Statute.[172] Similarly, a joint communiqué issued to the press in which two states confirm their common position or transaction may also constitute evidence of an international agreement.[173]

The law of treaties evolved during several centuries. Many of its fundamental principles became recognized as rules of international customary law. In 1949, the International Law Commission selected

169 Thirlway, *Sources*, above note 163 at 37.

170 *Customs Régime between Germany and Austria* (1931), Advisory Opinion, PCIJ (Ser A/B) No 41 at 47. Philip Gautier, "Article 2: Use of Terms" in Olivier Corten & Pierre Klein, eds, *The Vienna Conventions on the Law of Treaties: A Commentary*, Vol 1 (Oxford, UK: Oxford University Press, 2011) at 35.

171 *South West Africa (Ethiopia v South Africa; Liberia v South Africa)*, Preliminary Objections, [1962] ICJ Rep 319 at 331; *Maritime Delimitation and Territorial Questions between Qatar and Bahrain*, Jurisdiction and Admissibility, Judgment, [1994] ICJ Rep 112 at paras 23–24 [*Maritime Delimitation*].

172 *Maritime Delimitation*, *ibid* at para 23.

173 *Aegean Sea Continental Shelf (Greece v Turkey)*, Judgment, [1978] ICJ Rep 3 at paras 95–96.

the law of treaties as a topic for codification and appointed reputable international law experts to develop a document codifying customary rules that governed the law of treaties. In 1969—twenty years after the ILC had begun working on the codification of the law of treaties—the General Assembly adopted the *Vienna Convention on the Law of Treaties*.[174] This convention, which came into force on 27 January 1980, regulates the manner in which states conclude treaties, formulate reservations, express their consent, and observe, apply, and interpret international agreements. Essentially, the Vienna Convention is a treaty on treaties. The majority of the provisions found in it existed as international customary rules, while others clarified or crystalized imprecise or uncertain rules. The Vienna Convention has become an essential tool in applying and interpreting treaties. It defines the term "treaty" as "an international agreement concluded between States in written form and governed by international law, whether embodied in a single instrument or in two or more related instruments and whatever its particular designation."[175] This provision refers to agreements "in written form." This, however, does not mean that international conventions must always be in writing; it only means that the Vienna Convention of 1969 does not apply to or govern treaties that are not in written form. In fact, the Vienna Convention itself specifies that "the fact that [the Vienna] Convention does not apply to ... international agreements not in written form, shall not affect the legal force of such agreements."[176] The only restriction the Vienna Convention imposes on the freedom of states to conclude international agreements is not to conflict with a peremptory norm of general international law, which is defined as "a norm accepted and recognized by the international community of States as a whole as a norm from which no derogation is permitted and which can be modified only by subsequent norm of general international law having the same character."[177]

174 23 May 1969, 1155 UNTS 331 at art 53 (entered into force 27 January 1980).
175 *Ibid*, art 2.
176 *Ibid*, art 3.
177 *Ibid*, art 53.

Some treaties create international legal norms and are intended to have a general application.[178] The *UN Charter*, the *Vienna Convention on the Law of Treaties*, the *Geneva Convention relating to the Status of Refugees*, the *Convention on registration of objects launched into outer space*,[179] and the *Convention on the Elimination of All Forms of Discrimination against Women*[180] are examples of such "law-making" treaties. This type of treaty is concluded by a large number of states and fulfill a quasi-legislative function. In that sense, they constitute a source of international legal norms. Although these treaties are the most known types of international agreements, they are not the most prevalent type of legal instruments. A much larger number of treaties are bilateral or multilateral agreements that do not generate any international legal norms. Like contracts between two or more individuals, these treaties and conventions merely create very specific rights and obligations for a small number of states. For example, states often sign bilateral conventions for the avoidance of double taxation and the prevention of fiscal evasion with respect to taxes on income and capital gains. Such agreements create legal obligations only for the states that are parties to them. They are not opposable to any third party. Therefore, characterizing such international treaties as a source of international law is confusing. They should be referred to as sources of rights and obligations of the parties to a dispute.

2) International Custom

Customary international law refers to a set of rules that emerge from a constant and uniform practice of states, and in some cases of international organizations, that are regarded as binding on states and international organizations. Customary rules used to be the main source of public international law. Treaties played only a limited role

---

178 Malcolm N Shaw, *International Law*, 6th ed (New York: Cambridge University Press, 2008) at 94.

179 *Convention on registration of objects launched into outer space*, 12 November 1974, 1023 UNTS 15 (entered into force 15 September 1976).

180 *Convention on the Elimination of All Forms of Discrimination against Women*, 18 December 1979, 1249 UNTS 13 (entered into force 3 September 1981).

in public international law. This began to change at the beginning of the twentieth century when a large number of sovereign states became parties to important law-making treaties of general application, which either codified customary law or progressively developed it. As the number of such treaties increased, the relevance of customary law decreased. Nevertheless, customary international law still plays an important role in international law. First, the vast majority of treaties have not been adhered to by all sovereign states. Customary law may extend the application of treaty-based rules to states that are not parties to these treaties. Second, some areas or fields of international law have not yet been codified through treaties. For example, the law of jurisdictional immunities of a state is still primarily customary.[181] Finally, like any legislative act or contract, treaties may have gaps. Customary law can be useful in complementing or interpreting treaties. For instance, although the *UN Charter* requires the affirmative vote of all five permanent members of the Security Council for a substantive resolution to be adopted, it does not specify the effect of a permanent member's absence or abstention during a vote. A customary rule emerged as a result of a practice that the absence or abstention of a permanent member of the Security Council during a vote does not count as a veto and does not prevent the adoption of a resolution.

To determine the existence and scope of a rule of customary international law the following two elements must exist. First, there must be a general or settled practice (material or objective element). Second, this general or settled practice must be regarded as binding (subjective element). Each of these two constituent elements must be ascertained separately based on the evidence available to the Court.

The material element is a settled practice by states[182] or, in some cases, by international organizations.[183] Practice may include actions, such as diplomatic acts, correspondence, voting patterns in the General Assembly or the Security Council, or official statements. Inaction

181 *Jurisdictional Immunities of the State (Germany v Italy: Greece intervening)*, [2012] ICJ Rep 99 at para 54 [*Jurisdictional Immunities*].

182 *Ibid* at para 55.

183 *Identification of customary international law*, GA Res 73/203, UNGAOR, 73rd Sess, UN Doc A/Res/73/203 (2018) 1 [*Identification of customary international law*].

or failure to act may also be regarded as practice and lead to a formation of a customary rule. State practice can be observed in the exercise of its executive, legislative, judicial, or other functions.[184] While actions or conduct of other actors, such as individuals, corporations, or NGOs, cannot lead to the formation or expression of rules of customary international law, they may be relevant in assessing whether certain practices by states and international organizations actually exist.[185]

Not every form of practice can give rise to a formation of customary rules. The practice must be general, which means sufficiently widespread and representative, as well as settled, which means consistent or constant.[186] How many states does it take for practice to be sufficiently widespread and representative? Unfortunately, there is no rule of thumb. This factor depends on the overall context, the nature of the rule, and the particular circumstances in which the evidence in question is to be found. An isolated act by a single state or consistent acts by a minority of states would not constitute evidence of state practice.[187] Nevertheless, "long continued practice between two States accepted by them as regulating their relations [may] form the basis of mutual rights and obligations between the two States."[188] Also, occasional inconsistencies or violations of a customary rule do not negate the existence of a general and settled practice:

> It is not to be expected that in the practice of States the application of the rules in question should have been perfect, in the sense that States should have refrained, with complete consistency, from the use of force or from intervention in each other's internal affairs. The Court does not consider that, for a rule to be established as customary, the corresponding practice must be in absolutely rigorous conformity with the rule. In order to deduce the existence of customary rules, the Court deems it sufficient that the conduct of States should,

---

184 *Jurisdictional Immunities*, above note 181 at para 56.
185 *Identification of customary international law*, above note 183.
186 *Case concerning Right of Passage over Indian Territory*, Merits, [1960] ICJ Rep 6 at 40 [*Right of Passage over Indian Territory*].
187 Thirlway, *Sources*, above note 163 at 73.
188 *Right of Passage over Indian Territory*, above note 186 at 39.

> in general, be consistent with such rules, and that instances of State conduct inconsistent with a given rule should generally have been treated as breaches of that rule, not as indications of the recognition of a new rule. If a State acts in a way prima facie incompatible with a recognized rule, but defends its conduct by appealing to exceptions or justifications contained within the rule itself, then whether or not the State's conduct is in fact justifiable on that basis, the significance of that attitude is to confirm rather than to weaken the rule.[189]

Although no particular duration is required for a practice to exist, the passage of time is a significant factor in establishing the existence of a consistent practice. The longer the length of time during which a certain state practice can be observed, the easier it is to prove the existence of a rule of customary law. Conversely, the shorter the length of time during which the alleged state practice can be observed, the harder it is to prove the existence of a customary rule.

The second component of a customary rule is a subjective element known as *opinion juris sive necessitatis,* which can be translated from Latin as "an opinion of the law or of necessity." It requires that the general practice be accepted as law that the practice be followed with a sense of legal right or obligation.[190] *Opinio juris* is some sort of a conviction that a certain practice is binding as opposed to being followed as a matter of convenience. To prove the existence of such a conviction, one may rely on a state's public statements, official records, diplomatic correspondence, decisions of national courts, and other sources of information. A state's failure to react over time to a forming practice may serve as evidence of acceptance of that practice as law.

A state may consistently object to a rule of customary international law while that rule is in the process of formation. In such a case, the customary rule will be unopposable to the objecting state for as long as it maintains its objection. This is known as the "persistent objector" rule, which requires that the objection be clearly expressed,

---

189 *Case concerning Military and Paramilitary Activities in and against Nicaragua (Nicaragua v United States of America)*, Merits, [1986] ICJ Rep 14 at para 186.

190 *North Sea Continental Shelf (Federal Republic of Germany/Denmark; Federal Republic of Germany/Netherlands)*, [1969] ICJ Rep 3 at para 74.

made known to other states, and maintained assiduously.[191] Nonetheless, no state may object to the formation of a customary rule of peremptory character known as *jus cogens* rules. For instance, no persistent objector may oppose a customary rule that prohibits slavery or genocide. Rules of this nature are opposable to all states at all times.

3) General Principles of Law

The meaning to be ascribed to the concept of "general principles of law" as a source of international law was one of the most debated issues within the Advisory Committee of Jurists entrusted with the drafting of the Statute of the old Permanent Court of International Justice (PCIJ) in 1920.[192] The drafters of Article 38 of the Statute did not want to restrict the Permanent Court of International Justice to two sources of international legal norms. They were concerned that in cases where treaties and customary rules were silent on a specific point or subject, the Court would be unable to adjudicate a dispute since there would be no law governing the point in issue.[193] It was also thought that it would be inappropriate for the Court to legislate since the tribunal's role is to discover what the law is rather than to create legal norms and rules. Therefore, they added in Article 38.1(c) of the ICJ Statute a third source of international law, which is "the general principles of law recognized by civilized nations." Before we examine the meaning of the term "general principle," it is important to mention that the phrase "civilized nations" is now outdated, as most nations are considered civilized. This unfortunate and politically incorrect expression has long served to distinguish European states from states that did not possess similar legal systems and had values that were described as "uncivilized," "rude," or that were "enslaved" nations.[194]

---

191 *Identification of customary international law*, above note 183.

192 *Pulp Mills on the River Uruguay (Argentina v Uruguay)*, Separate Opinion of Judge Cançado Trindade [2010] ICJ Rep 137 at para 8 [*Pulp Mills*].

193 Thirlway, *Sources*, above note 163 at 106.

194 James Sloan, "Civilized Nations" in R Wolfrum, ed, *The Max Planck Encyclopedia of Public International Law* (Oxford, UK: Oxford University Press, 2012) 211.

There are disagreements over the meaning of the term "general principles of law." Some writers argue that they refer to principles of natural law, which is a system of justice based on morality and ethics that derives from nature and which all humans share irrespective of their legal and political systems. Others regard them as broad legal principles that can be found in all major legal systems, including the Anglo-American, French, and Germanic systems, which means principles of comparative law or analogies to private law. In the *Corfu Channel* case, the ICJ gave credence to the latter interpretation by ruling that direct proof of facts giving rise to responsibility is not always possible and not necessary; therefore, "indirect evidence is admitted in all systems of law and its use is recognised by international decisions."[195]

An example of a general principle of international law is the idea that a party must honour its contractual obligations because this basic rule exists in all legal systems. Similarly, the defense of necessity as a possible justification or exculpation for breaking the law is also a concept known to all legal systems. Other examples of general principles are listed in Article 2 of the *UN Charter* (see Chapter 2). The Permanent Court of International Justice and the International Court of Justice relied on general principles of law on a few occasions.[196] For instance, in the *Case concerning the Factory at Chorzòw*, the PCIJ concluded that "it is a principle of international law that the breach of an engagement involves an obligation to make reparation in an adequate form."[197] The ICJ held that "a judgment rendered by . . . a judicial body is res judicata and has binding force between the parties to the dispute."[198]

4) Subsidiary Sources

Unlike treaties, international customs, and general principles of law, judicial decisions and the teachings of the most highly qualified

195 *Corfu Channel Case (United Kingdom v Albania), Merits, Judgment*, [1949] ICJ Rep 4 at 18.

196 For a detailed analysis, see the separate opinion of Judge Cançado Trindade in *Pulp Mills*, above note 192.

197 *Case concerning the Factory at Chorzòw* (1927), PCIJ (Ser A) No 8 at 21.

198 *Effect of awards*, above note 139 at 53.

publicists are not autonomous sources of law. They are subsidiary means for determining the material contents of international rules. They cannot create new rules; they can only derive them from existing rules. Courts and tribunals are not legislative organs and their role is not to assert the law. They merely find the law. In practice, however, the act of finding and interpreting the law may often be extensive enough to resemble a legislative function. Judges provide very detailed reasons in support of their legal conclusions in order to convince the reader that they are not legislating but merely finding the law. Often, dissenting judges write just as much or even more to justify an opposite conclusion. Thus, the act of determining the contents of a legal norm to a certain extent amounts to creating law.

The ICJ frequently refers to its previous judgments and to the judgments of other courts and tribunals in reaching conclusions. This, however, does not mean that the doctrine of precedent or *stare decisis* that exists in the common law legal tradition applies also in international law. In fact, Article 59 of the ICJ Statute expressly states the opposite—that the decisions of the Court have no binding force except as between the parties and in respect of the case under consideration. The Court strives to follow its own jurisprudence not as much because it feels bound by it but more because it wants to ensure some consistency and foreseeability. Where a party requests the Court to overturn its jurisprudence, it must show "cause not to follow the reasoning and conclusions of earlier cases."[199]

Judicial decisions within the meaning of Article 38 of the ICJ Statute may emanate either from international or national courts and tribunals. The jurisprudence of the International Court of Justice has the highest authority.[200] However, the ICJ is not the only international court that generates jurisprudence. The International Criminal Court, the International Tribunal for the Law of the Sea, the *ad hoc* international criminal tribunals, arbitral tribunals, and the Appellate Body of the World Trade Organization have also issued judgments and awards relating to important international law concepts

199 *Maritime Boundary*, above note 172 at para 28.
200 Thirlway, *Sources*, above note 163 at 136.

and notions. In addition to international tribunals, the ICJ may also take into account the jurisprudence of regional and national courts. If the judgments emanating from domestic courts are invoked for the purposes of establishing the existence or inexistence of a treaty-based rule, international custom, or general principle of law, then it would be reasonable to rely on the jurisprudence of the highest national courts only. Such courts could include supreme courts, the House of Lords, or *Cour de cassation*. Relying on judgments emanating from low-level courts in order to establish the existence of an international legal norm would probably not be appropriate or reasonable. If, however, the domestic jurisprudence is invoked to establish the practice or the *opinion juris* of that state, then judgments of any judicial body of that state can be helpful.

The second subsidiary means for the determination of rules of law are the teachings of the most highly qualified publicists. This qualification is too subjective; consequently, it would be arbitrary to designate some authors as "most highly qualified" and others "unqualified" or "less qualified." Hence, it is not surprising that the ICJ rarely relies on doctrinal works in support of its legal conclusions.

Chapter 7

THE SECRETARIAT OF THE UNITED NATIONS

With the creation of the first permanent international institutions in the 1800s, such as the Danube and Rhine River commissions, there appeared the need to have permanent secretariats with staff. Initially, the main reason for establishing permanent secretariats was to ensure that member states received uninterrupted secretarial services, such as production of documents, recording of decisions, translation services, and other housekeeping tasks during their multilateral conferences.[1] Another motivation for setting permanent secretariats was to equip international organizations with some institutional memory in order to ensure consistency and foreseeability. The necessity to shield international organizations from the political influences of their member states was not a decisive consideration in establishing permanent secretariats. Despite the international nature of their work, staff of river commissions were appointed directly by their nations, took instructions from their governments, and owed a degree of allegiance to their countries of citizenship. International public servants enjoyed very limited immunities from the local jurisdiction of the host state.[2] Thus, the earliest forms of permanent secretariats had little in common with the modern-day secretariats of international organizations.

1 Leon Gordenker, *The UN Secretary-General and Secretariat*, 2d ed (New York: Routledge, 2010) at 4.

2 Maxwell Cohen, "The United States and the United Nations Secretariat: A Preliminary Appraisal" (1953) 1:3 *McGill LJ* 169 at 171.

Permanent secretariats underwent an important change with the establishment of the League of Nations. The first Secretary-General of the League, Sir Eric Drummond, was the architect of the League's Secretariat.[3] He tried to introduce a model similar to the Westminster system of public administration, in which public servants are entirely independent from the political apparatus. More specifically, the League's staff had to avoid any action that could lead to perceptions that its advice and work were affected by political factors. Public servants had a career path that did not depend on political patronage and was based exclusively on merit. Sir Drummond delineated deliberating bodies, namely the League's Assembly and Council, from the permanent secretariat, whose chief role was to implement policies adopted by the deliberating organs. For the first time, staff members of a secretariat of an international organization were required to take instructions from the Secretary-General and not from national governments. Since then, this clear division of roles and responsibilities between policy-shaping organs and the secretariat has become the main feature of the institutional structure of contemporary international organizations, including the United Nations.[4]

The UN perfected the League's model of international public service. The *UN Charter* recognizes the importance of the Secretariat by stating expressly that it is one of the main organs of the organization.[5] This recognition is significant because the Secretariat is not a mere clerical apparatus or subordinate body of the main organs, but an essential component of the organization. The Secretariat of the United Nations comprises a "Secretary-General and such staff as the Organization may require."[6] The Secretary-General is appointed by the General Assembly upon the recommendation of the Security Council.[7] The Secretary-General is the chief administrative officer

3 Gordenker, above note 1 at 5.

4 Egon F Ranshofen-Wertheimer, "The International Civil Service of the Future" (1946) 24 *Int'l Conciliation* 60 at 63.

5 *Charter of the United Nations*, 26 June 1945, Can TS 1945 No 7, art 7.1 [*Charter of the United Nations*].

6 *Ibid*, art 97.

7 *Ibid*.

of the organization[8] and acts in that capacity in all meetings of the General Assembly, the Security Council, and the Economic and Social Council.[9] The Secretary-General prepares an annual report to the General Assembly on the work of the organization[10] and brings to the attention of the Security Council any matter that may threaten the maintenance of international peace and security.[11] The Secretary-General is empowered to select and recruit members of personnel known as staff, appoints staff in accordance with the United Nations Staff Regulations established by the General Assembly,[12] and assigns appropriate staff to various organs of the United Nations.[13] On the basis of UN Staff Regulations endorsed by the General Assembly, the Secretary-General promulgates UN Staff Rules, which contain more detailed legal norms regulating the management of human resources in the UN Secretariat. While Staff Rules are more detailed than Staff Regulations, the two statutory documents must always remain consistent with one another. The paramount consideration in the employment of the staff and in the determination of the conditions of service must be the necessity of securing the highest standards of efficiency, competence, and integrity.[14] It is, however, not the sole consideration; "it is simply a consideration to which greater weight is normally to be given than to any other."[15] The importance of recruiting the staff on a wide geographical basis must also be a consideration when recruiting staff members.[16] In 2018, the UN Secretariat consisted of approximately 35,000 members of the staff,[17] based in over 210 locations called "duty stations."

8 *Ibid.*

9 *Ibid*, art 98.

10 *Ibid.*

11 *Ibid*, art 99.

12 *Ibid*, art 101.1.

13 *Ibid*, art 101.2.

14 *Ibid*, art 101.3.

15 *Application for Review of Judgment No 333 of the United Nations Administrative Tribunal*, Advisory Opinion, [1987] ICJ Rep 18 at para 81 [*Review of Judgment No 333*].

16 *Charter of the United Nations*, above note 5, art 101.3.

17 *Personnel Statistics as at 31 December 2018*, Chief Executive Board for Coordination, UN Doc CEB/2019/HLCM/HR/17 (2019).

The staff of the Secretariat are international civil servants who serve in their personal capacity. Consequently, in the performance of their duties, UN staff members are not permitted to seek or receive instructions from any government or from any other authority external to the organization.[18] They must refrain from any action that might negatively reflect on their position as international officials responsible only to the organization.[19] Each member state of the UN also has an obligation to respect the exclusively international character of the responsibilities of the Secretary-General and staff, and not to seek to influence them in the discharge of their responsibilities.[20]

A. THE HEADQUARTERS

The League of Nations had its headquarters in Geneva, Switzerland.[21] Naturally, member states wanted to establish the United Nations headquarters in the same city. However, the Swiss government was prepared to host the new organization only on one essential condition. "Switzerland would welcome the establishment of United Nations organs in Swiss territory; but it would demand that any decision by the Security Council involving the use of military forces be taken outside the proposed Geneva headquarters and beyond the Swiss borders."[22] Switzerland did not have this concern with respect to the League of Nations because, unlike the Security Council of the UN, the Council of the League had no power to authorize the use of force. The

18 *Charter of the United Nations*, above note 5, art 100.1.

19 *Ibid.*

20 *Ibid*, art 100.2.

21 The Hague and Brussels were also among the options considered for the seat of the League. However, The Hague was rejected because nations wanted a fresh start. They were disappointed by the broken promises of The Hague Peace Conference and, in particular, the Permanent Court of Arbitration's inability to prevent the First World War. President Wilson was opposed to the idea of establishing the League in Brussels. Geneva was a suitable location because the International Red Cross was already based there, because international treaties guaranteed Switzerland's neutrality, and because it was in the heart of Europe.

22 Trygve Lie, *In the Cause of Peace: Seven Years at the United Nations* (New York: Macmillan, 1954) at 59.

United Nations could not accept the condition and therefore began looking for alternative locations to establish the permanent seat of the UN. The organization's first temporary location was London, where member states had established the Preparatory Commission of the United Nations.[23] The British government hosted the United Nations during the first few weeks of 1946 while the organization was looking for a permanent seat.[24]

The decision of choosing a site for the future headquarters of the UN was a deeply politicized debate. The United States secretly hoped to host the organization but did not lobby for it for ethical considerations. Curiously, the Soviets favoured the establishment of the UN in the United States, arguing that the Old World had it once, and it was time for the New World to have it.[25] The French, however, strongly opposed the decision to locate the UN headquarters in the United States.[26] Following intense negotiations, member states agreed to base the headquarters of the organization in the United States. San Francisco, where the main conference took place, was not a viable option because travelling to the west coast of the United States from most parts of the world would have been too arduous for heads of states and delegates. New York seemed to be the most suitable location on the east coast of the United States because "its technical facilities were far superior to those of any other American city."[27] In March 1946, the small Secretariat of the newly established organization moved into its first temporary offices situated in Hunter College in the Bronx. When

---

23 The Preparatory Commission of the United Nations was established on 26 June 1945 by way of the Agreement on Interim Arrangements signed in San Francisco by the founding members of the United Nations. The purpose of this entity was to make provisional arrangements for the first sessions of the General Assembly, the Security Council, the Economic and Social Council, and the Trusteeship Council, as well as to establish the Secretariat and to convene the International Court of Justice. It ceased to exist on 2 February 1946 when the first Secretary-General of the United Nations, Trygve Lie, was appointed.

24 Stanley Meisler, *United Nations: A History* (New York: Grove Press, 1995) at 26.

25 *Ibid.*

26 Douglas G Anglin, "Lester Pearson and the Office of the Secretary-General" (1962) 17:2 *International Journal* 145.

27 Lie, above note 22 at 60.

the academic year began and students returned to school, the UN moved to a factory in Long Island. In December 1946, John D Rockefeller Jr purchased and donated to the UN the land in the Turtle Bay neighbourhood of Manhattan where the organization currently has its headquarters. The United States government advanced an interest-free loan of USD$65 million for the construction of the thirty-nine-storey skyscraper.[28] The construction was completed in 1952 and the UN Secretariat moved into its new headquarters.

B. FUNCTIONS OF THE SECRETARIAT

While the responsibility for agreeing on and devising international policies rests with the main organs that consist of member states — the General Assembly, the Security Council, and the Economic and Social Council — the execution of these policies devolves largely on the Secretariat.[29] The roles and responsibilities of UN staff members range from simple tasks of agenda-setting for the various deliberating UN organs to very complex responsibilities of managing peacekeeping operations. The Secretariat is the invisible hand that drives the decision-making process in the United Nations. It enables the deliberating organs of the UN to make policy decisions by collecting and providing information and knowledge. The functions of the Secretary-General and staff can be grouped under six categories or headings. These are political functions, representational functions, secretarial and executive functions, technical functions, financial functions, and functions relating to the organization and administration of the Secretariat.

1) Political Functions

The Secretary-General is the Secretariat's top diplomat. The unique nature of the "position lies not in the power to run an organization or

---

28 *Headquarters of the United Nations*, GA Res 182 (II), UNGAOR, 2nd Sess, UN Doc A/Res/182(II) (1947) 151 at para 3(b).

29 *Report of the Preparatory Commission of the United Nations*, PC/20 (1945), Chapter VIII, Section 2, at para 1 [*Report of the Preparatory Commission of the United Nations*].

to trump the interests of member states, but to transcend those interests."[30] The tools that the Secretary-General disposes are "reasonable persuasion and skill in negotiation, and the moral authority of [the] office—where it is recognized."[31] The powers given to the Secretary-General under the *UN Charter* go "beyond any power previously accorded to the head of an international organization,"[32] therefore the responsibility that the *UN Charter* confers upon the Secretary-General requires the exercise of the highest qualities of political judgment, tact, and integrity.[33] The Secretary-General may perform political functions by bringing to the attention of the Security Council any matter that may threaten the maintenance of international peace and security.[34] The Secretary-General is authorized to include items in the agenda of United Nations organs[35] and to make oral or written statements to these organs on any matter under consideration.[36] This authority enables the Secretary-General to intervene in the deliberations of any United Nations organ and to formulate and present proposals to it.

The Secretary-General and staff may also fulfill their political functions by attempting to resolve international conflicts or by de-escalating volatile situations. The range of political activities carried out by the Secretary-General and staff have included good offices, mediation,

---

30 Simon Chesterman & Thomas M Franck, "Resolving the Contradictions of the Office" in Simon Chesterman, ed, *Secretary or General?* (New York: Cambridge University Press, 2007) at 238.

31 Kurt Waldheim, *In the Eye of the Storm: The Memoirs of Kurt Waldheim* (London: George Weidenfeld & Nicolson Limited, 1985) at 4.

32 *Report of the Preparatory Commission of the United Nations*, above note 29 at para 16.

33 *Ibid.*

34 *Charter of the United Nations*, above note 5, art 99.

35 See Rules of Procedure of the General Assembly, UN Doc A/520/Rev.18, Rule 13(g) and 14 [Rules of Procedure of the General Assembly]; Provisional Rules of Procedure of the Security Council, UN Doc S/92/Rev.7, Rules 6 & 7 [Provisional Rules of Procedure of the Security Council].

36 See Rules of Procedure of the General Assembly, above note 35 at Rule 70; Provisional Rules of Procedure of the Security Council, above note 35 at Rule 22.

facilitation, dialogue processes, and even arbitration.[37] Specifically, Secretaries-General were directly involved in negotiating the release of US prisoners of war detained in China, facilitating negotiations of ceasefire deals in the Democratic Republic of the Congo, mediating the Cuban missile crisis, negotiating the release of US hostages in Iran, arbitrating a dispute between France and New Zealand, mediating the Falkland Islands dispute between Argentina and the United Kingdom, and providing good offices to the Syrian government and opposition groups.

Rainbow Warrior Affair

In 1986, the Secretary-General of the United Nations, Javier Pérez de Cuéllar, arbitrated a highly political dispute between France and New Zealand. In July 1985, the French military intended to conduct nuclear tests on the islands of French Polynesia. A Greenpeace vessel named "Rainbow Warrior" was planning to disrupt the tests. To prevent the Greenpeace vessel from sabotaging the nuclear tests, the French government sanctioned a covert operation with the view of sinking the ship. On 10 July 1985, officers of the French foreign intelligence services, called la Direction générale de la securité extérieure, detonated explosives and sank the Rainbow Warrior, killing a Dutch citizen. Following an investigation by the authorities of New Zealand, two French intelligence officers—Alain Mafard and Dominique Prieur—were apprehended. The remaining members of the French team had successfully fled New Zealand before the police had time to arrest them.

The two French officers pled guilty to charges of manslaughter and were convicted to ten years of imprisonment by the national courts of New Zealand. In September 1985, the French prime minister informed the authorities of New Zealand that the Rainbow Warrior was sunk at the

37 For a more detailed analysis, see Kjell Skjelsboek & Gunnar Fermann, "UN Secretary-General and Mediation of International Disputes" in Jacob Berkovitch, ed, *Resolving International Conflicts: The Theory and Practice of Mediation* (Boulder, CO: Lynne Rienner Publishers, 1995) 75; Roberto Lavalle, "The Inherent Powers of the UN Secretary-General in the Political Sphere: A Legal Analysis" (1990) 37 *Neth Int'l LR* 22.

instructions of the French government and that France was prepared to make reparations. In September 1986, the governments of France and New Zealand jointly requested the Secretary-General of the UN to arbitrate the dispute between them and agreed to abide by his ruling.

The Secretary-General ordered the prime minister of France to convey to the prime minister of New Zealand a formal and unqualified apology for the attack, contrary to international law, on the Rainbow Warrior by French service agents. He also decided that France had to pay a monetary compensation equivalent to seven million dollars. The Secretary-General also concluded that the government of New Zealand should transfer the two French officers to French military authorities so that they could be transferred to a French military facility on an isolated island for a period of three years. The French government had to ensure that the two officers did not leave the island for any reason, except with the mutual consent of the two governments. Mafard and Prieur were assigned to serve on Hao coral atoll in French Polynesia. Before the expiration of the three-year period and in violation of the Secretary-General's arbitral award, the government of France repatriated both officers. New Zealand submitted a new claim against France alleging a breach of treaty obligations. An arbitral tribunal found that France had failed to comply with its obligations but refused to order the return of the two officers to the Hao island or to award monetary damages.

Eleven years after the Rainbow Warrior bombing, France ended its nuclear tests in Polynesia, following further protests by Greenpeace and Pacific interests.

2) Representational Functions

Very early in its history, the UN was confronted with a situation in which it had to exercise its own legal rights against a state. The incident that triggered this situation was the assassination by Jewish radical fighters of the Swedish envoy, Count Folke Bernadotte, appointed by the Security Council to mediate the Arab–Israeli conflict. The Jewish Zionist group responsible for the act regarded the UN mediator as a British lackey and a supporter of Arabs. The Security Council condemned the attack and noted the failure of Israel's provisional government to report on the progress of the investigation into the assassination.[38] This case raised a number of novel questions for the UN. The fundamental question pertained to the UN's capacity to bring an international claim against a state. Specifically, in the event of an agent of the UN suffering injury in the performance of his duties attributable to a state, does the UN have the capacity to bring a claim against the government of the responsible state? In an advisory opinion sought by the General Assembly, the International Court of Justice answered this question in the affirmative. The Court concluded that the functions of the organization were of such a character that they could not be effectively discharged if they involved the concurrent action, on the international plane, of all member states of the UN. Therefore, the ICJ held that the UN had the capacity to bring international claims on its own, without which the organization would be unable to discharge its functions.[39] It is no longer disputed that the United Nations is an institution with a legal personality distinct from that of its member states[40] and that it may acquire and dispose of property, enter into legal agreements, and institute legal proceedings. This legal capacity and personality are exercised by the Secretary-General and staff on behalf of the UN.

The Secretary-General is also the chief spokesperson of the UN. The Office of the Spokesperson provides information to the public and to the media on the activities of the UN system through daily briefings, direct responses to media enquiries, press conferences, background briefings, and interviews. The Secretary-General informs the General Assembly, the Security Council, and the Economic and Social Council of the activities of the UN. The Secretary-General represents the UN in all forums where international organizations and UN entities

---

38 *The Palestine Question*, SC Res 57 and 59 (1948), UNSCOR, 3rd Year, UN Doc S/Res/57 (1948) and UNSCOR, 3rd Year, UN Doc S/Res/59 (1948) 26.

39 *Reparation for Injuries Suffered in the Service of the United Nations*, Advisory Opinion, [1949] ICJ Rep 174 at 180 and 184 [*Reparation for Injuries*].

40 *Convention on the Privileges and Immunities of the United Nations*, 13 February 1946, 1 UNTS 15, art I, s 1 (entered into force 17 September 1946) ("General Convention") [*Convention on the Privileges and Immunities of the United Nations*].

meet to agree on common approaches and strategies. The Secretary-General is also the official to whom member states address their communications with the United Nations.

3) Secretarial and Executive Functions

The Secretary-General and staff also perform secretarial and executive functions. They facilitate meetings of principal and subsidiary organs of the organization, facilitate communications between member states, coordinate activities of funds, programs, and specialized agencies, perform the role of a depository of international treaties, provide postal and telecommunications services, maintain documentary records and archives of meetings and communications, and prepare annual reports to other organs of the UN. Most secretarial and executive functions of the Secretary-General and staff are contained in the Rules of Procedure of the principal organs of the UN.

In relation to meetings of the General Assembly, some executive functions are performed by the Secretary-General personally, while other secretarial and administrative tasks are provided by the Secretariat's Department for General Assembly and Conference Management. The vast majority of housekeeping tasks are found in the Rules of Procedure of the General Assembly. For instance, the Secretary-General, or staff, notifies member states at least sixty days in advance of the opening of a regular session,[41] receives and communicates requests to convene special sessions,[42] draws up the provisional agenda for the regular session,[43] receives credentials of delegation representatives,[44] acts as the secretary in all meetings of the General Assembly,[45] and translates, prints, and distributes documents, reports, and resolutions of the General Assembly.[46]

41 Rules of Procedure of the General Assembly, above note 35 at Rule 5.
42 *Ibid* at Rule 9.
43 *Ibid* at Rule 12.
44 *Ibid* at Rule 27.
45 *Ibid* at Rule 45.
46 *Ibid* at Rule 47.

In relation to meetings of the Security Council, the Secretariat provides substantive and secretarial support through its Security Council Affairs Division, which is part of the Department of Political and Peacebuilding Affairs. Specifically, this division is responsible for supporting the daily work of the Council. It facilitates the holding of its meetings, manages the Security Council's program of work, and provides procedural advice. Staff members of the Security Council Affairs Division transmit on behalf of the Secretary-General communications concerning any matter for the consideration of the Security Council,[47] prepare the provisional agenda of the Security Council,[48] communicate the agenda to the members of the Security Council at least three days before the meeting,[49] transmit each week to the representatives on the Security Council a summary statement of matters of which the Security Council is seized and of the stage reached in their consideration, receive credentials of delegation representatives,[50] give to the representatives of the Security Council notice of meetings,[51] prepare documents required by the Security Council,[52] and other functions that facilitate meetings. This division also supports the Security Council's subsidiary bodies, such as various sanctions committees and the Counter-Terrorism Committee. Some important tasks can be performed by the Secretary-General only. For example, only the Secretary-General may propose that a meeting be held in a location other than the seat of the United Nations,[53] or bring to the attention of the Security Council any matter that threatens the maintenance of international peace and security.[54]

The Economic and Social Council is supported by the ECOSOC Affairs Branch, which is part of the Department for the General Assembly and Conference Management of the Secretariat. This branch

---

47 Provisional Rules of the Security Council, above note 35 at Rule 6.
48 *Ibid* at Rule 7.
49 *Ibid* at Rule 8.
50 *Ibid* at Rule 13.
51 *Ibid* at Rule 25.
52 *Ibid* at Rule 26.
53 *Ibid* at Rule 5.
54 *Charter of the United Nations*, above note 5, art 99.

provides conference management services to ECOSOC and two of the main committees of the General Assembly, which deal with economic and financial matters (Second and Third Committees). Under ECOSOC's Rules of Procedure, either the Secretary-General or staff are empowered to request an alteration of the date of the substantive session,[55] to draw up the provisional agenda,[56] to propose the inclusion of supplementary items in the provisional agenda,[57] to examine the credentials of representatives,[58] to act as the secretary,[59] to keep the members of the Council informed of any questions that may be brought before it for consideration,[60] to make oral or written statements,[61] to prepare and circulate a draft four-year medium-term plan and a biennial program budget,[62] and to place an item proposed by a specialized agency on the provisional agenda.[63] In addition, the staff of the Secretariat interprets speeches made at meetings,[64] receives, translates, and circulates documents,[65] maintains records of the sessions,[66] and keeps archives.[67]

Further administrative and executive functions of the Secretariat can be found in General Assembly, Security Council, or ECOSOC resolutions,[68] or other statutory instruments or agreements.

---

55 Rules of Procedure of the Economic and Social Council, UN Doc E/5715/Rev.2, art 3.
56 *Ibid* at Rule 9.1.
57 *Ibid* at Rule 12.
58 *Ibid* at Rule 17.
59 *Ibid* at Rule 28.1.
60 *Ibid* at Rule 28.3.
61 *Ibid* at Rule 30.
62 *Ibid* at Rule 31.1.
63 *Ibid* at Rule 76.
64 *Ibid* at Rule 29(a).
65 *Ibid* at Rule 29(b).
66 *Ibid* at Rule 29(c).
67 *Ibid* at Rule 29(d).
68 See *Results of the review by the Commission on Sustainable Development of the sectoral theme of "Oceans and seas": International coordination and cooperation*, GA Res 54/33, UNGAOR, 54th Sess, UN Doc A/Res/54/33 (1999) 1; SC Res 1874 (2009), UN Doc S/RES/1874 (2009) 1 para 26.

4) Technical Functions

The principal organs of the United Nations would be unable to achieve their purposes without the technical assistance that the Secretary-General and staff provide to them on a daily basis. The Secretariat consists of several departments and offices, including the Department of Political and Peacebuilding Affairs, the Department of Peace Operations, the Department of Operational Support, the Department of Economic and Social Affairs, the Department for General Assembly and Conference Management, the Department of Global Communications, the Department of Safety and Security, the Department of Management Strategy, Policy, and Compliance, the Office of Legal Affairs, the Office of Internal Oversight Services, the Office for Disarmament Affairs, the Office for the Coordination of Humanitarian Affairs, and the Office of Counter-Terrorism. Staff members of the Secretariat working in these departments and offices are often called upon to collect information and data, prepare reports and studies, provide technical advice, provide legal opinions, and make recommendations on a wide range of matters and issues.

The UN Secretariat also includes five regional commissions (for Latin America and the Caribbean, Asia Pacific, Africa, Europe, and Western Asia) that act as repositories of knowledge, technical expertise, and data on socio-economic issues in their respective regions. They conduct research and in-depth analytical studies on sustainable development, employment, demographics, women's rights, and other fields relevant to their regions. They provide technical assistance and training to their member states and regional organizations. To this end, regional commissions employ statisticians, IT experts, economists, advisors on gender affairs, and other subject matter experts who fulfill the technical functions of the UN Secretariat.

The Secretariat also has offices and experts specializing in human rights, peacekeeping and peacebuilding, terrorism, transnational crime, international trade, and coordination of humanitarian activities. The Secretariat's technical assistance has also been frequently sought with regard to procedural questions and legal matters. Specifically, the legal counsel of the United Nations may be called upon to interpret the *UN Charter*, the rules of procedure of a main organ or another instrument relevant to the functioning of various organs of the UN, or asked to prepare agreements regulating relations of the UN with its member states, other international organizations, and NGOs.

5) Financial Functions

As the chief administrative officer, the Secretary-General, with the help of staff, prepares the budget of the organization,[69] allocates funds, controls expenses, collects contributions from member states, manages various funds, and handles the financial administration and day-to-day operations of the organization. The Secretariat carries out these responsibilities based on the broad guidelines and directives provided by the General Assembly through the Financial Regulations. This legislative instrument contains directives for planning, programming, monitoring, and evaluating all activities undertaken by the United Nations, irrespective of their source of financing. In addition to the Financial Regulations, the UN also has the Financial Rules, which steer the Secretary-General and staff in implementing the Financial Regulations.

To obtain funds from UN member states, the Secretariat must submit to the General Assembly a budget proposal and receive from it an approval. The preparation of the budget proposal is a lengthy process that requires the participation of all departments and offices of the UN Secretariat. Heads of all departments and offices first prepare budget plans for the forthcoming budget period for their respective departments and offices and transmit them to the Office of Programme Planning, Finance and Budget (headed by the UN Financial Controller). This office administers the Financial Regulations and Rules, ensures compliance therewith, and provides the Secretary-General with advice and support on all matters pertaining to budgets, planning, and

69 In accordance with Rule 153 of the General Assembly Rules of Procedure, "no resolution involving expenditure shall be recommended by a committee for approval by the General Assembly unless it is accompanied by an estimate of expenditures prepared by the Secretary-General."

finances. It compiles budget proposals from different departments and offices into a single document,[70] which becomes the budget proposal. This voluminous document is then transmitted to the Advisory Committee on Administrative and Budgetary Questions (ACABQ), where sixteen financial experts appointed by the General Assembly in their individual capacities scrutinize the budget proposal and formulate recommendations to the Fifth Committee. The recommendation of the ACABQ carries enormous weight. The Fifth Committee (also known as the Administrative and Budgetary Committee) of the General Assembly may either approve or reject the recommendation of the Advisory Committee. If it approves the recommendation of ACABQ, it forwards the proposal to the General Assembly for a final endorsement.

6) Administration of the International Secretariat

The duties of the Secretariat also involve handling human resources within the organization. Managing the human resources of the Secretariat is an extremely difficult task due to the following five elements.

First, the UN Secretariat employs several types of personnel, such as staff members, consultants, individual contractors, UN Volunteers, interns, and Gratis Personnel. Each type of personnel has a different contractual arrangement with the United Nations. For instance, staff members have a letter of appointment. The terms and conditions of their employment are governed by United Nations Staff Regulations

70 *Financial Regulations and Rules*, Secretary-General's Bulletin, UN Doc ST/SGB/2013/4. After preparing their respective portions of the proposed program budget, departments submit their parts of the budget to the Office of Programme Planning, Budget and Accounts (OPPBA), which carries out activities pertaining to the financial and budgetary operations of the organization. OPPBA is part of the Department of Management and is headed by the Controller, who has the level of an Assistant Secretary-General. OPPBA is responsible for establishing and applying budgetary and accounting policies and procedures. It is responsible for the financial management of all resources of the organization, for accounting and reporting, as well as for facilitating intergovernmental deliberations on financial and budgetary matters.

and Rules[71] and other legal instruments, such as Secretary-General's Bulletins, Administrative Instructions, and Information Circulars.[72] Such is not the case for other types of personnel. Specifically, consultants and individual contractors sign a commercial service contract with the UN. This contract has terms and conditions different from those set out in UN Staff Regulations and Rules. UN Volunteers sign an entirely different type of contract with the United Nations Development Programme (UNDP), which administers the UN Volunteers Programme.

Second, there are different groups and categories of staff members. The two major groups of staff are internationally recruited staff and locally recruited staff. Within these two broad groups, there are several categories. Specifically, internationally recruited staff include political appointees at the Under-Secretary-General and Assistant Secretary-General levels, the Professional and higher category (from P-2 to D-2 grades), and the Field Service category. Locally recruited staff members consist of the General Services category (from G-1 to G-7) and National Professional Officers (NO-A to NO-D). Different categories and subcategories of staff have different conditions of service, benefits, and entitlements.

The third source of complexity is the type of appointments that UN staff members may hold under the UN Staff Regulations. The Secretariat may grant three types of appointments to its staff.[73] The most privileged class of staff hold continuing appointments. Continuing appointments are open-ended and do not have a date of expiration. To be eligible for a continuing appointment, a staff member needs to have accrued at least five years of continuous service under a fixed-term appointment.[74] A continuing appointment offers better job

---

71 *Staff Regulations and Rules of the United Nations*, Secretary-General's Bulletin, UN Doc ST/SGB/2018/1 [*UN Staff Regulations and Rules*].

72 The most authoritative document that the Secretary-General is empowered to issue is called "Secretary-General's Bulletin." The second most authoritative instrument (and the most frequent way of issuing legal norms internally) is known as "Administrative Instructions." The UN also issues "Information Circulars," but these are non-binding legal instruments.

73 *UN Staff Regulations and Rules*, above note 71 at Rule 4.11.

74 *Administrative Instruction, Administration of Continuing Appointments*, UN Doc ST/AI/2012/3 at para 2.9.

security than a fixed-term appointment and significantly better job security than a temporary appointment. A fixed-term appointment is granted for a period of one year or more, up to five years at a time.[75] They have an expiration date that is specified in the letter of appointment. A fixed-term appointment may be renewed for any period up to five years at a time.[76] Although a fixed-term appointment does not carry any expectancy of renewal, irrespective of the length of service,[77] decisions not to renew a staff member's appointment cannot be arbitrary. Such decisions must be based on objectively verifiable reasons, which may include an abolition of the staff member's post, insufficiency of funding (for project posts with limited budget), unsatisfactory performance, or as a result of a disciplinary measure that results in a staff member's separation from service. The least appealing type of appointment is called a temporary appointment, which is granted for a period of less than one year to meet seasonal or peak workloads and specific short-term requirements, having an expiration date specified in the letter of appointment.[78] A temporary appointment may be renewed for up to one additional year.[79] It cannot be converted to any other type of appointment. Therefore, a staff member who holds a temporary appointment will invariably leave the United Nations after a maximum of two years of service.

The fourth source of complexity is the diversity of benefits and entitlements that certain categories of staff members have. For example, internationally recruited staff members are eligible for such benefits and entitlements as education grant, home leave, rental subsidy, hardship allowance, mobility allowance, relocation grant and allowance, security allowance, etc. The General Assembly carried out several in-depth reviews and reforms of the Secretariat aimed at simplifying benefits and entitlements of all staff. The most recent reform took place in 2018. While each reform simplifies some of the benefits and entitlements, it also unnecessarily adds complexities to other

---

75 *UN Staff Regulations and Rules*, above note 71 at Rule 4.13(a).
76 *Ibid* at Rule 4.13(b).
77 *Ibid* at Rule 4.13(c).
78 *Ibid* at Rule 4.12(a).
79 *Ibid* at Rule 4.12(b).

benefits and entitlements. The UN can make significant savings by introducing a simplified remuneration package, which makes no distinction between staff with or without dependents.

Finally, UN staff members work in different parts of world. The cost of living and currency varies from one country to another. Therefore, staff members have different salary scales and exchange rates paid in different currencies.

This diversity of contractual arrangements, categories of personnel, benefits and entitlements, and geographic locations presents considerable difficulties in the management of human resources in the UN Secretariat. Not surprisingly, this diversity leads to frequent mistakes and generates work-related grievances and disputes between staff members and the United Nations Secretariat. Such disputes are settled through the internal justice system of the UN, which will be described below. The organizational unit of the Secretariat responsible for managing personnel is the Office of Human Resources, which is part of the Department of Management Strategy, Policy, and Compliance.

C. INDEPENDENCE OF THE UN SECRETARIAT

When the *UN Charter* was being developed, the idea of independence of secretariats from member states of international organizations had not yet fully matured. Indeed, under Article 6.3 of the Covenant of the League of Nations, staff members of the League's Secretariat were to be appointed by the Secretary-General with the approval of the Council. This meant that the League's Council could block the appointment of a candidate of whom it disapproved. This made the Secretariat of the League vulnerable to political influences. The founding fathers of the UN did not want to repeat the mistakes of the League. They knew that the Secretariat of an organization with a principally political vocation would be constantly exposed to political pressures from various stakeholders. For this reason, they made impartiality and independence cornerstones of the UN's Secretariat. First, they entrusted the authority to appoint even the most senior officials of the Secretariat to the Secretary-General. The political organs of the UN do not normally get involved in the recruitment and appointment process of UN officials. Second, they expressly prohibited any allegiance of UN staff members to their national governments. UN staff members are international civil servants. As such, their responsibilities are not national but exclusively international.[80] Third, member states expressly agreed to respect the international character of the UN Secretariat and to abstain from exerting any form of pressure on UN personnel. They adopted the *Convention on the Privileges and Immunities of the United Nations*,[81] which provides that officials of the United Nations shall: (a) be immune from legal process in respect of words spoken or written and all acts performed by them in their official capacity; (b) be exempt from taxation on the salaries and emoluments paid to them by the United Nations; (c) be immune from national service obligation; (d) be immune, together with their spouses and relatives dependent on them, from immigration restrictions and alien registration; (e) be accorded the same privileges in respect of exchange facilities as are accorded to the officials of comparable ranks forming part of diplomatic missions to the government concerned; (f) be given, together with their spouses and relatives dependent on them, the same repatriation facilities in time of international crisis as diplomatic envoys; and (g) have the right to import free of duty their furniture and effects at the time of first taking up their post in the country in question.[82] The highest-ranking officials of the Secretariat, including the Secretary-General, the Deputy Secretary-General, and all other officials at the Under-Secretary-General and Assistant Secretary-General levels, are accorded more generous privileges and immunities. They are treated like diplomatic envoys under international law.[83]

The Secretary-General has a duty to ensure that the independence and neutrality of UN staff members, as set out in the *UN Charter*, UN Staff Regulations, and relevant resolutions of the General Assembly,

---

80 *Ibid* at Regulation 1.1(a).

81 *Convention on the Privileges and Immunities of the United Nations*, above note 40.

82 *Ibid*, art V, s 18.

83 *Ibid*, s 19.

are respected.[84] The Secretary-General must resist political pressures from member states when making decisions affecting staff. The Secretaries-General did not always succeed in complying with this obligation. The independence of the Secretariat from the UN member states was first put to the test in the 1950s. During this period, US Senator Eugene McCarthy led a series of investigations against suspected communists in the UN. The UN Secretariat was accused of giving jobs to disloyal US citizens. A federal grand jury was set up in New York to investigate the alleged subversive activities by US citizens working in the United Nations. A number of Americans employed by the United Nations Secretariat appeared before the grand jury. Some of these staff members chose to testify, while others invoked their privilege under the Fifth Amendment of the US Constitution. The US government was displeased with twenty individuals who refused to testify before the grand jury and requested the then Secretary-General of the UN, Trygve Lie, to terminate their appointments. The Secretary-General yielded to the pressure and dismissed these twenty staff members on the basis that their refusal "to answer whether you are now engaged in any subversive activities against the United States Government" constituted a "fundamental breach of the obligations laid down in the Staff Regulations."[85] These staff members contested their dismissal before the former United Nations Administrative Tribunal—a judicial body that was responsible for adjudicating labour disputes between the UN and its staff.[86] The Administrative Tribunal

---

84 *UN Staff Regulations and Rules*, above note 71 at Regulation 1.1(c). See *Stepanenko v Secretary-General*, United Nations Administrative Tribunal, Judgment 763 (26 July 1996); *Gaskins v Secretary-General*, United Nations Dispute Tribunal, UNDT/2010/119; *Diop v Secretary-General*, United Nations Dispute Tribunal, UNDT/2012/029.

85 *Gordon v Secretary-General*, United Nations Administrative Tribunal, Judgment 29 (21 August 1953) at 121.

86 *Wallach v Secretary-General*, United Nations Administrative Tribunal, Judgment 28 (21 August 1953); *Gordon v Secretary-General*, United Nations Administrative Tribunal, Judgment 29 (21 August 1953); *Svenchansky v Secretary-General*, United Nations Administrative Tribunal, Judgment 30 (21 August 1953); *Harris v Secretary-General*, United Nations Administrative Tribunal, Judgment 31 (21 August 1953); *Eldridge v Secretary-General*, United Nations Administrative Tribunal, Judgment 32 (21 August 1953); *Glassman v Secretary-General*, United

ruled in favour of UN staff members and awarded a hefty monetary compensation. Since the Secretariat did not have sufficient funds to pay the damages awarded by the tribunal, the Secretary-General turned to member states for a supplementary appropriation to cover these unanticipated expenses. Some member states objected, arguing that they had no obligation to pay for unexpected expenses that they neither authorized nor caused. The Secretary-General was in a difficult position. On the one hand, the UN Administrative Tribunal had ordered him to pay a monetary compensation to staff members he had dismissed, and, on the other hand, he had no available funds to comply with the judgment. This deadlock led the General Assembly to seek an advisory opinion from the International Court of Justice. The World Court was asked whether the General Assembly could refuse to give effect to an award of compensation made by the UN Administrative Tribunal in favour of UN staff members whose contracts of service had been unlawfully terminated. The Court concluded that as the final judgment of the Administrative Tribunal had binding force on the United Nations, the General Assembly, as an organ of the United Nations, must likewise be bound by the judgment.[87] Consequently, member states had an obligation to increase their contributions so that the Secretary-General could compensate the aggrieved individuals. This incident underscored the importance of not interfering with the appointment process of UN staff members.

The impartiality and independence of UN staff members came under attack again when member states began exerting pressure on the Secretary-General to recruit their nationals for key positions. Initially, some senior posts in the UN Secretariat were earmarked for

---

Nations Administrative Tribunal, Judgment 33 (21 August 1953); *Older v Secretary-General,* United Nations Administrative Tribunal, Judgment 34 (21 August 1953); *Bancroft v Secretary-General,* United Nations Administrative Tribunal, Judgment 35 (21 August 1953); *Elveson v Secretary-General,* United Nations Administrative Tribunal, Judgment 36 (21 August 1953); *Reed v Secretary-General,* United Nations Administrative Tribunal, Judgment 37 (21 August 1953); *Glaser v Secretary-General,* United Nations Administrative Tribunal, Judgment 38 (21 August 1953).

87 *Effect of awards of compensation made by the UN Administrative Tribunal,* Advisory Opinion, [1954] ICJ Rep 47.

certain nations. However, pursuant to the *UN Charter*, the paramount consideration in the employment of the staff is not their nationality but the necessity of securing the highest standards of efficiency, competence, and integrity.[88] Consequently, earmarking some positions for specific nations was incompatible with the requirements of the *UN Charter*. For this reason, the General Assembly passed a resolution clarifying that "the principle that there should be no monopoly on senior posts by nationals of any State or group of States should be strictly observed and implemented."[89] In addition, the former Administrative Tribunal of the United Nations cautioned the Secretary-General against taking decisions pertaining to staff in order to please member nations. The tribunal pointed out that while the Secretary-General has the right to consult member states when exercising the power of appointment or renewal of contract, such consultations should not contravene the principles of independence and neutrality referred to in Article 100 of the *UN Charter*.[90] In other words, the purpose of the consultative process must be analogous to a reference check rather than an endorsement of his choice by a member state.

For these same reasons, the Secretary-General is not permitted to separate a staff member from service in order to please a member state. Disputes on this specific point arose on several occasions. In the *Gaskins* case,[91] a staff member of the UN Development Programme was in charge of managing a training program for the Sudanese judiciary. In carrying out his activities, Mr Gaskins made administrative decisions that upset some Sudanese judges. The Sudanese judiciary sent a letter to UNDP requesting the replacement of Gaskins by another official. UNDP complied with this request, which prompted Gaskins to challenge his replacement before the United Nations

88 *Charter of the United Nations*, above note 5, art 101.3.

89 *Strengthening of the United Nations System*, GA Res 51/241, UNGAOR, 51st Sess, UN Doc A/Res/51/241 (1997) 1 at para 66 [*Strengthening of the United Nations System*]. See also *Revitalization of the United Nations Secretariat*, GA Res 46/232, UNGAOR, 46th Sess, UN Doc A/Res/46/232 (1992) 3 at para 3(e) [*Revitalization of the UN Secretariat*].

90 *Qiu v Secretary-General*, United Nations Administrative Tribunal, Judgment 482 (25 May 1990).

91 *Gaskins v Secretary-General*, United Nations Dispute Tribunal, UNDT/2010/119.

Dispute Tribunal. The tribunal held that it was inconsistent with the high standards set by the *UN Charter* and the UN Staff Regulations to remove a staff member from his position solely as a response to an ultimatum by national authorities.

A similar dispute arose in the *Diop* case.[92] Mr Diop worked in the UN Office for Drugs and Crime (UNODC) in close collaboration with the ministry of justice of Mali. UNODC received a written complaint in which the minister of justice of Mali expressed his dissatisfaction with Mr Diop's performance. UNODC decided not to extend Mr Diop's contract on the basis of this complaint. Mr Diop contested the decision before the UN Dispute Tribunal and prevailed. The tribunal ruled that the Secretary-General should not yield to political pressures from member states when taking personnel decisions. The performance of a UN staff member should be assessed by his superiors and not by national authorities of member states. The tribunal held that UNODC's decision not to renew Mr Diop's contract and to separate him from service contravened Article 100 of the *UN Charter*.

The obligation of the Secretary-General to protect the independence of his staff from national governments is far-reaching. Specifically, when the government of a member state declares a UN staff member undesirable or *persona non grata* and requests their immediate removal, the Secretary-General has an obligation to demand an explanation or reasons from the member state. If the evicting state refuses to provide an explanation or provides an inadequate explanation, the Secretary-General has a duty to ensure that the staff member's rights under his employment contract are not adversely affected. This may entail a duty to relocate the staff member to another duty station and assign to him duties until the end of his contract.[93]

1) The Particular Case of Secondments

The independence and neutrality of UN staff were questioned again in relation to the practice of some member states to second individuals

92 *Diop v Secretary-General*, United Nations Dispute Tribunal, UNDT/2012/029.

93 *Hassouna v Secretary-General*, United Nations Dispute Tribunal, UNDT/2014/094.

from their national governments. Before the dissolution of the USSR, the only way for Soviet nationals to work for the UN Secretariat was to be seconded to the UN by their government. The secondment arrangement with the government of the USSR compelled Soviet citizens to return a large portion of their UN salary to the Soviet government. Other member states of the UN frequently questioned the independence of these individuals until the matter was formally brought to the attention of the General Assembly. The Assembly decided that "[t]he practice of secondment of staff from government public service is consistent with Article 100 of the UN Charter."[94] The secondment arrangement in and of itself does not affect a staff member's ability to act in the exclusive interests of the UN. It is important to emphasize that although secondment is a tolerated practice, under no circumstances can the Secretariat be composed, even in part, of national representatives responsible to their respective governments. When seconded to the United Nations by their governments, staff members become the servants only of the United Nations for the duration of their appointments. In this particular scenario, this meant that the nationals of the USSR seconded to the UN owed no allegiance to the Soviet Union and had to act in the interests of the UN only. Secondment from national administrations is not uncommon in international organizations. It is generally understood that a staff member seconded from its government would embrace and act in accordance with the principles of neutrality expected of all staff members. Nevertheless, the practice of secondment is problematic because it allows the member state to retain some control over the seconded staff member. In particular, the member state has the discretion not to extend the secondment of its citizen and to recall the staff member. This occurred in the *Yakimetz* case. In 1977, Mr Yakimetz, a national of the USSR, was offered a five-year fixed-term appointment, on secondment from the Soviet Government as Reviser in the Russian Languages Service. When Mr Yakimetz found out that the Soviet government was contemplating replacing him with another individual, he claimed asylum in the United States, resigned from the Ministry of Foreign

94 *Human Resources Management*, GA Res 51/226, UNGAOR, 51st Sess, UN Doc A/RES/55/226 (1997) 1 at 8 [*Human Resources Management*].

Affairs of the USSR and requested the Secretary-General to renew his appointment with the United Nations. Essentially, he attempted to change his employment status from "seconded staff member" to a regular staff member. The UN refused to renew Yakimetz's contract and Mr Yakimetz challenged the refusal before the UN Administrative Tribunal. The tribunal held that a staff member cannot unilaterally extract himself from a secondment, which is a tripartite agreement. The staff member presented an application for review of the Administrative Tribunal's judgment to the Committee on Applications for Review of Administrative Tribunal Judgments, in which he asked the Committee to request an advisory opinion of the International Court of Justice.[95] The World Court upheld the administrative tribunal's judgment. It ruled that while the Secretary-General was not precluded from renewing the appointment of Mr Yakimetz, despite the objection of the Soviet government, he did not have an obligation to do so. The Secretary-General was entitled to take into consideration the wishes of a member state and the adverse consequences that the renewal of Mr Yakimetz's contact could have on the UN.[96]

This case illustrates that member states can use secondment as a tool to retain control over and exert pressure on their nationals working in the UN. The fear of losing their employment with the UN exposes seconded staff members to improper interference by their country of nationality. For this reason, the practice of seconding staff from national governments has become rare in the United Nations.

---

95 The Statute of the UN Administrative Tribunal contained a provision that allowed a UN member state, the Secretary-General, or the person in respect of whom a judgment has been rendered by the Administrative Tribunal to make a written application to a committee established for these purposes to request an advisory opinion of the International Court of Justice on the matter. The ICJ had jurisdiction to review the judgment on the ground that the tribunal had exceeded or failed to exercise its jurisdiction, or had erred on a question of law relating to the provisions of the *UN Charter*, or had committed a fundamental error in procedure, which has occasioned a failure of justice.

96 *Review of Judgment No 333*, above note 15. See also *Stepanenko v Secretary-General*, United Nations Administrative Tribunal, Judgment 763 (26 July 1996).

D. SECRETARY-GENERAL

The UN Secretary-General is arguably the most important public service position in the world. The succinct description provided by the *UN Charter* of the Secretary-General's responsibilities does not do justice to this critical role. At the inception of the United Nations, the role of the Secretary-General was perceived to be more secretarial than political. In fact, in 1946, the first Secretary-General, Trygve Lie, was strongly rebuked by the president of the Security Council merely for circulating a legal opinion from the UN legal counsel in which he proposed to remove from the Security Council's agenda a moot point.[97] The permanent members of the Security Council expected the Secretary-General to be no more than a silent observer of Security Council meetings. Trygve Lie recalled in his memoirs that when he was handing over his responsibilities to his successor, Dag Hammarskjöld, he had described the role of the Secretary-General as the most impossible job on earth. However, the second Secretary-General was politically more astute than his predecessor. He began seeking opportunities that could allow the function of the Secretary-General to expand. Dag Hammarskjöld identified crises and situations that member states had difficulty tackling and offered his assistance. For instance, he offered to participate personally as a mediator in a conflict between Israel and Jordan.[98] He also offered to negotiate the release of American pilots who were under the UN command when they were captured by the Chinese forces and convicted on charges of spying.[99] These initiatives led to a progressive expansion of the Secretary-General's function. The role of the Secretary-General continued to evolve as member states entrusted him with more demanding tasks. Some argue that the first three Secretaries-General molded

---

97 Lie, above note 22 at 83.

98 See SC Res 101 (1953), UNSCOR, 8th Year, UN Doc S/3139/Rev.2 (1953) 1.

99 *Complaint of detention and imprisonment of the United Nations military personnel in violation of the Korean Armistice Agreement*, GA Res 906 (IX), UNGAOR, 9th Sess, UN Doc A/RES/906(IX) (1954) 56.

and shaped the office of the Secretary-General.[100] A factor that contributed to the development of the Secretary-General's role was the UN's rapid expansion after the Cold War.

1) Method of Appointment

The *UN Charter* provides that the Secretary-General is appointed by the General Assembly upon the recommendation of the Security Council.[101] For the nomination of the Secretary-General by the Security Council, an affirmative vote of the majority of its members, including the concurring votes of the permanent members, is required. In the General Assembly, a simple majority of the members is sufficient to appoint a Secretary-General, unless the General Assembly decides that a two-thirds majority is called for. A vote in either the Security Council or the General Assembly is taken by secret ballot.[102] When describing the process for appointing a Secretary-General, the *UN Charter* implies that the Security Council merely recommends candidates and that the final decision rests with the General Assembly. In practice, it is the exact opposite; the decisive element in the appointment of the Secretary-General is the recommendation of the Security Council. The endorsement of this recommendation by the General Assembly is a mere formality. Once the Security Council makes its recommendation, the General Assembly automatically approves the appointment of the recommended candidate. In fact, the General Assembly has never refused to appoint a candidate recommended by the Security Council. This practice resulted from a resolution of the General Assembly adopted in 1946 when the Assembly decided that "it would be desirable for the Security Council to proffer one candidate only for the consideration of the General Assembly, and for debate on the nomination in the General Assembly to be avoided."[103] This practice gives

100 Marcus Franda, *The United Nations in the Twenty-First Century* (Lanham: Rowman & Littlefield Publishers, 2006) at 27.

101 *Charter of the United Nations*, above note 5, art 97.

102 *Terms of Appointment of the Secretary-General*, GA Res 11 (I), UNGAOR, 1st Year, UN Doc A/RES/11(I) (1946) 14 [*Terms of Appointment*].

103 *Ibid.*

the permanent members of the Security Council the power to block the appointment of a Secretary-General by vetoing a recommendation. A more appropriate and democratic solution would have been for the General Assembly to instruct the Security Council to recommend not one candidate but a list of candidates. This way, the General Assembly would retain the authority to choose the Secretary-General. While a permanent member of the Security Council has always had the ability to veto the recommendation of a candidate for the Secretary-General's post, it is politically much easier to object to a recommendation of only one candidate than to an entire list of candidates.

In identifying the best candidate for the post of Secretary-General, regional rotation and gender equality are important factors to consider.[104] These factors are not formal requirements that can be found in any written document (and so far, gender equality has been purely theoretical). They have been established through consistent practice. The regional rotation of the post of Secretary-General to date can be described as follows: four Secretaries-General from Western Europe (Trygvie Lie, Dag Hammarskjöld, Kurt Waldheim, and Antonio Guterres); two Secretaries-General from Asia (U Thant and Ban Ki Moon); two Secretaries-General from Africa (Boutros Boutros-Ghali and Kofi Annan) and one Secretary-General from Latin America (Javier Pérez de Cuéllar). Traditionally, nationals of the five permanent member states of the Security Council are not considered for the position of Secretary-General in order to avoid further concentration of power within the UN.

The recommendation of a Secretary-General by the Security Council has always been an intensely politicized process. During the Cold War, instead of identifying the most suitable and qualified candidate for the position, permanent members of the Security Council used to examine the ideological convictions of candidates. Western powers would block a candidate supported by the Soviet Union and/or China and the East would block candidates proposed by the United States,

---

104 *Strengthening of the United Nations System*, above note 89 at para 59; *Revitalization of the General Assembly*, GA Res 60/286, UNGAOR, 60th Sess, UN Doc A/RES/60/286 (2006) 1 at Annex II, para 18.

the United Kingdom, and France. After the Cold War, an important consideration in excluding a candidate became the candidate's resolve to defy or challenge the authority of permanent members of the Security Council. As a result, the least objectionable contender has always had the strongest chance of being selected. Of course, this does not mean that former Secretaries-General were not qualified. It simply means that the United Nations could have attracted better and more qualified candidates for the position if the selection process had not been so heavily politicized and opaque.

Many viewed this seventy-year-old process for selecting a Secretary-General as outdated and not fit for purpose. It was often compared to a papal concave. Member states and civil society organizations from across the globe argued that the appointment process lacked transparency and could not guarantee the selection of the best possible candidate. The overall perception was that the General Assembly could and should play a more active role in the selection process. Member states demanded that the Assembly and its president engage directly with candidates. They also set expectations on the selection criteria and encouraged the Security Council to be more inclusive and transparent in its discussions and deliberations. Consequently, in 2015, the process was significantly improved.

The current selection process begins with a joint letter from the president of the General Assembly and the president of the Security Council to all member states encouraging them to nominate qualified candidates. This letter is sent during the year preceding the appointment. Once member states appoint their candidates,[105] the General Assembly conducts hearings with all the candidates. While due regard is still given to fair geographical distribution through rotation and to gender balance, personal qualifications constitute the most important criterion for identifying the strongest candidate.[106]

---

105 See *Letter dated 29 February 2016 from the prime minister of Portugal addressed to the president of the General Assembly and the president of the Security Council*, UN Doc A/70/768 and S/2016/206 (2016).

106 At para 40 of its Resolution 70/305, UN Doc A/Res/70/305, the General Assembly stressed "the need to ensure the appointment of the best possible candidate for the post of Secretary-General, who embodies the highest standards of

In the Security Council, the selection process is rather original. The viability of each candidate is assessed by means of a straw poll. Two types of papers are distributed to the members of the Security Council. White papers for non-permanent members and red papers for permanent members. Each paper contains the name of candidates next to which member states may mark either "encouraged" or "discouraged." After each round, candidates with the fewest votes are gradually eliminated. This straw poll exercise may be repeated until the most acceptable candidate is identified. Between each straw poll, members of the Security Council may hold informal consultations on the result of the straw poll and explore possible compromises.

SECRETARIES-GENERAL OF THE UN

Antonio Guterres (Portugal) was born in Lisbon in 1949. He holds a degree in engineering. Prior to his appointment as Secretary-General of the United Nations, Mr Guterres served as a member of parliament and subsequently prime minister of Portugal. He then served as the UN High Commissioner for Refugees (UNHCR) for a period of ten years. He took office as the Secretary-General on 1 January 2017.

Ban Ki Moon (South Korea) was born in the Republic of Korea in 1944. He holds a degree in international relations. He was a career diplomat in the Korean public service. He rose through the ranks and became South Korea's minister of foreign affairs and trade, the post he held at the time of his election as Secretary-General. Mr Ban held office from 1 January 2007 to 31 December 2016.

Kofi Annan (Ghana) was born in Kumasi, Ghana, in 1938 and died in Bern, Switzerland, in 2018. He held degrees in economics and international relations. Mr Annan was the only Secretary-General to emerge from the ranks of United Nations staff. Prior to his appointment as

---

efficiency, competence and integrity and who demonstrates a firm commitment to the purposes and principles of the United Nations, proven leadership and managerial abilities, extensive experience in international relations and strong diplomatic, communication and multilingual skills."

Secretary-General, Mr Annan was the Under-Secretary-General for Peacekeeping. He held office from January 1997 to December 2006.

Boutros Boutros-Ghali (Egypt) was born in Cairo, Egypt, in 1922 and died in 2016 at the age of 93. Mr Boutros-Ghali held several degrees in law. He served as Egypt's minister of state for foreign affairs for fourteen years. Prior to his appointment as Secretary-General, Mr Boutros-Ghali worked as the deputy prime minister for foreign affairs of Egypt. He is the only UN Secretary-General not to be elected for a second term. He held office from January 1992 to December 1996.

Javier Pérez de Cuéllar (Peru) was born in Lima, Peru, in 1920 and died in 2020 at the age of 100. A lawyer and career diplomat, he held several ambassadorial positions for the government of Peru. He was also Peru's deputy minister of foreign affairs and a member of the Peruvian delegation to the UN. He also held several senior posts in the United Nations, including the position of Under-Secretary-General for Special Political Affairs. He served as the UN Secretary-General from January 1982 to December 1991.

Kurt Waldheim (Austria) was born in a small town near Vienna, Austria, in 1918. Lawyer by education, Mr Waldheim was a seasoned politician and diplomat. He was the permanent representative of Austria to the United Nations for over five years. He was the federal minister for foreign affairs of Austria. He held office from January 1972 to December 1981. After the expiration of his second term, allegations arose that Mr Waldheim took part in atrocities against civilians during the Second World War.

U Thant (present-day Myanmar) was born in Burma (present-day Myanmar) in 1909. He was educated at University College Rangoon. Before his appointment as Acting Secretary-General, U Thant was Burma's permanent representative of Burma to the United Nations. He was first appointed as Acting Secretary-General after Dag Hammarskjöld was killed in an air crash in September 1961. He was formally appointed Secretary-General in November 1962 and served until 31 December 1971.

Dag Hjalmar Agne Carl Hammarskjöld (Sweden) was born in Sweden in 1905. He held degrees in economics and law. The son of Sweden's former prime minister, Dag Hammarskjöld was an accomplished public servant in the Swedish government. He was appointed as the Secretary-General of the United Nations in April 1953 after Trygve Lie unexpectedly resigned. He served until his death in a plane crash in Africa in September 1961.

Trygve Halvdan Lie (Norway) was born in Oslo, Norway in 1896. He held a law degree and worked in the Norwegian public service. Mr Lie was minister of foreign affairs of Norway and led the Norwegian delegation to the United Nations Conference in San Francisco. He led the commission responsible for drafting the Security Council provisions of the *UN Charter*. On 1 February 1946, Mr Lie was elected the first Secretary-General of the United Nations. After the Security Council authorized the UN armed forces, consisting primarily of US troops, to aid the Republic of Korea against North Korea, the Soviet Union ceased to recognize him as Secretary-General. Lie resigned in the interests of the organization.

2) Term

The *UN Charter* is silent on the length of the Secretary-General's term in office. This matter is regulated by a General Assembly resolution that states that a Secretary-General is appointed for five years, the appointment being open at the end of that period for a further five-year term.[107] The resolution does not expressly prohibit a third term, it merely provides that the appointment can be extended by a further five-year term. However, it has been interpreted to impose a limit of two terms. Customarily, a Secretary-General serves only two terms. Kurt Waldeim (the fourth Secretary-General) unsuccessfully sought an unprecedented renewal for a third term. China vetoed his reappointment after the expiration of his second mandate. U Thant was asked to serve a third term, but he declined. All other Secretaries-General of the

107 *Terms of Appointment*, above note 102.

UN, except one, served for two consecutive terms in office. Boutros Boutros-Ghali (the sixth Secretary-General) is the only Secretary-General who served for a single term. He was not re-elected for a second term because the United States vetoed the renewal of his mandate. In cases where the Security Council cannot agree on any candidate, the General Assembly may extend the mandate of the exiting Secretary-General until a successor is found. This occurred in 1950, when the members of the Security Council were unable to agree on a recommendation of a candidate as the successor to the first Secretary-General, Trygve Lie. The expiration of Lie's first term had coincided with the Security Council resolution authorizing UN armed forces, consisting primarily of US troops, to aid the Republic of Korea (South Korea). The Soviet Union held Lie responsible for this and vetoed his re-election for a second mandate. The United States vetoed all other candidates. As a result, the Security Council informed the General Assembly of its inability to formulate a recommendation. The General Assembly itself initiated a discussion regarding the appointment of the Secretary-General. Some argued that the General Assembly was exceeding its powers under Article 97 of the *UN Charter* by including on its agenda an item relating to the appointment of the Secretary-General without any recommendation from the Security Council. However, this objection did not propose an alternative solution. The UN needed a Secretary-General and the Security Council was unable to recommend a candidate. Therefore, to ensure the uninterrupted exercise of the Secretary-General's functions, the General Assembly decided to extend Trygve Lie's term for a period of three years without a recommendation from the Security Council.[108] The limitation of a Secretary-General's appointment to two terms is an excellent illustration of how certain UN practices become unwritten law. This practice may change; there being no stipulation on the subject in the *UN Charter*, the General Assembly and the Security Council are free to allow a third term or to modify the term of office of future Secretaries-General. Nevertheless, a wiser solution would be to limit the term of the

108 *Continuation in office of the Secretary-General of the United Nations*, GA Res 492 (V), UNGAOR, 5th Sess, UN Doc A/RES/492(V) (1950).

Secretary-General to a single non-renewable period of eight or ten years. This would ensure that decisions made by the Secretary-General are not influenced by their desire to please the permanent members of the Security Council in order to secure their support for a second term.

3) Conditions of Service

The Secretary-General's emoluments are established and periodically reviewed by the General Assembly. The emoluments of the Secretary-General were fixed for the first time in a General Assembly resolution, which states that

> the Secretary-General shall receive a salary of an amount sufficient to bring him in a net sum of 20,000 dollars (U.S.), together with a representation allowance of 20,000 dollars (U.S.), per annum. In addition, he shall be provided with a furnished residence, the repairs and maintenance of which, excluding provision of household staff, shall be borne by the Organization.[109]

The current gross salary of the Secretary-General is approximately USD$290,000 per annum.[110] In addition to this salary, the Secretary-General receives a representation allowance of USD$25,000 per annum, the purpose of which is to "enable a man of eminence and high attainment to accept and maintain the position."[111] The retirement benefit of the Secretary-General was fixed for the first time in General Assembly Resolution 13(I) to one-half of the net salary.[112] The

---

109 *Terms of Appointment*, above note 102.

110 See *Salary and retirement allowance of the Secretary-General and salary and pensionable remuneration of the Administrator of the United Nations Development Programme*, Report of the Advisory Committee on Administrative and Budgetary Questions, UNGAOR, 58th Sess, UN Doc A/57/7/Add.25 (2003); *Salary and retirement allowance of the Secretary-General and salary and pensionable remuneration of the Administrator of the United Nations Development Programme*, GA Res 57/310, UNGAOR, 57th Sess, UN Doc A/RES/57/310 (2003) 1, endorsing the recommendations of ACABQ.

111 *Terms of Appointment*, above note 102.

112 *Organization of the Secretariat*, GA Res 13 (I), UNGAOR, UN Doc A/RES/13(I) (1946) 14 [*Organization of the Secretariat*].

current retirement benefit of the Secretary-General is USD$137,710 per annum, which represents 50 percent net remuneration. The Secretary-General is also provided with a furnished residence, the repairs and maintenance of which, excluding provision of household staff, is borne by the organization. The Secretary-General lives in a mansion owned by the United Nations, which is situated on Sutton Place, in an exclusive neighbourhood in Manhattan's East Side, within walking distance of the UN headquarters. After retirement, the Secretary-General cannot accept any government position "because a Secretary-General is a confidant of many governments, [thus] his confidential information might be a source of embarrassment to other Members."[113] The position enjoys privileges and immunities identical to those granted to diplomatic envoys. These privileges and immunities can be waived only by the Security Council.

E. STAFF OF THE SECRETARIAT

As mentioned above, Article 97 of the *UN Charter* grants the Secretary-General the power to appoint such staff as the organization may require. The paramount consideration in the employment of staff is the necessity to secure the highest standards of efficiency, competence, and integrity.[114] Another important consideration in employing staff is the importance of recruiting the staff on as wide a geographical basis as possible. The word geographical was meant to include more than mere geography. The intention was to bring together men and women who speak different languages, belong to different races, have different nationalities, come from different cultures, and hold different religious beliefs. In recent years, an equal representation of men and women has also become an important factor in competitive selection processes for UN jobs.

The *UN Charter* does not define the word "staff" found in Article 97. This term may have two meanings. In its broadest sense, the word staff includes all members of the United Nations personnel

---

113 *Terms of Appointment*, above note 102.

114 *Charter of the United Nations*, above note 5, art 101.3.

irrespective of their contractual relationship with the organization, including consultants[115] or persons employed on special service agreements, individual contractors,[116] UN volunteers, interns, and regular staff members of the United Nations. Such a broad interpretation of the term staff appears to be inconsistent with Article 101.1 of the *UN Charter*, which provides that "[t]he staff shall be appointed by the Secretary-General under regulations established by the General Assembly." Interns, service agreement holders, or individual

115 The Administrative Instruction ST/AI/2013/4 on Consultants and Individual Contractors defines the term consultant as "an individual who is a recognized authority or specialist in a specific field, engaged by the United Nations under a temporary contract in an advisory or consultative capacity to the Secretariat. A consultant must have special skills or knowledge not normally possessed by the regular staff of the Organization and for which there is no continuing need in the Secretariat. The functions of a consultant are results-oriented and normally involve analyzing problems, facilitating seminars or training courses, preparing documents for conferences and meetings or writing reports on the matters within their area of expertise on which their advice or assistance is sought." In accordance with the Administrative Instruction ST/AI/1999/7 "Consultants and Individual Contractors," consultants engaged under "Consultant Contracts" and individual contractors engaged under a "Contract for Individual Contractor" serve in their personal capacity. They are neither UN "staff members" under the Staff Regulations nor "officials" for the purposes of the Convention on Privileges and Immunities of the United Nations.

116 The Administrative Instruction ST/AI/2013/4 on Consultants and Individual Contractors defines the term individual contractors as "an individual engaged by the Organization from time to time under a temporary contract to provide expertise, skills or knowledge for the performance of a specific task or piece of work, which would be short-term by nature, against the payment of an all-inclusive fee. The work assignment may involve full-time or part-time functions similar to those of staff members, such as the provision of translation, editing, language training, public information, secretarial or clerical and part-time maintenance services or other functions that could be performed by staff. An individual contractor need not work on United Nations premises." In accordance with the Administrative Instruction ST/AI/1999/7 "Consultants and Individual Contractors," consultants engaged under "Consultant Contracts" and individual contractors engaged under a "Contract for Individual Contractor" serve in their personal capacity. They are neither UN "staff members" under the Staff Regulations nor "officials" for the purposes of the Convention on Privileges and Immunities of the United Nations.

contractors are neither appointed by the Secretary-General nor governed by Staff Regulations.

A narrower and more correct interpretation of the word staff includes only staff members appointed by the Secretary-General through a "letter of appointment," which in UN parlance means the contract of employment between the UN and its staff members. It is the legal act signed by the Secretary-General or an official acting on behalf of the Secretary-General by which the organization legally undertakes to employ a person as a staff member.[117] Under this definition, the term *staff* would exclude members of personnel who do not hold a letter of appointment and whose conditions of service are not governed by the United Nations Staff Regulations. The United Nations Dispute Tribunal retained this narrower interpretation. It concluded that the word staff within the meaning of Article 97 of the *UN Charter* refers only to members of the personnel whose employment relationship with the UN is governed by a letter of appointment issued pursuant to UN Staff Regulations.[118] Therefore, personnel employed on special service agreements,[119] individual contractors,[120] UN Volunteers, and interns cannot be regarded as staff members within the meaning of the *UN Charter*.[121] UN military and police personnel were also held not to be staff members because they were not under the UN command and control.[122] Conversely, the type of letter of appointment a staff member holds is not a relevant consideration when determining if one is a staff member within the meaning of Article 97 of the *UN Charter*. In particular, personnel holding temporary

117 *Gabaldon v Secretary-General*, United Nations Appeals Tribunal, 2011-UNAT-120 [*Gabaldon*].

118 *Turner v Secretary-General*, United Nations Dispute Tribunal, UNDT/2010/170.

119 *Akoa v Secretary-General*, United Nations Dispute Tribunal, UNDT/2013/118; *Ndjadi v Secretary-General*, United Nations Dispute Tribunal, UNDT/2011/007 affirmed by the United Nations Appeals Tribunal in 2012-UNAT-197 [*Ndjadi*]; *Njenga v Secretary-General*, United Nations Dispute Tribunal, UNDT/2014/065.

120 *Kimugui v Secretary-General*, United Nations Dispute Tribunal, UNDT/2014/147.

121 See *Mindua v Secretary-General*, United Nations Dispute Tribunal, UNDT/2018/097, para 28.

122 *El Moctar v Secretary-General*, United Nations Dispute Tribunal, UNDT/2012/113.

appointments with the United Nations are as much staff members as those holding fixed-term, continuing, or permanent appointments.[123]

1) Categories of Staff

The staff of the UN Secretariat can be grouped into the following four categories: (a) political appointees;[124] (b) Professional and higher category; (c) Field Service category; and (d) General Service and related category.[125] The first three categories are internationally recruited staff. The last category consists of locally recruited staff members, which means that they are recruited in the duty station where the relevant UN office is located.

a) Political Appointees

The first category of staff are political appointees. These are senior executives of the UN. They can be appointed without any formality and outside the normal competitive process.[126] Political appointees include the following positions:

a) Deputy Secretary-General;[127]
b) Heads of Departments (rank of an Under-Secretary-General);

---

123 *Gabaldon*, above note 117.

124 *UN Staff Regulations and Rules*, above note 71 at Rule 2.1.

125 *Ibid.*

126 *Staff Selection and Managed Mobility System*, Administrative Instruction, UN Doc ST/AI/2016/1 at para 2.5(a) [*Staff Selection System 2016*].

127 In its resolutions *Renewing the United Nations: A programme for reform*, GA Res 52/12 and GA Res 52/520, UNGAOR, 52nd Sess, UN Doc A/RES/52/12B and *Questions relating to the proposed programme budget for the biennium 1998–1999*, GA Res A/RES/52/220 (13 February 1998), the United Nations General Assembly established the post of the Deputy Secretary-General (DSG). There is only one such post. The resolution that created this post defined the five primary responsibilities of the position as follows: (1) to assist the Secretary-General in the management of operations in the Secretariat, (2) to act for the Secretary-General in absentia (or in other cases decided by the Secretary-General), (3) to assist the Secretary-General in ensuring a coherence of activities and programmes between sectors and institutions and elevating the leadership of the United Nations in the economic and social realms (with a specific focus on developing a reputation in the development field), (4) to represent the Secretary-General at official functions (including conferences, ceremonial occasions and

c) Deputy Heads of Departments (rank of an Assistant Secretary-General);
d) Special Representatives of the Secretary-General, Deputy Special Representatives of the Secretary-General, Special Envoys, Envoys, and other officials such as Special Advisors (ranks of Under-Secretary-General or Assistant Secretary-General).

Under-Secretary-General (USG) usually refers to a rank or level. For instance, Executive Secretary is the functional title of the highest ranking official or head of all five UN regional commissions. The rank of Executive Secretary of all five regional commissions is that of Under-Secretary-General. Similarly, the UN High Commissioner for Human Rights is the official title of the individual, but the hierarchical rank is that of Under-Secretary-General.[128] Nevertheless, for some headquarters-based posts, it may be used to describe the official's functional title. The rank of the highest-ranking official of the Department of Peace Operations is also that of a USG. The official title for this post is Under-Secretary-General for Peace Operations. In this specific case, Under-Secretary-General is not only the official's rank but also a part of the functional title. In other words, Under-Secretary-General is used in some cases to describe the functional title of an official and in other cases the rank or seniority of the official.

The influence and power that different USGs wield in the UN vary dramatically. For instance, USGs who control budgets, programs, or key activities tend to be more influential. Similarly, USGs who head large departments, such as the Department of Peace Operations, or who are members of the Secretary-General's Senior Management Group,[129] are also influential. Officials who have the rank of a USG

---

other events) as determined by the Secretary-General, and (5) to undertake assignments determined by the Secretary-General.

128 *High Commissioner for the promotion and protection of all human rights*, GA Res 48/141, UNGAOR, 48th Sess, UN Doc A/Res/48/141 (1993) 1 at para 2(c).

129 The Senior Management Group (SMG) is a high-level body, chaired by the Secretary-General, which brings together leaders of United Nations departments, offices, funds, and programs. It is a forum for policy-related matters, planning and information sharing with respect to emerging challenges, and cross-cutting issues.

include the executive secretaries of all five regional commissions,[130] the heads of all three offices away from headquarters,[131] the heads of all departments[132] of the Secretariat, Special Representatives or Special Envoys of the Secretary-General for Security Council-mandated peacekeeping, peacebuilding, and special political missions. The UN Secretariat has over 130 USGs and Assistant Secretaries-General (ASG) combined.[133] This number does not include senior officials or heads of Funds and Programmes and Specialized Agencies.

All USGs of the Secretariat report to the Secretary-General. The only exception is the top watchdog of the UN, the USG for the Office of Internal Oversight Services (OIOS). This official reports to the General Assembly through the Secretary-General. OIOS conducts internal audits and investigations into allegations of misconduct. Since the Secretary-General may be the subject of an investigation, it was deemed more appropriate to have the USG for OIOS report directly to the General Assembly. Some USGs live and work in a headquarters location while others must reside in the relevant field mission. In particular, a Special Representative of the Secretary-General is the highest-ranking UN official in a peacekeeping mission, and is expected to live and work in the location where the peacekeeping mission is based. Special Envoys and Envoys of the Secretary-General, who deal with specific thematic issues, only visit the area they are responsible

---

130 Economic Commission for Africa (ECA); Economic Commission for Latin America and the Caribbean (ECLAC); Economic Commission for Europe (ECE); Economic and Social Commission for Asia and the Pacific (ESCAP); Economic and Social Commission for Western Asia (ESCWA).

131 The United Nations Secretariat has three offices away from headquarters. They are the United Nations Office in Geneva (UNOG), the United Nations Office in Vienna (UNOV), and the United Nations Office at Nairobi (UNON).

132 For instance, Department of Economic and Social Affairs, Department of Field Support, Department for General Assembly and Conference Management, Department of Management, Department of Political Affairs, Department of Public Information, Department of Peacekeeping Operations, Department of Safety and Security, Office for the Coordination of Humanitarian Affairs, Office of the United Nations High Commissioner for Human Rights, Office of Internal Oversight Services, Office of Legal Affairs.

133 *Personnel Statistics as at 31 December 2012*, Chief Executive Board for Coordinations, CEB/2013/HLCM/HR/12 (2013) at Table 3A.

for from time to time. Irrespective of where they work or how influential they are, all USGs and ASGs have a diplomatic rank equivalent to that of a diplomatic envoy or a national cabinet minister.

The General Assembly has entrusted the Secretary-General with the discretionary authority to appoint most staff at the level of USG and ASG, as well as Special Envoys at all levels.[134] In most cases, the Secretary-General has the ultimate authority to make the final selection, taking into account other factors, such as geographical distribution and gender balance. A few senior appointments are governed by specific resolutions of the General Assembly. These include the appointment of the High Commissioner of UNRWA, the High Commissioner for Refugees, Executive Director of UN Environment, the head of the Internal Oversight Services, and a few other senior officials. The appointment of these officials may be subject to certain conditions, procedural requirements, or endorsements such as term limits or a requirement to obtain the approval of the General Assembly.[135]

The appointment of USGs and ASGs is normally for a period of up to five years, subject to prolongation or renewal. As a general rule, no national of a member state should succeed a national of that state on a senior post and there should be no monopoly on senior

---

134 *Human Resources Management*, above note 94.

135 See *Assistance to Palestine refugees*, GA Res 302 (IV), UNGAOR, 4th Sess, UN Doc A/Res/302(IV) (1949) 23 for UNRWA; *Statute of the Office of the United Nations High Commissioner for Refugees*, GA Res 428 (V), UNGAOR, 5th Sess, UN Doc A/Res/428(V) (1950) 46 for UNHCR; *Establishment of the United Nations Conference on Trade and Development as an organ of the General Assembly*, GA Res 1995(XIX), UNGAOR,19th Sess, UN Doc A/Res/1995(XIX) (1964) 1 for UNCTAD; *Institutional and financial arrangements for international environmental cooperation*, GA Res 2997 (XXVII), UNGAOR, 27th Sess, UN Doc A/Res/2997(XXVII) (1972) 43 for UNEP; *High Commissioner for the promotion and protection of all human rights*, GA Res 48/141, UNGAOR, 48th Sess, UN Doc A/Res/48/141 (1993) 1 for OHCHR; *Review of the efficiency of the administrative and financial functioning of the United Nations*, GA Res 48/218B, UNGAOR, 48th Sess, UN Doc A/Res/48/218B (1994) 1 for OIOS; *Strengthening the mandate and status of the Commission on Human Settlements and the status, role and functions of the United Nations Centre for Human Settlements (Habitat)*, GA Res 56/206, UNGAOR, 56th Sess, UN Doc A/Res/56/206 (2002) 1 for UN Habitat.

posts by nationals of a state or group of states.[136] Nevertheless a historical analysis suggests that the nationals of some states are more likely to be appointed to certain senior posts. For instance, the executive director of UNICEF has always been an American national, the Under-Secretary-General in charge of the Office of Coordination for Humanitarian Affairs (OCHA) is frequently a British national, and the Under-Secretary-General for the Department of Peacekeeping Operations has been a French national since 1997.

Member states view the employment of their nationals in international organizations, especially in the UN, as an opportunity to influence the work of those organizations. Therefore, the recruitment of senior officials is often seen as a matter of national interest. It is common for member states to exert pressure on the Secretary-General (directly or through the senior management team) in order to have one of their nationals appointed to an influential post. Normally, large nations do not call in favours for positions at levels other than USG or ASG. The power struggle is intense for posts of executive heads of UN Funds, Programmes, and related organizations.

There are several notable differences between political appointees and the other categories of staff described below. First, the selection and recruitment process of political appointees are not governed by any specific rules. More specifically, procedures governing competitive selection processes that apply to UN staff members in general do not apply to political appointees.[137] The appointments at these levels are discretionary. Second, the remuneration scale that applies to USGs and ASGs works differently from the scale that applies to the remaining categories of staff members. The salary scale of UN staff members is determined not only by their grade (G-1 to G-7, P-1 to P-5, D-1 and D-2, etc.) but also by their step. For instance, the salary of a staff member at the P-5 grade will gradually increase, progressing from step I to step X. The normal qualifying period for in-grade movement between consecutive steps is one year or two years. Step increments do not exist for USGs and ASGs—they do not change steps. Third,

---

136 *Revitalization of the UN Secretariat*, above note 89.

137 *Staff Selection System 2016*, above note 126 at para 2.5 (a).

the appointment of political appointees may be terminated at will or in the interest of the organization. Indeed, Letters of Appointment of Assistant Secretaries-General and Under-Secretaries-General contain a contractual clause that provides that their "appointment is also subject to termination in the interest of the organization, as determined by the Secretary-General."[138] A similar clause is not part of an employment contract of regular staff members. The termination of appointment of all other categories of staff must have a valid legal basis supported by objectively verifiable reasons.[139]

b) Professional and Higher Categories

The second category of staff is known as Professional and higher categories.[140] They range from junior professionals at the P-1 level to executive directors at the D-2 level. The word professional refers to staff members at the P-1 to P-5 levels whereas the word higher refers to director-level positions at the D-1 and D-2 levels. Professional staff carry out the day-to-day substantive work of the organization. Applicants for Professional and higher-level positions are required to have an advanced university degree such as Master's degree or equivalent

---

138 See *Galbraith v Secretary-General*, United Nations Dispute Tribunal, UNDT/2013/102.

139 *UN Staff Regulations*, above note 71 at Regulation 9.3, states that the

> Secretary-General may, giving the reasons therefor, terminate the appointment of a staff member who holds a temporary, fixed-term or continuing appointment in accordance with the terms of his or her appointment or for any of the following reasons: (i) If the necessities of service require abolition of the post or reduction of the staff; (ii) If the services of the staff member prove unsatisfactory; (iii) If the staff member is, for reasons of health, incapacitated for further service; (iv) If the conduct of the staff member indicates that the staff member does not meet the highest standards of integrity required by Article 101, paragraph 3, of the Charter; (v) If facts anterior to the appointment of the staff member and relevant to his or her suitability come to light that, if they had been known at the time of his or her appointment, should, under the standards established in the Charter, have precluded his or her appointment; (vi) In the interest of the good administration of the Organization and in accordance with the standards of the Charter, provided that the action is not contested by the staff member concerned.

140 *UN Staff Regulations and Rules*, above note 71 at Rule 2.1(b).

or a first-level university degree combined with additional qualifying experience. They also need to have strong analytical and communications skills, substantial experience, and, in some cases, leadership ability. There is a large variety of jobs within the Professional category, including medical officers, legal officers, procurement specialists, program specialists, statisticians, IT experts, and social scientists. Directors, on the hand, are required to be strategic thinkers who manage teams, determine priorities, and allocate resources for an entire office. Appointments of staff at the D-1 and D-2 levels require the endorsement of the Secretary-General himself.[141]

Staff members in the Professional and higher categories are recruited internationally through competitive selection processes. Staff members are considered internationally recruited even when they are hired in the country where they work and subject to local recruitment.[142] Their salaries (emoluments) are determined on the basis of the Noblemaire principle,[143] which states that the international civil service should be able to recruit staff from its member states, including states where public service pays well. Therefore, the emoluments of staff in the Professional and higher categories are set by reference to the highest-paying national civil service. The International Civil Service Commission (ICSC) periodically identifies the national civil service of the member state that has the highest pay levels and that by its size lends itself to a comparison. The federal civil service of the United States has thus far been taken as the highest paid national civil service. In addition to a fixed salary for a specific level or grade, staff members in the Professional and higher categories also receive post adjustment, which is a percentage of the fixed salary that is paid to ensure equity in purchasing power of staff members in various duty stations or cities.[144] The amount of the post adjustment varies from city to city. For instance, the cost of living in Geneva, New York,

---

141 *Staff Selection System 2016*, above note 126 at para 12.2.

142 *UN Staff Regulations and Rules*, above note 71 at Rule 4.5(a) and (b).

143 Named after a French diplomat, Georges Noblemaire, who chaired a committee established under the auspices of the League of Nations to set the salaries of the League's staff.

144 *UN Staff Regulations and Rules*, above note 71 at Rule 3.7(a).

or Tokyo is significantly higher than the cost of living in Amman, Budapest, or Montreal. Therefore, the post adjustment is different in all six cities, which means that the net salary of UN staff members is also different in each city.

All posts in the Professional and higher categories must be properly and accurately classified,[145] which means that the seniority or level of the post must correspond to the complexity of the responsibilities listed in the vacancy announcement of the staff member. If the level of the post is not consistent with the responsibilities of the post or if a staff member is asked to perform duties not listed in a vacancy announcement, the staff member may request a monetary compensation and that the post be reclassified upwards.[146] The methodology for classifying posts in the UN Secretariat is unfortunately not rigorous. Many posts are either under-classified or over-classified. As a result, a significant number of staff members perform duties and responsibilities that are above their paygrade. Regrettably, budgetary constraints often dictate the outcome of a classification process, even though the only relevant factor must be the nature, roles, and responsibilities of the post.

c) Field Service Category

The third category is the Field Service (FS) category. These staff members are based mostly in a peacekeeping environment. The FS category was created to ensure that the United Nations has a pool of qualified support staff for deployment or assignment to peacekeeping missions. Very often, peacekeeping missions are situated in places where it is not possible to recruit locally qualified personnel. The Field Service category was created to fill that void. Staff members who belong to this category are either General Service staff, assigned outside their duty stations for a limited period of up to two years to

---

145 *Ibid* at Rule 2.1; *System for the Classification of Posts*, Administrative Instruction, UN Doc ST/AI/1998/9.

146 *System for the Classification of Posts*, Administrative Instruction, UN Doc ST/AI/1998/9 at para 1.1; *Zhouk v Secretary-General*, United Nations Dispute Tribunal, UNDT/2011/102 affirmed in 2012-UNAT-224; *Hosang v Secretary-General*, United Nations Dispute Tribunal, UNDT/2019/008 at para 24.

perform functions that would in normal circumstances be performed by locally recruited staff, or internationally recruited civil servants hired to perform specialized functions.

The Field Service category as we know it today is significantly different from the Secretary-General's initial idea. In 1949, the Secretary-General proposed to create the Field Service category for the following purpose:

> The Field Service would be a part of the Secretariat, but would be recruited by secondment from national Governments. It would consist of a maximum of 500 men. Personnel would, as far as possible, be physically fit men between the ages of 22 and 30, with field experience and the necessary technical background. The term of service would be from one to three years, except for a small number of supervisory personnel who would be regular Secretariat members. The Field Service would be stationed at headquarters for training.[147]

Some delegations were of the view that the Field Service category proposed by the Secretary-General had the character of a military unit because it would consist solely of physically fit men between the ages of twenty-two and thirty with special military training.[148] These delegations were opposed to the creation of this category because the *UN Charter* does not provide the Secretary-General with the authority to create military units. As a result, a compromise was reached, and the Secretary-General was allowed to create a Field Service category that could neither be considered as an armed force under Article 43 of the *UN Charter* nor ever be used for enforcement purposes under Chapter VII. The sole function of the Field Service as authorized by the General Assembly would be to render technical services to missions operating under the provisions of the *UN Charter*.[149]

---

147 *Report of the Special Committee on a United Nations Guard*, UNGAOR, 4th Sess, Supp 13, UN Doc A/959 (Supp) (1949), 6 at Annexes.

148 *Ibid* at para 48 (iii).

149 *United Nations Field Service and United Nations Panel of Field of Observers*, GA Res 297A (IV), UNGAOR, 4th Sess, UN Doc A/RES/297A (IV) (1949) 21.

d) General Services and Related Categories

The fourth category is the "General Service and related categories."[150] Staff members in the General Services category provide administrative, secretarial, and clerical support as well as building maintenance. The General Service category ranges from levels G-1 to G-7. The higher the level of the job, the more complex the functions become. Typically, a senior administrative assistant would incumber a G-7 post. The minimum standard education requirement is a high school diploma. Candidates for vacant posts in this category are also required to have successfully passed the United Nations Administrative Support Assessment Test (UNASAT).

Staff members in the General Service and related categories are recruited locally even when they do not hold the nationality of the state in which they have been recruited. For instance, the United Nations Office in Geneva recruits its General Service staff members in Switzerland, but the candidates do not need to have a Swiss citizenship; they can be Italian, French, or British. In some parts of the world, the United Nations often has difficulty attracting nationals of wealthy member states into the General Service category. For example, the Joint Support Office for the United Nations Assistance Mission for Iraq (UNAMI) and for the United Nations Assistance Mission for Afghanistan (UNAMA) was based in Kuwait. This office provided administrative services to peace operations and employed hundreds of individuals in Kuwait. Only a handful of staff members in the General Service category held Kuwait's nationality. Most employees were foreigners from neighbouring countries living and working in Kuwait. The salaries offered by the UN in Kuwait were not sufficiently attractive for Kuwaiti citizens.

In addition to the General Service category, the UN also has a related category known as National Professional Officers (NPO). This category consists of professional staff members recruited locally whose functions require national experience or knowledge of culture, language, governmental structures, or institutions. These staff members may be experts in their field, i.e., lawyers, engineers, and

---

150 *UN Staff Regulations and Rules*, above note 71 at Rule 2.1(b).

accountants, but their expertise is local or limited to their country of nationality. Applicants for NPO level positions must have as a minimum a first-level university degree. Typically, National Officers are paid significantly less than their counterparts in the Professional category. There are five levels within the NPO category, and they range from NO-A (which requires one year of professional experience) to NO-E (which requires over seven years of experience).

While the emoluments of staff members in the Professional and higher categories are determined in accordance with the Noblemaire principle, those of staff members in the General Services and related categories are determined in accordance with the Flemming principle. Essentially, the Flemming principle requires that the salaries of this category of staff be established by the Secretary-General on the basis of the best prevailing conditions of employment in the locality where the specific United Nations office is situated. The best prevailing conditions of employment are determined by surveying the local labour market, namely, the best paying employers in the relevant city.

e) Other Categories of Personnel

The United Nations also regularly employs personnel that do not constitute staff within the meaning of the *UN Charter*. They include *gratis* personnel,[151] UN Volunteers,[152] Interns, Consultants, and Individual

---

151 The Administrative Instruction ST/AI/1999/6 on *Gratis* Personnel defines this category of individuals as "personnel provided to the United Nations by a Government or other entity responsible for the remuneration of the services of such personnel and do not serve under any other established regime such as that applicable to interns, associate experts, personnel provided on a non-reimbursable loan [. . .]."

152 UN Volunteers are individuals of twenty-five years of age or older with professional skills and academic qualifications or training, who contribute their time and expertise as international volunteers, outside their own countries, or where UN programs exist in their own countries, as national volunteers. Volunteers have proven specialized experience in their professional fields and serve in assignments with diverse UN agencies to support peace and development. On average, UN Volunteers serve for thirty months. Eighty percent are citizens of developing and transition countries and the remaining 20 percent come from the industrialized world. United Nations Volunteers is also an entity that is headquartered in Bonn, Germany, and administered by United Nations Development

Contractors.[153] These classes of personnel play very important roles in fulfilling the mandate of the organization. Their roles, responsibilities, and emoluments are spelled out in their contracts of service.

2) Basic Obligations of UN Staff

In February 1946, the General Assembly called for the establishment of an international civil service commission to advise on the methods of recruitment of UN staff members.[154] As a result, in 1948, the International Civil Service Advisory Board (ICSAB) was established with terms of reference related chiefly to questions of recruitment and personnel administration. In 1954, the ICSAB issued Standards of Conduct expected of international civil servants. For all means and purposes, this document was a code of conduct for international public servants. It contained several broad principles that all staff members had to comply with. These standards of conduct were ultimately incorporated into UN Staff Regulations and Rules as basic obligations applicable to all UN staff. The obligations imposed on all UN staff members can be grouped into two categories: those that seek to ensure that UN staff members uphold the core values of the organization, which are integrity, professionalism, and respect for diversity; and those that aim at preserving their independence and impartiality.

Arguably, the most important obligation is to exhibit faith in fundamental human rights, in the dignity and worth of the human person, and in the equal rights of men and women.[155] This basic obligation aims at preventing and addressing sexual offences, abusive behaviours, and discriminatory practices by UN staff members. The United Nations has been plagued by incidents of sexual exploitation and abuse for the past two decades. These occurrences have caused significant reputational damage to the organization. The

---

Programme (UNDP). It adheres to UNDP policies and procedures for recruitment and staffing.

153 The Administrative Instruction on Consultants and Individual Contractors, UN Doc ST/OI/2013/4 defines these two roles.

154 *Organization of the Secretariat*, above note 112.

155 *UN Staff Regulations and Rules*, above note 71 at Regulation 1.2(a).

UN introduced a strict policy against sexual exploitation and sexual abuse,[156] prohibiting its staff from engaging in any sexual act with a person under the age of eighteen regardless of the age of majority or the age of consent. Mistaken belief in the age of a minor is not a valid defence for staff. The exchange of money, employment, goods, or services for sex, including sexual favours or other forms of humiliating, degrading, or exploitative behaviour, is also prohibited. Unfortunately, the organization's attempts to eradicate sexual offences have not been successful. Allegations of sexual exploitation and abuse by UN staff are still prevalent,[157] particularly in peacekeeping missions where the local population is vulnerable.

Another essential component of this obligation is to show respect for all cultures and not to discriminate against any individual or group of individuals.[158] Any form of discrimination, harassment, including sexual harassment, as well as abuse of authority at the workplace or in connection with work are prohibited. In September 2019, the Secretary-General issued a new policy that defines and prohibits discrimination, harassment, sexual harassment, and abuse of authority.[159] The policy also provides mechanisms for reporting, investigating, and, if necessary, sanctioning such behaviour.

---

156 *Special measures for protection from sexual exploitation and sexual abuse*, Secretary-General's Bulletin, UN Doc ST/SGB/2003/13 (2003).

157 *Special measures for protection from sexual exploitation and abuse*, Report of the Secretary-General, UN Doc A/73/744 (2019); Practice of the Secretary-General in disciplinary matters and cases of criminal behaviour, 1 July 2016 to 30 June 2017, Information Circular, UN Doc ST/IC/2017/33 (2017), at paras 58–59; Practice of the Secretary-General in disciplinary matters and cases of criminal behaviour, 1 July 2015 to 30 June 2016, Information Circular, UN Doc ST/IC/2016/26 (2016), at paras 67–69; Practice of the Secretary-General in disciplinary matters and cases of criminal behaviour, 1 July 2013 to 30 June 2014, Information Circular, UN Doc ST/IC/2014/26 (2014), at paras 41–44. See also *Erefa v Secretary-General*, United Nations Dispute Tribunal, Order No 002 (NBI/2019) (7 January 2019); *Gisage v Secretary-General*, United Nations Dispute Tribunal, UNDT/2019/059 (17 April 2019); *Kramo v Secretary-General*, United Nations Dispute Tribunal, UNDT/2018/122 (5 December 2018).

158 *UN Staff Regulations and Rules*, above note 71 at Regulation 1.2(a).

159 *Addressing discrimination, harassment, including sexual harassment, and abuse of authority*, Secretary-General's Bulletin, UN Doc ST/SGB/2019/8 (2019) replacing an earlier policy on the same topic, UN Doc ST/SGB/2008/5 (2008).

UN staff members must uphold the highest standards of efficiency, competence, and integrity, which includes probity, impartiality, fairness, honesty, and truthfulness in all matters affecting their work and status.[160] The efficiency, competence, and integrity of staff members are evaluated through annual performance appraisals.[161] Each UN staff member is entitled to an annual performance appraisal report in which the staff member's supervisor evaluates the quality of the member's work. If a staff member fails to uphold the highest standards of efficiency, competence, and integrity, that person may be separated from service for unsatisfactory performance.[162] In practice, the performance appraisal system of the UN is cumbersome and managers are often reluctant to give a negative appraisal to their subordinates because they are afraid that it would trigger a lengthy and time-consuming rebuttal process.

Staff members who fail to uphold the highest standards of integrity may also face disciplinary proceedings and sanctions, including dismissal. For instance, it is a disciplinary offence for UN staff members to intentionally misrepresent their functions, official title, or the nature of their duties.[163] Similarly, staff members who intentionally alter, destroy, falsify, misplace, or render useless any official document, record, or file entrusted to them by virtue of their functions commit misconduct. Upholding the highest standards of integrity also requires staff members to use the property and assets of the organization only for official purposes[164] and to respond fully to requests for information from staff members and other officials of the organization authorized to investigate the possible misuse of funds, waste, or abuse.[165]

Staff members are subject to the authority of the Secretary-General and to assignment to any of the activities or offices of the United

160 *UN Staff Regulations and Rules*, above note 71 at Regulation 1.2(b).
161 *Ibid* at Rule 1.3(a).
162 *Ibid* at Rule 9.3(a)(ii); *Performance management and development system*, Administrative Instruction, UN Doc ST/AI/2010/5 (2010).
163 *UN Staff Regulations and Rules*, above note 71, at Rule 1.2(h).
164 *Ibid* at Rule 1.2(q).
165 *Ibid* at Rule 1.2(r).

Nations.[166] Hence, in theory, UN staff members cannot refuse a reassignment by the Secretary-General to different functions or a different location as long as the Secretary-General makes all necessary safety and security arrangements for the staff members to carry out the responsibilities entrusted to them. Nevertheless, the United Nations Appeals Tribunal identified some parameters for determining whether the reassignment of a staff member is lawful:

> [T]he decision must be properly motivated, and not tainted by improper motive, or taken in violation of mandatory procedures. An accepted method for determining whether the reassignment of a staff member to another position was proper is to assess whether the new post was at the staff member's grade; whether the responsibilities involved corresponded to his or her level; whether the functions to be performed were commensurate with the staff member's competence and skills; and, whether he or she had substantial experience in the field.[167]

Staff members also have an obligation to follow the directions and instructions properly issued by the Secretary-General and by their supervisors.[168] Where they believe that their supervisors' instructions are unlawful, they can request that the instructions be provided in writing. However, they cannot unilaterally determine that the instructions are unlawful and refuse to comply with them because this could constitute insubordination. It is prohibited for staff members to use their office or knowledge gained from their official functions for private gain, financial or otherwise, or for the private gain of any third party, including family, friends, and those they favour.[169] Similarly, staff members cannot use their office for personal reasons to prejudice the positions of those they do not favour.[170] UN staff should also

166 *Ibid* at Rule 1.2(c).

167 *Rees v Secretary-General*, United Nations Appeals Tribunal, 2012-UNAT-266 at para 58; *Chemingui v Secretary-General*, United Nations Appeals Tribunal, 2019-UNAT-930 at para 40.

168 *UN Staff Regulations and Rules*, above note 71 at Rule 1.2(a).

169 *Ibid* at Rule 1.2(g).

170 *Ibid.*

avoid any real or apparent conflict of interest. The United Nations defines a conflict of interest as a situation in which a staff member's personal interests interfere with the performance of official duties and responsibilities or with the integrity, independence, and impartiality required by the staff member's status as an international civil servant.[171] In such cases, the conflict must be disclosed by staff members to their supervisors and resolved in favour of the interests of the organization. In particular, the conflicted staff member is expected to formally excuse itself from participating in any activity that may give rise to a conflict of interest.[172] Consequently, staff members are not allowed to engage in any outside occupation or employment, whether remunerated or not, without the approval of the Secretary-General.[173] The Secretary-General may authorize an outside occupation or employment only if the outside employment does not conflict with the staff member's official functions or the status of an international civil servant, is not against the interest of the United Nations, and is permitted by local law where the occupation or employment occurs.[174] UN staff must conduct themselves at all times in a manner befitting their status as international civil servants and cannot engage in any activity that is incompatible with the proper discharge of their official duties. They must comply with local laws and honour their private legal obligations, including, but not limited to, the obligation to honour orders of competent courts.[175] They are not allowed to make any kind of public pronouncement that may adversely reflect on their status or on the integrity, independence, and impartiality that are required by their status.[176]

A significant number of obligations are imposed on UN staff members to preserve their impartiality and independence. Upon appointment, UN staff members must make a written declaration

---

171 *Ibid* at Rule 1.2(m).

172 *Ibid* at Rule 1.2(q).

173 *Ibid* at Regulation 1.2(o).

174 *Ibid* at Regulation 1.2(p).

175 *Ibid*, art 1.2(b); *Benamar v Secretary-General*, United Nations Appeals Tribunal, 2017-UNAT-797 (27 October 2017).

176 *UN Staff Regulations and Rules*, above note 71 at Regulation 1.2(f).

witnessed by the Secretary-General or his authorized representative in which they promise to exercise in all loyalty, discretion, and conscience their official functions.[177] In the performance of their duties, staff members shall neither seek nor accept instructions from any government or from any other source external to the organization.[178] By accepting an appointment, staff members pledge themselves to discharge their functions and regulate their conduct with only the interests of the organization in view. Loyalty to the aims, principles, and purposes of the United Nations, as set forth in its *UN Charter*, is a fundamental obligation of all staff members by virtue of their status as international civil servants.[179] It is prohibited for staff members to seek to influence member states, principal or subsidiary organs of the United Nations, or expert groups in order to obtain a change from a position or decision taken by the Secretary-General, including decisions relating to the financing of the Secretariat, or in order to secure support for improving their personal situations or the personal situations of other staff members or for blocking or reversing unfavourable decisions regarding their status or their colleagues' status.[180]

While staff members may exercise the right to vote, they cannot participate in any political activity that could reflect adversely on their independence and impartiality.[181] For instance, the United Nations sanctioned a UN staff member who was involved in political partisanship and civil strife in Rwanda.[182] The staff member contested the disciplinary measure before the former Administrative Tribunal of the UN. The tribunal held that this conduct created at the minimum an apprehension of political involvement in domestic affairs, which constitutes a failure of the duty to remain impartial. Therefore, the tribunal upheld the disciplinary measure. Staff members may, of

177 *Ibid* at Rule 1.1(b), which codifies existing practice under which staff members subscribe to a written declaration but do not make a sworn statement, since the concept of sworn statement depends upon the operation of local law.

178 *Ibid* at Regulation 1.2(d).

179 *Ibid* at Regulation 1.2(e).

180 *Ibid* at Rule 1.2(j).

181 *Ibid* at Regulation 1.2(h).

182 *Nkubana v Secretary-General,* United Nations Administrative Tribunal, Judgment 738 (21 November 1995).

course, have personal views and convictions, including their political and religious convictions. However, these views and convictions should not adversely affect their official duties or the interests of the United Nations or influence their decisions or actions when carrying out their official duties. Staff members have an obligation not to give the impression that their actions or decisions are influenced by their personal views. UN personnel must exercise the utmost discretion with regard to all matters of official business and cannot communicate to any government, entity, person, or any other source any information known to them by reason of their official position that they know or ought to have known has not been made public.[183] UN staff members are not permitted to accept any honour, decoration, favour, gift, or remuneration from any government.[184] If, however, by refusing an unanticipated honour, decoration, favour, or gift from a government, the staff member can cause embarrassment to the UN, he or she may receive it on behalf of the organization and entrust it to the Secretary-General, who will either retain it for the organization or arrange for its disposal for the benefit of the organization or for a charitable purpose.[185] A similar prohibition applies to honours, decorations, favours, or gifts from non-governmental sources.[186] However, the Secretary-General may authorize staff members to accept from a university or a related institution academic awards, distinctions, and tokens of a commemorative or honorary character, such as scrolls, certificates, trophies, or other items of essentially nominal monetary value. The prohibition to accept any gift, remuneration, or favour is even stronger when its source is an individual or company that has or is seeking to have any type of contractual relationship with the UN. Further, it is prohibited for staff members to offer, promise, request, or receive any favour, gift, remuneration, or any other personal benefit to another staff member or to any third party with a view to causing

---

183 *UN Staff Regulations and Rules*, above note 71 at Regulation 1.2(i).
184 *Ibid* at Regulation 1.2(j).
185 *Ibid* at Regulation 1.2(k).
186 *Ibid* at Regulation 1.2(l).

that member to perform, fail to perform, or delay the performance of any official act.[187]

When a staff member fails to comply with these obligations or loses the ability to remain impartial and independent, the UN may institute disciplinary proceedings which may culminate in disciplinary measures ranging from a written censure to dismissal. In determining whether the conduct of a staff member warrants a disciplinary measure, the Secretary-General must be satisfied that the alleged facts have been established at least on a preponderance of evidence,[188] and that the established facts constitute a breach of the staff member's basic obligations. In determining the severity of the disciplinary measure, the Secretary-General must take into account mitigating and aggravating circumstances and must opt for a sanction that is proportionate to the gravity of the offence.[189] Staff members may then either accept the disciplinary measure or challenge it before the United Nations Dispute Tribunal. The legal process for challenging adverse decisions is described below in Section E(5).

3) Privileges and Immunities of UN Staff

To guarantee the independence of UN staff members, paragraph 105.2 of the *UN Charter* provides that representatives of the members of the United Nations and officials of the UN shall enjoy such privileges and immunities as are necessary for the independent exercise of their functions in connection with the organization. This provision does not elaborate further on the scope of these privileges and immunities. The *UN Charter* gave the General Assembly the authority to propose conventions to the UN member states with a view to determining the

---

187 *Ibid* at Rule 1.2(k).

188 Where the Secretary-General intends to impose the disciplinary measure of dismissal, the alleged facts must be established to an American standard of proof known as "clear and convincing evidence," which is higher than a balance of probabilities but lower than beyond a reasonable doubt.

189 *Masri v Secretary-General*, United Nations Appeals Tribunal, 2010-UNAT-098; *Shahatit v Secretary-General*, United Nations Appeals Tribunal, 2012-UNAT-195; *Portillo Moya v Secretary-General*, United Nations Appeals Tribunal, 2015-UNAT-523.

extent and limits of privileges and immunities. The General Assembly exercised this power at its first session and adopted the *Convention on the Privileges and Immunities of the United Nations.*[190] This convention, frequently referred to as the "General Convention," was drafted by the United Nations Preparatory Commission.[191]

The General Convention contains privileges and immunities applying to three categories of individuals who perform duties for the United Nations. They are: (a) representatives of member states to the UN; (b) United Nations officials; and (c) experts on missions for the United Nations. The privileges and immunities accorded to all three categories of individuals are not personal benefits, even though they attach to them.[192] The primary purpose of granting privileges and immunities to UN officials was the desire to protect the organization from improper political influence by national governments over its staff members. This, however, does not mean that privileges and immunities do not benefit the UN officials to whom they are accorded. It simply means that these officials receive privileges and immunities so that they can carry out their functions without any fear of political influence or retaliation. They must abstain from any action that could be viewed as an abuse of privileges and immunities. The International Court of Justice offered the following rationale for granting privileges and immunities to UN officials:

> In order that the agent may perform his duties satisfactorily, he must feel that this protection is assured to him by the Organization, and that he may count on it. To ensure the independence of the agent, and, consequently, the independent action of the Organization itself, it is essential that in performing his duties he need not have to rely on any other protection than that of the Organization.[193]

---

190 *Convention on the Privileges and Immunities of the United Nations*, above note 40.

191 Convention on the Privileges and Immunities of the United Nations, United Nations Audio-visual Library of International Law, 2008 at 1, online: http://legal.un.org/avl/pdf/ha/cpiun-cpisa/cpiun-cpisa_ph_e.pdf.

192 Anthony J Miller, "Privileges and Immunities of United Nations Officials" (2007) 4:2 *Intl Organizations L Rev* 169 at 188–89 [Miller, "Privileges"].

193 *Reparation for Injuries*, above note 39 at 183.

Neither the *UN Charter* nor the General Convention define the term "United Nations official." Article V, Section 17 of the General Convention deliberately left this to the Secretary-General's discretion, subject to the General Assembly's approval. The term "UN officials" was described in a General Assembly resolution as "all members of the staff of the United Nations, with the exception of those who are recruited locally and are assigned to hourly rates."[194] Although staff members in the General Service and related categories are recruited locally, they nevertheless enjoy privileges and immunities of a UN official because they are not assigned to hourly rates.[195] Personnel provided by the organization's contractors to a UN operation,[196] individual contractors,[197] and personnel supplied on a voluntary basis by a government are not UN officials within the meaning of the General Convention.[198]

Although the General Assembly resolution defines UN officials as staff members, it provides no definition of the term "staff member." The United Nations Staff Rules and Regulations[199] do not define this term either. As we have already pointed out above, the term "staff members" is understood within the UN system as those officials who hold a valid letter of appointment, which is another term for describing the contract of employment between the UN and its staff members.[200]

---

194 *Privileges and immunities of the Staff of the Secretariat of the United Nations*, GA Res 76 (I), UNGAOR, 1st Sess, UN Doc A/RES/76 (I) (1946).

195 *Ibid.*

196 Office of Legal Affairs, "Question whether locally recruited staff of the United Nations peace-keeping force in Cyprus are exempted from taxation on their salaries and emoluments" in *UN Juridical Yearbook* (New York: UN, 1987) at 216–17.

197 Office of Legal Affairs, "Obligations of the United Nations with respect to income tax levied by a Member State—Article II, Section 2, and Article V, Section 18, of the Convention on the Privileges and Immunities of the United Nations—Status of consultants" *UN Juridical Yearbook* (New York: UN, 1996) at 440–41.

198 Office of Legal Affairs, "Contractual relationship between the United Nations and individuals whose services are directly remunerated by their Government or other donor entity" *UN Juridical Yearbook* (New York: UN, 1998) at 475–77.

199 *UN Staff Regulations and Rules*, above note 71.

200 *Ibid* at Regulation 4.1.

This category of individuals excludes consultants, individual contractors, United Nations Volunteers, and interns. It includes staff in the Professional and higher categories, staff in the Field Service category as well as staff in the General Service and related categories. The Deputy Secretary-General, Under-Secretaries-General, Assistant Secretaries-General, and officials of equivalent rank are also considered as UN staff members. However, these senior officials as well as their spouses and minor children enjoy full diplomatic privileges and immunities similar to those granted to member states' diplomatic and consular agents.[201] Some categories of UN personnel were accorded the same privileges and immunities as those enjoyed by UN staff members. For instance, UN Volunteers[202] and officials who serve on a full-time basis as members of a body directly responsible to the General Assembly were afforded privileges and immunities of UN officials even though they are not considered staff members.[203] Privileges and immunities protect UN officials even after their separation from service. However, the protection is limited to actions carried out by staff while they were still employed by the United Nations.[204]

Most UN officials enjoy functional immunity as opposed to diplomatic immunity. As we have already mentioned, only the most senior

---

201 *Convention on the Privileges and Immunities of the United Nations*, above note 190, art V, s 19. The General Convention does not explicitly refer to Under-Secretaries-General because such a rank did not exist when the General Convention was adopted. Nevertheless, since this rank is higher in the UN's hierarchy than that of the Assistant Secretaries-General, it is only reasonable to infer that they should enjoy privileges and immunities at least similar to those granted to Assistant Secretaries-General. For the scope of diplomatic and consular privileges and immunities, see the Vienna Convention on Diplomatic Relations of 18 April 1961, the Vienna Convention on Consular Relations of 24 April 1963, and the ICJ judgment *Case Concerning the Arrest Warrant of 11 April 2000 (Democratic Republic of the Congo v Belgium)*, [2002] ICJ Rep 3.

202 Office of Legal Affairs, "Status of United Nations Volunteers—Article 105, Paragraph 1, of the Charter of the United Nations" *UN Juridical Yearbook* (New York: UN, 1998) at 474.

203 Office of Legal Affairs, "Convention on the Privileges and Immunities of the United Nations—Inclusion of additional categories of personnel among the categories of officials to which the provisions of articles V and VII of the Convention shall apply" *UN Juridical Yearbook* (New York: UN, 1973) at 164–66.

204 Miller, "Privileges," above note 192 at 192.

staff members at the Assistant Secretary-General rank and higher enjoy diplomatic immunity. Functional immunity means immunity "from legal process in respect of words spoken or written and all acts performed by them in their official capacity."[205] This is a necessary corollary of the immunity of legal proceedings accorded to the organization itself. In addition to jurisdictional immunity, United Nations officials are exempt from direct taxes on their UN emoluments. They do not pay income taxes on their UN salary. The reason for these exemptions and privileges is not to provide a personal benefit to staff members, but to ensure equality of treatment for all officials, irrespective of their nationality.[206] However, UN staff members pay a "staff assessment," which is a deduction from their salaries credited to the Tax Equalization Fund of the United Nations. Member states receive a portion of this Tax Equalization Fund as an offset against their assessments for the UN regular budget. Some UN staff members—namely, permanent residents and citizens of the United States—have to pay national income taxes on their UN earnings because the United States government made reservations to the provision of the General Convention that exempt UN staff members from direct taxation of their emoluments. US permanent residents and citizens pay their income taxes in the United States and claim a reimbursement from the United Nations. The UN reimburses US nationals the amount of taxes paid to the US government from the Tax Equalization Fund.

UN officials also enjoy travel and residence privileges.[207] Travel and residence privileges extend to immediate family members of UN

---

205 *Convention on the Privileges and Immunities of the United Nations*, above note 190, art V, s 18(a).

206 Office of Legal Affairs, "Privileges and immunities of locally recruited staff members of the United Nations—Obligation of Member States under Article 105 of the Charter to accord all staff members whether internationally or locally recruited such privileges and immunities as are necessary for the independent exercise of their functions" *UN Juridical Yearbook* (New York: UN, 1972) at 191, and UN General Assembly, *Tax Equalization*, 7 December 1946, A/RES/78(1).

207 *Convention on the Privileges and Immunities of the United Nations*, above note 190, art V, s 18. Some of these privileges can also be found in specific host-country agreements entered between the organization and a specific country in which it operates. It is to be noted that the General Convention does not

officials. For instance, while a receiving state is entitled to require UN officials to obtain visas in order to enter its territory, this requirement should not become a barrier to the official's travel.[208] The category or type of visa to be issued remains a matter of national jurisdiction and the prerogative of the receiving state. However, the immigration process should not impede or interfere with the work of the organization.[209]

Since privileges and immunities are granted to officials in the interests of the United Nations and not for the personal benefit of the individuals themselves,[210] the Secretary-General has the authority to waive the immunity of United Nations officials where it would "impede the course of justice and can be waived without prejudice to the interests of the United Nations."[211] The concerned official need not be consulted in the procedure of determining whether the immunity should be waived.[212] The waiver of privileges and immunities is intended to prevent the abuse of privileges and immunities by UN officials. Neither the General Convention nor UN Staff Rules and Regulations draws a distinction between the procedure for waiving full diplomatic immunities and that for waiving functional immunities. Therefore, it is reasonable to assume that the procedure is identical. The distinction between acts performed in an official capacity and those performed in a private capacity is a question of fact. The official position of the United Nations is that it is exclusively for the Secretary-General to determine the extent of the duties and functions of United Nations officials and of experts on mission of the UN.[213]

---

contain a definition of spouses or dependents. However, it is the practice of the organization to rely on the definition of those terms provided in the Staff Rules and Regulations, under Rule 3.6. Miller, "Privileges," above note 192 at 211–12.

208 Miller, "Privileges," above note 192 at 233.

209 *Ibid.*

210 *UN Staff Regulations and Rules*, above note 71 at Regulation 1.1(f).

211 *Convention on the Privileges and Immunities of the United Nations*, above note 40, art V, s 20.

212 Miller, "Privileges," above note 192 at 238.

213 *Memorandum of the United Nations Legal Rights When a Staff Member or Other Agent of the United Nations, or a Member of Their Family, Is Arrested or Detained*, Annex I to Administrative Instruction on Reporting of Arrest or Detention of Staff Member, UN Doc ST/AI/299 (1982) at para 3.

Therefore, even when the acts are clearly not performed in an official capacity, some national authorities request an explicit waiver of immunity.[214]

Another category of official that enjoys privileges and immunities is experts on mission for the United Nations. As opposed to UN staff members, experts on missions for the United Nations serve under a temporary and specific mandate. Therefore, the privileges and immunities accorded to them are not only functionally limited, as are necessary for the independent exercise of their functions,[215] but also limited in duration for the period of their missions.[216] An individual may become an expert on mission in a wide range of circumstances. Consultants and individual contractors may be afforded the status of experts on mission within the meaning of Article VI, Section 22 of the General Convention.[217] Special Rapporteurs and members of the International Law Commission[218] are normally regarded as experts on mission. The status of experts on mission also applies to some categories of personnel in peacekeeping missions, such as "military observers, military liaison officers, military advisers, arms monitors, members of formed police units, seconded individual United Nations police and seconded correction officers."[219] Under certain circumstances, participants in UN seminars and symposia may also be afforded the status of experts on mission.[220] In a seminal advisory opinion on privileges and immunities, the International Court of Justice ruled that experts on mission

---

214 Miller, "Privileges," above note 192 at 239.

215 *Convention on the Privileges and Immunities of the United Nations*, above note 40, art VI, s 22.

216 Bruno Simma et al, eds, *The Charter of the United Nations: A Commentary*, 3rd ed (Oxford, UK: Oxford University Press, 2012) at 2176 [Simma et al, eds].

217 *Consultants and Individual Contractors*, Administrative Instruction, UN Doc ST/AI/2013/4 at para 5.4.

218 *Information-sharing practices between the United Nations and national law enforcement authorities as well as referrals of possible criminal cases related to United Nations staff, United Nations officials and experts on mission*, Report of the Secretary-General, UNGAOR, 63rd Sess, UN Doc 63/331 (2008).

219 *Ibid* at para 9.

220 *Reporting of Arrest or Detention of Staff Members, Other Agents of the United Nations and Members of their Families*, Administrative Instruction, UN Doc ST/AI/299 (1982), Annex 1.

may be either appointed or elected individuals.[221] The Court added that an individual need not be remunerated or have a valid contract with the UN to be granted the status of an expert on mission and to enjoy the associated privileges and immunities.[222] When assessing the status of an official, the decisive factor must be the nature of the mission rather than technical arrangements or organizational aspects.[223] The Court also determined that there was no requirement for the individual to be travelling in relation to the mission in order to be considered an expert on mission.[224] Finally, the Court decided that the officials and experts on mission enjoyed privileges and immunities even in their countries of nationality, unless that country made a reservation specifying that the General Convention does not apply to its citizens.[225]

There are two important differences between the privileges and immunities of experts on missions and those of UN officials. First, experts on mission enjoy quasi-diplomatic privileges and immunities because it was foreseen that they would often operate away from UN offices and would not benefit from the protection of inviolability of UN premises.[226] Therefore, unlike UN officials, experts on mission are granted an express immunity from personal arrest or detention.[227] Another important distinction is exemption from income taxes. While UN officials are exempt from income taxes on the salaries and emoluments paid to them by the UN, experts on mission are accorded no such exemptions.[228]

---

221 *Applicability of Article VI, Section 22, of the Convention on the Privileges and Immunities of the United Nations*, Advisory Opinion [1989] ICJ Reports 177 at 194 [*Applicability of Article VI, Section 22*].

222 *Ibid.*

223 Simma et al, eds, above note 216 at 2176.

224 *Applicability of Article VI, Section 22*, above note 221 at 195.

225 *Ibid.*

226 Anthony J Miller, "United Nations Experts on Mission and Their Privileges and Immunities" (2007) 4 *Int'l Org L Rev* 11 at 11 [Miller, "United Nations"].

227 Serguei Tarassenko & Ralph Zacklin, "Independence of International Civil Servants (Privileges and Immunities)" in Chris De Cooker, ed, *International Administration—Law and Management Practices in International Organizations* (Leiden: Martinus Nijhoff Publishers, 2009) 483 at 489.

228 Miller, "United Nations," above note 226 at 42.

4) Benefits and Entitlements of UN Staff

As we have seen above (Section E.2), in February 1946, the General Assembly called for the establishment of an international civil service commission to advise on the methods of recruitment of UN staff members.[229] In 1948, the International Civil Service Advisory Board (ICSAB) was established with terms of reference related chiefly to questions of recruitment and personnel administration. In December 1974, the General Assembly replaced the International Civil Service Advisory Board (ICSAB) with the International Civil Service Commission (ICSC).[230] This commission is an independent expert body composed of fifteen members who serve in their personal capacity and who are appointed by the General Assembly for four-year terms. The ICSC provides advice or makes decisions on all aspects of UN staff employment conditions. It has the authority to make decisions on some questions and to make recommendations to the General Assembly on other questions. For instance, it determines the amount of daily subsistence allowance payable to UN staff members who travel on duty. It determines the postadjustment in various duty stations based on the cost of living. However, it only makes recommendations to the General Assembly on such matters as salary scales of staff in the Professional and higher categories and education grants payable to staff members residing and serving outside their recognized home countries whose dependent children are in full-time attendance at a school or university.[231]

The main component of the emoluments of internationally recruited staff members is the basic salary set out in Annex I to the United Nations Staff Regulations. The basic salary is only one part of a staff member's total compensation. In addition to this amount, staff members also receive post adjustment, which is an amount paid to staff members serving in the Professional and higher categories and in the Field Service category to ensure equity in purchasing power of

229 *Organization of the Secretariat*, above note 112.

230 *Statute of the International Civil Service Commission*, GA Res 3357(XXIX), UNGAOR, 29th Sess, UN Doc A/RES/3357(XXIX) (1974) 127.

231 *UN Staff Regulations and Rules*, above note 71 at Regulation 3.2(a).

staff members across duty stations.[232] The post adjustment is a percentage of the basic salary. For instance, if the post adjustment in a specific duty station is 50 percent, then the staff member will receive 150 percent of basic salary. Furthermore, staff members may also be entitled to dependency allowance if the income of their spouse does not exceed a certain threshold or if they have dependent children.[233] In duty stations where UN staff are obliged to rent housing accommodation at substantially higher commercial rates, staff members are entitled to a rental subsidy.[234]

Staff members who do not reside or work in their country of nationality or residence may receive an education grant for each dependent child in full-time attendance at a school or university. The education grant is normally payable up to the end of the school year in which the child completes four years of post-secondary studies or attains a first post-secondary degree, whichever comes first. The grant is normally not payable beyond the school year in which the child reaches the age of twenty-five years.[235] The education grant covers a percentage of tuition and other education-related fees up to a maximum of 86 percent.[236] The exact percentage depends on the amount of tuition fees paid. For children with disabilities, the UN pays a special and more generous education grant.[237]

Furthermore, the UN encourages its staff to move at least every five years. Staff members who accept assignments of one year or longer in another geographical location receive a mobility incentive. This incentive is paid to staff members who hold a continuing or fixed-term appointment and have more than five years of uninterrupted service with the UN. The incentive is paid as of the staff member's first move and is discontinued upon five continuous years in

232 *Ibid* at Rule 3.7(a).

233 *Ibid* at Rule 3.6.

234 *Ibid* at Rule 3.7(c).

235 *Ibid* at Rule 3.9(d).

236 *Education Grant and Related Benefits*, Administrative Instruction, UN Doc ST/AI/2018/1/Rev.1 (2018).

237 *UN Staff Regulations and Rules*, above note 71 at Rule 3.9(i).

the same duty station.[238] The amount of the mobility incentive and the conditions under which it is paid depend on the number of duty stations at which the staff member has previously served for a period of one year or longer, the staff member's category and grade, and the hardship classification of the new duty station to which the staff member is assigned.[239]

The mobility incentive described above is closely related to the hardship allowance for which certain staff members may be eligible. The International Civil Service Commission places all duty stations where the UN has a presence in one of six categories: H and A to E. Duty stations in category H are headquarters and similarly designated locations where the United Nations has no development or humanitarian assistance program, or locations in countries that are members of the European Union. New York, Vienna, and Geneva are H duty stations. Staff members in these locations do not receive any hardship allowances or mobility incentives. The A to E categories comprise all other duty stations, classified by order of difficulty of conditions of life and work. Hardship E duty stations are the most difficult places and where the families of UN staff members are not even allowed to be. Staff based in duty stations classified as Hardship E receive the highest hardship allowance, which ranges from USD$18,000 to USD$24,000 per year.[240] They also receive a non-family service allowance to compensate for the fact that they are separated from their families.[241] Staff are informed of the category of their duty station on an annual basis or more frequently if there is a change in classification.[242]

Finally, UN staff members are entitled to generous retirement, death, disability, and related benefits upon cessation of their services with the UN. The General Assembly established a separate entity called the United Nations Joint Staff Pension Fund (UNJSPF) to administer these benefits. The fund operates under its own regulations approved

---

238 *Ibid* at Rule 3.13(a).

239 *Mobility and Hardship Scheme*, Administrative Instruction, UN Doc ST/AI/2016/6 (2016) [*Mobility and Hardship Scheme*].

240 *Ibid*, Annex.

241 *UN Staff Regulations and Rules*, above note 71 at Rule 3.15.

242 *Mobility and Hardship Scheme*, above note 239 at para 1.6.

by the General Assembly and is governed by a board that consists of thirty-three members representing the twenty-four UN organizations.[243] The UNJSPF board reports to the General Assembly on the operations of the fund and on the investment of its assets. Over 70,000 retirees receive benefits from the fund and more than 126,000 participants pay monthly contributions to it.

5) Administration of Justice in the United Nations

Because the UN enjoys immunity from every form of legal process before national courts, UN staff members cannot challenge decisions that affect their employment rights in domestic courts. For this reason, the UN has put in place an internal dispute settlement mechanism that its staff can exercise for legal recourse against the organization. The internal justice system of the United Nations is reserved exclusively for labour law disputes between the organization and its staff members. The main components of the internal justice system are the administrative tribunals composed of experienced judges who hear grievances of UN staff and adjudicate cases. The UN is not the only international organization that has its own internal justice system. Large organizations such as the World Bank, the IMF, NATO, and the EU have administrative tribunals. Nevertheless, the UN's internal justice system is the largest and arguably the most advanced of them all.

a) History of International Administrative Tribunals

The first international administrative tribunal was created for the League of Nations in 1927. The number of disputes this tribunal settled was insignificant because the Secretariat of the League was very small.[244] Between 1929 and 1940, the tribunal held seven sessions during which it rendered thirty-seven judgments. This tribunal also

243 The Regulations of the United Nations Joint Staff Pension Fund were adopted by the General Assembly by Resolution 248 (III) of 23 January 1949 and have been amended several times since then on the basis of recommendations by the United Nations Joint Staff Pension Board.

244 In 1920, the League's Secretariat consisted of approximately 160 civil servants. In 1930, it had approximately 700 civil servants.

serviced the International Labour Organization (ILO). It adjudicated cases filed by ILO staff members against their employer for alleged breaches of their contractual rights.[245] When the League of Nations was formally dissolved in 1946, the ILO remained fully operational and continued to employ staff. Therefore, it was imperative to keep the League's administrative tribunal so that it could continue arbitrating disputes between the ILO and its staff. Member states of the League decided to transfer the League's administrative tribunal to the ILO. The new tribunal was renamed as the ILO Administrative Tribunal (ILOAT), which still exists today. It hears complaints from serving and former officials of the International Labour Organization (ILO). Many other international organizations recognized the jurisdiction of the ILOAT. Instead of creating their own internal administrative tribunals, approximately sixty international organizations and specialized agencies of the United Nations, employing over 45,000 international public service employees and officials, entrusted the adjudication of their internal disputes to the ILOAT.

In 1949, UN member states decided to create another administrative tribunal for the newly created United Nations. They firmly believed that the United Nations deserved an administrative tribunal of its own and that it should not rely on a tribunal of another organization. As a result, the General Assembly established the United Nations Administrative Tribunal (UNAT).[246] The tribunal was tasked with hearing and passing judgment on applications alleging non-observance of contracts of staff members of the UN Secretariat. It became the UN's first forum for adjudicating employment disputes arising between the organization and its staff members.

The competence of the tribunal quickly expanded to the secretariats of funds and programs of the United Nations that are financed from voluntary contributions, such as the United Nations Children's

---

245 S Bastid, "Les Tribunaux administratifs internationaux et leur jurisprudence" 92(II) RCADI, 364–76; F Wolf, "Le tribunal administratif de l'OIT" 63 RGDIP (1954) 794; Frank Gutteridge, "The ILO Administrative Tribunal" in de Cooker, ed, *International Administration*, V.2/1-33.

246 *Establishment of a United Nations Administrative Tribunal*, GA Res 351 (IV), UNGAOR, 4th Sess, UN Doc A/RES/351(IV) (1949) 49.

Fund (UNICEF), United Nations Development Programme (UNDP), United Nations Population Fund (UNFPA), United Nations High Commissioner for Refugees (UNHCR), United Nations Relief and Works Agency for Palestine Refugees in the Near East (UNRWA), as well as the International Maritime Organization (IMO), International Civil Aviation Organization (ICAO), International Seabed Authority (ISA), and the registries of the International Court of Justice (ICJ) and the International Tribunal for the Law of the Sea (ITLS). Between 1 January 1950 and 31 December 2009, the UN Administrative Tribunal adjudged 1,500 cases.

Consequently, agencies and various organizations that are part of the United Nations common system split into two groups. One group of UN entities (primarily specialized agencies and related organizations) accepted the jurisdiction of the ILOAT, whereas the other group of entities (mainly UN Funds and Programmes) chose to adhere to UNAT. This separation still exists today.

The UN Administrative Tribunal was less successful and efficient than its ILO counterpart. It could take the UN Administrative Tribunal as long as ten years to resolve disputes. For decades, UN staff members complained to the Secretary-General about the inadequacy of the UNAT and the Secretary-General complained to the General Assembly about the high costs associated with the tribunal. The system was slow, cumbersome and costly, and needed a complete overhaul.[247] In 2005, the General Assembly noted the continuing backlog of appeals in various parts of the system and finally recognized that the internal justice system of the UN urgently needed a fundamental reform. Consequently, it requested the Secretary-General to form a panel of external and independent experts to consider redesigning the system of administration of justice.[248] The panel was to be composed of a pre-eminent judge with administrative law experience, an expert in alternative dispute resolution methods, a leading legal academic in international law, a person with senior management and administrative experience

247 *Administration of justice at the United Nations*, GA Res 59/283, UNGAOR, 59th Sess, UN Doc A/RES/59/283 (2005) 1.

248 *Ibid* at para 47.

in an international organization, and a person with United Nations field experience.[249] This group of experts was called the Redesign Panel.

In July 2006, the panel submitted its findings and recommendations.[250] It confirmed the complaints of staff that the UN internal justice system was outmoded, dysfunctional, and ineffective, and that it lacked independence. It concluded that the financial, reputational, and other costs to the organization were enormous. The panel came to the conclusion that a new redesigned system of internal justice would be far more effective than an attempt to improve the current system. The Redesign Panel identified a large number of specific deficiencies in the old system and made comprehensive recommendations. It proposed a model for a new system for resolving staff grievances. The proposed model was to be independent, transparent, effective, efficient, and adequately resourced. It had to ensure managerial accountability. The Secretary-General submitted the Redesign Panel's recommendations to the General Assembly, which voted in favour of introducing a new system of administration of justice. The General Assembly wanted the new system to put a stronger emphasis on resolving disputes through informal means before resorting to formal litigation. The new system of administration of justice became operational on 1 July 2009.

b) The Redesigned System of Administration of Justice of the UN

The current dispute settlement framework has two pillars: formal and informal. The resolution of disputes through the informal system consists of mediation. The Office of the Ombudsman and Mediation Services of the UN helps staff to address their workplace issues and grievances confidentially and informally. UN ombudspersons and mediators are based in many duty stations and regularly travel to other duty stations, including peacekeeping missions, to ensure an equal access to their services by all staff. The Office of the Ombudsman and Mediation Services is funded entirely from the budget of the United

---

249 *Ibid* at para 48.

250 *Report of the Redesign Panel on the United Nations system of administration of justice*, UNGAOR, 1st Sess, UN Doc A/61/205 (2006).

Nations and provides services free of charge. It functions independently from all UN organs and officials. Ombudspersons and mediators are not supposed to take instructions from any official, including the Secretary-General. They have an obligation to preserve the confidentiality of the informal dispute settlement and to remain neutral at all times.

If the informal dispute settlement mechanism fails or does not lead to a satisfactory outcome, the staff member may resort to the formal route, which entails litigation. In most cases, a staff member who wishes to contest an administrative decision is required as a first step to request a management evaluation of the administrative decision within sixty days of being notified of the impugned decision.[251] In certain cases, a staff member is not required to submit a request for a management evaluation. For instance, if the contested decision concerns the imposition of a disciplinary measure or if it was taken by management based on the advice of an expert or advisory board, such as the Advisory Board on Compensation Claims, the aggrieved staff member can submit his grievance directly to the UN Dispute Tribunal.[252]

A management evaluation request is a written document in which a staff member exposes the facts that led to the impugned decision and provides its views about why the contested decision is unlawful. Although management evaluation requests are addressed to the Secretary-General, they are normally reviewed by the official who made the decision and a group of lawyers working for the Secretariat in an office known as the Management Evaluation Unit (which is part of the Department of Management Strategy, Policy, and Compliance). The purpose of the management evaluation request is to give the UN a chance to rescind the unlawful decision or to provide adequate remedies before the matter reaches the UN administrative tribunals. This initial review, which normally should be concluded within forty-five days (thirty days if the staff member is based in a headquarters location), requires an objective and reasoned assessment of the contested decision.[253] If, during the management evaluation, it is deter-

---

251 *UN Staff Regulations and Rules*, above note 71 at Rule 11.2(c).

252 *Ibid* at Rule 11.2(b).

253 *Ibid* at Rule 11.2(d).

mined that an improper decision has been made, the UN Secretariat must rescind the impugned decision or provide an adequate remedy. Unfortunately, the Management Evaluation Unit often upholds manifestly unlawful decisions on the basis of untenable legal positions.[254] This leads to unnecessary litigation.

If the Management Evaluation Unit agrees with the staff member, rescinds the impugned decision, and grants an appropriate remedy, the case is closed. If, on the other hand, the Management Evaluation Unit disagrees with the staff member and upholds the impugned decision, the staff member may pursue the formal dispute resolution process by filing an application before the United Nations Dispute Tribunal (UNDT). The UNDT is the UN's tribunal of first instance. It has a permanent presence in New York, Geneva, and Nairobi. Unlike the vast majority of international administrative tribunals, the UNDT holds hearings and hears witnesses. The hearings are presided by a single judge. Only staff members can bring cases before the UNDT because only they can challenge administrative decisions. The Secretary-General has no reason to challenge his own decisions; he has an opportunity to correct his own improper decisions when reviewing management evaluation requests submitted by staff. Hence, the Secretary-General can only be the respondent party before the UNDT.

The UNDT is competent to hear and pass judgment on an application filed by an individual against the Secretary-General in relation to the following three elements:

- an administrative decision that is alleged to be in non-compliance with the terms of contract of employment, which include all pertinent UN regulations and rules and all relevant administrative issuances in force;
- an administrative decision imposing a disciplinary measure;
- to enforce the implementation of an agreement reached through mediation.[255]

---

254 See *Dalgamouni v Secretary-General*, United Nations Dispute Tribunal, UNDT/2016/094 (30 June 2016) at para 92.

255 Article 2.1 of the *Statute of the United Nations Dispute Tribunal*, as adopted by the General Assembly in Resolution 63/253 on 24 December 2008, amended

The UNDT is also competent to order interim measures. More specifically, the tribunal may suspend, during the pendency of the management evaluation or at any time during the proceedings, the implementation of a contested administrative decision.[256] For instance, the tribunal may suspend the transfer of a staff member from one post to another while the lawfulness of the decision to transfer is being reviewed. To succeed on an application for a suspension of action, the staff member must demonstrate that the contested decision is *prima facie* unlawful, that implementation before the tribunal has had a chance to review would cause irreparable harm, and that there is urgency.[257] UNDT's orders suspending the implementation of a decision are final and not subject to appeal[258] unless the tribunal exceeds its jurisdiction.[259]

Judgments of the UNDT can be appealed to the United Nations Appeals Tribunal (UNAT). The appellate tribunal is composed of seven judges appointed by the General Assembly. The appeals tribunal holds hearings in approximately 10 percent of the cases only. The vast majority of cases are decided on the basis of written proceedings. Cases before the appeals tribunal are normally reviewed by a panel of three judges. Where the case raises a significant question of law, the case may be referred for consideration by the entire appeals tribunal.

One of the most innovative elements of the internal justice system of the United Nations is the Office of Staff Legal Assistance (OSLA). This Office was established in 2009 to provide professional legal

---

by Resolution 69/203 adopted on 18 December 2014, amended by Resolution 70/112 adopted on 14 December 2015, amended by Resolution 71/266 adopted on 23 December 2016, and amended by Resolution 73/276 adopted on 22 December 2018 [*Statute of the United Nations Dispute Tribunal*].

256 *Ibid*, art 2.2.

257 *Koura v Secretary-General*, United Nations Dispute Tribunal, Order No 7 (NBI/2019) (30 January 2019).

258 *Statute of the United Nations Dispute Tribunal*, above note 255, arts 2.2, 10.2.

259 *Bertucci v Secretary-General*, United Nations Appeals Tribunal, 2010-UNAT-062 at para 21, quoting *Kasmani v Secretary-General*, United Nations Appeals Tribunal, 2010-UNAT-011; *Onana v Secretary-General*, United Nations Appeals Tribunal, 2010-UNAT-008; *Tadonki v Secretary-General*, United Nations Appeals Tribunal, 2010-UNAT-005.

advice and representation to United Nations staff members, and in particular those working in remote and secluded areas where legal services may not be easily accessible. It is very similar to the legal aid services available in many countries. In particular, OSLA provides legal assistance and representation to UN staff members free of charge. It employs eight litigation lawyers who are also UN staff members. OSLA legal officers prepare management evaluation requests on behalf of their clients, draft legal briefs and proceedings for UN administrative tribunals, plead cases before both tribunals, negotiate out-of-court settlements with the lawyers acting for the Secretary-General, assist staff members accused of misconduct in responding to allegations and charges, etc. OSLA is largely funded by the budget of the United Nations. However, a small part of its funding comes from voluntary contributions by UN staff members. OSLA is not obliged to provide legal assistance and representation to all UN staff members. It carries out a preliminary review of requests for legal assistance and offers legal services only when there are reasonable prospects of success.[260] OSLA is functionally independent from the Secretary-General. It is not affiliated with the UN Staff Association, UN Ombudsman and Mediation Services, or the other UN offices.

The formal dispute settlement mechanism of the UN is open only to current or former staff members of the UN.[261] Consultants, workers on a service contract,[262] and interns[263] do not have standing before the UN Dispute Tribunal and the UN Appeals Tribunal. This jurisdictional limitation excludes approximately 35,000 individuals who are engaged by the UN Secretariat and the UN Funds and Programmes

---

260 *Staedtler v Secretary-General*, United Nations Appeals Tribunal, 2015-UNAT-577.

261 *Ndjadi*, above note 119.

262 *Megerditchian v Secretary-General*, United Nations Dispute Tribunal, UNDT/2010/035, affirmed by the United Nations Appeals Tribunal in 2010-UNAT-088; *Mialeshka v Secretary-General*, United Nations Dispute Tribunal, UNDT/2011/055.

263 *Basenko v Secretary-General*, United Nations Dispute Tribunal, UNDT/2010/145, affirmed by the United Nations Appeals Tribunal in 2011-UNAT-139; *Roberts v Secretary-General*, United Nations Dispute Tribunal, UNDT/2010/142.

as individual consultants, service contractors, or UN Volunteers.[264] Some of these UN personnel have no meaningful recourse and cannot seek justice either before the domestic courts (due to the UN's jurisdictional immunities) or before the UN's internal tribunals. Arbitral proceedings before the Permanent Court of Arbitration may be available to consultants and contractors if their specific contracts contain a dispute resolution clause. Such proceedings are prohibitively expensive, which dissuades most individuals from instituting legal proceedings against the UN. The Redesign Panel and the Secretary-General had recommended to the General Assembly to open the internal justice system to all individuals performing work for the organization by way of personal services.[265] Unfortunately, member states voted against this recommendation in the General Assembly.

264 *Report of the Redesign Panel on the United Nations system of administration of justice*, UNGAOR, 61st Sess, UN Doc A/61/758 (2007) at footnote 2 [*Report of the Redesign Panel 2007*].

265 *Report of the Redesign Panel on the United Nations system of administration of justice*, UNGAOR, 61st Sess, UN Doc A/61/205 (2006) at paras 19–20; *Report of the Redesign Panel 2007*, above note 264 at paras 10–12.

CONCLUSION

When the Security Council held its first meeting in the Bronx campus of Hunter College in March 1946, it found in the newly built ballot box of the Council a note on which was written:

> May I, who have had the privilege of fabricating this ballot box, cast the first vote?
>
> May God be with every member of the United Nations Organization and through your noble efforts bring lasting peace to us all—all over the world.
>
> Paul Antonio, Mechanic[1]

This message embodied humankind's hopes and expectations for the recently established United Nations Organization and for a better world through the prevention of conflict. The perennial question is whether or not the UN lives up to these expectations. To measure the UN's success, we first need to determine the evaluation criteria or yardsticks. As we have seen in Chapter 2 of this book, Article 1 of the *UN Charter* identifies the following four purposes of the United Nations:

1. To maintain international peace and security . . . ;
2. To develop friendly relations among nations based on respect for the principle of equal rights and self-determination of peoples . . . ;

---

1 Trygve Lie, *In the Cause of Peace* (New York: Macmillan Company, 1954) at 67.

3. To achieve international co-operation in solving international problems of an economic, social, cultural, or humanitarian character, and in promoting and encouraging respect for human rights and for fundamental freedoms for all without distinction as to race, sex, language, or religion; and
4. To be a centre for harmonizing the actions of nations in the attainment of these common ends.

These four purposes should serve as performance indicators against which the UN's success can be assessed. The first purpose—to maintain international peace and security—is the UN's primary responsibility. The remaining three purposes deal with self-determination of peoples, human rights, and development. These were the UN's secondary purposes. We will appraise the UN's performance against these two broad categories under a separate heading.

A. ASSESSING THE UN'S SUCCESS IN MAINTAINING INTERNATIONAL PEACE AND SECURITY

It is important to recall that the organization was created primarily "to save succeeding generations from the scourge of war, which twice in our lifetime brought untold sorrow to mankind."[2] As the second Secretary-General of the UN, Dag Hammarskjöld, famously once remarked "the United Nations was not created in order to bring us to heaven but in order to save us from hell."[3] The organization has thus far averted World War III and therefore fulfilled its principal mandate. While it is true that armed conflicts continue to occur in many parts of the world, these human tragedies are not the type of conflicts that the UN was set up to prevent.

What is more, fatalities resulting from armed conflicts have been continuously declining since 1946 and the vast majority of

2 *Charter of the United Nations*, 26 June 1945, Can TS 1945 No 7 at Preamble.

3 Address by Dag Hammarskjöld at University of California Convocation, Press Release SG/382 (13 May 1954), online: https://ask.un.org/loader.php?fid=11125&type=1&key=6bf400a0db526933d8577cce49f39ad2 at 7.

battle-related deaths result from intrastate conflicts or civil wars,[4] albeit with occasional foreign state intervention.

When measuring the UN's success in the field of international peace and security, the academic literature invariably focuses on UN peace operations. However, the UN's contribution to the maintenance of peace is not limited to peacekeeping activities. Many other important functions of the organization have a direct or indirect impact on preserving the peace. Preventive diplomacy is one mechanism that the UN uses to address threats to international peace and security. UN Secretaries-General have personally mediated and brokered peace pacts during major international conflicts. Chapter One described several instances where a Secretary-General of the UN played a key role in resolving an international conflict. The release of American airmen captured by China during the Korean war in 1955, the resolution of the Cuban missile crisis of 1961 opposing the USA and USSR, and the cessation of hostilities between Iran and Iraq in 1988 are just a few examples of how Secretaries-General of the UN contributed to international peace through mediation and preventive diplomacy. Where the Secretary-General is unable to act himself, he may appoint representatives and envoys to represent him and to carry out good offices, mediation, facilitation, and other dialogue processes.

The UN also contributes to international peace through its judicial dispute resolution organ, the International Court of Justice. The Court adjudicated an impressive number of cases, particularly territorial and maritime disputes between neighbouring countries, thereby reducing tensions and the likelihood of armed conflicts. Some UN agencies and bodies help maintain peace by controlling the use of weapons of mass destruction. Specifically, the Organisation for the Prohibition of Chemical Weapons oversees the efforts of states to eliminate chemical weapons, whereas the International Atomic Energy Agency and the Comprehensive Nuclear Test Ban Treaty Organization strive to ensure that nuclear technologies are used for peaceful means and that nations do not test or develop nuclear weapons.

---

4 See Therese Pettersson, Stina Högbladh & Magnus Öberg, "Organized Violence, 1989–2018 and Peace Agreements" (2018) 56:4 *Journal of Peace Research* 589.

The UN contributes to international peace and security in many other ways, including by promoting the rule of law at national and international levels, by holding accountable individuals responsible for war crimes and crimes against humanity, by stimulating development, and by assisting countries to conduct democratic elections.

With respect to peacekeeping activities, the success of the organization is a mixed bag. Measuring the UN's overall performance in a systemized manner by using objective yardsticks is not an easy task as there is no agreed definition of what constitutes success or failure. Between 1945 and 2020, the UN has operated approximately seventy peace operations. It currently runs fourteen peace operations with 100,000 peacekeepers worldwide. Some missions were so disastrous that calling them failures would not be controversial. However, in most cases, a binary assessment of peace operations—stating that the operation was either a complete success or a total failure—would neither be accurate nor fair. Several factors make the assessment of peace operations difficult. First and foremost, from whose perspective should one gauge the UN's success? When establishing a peacekeeping mission, the Security Council articulates the goals that the international community of states expects the UN to achieve in a specific conflict area. These expectations may not always be in line with those of the local community affected by the conflict. Hence, the UN may, in the eyes of the international community, successfully implement its mandate and nevertheless fail in the eyes of the local community or vice versa. A global research consortium, known as the Effectiveness of Peace Operations Network (EPON), assessed the effectiveness of specific peace operations in Somalia, the DRC, Mali, and South Sudan from the perspective of local communities and found that, in most cases, UN peace operations made significant contributions to preventing large-scale conflicts. The level of violence in these countries would have been significantly worse if the peace operations had not existed.[5] However, this view is not shared by all scholars and practitioners.

---

5 EPON, "The Effectiveness of Peace Operations Network," online: https://effectivepeaceops.net.

Another difficulty in appraising the UN's peacekeeping activities is the period that the evaluation should cover. A peacekeeping operation may exist for several decades. For instance, the UN Truce Supervision Organization (UNTSO) and the UN Military Observer in India and Pakistan (UNMOGIP) were established in 1948 and 1949 respectively and still operate. The performance of a peace operation is not always consistent and linear. During some years of its existence, the performance may be better than other years. The successive peacekeeping missions in the DRC and Somalia are just two examples of long-lasting interventions with considerable vicissitudes. Since the vast majority of peacekeeping missions are protracted endeavours, it is not always possible to measure accurately their performance for the entire period or to give them an overall score.

Finally, the intended purpose of the mission is equally important when evaluating its success. Some peace operations, namely legacy peacekeeping missions such as the UN Interim Force in Lebanon (UNIFIL) and the UN Disengagement Observer Force (UNDOF) in the Golan Heights, were given a very narrow mandate. UNDOF was established in 1974 to maintain the ceasefire between Israel and Syria and to supervise the disengagement of Israeli and Syrian forces. Its mandate does not authorize it to get involved in the civil war in Syria or to take any action in relation to it. Hence, it would be a mistake to assess UNDOF's success by examining the security situation in Syria, as these two elements are entirely unrelated. Similarly, UNIFIL was established in 1978 to confirm Israeli withdrawal from Lebanon, restore international peace and security, and assist the Lebanese government in restoring its effective authority in the area. During the armed conflict between Hezbollah and Israel in July and August 2006, UNIFIL's mandate had to be extended to monitor the cessation of hostilities. UNIFIL did not fail in its mission to maintain international peace and security when armed hostilities began under its watch because neither its mandate nor its resources allowed it to intervene to end the conflict.

Determining the underlying causes for the UN's inability to restore peace and security in a specific conflict zone is even more challenging than assessing its performance. An infinite number of circumstances beyond the UN's control may hinder its ability to intervene effectively and efficiently. One of the main and obvious reasons is the lack of consensus in the Security Council. The proper functioning of the UN collective security system was predicated on the continuing cooperation of the permanent members of the Security Council. The UN has often been feckless in the face of major conflicts in which permanent members have a stake. Recent cases dealt with by the Security Council prove that the collective security mechanism envisaged in the *UN Charter* is paralyzed as long as at least one of its permanent members is opposed to any preventive or remedial action by the United Nations. The Security Council's starkest failure has been its handling of the conflict in Syria, with Russia backing the regime in power and the United States, United Kingdom, and France supporting opposition groups. Despite several credible reports of war crimes, the Security Council's attempts to take decisive action on Syria were vetoed by Russia. The permanent members disagree on almost every conflict or situation that poses a threat to international peace and security, including in Yemen and Venezuela. Most recently, the Security Council was unable to agree on any action or measure that could halt the atrocities against the Rohingya ethnic group in Myanmar. The Gambia brought the matter before the International Court of Justice and sought provisional measures against Myanmar.

Another cause for failure is the lack of adequate resources. Even if the Security Council authorizes the UN to establish a peacekeeping mission, the UN will nevertheless need adequate resources to take effective action. Peacekeeping is no longer about monitoring ceasefires. It has become a multidimensional activity requiring adequate expertise in and technology for counterinsurgency, intelligence gathering, policing, and peacebuilding. Peacekeeping troops often engage against well-equipped hostile forces. Industrialized states with robust and well-resourced armed forces have been reluctant to contribute troops to UN peace operations after the fiascos in Somalia and Bosnia. Developing countries readily filled the gap because peacekeeping presents an attractive source of additional revenue for their armed forces. However, their troops are often either poorly trained, inadequately equipped, or both.[6]

---

6 See UNSCOR, 72nd Year, 8051st Mtg, UN Doc S/PV.8051 (2017).

B. ASSESSING THE UN'S SUCCESS IN THE FIELDS OF SELF-DETERMINATION, HUMAN RIGHTS, AND DEVELOPMENT

The UN achieved its goal to "develop friendly relations among nations based on respect for the principle of equal rights and self-determination of peoples" so well that one of its principal organs became redundant. After the independence of Palau in 1994, the Trusteeship Council had no colonial territories to administer and therefore suspended its operations. Under the UN's watch, nearly one-third of the world's population gained independence through the decolonization process. Of course, the determination of colonized peoples who fought for their independence was important and cannot be ignored. Nevertheless, decolonization would not have occurred so quickly without the UN. The General Assembly was the ideal shaming platform that the USSR and its allies used to exert pressure on the colonial powers of Europe to divest themselves of the colonies.

A good dose of political realism is required when appraising the UN's efficacy in the field of human rights.[7] Human rights still remain a highly politicized topic in the UN. In 2005, Secretary-General Annan made a recommendation to UN member states to replace the Commission on Human Rights with a smaller standing Human Rights Council. He expressed the view that the commission's ability to fulfill its mandate had been increasingly undermined by its declining credibility and professionalism. In particular, human rights abusers sought membership of the commission not to strengthen human rights but to protect themselves against criticism or to criticize others, which led to a credibility deficit and cast a shadow on the reputation of the UN system as a whole.[8] However, the replacement of the commission with a Human Rights Council did not correct the problem; member states continued to politicize human rights. Nevertheless, despite the difficult political context, the UN has come a long way in the past

---

7 Markus G Schmidt, "Does the United Nations Human Rights Program Make a Difference" (1997) 91 *American Society of Intl L Proceedings* 461 at 466.

8 *In Larger Freedom: Towards Development, Security and Human Rights for All,* Report of the Secretary-General, UNGAOR, 59th Sess, UN Doc A/59/2005 (2005) at para 182.

seventy-five years. First, it played a crucial role in creating a body of law enshrined in nine international human rights treaties. These legal instruments protect three categories of human rights: (a) civil and political rights, namely those listed in the International Covenant on Civil and Political Rights, such as freedom of expression and the right to vote; (b) economic, social, and cultural rights, particularly those contained in the International Covenant on Economic, Social, and Cultural Rights, such as the rights to decent standards of living, education, food, and social security; and (c) solidarity rights that can be found in, *inter alia*, the International Convention on the Elimination of All Forms of Racial Discrimination.[9] The rights contained in these legal instruments are universal, interdependent, interrelated,[10] and indivisible.[11] They have become so important that national courts and tribunals regularly invoke these instruments when adjudicating cases. Some member states have translated UN human rights treaties into domestic legislation.

In addition to the treaties, the UN also established a machinery of human rights bodies whose role includes the promotion and protection of human rights and the monitoring of the implementation of human rights instruments by UN member states. Currently, in addition to the Human Rights Council, OHCHR, and the General Assembly's Third Committee, the UN has ten human rights bodies created by treaties and composed of independent experts in human rights, who are nominated and elected by member states for fixed renewable terms of four years. Thus, the UN's overall performance in human rights deserves a positive assessment.

In the area of international cooperation, the organization has an impressive network of agencies specializing in virtually every field of human activity. As discussed in Chapter Five on the Economic and

---

9 Karel Vasak, "Human Rights: A Thirty-Year Struggle" (1977) 30 *UNESCO Courier* 11, 29 (1977); see also Patrick Macklem, *Sovereignty of Human Rights* (Oxford, UK: Oxford University Press, 2015) at 51–61.

10 The Vienna Declaration and Programme of Action, World Conference on Human Rights, UN Doc A/CONF.157/23 (1993).

11 Proclamation of Tehran, International Conference on Human Rights, UN Doc A/CONF.32/41 (1968), at para 13.

Social Council, under the UN umbrella, dozens of funds, programs, specialized agencies, and related organizations carry out activities that contribute to solving international problems of an economic, social, or humanitarian nature. With its thirty-four bodies and entities and annual revenue of approximately USD$30 billion, the UN development system is the biggest arm of the UN. The work of these numerous agencies and bodies is harmonized through a coordination machinery. This machinery does not always operate smoothly because the UN system is too fragmented to be fully efficient. Each UN entity and agency has its own governing body, chief administrative officer (head of agency), budget, and personnel. In addition, their functions and responsibilities often overlap. Nonetheless, the UN and its network of agencies manage to implement their mandates relatively well, albeit at a slightly higher cost than required. In particular, UNICEF continues to provide vaccines to 45 percent of the world's children, saving three million lives each year. It has saved an estimated ninety million children since its creation in 1946. WHO, a UN specialized agency, has played a key role in eradicating smallpox and other infectious diseases. It coordinates the efforts of member states in fighting pandemics. Each year, UNFPA helps twenty-five million pregnant women give birth without childbirth complications. WFP provides food to over ninety million individuals. The UN refugee agency, UNHCR, provides shelter to seventy million refugees. It is also the only intergovernmental organization that works with national governments to keep the global temperature rise below a certain threshold.

Despite UN's efforts, close to 300,000 children under five die every year due to poor sanitation, inadequate hygiene, or unsafe drinking water. Almost one billion individuals do not have enough to eat and live below the poverty line of USD$60 a month. Millions of people are forced to migrate due to natural disasters and poverty. In some parts of the world, slavery and forced labour still exist. Terrorism, transnational and organized crime, as well as drug trafficking continue to pose a major threat to the safety and security of all nations. These phenomena cannot be tackled alone by any single nation. They require concerted and well-coordinated action by the international community. The UN and its intricate web of agencies remain the only suitable actors to coordinate the actions of all countries. It is still the only intergovernmental organization with a truly universal membership that addresses all global issues, including health pandemics, protection of children and refugees, hunger and malnutrition, poverty, proliferation of weapons of mass destruction, deforestation and desertification, protection of intellectual property, standardization of aviation rules, protection of cultural heritage, and so on.

UN critics often blame the organization for being ineffective and slow. Typically, they evoke the UN's notorious failures in Rwanda and Bosnia, and the cholera pandemic its peacekeepers caused in Haiti. They focus on the organization's inability to prevent the genocide of Muslim Rohingyas of Myanmar, to stop the conflicts in Syria, Libya, and Yemen, to tame North Korea's and Iran's nuclear aspirations, to tackle the refugee problem, to find a lasting solution to the Israeli–Palestinian conflict, to eradicate HIV and malaria, to eliminate extreme poverty and inequalities, and to find a solution to recurrent tensions in the Security Council. UN critics tend to concentrate more on what the UN has failed to do as opposed to what it has done or could do better. This criticism is based on a fundamental misunderstanding of what the UN can do as an institution set up to serve the interests of its member states. The organization cannot be held responsible for decisions made by sovereign nations. As long as the international legal order is primarily founded on the deep-rooted yet very malleable principle of sovereign equality of states, as opposed to the rule of law, the UN's success will depend entirely on the support of its member nations.

TABLE OF CASES

International Cases

Other Jurisdictions

TABLE OF INTERNATIONAL MATERIALS

Treaties

UN General Assembly Resolutions

General Assembly Decisions

UN Security Council Resolutions

UN Economic and Social Council Resolutions

Economic and Social Council Decisions

Human Rights Council Resolutions

Other Instruments

INDEX

T after a page number indicates a table
F after a page number indicates a figure

ABOUT THE AUTHOR

Alexandre Tavadian is the principal legal advisor of a large NATO agency headquartered in Luxembourg. Prior to joining NATO, he worked in the Office of Administration of Justice of the UN Secretariat and in the Legal Affairs Service of UNHCR in Beirut, Nairobi, and Bangkok. He appeared as counsel of record before national and international courts and tribunals at all levels, including the UN Dispute Tribunal, the UN Appeals Tribunal, NATO Administrative Tribunal, and the Permanent Court of Arbitration in The Hague. Prior to joining the United Nations System, he worked as legal counsel in the Department of Justice of Canada, where he represented the interests of the Canadian government before the Federal Courts. He also worked as a lecturer in the Faculty of Law of the Université de Montréal.

FSC
www.fsc.org
MIX
Papier | Fördert
gute Waldnutzung
FSC® C083411

Kolibri 360 GmbH
Ferdinand-Jühlke-Straße 7
99095 Erfurt, Deutschland
produktsicherheit@kolibri360.de